Economic Report of the President

Transmitted to the Congress February 1994

TOGETHER WITH
THE ANNUAL REPORT
OF THE
COUNCIL OF ECONOMIC ADVISERS

UNITED STATES GOVERNMENT PRINTING OFFICE

WASHINGTON : 1994

For sale by the U.S. Government Printing Office
Superintendent of Documents, Mail Stop: SSOP, Washington, DC 20402-9328
ISBN 0-16-043028-3

CONTENTS

	Page
ECONOMIC REPORT OF THE PRESIDENT	1
ANNUAL REPORT OF THE COUNCIL OF ECONOMIC ADVISERS*	9
CHAPTER 1. A STRATEGY FOR GROWTH AND CHANGE	21
CHAPTER 2. THE U.S. ECONOMY IN 1993 AND BEYOND	55
CHAPTER 3. TRENDS AND RECENT DEVELOPMENTS IN THE U.S. LABOR MARKET	97
CHAPTER 4. HEALTH CARE REFORM	131
CHAPTER 5. MICROECONOMIC INITIATIVES TO PROMOTE EFFICIENCY AND PRODUCTIVITY	169
CHAPTER 6. THE UNITED STATES IN THE WORLD ECONOMY	205
APPENDIX A. REPORT TO THE PRESIDENT ON THE ACTIVITIES OF THE COUNCIL OF ECONOMIC ADVISERS DURING 1993	249
APPENDIX B. STATISTICAL TABLES RELATING TO INCOME, EMPLOYMENT, AND PRODUCTION	261

*For a detailed table of contents of the Council's Report, see page 13.

**ECONOMIC REPORT
OF THE PRESIDENT**

Economic Report of the President

To the Speaker of the House of Representatives and the President of the Senate:

America has always thrived on change. We have used the opportunities it creates to renew ourselves and build our prosperity. But for too long and in too many ways, our Nation has been drifting.

For the last 30 years, family life in America has been breaking down. For the last 20 years, the real compensation of working Americans has grown at a disappointing rate. For 12 years a policy of trickle-down economics built a false prosperity on a mountain of Federal debt. As a result of our national drift, far too many American families, even those with two working parents, no longer dream the American dream of a better life for their children.

In 1992, the American people demanded change. A year ago, I sought your support for a comprehensive short-term and long-term strategy to restore the promise of our country's economic future. You responded, and together we replaced drift and gridlock with renewal and reform. Together we have taken the first necessary steps to restore growth in the living standards of all Americans. We have created a sound macroeconomic environment and strengthened the foundations of future economic growth. As a result of our efforts, the economy is now on a path of rising output, increasing employment, and falling deficits.

Establishing the Fiscal Conditions for Sustained Growth

For more than a decade, the Federal Government has been living well beyond its means—spending much more than it has taken in, and borrowing the difference. The resulting deficits have been huge, both in sheer magnitude and as a percentage of the Nation's output. Since 1981 the Federal debt has been growing faster than the economy, reversing the trend of the previous three decades. As a consequence of this binge of deficit financing, Federal budget deficits have been gobbling up an inordinate share of the Nation's savings, driving up real long-term interest rates, discouraging private investment, and impeding long-run private sector growth.

On August 10, 1993, I signed the historic budget plan that you passed several days earlier. It will reduce Federal deficits by more than $500 billion. The plan is a balanced package of cuts in spending and increases in revenues. The spending cuts are specific, far-reaching, and genuine. They will reduce discretionary spending by over 12 percent in real terms in 5 years. The plan increases income tax rates for only the top 1.2 percent of taxpayers, the group of Americans who gained the most during the 1980s and are most able to pay higher taxes to help reduce the deficit. At the same time, a broad expansion of the earned income tax credit will help make work pay for up to 15 million American families. Nine out of ten small businesses will benefit from more-generous tax breaks that will help them invest and grow. And new, targeted capital gains tax relief will encourage investment in new small businesses.

Our deficit reduction plan has been the principal factor in the dramatic decline in long-term interest rates since my election in November 1992. Lower interest rates, in turn, have sparked an investment-driven economic expansion that has created more private sector jobs during the last year than were created during the previous four. The fact that investment is leading the recovery is good news for living standards, because investment is the key to productivity growth and hence to growth in real incomes for all Americans.

Investing in Our Nation's Future

Laying the macroeconomic groundwork for sustained growth is the government's first responsibility, but not its only responsibility. Government also has a vital role to play in providing some of the critical raw materials for economic growth: science and technology, an educated and well-trained work force, and public infrastructure. For much too long we have underinvested in these areas, in comparison both with our global competitors and with our own economic history. Our overall budget deficit has masked another, equally disturbing deficit—a deficit in the kinds of public investments that lay the foundations for private sector prosperity.

Like private investments, well-chosen public investments raise future living standards. As a consequence, deficit reduction at the expense of public investment has been and will continue to be self-defeating. That is why our budget package increases much-needed public investment even as it takes steps to reduce the budget deficit. One without the other will not work.

With the help of the Congress, our public investment initiatives in the areas of technology, infrastructure, the environment, and education and training received about 70 percent of the funding we requested in fiscal year 1994. We increased funding for such proven successes as Head Start and the WIC program in the human resources area, and the Advanced Technology Program of the National Institute of Standards and Technology in the area of technological research. We also launched a number of new initiatives, including the National Service program, a new program of empowerment zones and enterprise communities for urban and rural development, and several new technology programs, including the Technology Reinvestment Project, designed to help defense contractors retool to serve civilian markets. We increased funding for research into new environmental technologies. In addition, we developed a comprehensive, cost-effective Climate Change Action Plan, comprising nearly 50 initiatives to reduce U.S. greenhouse gas emissions to 1990 levels by the year 2000.

As these examples bear witness, we have made significant progress on our investment agenda, but much more remains to be done. We will have to work together to find room to fund essential new investments even as we reduce real government outlays to meet tight annual caps on discretionary spending. This will not be easy. But it is essential, for we face a dual challenge—we must fundamentally change the composition of discretionary spending even as we reduce it in real terms.

This year my Administration is requesting funding for several new investment initiatives. Our Goals 2000 proposal will encourage local innovation in and accelerate the pace of school reform. It will link world-class academic and occupational standards to grassroots education reforms all across America. Our School-to-Work initiative will provide opportunities for post-secondary training for those not going on to college. Our reemployment and training program will streamline today's patchwork of training programs and make them a source of new skills for people who lose their jobs. Finally, our proposed welfare reform will provide the support, job training, and child care necessary to move people off welfare after 2 years. That is the only way we will make welfare what it ought to be: a second chance, not a way of life.

Reforming Our Health Care System

This year we will also make history by reforming the Nation's health care system. We face a health care crisis that demands a solution, both for the health of our citizens and for the health of our economy over the long run. The United States today spends more on health care relative to the size of its economy than any other advanced industrial country. Yet we insure a smaller fraction of our population, and we rank poorly on important overall health indicators such as life expectancy and infant mortality. Over 15 percent of Americans—nearly 39 million people—were uninsured throughout 1992. And tens of millions more have inadequate insurance or risk becoming uninsured should they lose their jobs. Meanwhile health care costs continue to climb, increasing premiums and medical bills for American families and aggravating budget crises at all levels of government. Both the Office of Management and Budget and the Congressional Budget Office have concluded that unless the system is reformed, rising health care costs will begin pushing the Federal budget deficit back upward as this century comes to a close.

Piecemeal approaches to solving our health care crisis will not work. If we simply squeeze harder on Federal health spending, without attempting systemwide reform, more of the costs of covering health services guaranteed by the government will be shifted to the private sector, and medical care for the elderly, the disadvantaged, and the disabled will be put at risk. Similarly, if we attempt to provide universal coverage without complementary measures to improve competition and sharpen incentives for cost-conscious decisions, costs will continue to escalate.

Our health care reform proposal, while bold and comprehensive, builds on the strengths of our current, market-based system. Our approach preserves consumer choice and our largely employer-based private insurance arrangements. It relies on market competition and private incentives, not price controls and bureaucracy, to provide health security for all Americans, to rein in health care costs, and to solve our long-run budget deficit problem.

Opening Foreign Markets

Raising the living standards of all Americans is the fundamental economic goal of my Administration. That is why all of our initiatives in international trade share a common purpose: to open markets and promote American exports. This emphasis on exports is driven by two simple facts. First, America is part of an increasingly integrated world economy and must adapt to this new reality if we are to stay on top. There is simply no way to close our borders and return to the insular days of the 1950s. To try to do so would be an exercise in futility, doomed not only to fail but to lower living standards in the process. Second, export industries offer the kind of high-wage, high-skill jobs the country needs. By shifting production toward more exports, we will shift the composition of employment toward better jobs. In short, to realize our goal of higher living standards for all Americans, we must compete, not retreat.

The year just past will go down in the history books as a watershed for trade liberalization. With your help, we enacted the North American Free Trade Agreement, which links the United States, Canada, and Mexico together in the world's largest marketplace. We also successfully completed the Uruguay Round of the General Agreement on Tariffs and Trade, which promises to add as much as $100 billion to $200 billion to the Nation's output by the end of a decade. And we are now on a course of increasing trade and investment liberalization with the rapidly growing economies of East Asia and the Pacific, which will be a major source of new export opportunities for American products in the coming years. At home we have eliminated much of our export control system and have rationalized our export promotion activities to help our producers, workers, and farmers increase their sales around the world.

Improving the Efficiency of Government

My Administration is committed to improving the Federal government's efficiency across the board. The National Performance Review (NPR), completed under the bold leadership of Vice President Gore, provides a road map for what must be done. The NPR's report shows how substantial budgetary savings can be realized by making existing programs more efficient and cutting those that are no longer necessary. As a result of our efforts to reinvent how the government performs, we will reduce the Federal bureaucracy by 252,000 positions, bringing it down to the lowest level in decades.

My Administration is also committed to reducing the burden of government regulations by improving the regulatory review process. My Executive Order on Regulatory Planning and Review requires that all new regulations carefully balance costs and benefits, that only those regulations whose benefits exceed their costs be adopted, and that in each case the most cost-effective regulations be chosen.

This year we will also work with the Congress to develop the new regulatory framework required to encourage the development of the national information superhighway. We must cooperate with the private sector to connect every classroom, every library, and every hospital in America to this highway by the year 2000. Rapid access to the most advanced information available will increase productivity and living standards, help to educate our children, and help health providers improve medical care for our citizens.

The Economic Outlook

An economic strategy built on long-run investments will not bear fruit overnight. But there are already signs that our policy initiatives are beginning to pay off. Prospects for sustained economic expansion look far brighter now than they did a year ago, when my Administration first asked for your support. Growth of real gross domestic product increased steadily over the course of 1993, and the economic expansion has continued into 1994. Consumer spending should remain healthy because of continued gains in employment and output, and investment spending should remain strong because of low long-term interest rates and increasing levels of demand. Low interest rates will also continue to support the recent expansion in residential construction. The Administration forecasts that the economy will grow at 3 percent in 1994 and will remain on track to create 8 million jobs over 4 years.

As 1994 begins, our economy is strong and growing stronger. With continued deficit reduction, more public investment, a reformed health care system, increased exports, and a reinvented government, we can create the foundations for an even more prosperous America.

William J Clinton

THE WHITE HOUSE
FEBRUARY 14, 1994

THE ANNUAL REPORT
OF THE
COUNCIL OF ECONOMIC ADVISERS

LETTER OF TRANSMITTAL

COUNCIL OF ECONOMIC ADVISERS,
Washington, D.C., February 4, 1994.

MR. PRESIDENT:

The Council of Economic Advisers herewith submits its 1993 Annual Report in accordance with the provisions of the Employment Act of 1946 as amended by the Full Employment and Balanced Growth Act of 1978.

Sincerely,

Laura D'Andrea Tyson
Chair

Alan S. Blinder
Member

Joseph E. Stiglitz
Member

CONTENTS

	Page
CHAPTER 1. A STRATEGY FOR GROWTH AND CHANGE	21
The Legacy of the Recent Past	22
Inadequate Recovery from Recession	22
Inadequate Productivity Growth	23
Worsening Income Inequality	25
Large Deficits, Mounting Debt	26
Inadequate Public Investment	29
Prosperity and Growth: The Benefits of Economic Change	30
Reducing the Deficit to Promote Capital Formation	31
Investing in People	39
Investing in Public Infrastructure	41
Investing in Technology	43
Trade Policy and Living Standards	45
Health Care Reform	48
Summary: Prosperity and Change	49
Creating Opportunity	50
Summary	53
CHAPTER 2. THE U.S. ECONOMY IN 1993 AND BEYOND	55
Struggling to Grow	56
The End of the Cold War	56
Weak Foreign Economies	57
The Debt Workout	59
Oversupply of Commercial Buildings	61
Credit Crunch	63
Corporate Downsizings	63
The Headwinds Are Mostly Calming	64
Overview of the Economy in 1993	64
Consumption Expenditures	65
Business Fixed Investment	66
Inventories	66
Residential Investment	68
Net Exports	68
Employment and Productivity	68
Incomes	69
Inflation	69
Monetary Policy	70
Fiscal Policies and the Timing of Output	70

	Page
The Federal Government's Fiscal Stance	75
Industrial and Regional Disparities	76
Deficit Reduction and the Real Interest Rate	78
How Deficit Reduction Reduces Long-Term Interest Rates	81
Short-Run Effects of Interest Rates	84
Long-Term Effects of Deficit Reduction	85
The Economy's Response to Higher Income Taxes	87
Do Taxes Change Behavior?	88
Do Higher Tax Rates Increase Tax Revenues?	89
The Economic Outlook	90
Risks to the Forecast	92
Sources of Long-Run Growth	93
Conclusion	95
CHAPTER 3. TRENDS AND RECENT DEVELOPMENTS IN THE U.S. LABOR MARKET	97
Employment Growth	98
A Slow Recovery	99
Sources of Job Growth	101
Unemployment and Nonemployment	103
Trends	103
Is the Natural Rate of Unemployment Increasing? ...	110
Direct Measures of the Natural Rate	112
The Magnitude and Costs of Job Loss	114
Slowing Wage Growth and Widening Inequality	115
Slow Income Growth	115
Growing Inequality	115
Explaining Slow Wage Growth	117
Explaining the Growth of Inequality	118
Job Quality	121
Hours of Work	121
Job Stability	123
Benefits	127
Toward a Comprehensive Work Force Policy	128
CHAPTER 4. Health Care Reform	131
Universal Coverage and Health Security	133
Insurance Market Reform	137
Insuring Major Risks and Preexisting Conditions	137
Community Rating	138
Reducing Administrative Costs	139
Creating a More Efficient Market and Containing Costs	140
Explaining Cost Increases	144
Who Pays for Health Care?	145
Health Care and Government Budgets	149
The Architecture of the Health Security Act	151
Elements of Reform	151

	Page
Providing Comprehensive Benefits	153
Organizing the Insurance Market	154
Paying for Insurance	155
Providing Discounts	157
Using Savings to Guarantee Health Security and Reduce the Deficit	159
Economic Effects of the Health Security Act	163
Macroeconomic Effects	163
Sectoral Effects	163
Conclusion	167
CHAPTER 5. MICROECONOMIC INITIATIVES TO PROMOTE EFFICIENCY AND PRODUCTIVITY	169
Promoting Efficiency in the Public and Private Sectors	170
Creating a More Effective Government	170
Promoting Competition	173
More Efficient Regulation of Natural Monopolies	175
Addressing Environmental Externalities	179
Managing Resources on Federal Lands	181
Climate Change Action Plan	184
Superfund Reauthorization: the Administration Position	186
Sustainable Development and Green Accounting	188
Promoting Technology	189
Principles of Technology Policy	190
The Administration's Technology Initiatives	194
Technology Policy, Growth, and Competitiveness	204
CHAPTER 6. THE UNITED STATES IN THE WORLD ECONOMY	205
Trends in U.S. Trade	206
Trade, Jobs, and Wage Inequality	212
The Administration's Trade Initiatives	214
Domestic Initiatives: The National Export Strategy	214
Bilateral Negotiations	215
Regional Initiatives	225
Multilateral Initiatives: The Uruguay Round	233
The Trade Policy Agenda	238
Trade and the Environment	238
International Trade and Competition Policy	239
Regionalism	240
Foreign Exchange Market Developments	240
The European Monetary System	243
The European Currencies in Turmoil	244
The Maastricht Treaty on Economic and Monetary Union	245
Conclusions	247

APPENDIXES
- A. Report to the President on the Activities of the Council of Economic Advisers During 1993 249
- B. Statistical Tables Relating to Income, Employment, and Production 261

LIST OF TABLES

	Page
1-1 Structural Budget Deficit as Percent of GDP	27
1-2 Effect of OBRA93 on Fiscal 1998 Budget	32
1-3 Distribution of the Change in Taxes Under OBRA93 by Income Category	33
1-4 Changes in Statutory Marginal Tax Rates Under OBRA93 for Married Individuals Filing Jointly	34
1-5 Contributions to Growth of Interest-Sensitive and Other Components of GDP	36
1-6 Structural Budget Deficits	37
1-7 Sources of U.S. Economic Growth	44
2-1 Foreign Country Real GDP Growth	59
2-2 Administration Forecasts	92
2-3 Accounting for Growth in Real GDP, 1960-99	94
4-1 Health Perception and Health Status by Type of Insurance Coverage, 1987	136
4-2 Distribution of Population and Health Spending by Spending Category, Estimates for 1994	145
4-3 Sources and Uses of Health Care Funds, 1991	147
4-4 Estimated Premiums in the Regional Alliance, 1994	156
4-5 Discounts Under the Health Security Act in 2000	158
4-6 Caps on Premiums by Firm Size	159
4-7 Allowed Growth Rates of Alliance Premiums	160
4-8 New Federal Spending and Savings Due to Reform	162
4-9 Sources and Uses of Federal Funds Under Reform, 2000	162
4-10 Employer Payments for Health Care: Baseline and Reform, 2000	166
6-1 U.S. Merchandise Trade by Industry, 1972 and 1992	209
6-2 U.S. Merchandise Trade by World Region, 1972 and 1992	210
6-3 Stock of U.S. Outward and Inward Foreign Direct Investment, 1992	212
6-4 U.S. Merchandise Trade Balances with Selected Countries, 1987-92	216
6-5 Selected Trade Indicators for Six Industrialized Countries, 1990	216
6-6 Intrafirm Trade as Share of Total U.S. Exports to and Imports from Europe and Japan, 1992	218

LIST OF CHARTS

		Page
1-1	Growth of Real GDP in Recoveries	23
1-2	Real Income, Productivity, and Compensation	24
1-3	Shares of Total After-Tax Income by Income Category	25
1-4a	Federal Budget Deficits With and Without 1993 Deficit Reduction Package	28
1-4b	Net Federal Debt as Percent of GDP	28
1-5	Federal Civilian Fixed Investment as Percent of GDP	30
1-6	Federal Deficits and Real Interest Rates	31
1-7	Correlation of Investment and Productivity	37
1-8	Ratio of Wages of College Graduates to Wages of High School Graduates	40
1-9	Ratio of Public to Private Net Nonresidential Capital Stock	43
1-10	Projected Real Growth Rates of Principal Federal Budget Components	49
1-11	Shares of Wages and Benefits in Compensation	50
1-12	Earned Income Tax Credit for Families with Two or More Children	52
2-1	Recovery Pattern of Nonfarm Payroll Employment	57
2-2	National Defense Purchases as Share of GDP	58
2-3	U.S. Merchandise Exports to Various Trading Partners	60
2-4	U.S. Exports Implied by Industrial Country GDP	60
2-5	Households: Credit Market Debt as Percentage of Disposable Income	62
2-6	Nonfinancial Corporate Business: Credit Market Debt as Percentage of Output	62
2-7	Defense Spending: Actual Versus Baseline	72
2-8	Effects of 1992 Tax Withholding Change on Personal Consumption	73
2-9	Alternative Measures of the Stance of Fiscal Policy	76
2-10		77
2-11		77
2-12	Ten-Year Treasury Note Yields	79
2-13	Real Interest Rates	80
2-14	Federal Debt as Percent of Nominal GDP	82
2-15	Dynamic Effects of Deficit Reduction	86
2-16	Personal Income Taxes as a Share of GDP	90
3-1	Changes in Output and Payroll Employment in First Eleven Quarters of Recovery	100
3-2	Employment and Output in Recoveries	101
3-3	Civilian Unemployment Rate	105
3-4	Long-Term Unemployment as Share of Total Unemployment	106

List of Charts—Continued

		Page
3–5	Long-Term Unemployment and the Unemployment Rate	106
3–6	Employment-to-Population Ratios of Women	107
3–7	Unemployment Rates by Educational Attainment, March 1993	108
3–8	Ratio of White-Collar to Blue-Collar Unemployment Rates	109
3–9	Real Hourly Compensation and Wages	116
3–10	Average Annual Growth of Mean Family Income by Income Quintile	117
3–11	Productivity Growth and Price Reductions, 1950–90	118
3–12	Average Weekly Hours of Production and Nonsupervisory Workers	122
3–13	Help Supply Industry Employment as Share of Total Employment	124
3–14	Part-Time Employment: Total and Voluntary	125
3–15	Reallocation of Employment Between Industries	126
4–1	Distribution of Population by Source of Health Insurance Coverage: 1991	134
4–2	Sources of Payment for Health Care by Insurance Status: 1994 Estimates	135
4–3	Administrative Expenses of Commercial Insurers as a Share of Claims Paid	140
4–4	Health Expenditure and Life Expectancy in Industrial Countries	141
4–5	Estimates of Inappropriate Care for Five Common Procedures	144
4–6	Sources of Health Care Financing as Percent of Total Expenditures	148
4–7	Government Spending on Health Care as Percent of Total Government Revenues	150
4–8	Health Expenditures as Percent of GDP	162
4–9	Business Spending on Health Insurance	165
6–1	U.S. Trade as Share of Real Gross Domestic Product	207
6–2	U.S. Exports of Goods and Services	208
6–3	Nominal and Real Effective Dollar Exchange Rates	241
6–4	Exchange Rates of the Dollar Against Selected Currencies	242
6–5	French Franc-Deutsche Mark Exchange Rates	246

List of Boxes

		Page
1–1	The New Measure of Unemployment	22
1–2	Saving, Investment, and Current Account Deficits	29

List of Boxes—Continued

		Page
1–3	Credible Deficit Reduction and Real Interest Rates	35
1–4	A Balanced Budget Amendment to the Constitution?	39
1–5	The National Service Program	42
1–6	How Does the Earned Income Tax Credit Work?	51
2–1	The Economic Effects of the Midwest Floods of 1993	67
2–2	The Economic Effects of Lower Oil Prices	71
2–3	Are Current Long-Term Interest Rates Sustainable?	81
2–4	Estimating the Long-Run Effects of Deficit Reduction	87
3–1	The New Current Population Survey	104
3–2	Growing Inequality of Employment and Unemployment	116
3–3	Consequences of Productivity Growth	119
3–4	Why Productivity Growth Does Not Cause Unemployment	120
4–1	Moral Hazard and Adverse Selection	137
4–2	Recent Reductions in Health Care Inflation	146
4–3	Capped Entitlements	164
5–1	Selected National Performance Review Recommendations	172
5–2	Market Power	174
5–3	Natural Monopoly	176
5–4	Externalities	180
6–1	U.S. Exports: More Than Peanuts	209
6–2	The Case of the Polish Golf Carts	224
6–3	Mexican Economic Reforms	226
6–4	The Asian "Miracle"	232
6–5	The Economic Impact of the Uruguay Round	234
6–6	The Uruguay Round and U.S. Trade Laws	237
6–7	Exchange-Rate Volatility and International Trade	244
6–8	Criteria for Joining the Economic and Monetary Union	247

CHAPTER 1

A Strategy for Growth and Change

ON ELECTION DAY 1992, the American economy faced a number of daunting challenges—both short term and long term. The principal short-term problem was that recovery from the 1990–91 recession had been disappointing in almost all respects. Real gross domestic product (GDP) had grown at only a 2.2-percent annual rate from the first quarter of 1991 through the third quarter of 1992, less than half the pace of a typical recovery. Payroll employment had actually fallen during the first year of recovery and had risen a scant 0.4 percent from March 1991 to October 1992. Furthermore, the seesaw pattern that had plagued the recovery raised fears that the weak economy might relapse into recession.

But America's long-run problems ran deeper and their causes were less well understood. While U.S. workers and firms remained the world's most productive, our productivity *growth* had been sluggish for almost two decades. In consequence, real hourly compensation and GDP per capita had advanced extremely slowly, and real median family income had barely increased at all. In addition, inequality had been rising for more than a decade, leaving the American economy with the most unequal distribution of income in its postwar history. The combination of stagnant average incomes and widening dispersion meant that many middle-class and low-income families had actually suffered declines in their real incomes.

Finally, the Federal budget deficit was large and rising, the national debt had been growing faster than GDP for about a decade, and huge amounts of foreign borrowing had transformed the United States from the world's biggest creditor nation into its biggest debtor.

National economic policy was the major cause of some of our economic difficulties, such as the Federal budget deficit, but only a contributing factor to others, such as growing income inequality. Although the economic policy agenda of the new Administration cannot cure all of these problems overnight, steps we have taken have already contributed to noticeable progress on several fronts. The recovery has solidified. Job growth has resumed. Fiscal policies that will reduce the Federal deficit substantially have been put in place. Although much more needs to be done, taxes have been made more progressive and starts have been made on education and labor market policies that will address the inequality problem.

And, perhaps most fundamentally of all, the Administration has embarked on a comprehensive investment agenda designed to raise productivity, which is the wellspring of higher living standards in the long run.

This chapter explains the Administration's economic strategy and examines some of the specific policy initiatives that have been undertaken to pursue that strategy. The chapters that follow provide much more detail.

THE LEGACY OF THE RECENT PAST

The policies of any new Administration are dictated in part by the challenges it faces and the problems it inherits from the past. Because America's current problems are both short run and long run in nature, the solutions must be, too.

INADEQUATE RECOVERY FROM RECESSION

Short-run cyclical problems are, almost by definition, transitory. But when the American macroeconomy performs poorly, that one fact seems to overwhelm all others and crowd out consideration of longer run problems. In fact, the U.S. economy has been operating well below its productive capacity for years now. From 1989 through 1992, real GDP grew only 1.5 percent per year, and the civilian unemployment rate (by what was the standard measure until this year—Box 1-1) has remained above 6 percent since November 1990. Under such circumstances, public concerns with economic policy tend to be summarized in a single word: jobs.

Box 1-1.—The New Measure of Unemployment

Beginning with its February 4 announcement of the January 1994 unemployment rate, the Bureau of Labor Statistics has changed its principal measure of joblessness. The changes, reflecting technical improvements in the household survey used to estimate unemployment (Chapter 3 contains more details), are expected to increase the measured unemployment rate by about 0.5 to 0.6 percentage point, although the precise amount is impossible to know. All unemployment numbers used in this *Report* are measured on the old, traditional basis.

As Chart 1-1 shows, the recovery that began in the second quarter of 1991 has been exceptionally slow by historical standards—so slow, in fact, that the unemployment rate was still rising more than a year into the "recovery." Only in mid-1993 did unemployment fall back to its rate at the recession trough. Growth has been not only slow but extremely uneven, proceeding in fits and starts which have left consumers and business people wondering how long the recovery would last.

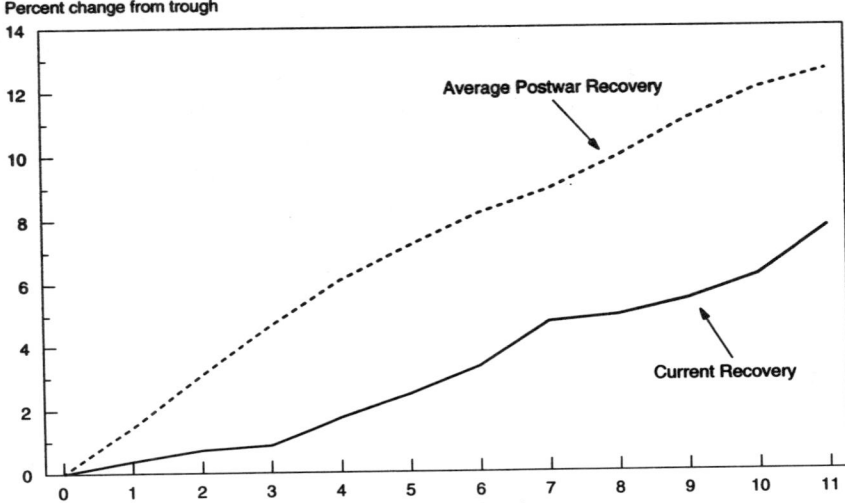

Chart 1-1 **Growth of Real GDP in Recoveries**
Real GDP in the current recovery has grown at only about half the rate of the typical post-World War II recovery.

Note: "Average" includes all recoveries from 1954 to 1982, except 1980. The trough quarter for the current recovery is first quarter 1991.
Sources: Department of Commerce and National Bureau of Economic Research.

Thus the Administration's first task was to put the recovery on a sound footing—not to produce a short-run burst of activity, but to lay the groundwork for a sustained expansion that would restore confidence and encourage firms to resume hiring. In large measure this task was accomplished in 1993. (Chapter 2 provides more details.) Sluggish economic growth in the first half of the year gave way to solid growth in the second half. More important, job growth began in earnest: Employers added about 2 million jobs to nonfarm payrolls between December 1992 and December 1993. As 1994 began, the outlook for sustained expansion looked brighter than it had in a long time.

INADEQUATE PRODUCTIVITY GROWTH

The economy's longer run problems will not be dealt with so quickly. They require sustained attention over a long period of time. Primary among them is the troubling fact that growth in productivity has been anemic for about two decades.

Chart 1-2 shows the remarkable slowdown in productivity growth that occurred around 1973—from an annual average of 3.1 percent in the 1947-73 period to just 1.0 percent since 1973. In part, this slowdown is exaggerated by the fact that the first few postwar decades were aberrant: There was much catching up to do after the Great Depression and the Second World War. But America's long-run average productivity growth rate over the century leading up to 1973 was slightly above 2 percent per year; since 1973 it has averaged about 1 percent. At 2-percent growth, productivity doubles in 35 years; at 1-percent growth, doubling takes 70 years. Even seemingly modest changes in productivity can have dramatic effects on living standards in the long run. Thus the Nation has much at stake in improving its productivity growth rate.

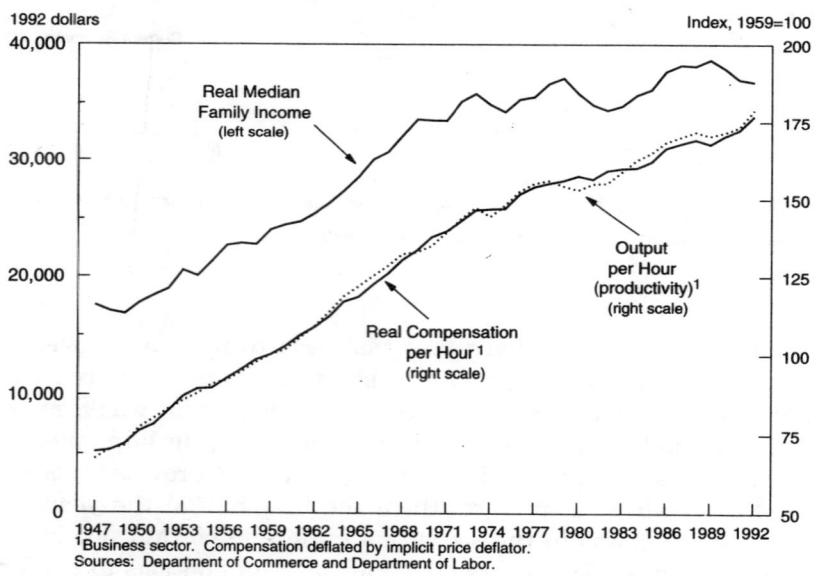

Chart 1-2 **Real Income, Productivity, and Compensation**
Productivity, real income, and real hourly compensation all slowed markedly around 1973.

[1] Business sector. Compensation deflated by implicit price deflator.
Sources: Department of Commerce and Department of Labor.

Labor productivity—output per hour of work—may seem an abstract concept, of more interest to analysts than to working men and women. But without productivity growth, higher real wages would lead directly to lower employment as profit-oriented firms reacted to higher labor costs by trimming their work forces. It is only steady productivity gains that enable the economy to generate more jobs and rising real wages at the same time. Chart 1-2 shows that growth in both real compensation per hour and real median family income slowed markedly at just about the time that productivity growth slowed. This coincidence in time is, of course, no coincidence at all. Productivity growth is the ultimate source of growing real wages and family incomes.

Nothing is more important to the long-run well-being of the U.S. economy than accelerating productivity growth. Most of the Administration's economic strategy is therefore devoted to that end.

WORSENING INCOME INEQUALITY

Starting some time in the late 1970s, income inequalities widened alarmingly in America. Chart 1-3 shows that the share of the Nation's income received by the richest 5 percent of American families rose from 18.6 percent in 1977 to 24.5 percent in 1990, while the share of the poorest 20 percent fell from 5.7 percent to 4.3 percent. Part of this change was due to the cuts in taxes and social spending of the early 1980s, the net benefits of which were heavily skewed toward the rich. But there was a much more powerful force at work, one not attributable to fiscal policy: The distribution of *wage rates* grew substantially more unequal. In real terms, wages at the bottom of the distribution fell while wages at the top rose.

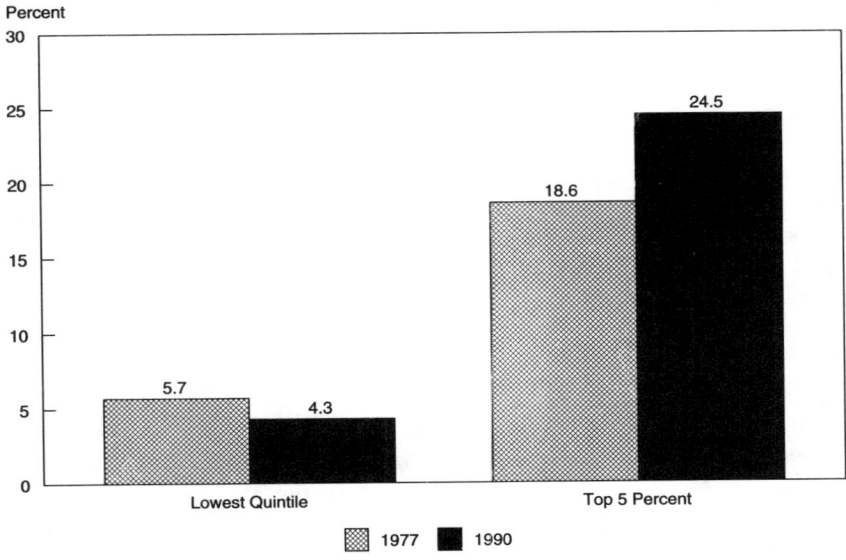

Chart 1-3 **Shares of Total After-Tax Income by Income Category**
The richest 5 percent of Americans saw their share of total income rise sharply in the 1980s, while the poorest 20 percent saw their share decline.

Source: Congressional Budget Office.

The forces underlying this widening of the wage distribution are not well understood. (More details are contained in Chapter 3.) But the facts are stark. Between 1979 and 1990, the real median income of males with 4 years of college fell about 1 percent, but that of males with only 4 years of high school fell a stunning 21 percent, and high school dropouts fared even worse. A similar pattern emerges almost any way one slices the data: Wages near the top of the distribution rose faster than wages near the bottom. Salaries of chief executive officers rose rapidly while the minimum wage fell in real terms. Wages of skilled workers rose faster than those of the unskilled. Wages of experienced workers grew faster than entry-level wages.

The widening dispersion of wages accounts for most of the squeeze on the middle class, because the middle 60 percent of the income distribution derives about three-quarters of its income from wages and salaries. And these people do not bring home the highest wages, but those nearer the middle. When middle-class wages stagnate, middle-class family incomes do, too. That is precisely what happened in the 1980s.

In sum, for whatever reasons, in the late 1970s our market economy began to dish out more-handsome rewards to the well-off and stingier ones to the middle class. Government policies compounded the problem by weakening the social safety net, lowering the tax burdens of the wealthy, and driving up real interest rates. In concert, the market and the government produced the greatest disequalization of incomes since at least before World War II.

This Administration sees the combination of stagnating average incomes and rising inequality as a threat to the social fabric that has long bound Americans together and made ours a society with minimal class distinctions. Although the underlying forces of the market are vastly more powerful than anything the government can do, the right kinds of policies can make a difference. For example, changes in Federal tax policy have already shifted the burden of taxation away from the working poor and toward the well-to-do. And several initiatives in the human investment arena, described later in this chapter and in Chapter 3, should help mitigate rising wage inequality.

LARGE DEFICITS, MOUNTING DEBT

Of all the Nation's economic problems, the one most directly traceable to government policy is the large Federal budget deficit. Although the Federal budget has been in deficit almost every year of the postwar period, until the 1980s these deficits were small enough that the ratio of public debt to GDP was stable or falling. In fact, the structural budget (that is, the one that would result if the economy were at a high level of employment) after adjustment for inflation was on average roughly balanced for decades (Table 1–1). This approximate balance was not achieved by any formal, legal requirement, but rather through an informal, unstated political consensus.

TABLE 1–1.—*Structural Budget Deficit as Percent of GDP*

Fiscal years	Adjusted deficit as percent of GDP[1]
1959–1982	−0.1
1983–1993	1.9
1994–1998 (forecast)	.8

[1] Adjusted deficit is unified structural budget deficit corrected for depreciation of the value of Federal debt due to inflation.

Sources: Office of Management and Budget, Congressional Budget Office, and Council of Economic Advisers.

The budget picture changed dramatically with the tax cuts of the early 1980s, and the structural, inflation-adjusted budget began to display chronic, large deficits for the first time. The deficit in fiscal 1992, the last year before the election of President Clinton, was a whopping $290 billion in the unified budget and $131 billion on a structural, inflation-adjusted basis. Worse yet, both the deficit and the debt-GDP ratio were expected to rise further (Charts 1–4a and 1–4b).

Deficits of this magnitude—around 5 percent of GDP—would have been far less worrisome if American households were saving enough to cover both the government budget deficit and the needs of business to finance investment. But, in fact, American household saving rates not only are among the lowest in the world, but actually fell in the 1980s. So for both of these reasons—declining household saving and rising budget deficits—*national* saving as a share of GDP dropped sharply in the 1980s.

Casual discussions often equate national saving with domestic investment, but the two can differ in an open economy (Box 1–2). And in the United States of the 1980s, they differed dramatically. While national saving was falling as a share of GDP, the share of domestic investment, although low by international standards, was roughly constant. To plug the gap between saving and investment, the United States had to import massive amounts of foreign capital. In consequence, our current account balance went from a small surplus to a large deficit in the 1980s.

All this foreign capital had its positive side: By limiting the rise of real U.S. interest rates, it partly shielded investment from the consequences of huge Federal deficits. But it left the United States the greatest debtor nation in the world. Even more disturbing, all this borrowing from abroad went to *maintaining* the Nation's comparatively meager investment rate, not to increasing it.

Chart 1-4a **Federal Budget Deficits With and Without 1993 Deficit Reduction Package**
Budget deficits will now reverse course. Deficits would have kept rising without the reduction package.

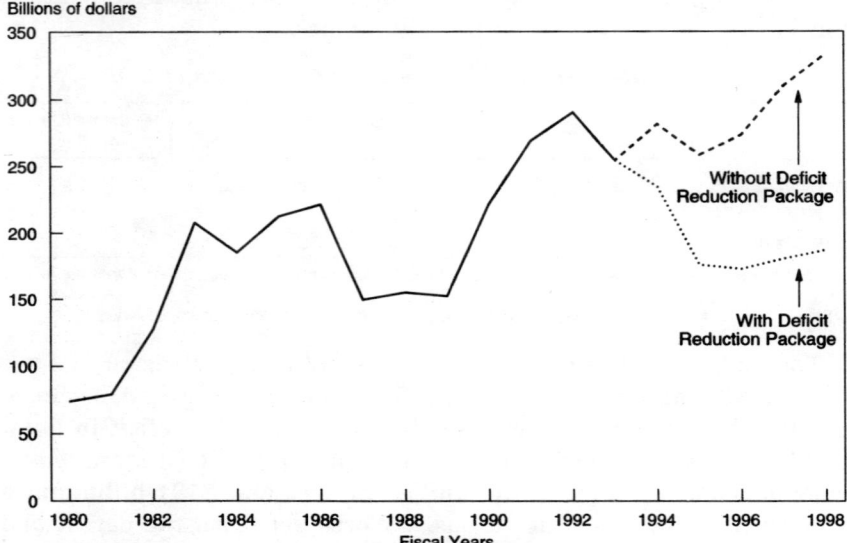

Note: Data exclude health care reform. Projected for fiscal years 1994-98.
Source: Office of Management and Budget.

Chart 1-4b **Net Federal Debt as Percent of GDP**
Federal indebtedness as a percent of GDP is expected to plateau after fiscal 1994 under OBRA93, instead of rising as estimated without deficit reduction.

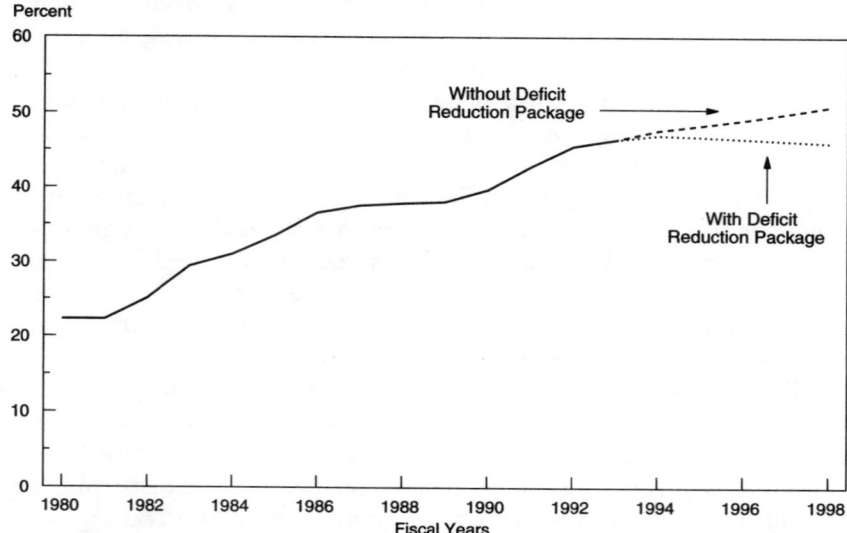

Note: Net federal debt defined as debt held by the public less debt held by the Federal Reserve. Data exclude health care reform. Projected for fiscal years 1994-98.
Sources: Council of Economic Advisers and Office of Management and Budget.

> **Box 1–2.—Saving, Investment, and Current Account Deficits**
>
> Private saving, whether generated by households or by businesses, can be used for one of three purposes: to finance domestic private investment, to purchase debt issued by the government, or to purchase foreign assets. If private saving is insufficient to cover the sum of the first two uses—private investment and the combined deficit of all levels of government—we must borrow the difference from abroad. Such a shortage of saving has characterized the United States for about a decade now.
>
> When Americans borrow from foreigners, we run a surplus in our international *capital account*. But, since the capital account and the current account must balance under floating exchange rates, the mirror image of this capital account surplus is an equally large *current account deficit*. Thus, a country that saves less than it invests and runs a large budget deficit is bound to have a large current account deficit. Indeed, chronic, large current account deficits date from precisely the time that the United States started running huge fiscal deficits. Between 1981 and 1984 the overall government budget deficit rose from 1.0 percent of GDP to 2.9 percent. During those same years the current account balance went from a surplus of 0.2 percent of GDP to a deficit of 2.6 percent of GDP.

The legacy of foreign debt was not the only cost of our addiction to foreign borrowing. To attract the needed capital to American shores, the United States had to offer interest rates higher than those prevailing in the other leading industrialized countries. This gap between U.S. and foreign interest rates, in turn, led to a sharp appreciation of the dollar, as foreign investors demanded more dollar-denominated assets. The sky-high dollar made life exceedingly pleasant for American tourists in Europe in the mid-1980s. But it handicapped portions of American industry by making many U.S. manufactured goods uncompetitive on world markets. It has taken years for our manufacturing sector to recover from this shock.

INADEQUATE PUBLIC INVESTMENT

The budget deficit and the trade deficit were major national concerns in the 1980s and on into the 1990s. But there was also a third deficit: a shortage of funds for public investment in critical national needs like education and training, transportation facilities, and environmental infrastructure.

The share of Federal civilian fixed investment in GDP is only about half what it was in the 1960s (Chart 1–5). Furthermore, the share of the Federal budget devoted to *all* types of public investment—including education and research and development, as well as civilian and military fixed investment—fell from 35 percent in 1963 to 17 percent in 1992. As the 1990s started, more and more Americans were becoming painfully aware that our public investment was not what it should be.

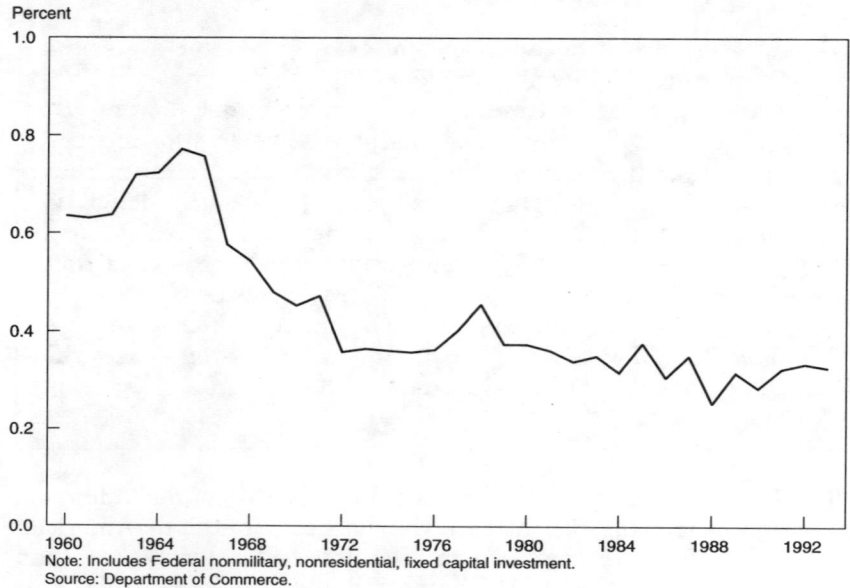

Chart 1-5 **Federal Civilian Fixed Investment as Percent of GDP**
Relative to GDP, the Federal government invested little more than half as much in nonmilitary infrastructure in the 1980s as it had in the 1960s.

Note: Includes Federal nonmilitary, nonresidential, fixed capital investment.
Source: Department of Commerce.

PROSPERITY AND GROWTH: THE BENEFITS OF ECONOMIC CHANGE

The economic strategy of this Administration follows logically from this legacy. We must secure the expansion and spur long-term economic growth. We must reverse the trend toward rising inequality. We must reduce Federal borrowing and shrink the trade deficit. We must invest more in both private and public capital. And we must bolster our human resources.

While the Administration's economic policy agenda is broad and varied, it can be summarized in a single word: *investment*—investment in private capital, investment in people, investment in public infrastructure, investment in technology, and investment in environmental preservation. Six major themes stand out and define the essence of the Administration's economic strategy: deficit reduction;

investments in human capital; investments in public infrastructure; investments in technology; expanding international trade; and health care reform.

REDUCING THE DEFICIT TO PROMOTE CAPITAL FORMATION

The legacy of large and growing Federal budget deficits required that first attention be devoted to their reduction, so as to free up resources for expansion of private physical capital—the machines, factories, and offices that make American labor more productive. For too long, Federal budget deficits have been gobbling up an inordinate share of the Nation's saving, thereby keeping real interest rates too high (Chart 1-6) and leaving the Nation with a Hobson's choice between lower domestic investment and higher foreign borrowing. Reducing the budget deficit was a necessary part of clearing away the financial underbrush that had grown up around us in the 1980s—so that economic growth could be put on a sounder and more sustained footing.

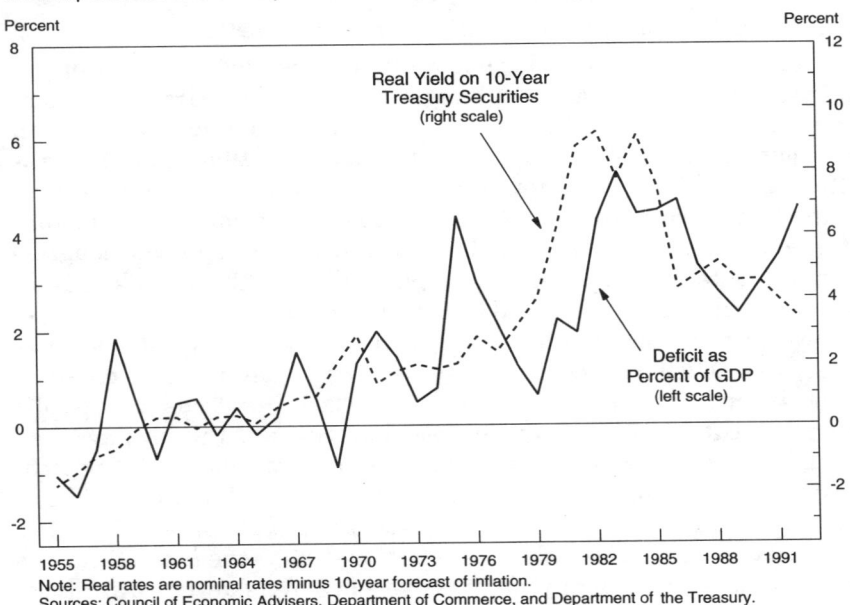

Chart 1-6 **Federal Deficits and Real Interest Rates**
Interest rates adjusted for inflation rose and fell sharply in the 1980s, in tandem with the sharp increase and subsequent decrease in the Federal budget deficit.

Note: Real rates are nominal rates minus 10-year forecast of inflation.
Sources: Council of Economic Advisers, Department of Commerce, and Department of the Treasury.

Deficit reduction is difficult and painful. But the President concluded that the Nation could not remain on the path bequeathed us by the previous Administration—a path on which the national debt was growing faster than GDP and deficits were threatening to explode (Chart 1–4). So he gave first priority to putting the Nation's fiscal house back in order.

Policy changes in the President's deficit reduction package will gradually reduce the Federal deficit after 5 years by 1¾ percent of GDP. By fiscal 1998, the last year of the program, the deficit is expected to be $146 billion below what it otherwise would have been: falling from $333 billion to $187 billion (Table 1–2). The ratio of debt to GDP at the end of fiscal 1998 falls from a projected 51 percent without the deficit reduction program to 46 percent with it.

TABLE 1–2.—*Effect of OBRA93 on Fiscal 1998 Budget*
[Billions of dollars]

Item	Before OBRA93	After OBRA93	Change
Outlays	1,825.5	1,738.2	−87.3
Discretionary	584.3	548.1	−36.2
Mandatory	970.6	945.0	−25.6
Debt service	270.5	245.0	−25.5
Revenue	1,492.2	1,550.8	58.6
Deficit	333.2	187.4	−145.8

Note.—Data exclude health reform.
Source: Office of Management and Budget.

The Omnibus Budget Reconciliation Act of 1993

Because the President did not want to delay deficit reduction for another year, the fiscal 1994 budget had to be prepared on a compressed schedule. The President introduced a detailed budget plan to a joint session of the Congress in February 1993, just 4 weeks after taking office. The House and Senate passed the final version of the budget resolution on April 1—the earliest date in the history of the modern congressional budget process. A spirited congressional debate followed, leading to enactment of the Omnibus Budget Reconciliation Act of 1993 (OBRA93) in August.

Several principles guided the design of OBRA93. First and foremost, the deficit reduction had to be large, genuine, and credible. To this end, the Administration proposed hundreds of specific spending cuts and increases in revenue. Second, the package had to be balanced between expenditure cuts and tax increases. Specifically, the $146 billion of deficit reduction in fiscal 1998 consists of $87 billion in net spending cuts—including $25 billion in lower debt service—and $59 billion in additional net revenue. Third, the tax increases were highly progressive—heavily skewed toward the people who are most able to pay and who benefited most from the large tax cuts of the early 1980s. Income tax rates were raised for only about the top 1.2 percent of taxpayers. Some 90 percent of the new taxes in OBRA93 will be borne by the upper 6.5 percent of the income distribution (Table 1–3). Fourth, even while cutting the deficit, room had to be found in the budget for a variety of critical public investments (more on this below).

TABLE 1–3.—*Distribution of the Change in Taxes Under OBRA93 by Income Category*

Family income (dollars)[1]	Share of families (percent)	Average change in taxes (dollars per family)	Share of total change in taxes (percent)
Less than 10,000	14.0	−68	−2.5
10,000–20,000	17.4	−86	−3.9
20,000–30,000	15.7	−41	−1.7
30,000–40,000	12.6	50	1.6
40,000–50,000	9.9	105	2.7
50,000–75,000	15.5	192	7.8
75,000–100,000	6.8	312	5.6
100,000–200,000	5.2	649	8.8
200,000 or more	1.3	23,521	81.3
All incomes[2]	100.0	382	100.0

[1] Pretax family income (CBO definition).
[2] Total includes negative incomes, not included in categories above.
Source: Congressional Budget Office (CBO).

The spending cuts touched virtually every part of the budget. On the discretionary side, the Congress imposed what amounts to a 5-year freeze on nominal spending, capping fiscal 1998 spending at $548 billion, or about $2.5 billion below the fiscal 1993 level. With inflation (as measured by the implicit deflator for GDP) projected to average about 2.8 percent per year over the period, the implied cut in *real* discretionary spending is about 13 percent. Furthermore, if inflation comes in lower than the forecast, the caps will be lowered commensurately. The budget cuts in OBRA93 include a reduction in the Federal work force by 100,000 positions (since raised to 252,000 positions), delay of the 1994 cost-of-living adjustment for Federal employees, defense cutbacks beyond those projected by the previous Administration, and a host of smaller cuts in discretionary programs.

On the mandatory side of the budget, the largest cuts were in the medicare program (about $18 billion by fiscal 1998). But there were also reductions in agricultural and veterans' programs, savings in the student loan program, new receipts from auctioning portions of the radio spectrum (discussed in Chapter 5), and savings from shortening the maturity structure of the national debt. Total cuts in mandatory spending other than debt service are expected to reach $25.6 billion by fiscal 1998.

OBRA93 also increased taxes. Higher income tax rates on the top 1.2 percent of households constitute the biggest source of new revenue by far: $27.2 billion by fiscal 1998. (The bracket structures before and after OBRA93 are compared in Table 1-4.) In addition, the 2.9-percent payroll tax for medicare, which formerly applied only to the first $135,000 of earnings, now applies to all earnings (raising $7.2 billion by fiscal 1998), the taxable portion of Social Security benefits was raised for the top 13 percent of recipients ($4.5 billion), and the motor fuels tax went up by 4.3 cents per gallon in October 1993 ($5 billion). Finally, OBRA93 increased the top corporate tax rate and closed a variety of business tax loopholes, but also enhanced or created several tax incentives for investment. The net effect of these increases and decreases in business taxes should yield about $8 billion in revenue by fiscal 1998.

TABLE 1-4.—*Changes in Statutory Marginal Tax Rates Under OBRA93 for Married Individuals Filing Jointly*

Taxable income (dollars)	Marginal rate (percent) Old law	Marginal rate (percent) OBRA93
0-36,900	15	15
36,900-89,150	28	28
89,150-140,000	31	31
140,000-250,000	31	36
Over 250,000	31	39.6

Source: Department of the Treasury.

OBRA93, Interest Rates, and Investment

As critical elements of the President's deficit reduction package started to become known, long-term interest rates began to fall—indicating that the financial markets viewed the proposals as substantial, genuine, and credible (Box 1-3). Rates fell dramatically between January and October 1993 before backing off a bit late in the year.

As documented more completely in Chapter 2, the medicine of low interest rates now seems to be taking hold. Business investment has been leading the economy's expansion, with consumer durables and housing important sources of strength. If we divide GDP into its interest-sensitive components (business fixed investment, housing, and consumer durables) and everything else, the data tell a fascinating story. While the three interest-sensitive pieces typically account for about 30 percent of GDP growth, in 1993 they accounted for virtually all of GDP growth. The rest of GDP barely increased over the year (Table 1-5).

It is important to understand *why* this Administration made deficit reduction a top priority and worked so hard to see it through the Congress. One important reason was the concern being expressed in many quarters that deficits were growing out of control and might threaten financial stability—and thereby macroeconomic stability.

Box 1-3.—Credible Deficit Reduction and Real Interest Rates

Long-term nominal and real interest rates dropped sharply in 1993. The decline in rates was closely linked to the proposal and enactment of the Administration's budget (as argued in Chapter 2).

Lower deficits reduce real bond yields through several channels:

- Lower Federal borrowing reduces interest rates directly, by reducing demand for credit.
- A more prudent fiscal policy reduces the likelihood that the Federal Reserve will need to pursue a restrictive monetary policy, and so reduces expected future short-term rates.
- As long as international capital mobility is not perfect, increased national saving leads to an increase in investment. In the long run, the consequent increase in the capital stock reduces the marginal product of capital and therefore the interest rate.

Because the plan had credibility, financial markets anticipated these effects. Since future expected short-term interest rates govern current long-term rates, long rates fell immediately in response to the proposal and enactment of the Administration's plan. There would have been no such market response if the plan had lacked credibility. What features of the Administration's plan account for its apparently high credibility?

- The plan is based on realistic economic assumptions; it does not presume that the economy can "grow its way out" of the deficit problem.
- The President proposed and the Congress enacted many specific spending cuts in the fiscal 1994 budget, thereby demonstrating the feasibility of maintaining the discretionary spending caps.
- The tax provisions of the plan by and large result in permanent increases in revenue; they do not merely shift future revenue into the current budget window.
- The President showed himself willing to make difficult choices to correct the fiscal imbalance: freezing total discretionary spending; increasing the taxation of Social Security benefits for recipients with the highest incomes; and proposing reform of the Nation's health care system.

TABLE 1–5.—*Contributions to Growth of Interest-Sensitive and Other Components of GDP*

[Average annual percent change]

Component	Historical average (1955–92)	Fourth quarter 1992 to fourth quarter 1993 [1]
Interest-sensitive components [2]	0.8	2.6
All other	2.1	.2
GDP	2.9	2.8

[1] Preliminary.
[2] Business fixed investment, housing, and expenditures on consumer durables.
Source: Department of Commerce.

But the central objective of deficit reduction was and remains *expenditure switching*—away from consumption and government purchases toward investment. The lower interest rates brought about by deficit reduction are the way the market accomplishes this expenditure switching.

The reasons for wanting to raise the investment share of GDP are straightforward: Workers are more productive when they are equipped with more and better capital, more-productive workers earn higher real wages, and higher real wages are the mainspring of higher living standards. Few economic propositions are better supported than these—or more important. As Chart 1–7 shows, investment rates and productivity growth rates correlate well across countries. Lower budget deficits that raise private investment are therefore critical to raising the economy's long-run growth rate.

However, some people worry that deficit reduction might retard growth in the short run by siphoning off aggregate demand. Such a concern is justified. Deficit reduction *by itself* certainly does tend to contract the economy. After all, raising taxes and cutting government spending reduce the demand for goods and services. But deficit reduction *accompanied by sufficient declines in long-term interest rates* need not be contractionary. It is, of course, the latter, not the former, that we experienced in 1993.

Economists judge the impact of fiscal policy on aggregate demand by looking at changes in the *structural* deficit. Table 1–6 shows that OBRA93 will reduce the structural deficit by about $65 billion from fiscal 1993 to fiscal 1995, after which it is expected to rise slightly. The large deficit reductions after fiscal 1995 serve to limit what would otherwise have been even larger increases in the structural deficit—mainly due to rising expenditures on health care. Analysis by the Council of Economic Advisers suggests that the declines in long-term interest rates that have occurred since the 1992 election, even after the backup late in 1993, are more than enough to offset the contractionary effects of this decrease in the structural

Chart 1-7 **Correlation of Investment and Productivity**
There is a close correlation between investment rates and productivity growth rates across countries.

Average annual per capita real GDP growth rate (1970-90)

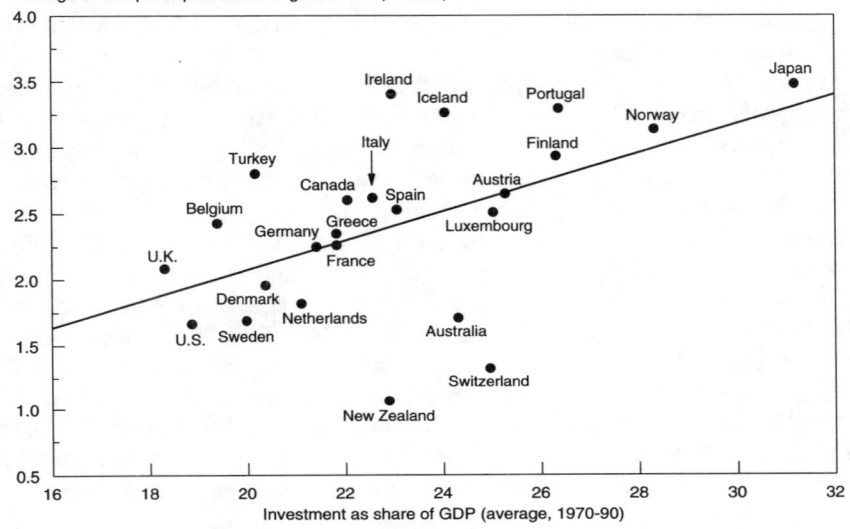

[Scatter plot showing countries plotted by Investment as share of GDP (average, 1970-90) on x-axis (16 to 32) versus Average annual per capita real GDP growth rate on y-axis (0.5 to 4.0). Countries shown include: Japan, Ireland, Iceland, Portugal, Norway, Italy, Finland, Turkey, Canada, Spain, Austria, Belgium, Greece, Luxembourg, Germany, U.K., France, Denmark, Netherlands, U.S., Sweden, Australia, Switzerland, New Zealand.]

Source: International Monetary Fund.

deficit. Hence the economy should be able to grow right through the deficit reduction period.

TABLE 1–6.—*Structural Budget Deficits*

Fiscal year	Structural deficit Billions of dollars	Percent of GDP
1992	206.0	3.5
1993	214.7	3.4
1994	190.8	2.9
1995	149.1	2.1
1996	156.1	2.1
1997	162.8	2.1
1998	171.4	2.1

Note.—Data for 1994–98 are forecasts excluding health reform.
Sources: Council of Economic Advisers, Congressional Budget Office, Office of Management and Budget, and Department of Commerce.

There are limits, however, to the amount of deficit reduction an economy can be expected to withstand within a short period without endangering economic growth. The Administration's judgment is that cutting the annual deficit by about $140 billion to $150 billion over a period of 5 years is roughly the right amount, given the current strength of our economy. Some critics dispute this judgment and call for much deeper cuts in spending than those provided in OBRA93, or for substantial increases in taxes. The Administration views this strategy of more aggressive deficit cutting in the near term as risky.

A *small* amount of additional deficit reduction would, of course, have only small effects on the economy. But further large spending cuts or tax increases at this time would require additional *large* declines in long-term interest rates to replace the lost aggregate demand. Should interest rates decline by less than the required amount, economic growth would slow and jobs would be lost. For example, a deficit reduction package substantially larger than OBRA93 would be needed to comply with the proposed balanced budget amendment to the Constitution (Box 1–4). The Council estimates that it would take a decline in long-term interest rates of roughly 3 percentage points to offset the contractionary effect of such a large fiscal package. Since a 3-percent long-term interest rate seems quite unlikely, complying with a balanced budget amendment seems likely to harm the economy—perhaps severely.

Deficit Reduction and Public Investment

Once it is understood that deficit reduction is not an end in itself, but a means to an end—the end of greater investment—two important principles become evident.

First, it is clear that deficit reduction is only a first step. We must start to build—to invest in our future. That is why the President's economic plan contains more than just deficit reduction; it also includes new proposals to encourage private investment and needed public investments in education and training, public infrastructure, and technology. We must worry about the debt we bequeath to our children, but we must also worry about the quality and quantity of capital—broadly conceived—that they will inherit.

Second, it is clear that squeezing worthwhile public investments out of the budget is the wrong way to reduce the deficit. After all, the main purpose of deficit reduction is to pave the way for more private investment. Cutting *public* investment to make room for more *private* investment is like running on a treadmill. America needs more of both, not a swap of one for the other.

Shifting Federal spending priorities from consumption to investment is one of the hallmarks of this Administration's approach to economic policy. We seek not only to constrain total government spending, but also to reorient it toward more productive uses. Doing so will take time and requires use of the surgical scalpel, not the meat-ax, in cutting the budget. As the Administration and the Congress struggle together over tight Federal budgets in fiscal

> **Box 1-4.—A Balanced Budget Amendment to the Constitution?**
>
> To argue that substantial deficit reduction was imperative in 1993 is not to argue that the budget deficit must be reduced even further in the short run—and certainly not to argue that we should mandate a balanced budget every year by constitutional amendment, as some have advocated.
>
> This Administration opposes the proposed balanced budget amendment to the Constitution for many reasons. First and foremost, the amendment would put fiscal policy in a straitjacket that might imperil macroeconomic stability, thereby abdicating one of the government's principal responsibilities and raising the specter of mass unemployment. Second, the proposed amendment would lead to budgetary gimmickry—such as mixing one-time asset sales with recurring income transactions—and would be almost impossible to enforce. It could push economic policy decisions into the courts, or even provoke a constitutional crisis.
>
> Third, there are many candidate definitions of "the budget deficit," making it both hazardous and unwise to enshrine any particular definition in the Constitution. For example, do we want to balance the unified budget or exclude Social Security? Why not the structural deficit, or even the inflation-adjusted structural deficit? Fourth, the amendment's call for a 60-percent congressional supermajority to waive the balanced budget requirement threatens to reinstall both gridlock and the tyranny of the minority.
>
> Fifth, and finally, the amendment by itself would not reduce the deficit by a single penny; all the hard choices that face us now would still face us. A deficit reduction package leading to a balanced budget would most likely have to include major new taxes on the middle class, substantial cuts in Social Security benefits, reductions in defense spending that go far beyond the Administration's proposals, and cuts in Federal spending on medical care large enough to imperil health reform. The Administration opposes all of these.

1995 and beyond, it is essential that we not allow fiscal myopia to lead to underinvestment in America's future.

INVESTING IN PEOPLE

The American work force remains the most productive in the world. Our aim should be simple: to keep it that way. But the rest of the world is not standing still; it is gaining on us, becoming ever more productive. And that is what compels change.

America has never competed on the basis of low wages, and we must not start doing so now. It is widely believed that modern industrial processes demand workers with higher levels of education and training; and evidence on the relative wages of, say, college-educated versus high school-educated labor (Chart 1-8) seems to bear this out. In 1981, workers with college degrees earned about 45 percent more than workers with only high school degrees; by 1992, this gap had reached almost 65 percent.

Chart 1-8 **Ratio of Wages of College Graduates to Wages of High School Graduates**
Workers with college degrees earn substantially more than workers without, and the gap between the two groups' wages grew during the 1980s.

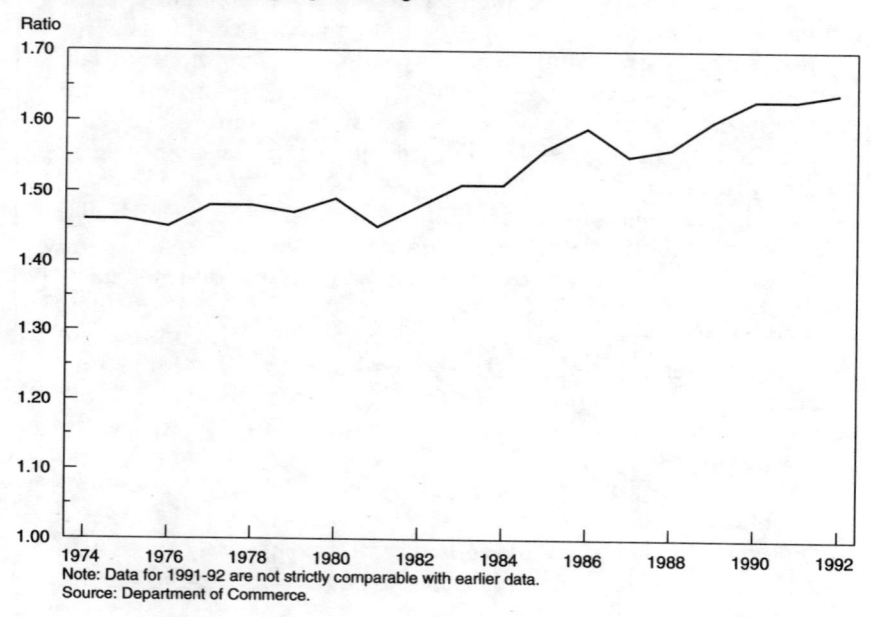

Note: Data for 1991-92 are not strictly comparable with earlier data.
Source: Department of Commerce.

Some observers claim that average work force quality may actually have deteriorated in the United States in recent decades. Whether or not this is true, few dispute that the supply of work force skills has failed to keep pace with the growing demand. Although Americans are, if measured by average years of schooling, among the most educated people on earth, the rate of illiteracy in our country has long been high. Tens of millions of adult Americans are either functionally illiterate or barely literate. International test scores suggest that our primary and secondary students are learning less science and mathematics than their counterparts in other countries.

This educational record is not good enough in a world economy that grows ever more competitive and ever more skill-intensive. American workers must build the additional human capital they need as a bridgehead to higher wages and living standards. Lifelong learning must cease being a slogan and become a reality.

In a fundamental sense, each American must be responsible for his or her own education and training. This Administration is committed to creating the requisite opportunities through a comprehensive agenda of education and training that starts before formal schooling and extends into the workplace. For example:

- Head Start will be expanded so that disadvantaged children have a chance to get ahead. Head Start has been proved effective in preparing these children for primary school, and has been estimated to save about six dollars in future government spending for every dollar invested today.
- Goals 2000 is a comprehensive legislative package that will set higher performance standards for American teachers and students.
- The Departments of Labor and Education are collaborating on a new School-to-Work transition program that will help students get hands-on, work-related training while still in high school. This is an area of our educational system that has been neglected for too long.
- The new National Service program (Box 1–5) will not only provide opportunities for community service and the acquisition of job-related skills, but also help send more Americans to college.
- The reformed student loan program will also help more of America's youth attend college by reducing borrowing costs and offering, for the first time on a national scale, loans whose repayment schedules depend on future earnings.
- The new program for dislocated workers will have an important retraining component, which will make opportunities available to displaced American workers. Some income support will be provided so that displaced workers can afford to take advantage of the training.

Each of these programs will help augment the Nation's stock of human resources, thereby raising the American standard of living.

INVESTING IN PUBLIC INFRASTRUCTURE

The most obvious kind of public investment is building new public infrastructure—the Nation's highways, bridges, airports, and water and sewage systems. The Administration believes the United States has underinvested in its public infrastructure. For example, the Department of Transportation estimates that almost 20 percent of our Nation's highways have poor or mediocre pavement and about 20 percent of our bridges are structurally deficient.

> **Box 1-5.—The National Service Program**
>
> In August 1993 the Congress passed the National and Community Service Trust Act of 1993, establishing the new National Service program. National Service provides participants both current compensation (at below-market wages) and educational grants of up to $4,725 per year to pay for college and other post-secondary education. Participants also receive valuable on-the-job training, accumulate employment skills, and acquire real-world work experience.
>
> The economic rationale for this program is threefold. First, employers may be reluctant to provide training in skills that can be utilized in a wide variety of employment applications because, if the employee leaves the firm soon thereafter, the firm will fail to recoup the cost of its investment. Since the accumulation of employment skills is socially desirable, it may be economically efficient for the government to finance part of this training.
>
> Second, the decline in Federal revenue sharing has reduced the intergovernmental resources available to State and local governments. These levels of government often know best what services their residents need most. Accordingly, the National Service program provides in-kind resources (labor services) to precisely those types of public and nonprofit organizations best able to determine what services are required.
>
> Third, the National Service program provides all Americans the opportunity to undertake community service positions by relaxing the tradeoff that workers often face between current compensation and the richness of an employment experience. The program ensures that valuable but low-paid public service positions will not be the province of the wealthy.
>
> The National Service program is funded through an initial appropriation of $300 million over previous funding for related programs. This is scheduled to rise to $500 million in 1995 and $700 million in 1996. At these funding levels, it is expected that the program will be able to support approximately 20,000 participants in 1994 and about 100,000 participants over the 3-year period covered by the legislation.

A variety of evidence indicates that there has been underinvestment. First, while the statistical evidence is not unequivocal, the weight of it points to handsome rates of return on well-planned investments in public infrastructure. Second, estimated benefit-cost ratios on specific infrastructure projects are often quite high. Third, the ratio of public to private capital has fallen markedly since the 1960s (Chart 1-9). Unless the data are grossly misleading, the principle of diminishing marginal returns leaves only two possible conclusions: Either America was overinvested in public capital in the early 1970s, or it is underinvested today.

Chart 1-9 **Ratio of Public to Private Net Nonresidential Capital Stock**
The ratio of public to private capital stock declined steadily and markedly in the 1970s and 1980s.

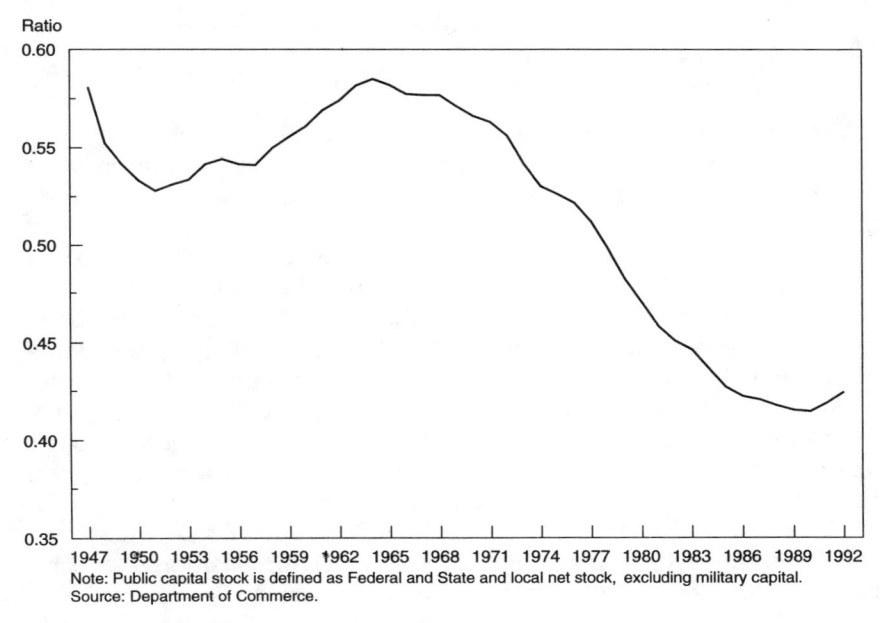

Note: Public capital stock is defined as Federal and State and local net stock, excluding military capital.
Source: Department of Commerce.

Finally, there is the evidence of the senses: America's roads and bridges are badly in need of repair, a number of our airports are overcrowded, and our sewage treatment facilities are overburdened. To many thoughtful observers, America's public infrastructure is simply not commensurate with our bounteous private wealth.

INVESTING IN TECHNOLOGY

But physical capital is not the only determinant of productivity, nor even the most important. Over long periods of time, rising productivity and hence advances in living standards depend on the upward march of technology. Indeed, studies of long-term economic growth attribute a large share of growth to improvements in knowhow (Table 1-7). The history of progress in the industrial world is working smarter, not working harder.

TABLE 1–7.—*Sources of U.S. Economic Growth*
[Average annual percent change]

Source	1947 to 1973	1973 to 1992
Labor inputs	1.01	0.88
Capital inputs	1.45	1.07
Total factor productivity (technological change)	1.63	.40
Adjustment from nonfarm business output to GDP	−.14	−.04
TOTAL (GDP growth)	3.94	2.30

Note.—Labor and capital inputs are measured for the nonfarm business sector.
Detail may not add to totals because of rounding.
Sources: Council of Economic Advisers, Department of Commerce, and Department of Labor.

Technological change does not come for free. Technology advances because scientists and engineers working in laboratories and on shop floors make new discoveries. And research is expensive.

Since the dawn of the industrial revolution, alarmists have argued that technology and automation threaten jobs. Such claims are still heard today. But history shows that they have never been right in the past and suggests that they are wrong again. Time after time, in epoch after epoch and country after country, technological advance has produced higher wages and living standards, not mass unemployment. That is exactly what we expect to happen again in the 21st century. And the government should be helping this process along—facilitating growth and change, not impeding it.

While the bulk of research and development (R&D) must and should be done by private industry, support for basic and generic research has long been recognized as a legitimate function of government because of informational externalities. New technology is expensive to *discover* but cheap to *disseminate*. So what one company learns passes quickly to others, making it impossible for the innovator to capture all the returns from its discovery. In fact, estimates find that innovating businesses capture less than half of the social returns to their R&D. Furthermore, estimated social rates of return on R&D range as high as 50 to 100 percent, suggesting that there is systematic underinvestment.

For this reason, the Administration asked the Congress to extend the research and experimentation tax credit, which was done in OBRA93. For the same reason, the Administration is increasing funding for research partnerships with industry, such as the Advanced Technology Program, and adding dozens of new manufacturing extension centers. Each of these initiatives and others are designed to speed the pace at which precompetitive technologies are invented and disseminated. Once that stage is passed, the market mechanism should and will take over. (Chapter 5 has more details on the Administration's technology policy.)

The development and deployment of new technology have long been of interest to the government. But technology policy is especially critical in a period of large-scale defense cutbacks, because more than half of total Federal support for R&D has traditionally been related to national defense. With less need for research on weaponry, the Federal Government must now make a choice. Will we reduce total research support, or will we shift the research dollars into civilian technologies? The President believes that the latter is the wiser course, which is why the Administration is reorienting the research capabilities of the Defense Department and the national laboratories toward R&D partnerships with industry.

Technology surely creates the wave of the future. America must be on the crest of that wave—with the technology, capital, and skilled work force needed to take advantage of tomorrow's economy.

TRADE POLICY AND LIVING STANDARDS

This Administration's policies toward private physical capital, human capital, public infrastructure, and technology all share a common objective: to raise the living standards of American families. Trade policy is yet another means toward that same end. This Administration vigorously supported the North American Free Trade Agreement (NAFTA), worked hard to complete the Uruguay Round of the General Agreement on Tariffs and Trade (GATT), streamlined the Nation's export promotion programs and eased restrictions on exports, and is striving to open the Japanese market through bilateral negotiations, all for the same reason—to open markets and boost American exports. (Chapter 6 contains more details on the Administration's trade policy.) The emphasis on trade expansion is, in turn, driven by two simple facts.

First, Americans now live in an increasingly integrated world economy and must therefore become increasingly outward-looking to stay on top. There is simply no way to close America's borders and return to the insular days of the 1950s and 1960s. Trying to do so would be an exercise in futility, doomed not only to fail but to lower living standards in the process. International competition through trade has long been a powerful engine of change and progress—for America and for the world. We must not let that engine idle. Instead, we must use it to power America up the technology ladder—by moving our workers into the jobs of the future, not keeping them mired in the jobs of the past. In the President's words, we must "compete, not retreat."

Second, jobs in export industries pay wages that are about 22 percent above the economy-wide average, according to the Council's latest estimates. The implication is that, if the Administration succeeds in shifting the composition of GDP toward more exports, we will automatically shift the composition of American employment toward better paying jobs. No government program or central direction is needed to accomplish this. The market will do the work for us.

Trade expansion is sometimes inaccurately characterized as "exporting jobs." Nothing could be further from the truth. A more accurate description is that international trade and investment lead low-skill, low-paid jobs that would inevitably migrate to poorer countries to go there in exchange for high-skill, better-paying jobs in the United States. American companies that compete successfully both at home and in foreign markets offer the best job opportunities for their workers. The history of capitalism throughout the world shows that companies and industries sheltered from the winds of competition tend to stagnate.

This Administration's focus on exports does not signal a revival of mercantilism. Rather, it reflects a belief that America's export promotion efforts have lagged behind those of other countries and that our markets are already among the most open in the world. The Administration fully expects trade liberalization—such as through NAFTA and the Uruguay Round of GATT—to raise *both* U.S. exports *and* U.S. imports. And we welcome both.

The North American Free Trade Agreement

Indeed, the recently ratified NAFTA illustrates the basic goals of Administration trade policy extremely well. NAFTA should boost trade with Mexico in both directions. In consequence, economic resources will be allocated more efficiently on both sides of the border. Inevitably, some American industries will therefore contract while others expand. Supported by the overwhelming preponderance of scholarly evidence, the Administration believes that NAFTA will lead to *net* job creation in the United States.

Equally important is the composition of those jobs, however. The new jobs that will arise in the United States will, on average, pay higher wages than the jobs that migrate south. It would be surprising indeed if anything else happened when a low-wage country and a high-wage country reduced trade barriers. In addition, the lower tariffs and reduced trade barriers from NAFTA will reduce prices for a variety of goods that American families buy. Together, the shift in the composition of employment toward higher paid jobs and the reduction in prices lead to a clear conclusion: NAFTA will raise the standard of living of the average American family—and the average Mexican family as well.

The Uruguay Round of GATT

The recently completed Uruguay Round of GATT was a landmark achievement for the entire world trading system. It literally rewrites the rules of trade for the start of the next century.

Earlier rounds of GATT talks had focused almost exclusively on tariff reductions. The market access component of the Uruguay Round continues this tradition by reducing tariffs on literally thousands of manufactured goods—by more than one-third on average. Such tariff reductions should be a tonic for world trade and growth, just as they have been in the past, and should increase specialization and economic efficiency around the globe. As usual, producers will gain from bigger markets and consumers will gain from lower prices.

But the most remarkable achievements of the Uruguay Round are to be found elsewhere. For the first time, trade in agricultural commodities has been brought under GATT—a goal that had eluded trade negotiators for decades. When fully effective, the agreement will reduce agricultural export subsidies by 21 percent in volume and 36 percent in value, saving taxpayers and consumers in many countries billions of dollars. Trade in agricultural goods will also be liberalized by reducing tariffs on certain commodities (like beef and fruits and vegetables), partially opening markets that were previously closed (like rice in Japan and the Republic of Korea), and prohibiting certain food "safety" measures that were really disguised trade barriers. America's farmers, consumers, and taxpayers all stand to gain handsomely from this agreement.

In addition, for the first time GATT disciplines have been extended to a variety of service industries. This achievement of the Uruguay Round is a vitally important precedent for the United States for two reasons. One is that production patterns both here and elsewhere have been shifting and will continue to shift toward services. The other is that the United States seems to have a strong comparative advantage in many service industries; in fact, our trade surplus in services is already three times larger than our trade surplus in agriculture.

The United States did not succeed in bringing all services into the agreement, and will continue to press for trade liberalization in sectors that were left out of the Uruguay Round. But the gains were still significant: Trade rules in such important industries as accounting, consulting, construction, and telecommunications will now require that foreign countries grant the same treatment to American firms operating abroad as they do to their own companies.

Finally, the path-breaking agreement will provide much stronger protection for a range of intellectual property rights including patents, copyrights, trademarks, and trade secrets. Since the United States is the home of so much commercial innovation, we will reap large gains from the agreement. Among the biggest industrial winners are software, pharmaceuticals, and biotechnology.

In sum, the Council estimates that the various provisions of the Uruguay Round, once fully phased in after a decade, will increase U.S. GDP by at least 1½ percent by raising real wages, lowering consumer prices, and protecting our national property rights.

HEALTH CARE REFORM

Successful health care reform will accomplish many things. Perhaps primary among them is health security for all Americans—a precious commodity that too many of our citizens have been denied for too long. In today's United States, workers who lose their jobs often lose their health insurance, too. Other people and businesses lose their coverage because a family member or employee becomes ill and incurs large medical bills. Still other people are afraid to take jobs that would lift them out of welfare because they cannot risk losing medicaid coverage. In total, nearly 39 million Americans lack health insurance, millions more are inadequately covered, and tens of millions live in fear of losing the coverage they have. Few people in other industrialized countries face such insecurity.

Under the President's health care reform proposal, which is described in detail in Chapter 4, none of this would ever happen again. Americans would know that their health insurance would never lapse, whether they changed jobs, moved, quit to start a new business, or had the misfortune of serious illness in the family. When effective health care reform is enacted, one of the major sources of economic insecurity facing Americans today will have been removed.

Health care reform is also fundamental to long-run budget control. It is often said that the fastest growing part of the budget is "entitlements." But the fastest growing part of the entitlement budget by far is health care spending (Chart 1-10). As the President has repeatedly emphasized, controlling the costs of medical care is the key to controlling entitlements, and therefore to long-run deficit reduction.

But health care reform will accomplish more than just budget control and security. The Administration also sees it as a route to higher standards of living.

For years, the rising cost of health care has forced a shift in the composition of the typical pay packet away from wages and salaries toward fringe benefits, especially health insurance. Chart 1-11 shows that the share of health benefits in total labor compensation rose from 1.8 percent in 1960 to 8.5 percent in 1992. Correspondingly, the share of cash wages fell. In absolute terms, in fact, real wages and salaries have barely increased in 20 years. Almost all the gains in compensation have been taken as fringe benefits. This means that working men and women have, for the most part, paid

Chart 1-10 Projected Real Growth Rates of Principal Federal Budget Components
From fiscal 1994 to fiscal 1998, health care spending is projected to grow four times as rapidly as any other major component.

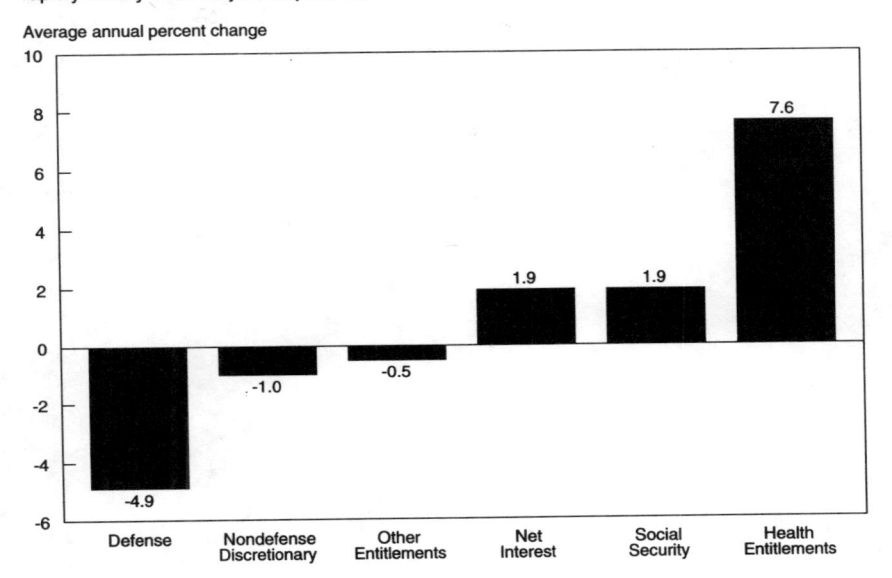

Average annual percent change

Component	Average annual percent change
Defense	-4.9
Nondefense Discretionary	-1.0
Other Entitlements	-0.5
Net Interest	1.9
Social Security	1.9
Health Entitlements	7.6

Source: Office of Management and Budget.

for their escalating health costs by taking home lower wages than they would have otherwise.

We can arrest this process only by containing medical costs. The President's health care reform is designed to do precisely that by making the market more competitive and making both consumers and providers more cost conscious. On the assumption that the future will look like the past, the Administration expects most of the benefits from effective health care cost containment to redound to working Americans in the form of higher take-home pay.

SUMMARY: PROSPERITY AND CHANGE

All of the policy initiatives described here—from deficit reduction, to public investments (both human and physical), to trade expansion, to health care—share a common goal: raising the standard of living of average American families. But all of them also require change, sometimes wrenching change. Deficit reduction required a host of painful changes in government programs and some increased taxes. Lifelong learning requires changes in the way we view education. Freer trade and export expansion mean that some jobs will disappear so that more and better jobs can be created.

Chart 1-11 **Shares of Wages and Benefits in Compensation**
Most of the decline in the wage share of total compensation has gone to increased health benefits.

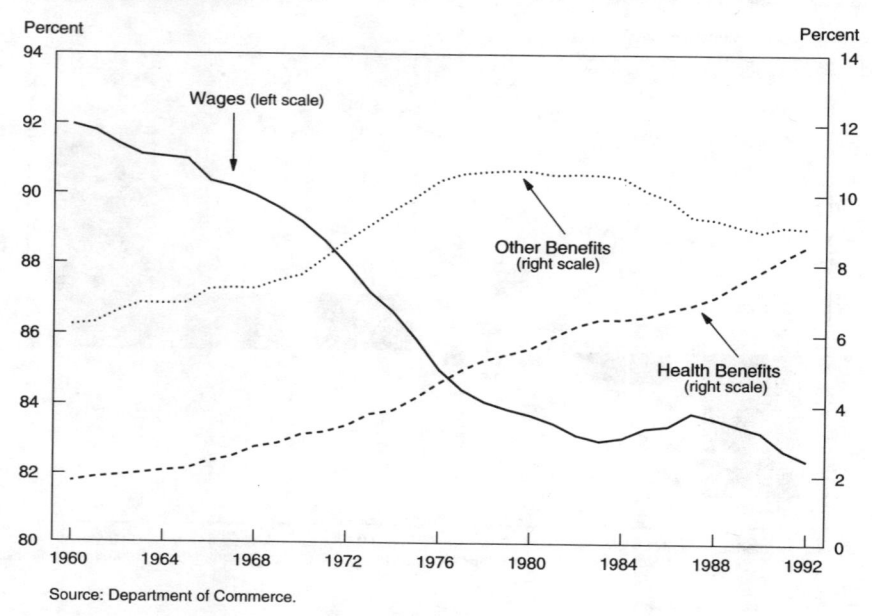

Source: Department of Commerce.

And health care reform requires nothing less than a major overhaul of one-seventh of our economy.

None of this will be quick or easy. Real change rarely is. But, in truth, we have no choice, for standing still is not an option that history allows. The secret to economic success is making change our friend, not our enemy—coming to view change as the opportunity for advancement that it is, not as the threat that it sometimes appears to be.

CREATING OPPORTUNITY

Our focus on raising the standard of living of middle-class Americans must not blind us to the fact that some of our fellow citizens have not managed to attain a middle-class living standard. And change is especially threatening to those at the bottom of the economic ladder.

When money incomes are corrected for purchasing power, America is the richest of the world's major nations in terms of per capita income. But a nagging poverty problem remains in this land of plenty. Millions of Americans have little or no earning power and are therefore on the public dole. Millions more work but do not earn enough to support their families. Two key policy initiatives enacted in 1993, the expansion of the earned income tax credit and the introduction of empowerment zones, were designed to help low-income workers by making work pay.

The earned income tax credit (EITC) provides needy families with both income support and greater rewards for working (Box 1–6). In part, the credit offsets income taxes that low-income working families would otherwise have to pay. But the credit is also *refundable,* meaning that if a family's credit exceeds its tax liability, the Internal Revenue Service sends a check for the difference. As part of OBRA93, the EITC was increased substantially, both by making payments more generous and by extending the credit to more families.

Box 1–6.—How Does the Earned Income Tax Credit Work?

The earned income tax credit is often thought of as a type of negative income tax, but in fact it is more complicated than that. The EITC has three ranges: a "credit range" in which it functions like a wage subsidy, a "plateau" in which it has no marginal effect, and a "phaseout" range in which the credit is paid back as earnings rise (Chart 1–12).

To illustrate, when the increases enacted in 1993 are fully effective (in 1996), the credit will work as follows for a family with two or more children. (Less generous schedules apply to one-child and childless families.) As earnings rise from zero to $8,425 (all dollar figures are in 1994 dollars), the EITC will provide a 40-percent wage subsidy, so that each $100 of additional earnings will net the family $140. The maximum credit is $3,370, which is therefore reached when earnings hit $8,425. The credit will then be constant as earnings rise from $8,425 to $11,000. Beyond $11,000, however, the family's tax credit is reduced 21 cents for each extra dollar earned. Benefits are thus exhausted when earnings reach $27,000.

Clearly, the EITC provides a marginal work incentive in the credit range (unlike a negative income tax), a marginal disincentive in the phaseout range, and neither in the plateau. However, to the extent that labor supply decisions involve whether or not to work, rather than how many hours to work, the credit provides a positive work incentive to *all* recipients.

As a first step toward welfare reform, the EITC has many virtues. It will lift many families with children out of poverty. It provides positive work incentives for many of the lowest-paid employees in our society. It is better targeted on the low-income population than is, say, an increase in the minimum wage, because minimum-wage workers are found in all family-income brackets. It is simple to administer, requiring no special bureaucracy. And, finally, it apparently reaches a larger fraction of the eligible recipients than is typical of other income-support programs, perhaps because it is easy to claim and carries no stigma.

Chart 1-12 **Earned Income Tax Credit for Families with Two or More Children**
The expanded earned income tax credit will substantially increase the credit for eligible families.

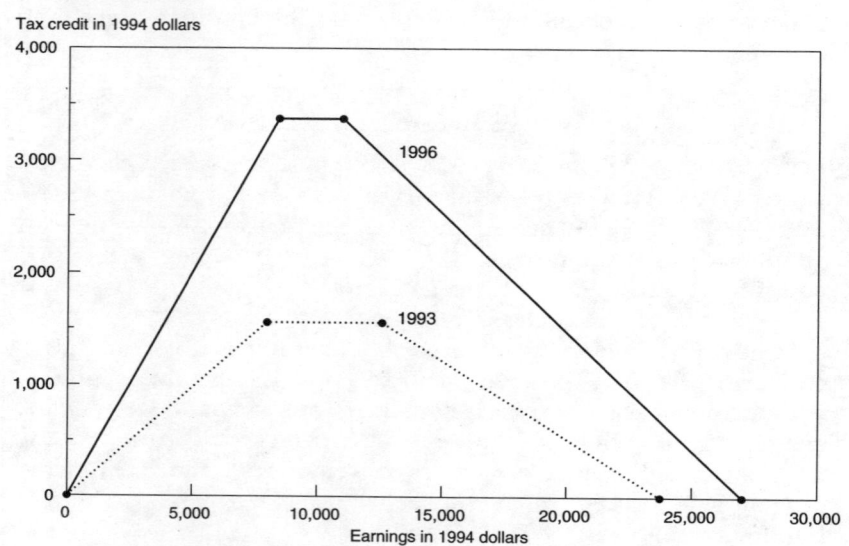

Source: Department of the Treasury.

The goal of the innovative empowerment zone program is to strengthen business activity in certain geographic areas that are extremely depressed, so that synergies from concentrated economic activity can help revive these areas. The program's main tax incentive is a 20-percent tax credit for wages up to $15,000 per year paid by a zone business to a zone resident. This should be a powerful incentive to create jobs in the zones. In addition, a variety of regulatory waivers may be granted to give communities greater flexibility, and several Federal agencies will direct spending toward the zones.

Beginning this year, nine empowerment zones, six urban and three rural, will be selected by a competitive process that should encourage both imaginative thinking and private-public partnerships. In addition, 95 other neighborhoods will be designated enterprise communities and be granted smaller benefits than the zones while sharing the relaxed regulatory environment. The program will be carefully monitored and evaluated over a 10-year period, during which time we should learn a great deal about what works and what does not.

No American should think that programs like empowerment zones, the EITC, and welfare reform serve *only* the poor. Every citizen benefits when the welfare rolls are reduced, when low-income families earn more, when blighted neighborhoods come to life, and when city streets once again become safe. We are, after all, one Nation.

SUMMARY

An economic strategy based on long-run investments, as ours is, will not bear fruit overnight. It takes time to see tangible results and patience to wait for them. The important thing is to get started down the right path—and soon. The Administration believes that 1993 marked a turning point in that regard. Recovery firmly took hold in 1993, and prospects for sustained economic expansion look far brighter now than they did a year ago. The long-run deficit problem, while not completely solved, looks far less threatening than it did then. The Congress has begun to fund the President's ambitious investment agenda—including infrastructure, human capital, technology, and environmental preservation. Two historic trade agreements whose negotiations began years ago—NAFTA and the Uruguay Round of GATT—were brought to a successful conclusion. And the stage has been set for a much-needed national debate on health care reform in 1994. All of these accomplishments set in place the foundation for a more prosperous America.

CHAPTER 2

The U.S. Economy in 1993 and Beyond

THE ECONOMIC EXPANSION consolidated in 1993, setting the stage for sustained growth in 1994. A sharp decline in long-term interest rates to 25-year lows, in large part the result of the Administration's deficit reduction package, was the major economic story of 1993. Momentum picked up in the second half, with interest-sensitive sectors like housing and consumers' and producers' durable goods leading the way. Continued advances in these sectors helped to create sustained employment and income gains that put real gross domestic product (GDP) on roughly a 3-percent-per-year growth path.

During 1992 the economy was widely described as being in a jobless recovery, advancing with a disconcerting seesaw quality. The combination of self-sustaining forces that typically appear in a recovery—strongly rising employment, accelerating incomes, sharply rebounding automobile sales and housing activity, markedly higher levels of consumer confidence, and a renewed willingness on the part of consumers to take on debt—was missing. Many of these forces did appear over the course of 1993. The economy experienced a sustained moderate expansion with healthier job creation. Payroll employment increased by 162,000 jobs per month in 1993, double the 81,000-job-per-month pace of 1992. The unemployment rate, higher at the end of 1992 than it had been at the beginning, fell by almost a full percentage point in 1993.

Many interest-sensitive sectors of the economy finally exhibited clear-cut improvements during 1993. Business spending for durable equipment increased at the fastest rate since 1972. Consumer spending for furniture and household furnishings, another leading sector in business cycle upswings, also posted one of the biggest gains in a decade. Motor vehicle sales rebounded smartly as consumers exhibited a newfound willingness to incur debt to finance a major purchase. Together these forces have put the economy on track for sustainable growth.

With a greatly improved outlook for the Federal budget deficit, the Council of Economic Advisers expects long-term interest rates to remain relatively low for the foreseeable future—which will help to keep economic growth on track. Low interest rates are the key ingredient that should allow the economy to grow in the face of future large deficit reductions, which would otherwise tend to contract the economy. Expected growth in the 2½- to 3-percent range for 4 years should create about 8 million new jobs and steadily reduce the unemployment rate from its currently unacceptable level toward a rate that is close to noninflationary full employment.

STRUGGLING TO GROW

GDP growth over the current expansion has been much slower than usual. In the first year after a recession trough, output typically grows by 6 percent in real terms; in this recovery, output growth over the first year after the trough was less than 2 percent. Even though potential GDP growth is lower today than it was in the 1960s and 1970s—mainly because of slower productivity growth—this factor can only explain a small part of the slower rebound.

Not surprisingly, given the well-established linkage between output growth and employment growth, job growth in this expansion has also been atypically slow. The decline in employment during the recent contraction did not bottom out with the rest of the economy, and no rebound in job growth was evident until a year after the recession's trough. By late 1993 the growth path of employment was still well below the typical postwar recovery path (Chart 2–1). After 11 quarters, we have had the employment gains normally expected after just three quarters. Adjusted for the sluggish pace of output growth, however, employment growth has been closer to normal. (For further discussion, see Chapter 3.)

A number of special factors have combined to induce this sluggish economic performance. These "headwinds" include defense cutbacks, weak foreign economies, an oversupply of commercial buildings in the wake of the 1980s, the credit crunch, debt overhang, and a wave of corporate downsizings. None of these factors by itself explains why the recovery has run so far behind historical levels, but there is evidence that together they have retarded economic growth significantly.

THE END OF THE COLD WAR

The end of the cold war was a major geopolitical event for the United States, and the ensuing defense builddown has had profound economic effects. In 1986 defense spending accounted for 6.5 percent of U.S. GDP. By 1993 its share had fallen to about 4.8 percent, and by 1997 it is predicted to drop to about 3.2 percent (Chart 2–2). This massive shift of national resources away from defense has meant numerous base closings, cancellations of major weapons programs, scaled-back procurement plans, and attendant layoffs in

Chart 2-1 Recovery Pattern of Nonfarm Payroll Employment
Employment growth in this recovery has been much weaker than in the average postwar recovery.

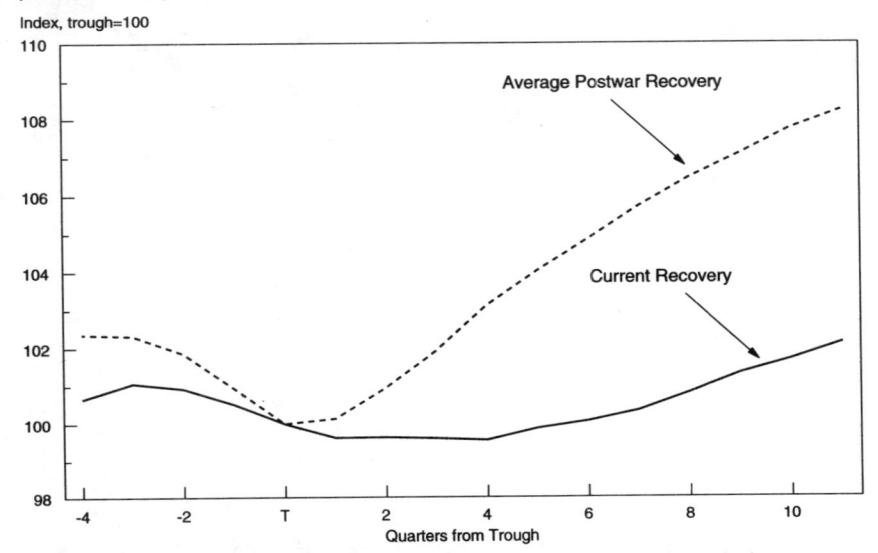

Note: "Average" includes all recoveries from 1954 to 1982, except 1980. The trough quarter for the current recovery is first quarter 1991.
Sources: Department of Labor and National Bureau of Economic Research.

the whole defense sector. For example, total defense-related jobs are projected to number 4.5 million by 1997, down from 7.2 million jobs in 1987. In a purely arithmetical sense, reduced defense spending subtracted roughly 0.5 percentage point off the real GDP growth rate in 1993. Moreover, the defense cutbacks have had a further adverse impact on aggregate demand through the expenditure multiplier. Moving resources out of the defense sector frees them up for use in the production of consumption and investment goods and services, improving living standards. But this is a longer term effect. The conversion process takes time, and although the defense scaledown is not as large relative to the size of the economy as it was at the end of several wars, reconversion will cause painful dislocations in the short run.

WEAK FOREIGN ECONOMIES

Weak economic performance in the rest of the industrialized world over the past few years has also taken a toll on the U.S. economy by slowing export growth. The period 1991–93 will go down in history as the *worst* for economic performance in foreign industrial countries since at least 1960. During this 3-year period,

Chart 2-2 **National Defense Purchases as Share of GDP**
Defense spending as a share of nominal GDP is projected to continue to fall steadily over the 1990s.

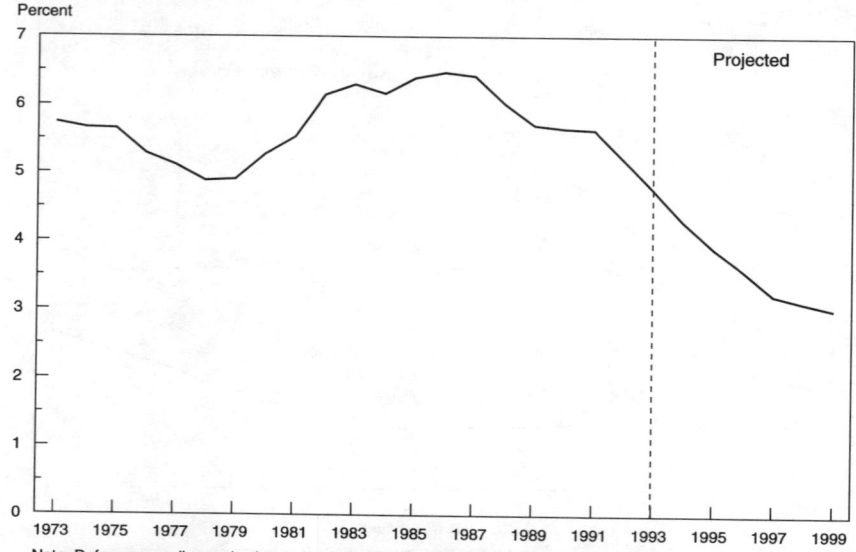

Percent

[Line chart showing defense spending as a percent of GDP from 1973 to 1999, starting near 5.8% in 1973, declining to about 4.9% in 1979, rising to a peak of about 6.4% in 1986-1987, then declining to about 4.7% in 1993, with projections continuing down to about 2.9% by 1999.]

Note: Defense spending projections taken from Mid-Session Review of the 1994 Budget.
Sources: Council of Economic Advisers, Department of Commerce, Department of the Treasury, and Office of Management and Budget.

output growth averaged just 0.6 percent per year in the European Community, 1.7 percent per year in Japan, and only 0.2 percent per year in the world's other industrial countries (Table 2-1). Even though U.S. growth has been sluggish over the past couple of years, it has been the fastest among all the Group of Seven major industrial market economies. The world's second- and third-largest industrial economies, Japan and Germany, both entered deep recessions in the latter part of 1992 and are now operating well below their capacities. During 1993, all of the Group of Seven countries had substantial output gaps (that is, actual GDP was well below potential), and growth was slowing in such developing-country markets for U.S. exports as Mexico and the Middle East.

In large part because of this global weakness, U.S. merchandise exports, which had increased by about 7 percent in nominal terms in 1991 and 5 percent in 1992, rose by only 2 percent in 1993. Merchandise exports to Japan and Western Europe, which together account for 35 percent of total U.S. merchandise exports, were especially hard hit, dropping by about 3 percent (Chart 2-3). Even exports to Mexico flattened in 1993 after half a decade of rapid increases. With excellent cost competitiveness in world markets, U.S.

TABLE 2-1.— *Foreign Country Real GDP Growth*
[Average annual percent change]

	1989	1990	1991	1992	1993
European Community	3.5	3.0	0.8	1.1	−0.2
Japan	4.7	4.8	4.0	1.3	−0.1
Other industrial countries	3.2	1.1	−1.1	0.6	1.2
Developing countries	4.1	3.7	4.5	5.8	6.1

Note.— 1993 figures are forecasts.
Source: International Monetary Fund.

exporters have been able to do better than a trade-weighted average of major industrial economies' GDP growth rates would suggest (Chart 2-4). Still, what had been a strong engine of growth from the mid-1980s until 1991 clearly shifted into neutral in 1993.

Meanwhile, growing U.S. reliance on foreign computers has led to a surge of imported capital goods. Office automation equipment, which now accounts for nearly 45 percent of real private investment in producers' durable equipment, has become the fastest growing major demand component in the U.S. economy, and imports have been filling a growing portion of this demand. Imports also account for about one-third of the nonautomotive, noncomputer portion of producers' durable equipment spending—up sharply over the past decade.

Together, the slowing of U.S. exports and the surge in imports have meant that net exports (the difference between them) are now working against U.S. growth, after making strong positive contributions from the mid-1980s to 1991. For example, according to a simple calculation holding other components of demand fixed, if net exports had simply not deteriorated in 1993 from their 1992 level, U.S. GDP growth would have been over 1 percentage point higher than it actually was in 1993.

THE DEBT WORKOUT

Working off the heavy indebtedness built up over the 1980s may also have retarded growth. During the 1960s and 1970s, households and firms only gradually increased their levels of indebtedness relative to their incomes. Over the 1984-90 period, this changed abruptly as individuals and businesses increased their indebtedness sharply (Charts 2-5 and 2-6). For the corporate sector, the proximate cause of increased indebtedness was a rise in debt-based financial restructurings, such as leveraged buyouts. A portion of new debt issues in the 1980s was used to purchase equity in existing companies, not to finance increases in plant and equipment investment. It is unclear exactly what motivated households to move further into debt during this period, although rapid appre-

Chart 2-3 Growth of U.S. Merchandise Exports
Continued weak economic growth in industrialized countries has depressed demand for U.S. exports.

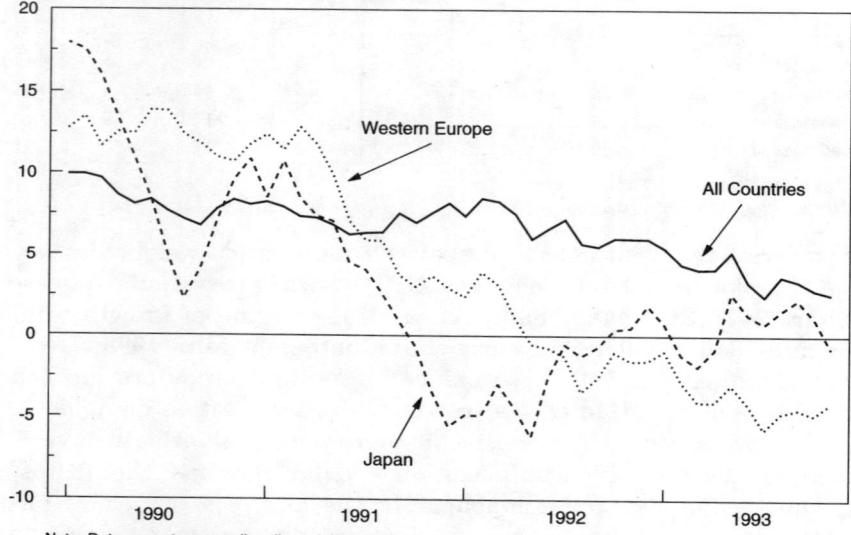

Percent change from year earlier, 6-month moving average

Note: Data are not seasonally adjusted, f.a.s. basis.
Source: Department of Commerce.

Chart 2-4 U.S. Exports Implied by Industrial Country GDP
U.S. export demand has been healthier than would be expected given the lackluster performance of the major foreign industrial economies.

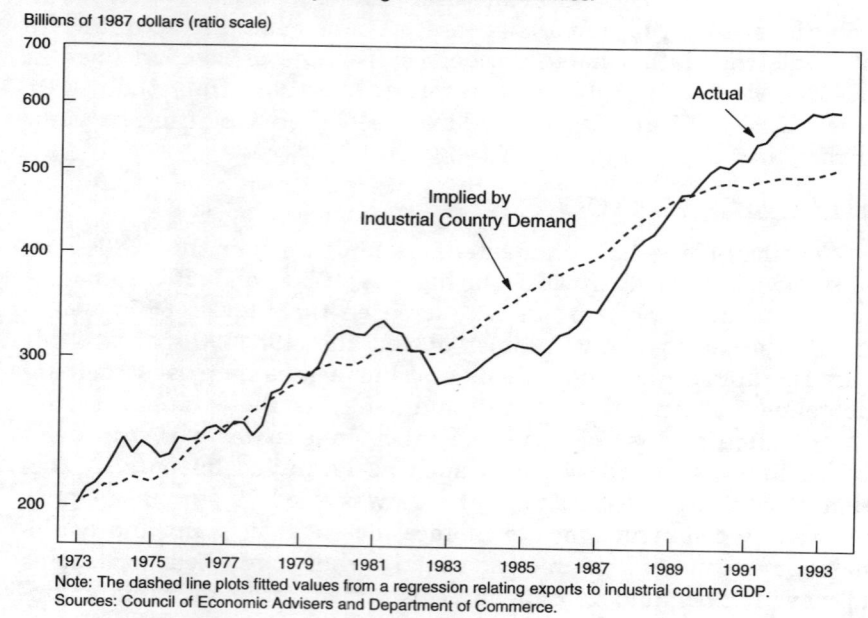

Billions of 1987 dollars (ratio scale)

Note: The dashed line plots fitted values from a regression relating exports to industrial country GDP.
Sources: Council of Economic Advisers and Department of Commerce.

ciation in the stock market and booms in numerous housing markets probably played a role. Higher asset values may have given consumers a greater sense of financial security to borrow and spend even in the face of modest personal income growth.

The debt-income ratios for both households and firms flattened as the 1980s came to a close. Beginning in 1991, firms initiated a dramatic reduction in their leverage. This balance sheet repair was presumably triggered by a reversal of the factors that led them to accumulate debt. Moreover, there were declines in firms' net worth, which might have caused them to reduce leverage out of fear of insolvency.

For a domestic debtor to repay a domestic creditor, there need not be any increase in national saving. Rather, such repayments represent—in the first instance—adjustments in the portfolios of domestic households, businesses, and financial institutions. Yet the recent balance sheet adjustments probably did stem in part from an increase in saving and therefore acted to slow growth in aggregate demand.

By what mechanism would such balance sheet adjustments affect national saving? If the households and firms who repaid debts had higher marginal propensities to spend than those who got the repayments, the balance sheet restructuring would have increased saving. By virtue of their indebtedness, we can infer that firms and households who retired debt had in the past shown much more eagerness to spend or to undertake investment projects. Extrapolation would suggest that they still had a high propensity to spend relative to the creditor firms and households. Therefore, balance sheet restructuring was probably a drag on aggregate demand in recent years.

Of course, the causality could be reversed. Indebted households and firms might have decided for reasons other than those based on the state of their balance sheets (e.g., reduced expectations of income or profitability of investment projects) to reduce expenditures, using their free cash flow to repay debt rather than to spend.

OVERSUPPLY OF COMMERCIAL BUILDINGS

Yet another headwind has been the glut of nonresidential structures that was built up over the 1980s. Investment in nonresidential structures soared in the early 1980s, fueled in part by high inflation and changes to the Tax Code in 1981 that made commercial real estate investment more attractive. As this overbuilding continued, vacancy rates rose sharply across the country.

The reversal of the 1981 tax provisions by the 1986 tax reforms, together with higher interest rates in the late 1980s, derailed the boom in commercial real estate. The decline in this sector was further exacerbated by the movement of the rest of the economy into

Chart 2-5   Households: Credit Market Debt as Percent of Disposable Income
After trending upward slowly over most of the 1960s and 1970s, the ratio of household credit-market debt to disposable personal income increased sharply in the 1980s.

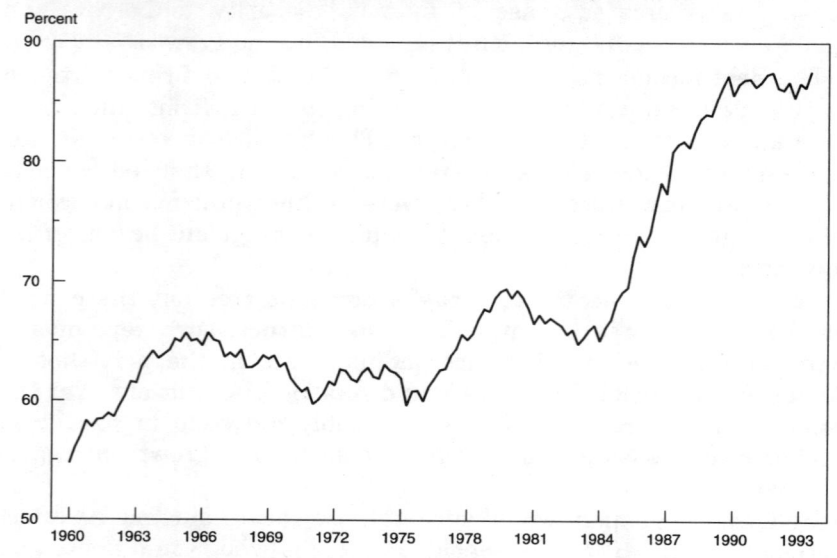

Sources: Department of Commerce and Board of Governors of the Federal Reserve System.

Chart 2-6   Nonfinancial Corporate Business: Credit Market Debt as Percent of Output
The ratio of nonfinancial corporate business debt to nonfinancial corporate GDP rose sharply in the 1980s. It has since begun to decline.

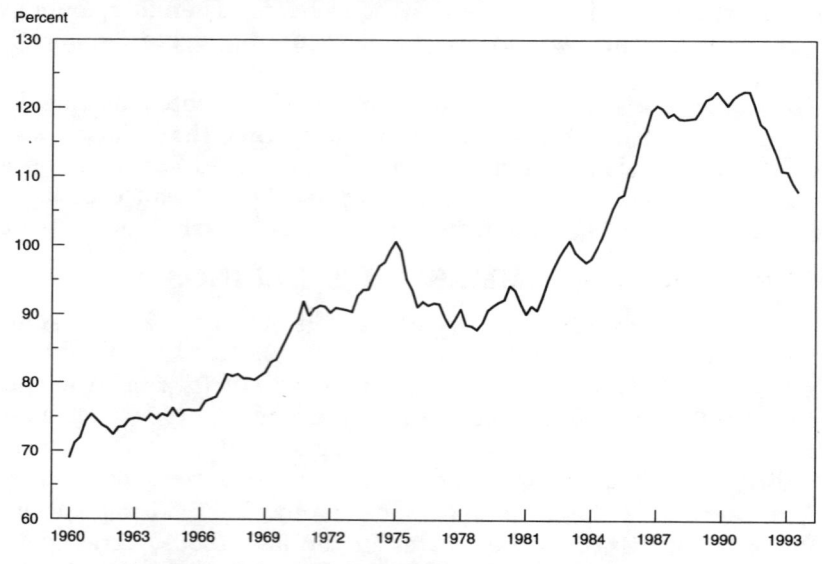

Sources: Department of Commerce and Board of Governors of the Federal Reserve System.

recession in 1990. Even by late 1993—more than 2 years into the recovery—the value of investment in nonresidential structures was more than 25 percent below its 1990 peak in real terms. Clearly this small but volatile sector of the economy has failed to provide its normal cyclical lift.

CREDIT CRUNCH

The credit crunch and its vestiges have also slowed economic activity over this recovery period. Many banks developed balance sheet problems in the 1980s as the developing-country debt crisis and widespread lending for speculative construction projects led to massive loan writeoffs and weak profitability. This weak profitability reduced the banks' ability to lend and probably aggravated the credit crunch. More-aggressive bank regulation, some of it a reaction to the 1980s savings and loan debacle, accentuated the problem. In 1991 and 1992 there were widespread reports that would-be borrowers were having difficulty obtaining funds, although these reports tended to be concentrated in certain industries (notably real estate) and regions (particularly the Northeast). A National Association of Home Builders survey of its members, for example, consistently ranked "obtaining financing for construction projects" as a top business problem over this period.

CORPORATE DOWNSIZINGS

Finally, corporations across the industrial spectrum have been restructuring their businesses and paring costs. The prolonged economic sluggishness apparently induced many firms to hunker down and reduce their breakeven points as much as possible, often by shedding workers. Foreign competition and cutbacks associated with debt workouts might also have been factors. Technological changes have played a role as well; some of the most notable layoffs have been at mainframe computer companies, for example. In addition, lower capital costs may have led some firms to substitute capital for labor.

Even though downsizing may well have made corporations more efficient and better poised to earn profits in the future, the widespread layoffs have helped to depress wage and salary growth and probably consumer confidence as well. In addition, although higher profits can imply higher incomes for corporate stockholders, this group's marginal propensity to consume is probably lower than it is among individuals whose primary source of income is wages. This would also have reduced consumption spending and overall economic growth.

THE HEADWINDS ARE MOSTLY CALMING

As the economy enters 1994, many of these headwinds are dissipating. The credit crunch is fading as banks show new signs of wanting to make business loans. The decline in yields on government bonds, where banks had parked large amounts of assets, and the improvement in overall business conditions are making such loans relatively more profitable. Aided by lower interest rates and greatly improved margins, banks have also been posting record profits for the past 2 years. Bank lending surveys by the Federal Reserve also suggest that credit conditions have eased. For these reasons, bank lending today is becoming less of a retardant to growth.

Meanwhile, the other industrial countries will not remain mired in recession forever. Indeed, the ones that entered recession first in this global slowdown—the United Kingdom, Canada, Australia, and New Zealand, for example—are all showing signs of economic rebound. Even Germany, a late arrival on the global recession scene, recorded positive GDP growth in the second and third quarters of 1993. By late 1993 there were increasing signs that the European recession was nearing bottom, and that at least modest growth would return in 1994. Even a small rebound in Europe would be welcome news to U.S. exporters. The odds of economic recovery in Japan, at least by 1995, seem good as well.

Commercial construction has also started to improve, although it will not be as bullish as it was in the mid-1980s. By late 1993 there were signs that vacancy rates for commercial real estate were posting significant declines, implying that the worst might be over for this sector.

The key exception to the forecast of diminishing headwinds is defense cutbacks. These seem almost certain to continue over the rest of the decade unless there is some major change in the world's geopolitical circumstances—which might have other, far less beneficial repercussions. Still, with most of these headwinds blowing less fiercely over the mid-1990s than they did earlier in the decade, the economy should be able to turn in a better performance.

OVERVIEW OF THE ECONOMY IN 1993

Although economic growth was sluggish in early 1993, substantial progress was made despite these headwinds. Employment increased steadily, the unemployment rate dropped, inflation remained subdued, and real GDP increased by 2.8 percent from the fourth quarter of 1992 to the fourth quarter of 1993. Claims early in the year that only a half-speed economic expansion was under way gradually gave way to the view that more-normal growth was returning. Fourth-quarter growth of 5.9 percent (annual rate)—the highest in 6 years—reinforced this view.

The 1993 economy actually exhibited more underlying strength than was reflected in press reports or in indexes of consumer and business confidence. Domestic demand and real final sales both posted healthy increases. Real final sales to domestic purchasers (that is, excluding inventories and exports but including imports) actually increased at an annual rate of 4 percent on average from mid-1992 until the end of 1993, and only dipped below 3 percent growth once over that period—in the first quarter of 1993. At least a portion of that dip was arguably caused by a policy of the previous Administration: increased tax liabilities in early 1993 owing to a reduction in withholding that began in March 1992. In addition, an early 1993 defense spending collapse caused a growth letdown in early 1993.

A look at economic performance sector by sector provides a clearer picture of the laggards and leaders in the present expansion.

CONSUMPTION EXPENDITURES

Because consumer spending represents about two-thirds of GDP, it is not surprising that the modest output growth in the expansion to date has been associated with sluggish consumption growth. Indeed, consumption as a whole has failed to show the kind of sharp rebound typical of postwar recoveries: 11 quarters after the recession's trough, consumption had advanced only two-thirds as far as would be expected from postwar experience. Consumer sentiment manifested a typical recovery pattern for only a short time; the sharp advance usually seen when a recession ends sputtered to a halt two quarters after the 1991 trough. Sentiment trended upward only slowly over 1992 and 1993, although there was a sharp acceleration late in 1993.

Weakness in consumer spending can also be seen in the behavior of the saving rate. Typically, the saving rate falls as a recovery begins, as consumers begin to spend ahead of income. Increases in spending on consumer durables, such as automobiles and household furnishings, typically follow. Such a drop in the saving rate did not occur after the 1991 trough, however; the saving rate actually trended *upward* slightly for almost 2 years into the recovery. Over 1992, real consumer spending lagged behind real income growth, suggesting that households were still getting their balance sheets in order.

Nineteen hundred and ninety-three saw belated reductions in the saving rate. Between the fourth quarter of 1992 and the third quarter of 1993, for example, the saving rate fell by more than 2 percentage points, and this provided much of the overall lift that the economy experienced. In fact, over the last three quarters of

1993, real consumer spending increased at a 3.9-percent average annual rate—not high by historical standards, but at least tending toward the normal range for a postwar expansion.

BUSINESS FIXED INVESTMENT

After a late start, several important components of investment spending have rebounded in line with typical recovery patterns. While investment in structures has remained weak for the reasons discussed earlier, producers' durable equipment has turned in a stellar performance. For about a year after the recession trough, equipment investment remained stagnant; then it spurted to a growth path *above* the postwar recovery average. Today, investment in producers' durable equipment remains one of the strongest components of the expansion. In fact, over the year ending in the fourth quarter of 1993, investment in these goods increased by about 18 percent—a growth rate more typical of a Japanese rather than an American business cycle expansion. Certainly as far as equipment investment spending is concerned, the weak portion of the recovery was limited to the first year after the trough. More recent activity has actually exceeded the postwar norm.

INVENTORIES

Businesses kept inventories at extremely low levels relative to sales throughout 1993, and a major swing in farm inventories resulting from the Midwest floods and Southeast drought influenced the quarterly GDP growth pattern over the year (Box 2–1). The inventory-to-sales ratio was under 1.5 throughout the year, and the ratio for manufacturing hit an all-time low during the fourth quarter as sales perked up faster than some businesses expected. Several factors were at work. First, the inventory-to-sales ratio in manufacturing industries is in secular decline. Second, businesses seemed to lack confidence in the strength of the recovery. Disappointing growth in the first and second quarters of 1993 and pessimism about the economy's future prospects probably made businesses extremely cautious about producing at a faster rate than was absolutely necessary. Third, production problems in some key sectors that did experience a sharp pickup in demand, especially automobiles, probably prevented some firms from achieving the level of inventories that they deemed optimal.

The extremely lean inventories of late 1993 are good news for 1994. As 1994 opens, manufacturers are in a position where they risk losing business because of inadequate inventories, and they are therefore under pressure to increase output. There seems to be relatively little risk that overaccumulation of inventories will lead to production cutbacks in 1994.

Box 2-1.—The Economic Effects of the Midwest Floods of 1993

Last summer's floods in the Midwest were a human tragedy whose immense scope was obvious to all. Measuring their economic effects is more difficult, however. The floods disrupted the day-to-day operations of businesses, destroyed inventories and crops, and wrecked a significant portion of the region's infrastructure and housing stock. But because the level of economic activity that would have occurred without the floods is unknowable, the effects of the flooding on third- and fourth-quarter economic performance cannot be definitively assessed.

The clearest effect of the floods on national economic performance was a decline in farm output. The Bureau of Economic Analysis (BEA) of the Department of Commerce judged that $2.5 billion worth of farm output was destroyed by the floods and the simultaneous drought in the Southeast. The BEA accounted for this crop loss by lowering its estimates of farm output by $7.5 billion (annualized) in the third quarter of 1993 and by a further $2.5 billion in the fourth quarter. The adjustments were reflected in the change in farm inventories. The result of these adjustments was that measured real GDP growth was lowered by about 0.6 percentage point in the third quarter of 1993 and increased by about 0.4 percentage point in the fourth quarter. The BEA also:

- reduced estimated farm proprietors' income to account for crop damage and uninsured losses to farm property
- lowered estimates of the rental income of persons and nonfarm proprietors' income to account for uninsured property losses.

Other flood effects are too embedded in the source data to be explicitly measured. These include:

- effects of reduced farm output on inflation
- the negative effect of the floods on nonfarm business output in affected areas
- potential stimulative effects from the rebuilding of flood-damaged roads, bridges, railways, and houses—especially if the rebuilding was funded from savings and not insurance company payouts (whose effects are more like a transfer from owners of insurance companies to policyholders)
- the effect of Federal disaster assistance, insurance payments, and emergency grants.

RESIDENTIAL INVESTMENT

Residential investment was an enigma over the first part of 1993. Mortgage rates fell to 20-year lows, affordability was at 20-year highs, yet housing starts were flat for the first half of the year. Finally, starting in August, housing activity began to respond to these favorable economic conditions and posted sharp additional gains. Housing starts rose a stunning 25 percent between July and December.

A healthy fraction of new homes being sold today are sold before construction has started. This suggests that the gains in residential construction are solid and that the upward trend in housing should continue without any likely inventory cycle. As 1993 ended, the inventory-to-sales ratio of new homes, as measured by the stock of homes for sale divided by the number actually sold in a month, was at its lowest level since 1986. Given the unfavorable underlying demographic factors for housing, especially the relatively low rate of household formation, housing turned in a very good performance late in the year and was a solid contributor to the economy's advance.

NET EXPORTS

As mentioned earlier, net exports shifted from being a major contributor to economic growth over the 1987–90 period to being a retardant in 1992 and 1993. Weak foreign economies severely crimped export growth, while imports surged with the capital equipment spending boom. Even the growth rate of service-sector exports, the brightest component of U.S. trade, was hit by slow foreign growth. In current dollar terms U.S. trade in services still posted a $68 billion surplus in 1993, however, illustrating the strong comparative advantage of U.S. firms in this sector. And exports of services represented about 25 percent of total U.S. real exports in 1993. By comparison, agricultural exports in 1993 represented only about 6 percent of the total.

EMPLOYMENT AND PRODUCTIVITY

The increases in consumer spending and investment and the general pickup in the economy over the past year and a half have finally led to a more acceptable pace of job creation—something that was completely missing over the first year of recovery. On average, the economy generated 162,000 jobs per month over 1993, compared with only 81,000 jobs per month over 1992, and the *loss* of 73,000 jobs per month over 1991.

One important development in 1993 was the lengthening of the factory workweek and the increase in manufacturing overtime. In November the workweek reached a postwar record high, and overtime reached its highest level since the data series was begun in the 1950s. Employers have apparently been concerned about the fixed costs of adding new workers and about the unsteady nature of the expansion. Many have apparently been concerned that another decline in orders might force new rounds of layoffs, and so they have been trying to squeeze the most output possible out of their existing work forces. The good news is that, with the workweek and overtime so high, there should be building pressure on businesses to add new workers as demand continues to increase.

Productivity growth was weak over the first half of 1993 but rebounded in the third quarter as the economy picked up speed. Employers kept a tight rein on labor costs as output increased. Given the moderate rates of wage increase, nonfarm unit labor costs (the cost of labor needed to produce one unit of output) increased by about 2 percent, about the same as the 1992 increase. These modest gains in unit labor costs helped to give a healthy boost to corporate profits and maintained the prospects for low inflation.

INCOMES

Real disposable income increased by a modest 1 percent in 1993. Pretax profits posted strong increases, and proprietors' income was up by over 7 percent. But wages and salaries increased by a more modest percentage, and interest income was stagnant as interest rates fell. Average weekly earnings of production workers barely kept up with inflation.

INFLATION

Nineteen hundred and ninety-three saw the best inflation performance in a generation. The implicit price deflator increased by the smallest percentage since 1964. During 1993 the consumer price index (CPI) registered its smallest increase since 1986, and the core CPI (excluding food and energy) increased by the smallest percentage since 1972. Meanwhile the producer price index (PPI) for finished goods showed virtually no increase over the course of the year. The producer price index for finished goods excluding food and energy, the so-called core PPI, showed its smallest annual increase since the government began compiling this series in 1973.

Measured inflation increased as 1993 began, as prices of apparel, public transportation, tobacco products, and motor fuels posted large increases. The GDP price deflator, the CPI, and the PPI for finished goods all accelerated from their previous quarter's rate of change. The increase in inflation was temporary, however; many analysts believe it was due to problems with seasonal adjustment. Lower measured inflation returned after the spring.

Wage gains remained modest, as mentioned, and showed no tendency to accelerate over the course of the year. Medical costs showed some signs of moderating over 1993 and recorded their smallest annual increase in 20 years. They still increased at roughly twice the pace of the nonmedical CPI, however. External price factors, such as commodity prices, remained generally tame throughout the year, and oil prices fell sharply, suggesting a flat commodity price trajectory as 1994 began. (Box 2–2 discusses the possible economic effects of lower oil prices.) Given that the economy remains below its potential output level, there appear to be few inflationary seeds from 1993 blowing into 1994.

MONETARY POLICY

Short-term interest rates were essentially constant over the course of 1993, and the Federal Reserve continued its vigilance on inflation. After indications of an acceleration of prices in the first several months of the year, the Fed adopted an asymmetrical policy tilt, poised to tighten monetary policy if inflation gained momentum. Over the summer, however, low inflation returned, and the Fed reverted to its neutral policy stance.

The tendency in recent years for the broad monetary aggregates to behave in atypical ways, given changes in interest rates and economic activity, led the Federal Reserve to place less emphasis on these money supply measures in 1993. Some of the change in the behavior of the monetary aggregates stems from massive portfolio shifts by American households. For example, the sharp decline in interest rates on bank certificates of deposit led many households to shift money into stock and bond mutual funds. The downward shift of M2 (the broad monetary aggregate) relative to income that resulted from this and other developments clearly reduced that aggregate's usefulness as a short-term policy indicator. The sluggish growth of M2 did not signal that the Fed was running a tight monetary policy: In 1993, growth rates of M1 (the narrow monetary aggregate) and the monetary base were up to 10 percentage points higher than M2 growth.

Another policy indicator in which the Federal Reserve has expressed some interest is the concept of a real short-term interest rate—the nominal rate less expected inflation. It is generally assumed that real short-term rates will gradually rise as the economy strengthens and the output gap shrinks. The Federal Reserve's shift toward reliance on a broader set of guidelines for setting monetary policy, including short-term interest rates, appears to be an appropriate adaptation to changing events. It should allow the overall condition of the economy to be carefully monitored, and an appropriate policy response to be crafted.

FISCAL POLICIES AND THE TIMING OF OUTPUT

The uneven pattern of strong growth in late 1992 and slowdown in early 1993 was attributable in part to tax and spending changes

> **Box 2-2.—The Economic Effects of Lower Oil Prices**
>
> Oil prices tumbled during 1993. Over the first half of the year, West Texas Intermediate crude oil averaged about $20 per barrel. By the middle of October the price was down to about $18.25 per barrel, and by late December the price had fallen to about $14.25—more than 25 percent lower than earlier in the year. Weak global economic conditions, including the recessions in Europe and Japan, the seeming inability of the Organization of Petroleum Exporting Countries (OPEC) to restrict its members' production levels, and the possibility that Iraq would soon be exporting substantial quantities of oil again were likely contributors to the price declines.
>
> A drop in the price of oil, like any relative price change, has microeconomic consequences: Some sectors benefit and others are hurt. Lower oil prices will likely bring painful dislocations in the U.S. oil industry and the regions where it is concentrated. If oil prices remain low, domestic oil output is likely to decline faster than it already has been. U.S. dependence on foreign oil would also be likely to increase. Lower oil prices would also cause more energy to be used and might lead to higher levels of pollution.
>
> Because oil is such an important input into the U.S. economy, however, lower oil prices will also have favorable effects on the U.S. macroeconomy in 1994—if prices stay in the $15-per-barrel range. There are several transmission channels. The main beneficial effect is that lower oil prices translate into lower inflation, which boosts real disposable income for consumers, giving them the wherewithal to make more nonoil purchases. Lower oil prices also mean that businesses have lower costs, which translate into higher cash flow and profit margins, leading in turn to more investment spending. Foreign industrial economies also get an upward boost from lower oil prices and in turn demand more U.S. exports.
>
> Some economic models suggest that if the 25-percent drop in oil prices in 1993 were sustained over 1994, real GDP growth would be between 0.3 and 0.4 percentage point higher in 1994. The same models predict that CPI inflation would be noticeably lower.

in 1992 that served to raise aggregate demand in 1992 and depress it in the first half of 1993. First, there was a temporary burst in defense spending in the second half of 1992. Second, a decrease in individual income tax withholding raised consumer spending in 1992 but reduced it in 1993 as households made their final settlements with the Internal Revenue Service (IRS). The Council estimates that these two factors added 0.2 percent to the level of GDP in the second quarter of 1992 and 0.4 percent in the third and fourth quarters. These gains were temporary, however. GDP growth was 0.3 percent lower in the first quarter of 1993 and 0.4 percent lower in the second quarter than it would have been without these fiscal factors. There were also effects on the timing of consumer spending arising from the expectation and misperception of 1993 tax changes.

Defense Spending

During the second half of 1992, defense spending temporarily increased well above its trend. Part of the change was in purchases of durables. The other portion was in "other services," whose increase was in part due to expenditures to close military bases. Chart 2–7 shows the temporary burst of spending relative to a baseline which is estimated as the trend in defense spending from the third quarter of 1989 to the third quarter of 1993, excluding the quarters of the Persian Gulf crisis and the last two quarters of 1992.

Chart 2-7 **Defense Spending: Actual Versus Baseline**
Although defense spending is falling in the post-Cold War era, two recent periods of relatively high defense spending stand out.

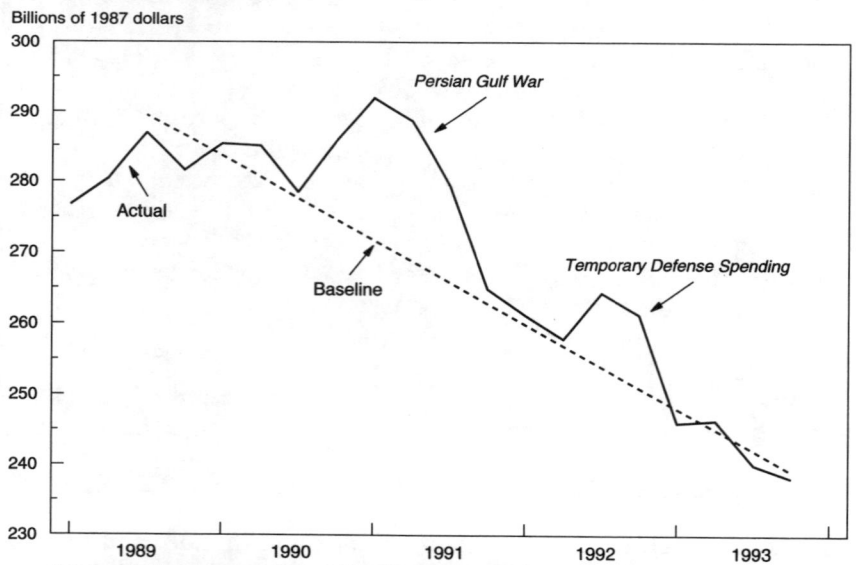

Note: Baseline is trend in spending from 1989:III to 1993:IV, excluding 1990:IV-1991:III and 1992:III-IV.
Sources: Council of Economic Advisers and Department of Commerce.

Change in Tax Withholding

The change in the withholding tables reduced income tax withholding for most taxpayers by an average of $25 a month beginning in March 1992. Taxpayers therefore owed the IRS an additional $250 (or received a smaller refund) in 1993. Households basically faced two choices: They could let the cash accumulate in their bank accounts and use it to make the extra $250 payment in April, or they could spend it. From both time-series and cross-sectional estimates of consumer behavior, the Council estimates that roughly 40 percent of households spent the extra cash because of either liquidity constraints, myopia, or inertia. Given their incomes, those households then had to reduce spending when they settled with the IRS in 1993. This shift in take-home pay led to the estimated shifting of consumption from 1993 to 1992 shown in Chart 2–8. The presumption is that households readjusted withholding and spending after their 1993 final settlements, so that this pattern will not repeat itself.

Chart 2-8 **Effects of 1992 Tax Withholding Change on Personal Consumption**
The reduction in personal income tax withholding in 1992 induced some households to shift consumption from 1993 to 1992.

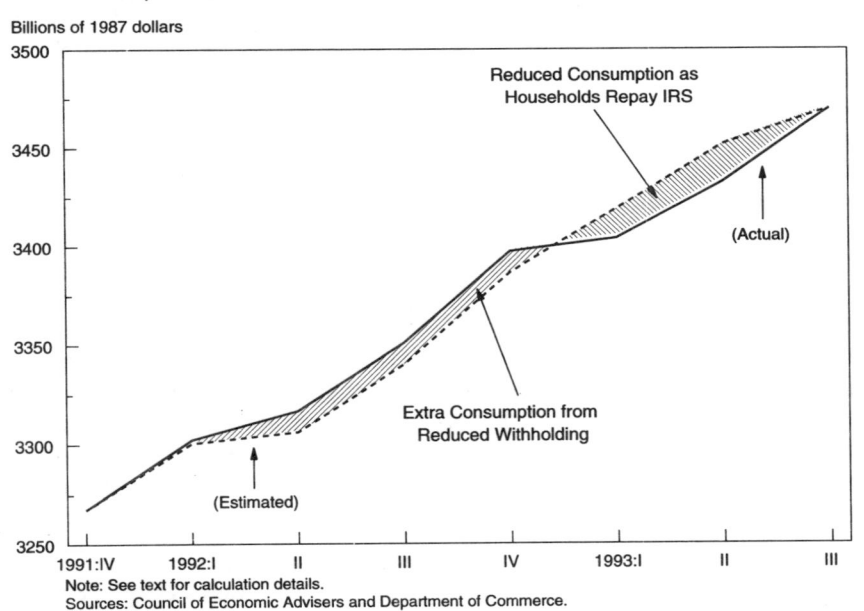

Note: See text for calculation details.
Sources: Council of Economic Advisers and Department of Commerce.

There have been other changes in tax rules that worked in an offsetting direction regarding tax payments, but not in an offsetting direction regarding consumption. Specifically, the change in the safe-harbor rules for underpayment of estimated tax probably caused some high-income taxpayers to move payments that they would have normally made in their April 1993 final settlements with the IRS to 1992 estimated tax payments. A household paying estimated tax is probably less likely to let changes in the timing of tax payments affect its consumption than is the typical household.

Expectations of 1993 Tax Changes

Anticipation and misperception of proposed 1993 changes in the tax law could have had further effects on the timing of demand. During his campaign for the Presidency, then-Governor Clinton proposed an investment tax credit. In December 1992, then-Senate Finance Committee Chairman Bentsen and House Ways and Means Committee Chairman Rostenkowski announced that any credit would be retroactive to December 3, 1992. Earlier in the quarter some firms may have delayed making investments in anticipation of receiving such a credit. Except for information-processing equipment, however, there was no discernable shift in investment spending during the fourth quarter of 1992. Given the lags in making investment decisions, it is not surprising that the anticipation of a possible credit appears to have had little effect on most components of investment. There was, however, a substantial deceleration in investment in computer and other information-processing equipment during the final quarter of 1992. It is probably relatively easy to change the scheduling of purchases of such equipment. Hence, this deceleration could well be explained in part by firms delaying purchases in anticipation of the credit.

Apparently there were also widespread misperceptions about the scope of the income tax increases in the Administration's economic plan. As late as the end of July 1993, over 70 percent of respondents to a Wall Street Journal/NBC News poll thought that middle-class taxpayers would bear most of the tax increases. In fact, the income tax increases apply only to families with taxable incomes over $140,000—the top 1.2 percent of households. Hence, it appeared for much of 1993 that many consumers incorrectly expected an income tax increase. This misperception may have accounted for some of the weakness of consumption in early 1993.

Do the 1993 Fiscal Measures Threaten 1994 Growth?

High-income households will have to make increased tax payments in April 1994 because of the increase in income tax rates enacted in 1993. There is reason to expect, however, that these extra payments by high-income individuals in 1994 will have a smaller effect on GDP than the extra payments made in 1993 by taxpayers affected by the 1992 change in withholding. One reason is that high-income taxpayers are presumably more likely to make the payments out of savings. Another is that many high-income taxpayers reduced their 1993 tax liability by shifting income from 1993 to December 1992. Moreover, under provisions of the Omnibus Budget Reconciliation Act of 1993 (OBRA93), these taxpayers can spread their increased 1993 payments over 3 years.

Nineteen hundred and ninety-four will also see an increase in the earned income tax credit (EITC). Payment of the EITC will tend to stimulate demand. Although households are entitled to collect the EITC during the tax year, most only claim it when they fill out their returns the following year, and they are likely to spend most of it.

THE FEDERAL GOVERNMENT'S FISCAL STANCE

The size of the budget deficit is an incomplete measure of the stance of fiscal policy. One important function of the budget is to act as an automatic stabilizer against economic fluctuations. When the economy enters a recession, tax collections fall as incomes decline, and there is an increase in government spending on such items as unemployment insurance and income maintenance programs. As a result, the budget deficit tends to increase in recessions and fall in recoveries, without any change to the tax system or in legislated expenditures. Chart 2–9 plots historical and predicted levels of the actual Federal budget deficit, which is expected to fall from 4 percent of GDP in fiscal 1993 to about 2.3 percent of GDP by the late 1990s.

The effects of the business cycle and inflation mask the true fiscal stance of the government. Declines in output from its full-employment level reduce revenue and increase expenditures. Inflation reduces the real interest cost to the government for a given level of nominal interest payments, which are included in the deficit. Chart 2–9 shows the actual deficit and the inflation-adjusted structural deficit. (The structural deficit is the one that would prevail at a high level of employment.) The estimates use the Congressional Budget Office's estimate of the cyclical adjustment. For the inflation adjustment, the outstanding Federal debt (bonds held by the private sector plus the monetary base) is multiplied by the inflation rate. As a result of the Administration's budget plan, the inflation-adjusted structural deficit falls to less than 1 percent of GDP after fiscal 1994—its lowest level since 1982. This share, moreover, remains constant for the remainder of the forecast period. The conclusion is that current fiscal policy—primarily as a result of the Administration's recently adopted deficit reduction plan—is following a more balanced and stable course than did the policies of the previous decade.

Chart 2-9 Alternative Measures of the Stance of Fiscal Policy
Fiscal policy as measured by the adjusted structural budget deficit is forecast to move to a more stable trajectory with the current deficit reduction plan.

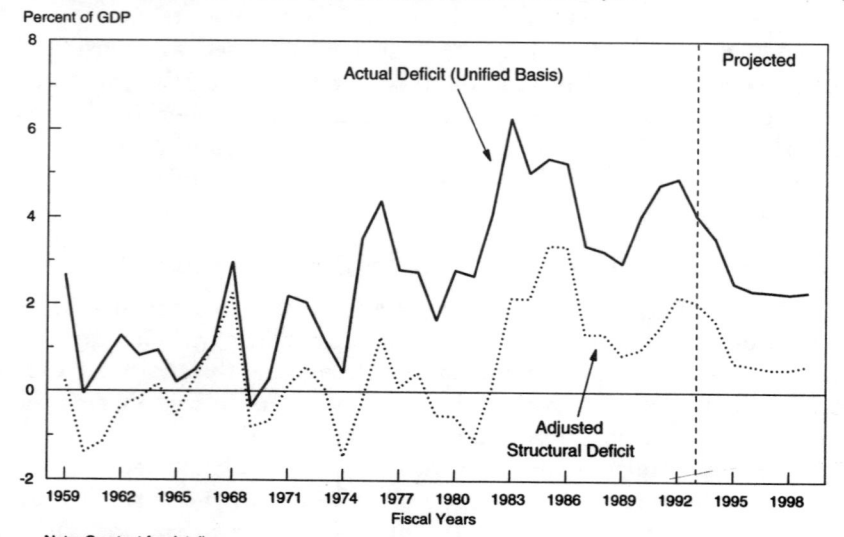

Note: See text for details.
Sources: Council of Economic Advisers, Congressional Budget Office, Office of Management and Budget, and Board of Governors of the Federal Reserve System.

INDUSTRIAL AND REGIONAL DISPARITIES

Disparities in growth across industries became more pronounced over 1993. Information-processing equipment benefited from heavy investment demand and experienced double-digit output gains. Certain interest-sensitive sectors of the economy, especially furniture, motor vehicles, and major appliances, were clearly helped by the sharply lower long-term interest rates and also posted large output gains. At the opposite end of the spectrum, the defense-related industries—aerospace, instruments, and ordnance—saw continued sharp production cutbacks.

These industrial disparities contributed to regional differences in economic activities. The State of California has been particularly hard hit by the defense builddown and has yet to start posting gains in nonagricultural employment, even though the rebound in the Nation as a whole began in March 1992. Aerospace jobs are a particularly acute problem: Of the 125,000 defense-related jobs that are projected to be lost in California from 1993 to 1997, 90,000 will be in the aerospace sector. California's 8.7-percent unemployment rate at year-end contrasted with a rate of just 6.4 percent for the Nation as a whole (Chart 2–10).

Chart 2-10 Unemployment Rates by State, December 1993
The national unemployment rate masks substantial regional differences. California is the only large state with an unemployment rate above 8 1/2 percent.

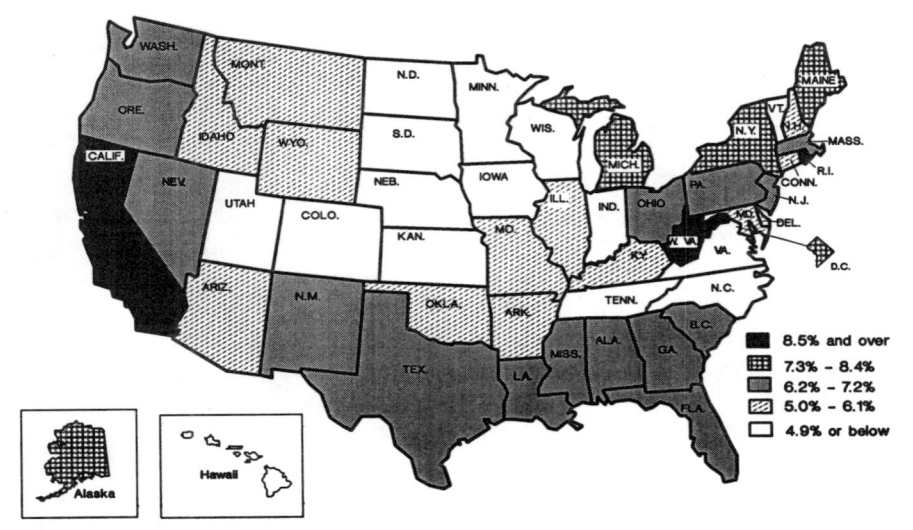

- 8.5% and over
- 7.3% – 8.4%
- 6.2% – 7.2%
- 5.0% – 6.1%
- 4.9% or below

Source: Department of Labor.

Chart 2-11 Nonfarm Employment Growth by State, November 1992 to November 1993
Employment gains are now widespread across the country. California remains a key exception.

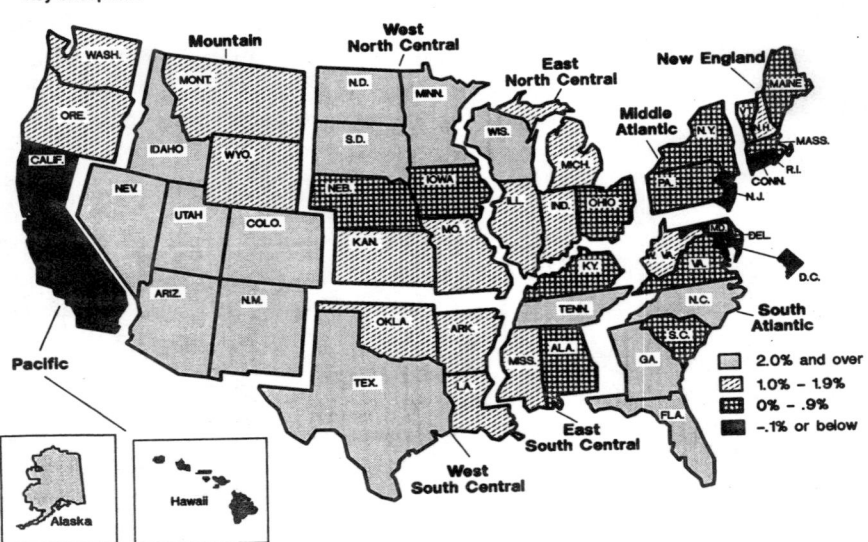

- 2.0% and over
- 1.0% – 1.9%
- 0% – .9%
- –.1% or below

Note: Chart shows percent change in nonfarm payroll employment.
Source: Department of Labor.

Meanwhile, the Mountain States were 1993's growth leaders. Strong income and employment gains were seen in Utah, Colorado, New Mexico, and Arizona (Chart 2–11).

DEFICIT REDUCTION AND THE REAL INTEREST RATE

As the new Administration took office, it appeared that the ratio of Federal Government debt to GDP was on an unsustainable upward path. The explosion of debt in the 1980s had kept real interest rates high throughout the decade. Hence, nominal rates did not fall by as much as the 1980s' victory against inflation warranted. Much of the recent reduction in long-term interest rates, it will be argued below, should be attributed to the change in budget policy in early 1993. The close linkage of the decline in long-term interest rates to the political and legislative events of the last 15 months gives strong support to the view that high Federal debt in the 1980s was responsible for the high real returns on long-term bonds, and that the change in Federal fiscal policy is responsible in large part for the declines in real interest rates.

The President's economic plan reoriented fiscal policy from consumption toward investment, both by reducing the size of projected budget deficits and by changing the composition of Federal spending from current expenditures to investment. The reduction in future Federal borrowing was well received by the financial markets. In the words of the Federal Reserve Board Chairman in his July 1993 Humphrey-Hawkins testimony, the financial markets "brought forward" the effects of future deficit reduction. The event analysis shown in Chart 2–12, linking the announcement and enactment of credible budget reduction to changes in the long-term interest rate, provides support for the view that the interest rate declines were largely due to budget policy.

Long-term interest rates are near the lowest they have been since the 1960s. On election day 1992, the 10-year Treasury yield was 6.87 percent. It has ratcheted down several times since then, with the declines closely tied to political and legislative events. The yield fell to 6.02 percent at the end of February, following Treasury Secretary Bentsen's announcement of the proposed energy tax and the President's speech announcing his economic plan. The decline stalled in April when the stimulus component of the President's plan was filibustered in the Senate. It resumed its downward movement when the House passed the President's budget in late May. It then fell to 5.51 percent at the end of August after the plan was finally enacted by the Congress.

Long-term rates did increase in late 1993, reversing some of the decline that followed the passage of OBRA93. Reports in the finan-

Chart 2-12 Yields on 10-Year Treasury Securities
Administration policy actions have had a noticeable effect in reducing interest rates.

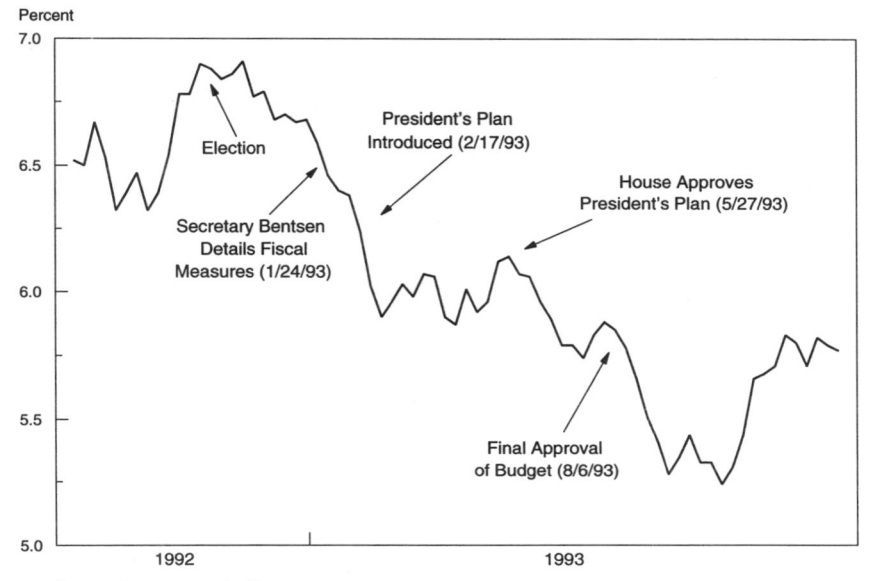

[Line chart showing yields from 1992 to 1993, with annotations: Election; Secretary Bentsen Details Fiscal Measures (1/24/93); President's Plan Introduced (2/17/93); House Approves President's Plan (5/27/93); Final Approval of Budget (8/6/93). Y-axis in Percent from 5.0 to 7.0.]

Source: Department of the Treasury.

cial press attributed the increase in yields to the release of favorable economic data and to speculation by some financial observers that the Federal Reserve would tighten monetary policy. But these data and statements did not actually signal much that was new about the state of the economy nor any change of monetary policy. Unobserved factors, psychological or otherwise, are important determinants of market prices. Still, despite large, unexplained fluctuations, the three major moves in yields shown in the chart have resulted in a cumulative reduction in yields on 10-year Treasuries of 104 basis points from the election to December 31, 1993.

The sharp decline in long-term interest rates in 1993 continued the downward trend that began in the early 1980s. Interest rates, both short- and long-term, had reached historic highs in the late 1970s and early 1980s, during the period of very high inflation and the subsequent period of very tight money. The latter period was characterized by a negative or slightly positive slope to the yield curve (which relates interest rates to lengthening maturities).

Long-term real rates remained high throughout the 1980s. Chart 2–13 decomposes the nominal yield on 10-year Treasuries into expected inflation and the implied *ex ante* real interest rate. Expected inflation is measured by the Blue Chip consensus forecast (a private sector survey of forecasts) for 10-year inflation, which has been compiled semiannually since 1980.

Chart 2-13 **Real Interest Rates**
Recent declines in the nominal long-term interest rate reflect declines in the *ex ante* real rate from its unusually high level over most of the 1980s.

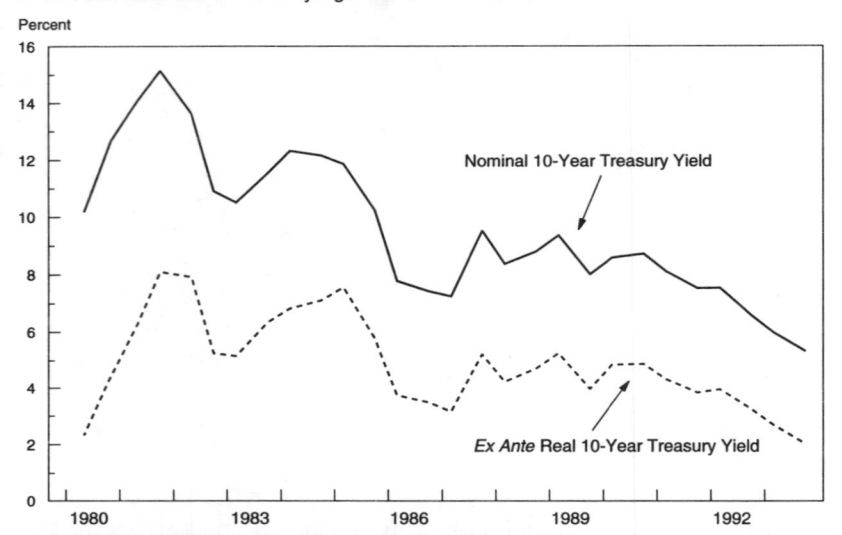

Note: Real rate is nominal rate minus a consensus forecast of 10-year inflation.
Sources: Council of Economic Advisers, Department of the Treasury, and Eggert's Blue Chip Economic Indicators.

Over the period shown in the chart, the *ex ante* real rate averaged almost 5 percent. Unfortunately, comparable data on long-term expected inflation are not available prior to 1980. *Ex post* real rates provide only an imperfect guide to *ex ante* rates, especially for long-term rates, because there are so few time periods over which to average the expectational errors. Over the second half of the 1950s, the average *ex post* real 10-year rate was about 1 percentage point, over the 1960s it was −0.4 percentage point, and over the 1970s it was about +0.7 percentage point. The low *ex post* real rates of the 1960s and 1970s were surely partly explained by the unexpected rise in inflation of the 1970s. For the 1960s and 1970s, the *ex post* 10–year real interest rate understates the *ex ante* real rate because of the unexpected inflation in the late 1960s and throughout the 1970s. Based on forecasts of 10-year inflation, the Council estimates that *ex ante* real 10-year interest rates averaged slightly above 0.5 percent in the 1960s and about 2.4 percent in the

1970s. Although higher than the *ex post* rates for the same periods, these rates are well below the *ex ante* rates of the 1980s.

Therefore, it appears that real rates were unusually high throughout the 1980s. Only with the declines in nominal rates over the last few years has the real rate begun to decline. With the most recent set of observations, those of October 1993, the 10-year Treasury yield was 5.33 percent and the Blue Chip consensus forecast for long-term inflation was 3.3 percent, so the real rate was close to 2 percent. This level of real rates is somewhat above historical norms (Box 2–3).

Box 2–3.—Are Current Long-Term Interest Rates Sustainable?

Long-term Treasury bonds now yield about 6 percent. These nominal interest rates are very low by the standards of the last decade. But given the expected rate of inflation and historical standards for real interest rates, they appear to be sustainable. Long-term expected inflation is probably between 3 and 3½ percent, implying a 2½- to 3-percent real yield on long-term Treasuries. A real interest rate in this range, although low relative to recent experience, is not low relative to historical experience.

From 1953 to 1982 the *ex post* real yield on 10-year Treasuries averaged about 1 percent. Over the period 1900–50, the *ex post* real yield on government bonds was under 1 percent, but these bonds are not wholly comparable to current Treasury notes because they were callable and had tax benefits.

Clearly, if inflation remains under control, bond yields have some way to fall to come into line with their historical real averages.

HOW DEFICIT REDUCTION REDUCES LONG-TERM INTEREST RATES

The previous section discussed the circumstantial evidence linking Federal deficit reduction to the decline in real long-term interest rates. Over the 1980s, which saw a growing and potentially explosive Federal debt, real long-term rates were unprecedentedly high. Over the last 15 months there have been sharp declines in real rates associated with policy changes that provide for credible deficit reduction. This section explores the four economic mechanisms that link Federal deficit reduction policy with the real rate: national saving, investment, and capital accumulation; the policy mix; short-run real activity; and inflation risk.

Saving, Investment, and Capital Accumulation

The Federal debt-GDP ratio doubled in the 1980s, jumping from 22 percent of GDP in 1980 to 46 percent currently (Chart 2-14). To the extent that Federal debt substitutes for productive capital in an individual's portfolio, the increase in debt reduces income and productivity and raises the marginal product of capital and therefore the real interest rate. The Administration's economic plan is meant to increase national saving and national investment. The cumulated additional investment will have a significant effect on the capital stock and therefore on future real interest rates. (See the section on "Long-Term Effects of Deficit Reduction" below for estimates of the impact of the plan on wages and the capital stock.)

Chart 2-14 Net Federal Debt as Percent of Nominal GDP
From the end of World War II until 1980, the debt-GDP ratio fell to about 20 percent. Since 1980 it has increased to over 45 percent.

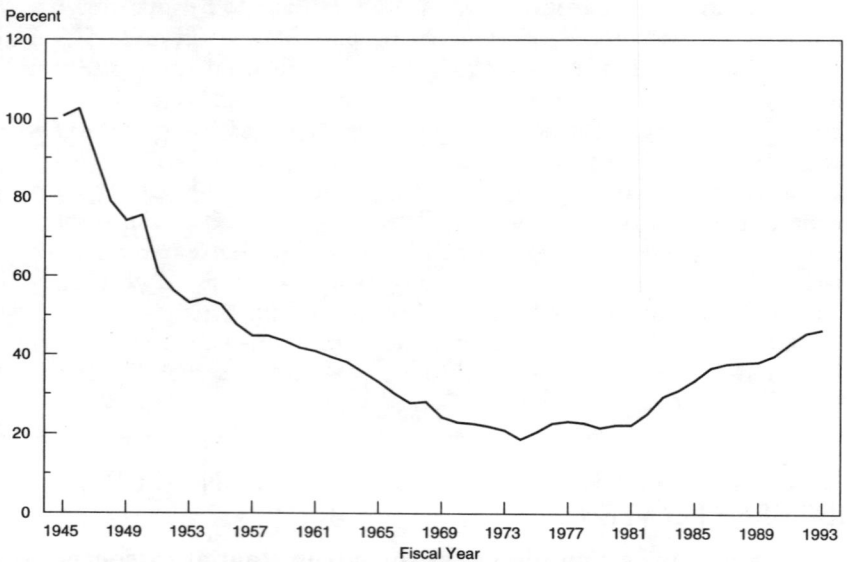

Note: Net Federal debt is defined as debt held by the public less debt held by the Federal Reserve.
Sources: Department of Commerce and Office of Management and Budget.

The policy changes in OBRA93 reduce the projected deficit for fiscal 1998 by 1¾ percent of GDP. Not all of this projected reduction in the deficit will go to national investment, however. Changes in either the current account or private saving could offset the decrease in Federal dissaving.

During the 1980s much of the Federal deficit was offset by increases in the current account deficit. As the budget deficit is reduced, there should be similar decreases in the current account deficit. The mechanism is simple. Deficit reduction is generally associated with an improvement in the price competitiveness of U.S. goods and services abroad, and therefore an increase in net exports. This expansion in net exports provides a stimulus that partially offsets the contractionary impact of spending cuts and tax increases on domestic demand. While it is difficult to determine the magnitude of this offset precisely, studies suggest that net exports will rise by approximately 40 percent of the initial deficit reduction.

Declines in private saving could also offset decreased Federal dissaving. However, the experience of the 1980s provides strong evidence on the reaction of private savers to government deficits. Personal saving did *not* act to offset ballooning Federal deficits in the 1980s, contrary to the predictions of neo-Ricardian theory. Therefore, we expect no decrease in private saving as deficits are reduced under the President's economic plan. After taking into account the reduction in the current account deficit, we estimate that the deficit reduction plan enacted in OBRA93 should increase the share of national investment in GDP by about 1 percentage point.

The deficit reduction package should increase the capital stock, as productive capital substitutes for government debt in private portfolios. An increase in the share of investment in GDP of 1 percentage point would have a substantial effect on the capital-labor ratio—raising it in steady state by about 10 percent (see below for details of the assumptions underlying this calculation). With conservative assumptions about the curvature of the production function (which governs how much output per worker will increase for a given increase in capital per worker), such a change in the capital-labor ratio would be expected to reduce the return on capital by about 2 percentage points—which is slightly higher than the decline in real long-term rates that we have seen to date.

It takes many years, however, to adjust to a new steady state. Along the transition path, the return on capital would fall only gradually. So, even if we accept the implied reduction in the steady-state return on capital, capital deepening alone cannot account for the sharp reduction of interest rates on long-term bonds that has already occurred.

Policy Mix

Credible deficit reduction also might affect long-term interest rates through the expectation of a changed mix of fiscal and monetary policy. In the 1980s, the Federal Reserve pursued a relatively restrictive policy to counter the stimulus engendered by loose fiscal policy. This mix resulted in high real interest rates. With credible deficit reduction, the Federal Reserve will be able to achieve a given level of nominal demand with a less restrictive monetary policy. This shift in the policy mix should reduce future real short-term interest rates. Expectations that short rates will be lower in the future should be reflected in lower real long-term rates. As a consequence, the composition of output will shift toward investment at the expense of consumption.

The Short-Run Level of Real Activity

Long-term rates might also fall because of bad news about expected future real economic activity. Real growth in the first half of 1993 was indeed disappointing. But both Administration and private forecasters believed, correctly as it turned out, that growth would be better in the second half of the year. Moreover, if there are fears of a future slump, why is the stock market at record highs? Presumably, market participants expect good earnings and dividends. The low bond yields and high stock values are consistent with the path of stable growth, low inflation, and decreasing unemployment that the Administration forecasts. Finally, the news of increasing growth that began to emerge in the fall was greeted by only modest increases in long-term rates.

Inflation Risk

A decline in expected inflation could also account for the decline in long-term bond rates associated with the deficit reduction plan. Chart 2–13 shows, however, that there is no break in inflation expectations associated with this decline in long-term bond rates. The difference between the nominal and real interest rates in Chart 2–13 gives a time-series of expected long-term inflation. In October 1992 the Blue Chip consensus expected an average annual GDP inflation of 3.3 percent for 1994–98 and 3.4 percent for 1999–2003. In October 1993, the consensus was again for 3.3-percent inflation for 1995–99, and 3.3 percent for 2000–2004. Hence, the consensus forecast implies that virtually all the recent reductions in nominal long-term rates were also reductions in real rates.

SHORT-RUN EFFECTS OF INTEREST RATES

The reduction in real long-term interest rates has been an important element powering the economic recovery. As discussed elsewhere in this chapter, reductions in Federal purchases—especially for defense—have been an important factor holding back the recovery. As the reductions in expenditures and increases in taxes built into the Administration's plan take effect, they—taken in isolation—would place a continued drag on the economy. But they should not be taken in isolation. Because long-term interest rates anticipate credible future fiscal consolidation, the effects of deficit reduction in long-term rates show up in advance of the actual deficit reduction. The resulting increases in interest-sensitive expenditures provide a boost to economic growth that works in the opposite direction of the direct fiscal effect. This increase in interest-sensitive spending is closely linked with the sustained reduction in long rates. In 1993, real GDP in the interest-sensitive sectors (business fixed investment, housing, and consumer durables) rose 11 percent, while the non-interest-sensitive sectors showed virtually no growth.

The interest-sensitive components of spending did not, however, increase uniformly throughout 1993. Producers' durable equipment was strong throughout the year, growing 18 percent from fourth quarter to fourth quarter. Expenditure on consumer durables was also strong throughout the year (with an 8-percent growth rate), but production of automobiles was irregular. Investment in nonresidential structures was weak for most of the year, most likely as a result of high vacancy rates in existing buildings, due in turn partly to overbuilding in the 1980s. The lags in the response of residential construction to the low interest rates were unusually long. Residential investment fell at a 4-percent annual rate in the first two quarters of 1993, but rose at a 21-percent rate in the last two quarters.

Net exports would appear on many economists' lists of interest-sensitive expenditures. Normally, low interest rates should lead to depreciation of the dollar and therefore to increased exports. This channel for interest rates was offset by other factors, however. Short-term rates fell around the world, not just in the United States, and the dollar has actually appreciated slightly on a multilateral basis. (A further discussion of the exchange rate is presented in Chapter 6.)

LONG-TERM EFFECTS OF DEFICIT REDUCTION

The key macroeconomic rationale for reducing the Federal deficit is to increase investment and therefore productivity and real incomes in the future. Changes in fiscal policy should exert sustained effects on national investment and saving. As discussed above, the President's economic plan should increase the share of domestic investment in GDP by about 1 percent once it is fully phased in. Chart 2–15 shows the projected impact of such an increase in the national investment rate on the marginal product of capital, the real wage rate, and the capital stock. (Box 2–4 contains details of the computation.) The data are expressed relative to the initial steady-state position.

All of the variables require several decades to adjust to their steady-state values. The ultimate reduction in the return to capital is about 2 percentage points. The reduction in long-term rates we have already seen is closer to 1½ percentage points. The reduction in the marginal product of capital takes place, however, over a very long period of time. Indeed, as presented in the chart, the marginal product of capital is down only 1 percentage point after 8 years. Moreover, since capital and bonds are not perfect substitutes, their

Chart 2-15 **Dynamic Effects of Deficit Reduction**
The real effects of raising the saving rate through deficit reduction include higher wages and investment and lower real interest rates.

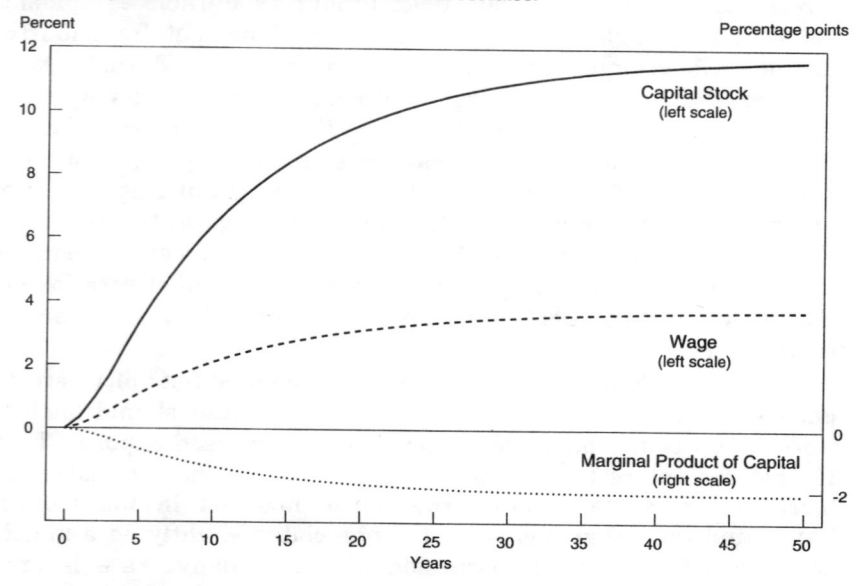

Source: Council of Economic Advisers.

rates will move by less than one for one. Other factors, such as expectations about the policy mix, therefore must explain the bulk of the rate reduction.

A small increase in the investment rate buys a substantial increase in the capital stock, again over a long period. This increase in the capital stock should ultimately raise real wages and productivity by about 3¾ percent.

Initially, consumption falls because of the direct effect of the Federal budget package. As output and productivity increase, however, so does consumption. It takes about 5 years for the change in fiscal policy to have a net positive effect on consumption. Thereafter, the effect of the economic plan is to raise consumption permanently, eventually by more than 2½ percent per year.

These calculations are quite conservative. They do not assume any externality from capital accumulation or any extra boost to productivity from embodied technological progress. If these factors are present, the gains from the increase in investment could be substantially higher.

> **Box 2–4.—Estimating the Long-Run Effects of Deficit Reduction**
>
> Chart 2–15 shows the results of applying a model of economic growth developed by Robert M. Solow to the change in the investment rate engendered by OBRA93. To carry out these calculations, we make several assumptions:
>
> - The production function is Cobb-Douglas with a capital share of one-third. (The Cobb-Douglas function presumes a fairly large degree of substitutability between capital and labor and will thus show a substantial output effect of increasing capital).
> - The rate of growth of the economy's potential output (a little below 2.5 percent) plus the rate of depreciation (a little above 9 percent) is 11.5 percent.
> - The initial investment rate is 13 percent, about the ratio of fixed investment to GDP in 1993. It is assumed to rise to 13.4 percent the first year, 13.7 percent in the second, 13.8 percent in the third, and is 14.0 percent thereafter.
>
> The magnitude and timing of the increases in investment reflect the increase in Federal saving from the deficit reduction package and the assumption (see text) that 40 percent of the increased Federal saving will be offset by a reduced current account deficit.
>
> These calculations are subject to a considerable degree of uncertainty. They are sensitive to the form of the production function and the assumed rates of depreciation and growth in potential.

THE ECONOMY'S RESPONSE TO HIGHER INCOME TAXES

Critics of the increase in income tax rates enacted in August 1993 make two related claims: first, that higher tax rates will have an adverse effect on the level of saving, investment, and employment in the economy, and second, that the higher tax rates on high-income taxpayers will not result in much (or any) increase in tax revenues. The arguments offered to bolster these claims have a common foundation, namely, that the disincentive effects of higher marginal tax rates have a profound influence on individuals' behavior.

We note first that economies can thrive under a wide range of top marginal tax rates—which already weakens the arguments of these critics. In fact, the U.S. economy has performed extremely well during periods of relatively high top marginal rates: We enjoyed healthy average real GDP growth of 4 percent per year over the decade of the 1960s, when the top marginal income tax rate on wage and salary income averaged 80.3 percent, but less impressive 2½-percent average annual growth in the decade of the 1980s, when the top rate on wages and salaries averaged 48.4 percent. Also, many people in the United States admired the investment-led economic boom that Japan enjoyed in the 1980s, when that country had much higher marginal income tax rates than did the United States. Obviously, many other important factors besides marginal tax rates determine saving and investment patterns and economic growth.

DO TAXES CHANGE BEHAVIOR?

A central tenet of economics is that relative prices matter. Taxes on capital and wage income change the relationships among the various prices that people face when deciding how much to save, invest, and work, and thus have an effect on the way people choose to allocate their time (between supplying labor and taking leisure) and their income (between current consumption and saving). This observation serves as the basis of the supply-side dictum that a reduction in taxes, by inducing people to work harder and save more, can induce higher rates of investment and economic growth.

The extent to which changes in the marginal tax rate on income affect labor supply and saving has been a subject of extensive research for many years. The preponderance of evidence seems to indicate that the changes are small. Saving rates seem to be little affected by movements in after-tax interest rates, and hours worked and labor force participation rates for most demographic groups show only limited sensitivity to changes in after-tax wages.

It is undeniable that the sharp reduction in taxes in the early 1980s was a strong impetus to economic growth. But it is unlikely that the principal source of this growth was people reacting to reductions in marginal tax rates by working and saving more. The expansion that took place over the 1980s was tax-induced mainly insofar as lower taxes raised disposable income, which led to increased consumption. For example, between 1981 and 1986, the consumption share of GDP increased from 64.5 percent to 67.4 percent. In other words, the 1980s' saw a classical Keynesian, demand-driven expansion—not the kind of expansion that supply-side theory predicted. Those who would point to the effects of the 1980's tax cuts as evidence of strong supply-side effects of taxation are grossly overstating the case.

The increases in the top marginal income tax rates enacted by the Congress in 1993 will affect directly only the top 1.2 percent of American families. Moreover, top marginal tax rates remain low by historical standards. While some individuals may alter their behavior because of the higher tax rates and, for example, cut back their hours worked, others may actually increase their work effort in order to meet saving or consumption objectives. Overall, it is unlikely that the Administration's plan will induce large responses in labor force participation, hours worked, or savings in the overall economy.

DO HIGHER TAX RATES INCREASE TAX REVENUES?

Some also argue that income tax collections do not vary much when top marginal tax rates increase or decrease. In this view, an increase in income tax rates provides such a strong incentive for people to reduce their taxable income that the tax base shrinks and no additional revenue is generated. For example, a worker facing higher taxes on wages might choose to take some compensation in the form of nonwage benefits, such as more vacation time or larger future pensions. Similarly, individuals facing higher tax rates on unearned income might change the composition of their savings (while keeping the level constant) by investing in tax-exempt bonds rather than stocks or corporate debt.

History can serve as a guide to determining whether these offsetting effects of a change in tax rates are strong enough to have a significant impact on revenues. For the United States, contrary to the supply-siders' claims, income tax cuts have generally *reduced* income tax revenues and tax increases have generally raised them. Chart 2–16 illustrates the effect that a number of changes in tax policy have had on personal income tax receipts. Several episodes stand out:

- The 1964 tax cut reduced the top marginal rate from 91 percent in 1963 to 77 percent in 1964 and then to 70 percent in 1965. Income tax revenue as a share of GDP dropped sharply.
- The special Vietnam war surtax imposed additional charges equal to 7.5 percent of tax in 1968, 10 percent in 1969, and 2.5 percent in 1970. The result was a sharp increase in revenues in 1968 and 1969, followed by a decline as the surtax was phased out.
- The 1981 tax cut reduced the top marginal rate from 70 percent to 50 percent in 1982 and cut tax rates for lower income individuals over the 1982–84 period. *Since then, personal income tax revenues as a share of GDP have never regained their 1981–82 levels.* Similarly, the 1986 tax reform reduced marginal rates in stages over 1987 and 1988, and revenues as a share of GDP in 1988 fell slightly below their 1986 level.

In short, evidence from postwar experience strongly suggests that personal income tax revenues rise when marginal rates are increased, and fall when marginal rates are reduced.

Chart 2-16 **Personal Income Taxes as Percent of GDP**
A number of historical changes in tax rates demonstrate the effect that rate changes have on revenues.

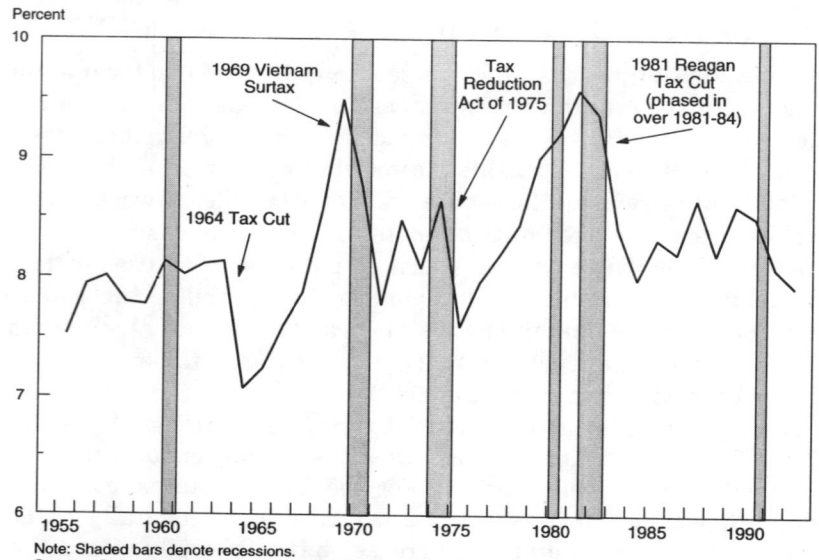

Note: Shaded bars denote recessions.
Sources: Department of Commerce and National Bureau of Economic Research.

THE ECONOMIC OUTLOOK

A credible deficit reduction plan and low long-term interest rates have set the stage for moderate but sustainable economic growth over the mid-1990s. As the ratio of the Federal budget deficit to GDP declines, financial markets should be reassured that inflation and interest rates can be sustained at the levels of the 1950s and 1960s. Interest-sensitive sectors of the economy, particularly business fixed investment, should thrive and provide a steady demand base. Housing and demand for household durable goods and automobiles should also do well and underpin a steady economic expansion.

The lean inventories that the economy was carrying as it entered 1994 suggest that manufacturers should face gradually increasing order levels. With the factory workweek and manufacturing overtime at postwar highs, there will be growing pressure on firms to add new workers to meet production demands. Higher employment should contribute to a steady increase in income and provide lift for all sectors of the economy. Income growth, which was outstripped by increases in consumer spending over the course of 1993, should gradually overtake spending growth over the next couple of years, leading to a slowly increasing saving rate.

Finally, foreign economies should recover over the next couple of years and provide an export lift for U.S. firms. By early 1995, net exports should once again be contributing to U.S. growth rather than subtracting from it. Strength in these sectors is expected to more than offset the continued declines in real Federal spending that are expected over the next 5 years.

The projected decline in the Federal budget deficit, from 4.0 percent of GDP in fiscal 1993 to about 2.3 percent of GDP by fiscal 1996, should have benefits for the economy that go beyond interest rates. First, with less government "crowding out," more funds will be available for private business investment. This higher investment level will increase the Nation's capital stock and hence increase its long-run potential output. Second, there is a linkage between the Federal budget deficit and the current account deficit. Because foreign savings have been steadily flowing into the United States to cover the imbalance between domestic saving and domestic investment, we have been running large capital account surpluses. These in turn have required large current account deficits, because the two accounts are mirror images. A steady reduction of the Federal budget deficit, therefore, should also translate into smaller current account deficits.

With these developments, GDP growth of 2½ percent to 3 percent per year—in line with 1993 growth—seems likely to continue over the rest of the 1990s (Table 2–2). This growth should be sufficient to reduce the unemployment rate steadily from the roughly 6½–percent level of late 1993 to about 5½ percent (under the old unemployment definition) by the end of 1998. (Box 3–1 in Chapter 3 contains a discussion of the relationship between the old unemployment rate, based on the historical Current Population Survey, and the new unemployment rate, based on the revised version of the survey.) These gains will be paired with healthy increases in real disposable income, which are as important as job growth to the American worker. After two decades of relative stagnation, real wages should post solid gains and allow American families once again to enjoy steadily improving living standards.

Within this macroeconomic environment, short-term interest rates are likely to drift slowly upward over the coming years as the economy strengthens. Long-term interest rates are not expected to increase appreciably, however, because inflation should remain subdued and budget deficits will continue to shrink. Healthy gains in productivity, the mainspring of rising living standards, will be the key to keeping inflation tame. The higher rate of business investment in the 1990s than in the 1970s and 1980s should keep productivity on a relatively fast track and prevent unit labor costs

TABLE 2-2.— *Administration Forecasts*

Item	1993	1994	1995	1996	1997	1998	1999
	Percent change, fourth quarter to fourth quarter							
Real GDP	2.8	3.0	2.7	2.7	2.6	2.6	2.5
GDP implicit deflator	2.2	2.7	2.8	2.9	3.0	3.0	3.0
Consumer price index (CPI-U)	2.7	3.0	3.2	3.3	3.4	3.4	3.4
	Calendar year average							
Unemployment rate (percent)							
Old basis	6.8	6.3	5.9	5.7	5.6	5.5	5.5
New basis	....	(6.6–7.2)	(6.2–6.8)	(6.0–6.6)	(5.9–6.5)	(5.8–6.4)	(5.8–6.4)
Interest rate, 91-day Treasury bills (percent)	3.0	3.4	3.8	4.1	4.4	4.4	4.4
Interest rate, 10-year Treasury note (percent)	5.9	5.7	5.7	5.7	5.7	5.7	5.7
Nonfarm payroll employment (millions)	110.2	112.3	114.3	116.2	118.2	120.0	121.9

Sources: Council of Economic Advisers, Department of the Treasury, and Office of Management and Budget.

from accelerating. Health care reform should help rein in the spiraling costs that have plagued that huge sector of the economy and thus help control overall inflation.

The Administration's forecast is in line with private sector forecasts for 1994 and the mid-1990s. It assumes no dramatic shift in aggregate economic performance beyond the trends clearly established over 1993—low inflation, low long-term interest rates, and healthy investment spending. It also assumes that the historical (Okun's law) relationship between output and unemployment continues to hold.

RISKS TO THE FORECAST

As always, there are risks to this forecast. First, foreign economic activity may not pick up as expected, especially if other governments remain reluctant to stimulate their economies by easing interest rates or pursuing countercyclical fiscal policies. It is also possible that the kind of industrial restructuring that the United States has endured over the past decade may prove to be a bigger hurdle than realized for key European trading partners and Japan. Also, the timetable for the correction of the Japanese speculative bubble of the late 1980s is unclear and could take longer than expected. The better the Group of Seven countries coordinate their macroeconomic policies over the next couple of years, the lower the risk of a prolonged pause in industrial-country growth.

A second risk is that long-term interest rates could take back more of their declines of 1993. Such a move could crimp the interest-sensitive sectors that provided the economy with most of its growth in 1993. Housing and business fixed investment would likely be the most vulnerable sectors.

A stalling out of consumer demand cannot be ruled out either. Consumers have been increasing their spending by a larger percentage than their incomes have been rising over the past year, and they could turn pessimistic about the future again. Indeed, they have already done so several times in this business cycle expansion. An unexpected cutback in consumer spending would lead to higher than desired inventory levels, which would in turn reverberate back through the economy in the form of lower orders and perhaps lower employment in manufacturing.

But economic growth could also exceed this forecast in the short run. The U.S. output gap widened sharply over the 1990–91 recession, and the economy could grow faster than its noninflationary potential for a couple of years as part of a catchup process. Certainly growth of 4 percent would not be unprecedented during such a phase. Among the factors that might contribute to faster than expected growth are a faster than expected rebound of economic growth in Europe, Japan, and the rest of the industrial world, which would sharply boost U.S. exports; oil prices remaining relatively low and giving a healthy boost to real disposable incomes; and the possibility that Americans have more pent-up demand than realized for houses, automobiles, and other durable goods.

SOURCES OF LONG-RUN GROWTH

The long-run rate of real GDP growth can be expressed as the sum of the individual growth rates of four components: (1) the number of available workers in the economy (the labor force); (2) the rate at which these workers are employed (the employment rate); (3) the number of hours worked per year (which is proportional to the average workweek); and (4) the quantity of goods and services produced by an hour of labor (labor productivity). Table 2–3 details the contribution of each of these components to real GDP growth over several historical time periods and as projected for the rest of the decade. Because many of these components vary with the business cycle, their growth rates are measured from cyclical peak to cyclical peak. Estimates in the fourth column are based on actual data through the fourth quarter of 1993 and forecasts by the Administration through 1999.

The projected growth of nonfarm business product from the business cycle peak in the third quarter of 1990 to the end of 1999 is 2.7 percent per year. Underlying this projection is a growth in output per hour of 1.5 percent per year and growth in hours of 1.2 per-

TABLE 2–3.— *Accounting for Growth in Real GDP, 1960–99*
[Average annual percent change]

	1960 II to 1981 III	1973 IV to 1981 III	1981 III to 1990 III	1990 III to 1999 IV
1) Civilian noninstitutional population aged 16 and over	1.8	1.8	1.1	1.0
2) PLUS: Civilian labor force participation rate	0.3	0.5	0.4	0.2
3) EQUALS: Civilian labor force	2.1	2.4	1.6	1.2
4) PLUS: Civilian employment rate	−0.1	−0.4	0.2	0.0
5) EQUALS: Civilian employment	2.0	2.0	1.8	1.2
6) PLUS: Nonfarm business employment as a share of civilian employment	0.1	0.1	0.2	0.0
7) EQUALS: Nonfarm business employment	2.1	2.1	2.0	1.2
8) PLUS: Average weekly hours (nonfarm business sector)	−0.6	−0.7	0.0	0.0
9) EQUALS: Hours of all persons (nonfarm business)	1.5	1.3	2.0	1.2
10) PLUS: Output per hour (productivity, nonfarm business)	1.7	0.6	0.9	1.5
11) EQUALS: Nonfarm business output	3.3	1.9	2.9	2.7
12) LESS: Nonfarm business output as a share of real GDP[2]	0.1	−0.2	0.2	0.4
13) EQUALS: Real GDP	3.2	2.1	2.7	2.4

[1] Line six translates the civilian employment growth rate into the nonfarm business employment growth rate.
[2] Line 12 translates nonfarm business output back into output for all sectors (GDP), which includes the output of farms and general government.

Note.——Data may not sum to totals due to rounding.
Time periods are from business cycle peak to business cycle peak to avoid cyclical variation.
Source: Council of Economic Advisers, Department of Commerce, Department of Labor, Department of the Treasury, and Office of Management and Budget.

cent per year. The share of nonfarm business in GDP is projected to grow at 0.4 percent per year, so the growth rate of GDP over this period is projected to be roughly 2.4 percent per year.

The forecast for nonfarm hours assumes a civilian labor force growth rate of 1.2 percent per year, which is about a percentage point lower than labor force growth during the 1960s and 1970s. Virtually all of this difference reflects the slower growth of the labor force. It also assumes no change in the average workweek. The return of the economy to full employment by 1998 implies zero peak-to-peak growth in the civilian employment rate over the forecast period.

More than half of the predicted growth in real GDP results from an assumed rate of nonfarm labor productivity growth of 1.5 percent per year. This rate is somewhat higher than the actual rate over the past two decades. While the sources of productivity growth are complex, and the causes of the well-documented "productivity slowdown" of the 1970s remain under debate, we believe there is justification for assuming an increase in labor productivity growth over the near term.

First, the baby-boom generation, which entered the labor market *en masse* during the 1970s, has now been fully assimilated. The workforce of today is thus older, more educated, and more experienced than in previous years. Second, capital deepening (see above) is likely to occur. As business continues to respond to low real interest rates, the level of investment in the economy should rise, leading to an increase in capital intensity. Third, the Administration's programs of promoting public investment—including better transportation and communications infrastructure—and human capital formation should enhance private sector productivity. The implication of all these factors is that some improvement in the rate of productivity growth over the next several years is likely.

CONCLUSION

The performance of the U.S. economy was unsatisfactory from early 1990 until the second half of 1992. Job creation was lackluster, unemployment was higher than it should have been, and real output failed to manifest the gains that are usual for an economic recovery. Even today the economy is operating below its potential level of output. Some of the sluggishness over this period was payback for a decade of debt-financed growth. Over the 1980s and early 1990s, the Federal Government ran massive budget deficits even in years of strong economic growth, and the level of net Federal debt jumped from about $800 billion in 1982 to about $2.7 trillion in 1992. A key result was historically high real interest rates.

Corporations followed suit, heavily leveraging their operations. Even individuals got into the act and allowed debt levels to rise markedly. Meanwhile, large budget deficits contributed to the remarkable transformation of the United States, from a country that lent more to foreigners than it borrowed, into the world's largest debtor.

Many necessary corrections have now taken place, including new, more responsible fiscal policy. The Federal budget deficit should fall roughly in half as a share of GDP over the next 4 years. This anticipated deficit reduction has already caused long-term real interest rates to tumble. With inflation likely to remain subdued, these lower interest rates poise the economy for a period of sustained growth in the mid-1990s. This growth should be sufficient to generate 8 million new jobs within 4 years.

Lower interest rates should also boost the share of the economy going to investment. More investment should lead to capital deepening, higher labor productivity, and higher real American wages. As the government share of the economy falls, the net export share should increase. A higher level of exports should give a boost to real wages, too, partly because export jobs on average pay better wages than average U.S. jobs, and partly because of increasing specialization by American industry. Real income gains, in the final analysis, are the ultimate payoff from economic growth.

CHAPTER 3

Trends and Recent Developments in the U.S. Labor Market

THE CLINTON ADMINISTRATION has made increasing both the quantity and the quality of jobs its highest priority. Providing a stable macroeconomic foundation for private sector activity is essential to achieving this goal, but it is not enough. Sound macroeconomic policies are necessary but not sufficient for the task at hand. They must be complemented by labor market policies to remedy a number of deep and longstanding impediments to the maintenance of high employment and to improvements in the quality of jobs. This chapter discusses these impediments and the Administration's proposals for addressing them.

The 1990–91 recession and the first year of the recovery witnessed rising unemployment. Even though output and employment have since been increasing, the news has been filled with stories of corporate downsizings and the increasing use of "contingent workers." These reports have sharpened fundamental fears about the security of employment. Popular accounts of recent events also allege that technical change is reducing employment throughout the economy.

After rising steadily for several decades, U.S. real wages have hardly grown since the early 1970s, while the growth of total real compensation (wages plus benefits) has slowed considerably. At the same time, the income gap between rich and poor has been growing, so that the poor are worse off in real terms now than they were two decades ago. Incomes of those in the middle have stagnated. The unemployment rate, both at peaks and troughs of the business cycle, has tended to be higher in the last two decades than in the first half of the postwar period. Employment-to-population ratios have risen for women, but fallen for men—especially for black men, whose employment prospects are particularly bleak. Further, although there is little evidence of any large increase in job instability, turnover rates in the U.S. labor market have long been very high, and job displacement is often very costly for those unlucky enough to lose a job they have held for many years. High turnover rates combined with rising inequality imply increasing uncertainty about future income for many Americans.

In response to these problems in the Nation's labor market, many of which have been with us for several years, this Administration has set out a long-term work force strategy to help the economy create more jobs—at least 8 million over 4 years. To reduce job insecurity, the Administration aims to ease labor market transitions in a number of ways. By making sure that people have health insurance whether or not they are employed, the Administration seeks to reduce the trauma of job loss. The strategy also includes plans to help young workers enter the labor market more smoothly by providing a bridge between school and work. The Work Force Security Act will help experienced workers who have lost jobs find new employment more quickly, and will provide support for training for those who cannot.

Finally, and importantly, the Administration's strategy seeks to improve worker productivity and increase earnings. To this end, the Administration is pursuing policies to increase investment in research and development, to spur private investment in plant and equipment, and to facilitate the spread of modern cooperative employment practices (such as total quality management and quality circles). These initiatives address the general problem of slow wage growth, but growing inequality and real wage declines for the least advantaged are problems that require specific attention. Since growing inequality is due in large part to the growing mismatch between the demand for trained labor and its supply, the Administration aims to provide more and higher quality training so that wages may rise—particularly for the middle-class and the least advantaged. Income inequality has also been directly addressed by an increase in the earned income tax credit.

EMPLOYMENT GROWTH

U.S. employment grew rapidly from 1950 to 1990, with the number of nonfarm jobs increasing on average by over 2.2 percent a year. In contrast, from the end of 1990 to the end of 1992, job growth was virtually nonexistent. During 1993, employment growth improved considerably to an annual rate of 1.8 percent, but job creation remains low compared with past recoveries. As of the fourth quarter of 1993, the U.S. economy had been in recovery for 11 quarters. The unemployment rate fell from its postrecession high of 7.7 percent in June 1992 to 6.4 percent in December 1993. Yet despite these signs of recovery there has been widespread concern about the pace of job growth.

A SLOW RECOVERY

Without question, job growth has been relatively weak since the trough of the recent recession. During the 11 quarters after the first quarter of 1991, nonfarm payroll employment grew by 2.3 million, an increase of only 2.1 percent. In fact, employment did not begin to rebound until the first quarter of 1992. In previous recoveries employment growth was much stronger. For example, during the first 11 quarters after the recession of 1981–82, nonfarm employment grew by 10.1 percent. In seven previous postwar recoveries, employment increased, on average, by 8.8 percent over the first 11 quarters of recovery and expansion.

A key difference between the current and past recoveries, however, is the extraordinarily slow pace of output growth. Real gross domestic product (GDP) grew only 7.7 percent during the first 11 quarters of this recovery, compared with an average increase of 14.3 percent during the previous postwar recoveries. Possible reasons for the slow growth of output are discussed in Chapter 2. They include balance sheet adjustments by firms and consumers, cutbacks in defense purchases, slow growth of construction spending, the credit crunch, and slower export growth due to weak economies abroad. Given the slow rate of output growth, it should not be surprising that employment growth has also been slow.

Nevertheless, the current recovery still stands out relative to other recoveries when one compares the ratio of total employment growth to output growth. By the 11th quarter of previous recoveries, that ratio was about 0.62, compared with 0.27 in the current recovery (Chart 3–1). It is comparisons such as this that have led observers to claim that corporate restructuring and rapidly rising productivity have allowed output to grow without commensurate increases in employment. Some critics see deeper forces at work. For example, it has been argued that productivity growth—strongest in the manufacturing sector—is now proceeding at a rapid pace in the service sector as well. Historically, job losses in manufacturing were offset by rapid growth in the service sector, but with strong productivity growth in the service sector this is alleged to be no longer possible.

However, simple comparisons of total labor force growth to total output growth miss an essential point. As output rises during the early stages of a recovery, the ratio of employment growth to output growth is usually low. This is because employers keep more workers on their payrolls than are needed during downturns, and therefore do not hire more workers until their existing work force is fully employed and they are confident of continued growth. Consequently, employment grows slowly, and may even continue to decline, for the first few quarters after GDP begins to recover.

Chart 3–2 compares the *cumulative* growth of employment and output during the most recent recovery with that in previous recoveries. The boxes show how output and employment have grown together historically. The circles show how output and employment

Chart 3-1 Changes in Output and Payroll Employment in First Eleven Quarters of Recovery
The ratio of employment to output growth is much lower in the current recovery than in the past. Output growth is much slower, too.

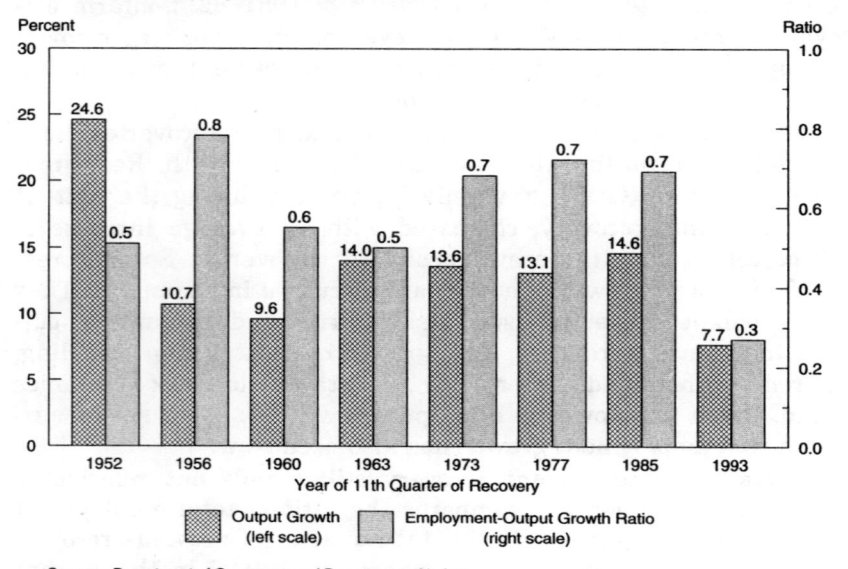

Year of 11th Quarter of Recovery	Output Growth (Percent)	Employment-Output Growth Ratio
1952	24.6	0.5
1956	10.7	0.8
1960	9.6	0.6
1963	14.0	0.5
1973	13.6	0.7
1977	13.1	0.7
1985	14.6	0.7
1993	7.7	0.3

Sources: Department of Commerce and Department of Labor.

have grown together in the most recent recovery. Although the cumulative growth of output and that of employment have both been extraordinarily slow in this recovery, *the relationship between them is consistent with historical experience.* Using the historical relationship between output and employment growth, one can estimate what employment growth *should have been* during the most recent recovery given output growth. This exercise yields estimates of cumulative employment growth that are larger than actual employment growth during this recovery by as much as 1 percent of total employment. This is a large difference, but not a statistically significant one. In other words, employment growth in the most recent recovery appears to have been at the low end of the range of historical experience, but is nonetheless consistent with it.

A similar conclusion applies to the behavior of manufacturing employment. Analysis of past experience shows that the actual growth of manufacturing employment during the most recent recovery is not statistically different from what would have been predicted based on GDP growth and long-term trends. (Manufacturing employment has been declining as a fraction of the labor force since 1953 and reached its postwar peak in 1979.) This is surprising because defense cutbacks have caused large job losses in manufacturing in the most recent recovery. Evidently, growth in demand for manufactured goods in other parts of the economy was strong enough to offset the depressing effects of these cutbacks on manufacturing employment.

Chart 3-2 Employment and Output in Recoveries
Employment growth in the recent recovery is in line with past experience given the slow growth of output.

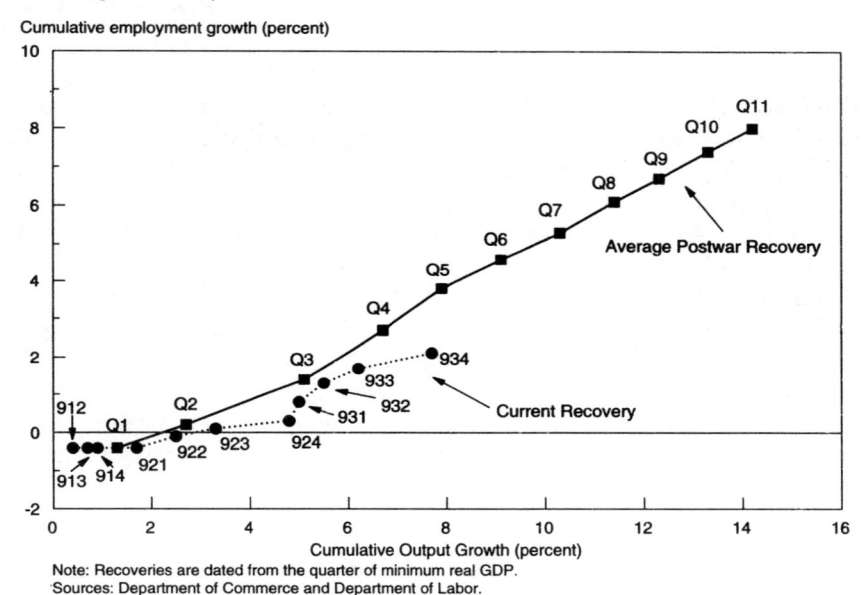

Note: Recoveries are dated from the quarter of minimum real GDP.
Sources: Department of Commerce and Department of Labor.

SOURCES OF JOB GROWTH

Although much has been written about the sources of job growth, it is hard to get an accurate picture from the pastiche of popular accounts. Are new jobs good jobs or bad jobs? What does the future hold?

Industry and Occupation

The service sector—defined to include personal and business services but exclude trade and finance—was the economy's job engine in 1993. Although these industries account for less than 30 percent of total employment, they were responsible for more than 60 percent of total job growth in that year. Many of these jobs—about 350,000—were created in the personnel supply industry (mainly temporary agencies), which represented almost 20 percent of total payroll job growth. Other sectors registering strong job creation over 1993 included retail trade (more than 400,000 jobs) and construction (about 200,000 jobs). In contast, manufacturing employment declined by about 180,000 during the year.

These sectoral patterns are not new, however. Since January 1983, service sector employment has grown by 11.5 million and has accounted for 52 percent of total nonfarm job growth. And, jobs in retail trade have accounted for an additional 21 percent of all jobs created over this period. Since January 1983, construction employment has risen by 785,000, but manufacturing payrolls have shrunk by 325,000.

A common misconception identifies manufacturing jobs as "good jobs" and service jobs as "bad jobs." However, growth in high-end services such as various kinds of business services have led to increased demand for high-level white-collar workers. During 1993, 48 percent of the increase in employment occurred in the managerial and professional occupations. The large increases in these relatively well-paying occupations belie the criticism that most employment growth has been in "bad jobs."

The recent occupational pattern of employment growth is largely in line with the experience of the last 10 years, during which managerial and professional jobs accounted for 49 percent of new employment. Both over the last year and over the last decade, new employment has shifted toward better paying jobs requiring more skills and education, not toward low-paid, low-skilled jobs.

Outlook for the Future

One of the major goals of this Administration is to increase employment by at least 8 million jobs in 4 years. Progress toward this goal has been moderate but steady. Between January and December 1993, nonfarm payroll employment grew by 1.8 million jobs, and the number of unemployed fell by 809,000, lowering the unemployment rate from 7.1 percent to 6.4 percent. With a higher growth rate of output expected next year, the pace of job creation should accelerate.

The Bureau of Labor Statistics (BLS) projects employment to grow between 1.1 and 1.9 percent per year through 2005. Most of this growth is expected in service-producing industries, which the BLS expects will add between 1.4 million and 2.1 million jobs per year. Employment in manufacturing is expected to fall or to rise only modestly, with losses or gains of fewer than 160,000 workers per year. Many new jobs (about 500,000 a year) will be in service occupations such as food service workers and home health aides, but even more will be in the comparatively higher-paying managerial, professional, and technical occupations (about 825,000 a year).

UNEMPLOYMENT AND NONEMPLOYMENT

The United States has a history of strong job growth, and the outlook for job creation over the next decade is good. But how many new jobs are enough? The best indicator of how well we are doing is how many of the people who want jobs are able to get them. The unemployment rate is one measure of this. The unemployed are defined as people who are not working but are either waiting to return to a job or looking for a new one. If jobs are sufficiently difficult to find, however, some people may give up looking. Then they are counted not as unemployed but as "discouraged workers." Thus, both unemployment rates and the employment-to-population ratio need to be examined to determine if the economy is providing enough jobs.

TRENDS

The National Bureau of Economic Research, the private organization that dates the beginning and endpoints of U.S. business cycles, fixed the trough of the 1990–91 recession at March 1991. Yet unemployment did not reach its peak of 7.7 percent until June 1992. Since then the unemployment rate has fallen steadily to 6.4 percent in December 1993. (In January 1994 the BLS began measuring unemployment in a new way: Box 3–1 describes the changes). This represents a considerable improvement, but the economy has a way to go before unemployment reaches normal levels. Unemployment was below 6.4 percent from April 1987 to January 1991, and from February 1978 to March 1980. After World War II and prior to 1974, unemployment topped 6.4 percent for only three brief periods, each of less than a year.

Chart 3–3 shows the time path for unemployment since 1948. Besides the ups and downs that correspond to business cycles, the outstanding feature is the apparent ratcheting up in the level of unemployment in the 1970s. Since the early 1970s, unemployment has never returned to the levels typical of recoveries in the 1950s and 1960s, and has peaked at much higher rates. It is widely believed that this long-term increase in unemployment is at least in part due to an increase in the minimum level to which unemployment can be reduced without causing increasing inflation—the so-called natural rate of unemployment. The natural rate in turn is thought to depend on labor market frictions, and skill and geographic mismatches, between labor supply and labor demand.

There have also been changes in the incidence of long-term unemployment. As of December 1993, 1.7 million workers, comprising 21.0 percent of the unemployed, had been unemployed for 27 weeks or longer. This is a reduction from September 1992, when the number of long-term unemployed reached 2.1 million and comprised

> **Box 3-1.—The New Current Population Survey**
>
> The Current Population Survey (CPS), a national survey of 60,000 U.S. households, provides a monthly picture of the Nation's labor force, employment, and the unemployment rate. Beginning in January 1994, that picture is being taken through a new lens. For the first time since 1967, the CPS has undergone a major redesign. Changes in the patterns of employment by industry, the increased labor force participation of women, and several other factors have made the pre-1994 survey less accurate as a guide to the Nation's work force. The new survey includes new and revised questions that reflect these changes and incorporates new procedures (including the use of portable computers to conduct the survey rather than pencil and paper) designed to lead to more-accurate and consistent responses.
>
> Between July 1992 and December 1993, a pilot version of the new survey was conducted in parallel with the old CPS to determine the effects of the new questions and data collection procedures. Results of the parallel survey indicate significantly different estimates for key statistics, including the unemployment rate. Specifically, the unemployment rate as measured by the parallel survey averaged a half a percentage point higher than the estimates from the old CPS. In addition, the use of new population weights increased the measured unemployment rate another 0.1 percentage point. The unemployment rate is expected to rise for all demographic groups, but particularly for women, since the old CPS questionnaire may have tended to classify women who were unemployed as out of the labor force.
>
> The new survey is expected to produce several other changes as well. For example, measured labor force participation rates and employment-to-population ratios are expected to rise for women and fall for men. Changes in the questions defining discouraged workers and people working part-time for economic reasons are expected to lead to a decline in numbers of discouraged workers of 60 percent and part-time workers for economic reasons of 20 to 25 percent.

21.7 percent of all unemployed workers. There is still a sense, however, that long-term unemployment is unusually high today. The peak share of long-term unemployed workers during the current recovery was higher than during most previous postwar recoveries (Chart 3-4). In addition, the share of long-term unemployment is high given the overall unemployment rate (Chart 3-5).

Chart 3-3 **Civilian Unemployment Rate**
Unemployment rate peaks and troughs have been higher since 1973.

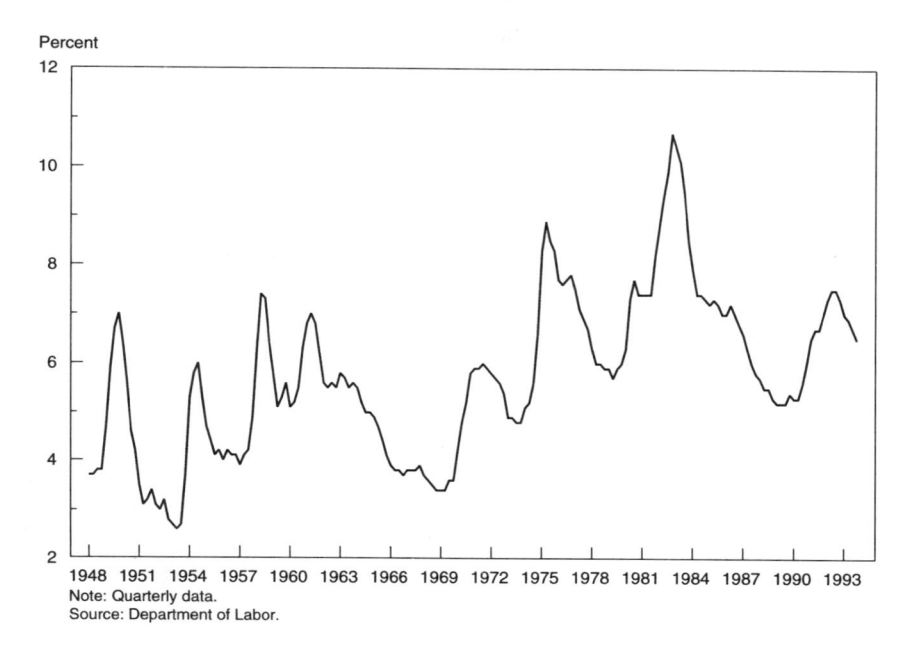

Note: Quarterly data.
Source: Department of Labor.

While average unemployment rates have risen, they have risen more for some groups than for others. The unemployment rate for women, which used to be consistently above the unemployment rate for men, is somewhat lower (6.2 percent for women, 6.5 percent for men in December 1993). In contrast, the black unemployment rate has risen more than the white unemployment rate (1.5 percentage points for whites between 1970 and 1993, and 3.5 percentage points for blacks and others).

Employment-to-population ratios show some of the same patterns of relative distress for different groups. While black women had a higher employment ratio than white women in the 1970s, the reverse is now true (Chart 3-6). Both black and white men have had falling employment-to-population ratios since the early 1970s; but the decline for black men has been larger than for white men (10 percentage points for black men from 1972 to 1993; 6 percentage points for white men).

The unemployment rate for teenage workers (aged 16 to 19 years) has always been higher than the rate for all workers, and the current situation is no exception. While the unemployment rate for all workers during 1993 averaged 6.8 percent, the rate for teen-

Chart 3-4 Long-Term Unemployment as Share of Total Unemployment
The share of the unemployed who have been out of work 27 weeks or more approached historical highs in the last downturn.

Note: Quarterly data.
Source: Department of Labor.

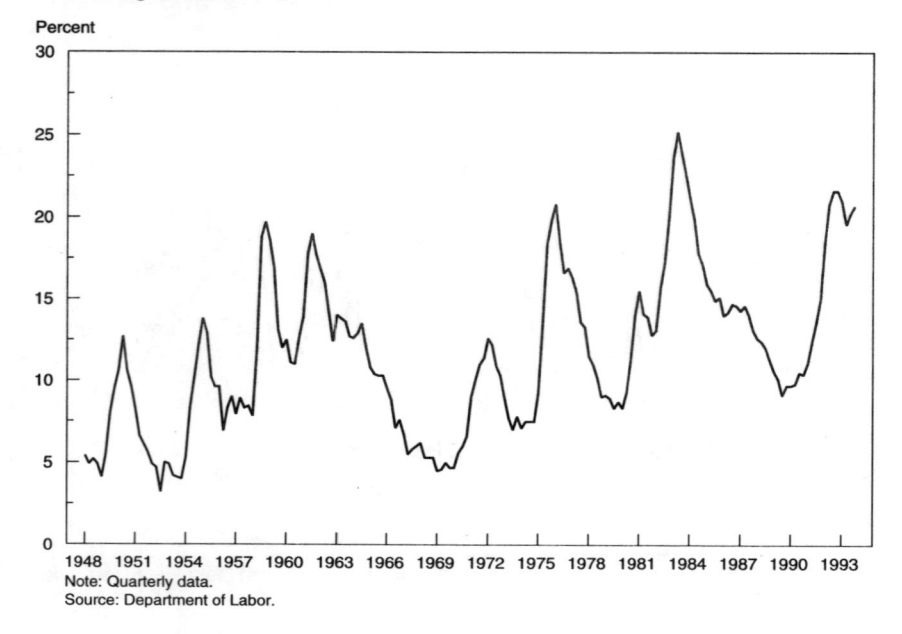

Chart 3-5 Long-Term Unemployment and the Unemployment Rate
The share of long-term unemployment in total unemployment has been high recently, given the unemployment rate.

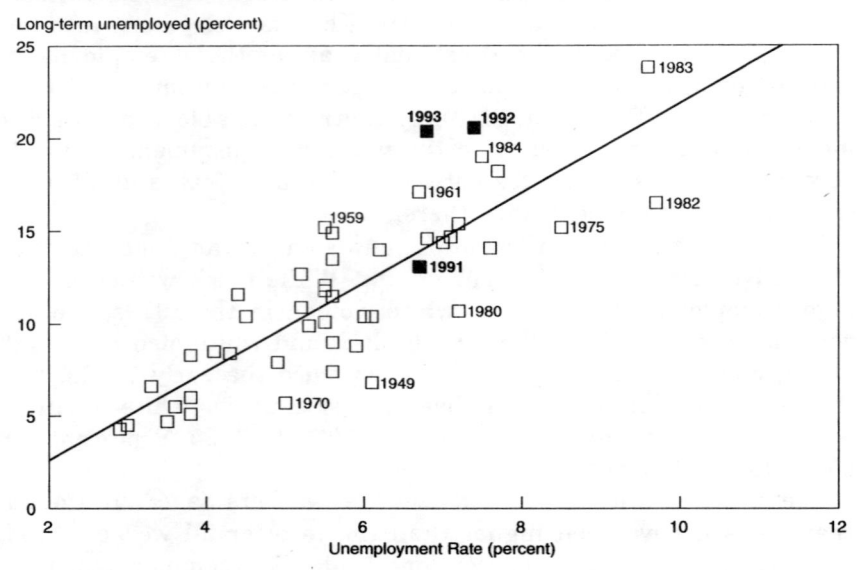

Source: Department of Labor.

Chart 3-6 Employment-to-Population Ratios of Women
The employment rate of black women fell below that of white women in the last recession.

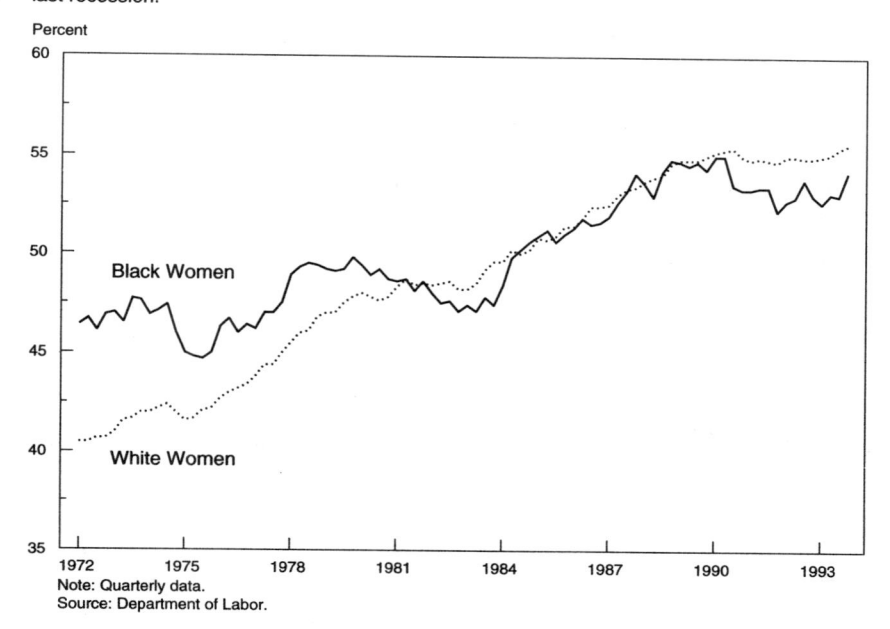

[Line chart showing Black Women and White Women employment-to-population ratios, quarterly data, 1972-1993. Black Women start around 46-47% in 1972, rising to about 53-54% by 1993. White Women start around 40% in 1972, rising steadily to about 55% by 1993.]

Note: Quarterly data.
Source: Department of Labor.

agers was nearly three times as high at 19 percent. Teenage unemployment rates were 17.6 percent and 14.6 percent for white males and females, respectively. The unemployment rates for black teenage workers were more than twice as high at 40.1 percent for males and 37.5 percent for females. Over the last 20 years, the teenage unemployment rate rose along with the overall unemployment rate. Unemployment rates also differ by education. Chart 3–7 compares the unemployment rates of those without a high school diploma, high school graduates, those with some college, college graduates, and those with advanced degrees.

According to popular accounts, another distinguishing feature of recent labor market developments is the "white-collar recession." That expression implies that the recent unemployment experience of white-collar workers relative to that of blue-collar workers has been significantly worse than in past recessions.

In fact, as in the past, the unemployment rate among white-collar workers has been significantly below that of blue-collar workers in the most recent recession and recovery (3.2 percent versus 9.9 percent in 1992). However, the white-collar unemployment rate *relative* to the blue-collar rate has been rising (Chart 3–8). The ratio

Chart 3-7 Unemployment Rates by Educational Attainment, March 1993
Unemployment is generally lower for more-educated workers.

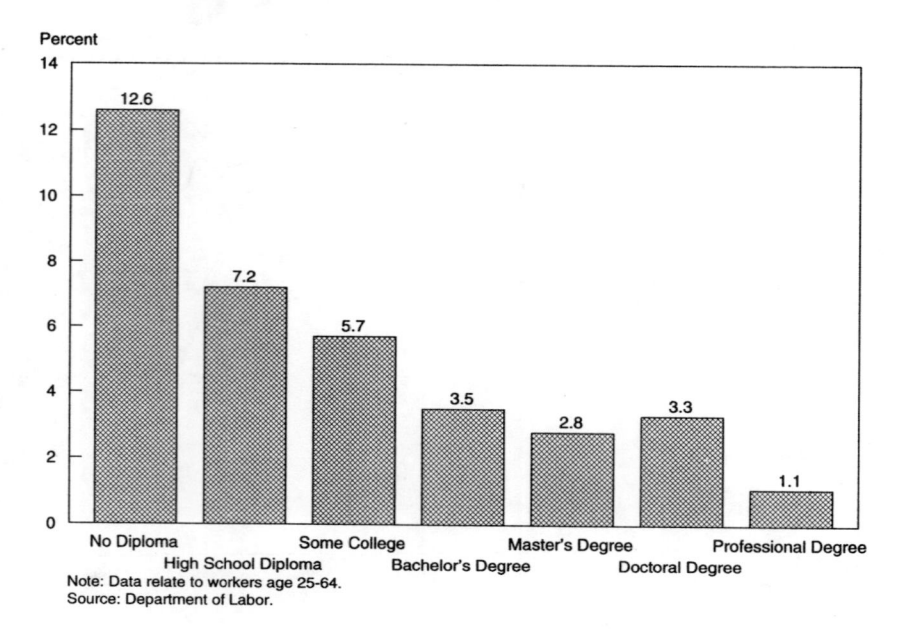

Percent

No Diploma	12.6
High School Diploma	7.2
Some College	5.7
Bachelor's Degree	3.5
Master's Degree	2.8
Doctoral Degree	3.3
Professional Degree	1.1

Note: Data relate to workers age 25-64.
Source: Department of Labor.

of the two rates in 1992 was 0.33, the highest since 1979. The ratio of the *number* of unemployed white-collar workers to the number of unemployed blue-collar workers has been rising since 1982, the first year for which we have consistent occupational estimates. By 1992, the ratio of the number of white-collar unemployed to that of blue-collar unemployed was about one-third, compared with only one-fifth in 1983. This happened both because the *ratio* of the white-collar to the blue-collar unemployment rate has increased, as already noted, and because white-collar workers now make up a larger fraction of the work force than they did before.

Just as the rate of overall employment growth is not out of line with past experience given output growth, the level of unemployment in the most recent recession is within the bounds of what we would expect given GDP growth. Further, as already noted, unemployment has fallen by 1.3 percentage points from its June 1992 peak, with nearly a percentage point of the drop coming in 1993. However, three concerns are raised by trends and recent experience.

The first problem is increasing disparities between black and white rates of both employment and unemployment. These changes

Chart 3-8 Ratio of White-Collar to Blue-Collar Unemployment Rates
The ratio of white-collar to blue-collar unemployment rates has been rising but is still below historical highs.

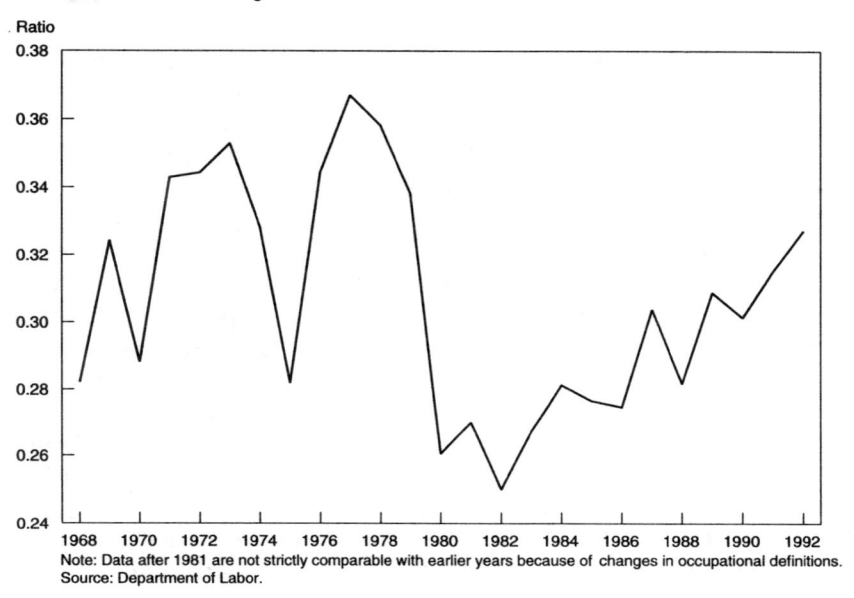

Note: Data after 1981 are not strictly comparable with earlier years because of changes in occupational definitions.
Source: Department of Labor.

are linked to equally disturbing changes in the distribution of income and job security, discussed later in this chapter. The second concern is the long-term increase in the average level of unemployment. The third concern is that recent high levels of long-term unemployment suggest that we may be seeing an increase in the share of unemployment caused by mismatches between workers' skills and job demands. If this is the case, it is argued, it may be difficult to lower the unemployment rate much further without causing labor market bottlenecks. As we will see below, little evidence can be found that skill mismatches have contributed much to recent increases in unemployment, but they do seem to have been a major cause of growing income inequality.

IS THE NATURAL RATE OF UNEMPLOYMENT INCREASING?

How would we know if there had been an increase in what economists call the natural rate of unemployment? A sustained increase in long-term unemployment might be one indication, an increase in the number of people who have given up looking for work might be another, and an increase in the fraction of job losers among the unemployed yet another. These are all indirect indicators of an increase in the natural rate of unemployment. The problem is that these indicators also respond to cyclical conditions—they increase when the economy is in recession, and they can be slow to decline, or may even increase, in periods of slow recovery.

Not surprisingly, therefore, concerns that mismatch unemployment is increasing are likely to develop in recessionary times. Less skilled workers are more likely to find themselves unemployed than better skilled workers. During recessions, labor market slack makes it easier for employers to find better qualified employees, allowing them to raise job qualifications without raising compensation. Thus recessions may create the appearance of increasing mismatch unemployment. Once a recovery is under way, however, more jobs of all types are created, and the unemployment rate for the less skilled usually declines. Thus indirect indicators of increasing skill mismatch are not enough to determine whether the natural rate is increasing. We must consider additional evidence.

If most new jobs require skills that many workers do not have, they might experience lengthening periods of unemployment as they wait for jobs appropriate to their skills to become available. On the other hand, the available statistical evidence does not rule out the possibility that relatively slow output growth since the recession trough in 1991 is the major reason why recent levels of long-term unemployment have been so high. Since high levels of overall unemployment have persisted for so long, the number of people looking for work for a long period of time has also increased. A statistical analysis relating the percentage change in the number of workers unemployed for 27 weeks or more to the percentage change in output indicates that the behavior of long-term unemployment in the most recent period of recession and recovery is not statistically different from that during previous recession-recovery cycles. Although the recent behavior of long-term unemployment may not be different, it is worth noting that the average number of long-term unemployed increased substantially during the 1970s and has remained high since then.

Another possible indicator of worsening mismatch unemployment is the number of discouraged workers. Because they have given up looking for work, they are not counted as unemployed. Yet large increases in the number of discouraged workers might be taken as indirect evidence that many people are having a very difficult time finding jobs. Again, however, the slow speed of the recovery could also explain such an increase. Although the number of discouraged workers is up, reaching 1.1 million in the fourth quarter of 1993 compared with fewer than 800,000 in the first quarter of 1990, the percentage increase in the number of discouraged workers is less than would be expected given its historical relationship with output growth.

In summary, after taking into account the effects of slow output growth, neither recent high levels of long-term unemployment nor recent increases in the number of discouraged workers suggest that there has been an abrupt worsening of mismatch unemployment or an abrupt increase in the natural rate of unemployment in the most recent period of recession and recovery.

A third indirect indicator of a changing natural rate of unemployment is the share of permanent job losers in total unemployment. If unemployment is truly cyclical, firms lay off workers for a while, but recall them when conditions improve. However, if mismatch is increasing, one might expect to see more permanent job losers among the unemployed rather than individuals on temporary layoff. Indeed, the share of permanent job losers among the unemployed hit an all-time high of 43.9 percent in the second quarter of 1992, and has fallen only slightly since then. However, this number must be interpreted with caution. Despite the image of cyclical unemployment as due to temporary layoffs, the fact is that the share of permanent job losers among the unemployed rises in every recession. Recessions bring not only temporary interruptions in employment due to slack demand, but also business failures and forced restructurings that cause permanent job loss at a higher rate than during normal times.

A statistical analysis relating the number of permanent job losers to output growth indicates that the relatively large number of permanent job losers in the most recent period of recession and recovery can be explained by relatively slow output growth. Thus there is little evidence of any recent increase in the natural rate of unemployment in this relationship, either. The predictions of this analysis for earlier periods do suggest that there was an abrupt increase in the number of unemployed permanent job losers in the early to mid-1970s, compared with what would have been expected given business conditions. This is consistent with other data which suggest an increase in the natural rate around that time.

DIRECT MEASURES OF THE NATURAL RATE

Traditionally, economists have used two methods to identify the natural rate, and two additional methods for evaluating how it might be changing. The simplest way to identify the natural rate is to look back and see at what unemployment rate the last acceleration of inflation began. Alternatively, a statistical model of inflation that embodies the assumption of a natural rate (an accelerationist "Phillips curve") can be used to estimate the natural rate.

Changes in the natural rate have been identified in two ways. Since different demographic groups have different unemployment rates, it has become a common procedure to assume that the natural rate changes whenever the composition of the work force changes. More recently, several authors have looked at the relation between unemployment and proxies for job vacancies. If increases in the natural rate are caused by an increasing mismatch of workers and jobs, then the job vacancy rate should be rising along with the unemployment rate.

All these approaches have serious shortcomings. Many factors other than the tightness of the labor market influence the rate of wage and price inflation. Taxes, raw material prices, exchange rates, expectations, and a host of other factors all come into play. Thus, determining the natural rate by looking back to see what the unemployment rate was the last time inflation picked up works only if inflation was caused by labor market tightness.

Some economists argue, however, that the principal causes of inflation since the early 1970s have been factors other than tightness in the labor market—for example, oil and other commodity price increases in the 1970s and the falling value of the dollar in the late 1980s. If this is true, estimating the natural rate by estimating models of inflation is a misleading exercise unless all causes of inflation besides tightness in the labor market are adequately controlled for. Moreover, even estimates of the natural rate obtained in this manner may be very sensitive to assumptions about the form of the Phillips curve relation. Without direct evidence of a rapidly increasing rate of inflation below a particular unemployment rate, estimates of a changing natural rate from statistical models of inflation are suspect at best.

Determining how the natural rate has changed by looking at demographic changes also poses problems. In the 1970s, the apparent increase in the natural rate was attributed in large part to increasing labor force participation of women and teenagers—both of whom had higher than average unemployment rates at the time. However, as women have changed their attachment to the labor force, their unemployment experience has also changed. In the recent past, women have had a lower unemployment rate than men. Should we therefore believe that the increased labor force participation of women has tended to decrease the natural rate below what it was prior to the surge in their participation? The share of teenagers in the labor force has also fallen in the last decade, and this too should have reduced the natural rate.

Further, why focus on these particular demographic changes to the exclusion of others? Black male labor force participation rates have been falling over the last two decades. Since black men have higher unemployment rates than white men, should we conclude that the natural rate is falling? More important, people with college educations have a much lower rate of unemployment than those with less education, and their share of the labor force has increased considerably over the last two decades. Again, this would suggest that the natural rate should be lower today than in 1970, before the ratcheting up of the unemployment rate.

Finally, although the U.S. Government does not collect the data on job vacancies that would allow us to examine directly whether there is an increasing mismatch of jobs and workers, the Conference Board does publish an index of help-wanted advertising. The relationship between this index and the unemployment rate has changed over time, but there is no evidence of any increase in the level of help-wanted advertising, given the unemployment rate, in the last decade. There is, however, a higher level of help-wanted advertising at all levels of unemployment since the early 1970s.

The increase in help-wanted advertising could be interpreted as evidence of an increase in mismatch unemployment, but many other things affect the level of help-wanted advertising. Different types of employers advertise in different ways for different types of jobs. Changes in the industrial and occupational mix of employment make an advertising index a questionable measure of long-term changes in job vacancies. Changes in advertising prices, the structure of media markets, and legal requirements for advertising certain jobs also change the relationship between vacancies and advertising in ways that call into question the meaning of any long-term changes.

Altogether, the various pieces of statistical evidence examined in the preceding discussion suggest that the increase in the unemployment rate since 1989 has been largely cyclical in nature. There is some evidence of an increase in the natural rate—possibly due to an increase in mismatch unemployment—in the early 1970s, but little evidence of any increase since then. The evidence also suggests that today's unemployment rate exceeds the natural rate by a significant amount. Therefore, wage-push price inflation is unlikely to be a factor constraining economic growth in the near future.

THE MAGNITUDE AND COSTS OF JOB LOSS

The U.S. economy is constantly in flux, and while there is no evidence that the rate of churning in the labor market has increased in recent years (see the discussion of job stability below), normal rates of structural adjustment are quite high and impose significant costs.

Estimates of the number of jobs created and destroyed each year in the United States are staggering. Data from various sources suggest that on average more than 10 percent of all jobs disappear every year, while even more new jobs are created. Luckily, not every job that is lost forces someone to become unemployed. Companies reducing the size of their operations can often do so using normal attrition—quits and retirements. When they cannot, workers given advance notice of an imminent layoff can sometimes find work before they lose their old job, allowing a seamless transition with no unemployment. But for the many workers who do not make such easy transitions, the costs of dislocation can be high.

Between 1981 and 1990, about 2 million full-time workers per year lost their jobs. These workers spent an average of nearly 30 weeks unemployed, and of those who found new employment, about a third suffered earnings losses of more than 20 percent.

Wage losses were most severe for those who had been with their employers the longest. For example, those with 10 or more years of tenure on their previous job were nearly four times as likely to see their earnings fall by 20 percent as to see them rise by 20 percent in their new jobs. They were also less likely than other displaced workers to find new employment at all. One set of surveys asking about job loss found that 73 percent of all job losers had obtained new jobs, but only 65 percent of those with 10 or more years of job tenure had found new work.

The special problems of workers with long job tenure are understandable. Those who work for the same employer for a long time build up skills that are most valuable to that employer. Further, many employers reward long job tenure with higher wages as a way of motivating employees and ensuring their loyalty. The loss of a job when one has obtained the privileges of long tenure can be particularly devastating.

SLOWING WAGE GROWTH AND WIDENING INEQUALITY

In the last two decades, family income growth has stagnated and incomes have become more unequally distributed. In fact, the real incomes of the bottom 60 percent of American families were lower in the early 1990s than for the analogous families at the end of the 1970s. Underlying the rising disparity in the fortunes of American families has been a rise in labor market inequality that has shifted wage and employment opportunities in favor of the more educated and the more experienced. Less educated workers suffered substantial losses in real earnings during the 1980s. Here we consider the dimensions, and some likely causes, of slow income growth and widening inequality.

SLOW INCOME GROWTH

Income trends have been discouraging for about two decades—the median family today has virtually the same real income as the median family 20 years ago. This stagnation is a marked departure from the substantial income growth that occurred over previous generations.

From 1947 to 1973 the real income of the median American family increased by a robust 2.8 percent a year, more than doubling. In contrast, from 1973 to 1992 the income of the typical American family was essentially stagnant, rising by only 0.1 percent a year after adjusting for inflation. (The trend from 1979 to 1989—roughly equivalent years in the economic cycle—is similar.) At the pace of income growth from 1973 to 1992, it would take centuries for real median family income to double.

Although the labor force participation decisions of women and changes in the composition of families have affected family income, the major trends in family income are dominated by trends in real wages. Chart 3-9 shows the changes in wages and total hourly compensation, adjusted for inflation, since 1948. Both wages and compensation suffered abrupt slowdowns in growth rates around 1973.

GROWING INEQUALITY

Families have been affected unevenly by recent income trends. Real incomes at the top have increased smartly, real incomes at the middle have essentially stagnated, and real incomes at the bottom have fallen. Box 3-2 discusses the implications of these developments for employment and unemployment.

From 1973 to 1992, the average real income of the upper 20 percent of families rose 19 percent, or about 1 percent per year. This is well below the rate for the 1950s and 1960s, but far better than for the rest of the population. Between 1973 and 1992, the average income of the middle 20 percent of families rose a paltry 4 percent in real terms. Lower income families fared even worse. Among the bottom 20 percent of families, mean real income fell by 12 percent from 1973 to 1992. Chart 3-10 shows the growth of mean family incomes for different income groups over the periods before and after 1973. It makes clear just how abrupt the changes in the distribution of income growth have been. A trend toward greater equality in the 1960s and toward greater inequality in the 1970s and 1980s is apparent in both income and consumption measures of economic well-being. Rising inequality of family incomes during the 1980s is apparent in both pretax and posttax income measures.

Chart 3-9 **Real Hourly Compensation and Wages**
The growth of real compensation per hour and of real hourly wages has declined since 1973.

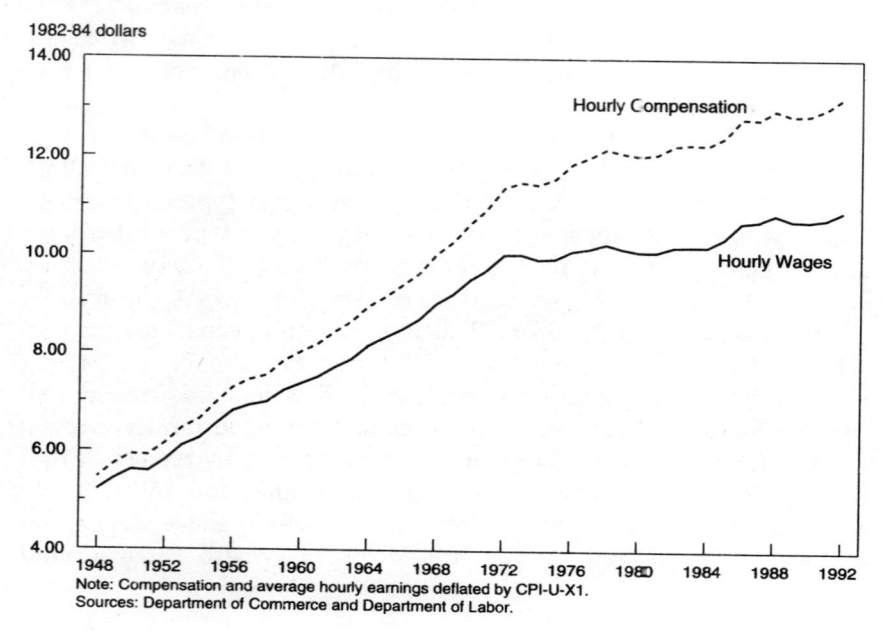

1982-84 dollars

[Line chart showing Hourly Compensation (dashed line) and Hourly Wages (solid line) from 1948 to 1992, both rising from around $5-6 in 1948 to about $13 and $10.50 respectively by 1992, with slower growth after 1973.]

Note: Compensation and average hourly earnings deflated by CPI-U-X1.
Sources: Department of Commerce and Department of Labor.

Box 3-2.—Growing Inequality of Employment and Unemployment

The falling relative wages of those with less experience and schooling may explain, at least in part, some of the observed changes in employment-to-population ratios for certain demographic groups. The black and teenage populations tend to have less schooling than the average for all Americans. Consequently, the wages they command have fallen, making work less attractive. To the extent that the shift in demand away from less-educated workers is manifest in fewer available jobs instead of lower wages, these groups face higher unemployment rates as well.

EXPLAINING SLOW WAGE GROWTH

Stagnant wages and slow total compensation growth since the early 1970s largely reflect a substantial slowdown in productivity growth. From 1947 to 1973 productivity rose at a compound annual rate of 3.1 percent, and inflation-adjusted compensation per hour

Chart 3-10 Average Annual Growth of Mean Family Income by Income Quintile
Family incomes in all income groups grew more or less evenly, but slightly faster for lower income groups, before 1973.

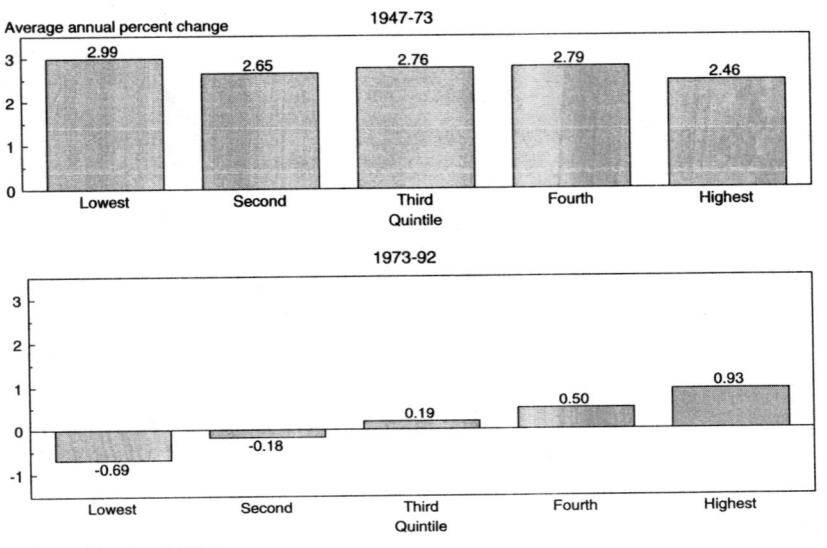

1947-73

Average annual percent change

Quintile	Lowest	Second	Third	Fourth	Highest
%	2.99	2.65	2.76	2.79	2.46

1973-92

Quintile	Lowest	Second	Third	Fourth	Highest
%	-0.69	-0.18	0.19	0.50	0.93

Source: Department of Commerce.

grew at a similar rate. From 1973 to 1979 the rate of productivity growth fell to an average of 0.8 percent a year, and compensation growth fell with it. Since 1979 the productivity growth rate has picked up only slightly, averaging 1.2 percent on an annual basis. Chart 3–11 shows the close relation between productivity and real compensation. Boxes 3–3 and 3–4 discuss some of the other effects of productivity growth.

The productivity slowdown has been intensely studied. Many partial explanations have been given, but no complete accounting has been made.

EXPLAINING THE GROWTH OF INEQUALITY

Several factors have contributed to widening inequality. One major factor is increasing returns to education and experience. The college–high school wage premium increased by over 100 percent for workers aged 25 to 34 between 1974 and 1992, while increasing 20 percent for all workers 18 years old and over (Chart 1–8). In addition, among workers without college degrees, the average wages of older workers increased relative to those of younger workers. Since the relative supply of educated workers has increased at the

Chart 3-11 Productivity Growth and Price Reductions, 1950-90
Productivity growth in an industry leads to lower relative prices.

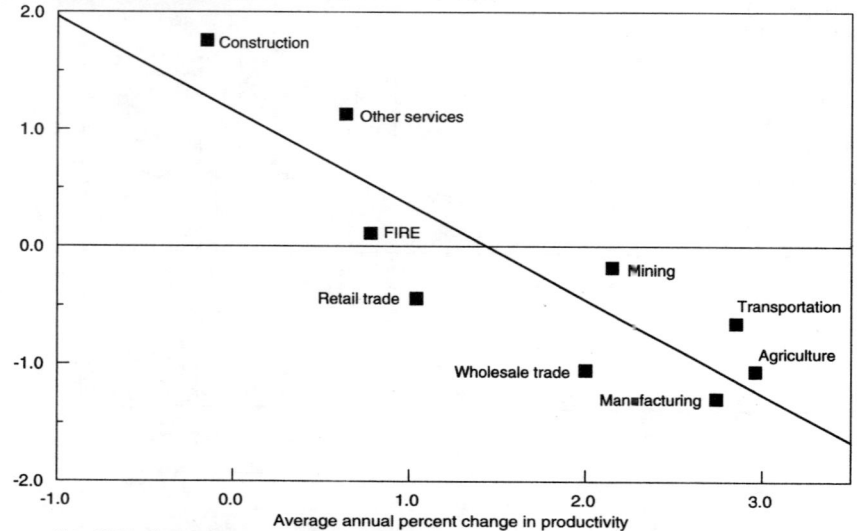

Average annual percent change in relative prices vs. Average annual percent change in productivity. Data points: Construction, Other services, FIRE, Retail trade, Mining, Wholesale trade, Transportation, Manufacturing, Agriculture.

Note: FIRE = finance, insurance, and real estate.
Source: Department of Commerce.

same time that wage disparities have grown, the demand for educated workers must have increased faster than their supply. Some have suggested that increasing trade has undermined demand for less educated workers in the United States, since they are plentiful elsewhere in the world. So far, however, several studies have been unable to discern any substantial impact of trade on wage inequality, however. If increased trade were the cause of growing wage inequality, the relative prices of goods that use highly educated labor would be rising relative to those of goods that use less highly educated labor. But studies have found no evidence of such a change in relative prices. Similarly, if increased trade were responsible for increased wage inequality, the growth of wage differentials would lead firms in all sectors to substitute less educated labor for more educated labor. Instead, studies find that virtually all manufacturing industries have increased their relative use of educated labor despite growing wage differentials. Rising wage differentials with greater use of educated labor suggest that demand for skilled labor has been rising broadly in the economy. Thus it appears that most of the demand shift toward highly educated workers must have originated domestically.

> **Box 3-3.—Consequences of Productivity Growth**
>
> Rising productivity has been shown to have a variety of beneficial effects:
>
> - *The prices of goods produced by industries that have had rapid productivity growth have fallen relative to those of goods from industries with slower productivity growth.* Chart 3-11 shows average productivity growth and price changes by industry for the 1950-90 period.
> - *Periods of rapid productivity growth have been accompanied by increases in real wages.* The prices of products in industries experiencing productivity growth also decline relative to wages. This decline in product prices means that real wages tend to rise during periods of rapid productivity growth.
> - *Periods of rapid productivity growth have also been periods of low inflation.* Productivity growth allows nominal wages to increase without putting pressure on prices.
> - *Periods of rapid productivity growth have not been associated with large increases in unemployment.* In periods when productivity growth was more rapid, such as the 1960s, unemployment rates have tended to be low. In contrast, periods with slow rates of productivity growth, such as the 1970s, have been periods of relatively high unemployment.

Since the use of more-educated labor has increased in all industries, a logical explanation of this trend is technical change. For example, one study shows that people who work with personal computers earn a substantial wage premium over those who do not, and that this can account for half of the increasing gap between the wages of college and high school graduates.

Although changes in labor demand induced by changes in the composition of trade do not appear to explain much of the increase in income inequality, the internationalization of the U.S. economy may affect wages in other ways. For example, the threat of increased import competition or of the relocation of a factory to another country may undermine worker bargaining power or cause a decline in the number of workers employed in unionized firms. At this time, no reliable studies have properly quantified how important such effects have been. In addition, there is no guarantee that the future will resemble the past. Trade could become a more important factor in bringing down the wages of less educated workers in the future. On the other hand, technical change could move in

> **Box 3–4.—Why Productivity Growth Does Not Cause Unemployment**
>
> Productivity growth need not cause an increase in unemployment because, as productivity rises, more goods can be produced with the same number of workers. This means a cost saving, which must result in either increased profits, increased wages, or lower prices. If profits or wages increase, those benefiting from the increase will increase their spending. If prices fall, consumers' incomes will go further and they will buy more. In any case, the increased spending will lead to the purchase of more goods and services, which will create new jobs offsetting losses from the productivity increase. If the new jobs created are not equal in number to the jobs lost, there will be a tendency for wages to change to equate supply and demand for labor. Nonetheless, in the short run some workers are likely to have to change jobs. As the discussion of the costs of job loss makes clear, this can be a traumatic experience for the established worker.

the direction of economizing on educated labor and making better use of less educated labor.

In addition to rapidly increasing demand for educated labor, two institutional factors seem to have contributed to rising wage inequality: the decline of unions and the erosion of the minimum wage by inflation. In the early 1970s, 27 percent of the work force were union members. By 1990 that fraction had declined to 16 percent, and it has probably fallen further since. Several studies conclude that this decline can account for about 20 percent of the increase in wage inequality.

In 1970 the minimum wage was 50 percent of the average hourly wage of private production and nonsupervisory workers. By 1992 it had fallen to 40 percent of the average. This erosion of the minimum wage has allowed a substantial fattening of the lower tail of the wage distribution and contributed to increasing wage inequality. The effect of the minimum wage on the distribution of income is less obvious, since it is possible that the decline in the inflation-adjusted minimum wage may have caused an increase in employment of low-wage workers.

Immigration has increased the relative supply of less educated labor and appears to have contributed to the increasing inequality of income, but the effect has been small. A study of the effects of immigration between 1980 and 1988 found that it explains less than 1 percent of the change in the college–high school wage differential. Although immigration flows were considerably larger in the late 1980s than the early 1980s, this study makes it seem unlikely that immigration could explain more than a few percent of the total change in this differential.

JOB QUALITY

The Administration is concerned about increasing the quality as well as the quantity of jobs in the American economy. Job quality encompasses a number of factors beyond wage levels—including job security, employer-provided benefits such as pensions and health insurance, and hours of employment.

HOURS OF WORK

Average weekly hours in manufacturing were consistently higher through December 1993 than during most previous recoveries since 1958 (excluding the short recovery in 1980–81), and they reached a post-World War II high of 41.7 hours per week in November 1993. This was slightly above the previous peak of 41.6 hours per week reached in February 1966 (Chart 3-12). Factory overtime hours also reached a record in November at 4.4 hours per week, the highest level since the data series began in 1956.

Chart 3-12 **Average Weekly Hours of Production and Nonsupervisory Workers**
Average weekly hours in manufacturing are at a postwar high, while average hours for all industries show a long-term decline.

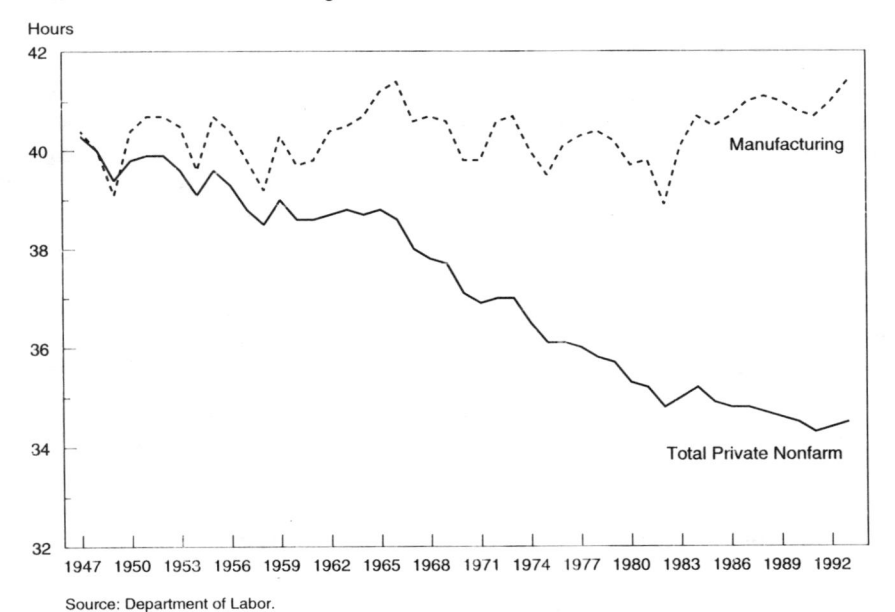

Source: Department of Labor.

In contrast, over the past half-century, average weekly hours worked by production and nonsupervisory employees on nonfarm private payrolls have declined significantly from 40.3 hours per week in 1947 to 34.5 hours per week in 1993. The patterns of average weekly hours of all private sector workers and those in manufacturing have diverged over the last 50 years.

In keeping with their long-term trend, average weekly hours of all private nonfarm workers have been lower since the trough of the last recession than during comparable periods following the three previous recessions after 1970. Average hours typically rise during recoveries, as employers respond to rising demand by using their existing work forces more intensively before they begin significant hiring of new employees. The increase in average hours since the 1991 recession trough has generally been in line with previous recoveries since 1970—although in recent months the increase in hours has been higher than in recent recoveries.

Popular accounts have suggested that Americans are working more. How can this be if hours worked on the average job are declining? The answer is that women's labor force participation is up, so that average hours of paid work *per person* are up. How do workers feel about their hours of work? Most studies find that, on average, people would like to work more hours if they were paid their hourly rate for the additional hours.

JOB STABILITY

The slow pace of job creation and the relatively high unemployment rate in the current recovery, along with continuing corporate downsizing and increased use of part-time and temporary workers, have led to the perception that employment is becoming less stable than in the past. The fear is that a decline in permanent employment will lead to a largely "contingent" work force, meaning that there will no longer be an understanding between worker and employer that a job will last for a long time. Is the current sense of less stable employment the result of the recent recession, or are long-term forces at work?

There are several different approaches to measuring the stability of employment. To some extent, growth of the contingent work force can be measured directly. We can also look at how likely individuals are to stay with an employer, at the dynamics of firm size, and at changes in the industrial composition of employment.

No official statistics are kept on the number of workers employed on a contingent basis. One study that examined employment practices at a number of large firms in 1985 found that slightly less than 1.5 percent of the labor they used was explicitly hired on a temporary basis.

We do, however, know how many workers are employed in the personnel supply industry (largely temporary workers). This number has increased dramatically since the early 1970s, and particularly rapidly in the current recovery. From the trough of the recession in March 1991 to December 1993, employment in the personnel supply industry grew by 687,000 workers. This was 26 percent of all employment growth over this period.

Taking a longer perspective, employment in the temporary help industry has grown from less than one-third of 1 percent of total employment in the early 1970s to nearly 1.3 percent today (Chart 3-13). While growth has been explosive, the fraction of the work force employed on a contingent basis is probably still less than 3 percent.

Chart 3-13 **Help Supply Industry Employment as Share of Total Employment**
Temporary workers are a small but increasing share of total employment.

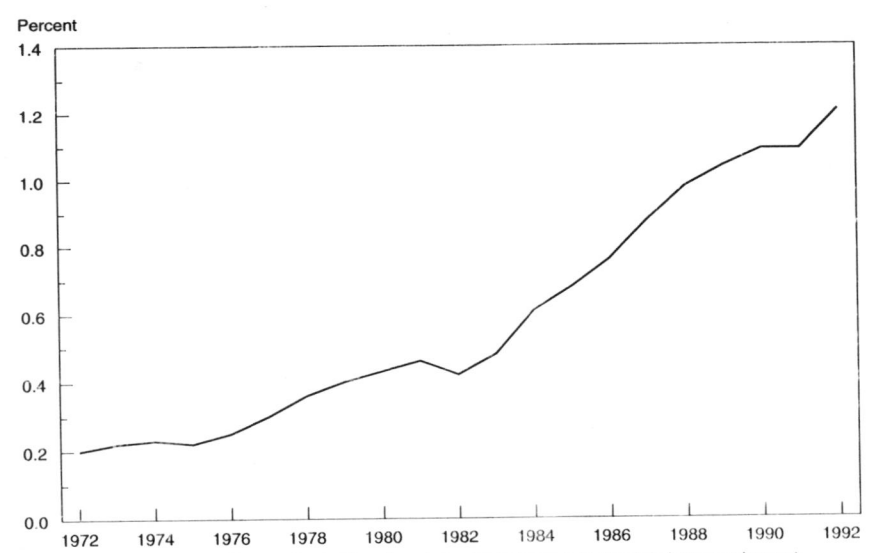

Note: Values before 1982 are estimated from the relationship between help supply industry employment and personnel supply industry employment after 1982.
Source: Department of Labor.

Another potential indicator of declining job stability is the growing use of part-time workers. Like temporary workers, part-time workers usually do not receive pension and health benefits and tend to have a weak attachment to their firms. Several authors have included them when enumerating the contingent work force.

Between August 1990 and December 1993, part-time employment increased by 6.4 percent, compared with only a 1.7-percent increase for full-time employment. But part-time employment always expands during recessions, and the increased use of part-time workers during this recession is not significantly different from the pattern of past recessions, given sluggish output growth. Over the last several decades, however, there has been a small secular increase in the fraction of the labor force working part-time, but it has not been a steady increase. The fraction grew considerably from the late 1960s through the early 1980s, reaching a peak in 1983. It then declined through the rest of the 1980s and increased moderately in the 1990 recession. The fraction of workers working part-time by choice has remained nearly constant since the early 1970s (Chart 3–14).

Chart 3-14 **Part-Time Employment: Total and Voluntary**
Since the late 1960s the use of part-time workers has grown, but the number working part-time by choice has not.

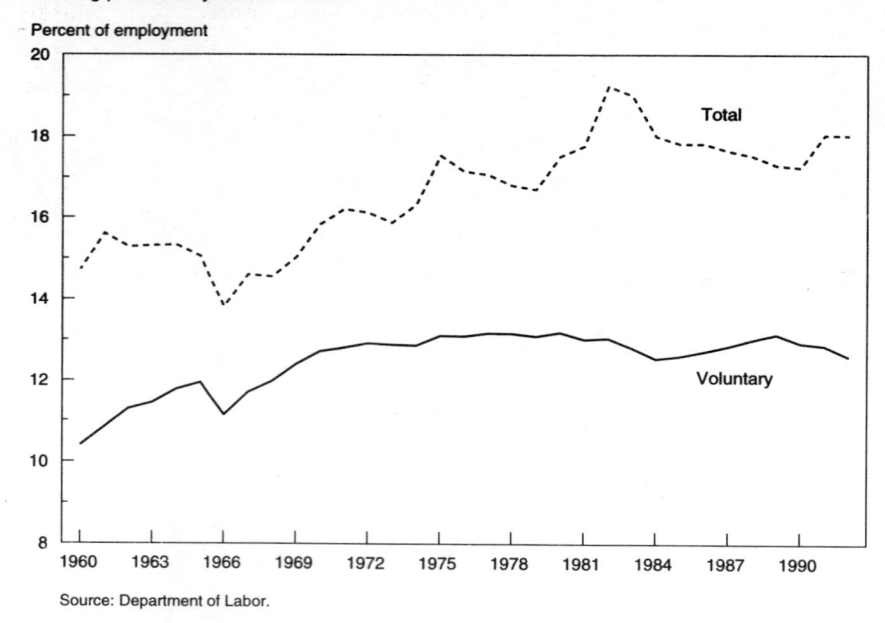

Source: Department of Labor.

What accounts for the secular shifts toward temporary and part-time employment? One possibility is that the underlying demand for goods and services has become more volatile, leading firms to desire less permanent work forces so that they can more easily respond to shifting needs. If this were so, we should observe greater volatility in the industrial composition of employment or in firm size. Such evidence is lacking, however. Data from the Census of Manufactures show no long-term increase in variability of firm size. No data are available on volatility of firm size in the rest of the economy.

A simple measure of the amount of reallocation of labor between industries is the sum of changes in the share of each industry's employment in total employment for those industries that are increasing their employment share. (This is equal to the absolute value of the sum of the decreases in the share of employment in each industry with a shrinking share.) When total employment is constant, this measure is simply interpreted as the fraction of the work force being reallocated between industries. According to this measure, the rate of change in the industrial structure across all industries increased in 1990 and 1991, which is typical for a recession. The rate of change in industry composition typically declines during recoveries, and the current recovery fits this pattern, with churning declining in 1992 and 1993 (Chart 3–15).

Chart 3-15 **Reallocation of Employment Between Industries**
The rate of reallocation of employment between industries follows business conditions but shows no upward trend.

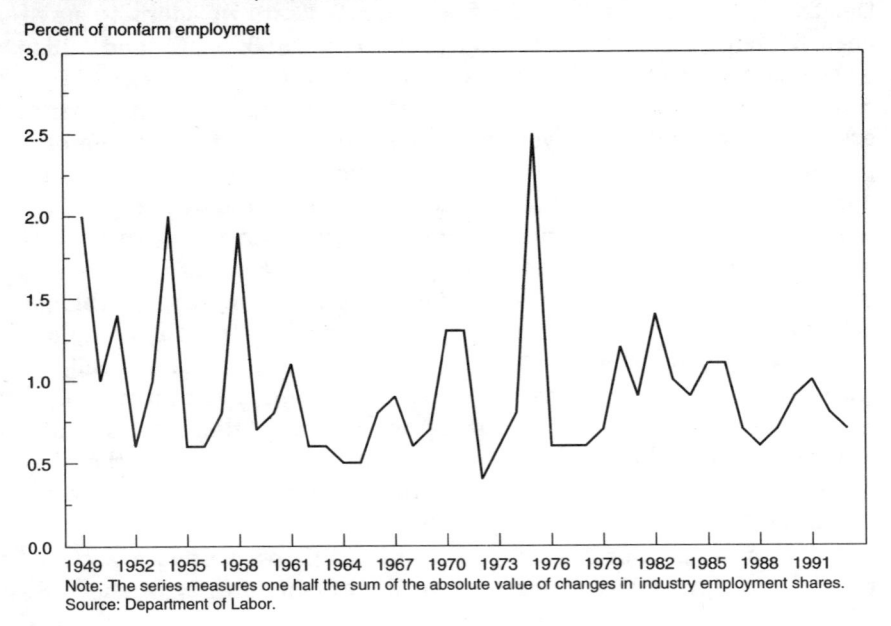

Percent of nonfarm employment

Note: The series measures one half the sum of the absolute value of changes in industry employment shares.
Source: Department of Labor.

Has the rate of change of the industrial composition of employment trended upward over time? Chart 3–16 shows that the answer is no. There is a big spike in 1975 after the first oil shock, but no trend. Over the entire 1949–93 period, the average rate of reallocation was 0.9 percent per year. Recent experience appears consistent with the past. Since 1980, the average rate of reallocation has also been 0.9 percent per year.

How are we to reconcile what we know to be major changes in the industrial composition of employment (such as those due to defense cutbacks) with the fact that there has been no apparent increase in the rate of industrial change? Evidently the economy is typically experiencing significant changes in its structure. Just as horseshoes gave way to tires and mechanical adding machines gave way to electronic calculators, industries today continue to grow and die.

If job instability is increasing, it does not appear to be because of changes in the volatility of firm size or industry demand. If there are significant changes in job stability, apparently they are happening at the individual level. If individuals' attachments to their jobs are becoming more tenuous, we should observe a drop in the length of time workers spend with each employer, and an increase in the probability that a worker will leave his or her firm in any given year. But analysis of the Current Population Survey shows the fraction of workers holding jobs for 8 years or more to have been 30 percent in 1979, and 31 percent in 1983, 1987, and 1991.

A constant fraction of workers holding long-term jobs might hide changes in the experience of individuals. For example, older workers are more likely than young workers to stay with the same employer. The aging of the work force might therefore have brought about an increase in average job tenure, even if individuals at any particular age were experiencing greater job instability. Two studies that have attempted to examine this question provide mixed evidence. Both find that employment for nonwhites and college graduates has become less stable, but both also find that employment stability for some groups has increased. No strong trend toward increasing overall instability can be found in either study. It is impossible to rule out increasing overall instability on the basis of these studies, but if there has been an increase it is either too recent or too subtle to be reflected in the aggregate tenure statistics discussed in the previous paragraph.

Whether or not job security is decreasing, two things are clear. First, there has always been a great deal of instability in the U.S. labor market. Second, there is no question that there is a *perception* that job security is decreasing. This may be due entirely to the normal increase in job losses during the recent recession, to media accounts of mass layoffs at companies that used to offer unusually stable jobs, or to increases in job instability that simply are not reflected in aggregate statistics. Alternatively, a constant rate of job loss combined with greater income inequality has meant an increase in *income* (as opposed to employment) insecurity.

BENEFITS

One of the concerns raised by the growing use of contingent workers is that fewer workers will be covered by employer-provided health insurance and retirement income programs. In fact, there is some evidence that this has occurred, at least for some recent periods. The timing of these changes, however, does not appear to correspond to the timing of increases in temporary or part-time work, but the changes are troubling nonetheless.

After rising for several decades, the fraction of workers covered by employer-provided health insurance has fallen since the mid-1980s. However, it is likely that this fall represents less than 10 percent of all workers. Nonetheless, since 1985 the fraction of the population covered by job-related health insurance has remained roughly constant (around 60 percent). Evidently the decline in coverage per worker is being offset by the increase in the number of households with more than one person working.

Retirement income is another area where different surveys suggest different conclusions. Business tax records show no decline in the fraction of workers covered by retirement income programs; however, studies examining defined-benefit pension coverage find a decline in the late 1980s. The difference is at least in part due to the growth of tax-exempt retirement savings plans provided by employers. These tend to be less generous than defined-benefit retirement plans, so that there has at least been a decline in the *quality* of retirement security plans, if not in the quantity. Even here the story is mixed. At least one recent study finds that pension coverage has begun to increase again in the 1990s.

TOWARD A COMPREHENSIVE WORK FORCE POLICY

The labor market has changed. Although there is little evidence of any recent abrupt changes in the fundamental behavior of the labor market, three aspects of the longer term picture are worthy of concern: (1) the slow growth of incomes and increasing income inequality; (2) increasing unemployment and nonemployment, particularly for certain groups; and (3) the high rates of job loss and dislocation that are normal for our economy.

Real income has grown very slowly since the early 1970s, and the real incomes of the least well-off have actually fallen. The Administration's policies address these problems at four levels.

First, the primary source of income growth is productivity growth. To increase productivity growth, we must invest more in research and development of new technologies. To take advantage of technical progress, we must invest more in new plant and equipment. Second, U.S. employers have learned new ways to organize work that make better use of the vast pool of talent in our work force. These participatory techniques are particularly effective in organizations adapting to rapid technical change but have wider applicability as well. Third, to deal with the problems of income growth and inequality, we must invest more and invest more equitably in education and training for our work force. Finally, in order to promote investment and to ensure that incomes grow with increasing productivity, the Administration's macroeconomic policies aim to encourage full employment built on a sound fiscal foundation.

The Administration's main vehicle for encouraging investments of all sorts has been to reduce Federal borrowing so as to make room in credit markets for private borrowers. As noted in Chapter 2, deficit reduction has resulted in much lower interest rates, making it easier for firms and individuals to undertake productivity-enhancing investments. As the recovery continues, we expect to see more individuals and firms taking advantage of these opportunities. Funding for research is also a high priority for this Administration.

In addition to promoting capital formation and technical change, the Administration aims to increase the productivity of the work force by helping employers make better use of their workers through increased worker participation. Numerous studies have now demonstrated that cooperative techniques increase productivity substantially in a wide range of enterprises. By helping to disseminate information on what successful firms have been able to accomplish, the Administration hopes to speed the adoption of these practices throughout the economy.

Improvements in education and training to boost the skills and enhance the flexibility of the U.S. work force are top priorities. To this end, the Administration is increasing spending and reorganizing programs to increase effectiveness. From increasing funding for Head Start to proposals for developing "lifelong learning," the Administration hopes to address education and training needs everywhere in our society. The Administration's Goals 2000: Educate America Act and the Improving America's Schools Act aim to ensure a quality education for all students, first by guaranteeing all students a safe environment for learning, and then by setting national standards for students and teachers. To ensure that all postsecondary students have access to the means to finance their higher education, the Congress has passed legislation proposed by this Administration establishing a direct lending program where the rate at which the loan will be paid back will depend on the recipient's income.

Recognizing the need to coordinate education and job training, the Departments of Education and Labor have joined in an unprecedented partnership to develop a number of new programs. Government programs have traditionally provided extensive support for those going to college. The School-to-Work initiative of the Departments of Education and Labor will help those who begin their careers with a high school diploma to obtain meaningful work-based training. This training will go hand in hand with a new system of skill standards and certification, which will make the skills workers learn more portable and consequently more valuable. The Administration's Workforce Security Act will provide training and job search assistance to dislocated workers who are having difficulty finding new work. The aim is to transform our unemployment system into a reemployment system. The Administration's proposed welfare reform plan will provide funds for training to some of the most disadvantaged in our society: mothers and fathers with children in poverty.

Another part of the Administration's answer to the problem of growing inequality is the substantial increase in the earned income tax credit that has been put in place. This tax credit, primarily for low-wage workers with children, along with the full range of other government transfer programs, will lift many families with a full-time worker out of poverty. It is described in detail in Chapter 1.

Increased productivity growth is the answer to stagnant real wages, and improved training and education—particularly for the least advantaged—is a major part of the solution to growing inequality. But we cannot expect firms to purchase new equipment unless there is demand for more products, and we cannot expect workers to train for jobs that do not exist. Therefore, an integral goal of the Administration's economic policies is the return to full employment.

Maintaining a high rate of economic growth is also essential for dealing with the second major labor market trend of the last two decades: increased unemployment. The analysis presented above suggests that most of the increase in average unemployment over the 1970s and 1980s was due to slack aggregate demand. There is also some indication of a permanent increase in the natural rate of unemployment in the 1970s. Whatever the cause of the increase in the natural rate, the Administration's Workforce Security Act should help reduce the natural rate by facilitating a more efficient matching of workers and employers.

An initial step toward the establishment of a reemployment system was taken last fall with the passage of legislation extending Federal emergency unemployment benefits. That legislation put in place for the first time a system of worker profiling to help identify workers who are likely to experience long-term unemployment, and to provide them with a package of job search assistance services. Several controlled experiments have now shown such services to be effective in reducing the duration of unemployment. Once fully in place, the Workforce Security Act will provide both job search assistance and long-term training to those who lack the skills necessary to secure good employment. This will help reduce mismatch unemployment and the natural rate of unemployment.

Existing training programs for dislocated workers have been criticized as ineffective. The new programs proposed by the Administration address this problem by emphasizing long-term training and continuing postsecondary education. The large human capital literature shows substantial potential benefits from this approach to increasing worker skills.

Dislocated workers have always faced problems with income security and health care. With growing income inequality, the normally high rates of dislocation in our economy mean greater income insecurity. The Administration is moving to make job transitions easier for displaced workers in a number of ways. The Workforce Security Act will help ease transitions and help those who need it with retraining for a new career. The Administration's health care plan will provide universal coverage, relieving one of the major worries of a dislocated worker—what to do if a family member becomes ill after health coverage from the lost job has lapsed.

Overall, the labor, education, health, and welfare programs proposed by the Clinton Administration hold out the hope of lower unemployment rates, reduced inequality, and stronger income growth for American workers and their families.

CHAPTER 4

Health Care Reform

THE UNITED STATES SPENDS far more per capita on and devotes a much larger share of its income to health care than does any other country. In 1993, one out of every seven dollars that Americans spent—14.3 percent of gross domestic product (GDP)—went to health services. In 1991, the most recent year for which comparable international data are available, the United States spent 13.2 percent of GDP on health care, while no other industrialized country spent more than 10 percent. Indeed the average for all the industrialized countries of the Organization for Economic Cooperation and Development (OECD) was only about 8 percent. Yet despite this massive commitment of resources, the United States insures a much smaller fraction of its population than do most other industrial countries, and ranks comparatively poorly on such important overall indicators of health outcomes as life expectancy and infant mortality. Tens of millions of Americans remain uninsured and live in constant fear of bankruptcy should they become ill. Tens of millions more have inadequate insurance or risk becoming uninsured if they lose their jobs.

For the lucky Americans who have comprehensive benefits and little worry about becoming uninsured, the current system buys care of high quality and provides genuine health security. For others less fortunate, the system works less well or not at all. And even the lucky suffer from the shortcomings of the current system, as the costs of covering services for the uninsured and some of the costs for those served by government programs are shifted onto hospitals and other providers and ultimately onto private sector insurance premiums.

Health care spending is not only high but growing rapidly. In almost every year of the last three decades, health care costs have increased at more than twice the rate of total income. In the 1980s, real per capita health care spending increased at an annual rate of 4.4 percent in the United States, compared with an average of only 3.2 percent in Canada, France, Germany, Japan, and the United Kingdom. Current projections indicate that, without reform, the United States will devote nearly 18 percent of its GDP to health care by the turn of the century.

At the level of the individual, the family, and the firm, the inexorable growth in health care spending means ever-increasing insurance premiums and ever-higher medical bills. And at the level of Federal and State and local governments, rising health care costs mean that health expenditures claim larger and larger budget shares, with less left over for essential competing demands like public safety, infrastructure maintenance and expansion, and improvements in education and training. Despite a sustained reduction in real discretionary spending, the Congressional Budget Office projects that escalating health care costs will be the dominant force pushing Federal budget deficits back up as the 20th century nears its end.

The facts speak for themselves: The United States faces a health care crisis that demands a solution, both for the health of its citizens and for the health of its economy over the long run.

For analytical purposes, this crisis can be divided into four separate but interrelated parts. First, the current system fails to provide health security for millions of Americans, both insured and uninsured. Insured Americans do not have health security when they face the prospect of losing their coverage if they lose or change their jobs. Some estimates suggest that such worries may reduce job mobility by as much as 25 percent. The health security of the uninsured is still more precarious: Even when they do manage to obtain care, the evidence indicates that they receive less treatment, are sicker, and suffer higher mortality rates than the insured. It is simply not true, as some claim, that all Americans get decent care when they need it.

Shortcomings in private insurance markets are a second and related problem. Under the current system people who are less healthy pay more, sometimes much more, for insurance than people who are healthy. Insurance for those with preexisting conditions is often either unavailable or available only at prices that put it out of reach for many Americans. And many insurance policies simply do not cover a variety of large financial risks—exactly the kinds of risks that insurance is designed to address in the first place.

The third problem in our current health care system is the lack of effective competition, which in turn weakens the incentives for both providers and consumers to make cost-conscious decisions. Inadequate competition is a major reason why the costs of the American health care system are so high. Studies suggest that a variety of common procedures are often performed in circumstances where they are inappropriate or of equivocal value on purely medical grounds. Fee-for-service providers clearly have an incentive to provide more care, including care that is inappropriate, because they are generally reimbursed for each additional test or procedure they perform. Consumers often do not have the information they need to evaluate whether a particular service is indicated, and some do not have the choice among providers that might allow them to make cost-conscious decisions. In addition, many consumers have weak incentives to choose among health care services on the basis of cost, and among health care plans on the basis of price. Finally, because many insurance policies do not cover preventive care, consumers may underutilize cost-effective services at earlier stages of medical need.

The fourth problem with our current system is the burden it places on public sector budgets. Large and growing public health care expenditures force governments to make painful choices among cutting other spending programs, increasing revenues, or increasing budget deficits—each of which can have adverse consequences for long-term economic growth.

None of these four problems can be solved in isolation. For example, in the absence of systemwide reform, arbitrary caps on Federal health care programs, which some have proposed, would simply shift still more of government program costs onto the private sector. According to one recent estimate, uncompensated care and government programs that reimbursed hospitals below market prices shifted $26.1 billion onto the private sector in 1991. Caps on government programs would simply aggravate this problem. Similarly, any attempt to provide universal coverage without complementary measures to improve competition and sharpen the incentives for more cost-conscious decisions would mean even more dramatic increases in systemwide costs. And reforms designed only to address the most glaring shortcomings of private insurance markets would not solve either the problem of providing health security for all Americans or the problem of escalating public health care bills.

In short, a piecemeal approach will not work. Health care reform requires a comprehensive solution. At the same time, it requires a solution that preserves what is good about the current system and that maintains choice at all levels. This is indeed a daunting challenge, but one that the Nation can ill afford to ignore.

UNIVERSAL COVERAGE AND HEALTH SECURITY

Providing universal health coverage and security for all Americans is an essential objective of health care reform. Chart 4–1 shows the sources of health insurance for the American population. According to the Current Population Survey, over 15 percent of Americans—nearly 39 million people—were uninsured throughout 1992. That is one of the highest shares in the industrialized world. While some people remain uninsured for long periods of time, many more experience brief episodes during which they lack coverage, for instance when they lose a job. The Survey of Income and Program Participation (SIPP) found that over three times as many people are uninsured at some time during a given year as are uninsured throughout the year. The SIPP estimates that more than one in four Americans were uninsured at some point in a 28-month period from 1987 to 1989.

Chart 4-1 **Distribution of Population by Source of Health Insurance Coverage: 1991**
Most Americans receive health insurance through their employers. Fifteen percent of Americans are uninsured.

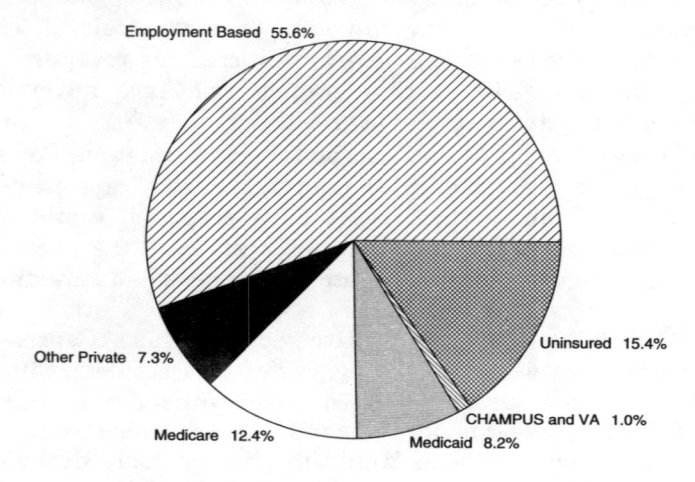

- Employment Based 55.6%
- Uninsured 15.4%
- CHAMPUS and VA 1.0%
- Medicaid 8.2%
- Medicare 12.4%
- Other Private 7.3%

Note: Detail does not sum to 100 percent due to rounding.
Source: Employee Benefit Research Institute.

The fact that so many people are uninsured at least some of the time means that the prospect of being uninsured may influence the behavior of a large number of Americans. As long as people can lose their health coverage simply by changing employment, health insecurity will remain a barrier to changing jobs or starting new businesses. An important rationale for universal coverage is therefore to increase mobility and employment opportunities for those who already have insurance but do not have health security.

Similarly, many people remain on welfare because they will lose their medicaid coverage if they take a job. Some estimates indicate that up to one-quarter of recipients of aid to families with dependent children (AFDC) would take a job if private health insurance equivalent to that provided by medicaid were available to them. A second rationale for universal coverage is thus to reduce the number of people on welfare and to further the Administration's goal of welfare reform.

A third rationale for universal coverage is to improve the health of the uninsured. The uninsured do use health care—they do not simply do without. It is estimated that those without insurance for all of 1994 will consume about $1,200 of medical care per capita—60 percent of which will be paid for by governments and private payers, not by the uninsured themselves (Chart 4-2). This expenditure is roughly half the over $2,300 per capita consumed by those who are currently insured.

Chart 4-2 **Sources of Payment for Health Care by Insurance Status: 1994 Estimates**
About 60 percent of care for the uninsured is financed by governments, other private payers, bad debt, free care, or workers' compensation.

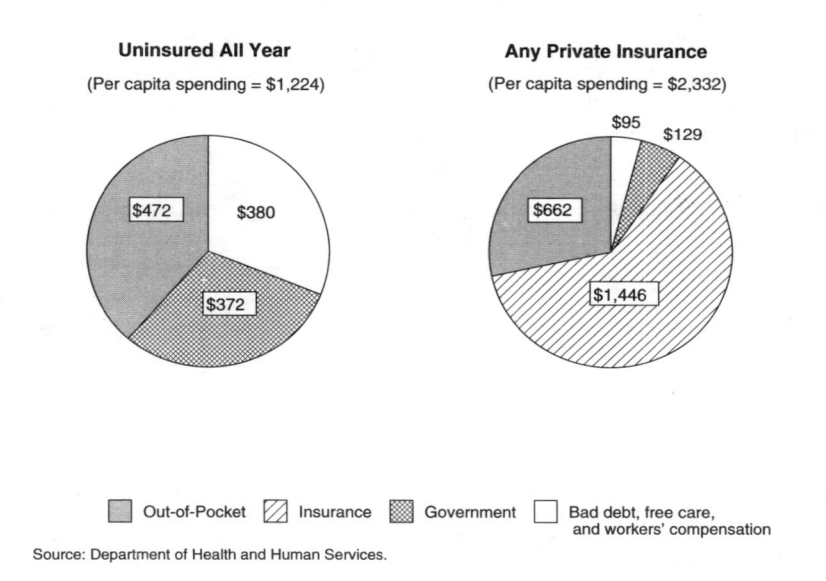

Uninsured All Year
(Per capita spending = $1,224)
- $472
- $380
- $372

Any Private Insurance
(Per capita spending = $2,332)
- $95
- $129
- $662
- $1,446

☐ Out-of-Pocket ▨ Insurance ▨ Government ☐ Bad debt, free care, and workers' compensation

Source: Department of Health and Human Services.

While the uninsured do receive care, it is often neither timely nor appropriate. The uninsured are more likely than the insured to receive care in the emergency room, are less healthy when they are admitted to a hospital, and receive less treatment than people with similar diagnoses once admitted. Some studies indicate—and common sense suggests—that the health of the uninsured suffers as a result.

Indeed, without reform, the problem of adverse health outcomes for the uninsured is likely to worsen over time. Historically, governments and private payers have shouldered the burden of financing care for the uninsured. As health care costs continue to escalate, however, these payers may become less willing to bear this burden.

Perhaps surprisingly, providing universal health insurance to cover those currently uninsured will not require a large increase in total health expenditures. While the uninsured are poorer than the population as a whole, they are also younger and healthier. Almost all of the elderly already have insurance—through medicare. Among the nonelderly population, 24 percent of those with employer-sponsored insurance are between the ages of 45 and 64, compared with only 17 percent of the uninsured. Only 9 percent of the privately insured are between the ages of 18 and 24, compared with 18 percent of the uninsured. And while uninsured adults often perceive themselves to be in poorer general health than the population as a whole, they are less likely than the insured to have chronic conditions (Table 4–1). Estimates that account for these demographic and health factors generally find that insuring the uninsured would increase national health spending by less than 10 percent.

TABLE 4–1.—*Health Perception and Health Status by Type of Insurance Coverage, 1987*

[Percent]

Characteristic	Private, employment related	Uninsured
Self-reported general health perception:		
Fair	10.6	18.1
Poor	1.3	2.4
Any chronic condition	33.1	26.1

Note.—The sample is composed of adults aged 18 to 64.
Source: Department of Health and Human Services.

A fourth rationale for universal coverage is to solve the "free rider" problem. At least some of the uninsured could afford to purchase insurance but choose to go without because they feel they do not need it, and because they know that if they do become sick they will be cared for on an emergency basis at little cost to themselves. For some, relying on such "free" catastrophic insurance can be more attractive than purchasing insurance in the private market. By requiring that all individuals pay something for coverage, health reform can help eliminate this problem.

Finally, as discussed below, universal coverage is essential if everyone in the population is to share equally in the costs of insurance (Box 4–1).

> **Box 4-1.—Moral Hazard and Adverse Selection**
>
> All insurance markets face two potential problems. The first, called moral hazard, involves incentives. Insurance may encourage those who are covered to use insured services more than they otherwise would, or it may discourage the insured from taking steps to lower their need for such services. Insurance against any kind of risk—including health risks—always involves some element of moral hazard. When people use health services more than they would without insurance, the total amount insurers must pay increases, and they in turn must increase their prices. Furthermore, because individuals pay less than the full social cost of the services they receive, too much of society's resources will be devoted to such services.
>
> The second problem is adverse selection. People who know that they are more at risk than others of falling ill are more likely to purchase health insurance. Therefore, insurers who set their prices at the average cost for the population as a whole are likely to discover that their prices do not cover their costs, because their customers are on average sicker than the population at large. To address this problem, insurers have incentives both to charge prices that exceed the cost of covering the average person and to select risks as best they can. The higher prices of insurance that result from adverse selection have the perverse effect of discouraging some healthy people from purchasing insurance. Because of the adverse selection problem, all people must be required to purchase insurance if each of them is to be charged the average cost of providing insurance.

INSURANCE MARKET REFORM

Private insurance markets have a number of shortcomings that impede the realization of universal coverage.

INSURING MAJOR RISKS AND PREEXISTING CONDITIONS

Economic theory suggests that *at a minimum* well-functioning insurance markets should insure against the expenses that accompany large medical risks because those are precisely the ones that cause the most financial hardship to individuals and families, are the least susceptible to moral hazard, and have the lowest administrative costs as a share of benefits. In our current system, however, private insurance markets often fail even when judged against this minimal standard.

About 80 percent of conventional health insurance policies have limits—generally ranging from $250,000 to over $1 million—on the amount that the insurer will pay over the policyholder's lifetime. Many insurers also initially exclude coverage of "preexisting conditions"—health problems that exist before the policy takes effect. A typical rule, for example, is to exclude for 6 months a condition that was present in the 6 months prior to joining a plan. Some estimates suggest that up to 80 million Americans have preexisting conditions that could be excluded from any new coverage or would require payment of a higher premium.

Both the exclusion of coverage for preexisting conditions and the limitations on maximum lifetime payments are ways that insurers respond to the adverse selection problem discussed in Box 4–1. Such practices also reflect the fact that insurers who know in advance about the likely health status of their potential policyholders can choose which risks they are willing to insure and which they are not, and can choose to charge different prices to different individuals based on this assessment.

Such common insurance practices may be privately optimal for individual insurers, but they are not socially efficient. People with preexisting conditions and people who have exhausted their lifetime insurance limits may still require care, and someone must bear the costs. If they cannot obtain private insurance and they have exhausted their own funds, either they will get insurance through public sector programs, such as medicaid, or the costs of their care will be shifted onto the premiums of those who are able to obtain insurance. By compelling all insurers to cover preexisting conditions and by eliminating limitations on lifetime payments, the government could reduce the adverse selection problem in private insurance markets and thereby improve how they function.

COMMUNITY RATING

A second essential component of insurance reform is "community rating"—charging everyone in a large group the same price regardless of individual differences in demographic or health status. Currently, health insurance is often experience rated—the price for members of a particular group is based in whole or in part on that group's expected utilization of insured services. However, there are strong reasons for requiring community rating.

The rationale for any kind of insurance is to spread costs throughout the insured population. Complete health insurance would spread the cost of care across everyone in the population, regardless of their health status. Similarly, complete insurance would guarantee that the price paid by each individual for coverage would be the average cost of such coverage for the population. In contrast, experience rating means that the price one pays for insurance varies depending on one's health status. But at least for those health problems and their associated costs that individuals cannot influence by their behavior, experience rating is at odds with the basic function of insurance—to insure against risk.

In principle, of course, one can distinguish between those health risks that individuals can influence and those that they cannot, and apply experience rating to the former. In practice, however, this is often difficult to do, because it would require detailed monitoring of personal behavior. In addition, many major health risks, with the obvious exception of those associated with smoking, are linked quite imperfectly to individual behavior, or the medical profession's understanding of the linkage remains rudimentary. Based on these considerations, community rating of health insurance, and continued public programs to deter smoking, are appropriate elements of health insurance reform.

However, community rating is difficult to enact without complementary reforms. The adverse selection issue described in Box 4–1 is one potential problem, which universal coverage could address by requiring people to have coverage. A related problem stems from the fact that insurers who are compelled to charge a community rate will have incentives to seek out the healthiest consumers, because they can be covered for the lowest cost and thus are likely to yield insurers the highest profits. This risk selection may involve high administrative costs, for example in determining the medical history of each member of a group. Resources devoted to this activity increase the overall costs of health care without providing any additional health benefits.

Several steps could be taken to minimize the possibility of such selection. First, a system of "risk adjustment payments" could be designed—monetary transfers from plans that have a healthier mix of enrollees to plans with a sicker mix of enrollees. If risk adjustment perfectly compensated for true differences in health risk, it would eliminate the incentives for selection on the part of insurers.

Second, all insurers could be required to offer the same package of benefits, thereby eliminating the opportunity to use the variations in the benefits package to attract better risks. Finally, "guaranteed issue" and "guaranteed renewability" of insurance could be required—that is, people could not be denied the right to enroll initially or renew enrollment in a health plan because of demographic or health status.

REDUCING ADMINISTRATIVE COSTS

In part because of the experience rating practices of insurance companies, there is insufficient standardization across insurers. Providers must deal with different insurers using different claim forms and covering different sets of services. Lack of standardization results in high administrative expenses. In 1991 over 6 percent of all health care expenditures went for administrative expenses. This exceeds total spending on all public health service programs.

Standardizing benefits and billing procedures and increasing the automation of bill payment could produce substantial administrative savings. Grouping small firms and individuals into larger purchasing pools would have the same effect. As Chart 4-3 shows, the administrative load charged by commercial insurers for small groups (1 to 4 employees) averages about 40 percent of claims paid—in contrast to only about 5½ percent for large groups (over 10,000 employees).

Chart 4-3 **Administrative Expenses of Commercial Insurers as Percent of Claims Paid**
Administrative expenses are much higher in proportion to claims paid for small groups than for large groups.

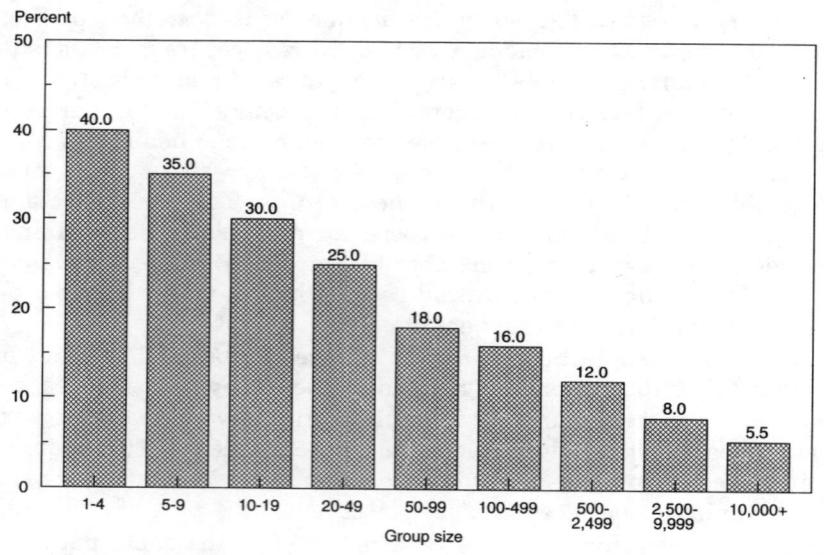

Group size	Percent
1-4	40.0
5-9	35.0
10-19	30.0
20-49	25.0
50-99	18.0
100-499	16.0
500-2,499	12.0
2,500-9,999	8.0
10,000+	5.5

Source: Hay/Huggins Company, Inc.

CREATING A MORE EFFICIENT MARKET AND CONTAINING COSTS

The third problem with the current health care system is that it appears to be far from efficient. As already noted, the United States spends a larger share of its GDP on health care than any other industrialized nation. If Americans valued medical care more than people in other countries do, this might not be cause for concern. But the facts suggest otherwise.

Although the fraction of national resources devoted to health care in the United States is partially explainable by our higher income, Chart 4-4 reveals that the United States is an outlier—we spend considerably more per capita on health care yet achieve a somewhat lower life expectancy than our higher income would predict. Nor can these differences be explained away by the age of the American population. In fact, the percentage of the population over 65 is lower in the United States than in most of the other OECD countries. Since older people tend to use more medical care than younger people, the age distribution of the American population suggests that the United States should spend a smaller rather than a larger fraction of GDP on health care than do other industrialized countries.

Chart 4-4 **Health Expenditure and Life Expectancy in Industrial Countries**
The United States spends more on health care yet has lower life expectancy than would be expected given its level of income.

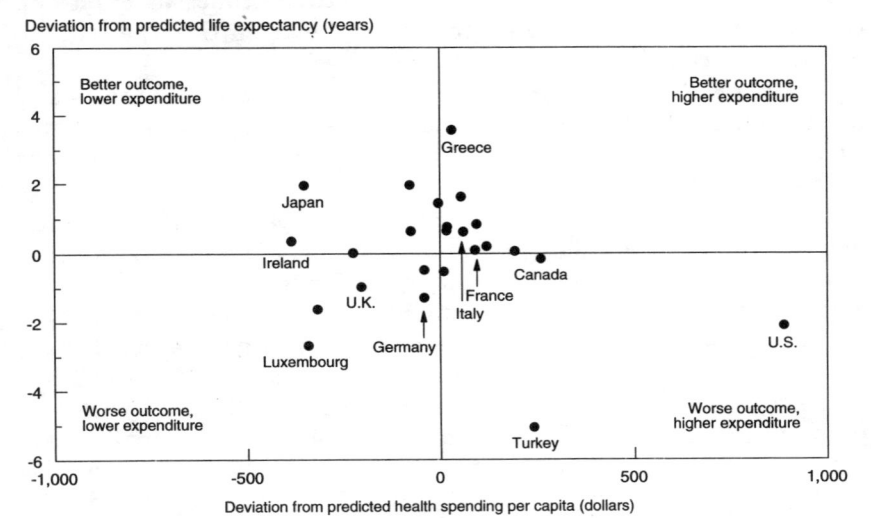

Note: Health spending and life expectancy are deviations from what would be expected given per capita income. The sample consists of the member countries of the OECD.
Sources: Organization for Economic Cooperation and Development and the World Bank.

It has been suggested that sociodemographic factors such as the greater prevalence of violence in American life may explain why health care spending in the United States is comparatively high. Existing research based on partial estimates suggests, however, that violent crime may add only about 2 percent to national health expenditures. No comparative studies have assessed whether violence is a more important determinant of health care spending in the United States than elsewhere.

At least part of the higher health care costs in America stem from inefficiencies of various sorts. First, there are the administrative inefficiencies in the insurance market discussed earlier. Inadequate competition among providers and inadequate incentives for cost-conscious behavior by both providers and consumers are a second major source of inefficiency in the current health care system. Traditional fee-for-service plans, which pay providers for each test and procedure they perform, are used by 58 percent of private sector employees who receive health insurance through their employers. Such plans have built-in incentives encouraging providers to perform more care than may be appropriate. These incentives are sometimes reinforced by self-referral arrangements whereby providers prescribe tests or other services from laboratories or clinics in which they have a direct financial interest. For example, one study found that doctors who performed and charged for their own radiological tests prescribed them at least four times as often and charged higher fees than did doctors who referred their patients to unaffiliated radiologists.

Providers sometimes have an incentive to overprescribe tests and procedures because they fear malpractice suits. Available estimates suggest that such "defensive medicine" accounts for about 3 percent of total health spending.

Even when there are many providers in a particular health care market, competition among them is often weak. Only 53 percent of people insured through an employer, for example, can choose among alternative health care plans, and often the choice of a capitated plan, such as a health maintenance organization (HMO), is not available. Many small firms do not offer multiple policies. One study found that only 5 percent of workers in firms with less than 25 employees were offered any choice among health care plans. As a result, many consumers have only limited choices among both plans and providers. Consumers also may not have a choice of hospitals, since hospital selection is usually left to doctors, who choose on the basis of where they practice and may not choose on the basis of price.

Moreover, effective consumer choice depends on adequate consumer information. But many consumers rely primarily on their providers for advice about what services are indicated in a particular situation. Consumers often do not even know the prices of medical goods and services, and they seldom have the information they would need to evaluate the quality of the services they receive. This means that providers are often in a position to influence both the supply and the demand sides of their markets. In short, consumers are ill equipped to bring strong competitive pressures to bear on providers to make cost-conscious decisions.

Nor do consumers themselves have strong incentives to exert such pressure. Even when they have a choice, consumers usually face weak incentives to opt for a low-cost health care plan. Many employers pay a fixed percentage—generally 80 percent—of whatever plan an employee chooses. Thus, when an employee selects a less expensive plan, 80 cents of each dollar saved goes to the employer and only 20 cents to the employee.

As the earlier discussion of moral hazard suggested, the current system of insurance may also encourage some consumers to use more care or more-expensive care options than they would if they were forced to pay higher out-of-pocket costs for services. On the other hand, if consumer copayments or deductibles were increased to reduce utilization, some of the value of insurance would be lost. Higher copayments might also discourage utilization of preventive services, with potentially adverse effects on health outcomes. Furthermore, even drastic increases in deductibles would provide only limited incentives. Table 4–2 shows that even if all families had a $5,000 deductible, only 29 percent of health dollars would be spent by individuals or families paying the full marginal cost of care.

TABLE 4–2.—*Distribution of Population and Health Spending by Spending Category, Estimates for 1994*

Annual health spending (dollars)	Percent of population	Percent of spending
0	7.8	0.0
1–500	26.0	1.4
501–1,000	13.1	2.5
1,001–3,000	25.2	13.4
3,001–5,000	10.4	12.0
5,001–10,000	9.3	19.4
10,001–30,000	6.5	31.0
Over 30,000	1.6	20.3

Note.—Health spending is in 1994 dollars. The estimates pertain to the noninstitutionalized population under the age of 65, excluding people who receive aid to families with dependent children or supplemental security income. The distribution presented is for health insurance units.

Source: Department of Health and Human Services.

Available evidence indicates that the weakness of effective competition in the health care marketplace results in substantial fraud and abuse as well as inappropriate care or care of equivocal value. Some estimates suggest that fraud and abuse may account for about 10 percent of total health care spending. And, as noted above and summarized in Chart 4–5, as much as one-third of some common procedures may be performed in cases where they are inappropriate or of equivocal value on medical grounds.

Chart 4-5 **Estimates of Inappropriate Care for Five Common Procedures**
Studies have shown that as many as one-third of some procedures may be inappropriate or of equivocal value.

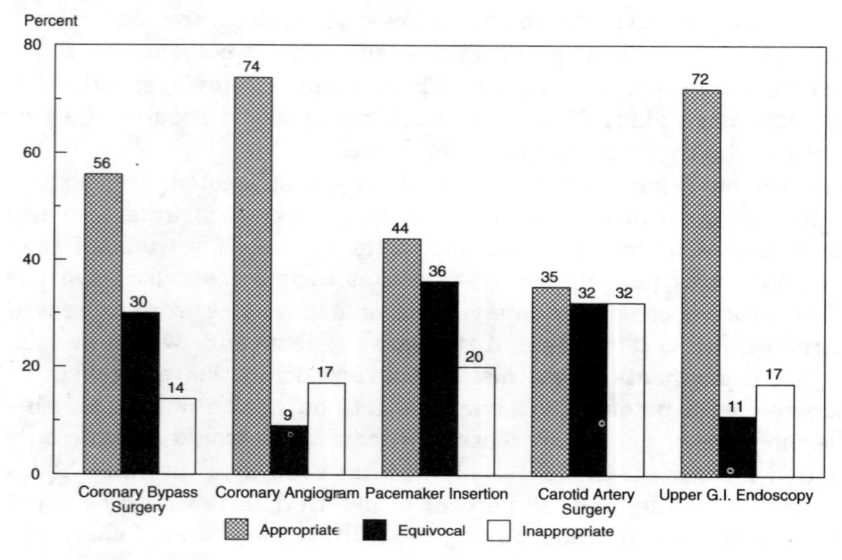

Procedure	Appropriate	Equivocal	Inappropriate
Coronary Bypass Surgery	56	30	14
Coronary Angiogram	74	9	17
Pacemaker Insertion	44	36	20
Carotid Artery Surgery	35	32	32
Upper G.I. Endoscopy	72	11	17

Source: The RAND Corporation.

There are often large differences in the amounts of medical care that people receive in different regions of the country, and even in different areas within the same region. These geographic differences may be evidence of resource misallocation. In 1989, for example, medicare physician payments per capita were 57 percent higher in Detroit than in New York City. Other research has found that the level of use of hospital beds in a community is determined primarily by the number of beds in that community. People in areas with more hospital beds are not any healthier than people who live in areas with fewer beds, but they are more likely to die in a hospital.

EXPLAINING COST INCREASES

Not only are the costs of the American health care system high, but they are rising rapidly as well (Box 4–2). Several factors have been identified as possible sources of cost growth, including the aging of the population; the growth in incomes and the reductions in cost sharing by consumers; slow productivity growth in most health care services; and technological change.

By itself, the aging of the population can explain about 5 to 10 percent of the growth in health care spending. Some estimates of individual behavior based on controlled experiments suggest that roughly another quarter can be explained by more-rapid income growth and the reduction in the cost-sharing component of health insurance over the last 40 years.

Health care costs may also have risen rapidly because so much medical care consists of personally provided services rather than goods. On average, over long periods of time, the prices of personal services rise faster than the prices of goods because productivity advances more rapidly in goods production than it does in services. Unfortunately, there is no reliable estimate of the magnitude of this factor. If there were no productivity growth at all in the health sector, the relative price of health care would be expected to rise, on average, at the economy-wide productivity growth rate—about 1 to 1½ percent per year in recent years, which is about one-quarter to one-third of the observed increase in relative prices. There is, however, almost certainly *some* productivity growth in health care, so the so-called cost disease factor cannot account for even this much extra health inflation.

Finally, many health economists believe that technological change itself drives health care costs upward. Once again, however, no reliable measures of its quantitative importance are available. In theory, the introduction of a new technology may increase or decrease health care costs, depending on whether it substitutes for or complements existing methods of treatment and, if the former, on whether it costs more or less than the technology currently available. In addition, some technological change may consist of applying previously existing technologies to different diagnoses.

Technology's influence on future trends in health care costs is difficult to predict. Medical science is on the brink of new technologies made possible by the revolution in genetic research, and these may prove to be less costly substitutes for existing technologies. In addition, as historians of technological progress have demonstrated, technological change is not entirely exogenous—its form depends on the incentive environment in which it occurs. A health care reform that encourages more cost-conscious decisions by providers and consumers may in fact encourage new technologies that are more cost effective. Finally, an increase in competitive pressure in health care markets will exercise greater price discipline on both existing and new technologies and thereby moderate their effects on the growth of health care spending.

WHO PAYS FOR HEALTH CARE?

Table 4–3 shows who paid for health care in 1991, and where the money was spent. The largest amount of health care spending (38

> **Box 4-2.—Recent Reductions in Health Care Inflation**
>
> The rate of inflation in the health sector slowed in 1993, largely as a result of slower growth in prices for health services, including physicians and hospital care:
>
> | Inflation rate of: | Average 1983-91 | Year ending December (percentages) 1992 | 1993 |
> |---|---|---|---|
> | Total CPI | 3.9 | 2.9 | 2.7 |
> | Health care | 7.3 | 6.6 | 5.4 |
> | Excess of health care inflation over total | 3.4 | 3.7 | 2.7 |
>
> Source: Department of Labor.
>
> Historically, health care inflation tends to move in parallel with inflation in the rest of the economy, but at a higher average level. In 1993 the gap between health care inflation and overall inflation narrowed somewhat, but the change does not appear to be statistically significant.
>
> Some have argued that the recent slowdown in health inflation is a sign that reform of the health care system is not required. But despite the slowdown, the relative price of health care continues to increase: The medical care component of the consumer price index grew at twice the rate of total consumer price inflation in 1993. Moreover, this argument overlooks several other important motives for health reform: the lack of health security and universal coverage, the failures of the insurance market, and the burden of health care expenditures on government budgets. The cost problem will not be solved without reforms that increase competition in the health care marketplace.

percent) is for hospital care. Payments to physicians and other health care professionals are the second-largest category, at 29 percent of total spending. The remainder of personal health care is for home and nursing home care (9 percent), and drugs and other personal care outside of hospitals and nursing homes (12 percent). The costs of insurance administration are estimated at 6 percent of health spending. Finally, public health activities and research and construction total 6 percent of spending.

Health spending is financed in four principal ways. Businesses pay for health care directly through health insurance premiums ($153 billion in 1991) and workers' compensation and disability insurance ($18 billion). Total business spending ($171 billion) was about 23 percent of total health spending and 6.3 percent of total

TABLE 4–3.—*Sources and Uses of Health Care Funds, 1991*
[Billions of dollars]

Uses of funds	Total	Private spending					Government			
		Business		Household		Nonpatient revenue	Medicare	Medicaid	Employer	Other
		Premiums [1]	Workers' compensation	Premiums	Out-of-pocket					
Total	752	153	18	52	144	33	123	101	40	91
Hospital care	289	64	8	22	10	15	73	43	17	38
Physician care	142	42	7	14	26	0	33	7	11	3
Other professionals, dental visits	73	18	1	6	30	4	4	4	5	1
Home health and nursing home care	70	1	0	0	27	2	7	31	0	1
Drugs, vision, other personal care	87	6	1	2	52	2	3	12	2	7
Administration	44	22	1	7	0	1	3	4	6	0
Public health	25	0	0	0	0	0	0	0	0	25
Research and construction	23	0	0	0	0	9	0	0	0	14

[1] Includes household and employer premiums.
Source: Health Care Financing Administration.

compensation. Households pay for health care through insurance premiums ($52 billion in 1991) and out-of-pocket expenses ($144 billion). Total household spending of $196 billion was 26 percent of national health spending. The average household spent about $2,100 on health care in 1991. The health care industry receives additional nonpatient revenues of $33 billion (4 percent of total spending) from such activities as parking lot receipts.

Finally, governments pay for 47 percent of all health spending ($355 billion), most of it for medicare and medicaid. There is additional spending on health insurance for government employees and on activities of the Department of Veterans Affairs, the Department of Defense, and the Public Health Service. About 21 percent of Federal Government revenues and over 21 percent of State and local government revenues are devoted to health care.

Governments also subsidize health care indirectly, by excluding employer-provided health insurance from taxable income. In 1991 this tax expenditure cost the Federal Government an estimated $36 billion in individual income taxes. The government lost Social Security revenues as well, although Social Security payments in the future will also be somewhat lower.

Chart 4–6 shows the evolution of these payment sources over time. Between 1965 and 1991, payments by health insurers, medicare, and medicaid increased from 24 percent to 62 percent of total health care spending. Other government spending fell from 25 to

14 percent, and out-of-pocket spending declined from 46 percent to 20 percent of the total. The dramatic extension of insurance coverage—in both the public and the private sectors—may be both a response to and a cause of increased costs.

Chart 4-6 Sources of Health Care Financing as Percent of Total Expenditures
Health insurance and government-financed expenditures have been rising as a share of total spending, while out-of-pocket expenditures have been falling.

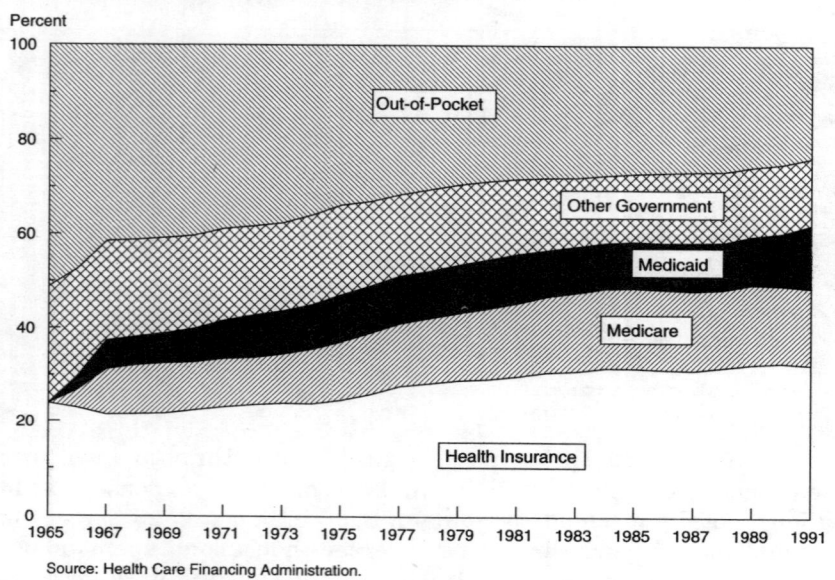

Source: Health Care Financing Administration.

While Table 4-3 shows who is responsible for paying for health care, it does not show the economic incidence—whose income is ultimately reduced because of high health care costs. In response to higher costs, businesses have several options: They can reduce health benefits; lower workers' wages or other benefits so that total compensation does not rise; reduce employment; lower returns to shareholders; reduce payments to other factors of production; reduce investment in plant and equipment or research and development; or raise prices to their customers.

Economic theory suggests that most of the increase in health care costs will be reflected in lower wages. The reason is simple. Firms are indifferent between spending a dollar on wages or on health premiums. But since wages are taxed while health insurance premiums are not, employees should be willing to "buy" increased health insurance by sacrificing wages until the marginal dollar of health insurance is worth one dollar of *after-tax* wages, or about 65 to 70 cents for a typical family. At this point, the worker should also be indifferent between contributing more to health insurance or to wages.

Empirical research suggests that the dominant long-run response of businesses to rising health care costs has indeed been to lower the rate of increase of workers' wages. Between 80 and 100 percent of increases in health care spending appears to be reflected in lower wages. As noted in Chapter 1, the share of wages in total compensation has been falling since 1960, while the share of business health insurance spending has increased markedly.

When firms slow wage increases to offset rising health insurance costs, they limit the increase in their total labor costs, and thus limit the job losses that might otherwise result. The slower wage growth due to rising business health expenditures has led to slower increases in incomes than would otherwise have occurred. If business spending on health care were the same share of compensation today as it was in 1975, wages per employee could be over $1,000 higher.

If increases in business spending on health insurance are not entirely balanced by reductions in other forms of labor payments, total compensation will rise. In this case, some other business decisions are likely to be affected, such as employment, pricing, or investment decisions. Empirical research, however, has not explored such alternative responses in any depth.

In summary, the economic literature on the incidence of health care costs suggests that employees eventually pay for most of their employer-provided health coverage by taking home lower cash wages. Reforms that enhance the efficiency of the health care market will allow employees to have both more health care coverage and higher take-home pay at the same time. Greater efficiency will therefore translate into an improvement in living standards for society as a whole.

HEALTH CARE AND GOVERNMENT BUDGETS

The final problem in the current health care system is the growing burden it places on government finances. Because governments pay for such a large share of health spending, increases in health costs contribute directly to pressures on Federal, State, and local budgets. Public sector spending on health care grew over 2 percentage points faster than private sector spending in the 1970s, and at about the same rate as private sector spending in the 1980s. The result has been an increasing share of health spending by governments. In addition, as was pointed out in Chapter 1, health spending is growing four times as rapidly as any other component of the Federal budget. Over the two decades ending in 1991, Federal health spending increased from 9 percent to 21 percent of total Federal revenues (Chart 4–7). Similar changes have occurred in State and local government spending.

Chart 4-7 Government Spending on Health Care as Percent of Total Government Revenues
Federal and State and local spending on health care account for increasing shares of total government revenues.

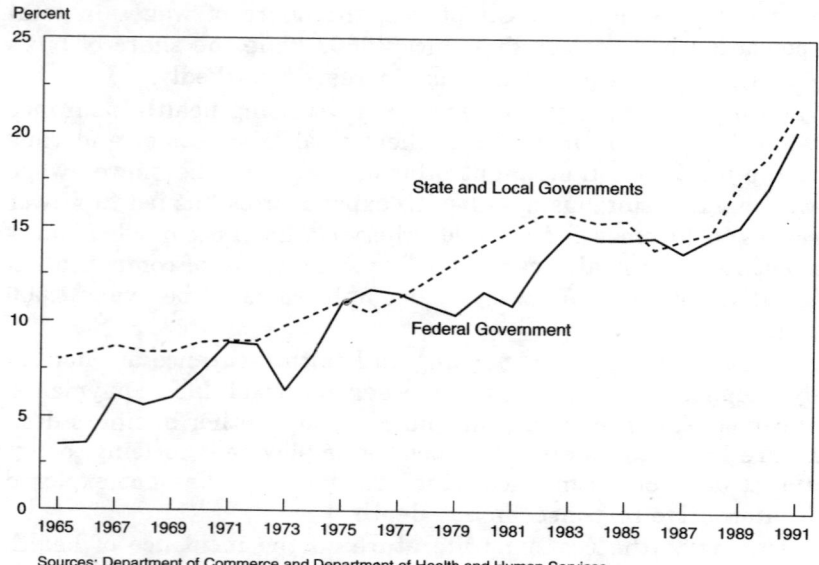

Sources: Department of Commerce and Department of Health and Human Services.

The Federal Government has responded to increasing health care costs in part by attempting to limit the reimbursement rates paid by public programs to health care providers. This approach in turn has resulted in the substantial shifting of costs to the private sector described earlier. In the absence of systemwide reform, the imposition of caps on Federal health care programs would either further aggravate the cost-shifting problem or gradually limit access to care.

Without health care reform, escalating health care costs will continue to confront the Federal Government—as well as State and local governments—with painful choices among additional taxes, cuts in spending on education and other programs that promote economic prosperity, or increases in budget deficits. As already noted, projected increases in Federal spending on medicare and medicaid are the main force behind a projected increase in the Federal deficit toward the end of this century.

THE ARCHITECTURE OF THE HEALTH SECURITY ACT

The Administration's approach to health care reform, while bold and comprehensive, builds on the strengths of the current market-based system. The Administration considered but rejected radical approaches such as a single-payer system or government-set health care prices in favor of restructuring the current system and relying on the forces of market competition. The Administration's framework preserves and expands consumer choice among providers and preserves the current employer-based system of health insurance. The Administration's plan also allows large firms to continue operating self-insured plans. Such firms generally provide comprehensive benefits, and many have managed to control health care spending. Indeed, the Administration's plan reflects many of the lessons learned from the experience of such firms.

ELEMENTS OF REFORM

To address the Nation's health care problems, meaningful reforms must address the four interrelated issues identified in the preceding discussion: universal coverage and health security; reform of the private insurance system; efficiency improvements and cost control; and sustained deficit reduction. The Health Security Act, which the Administration proposed in 1993, contains reforms that simultaneously meet these objectives. The principal features of the Administration's reforms are outlined in this section and discussed in greater detail in the remainder of this chapter.

Universal Coverage

The Health Security Act guarantees all Americans a health insurance package with a comprehensive set of benefits. The medicare program will be left largely unchanged, and medicare will remain the insurer for most Americans over the age of 65. Most medicaid recipients under 65 will be absorbed into the new system. With very few exceptions, all other Americans will receive their health insurance from the "health alliances" described below.

Universal coverage is essential for the reasons noted earlier. Comprehensive benefits are equally important if health security for all Americans is to be achieved. Some reform proposals promise universal coverage but guarantee coverage only for catastrophic expenses. In practice, people with high incomes may be able to afford additional coverage beyond catastrophic, but many other Americans cannot. Plans that guarantee only catastrophic coverage leave many people without genuine health security—subject to the risk that their insurance coverage will deteriorate if they lose their jobs, just when their incomes are falling.

Since the Administration's comprehensive benefits package includes a prescription drug benefit for the under-65 population, the Administration's proposal also calls for a comparable drug benefit to be added to the medicare program. In addition, the proposal includes funding for long-term care services, primarily to expand the amount of home- and community-based care.

Reforming Insurance Markets

Under the Health Security Act, individuals and families will receive coverage through regional or corporate "health alliances"—pools of individuals who purchase from a set of health plans. No insurer will be able to impose restrictions on preexisting conditions or lifetime limitations on insurance benefits, or to deny people the right to initiate or renew enrollment because of demographic or health status. Insurers will have to charge a community rate to everyone in an alliance.

Because there will be only one regional alliance in each geographic area, and coverage will be universal, healthy people in each area will naturally be pooled with sicker people. Pooling health risks makes insurance affordable for everyone. It also provides the healthy with the knowledge that their insurance premiums will not rise if they or a family member become ill.

Eliminating exclusions for preexisting conditions and lifetime limitations on benefits guarantees that large financial risks will be covered. Providing for guaranteed issue and guaranteed renewability allows individuals to exercise their choices among health plans.

Efficiency Improvements and Cost Savings

To encourage cost-conscious decisions, the Health Security Act allows consumers a choice among several plans with identical benefits, gives them information about the quality of competing plans and their customers' satisfaction, and allows them to receive more of the savings if they choose a less expensive health plan. In addition, the act sets a limit on the growth of premiums in the alliances.

Promoting choice among health plans is essential to controlling costs. By encouraging plan choice, the act attempts to create a more efficient health care delivery system and thus lower overall spending.

The act's proposed limits on the allowable growth of premiums are intended to guarantee control over the growth of costs, in case enhanced private incentives fail to have the anticipated effect. These limits are an important safeguard because they reduce the risk to the government of runaway health spending.

Deficit Reduction

Over time, cost savings from the provisions just described and from reimbursement changes in public programs will provide budgetary savings for the Federal Government. As noted above, long-run success in keeping the Federal deficit under control is directly tied to success in reducing the growth rate of Federal health care spending. In the short term, the Health Security Act entails some new Federal costs—discounts for the poor and for small and low-average-wage businesses, a new drug benefit for medicare, and coverage of long-term care. The savings from slowing the rate of growth of health care spending start right away, but they are small at first. Over time, these savings grow larger, and deficit reduction increases accordingly.

Maintaining Choice

The Health Security Act allows families, doctors, firms, and States to make significant choices about the nature of their involvement in the new health care system.

Households will get to choose their own doctors, and many families that currently have no choice over their health plan will be given several options. Doctors will get to choose the plan or plans in which they work, and may remain in the fee-for-service sector if they wish. Large firms may choose to form corporate alliances or to join regional alliances. And each State will be allowed to adjust its health care system to its particular circumstances—including the establishment of a single-payer system if it so chooses.

PROVIDING COMPREHENSIVE BENEFITS

All health plans organized under the Health Security Act must offer the same set of comprehensive benefits. These benefits include hospital services; services of health professionals; clinical preventive services; mental illness and substance abuse services; family planning services; hospice care; home health care; extended care services; ambulance services; outpatient laboratory, radiology, and diagnostic services; outpatient prescription drugs and biological agents; outpatient rehabilitative services; durable medical equipment and prosthetic and orthotic devices; vision care; and pediatric dental care. The guaranteed benefit package to be in effect through the year 2000 provides the level of benefits currently offered by a typical medium-sized to large firm. In the year 2001 the benefit package expands to include services not fully covered previously—principally, adult dental benefits and broader coverage for mental illness and substance abuse.

Health plans will offer one of three forms of cost sharing. The first is a "higher cost-sharing" option similar to those in traditional fee-for-service plans. There is a general deductible of $200 per year for a single individual and $400 per year for a family, with separate deductibles for mental illness and substance abuse treatment, prescription drugs, and dental services. After the deductible is met, the insured individual pays 20 percent of the cost of most services.

The second option is a "lower cost-sharing" option similar to those in HMOs. This option has only a $10 copayment for most services, a $5 copayment for prescription drugs, and higher copayments for services such as hospital emergency room services, inpatient mental illnesses services, outpatient psychotherapy, and orthodontic care. Preventive services are covered without cost sharing under either schedule. The final option is "combination cost sharing" similar to that in preferred provider organizations (PPOs). This option follows the lower cost sharing for services provided inside a network and the higher cost sharing for services outside of the network. Under all cost-sharing schedules, out-of-pocket payments will not exceed $1,500 per year for a single individual or $3,000 for a family. All of the cost-sharing limits are in 1994 dollars and are indexed in subsequent years to the rate of premium growth.

ORGANIZING THE INSURANCE MARKET

The organizing mechanism for health insurance under the Health Security Act is the health alliance. The alliance is the "broker" between consumers and plans—negotiating with health plans and offering choices to consumers, and accepting premium payments from consumers and distributing them to plans.

The act creates two types of health alliances: regional alliances and corporate alliances. Regional health alliances are designed for workers in firms with fewer than 5,000 employees, nonworkers, and most medicaid recipients. Each State will have one or more regional alliances, but alliances may not overlap geographically. Boundaries of the regional alliances may not be drawn to segregate people with high expected health care costs in one area. Firms with over 5,000 employees will have the option to form a corporate alliance, but they must provide the guaranteed package and will not receive any discounts on their premium contributions.

The alliance structure is designed to enhance competition and thus produce efficiency savings. Within an alliance, consumers have a choice of health plans. Plans will be either fee-for-service, PPOs, or HMOs. HMOs must offer consumers the opportunity to purchase a point-of-service option, allowing them to use care outside the HMO as in a fee-for-service plan if they choose. All plans will offer the same set of benefits, so individuals will not fear changes in covered services if they switch plans.

There will be an annual open enrollment period during which consumers can switch from one health plan to another without loss of coverage. To increase consumers' ability to evaluate competing plans, the alliance will also publish price and quality data about the different plans. Consumers are required to pay the cost of the plan they select, less the amount their employers are required to contribute. Employers are allowed to supplement their required contribution, within limits. Outside of collective bargaining agreements, employers must offer the same supplementation to every worker in a given rating pool (rating pools are described in the next section). The supplementation cannot cause the total employer contribution to exceed the premium of the highest cost plan for that rating pool in the alliance. Employers who choose to contribute more must give full rebates to employees who choose a plan that costs less. Thus, the consumer will realize the full savings (subject to taxes) from choosing a less expensive health plan.

Individuals may also use after-tax dollars to purchase health coverage for benefits beyond the guaranteed package or for supplemental policies to reduce out-of-pocket payments. The Health Security Act specifies a floor for coverage below which individuals should not fall, rather than a ceiling on the generosity of health benefits an individual can receive.

On the provider side, the health alliance solves many of the problems inherent in the current market. As a requirement for selling insurance in an alliance, plans must agree to community rating, guaranteed issue, and guaranteed renewability, and must cover individuals with preexisting conditions. The health alliance must accept all qualified health plans into the alliance, with the exception that the alliance can exclude plans that charge over 120 percent of the average premium.

Some economists have argued that the Federal Government should tax employer contributions for health insurance as if these benefits were paid as wages. Such a tax change would raise the price to consumers of more-expensive health plans, thereby providing an incentive to limit health care spending. There are several ways to reform the tax treatment of health benefits. First, employees could be prohibited from contributing pretax dollars to health insurance under certain employee benefit arrangements called "cafeteria plans." This limitation is a part of the Health Security Act. Second, employer payments for covered services beyond the guaranteed benefit package—whether in reduced cost sharing or in additional services—could be considered taxable income. This limitation is scheduled to occur in the year 2004 under the Health Security Act. Finally, all or part of the cost of a guaranteed benefit package above some level could be considered taxable income. This change is not part of the Health Security Act.

PAYING FOR INSURANCE

The Health Security Act classifies people into four rating pools: singles, couples with no children, families with children and one adult, and families with children and two adults. Table 4–4 shows the estimated premiums in 1994 for policies for these four pools. For a two-adult family with children, for example, the national average premium in 1994 is estimated to be $4,360. The actual premiums will vary by region of the country, as health spending does currently.

TABLE 4–4.—*Estimated Premiums in the Regional Alliance, 1994*

Rating pool	Average premium	Payments by:			
		Family (20 percent)	Employer		
			Per-family requirement (80 percent)	Average number of workers per family	Per-worker requirement
Singles	$1,932	$386	$1,546	1.00	$1,546
Couples (no children)	3,865	773	3,092	1.45	2,125
One-adult family	3,893	779	} 3,409	1.38	2,479
Two-adult family	4,360	872			

Note.—Premiums are national averages. Actual premiums will differ from alliance to alliance. Employer payments for one-adult and two-adult families are pooled.
Source: Administration estimates.

Employers are required to pay 80 percent of the average premium for each family. Single individuals are considered to have one worker per family. An employer of a full-time single worker therefore pays 80 percent of the $1,932 premium cost, or $1,546. In the case of childless couples, there are on average in the United States about 1.45 workers per family. Since 80 percent of the premium for childless couples is $3,092, the amount per worker is only $3,092 divided by the number of workers per family, or $2,125. Employers must pay this amount for each worker. Workers in families with children—whether the family has one adult or two—are pooled. The alliance computes total requirements ($3,409 per family) and divides this by the number of workers per family (about 1.38 as a national average). The employer payment for a full-time worker in a family with children is therefore $2,479. Because these amounts are independent of the number of workers in a family, employers do not have to coordinate payments with employers of other family members. This system is thus relatively simple to administer.

Employer payments for part-time workers are prorated, based on the percentage of a 120-hour month (about 30 hours per week) that the person works. If the employee works 60 hours per month, the employer would owe one-half of an employer premium. No employer payment is required if the individual works fewer than 40 hours per month. Thus, an employee who worked at two 60-hour-per-month jobs would be credited with two half-payments, or one full-time payment. An employee who did not work at any job for at least 40 hours per month is treated as a nonworker.

Self-employed people will make their own employer payments, as they do now. However, if a self-employed worker also has wage and salary income, payments from the employer will be credited against the amount owed on the worker's self-employment income. Thus, a worker who earns wages or a salary for half the year and is self-employed for the other half would owe only half of an employer payment on his or her self-employment earnings, with discounts available for those with low self-employment earnings. In addition, self-employed people will be able to deduct all their payments for health insurance in computing taxable income, compared with the 25-percent deductibility under current law.

The equivalent of at least one employer premium must be collected for each family. In cases where no family member receives employer coverage, or the family members worked less than 12 full-time months in a year, the balance of the premium is the responsibility of the family. If the family members worked 6 full-time months, for example, the family would owe one-half of an employer share, the employer having paid the other half.

Finally, each family owes any difference between the employer contribution and the price of the plan they select (but low-income families will be eligible for discounts on their share). For the average family, this difference will be 20 percent of the total premium, or $872 in the case of a family with children. If the family chooses a more expensive plan, it will pay the additional cost. If the family chooses a less expensive plan, it will keep the savings.

PROVIDING DISCOUNTS

The government provides discounts on the cost of insurance to small and low-wage businesses and low-income families. There are five types of discounts in the Health Security Act, which are detailed in Table 4–5: discounts to families on their 20-percent share of the premium; discounts to families that (for reasons just explained) owe some of the employer payment; discounts to early retirees; discounts to firms; and discounts to low-income families facing high out-of-pocket payments. The cost of providing these discounts is made up by government payments.

Low-income families in the regional alliances receive a discount on their 20-percent share of the premium. No payment at all is required on the first $1,000 of income. The discount phases out at 150 percent of the poverty line—about $23,000 for a family of four in 1994. Income for these purposes is defined as adjusted gross income plus tax-exempt interest income. The $1,000 disregard and the poverty line are indexed to the consumer price index.

Additional discounts are provided for families that owe part of an employer payment. No payment is required if nonwage income is below $1,000, and full payment is expected if nonwage income is greater than 250 percent of the poverty level, or about $39,000 for a family of four in 1994. Nonwage income is defined as adjusted

TABLE 4–5.—*Discounts Under the Health Security Act in 2000*
[Billions of dollars]

Discount	Purpose	Amount
Employer	Limit firm payments to 7.9 percent of payroll or less	29
Household		
Nonretiree	Limit payment for 20 percent share of premiums and for time spent not working	47
Nonworker discounts to retirees.	Limit employer payments for time spent not working	7
Early retirees	Eliminate remaining employer payment	5
Out-of-pocket	Lower cost sharing for poor families	3
Cushion	Allowance for behavioral effects and unfavorable economic circumstances	13
Total		103

Source: Administration estimates.

gross income less unemployment compensation and wage and salary and self-employed income (up to $60,000 per year), and including tax-exempt interest. Labor income is excluded from this calculation because it is assumed that families have already "paid" for their employer's contribution through lower wages and salaries.

Beginning in 1998, if a retired individual is between the ages of 55 and 64, has less than $90,000 in income, and meets the Social Security earnings test, the government pays the entire employer share of the retiree's premium. This discount supplants any payment for the employer share that the individual or his or her employer would have made. The largest benefit to corporations with early retirees, however, will come not from this special provision for retirees (which will save firms about $2 billion), but from community rating of premiums, which will save about $7 billion. From 1998 through 2000, firms that are currently providing health insurance to their retirees must pay the government 50 percent of the savings they realize from this provision.

Total household discounts are expected to be $59 billion in the year 2000. This total includes $47 billion in nonretiree discounts, $7 billion in low-income discounts given to retirees, and almost $5 billion in additional discounts to early retirees.

Some firms will also receive discounts on their required payments. Contributions from each firm in the regional alliances are capped at 7.9 percent of payroll. If a firm's required payments would be greater than 7.9 percent of payroll, the government pays the overage. Small, low-wage firms are capped at even lower percentages of payroll, as detailed in Table 4–6. Employer discounts total $29 billion in 2000 (Table 4–5), about three-quarters of which are for firms with fewer than 25 employees.

Finally, low-income individuals can receive discounts for their out-of-pocket payments if they live in areas where there are no

TABLE 4-6.—*Caps on Premiums by Firm Size*
[Percent of total payroll]

Average wage (dollars)	Firm size (number of workers)			
	Less than 25	25–49	50–74	75 and over
Less than 12,000	3.5	4.4	5.3	7.9
12,000–15,000	4.4	5.3	6.2	7.9
15,000–18,000	5.3	6.2	7.1	7.9
18,000–21,000	6.2	7.1	7.9	7.9
21,000–24,000	7.1	7.9	7.9	7.9
Over 24,000	7.9	7.9	7.9	7.9

Source: Administration estimates.

health plans that offer lower cost sharing or that charge premiums at or below the average-cost plan. These discounts end at 150 percent of the poverty level. The total cost of these discounts is estimated to be $3 billion in the year 2000.

Numerous behavioral effects could influence the discounts the government is obligated to pay. For example, firms that have high average wages, and therefore pay the full premiums for their workers, may find it in their interest to contract out for low-wage services from firms that receive discounts. To allow for this and other behavioral reactions, the projected discounts were increased by 15 percent above the static estimate, or $13 billion in the year 2000.

USING SAVINGS TO GUARANTEE HEALTH SECURITY AND REDUCE THE DEFICIT

At the broadest level, the Health Security Act is designed to finance new spending and deficit reduction out of savings from reduced expenditures relative to the no-reform baseline. Savings are expected to result from reduced administrative costs, consumers switching to less expensive plans, and lower costs from improved incentives.

Insurance reform will save money through lower underwriting costs. On net, the cost of insurance administration should decline by about 3.5 percent of claims paid. Since current premiums for the population that will be included in the health alliances are about $200 billion, the savings from the insurance reforms in the health alliances should be about $7 billion annually.

There are also likely to be savings from consumers switching to lower cost plans. Several studies have found that managed care arrangements have lower health spending than open-ended plans. The most comprehensive forms of managed care—group and staff model HMOs—save an estimated 15 percent on health spending by, for example, finding alternatives to hospitalization.

A number of governments and corporations have experimented with paying a fixed amount for health insurance, regardless of the plan the employee chooses, and have found that these payment rules have a large effect on individual choices. The State of Minnesota, for example, implemented a fixed-dollar contribution for public sector employees in 1989. Between 1988 and 1993, the share of employees in the highest cost plan fell from 42 to 17 percent, while the share in the lowest cost plan increased from 28 to 54 percent. The State of Wisconsin implemented a similar system for its public employees in 1984. In one year, enrollment in HMOs increased by over 60 percent. Similar responses have been observed in several private companies.

Finally, there is the case of California, which passed laws in the early 1980s increasing the ability of plans to contract selectively with providers. Since then, growth in health care costs has been much lower in California than in other States. Between 1982 and 1991, real per capita costs for hospitals, physicians, and prescription drugs increased 2.8 percent annually in California, compared with 4.8 percent annually in the rest of the United States. As a result, California's per capita costs fell from 18 percent above the average State in 1982 to 2 percent above the average in 1991.

As a backup to the market incentives it provides, the Health Security Act places a limit on the growth of premiums in regional and corporate alliances. Up to the year 2000, growth in total premiums is constrained to the growth of inflation and population, plus an adjustment factor ranging from 1.5 percent in 1996 to zero in 1999 and 2000 (Table 4–7). This reduction in growth rates is in anticipation of one-time savings in health expenditures. After 2000 the growth rate of spending is expected to increase, but not to the level in the current system.

TABLE 4–7.—*Allowed Growth Rates of Alliance Premiums*
[Percent]

Growth rate	1995	1996	1997	1998	1999	2000
Baseline	9.0	9.5	9.2	9.0	8.9	9.0
Reform [1]	9.0	5.8	5.3	4.8	4.3	4.2
Adjustment factor [2]		1.5	1.0	.5	.0	.0

[1] Projected average annual growth rates. Some alliances may experience higher annual growth rates prior to 1998.
[2] Adjustment factor added to inflation plus population growth to find reform growth limits.
Source: Baseline projections are from Congressional Budget Office, updated for higher estimates of inflation by the Administration. Reform projections are Administration estimates.

Each year, plans will submit bids on the premiums they propose for serving the alliance population. If an alliance's expected weighted-average premium is above the premium limit, and plans do not voluntarily reduce their bids, the premiums of the plans that exceed the limit will be reduced so that the cap is met.

An example will illustrate the process. If the average premium in one year is $4,000 and the target growth rate is 5 percent, the allowed increase in the average premium in the next year is $200. Suppose there are two plans with equal enrollments, one of which wants to increase the premium by $100 and the other by $400. Under the cap, the second plan would be allowed to increase its premium by only $300, so that the average increase would be $200.

Finally, if more people than expected join high-cost plans, so that actual premiums exceed the target, the premium target is reduced in the next 2 years to recoup the overage.

Chart 4-8 shows the projected change in national health expenditures under the act. Spending initially increases, because of the extension of coverage to the uninsured. By 1998, when universal coverage is complete, spending is above baseline by 0.3 percent of GDP. Over time, however, the savings from the market reforms—or, as a backstop, from the caps on premium growth—rise and spending falls relative to the baseline. In 1999 and 2000, spending is projected to grow at almost the rate of nominal GDP, so that health care as a share of GDP rises by only 0.2 percentage point. By the end of the decade, health expenditures with reform are projected to be below the level estimated to occur without reform.

Both the new Federal health spending and deficit reduction are financed out of savings in the existing system (Table 4-8). Spending rises with the implementation of universal coverage, but the slower growth of costs generates savings to the government. Health reform is essentially deficit-neutral in the first 4 years and deficit-reducing thereafter. By 2000, new Federal spending is projected to be $94 billion, and savings are projected to be $132 billion, yielding deficit reduction of $38 billion.

The new spending comes in five principal areas, detailed for the year 2000 in Table 4-9. First, net premium and other discounts total $42 billion. These discounts are the difference between $103 billion in gross spending and $61 billion in medicare and medicaid "offsets," as people leave these programs and receive coverage in the alliances instead. There is additional spending for the Department of Veterans Affairs, public health (including WIC [women, infants, and children] expansions and funding for academic medical centers), administration ($10 billion), the prescription drug benefit to the medicare program ($17 billion), and long-term care. Finally, allowing 100-percent tax deductibility of health insurance premiums for the self-employed will cost $3 billion in forgone revenues.

These new costs are financed by seven sources of funds. First, a tobacco tax will raise $11 billion, and a 1-percent payroll assessment on corporations that choose to form their own corporate alliances will raise $5 billion. There are also savings in public sector

Chart 4-8 **Health Expenditures as Percent of GDP**
Health expenditures will increase in the short term but will fall below baseline by the end of the decade.

Percent

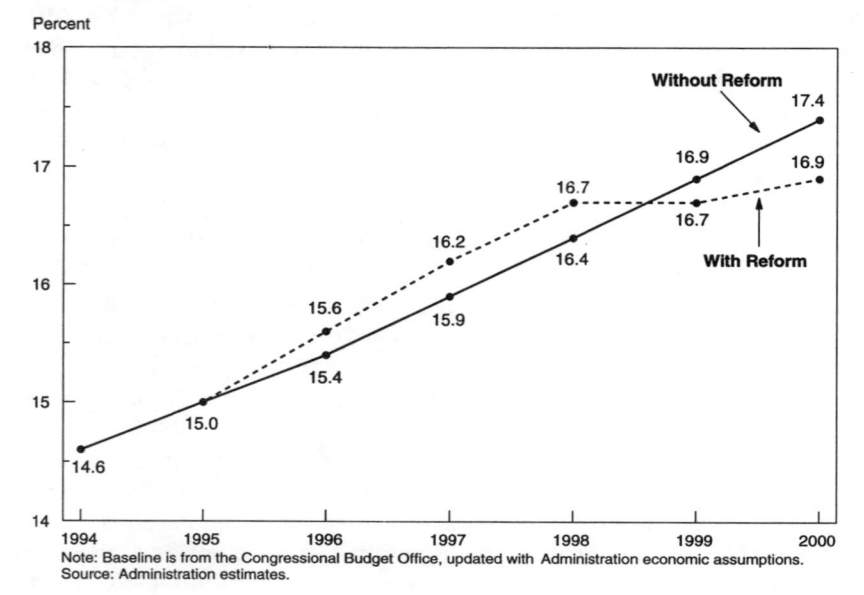

[Line chart showing two series from 1994 to 2000:
- Without Reform: 14.6 (1994), 15.0 (1995), 15.4 (1996), 15.9 (1997), 16.4 (1998), 16.9 (1999), 17.4 (2000)
- With Reform: 14.6 (1994), 15.0 (1995), 15.6 (1996), 16.2 (1997), 16.7 (1998), 16.7 (1999), 16.9 (2000)]

Note: Baseline is from the Congressional Budget Office, updated with Administration economic assumptions.
Source: Administration estimates.

TABLE 4–8.—*New Federal Spending and Savings Due to Reform*
[Billions of dollars]

Item	1995	1996	1997	1998	1999	2000
New spending	3.5	23.5	50.9	79.4	88.8	92.1
Savings	14.5	26.7	44.0	74.7	107.0	129.8
Change in deficit	−11.0	−3.2	6.9	4.8	−18.2	−37.7

Note.—A negative number for change in deficit denotes a reduction in the deficit.
Source: Administration estimates.

programs. Medicare savings are projected at $39 billion in the year 2000. These savings result from 28 specific changes, ranging from lower hospital payment updates to increased premiums for the high-income elderly. Medicaid savings are projected to be $27 billion in 2000, due to lower payments for hospitals that treat the uninsured (since everyone will be covered) and slower growth of costs for medicaid beneficiaries in the health alliances, resulting from the improved incentives. Other programs such as those of the Department of Veterans Affairs, the Department of Defense, and the Federal Employees Benefit Program are projected to realize sav-

TABLE 4–9.—*Sources and Uses of Federal Funds Under Reform, 2000*
[Billions of dollars]

Source	Amount	Use	Amount
Tobacco tax	11	Discounts:	
Corporate assessment	5	Gross spending	103
Medicare	39	Offsets	–61
Medicaid	27	Net	42
Other Federal programs	11	Veterans Administration, Public Health, New Administration	10
Other revenue effects	35	Medicare drug benefit	17
Debt service	2	Long-term care	20
		100 percent tax deduction for self-employed	3
Total	130	Total spending	92
		Deficit reduction	38

Source: Administration estimates.

ings of $11 billion from slower cost growth, the provisions related to early retirees, and the increase in payments from private payers. Additional revenue amounting to $35 billion comes from a combination of factors, including additional tax revenue from the reduction in employer health care costs over time, removing health insurance premiums from "cafeteria plans" offered by employers, payments from corporations with early retirees, dedicated premium revenue for academic health centers, and other tax changes. Finally, the plan generates $2 billion in lower debt service as a result of deficit reduction in years prior to 2000.

To protect the Federal budget against open-ended commitments, the Health Security Act sets a ceiling on discounts that can be paid (Box 4–3). Authorized discount payments that are not utilized in any one year can be carried forward into future years to increase the maximum payment. This reduces the probability that the limits will be exceeded.

ECONOMIC EFFECTS OF THE HEALTH SECURITY ACT

The Health Security Act is certain to have impacts both on the overall American economy and on the health care sector in particular.

MACROECONOMIC EFFECTS

One important concern about health care reform is its effect on employment. Because employer mandates to provide insurance may initially increase labor costs to firms that are not now providing or

> **Box 4–3.—Capped Entitlements**
>
> Both the premium discounts and the new long-term care program are "capped entitlements." The long-term care program is an entitlement to States, not to individuals. The amount of money that States may receive is specified explicitly. Federal liability is limited to that amount, even if demand is greater than predicted. Similarly, there is no authority to pay for premium discounts beyond what is provided in the Health Security Act. In the event that spending is projected to exceed the amount in the legislation, the President must submit to the Congress a plan for addressing the issue. The Congress will then act on this plan through an expedited process.
>
> The notion of a capped entitlement is not new. A number of Federal entitlement programs operate under a budget limit, including the social services block grant and payments to States for AFDC work programs. The legislated appropriation sets a limit on how much can be spent in total. Then, if spending is expected to be above projections, the government must change the eligibility requirements, change the benefits, or pass a supplementary appropriation.

are underproviding insurance, fears have arisen that labor demand might decline as a consequence of reform.

In fact, however, changes in employer-paid health insurance costs can have several effects on workers other than changes in employment. As noted earlier, the dominant effect of increases in health care costs in the past has been a reduction in the real wages received by employees.

Chart 4–9 shows projections of total employer health insurance payments with and without health reform. While reform will have different effects on different firms, total employer spending is essentially unchanged through 1998 and then declines relative to the baseline. This pattern reflects the balance of spending increases from the employer mandate and spending reductions from cost savings. Through 1998 these effects are roughly equal, resulting in little additional business spending. Between 1998 and 2000, the savings increase but there is no increase in spending. The result is a net savings in employer payments.

There are many things employers can do with the savings from reform: They can hire more workers, pay higher returns to shareholders, or increase employee compensation. Empirical evidence suggests, however, that as total employer payments fall over time, the likely result will be a corresponding increase in workers' wages. By the year 2000, wage and salary compensation could therefore

Chart 4-9 Business Spending on Health Insurance
Business spending will increase slightly after reform but will fall below baseline by the end of the decade.

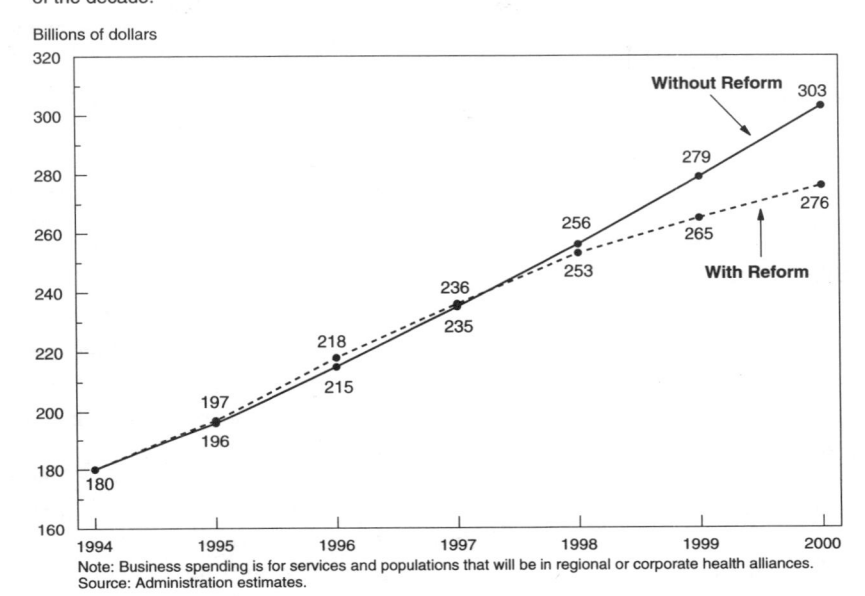

Billions of dollars

Year	Without Reform	With Reform
1994	180	180
1995	197	196
1996	215	218
1997	235	236
1998	256	253
1999	279	265
2000	303	276

Note: Business spending is for services and populations that will be in regional or corporate health alliances.
Source: Administration estimates.

increase by $20 billion to $30 billion, or about 0.6 percent of payroll.

Although reform is unlikely to lead to a large reduction in the demand for labor, it could affect the supply. Some individuals who work mainly to obtain health insurance may voluntarily leave the labor force after health reform is passed. Evidence from continuation of coverage (COBRA) laws passed by the Federal Government and many State governments suggests that the number of people deciding to retire is about 1 percent higher when they have the option to purchase coverage through their former employer after retirement. These estimates must be raised to account for the lower price of insurance under reform; with this adjustment, it is estimated that about 350,000 to 600,000 additional people will be retired as a result of the provisions in the Health Security Act.

On the other hand, some welfare recipients are likely to decide to enter the labor force when health benefits become universal. A welfare recipient currently receiving medicaid benefits who then takes a job incurs a "tax" of two-thirds or more on earnings because of the resulting reduction in AFDC benefits, food stamps, and medicaid benefits. Once health care is guaranteed universally, the loss of income associated with leaving welfare should fall by up to 10 percentage points. A number of studies suggest that many more welfare recipients will decide to work in response to these lower implicit tax rates.

Weighing all this evidence, several private sector economists have concluded, as has this Council, that the net effect of health reform on employment is likely to be small: at most plus or minus one-half of 1 percent of total employment. The reason is that a number of offsetting factors are in the plan, some of which will increase employment and some of which will reduce it. On net, these factors are likely to cancel out.

SECTORAL EFFECTS

Health reform will affect different firms differently (Table 4–10). Firms that are not now providing insurance will face increased costs after reform. Firms that are currently offering coverage, however, will on average enjoy cost reductions. These gains come from spreading the cost of universal coverage over everyone in the population, from premium discounts, and from slower growth of costs over time. Putting these two groups together, the average firm will experience cost reductions of about $230 per worker in 2000. There will also be changes in the distribution of spending across industries. Industries that have traditionally provided generous benefits to much of their work force, such as manufacturing, will see expenditure reductions compared with industries in which most firms do not currently provide insurance.

TABLE 4–10.—*Employer Payments for Health Care: Baseline and Reform, 2000*

Insurance status of firm	Number of workers (millions)	Average spending per worker (dollars)		
		Baseline	Reform	Change
All	122.7	2,478	2,245	−233
Currently offers insurance	96.3	3,092	2,482	−610
Does not offer insurance	24.4	0	1,292	1,292

Source: Urban Institute.

Employment is expected to increase in the health sector in the short run, because of increased spending on the uninsured and underinsured. Universal coverage by itself will increase health-related employment by more than 400,000 jobs, although employment will not increase uniformly throughout the sector. Resources are likely to shift from administration to providing care. As the growth rate of health spending falls, employment in health care will grow less rapidly than without reform. The number of employees will still increase over time, however.

Health care reform should set the stage for increased productivity growth. As administrative expense and inappropriate care decrease and the health care industry becomes more productive, the economy should be able to produce more output than it would have without reform. As a result, Americans will be able to consume health services of the same or better quality as before, as well as more of other goods and services. This productivity increase will raise living standards, which is the principal objective of this Administration's economic policies.

CONCLUSION

Reforming the Nation's health care system is integral to the health of both our citizens and our economy. One-seventh of the Nation's economy is currently characterized by weak competition, inadequate information, and inappropriate incentives. The Administration's health care reform proposal builds on the strengths of the current system while correcting its shortcomings. It preserves consumer choice and our employer-based private insurance system. It relies on enhanced market competition and improved incentives to provide health security for all Americans, slow rising health care costs, and address our long-run budget deficit problem.

CHAPTER 5

Microeconomic Initiatives to Promote Efficiency and Productivity

AS WORKERS AND CONSUMERS, we conduct our economic affairs through markets. These markets provide us with a vast array of products and services to purchase, and a host of different ways to earn our livelihoods.

Yet markets are not flawless. They may, for example, become controlled by monopolies, generate excessive pollution, or lead to insufficient investment in research and development. Through collective action, we can sometimes correct such "market failures," and thereby improve the ability of private markets to serve social goals. When targeted microeconomic policies are successful, they reduce the costs of production and distribution, place goods and services in the hands of those who value them most, and maximize the increase in social well-being that derives from trade in the private marketplace. For these reasons, well-chosen government initiatives are as important for microeconomic policy as they are for macroeconomic policy.

The United States has a long history of employing targeted microeconomic policies to improve the performance of private enterprise in significant industries. Roughly three-fourths of the Nation's investment in canal construction before the Civil War was publicly financed. Land grants and other subsidies encouraged the development of intercontinental railroads during the second half of the 19th century. Since 1914, the Extension Service of the Department of Agriculture, a cooperative venture of Federal, State, and local governments, has vastly improved the Nation's agricultural productivity by spreading information about modern farming techniques. Our massive national commitment to create high-technology industries critical to our defense, such as computers and jet aircraft, dates from the Second World War. Targeted microeconomic policies such as these have been employed throughout the history of the Republic, regardless of the political party in power.

The Administration's initiatives described in this chapter are aimed at both correcting failures of private markets and improving the functioning of the Federal Government. The initiatives are organized around three themes: promoting efficiency in the public and private sectors, addressing environmental externalities, and promoting technology.

PROMOTING EFFICIENCY IN THE PUBLIC AND PRIVATE SECTORS

In all modern industrialized nations, some goods and services are provided directly by the government, others almost entirely through unregulated private markets, and still others by the private sector through regulated markets. Because none of these methods of conducting our economic affairs is flawless, it is important to develop ways of improving the performance of each. For this reason, the Administration has developed initiatives to promote a more effective government, more competitive markets, and more efficient regulation.

CREATING A MORE EFFECTIVE GOVERNMENT

Governmental activities, however well-intended, are not always performed as efficiently as possible. There are two important sources of what might be termed "government failure."

First, as recognized by both the framers of the Constitution and modern scholars of public choice, all political systems provide interest groups with an incentive for "rent seeking," that is, manipulation of collective action for private benefit. Rent-seeking behavior can bias public actions away from maximizing aggregate social welfare. It can, for example, lead government agencies to make decisions that benefit a particular interest group even though they are costly to society as a whole.

Second, the government—in providing services to citizens, in hiring and managing personnel, in procuring supplies, and in making investments—generally does not face the same competitive pressures as private industry to serve customers well and minimize costs. Competition among the political parties; oversight by the Office of Management and Budget (OMB), by the Congress, and by heads of agencies; and public scrutiny through the media provide a partial but incomplete substitute for market competition. Frequently, internal governmental regulations, such as personnel and procurement rules or reporting requirements, are introduced to address these problems. But these are blunt instruments that may create significant managerial inefficiencies of their own.

The Administration has placed a high priority on governmental reform—or "reinventing government." A major objective is to improve the performance of government by introducing market-like mechanisms and benefit-cost tests wherever possible. Such mechanisms are designed to reduce rent seeking and the governmental inefficiencies resulting from the lack of competitive pressures.

The National Performance Review

The National Performance Review (NPR), directed by the Vice President, took a fresh look at the way the Federal Government performs its tasks, with less emphasis on the related issue, routinely considered in the budgetary process, of whether those functions should be performed at all.

The NPR identified 384 ways that the Federal Government could save money without reducing the level of service and, indeed, often while improving governmental performance. Its report concluded that, by shifting to a market-like focus on customer service, by introducing competition where possible, and by streamlining internal government processes to facilitate better management, we could have a government that "works better and costs less."

The Administration has moved rapidly to introduce the NPR reforms. One important element is a set of recommendations to improve the procurement process. These include changing laws and regulations to make it easier for the government to buy commercially produced goods and services, to raise the threshold for the use of simplified acquisition procedures, and to amend contract protest rules to streamline contracting and discourage frivolous protests. These reforms can be accomplished while preserving oversight by the Congress and OMB, which is necessary to protect against fraud and abuse. Other NPR recommendations identify ways to streamline management control; improve customer services; shift to mission-driven, results-oriented budgeting; improve financial and human resource management; integrate information technology into the business of government; and improve the functioning of every executive branch department (Box 5–1). In a similar effort, the Defense Department has conducted a "bottom-up" review of its activities.

A New Framework for Regulatory Review

The President's Executive Order 12866 on Regulatory Planning and Review provides a framework for developing regulations that serve the best interests of the American people without imposing unreasonable burdens on business. The order directs agencies to promulgate only those regulations made necessary by law or compelling public need, such as correcting market failures. The regulatory philosophy that underlies the order calls on agencies to assess all the costs and benefits of the available alternatives when deciding whether and how to regulate, including the alternative of not regulating. Further, the order requires that, to the extent permitted by statute, agencies select a regulatory approach that maximizes the net benefits to the public (benefits less costs). Applying this test to public regulation will lead affected firms in the private

> **Box 5-1.—Selected National Performance Review Recommendations**
> - Allow agencies to create innovation capital funds from retained savings to invest in innovations that can improve service and provide a return on investment.
> - Provide line managers with greater budget flexibility to achieve results by expediting the reprogramming of funds within agencies.
> - Use electronic funds transfer to pay and reimburse expenses for all Federal employees, to make payments to other agencies, and to pay for purchases from the private sector.
> - Create competitive enterprises within the government to manage real property on a fee basis, and give Federal managers the authority to choose their source of property management services.
> - Establish a corporation to provide air traffic control services.

sector to roughly mimic what a properly functioning market would do absent the market failure that necessitates regulation.

In conducting benefit-cost analyses of regulatory alternatives, the order directs agencies to consider *all* the benefits and costs—those that are easily measured as well as those that are not. This approach addresses one major criticism of centralized regulatory review in previous Administrations: that the use of a benefit-cost test was subject to bias against appropriate regulations whenever the costs of regulation were more readily quantified than the benefits—which happens frequently.

In addition, the order encourages agencies to act to limit any economic distortions their regulations cause. Agencies must, for example, design regulations to achieve their objectives in the most cost-effective manner. To the extent feasible, agencies must specify performance standards rather than specify a behavior or manner of compliance. Agencies must also consider alternatives to direct regulation that provide economic incentives to encourage the desired behavior.

This framework does not apply solely to new regulatory initiatives. The Executive order also sets forth a procedure for review of existing regulations to ensure that they too maximize the net benefits to society. This wide-ranging review of old and new regulations alike promises to improve the performance of the public sector by making regulation more effective.

PROMOTING COMPETITION

Competition among the providers of goods and services is the most effective method ever devised for organizing most economic activity. Competition simultaneously leads to low production costs, innovation in product design and production techniques, low prices for consumers, and the allocation of goods and services to those who value them most. For these reasons, our economy must rely upon competition to the maximum extent possible, and the government should act to promote and strengthen competition throughout the private sector. When market failures necessitate public regulation or public provision of services, the resulting public policies should rely on market-like mechanisms to the extent feasible, in order to realize the benefits of competition.

Antitrust Enforcement

For more than a century, the antitrust laws have been, in the words of the Supreme Court, "a comprehensive charter of economic liberty aimed at preserving free and unfettered competition as the rule of trade." The antitrust laws address market failures arising from the exercise of market power (Box 5–2). These laws are enforced directly by the Department of Justice, the Federal Trade Commission, the States, and private plaintiffs.

Over the past dozen years, Federal antitrust enforcement has emphasized challenges to mergers among competitors in concentrated industries and the prosecution of bid-rigging schemes by government contractors. Frequently, the defendants were small firms. Federal antitrust enforcement efforts are now being refocused to encompass harmful conduct by large firms, affecting broad sectors of the economy, through means in addition to merger or bid rigging.

For example, the Justice Department is vigorously pursuing a court case charging the major domestic airlines with widespread price fixing from 1988 to 1992. The conspiracies were allegedly accomplished in a novel way: through the computerized exchange of prospective fare information. In terms of the magnitude of the violation and the size of the firms involved, this alleged price-fixing scheme recalls the electrical equipment conspiracy of the 1950s.

The government's actions to promote and protect competition go beyond filing lawsuits. When appropriate, government agencies issue guidelines that will encourage procompetitive behavior and minimize the private costs of understanding and complying with the law. Merger guidelines are the best examples, but the two Federal antitrust agencies have also recently promulgated enforcement guidelines to promote competitive behavior among health care providers.

Box 5-2.—Market Power

Firms are said to exercise market power when they reduce output below what a competitive industry would sell, in order to raise prices above competitive levels. Firms may achieve market power collectively—for example, through an agreement among competitors to raise prices—or unilaterally, as by engaging in practices that inhibit the ability of current or potential rivals to compete. Firms may also obtain market power through government action, as when imports are blocked by tariffs or quotas.

The exercise of market power is harmful for several reasons. First, an industry in which market power is exercised produces less and employs fewer workers than would a competitive industry. Second, sellers who exercise market power in effect tax buyers unfairly, forcing them to pay more for their products than they would have paid under competition. Finally, firms exercising market power may tend to innovate less than competitors, because they recognize that a successful new product could cannibalize their existing market share and decrease the value of their capital. (In some industries, however, large firms exercising market power may be more likely than small or competitive firms to take the risk of investing in large-scale innovations.)

Although market power is costly to society, these problems are of limited concern in markets in which new competition can quickly and easily appear. Then the exercise of market power is likely to be nonexistent or temporary, and new entrants attracted by the opportunity to share monopoly profits will tend to shift resources into their most socially valuable uses. In some circumstances, moreover, society accepts some exercise of market power in order to achieve another economic benefit otherwise unavailable. For example, since the founding of the United States, the award of a patent monopoly as a prize for a successful invention has been the cornerstone of government policy to encourage research and promote innovation.

The antitrust guidelines for health care respond to the concern that health providers may have delayed cooperative cost-cutting arrangements because of uncertainty about antitrust restrictions. To give providers some security, the guidelines establish a number of "antitrust safety zones," which describe circumstances under which the government will not normally challenge cooperative ventures. One example is a safety zone for hospital mergers if either of the merging hospitals averages fewer than 100 beds and less than 40 patients per day over a 3-year period. Another is a safety zone for physician networks (such as preferred provider organizations, or PPOs) that comprise no more than 20 percent of the doctors in each specialty in the relevant geographic market, so long as the network members share substantial financial risk. Mergers or joint ventures by physicians that fall outside the safety zones are not necessarily antitrust violations but will be evaluated individually to determine their legality. The two Federal antitrust agencies have also committed to reduce uncertainty by providing advice to health care providers on an expedited basis.

Other government agencies have also taken steps to limit the exercise of market power. For example, a widely reported investigation by the Department of Transportation helped ensure that an established air carrier would not use anticompetitive practices to exclude a new entrant.

Government can go beyond simply preventing anticompetitive practices; it can act to stimulate competition directly. Thus, the Department of Transportation has provided new airlines with assistance in complying with its regulations. Partly as a result of the department's actions to promote competition, 18 new cargo, charter, and scheduled passenger carriers began service during 1993, and 20 more new carriers are awaiting certification to begin passenger jet service.

Spectrum Auctions

As the Transportation Department's efforts to foster new air carriers suggest, competition can be promoted by encouraging entry. The Federal Communications Commission (FCC) will soon seek to promote competition in this way by allocating portions of the electromagnetic spectrum for telecommunications services. Legislation enacted in August 1993 authorizes the FCC to auction most of the new licenses to use spectrum, and requires the FCC to begin issuing licenses for personal communications services (PCS) by May 1994. The allocation of spectrum to PCS will encourage competition between new firms offering PCS and existing cellular providers. The auction mechanism will ensure that the spectrum goes to those private parties who place the highest value on it. The auction will also raise billions of dollars for the government, by selling the right to the use of a scarce public resource instead of giving it away.

MORE EFFICIENT REGULATION OF NATURAL MONOPOLIES

Economists have long recognized that competition will perform poorly in certain industries that are "natural monopolies" (Box 5–3). In Europe, natural monopolies have often been turned into government enterprises. The traditional U.S. response is to impose rate regulation. For example, State public utility commissions typically regulate the local distribution of electricity, water, natural gas, and telephone service, and Federal agencies regulate interstate pipelines and long-distance telephone service.

Box 5–3.—Natural Monopoly

An industry is a natural monopoly if a single firm can serve the market at lower total cost than two or more firms. A natural monopoly may result when an industry's production technology is characterized by economies of scale, that is, when average production costs decline as output rises. A natural monopoly may also have economies of scope, in which two or more related products can be produced more cheaply by a single firm than by separate firms. The size of the market interacts with the production technology in determining whether an industry is a natural monopoly. For example, if most of the cost reductions from producing at scale are achieved at low levels of output relative to market demand, the market is not likely to be a natural monopoly.

In an unregulated market, some natural monopoly industries would be served by a single firm that exercises market power. Entry would be deterred, even though the incumbent firm charges a price in excess of its long-run average cost. Potential entrants, tempted by the opportunity to undercut the incumbent's price, would refrain from doing so because they would recognize that the incumbent would lower its price in response and could sustain that lower price profitably while the entrant could not. One way to avoid the exercise of market power in such a case is to regulate the natural monopolist's prices.

Oil Pipeline Rate Regulation

For nearly 90 years the Federal Energy Regulatory Commission (FERC) and its predecessors have regulated rates charged by interstate oil pipelines. Over this period, many if not most pipelines have likely been natural monopolies. Pipeline rates were set through a cost-of-service methodology, similar to the approach that State public utility commissions typically employ to determine rates for electricity, gas, water, and telephone service.

Under the cost-of-service approach, the regulated firm is allowed to earn enough revenues to cover its expected costs of operations plus a fair return on capital to its investors. The regulator sets prices on the regulated firm's individual services in such a way that the firm's expected revenues (based on forecasts of buyer demand) will reach the permitted level. Although this method is generally successful at preventing regulated firms from charging monopoly prices, it has been criticized on several grounds. Cost-of-service rate setting can be expensive to administer, as the regulatory commission typically engages in a trial-type hearing before determining rates. In addition, if the regulator adjusts rates rapidly when operating costs change, the regulated firm may lack a strong incentive to keep costs low, reduce costs further, or innovate.

Incentive methodologies for setting rates promise to reduce inefficiencies created by the cost-of-service methodology. One form of incentive regulation is a "price cap." The regulator sets a maximum price (or a price path, often set to decline over time) for a collection of regulated services, and permits the firm to set whatever rates it chooses for individual services so long as the price cap is not exceeded. If the regulator and the firm are willing to live by a price cap for a long time, the administrative costs of regulation are greatly reduced. In addition, the regulated firm is given a strong incentive to reduce costs and to innovate: As long as the price cap is not revised downward, the firm gets to keep any additional profits that result from cost savings. Finally, if the price cap applies to the average rate for a broad collection of services, this form of incentive regulation permits the regulated firm to exercise significant discretion in rate design. The resulting rates may distort consumer choice less than those set by regulators. For such reasons, in 1989 the FCC adopted price cap regulation for the long-distance telephone rates charged by American Telephone and Telegraph Co. (AT&T).

In 1993, FERC replaced cost-of-service rate setting for oil pipelines with an incentive methodology. The new approach generally starts with cost-of-service-based rates and caps rate increases for pipeline services at 1 percent below the increase in the producer price index for finished goods. Moreover, wherever the scope of the natural monopoly has narrowed, permitting the pipeline to demonstrate that it lacks significant market power, the regulatory constraint may be removed in favor of relying on competition to determine prices and output.

Telecommunications Regulation

The rapid pace of innovation in telecommunications is creating new industries, transforming old ones, and promising to change the way we live and work. In the coming years, American households and businesses will have access to a National Information Infrastructure (NII)—an interconnected web of networks linking computers, databases, consumer electronics, and communications devices that will put vast amounts of information at every user's fingertips. The technologies to create, manage, manipulate, and use information will fuel economic growth, promote the international competitiveness of U.S. industry, and create challenging, high-paying jobs.

Many of the innovations that are creating the new information infrastructure are also shrinking the scope of natural monopoly in the provision of telecommunications services. Microwave technology made competition in long-distance telephone service possible. The development of low-cost private branch exchange (PBX) technology has carved out a competitive market for carrying telephone calls within office buildings. For many business customers the local telephone monopoly now ends at the street rather than continuing into the building. Competitive access providers now sell alternative high-capacity services that allow some business customers to complete calls while bypassing some or all of the local telephone company's network. It is now feasible and increasingly practical for telephone lines to carry video programming, for cable lines to carry telephone calls, and for wireless providers to carry both. If and when these developments end the natural monopoly in local telephone and video service altogether, competition can replace regulation as the best economic mechanism for setting prices and providing telecommunications services to buyers.

The information highways that will be central to the emerging information infrastructure will be built in part with fiber optic lines, coaxial cable, and copper wire, and in part through wireless technologies such as cellular telephone, PCS, and direct broadcast satellites. The private sector will make the necessary investments, and the government will promote those investments by encouraging competition. In consequence, the market will determine, to the extent possible, which technologies provide the most value relative to cost and, accordingly, how the information highways will be built.

The Administration's regulatory policies will promote competition among the firms that build and operate the information highways, and among the firms that sell their services and programming through the network. Under the Administration's legislative proposals, for example, local telephone monopolies will be required to unbundle the services they offer and to interconnect with new entrants on a nondiscriminatory basis. This will facilitate new competition in local telephone service by allowing new providers to combine, for example, switching provided by the telephone company with their own transmission facilities. The legislative proposals will also set forth a process by which local telephone companies will be permitted to provide new competition in the interstate long-distance telephone market. The Administration's proposals will identify safeguards that will protect against regulatory evasion through transfer pricing (strategic pricing of goods and services sold to affiliates) and the abuse of monopoly power until the time that competition in local telephone service makes rate regulation unnecessary.

Rapid developments in technology and the marketplace will create new challenges for telecommunications regulation. Old regulatory structures based on the natural monopoly paradigm are not appropriate for a market now characterized by mixed elements of competition and monopoly. Accordingly, the Administration will propose adding a new title to the Communications Act of 1934, specifying a flexible regulatory framework for this new environment. The new framework can adapt to technological and marketplace developments, to protect consumers from monopolies without discouraging investment, innovation, or the growth of competition. In addition, the Administration's legislative initiative will give the FCC broad power to forbear from regulating when markets become effectively competitive, and the power to preempt State and local regulation made unnecessary by the emergence of competition.

The Administration's policies will also promote universal service, to avoid creating a permanent class of information "have-nots," and open access to the network, to allow all service and information providers to reach potential customers. The government will also encourage research and development designed to create new technologies and new applications, as discussed below along with other technology initiatives.

ADDRESSING ENVIRONMENTAL EXTERNALITIES

The notion of tradeoffs is among the most fundamental in economics: nothing is free; everything has an opportunity cost. In private markets, tradeoffs are handled automatically, as consumers choose among alternative goods and services and producers choose among alternative inputs. Prices guide these decisions. Tradeoffs involving the environment cannot be made so easily, however, because use of the environment is generally unpriced. As a result, firms and individuals, in their marketplace decisions, do not always make the best tradeoffs from the standpoint of society as a whole. The effects of failing to price environmental goods and services are examples of externalities (Box 5–4). When externalities are significant, the government can often design policies that improve the functioning of markets and thereby increase aggregate social welfare.

The Administration has sought to encourage the development of environmental technologies to mitigate tradeoffs and foster economic growth. Improvements in the technologies for preventing and treating pollution, and efforts to spread knowledge about technologies already available, can free resources for other socially ben-

> **Box 5-4.—Externalities**
>
> An externality, or spillover, is a type of market failure that arises when the private costs or benefits of production differ from the social costs or benefits. For example, if a factory pollutes, and neither the firm nor its customers pay for the harm that pollution causes, the pollution is an externality. In the presence of this negative (harmful) externality, market forces will generate too much of the activity causing the externality, here the factory's production, and too much of the externality itself, here the pollution. In the case of beneficial externalities, firms will generate too little of the activity causing the externality, and too little of the externality itself, because they are not compensated for the benefits they offer. For example, the development of laser technology has had beneficial effects far beyond whatever gains its developers captured, improving products in industries as diverse as medicine and telecommunications. Too little research and development and other activities generating positive externalities will take place in the absence of some governmental intervention.
>
> To remedy market failures and induce the market to provide the efficient level of the externality-causing activity, the private parties involved in the activity must face the full social costs and benefits of their actions. Policymakers may employ a variety of tools to accomplish this result, such as taxes, user fees, subsidies, or the establishment or clarification of property rights.

eficial purposes or permit the attainment of higher environmental goals without increasing the burden on the economy. Given the worldwide explosion in environmental regulatory activity—in the Far East, in eastern Europe, in Mexico, and elsewhere—the development of more-effective and lower cost pollution control technology can also increase our export competitiveness. In fact, we already enjoy considerable success in this area. The United States is now the world leader in exports of environmental equipment. In a global market for environmental technologies of $295 billion in 1992, the $134 billion U.S. share is the largest by far. Our trade surplus in pollution control equipment has been increasing and was $1.1 billion in 1991.

The Administration has also sought to improve the "technology" of regulating the use of natural and environmental resources. This effort involves seeking a better balance among conflicting interests in the use of natural resources, and developing approaches to regulate pollution that rely more on economic incentives and eliminate the economic distortions of some current regulations. Examples of improving the technology for regulating the environment are found in the Administration's plan for managing the old growth forests of the Pacific Northwest, in its approach to grazing on Federal lands, in the Climate Change Action Plan, and in the Administration's position favoring the reauthorization of the Comprehensive Environmental Response, Compensation, and Liability Act, better known as "Superfund." To better assess where interventions to improve the environment will benefit the economy, the Administration is also engaged in efforts to define sustainable development and develop "green" GDP accounts.

MANAGING RESOURCES ON FEDERAL LANDS

The Federal Government owns vast tracts of land, primarily in the West. These lands contain natural resources of economic importance to both local communities and the Nation, including timber and other forest products, forage for grazing livestock, and mineral deposits. They are also sources of extremely valuable environmental amenities, such as open space for recreational uses like wildlife viewing, scenery, camping, hiking, and hunting; fish and wildlife (including endangered species) habitat; watershed protection; and many others.

Improving the "technology" of regulating the use of these Federal lands is a centerpiece of Administration policy. Two principles guide that policy: (1) reducing inefficiencies caused by improper pricing and regulatory restrictions, and (2) ensuring that both pricing and regulation will achieve a better balance among competing uses of these resources, particularly between extractive (timber, grazing, mining) and environmental uses. These principles can be seen at work in the Administration's plans for managing old growth forests in the Pacific Northwest and for rangeland reform.

Old Growth Forests, Spotted Owls, and Timber

The controversy over logging in the old growth forests and spotted owl habitat of the Northwest provides a case study in reconciling environmental and economic objectives and illustrates how a careful balancing of competing interests can result in progress on all fronts.

The forest products industry is a major industry in the Pacific Northwest, where it is heavily dependent on timber from Federal lands. Much of the Federal land on which this logging has taken place consists of mature forest stands. Referred to as "old growth," this mature forest is the habitat of the northern spotted owl, a threatened species, and many other plants and animals.

For several years Federal forest policy in the Northwest failed to take appropriate account of impacts on environmental quality and biodiversity. In particular, timber harvests on Federal lands were accelerated substantially in the mid- and late 1980s: Such harvests in the habitat of the spotted owl rose from 2.4 billion board feet (bbf) in 1982 to 6.7 bbf in 1988. According to experts, these levels were too high to be sustained indefinitely. Legal challenges to Federal timber policy resulted in injunctions blocking the sale of timber on Federal forest lands in the spotted owl region, in part because agencies within the Federal Government had failed to work cooperatively to comply with environmental and forest management laws. The injunctions had a severe impact on the timber industry, albeit in large part because harvest levels had been extraordinarily and unsustainably large.

The Administration put a high priority on resolving the problems associated with forest management policy in the Pacific Northwest. Accordingly, in July 1993 the Administration announced a "Forest Plan for a Sustainable Economy and a Sustainable Environment." The plan attempts to end the uncertainty caused by legal wrangling and confusion and ameliorate the impact of economic dislocation, while achieving full compliance with existing laws. It also seeks to maintain and improve the ecosystem as a whole, balance the interests of competing uses of the ecosystem for environmental and economic purposes, and create a political consensus to avoid economic instability.

The plan provides for the maximum legally defensible harvest from Federal forests in the spotted owl region (about 1.2 bbf annually). The process of adjustment to the new, lower harvest levels will be smoothed by an economic adjustment plan that is expected to create more than 8,000 new jobs and 5,400 retraining opportunities in the region in 1994. Many of the new jobs will be in enterprises that improve water quality, expand the prospects for commercial fishing, and improve forest management in the region.

The plan focuses on maintaining and improving the environmental quality of watersheds in the region, recognizing how the complex interactions of flora, fauna, and human activities affect that ecosystem. It establishes old growth reserves and protects over 6.5 million acres of old growth forest (about 80 percent of existing old growth). It also establishes 10 "adaptive management areas" for experimentation into better ways of integrating ecological and economic objectives.

Rangeland Reform

The Federal Government owns extensive rangelands throughout the West. While these lands are used primarily for grazing cattle and sheep, increased demand for environmental uses has fueled controversy over Federal management. The controversy over rangeland reform shows the importance of integrating pricing with regulation to use the Nation's resources more efficiently and strike a better balance between economic and environmental objectives.

A central point of contention involves the fees that the Federal Government charges ranchers to graze animals on Federal land. These fees should reflect both the value of the forage used by an additional animal and the external environmental costs of grazing an additional animal (such as the value of reductions in recreation or water quality). Charging ranchers the marginal value of forage, the first component, encourages efficient use of the range. By preventing overgrazing, it protects the condition of the range for future grazing uses. It also promotes long-run efficiency in the livestock industry: Prices for forage that are too low encourage excessive investment in the industry. Forage value varies from tract to tract because of differences in forage productivity, location, proximity to roads and other transportation, rainfall, and access to water. But it can still be measured easily and reliably using the value of private rangelands in nearby locations. The second component, the external costs of grazing, cannot be determined from private market transactions. But economists have developed ways of inferring the value of open space or other environmental amenities from the costs people willingly incur to use them or from sophisticated survey methods.

Current Federal management policies are relics of an earlier era when the Federal Government used resource subsidies to encourage settlement of the West. One result is that grazing fees on Federal lands average only 17 to 37 percent of the value of grazing on comparable private lands. Moreover, the formula used to calculate Federal grazing fees has kept those fees from increasing along with private grazing lease rates. Promoting efficiency thus means both increasing grazing fees and ensuring that Federal grazing fees change from year to year in accordance with changes in rent on private grazing land. The Administration's plans for rangeland reform do both. The current proposal calls for phasing in a new fee structure that more than doubles current fees, and for using an updating formula that will adjust Federal fees at the same rate that private fees change.

Pricing reform must be accompanied by changes in regulation. For example, Federal grazing permits have "use-it-or-lose-it" provisions, under which decreases in the number of animals grazed may result in the loss of a grazing permit or a reduction in the number of animals that the permitholder may graze in the future. This policy prevents ranchers from temporarily reducing the number of animals grazed to improve range condition. The Administration's plan allows the terms of grazing permits to be rewritten to allow ranchers to vary the number of animals they graze in response to changes in weather or economic conditions. The plan also includes provisions to strengthen environmental management.

CLIMATE CHANGE ACTION PLAN

Certain gases emitted into the atmosphere by industrial, automotive, and other combustion have been implicated as a threat to the global climate: By preventing reflected solar radiation from escaping into space, these "greenhouse gases" may be causing a generalized warming of the planet. For this reason, an international agreement to reduce greenhouse gas emissions, the Framework Convention on Climate Change, was signed in 1992. The previous Administration had adopted what was called a "no regrets" policy; it was willing to take steps to reduce emissions only if those actions would be beneficial for other reasons—that is, even if greenhouse gas emissions were ultimately found unrelated to changes in the global climate. In contrast, this Administration sees cost-effective policies to reduce greenhouse gas emissions as appropriate "insurance" against the threat of climate change. Accordingly, the President, in his Earth Day speech on April 21, 1993, issued a "clarion call" for the creation of a cost-effective plan to reduce U.S. greenhouse gas emissions to 1990 levels by the year 2000.

The President's call resulted 6 months later in the Climate Change Action Plan, containing nearly 50 initiatives that cover reductions in all significant greenhouse gases and will affect most sectors of the economy. The plan was based on the understanding that the climate change threat results from *all* greenhouse gases, that it depends on *net* emissions (after accounting for greenhouse gas "sinks" such as forests and oceans), and that the problem is *global*. The strategies adopted to address the externalities associated with greenhouse gas emissions were chosen on the basis of a qualitative assessment of the cost-effectiveness of the alternatives, in part by selecting policies that make markets work better.

Some of the strategies expand upon initiatives of this and previous Administrations to promote energy-saving technology. For example, the Green Lights program improves the diffusion of technology by providing consumers and firms with information about environmentally friendly products such as energy-saving lights that promise to reduce electricity generation and the resulting emissions. Other strategies reduce emissions by making government more efficient. Two examples are (1) reform of regulations that block the seasonal use of natural gas (a low-polluting alternative to coal) by electric utilities, and (2) removal of regulatory impediments to private investments in upgrading Federal hydroelectric facilities.

Parking Cashout

Greenhouse gas emissions will also be reduced by improving the pricing of activities that generate externalities. The parking cashout policy attempts to correct a distortion in private incentives resulting from the tax treatment of employer-provided parking.

Currently, the Internal Revenue Code allows employers to deduct any costs for employer-provided parking as a business expense, and lets workers exclude the benefits from their taxable income (up to $155 a month). As a result, 95 percent of automobile commuters receive free or subsidized parking, more than half of them in central business districts. All told, U.S. companies claim $52 billion per year in parking-related deductions from this free or subsidized service.

The Climate Change Action Plan proposes that Federal tax laws be modified to require that firms offer employees the option of taking the cash value of their employer-provided parking benefit as taxable income rather than accepting their free parking space. The program would apply initially only to those firms with more than 25 employees that make monthly cash payments for their employees to park in lots owned by third parties. Thus, only about 15 percent of employer-provided parking would be covered at first, although the program would expand later as new parking leases are negotiated.

This policy change should reduce the overuse of automobiles for commuting resulting from the current parking subsidy, by making commuters face more of the social costs of driving. As consumers shift to carpools and public transportation, greenhouse gas emissions, other pollutants, and traffic congestion should all be reduced. Other distortions of the choice between commuting by car and by public transit will remain uncorrected, however, to the extent that current regulation of automobile emissions does not fully capture their environmental, congestion, and health costs.

International Strategies for Greenhouse Gas Reductions

One hundred and sixty-one countries signed the Framework Convention on Climate Change in 1992, agreeing that it is necessary to stabilize greenhouse gas concentrations at a level that will prevent "dangerous anthropogenic interference with the climate system." Because this is a global problem, the Climate Change Action Plan addressed what is termed "joint implementation"—the cooperative effort between countries or entities within them to reduce greenhouse gas emissions. The plan recognizes that there may be enormous cost savings to meeting global goals for greenhouse gas reductions if acceptable international strategies can be developed to reduce emissions where it is cheapest to do so, rather than have each country pursue its emissions reduction goals on its own. Some important questions need resolution, however, such as how reductions are to be identified, monitored, and enforced. To begin testing the joint implementation concept, the plan creates a pilot program that evaluates investments by U.S. firms and government assistance to foreign countries for new greenhouse gas emission reductions; measures, tracks, and scores these reductions; and, in general, lays a foundation for broader, more formal policy initiatives in the future.

SUPERFUND REAUTHORIZATION: THE ADMINISTRATION POSITION

The Comprehensive Environmental Response, Compensation, and Liability Act, better known as Superfund, was enacted in 1980 and amended in 1986 in response to widespread concerns that improperly disposed-of wastes threatened human health and valuable natural resources, such as groundwater aquifers. The act has been unsatisfactory in addressing this problem. Fewer than 20 percent of the 1,300 disposal sites on the priority list drawn up by the Environmental Protection Agency (EPA) have been fully "cleaned up," although 3,500 separate actions have been taken to remove wastes posing an immediate threat to health.

At the same time, the costs of the program have been substantial, running almost $7 billion per year. This figure includes direct draws on the Superfund trust fund collected from the oil and chemical industries to pay for EPA expenses (including $1.6 billion in spending on cleanups where no private parties can be assigned responsibility), $3.2 billion in spending by Federal agencies that own or contributed to hazardous waste sites, and $2 billion in spending by private parties, much of which goes to lawyers' fees and other transactions costs in an effort to escape or reduce liability. Some estimates put the total cost of cleaning up the 3,000 sites projected to be on the EPA's National Priority List (NPL) over the next 30 to 40 years at $130 billion to $150 billion, with $200 billion to $300 billion more needed for Federal facility cleanups.

In response to the poor cost-effectiveness and slow pace of this program, the Administration has proposed several significant reforms. The two most important involve the standards and processes governing the cleanup strategy chosen at a site, and the process for assigning and financing liability.

Remedy Selection

Under the current law, remedial measures at Superfund sites are chosen with a preference for treatment and permanent cleanup of soil and water. They are also selected to meet high standards of cleanliness: land generally must become suitable for residential use, and water often must achieve drinking quality. Costs have little weight in remedy selection; they come into play only to identify the cheapest of the set of remedies meeting other criteria.

The Administration's position establishes more-reasonable goals and processes for cleanup decisions. It sets uniform national goals for health and environmental protection to guide remedy selection. It substitutes a concern for long-term reliability as a factor to consider in remedy selection, in place of the preference for treatment and permanence (except for treatment of "hot spots"). It explicitly recognizes containment as a legitimate cleanup strategy. It limits the use of State and Federal standards designed for other pollution contexts. Finally, it introduces greater flexibility and community input into the determination of appropriate land use for the site, permitting some sites to be designated for industrial use, with appropriately lower levels of cleanup required.

The Administration's proposal also offers a streamlined approach to remedy selection at individual sites. With EPA approval, parties will be able to avail themselves of a set of cost-effective "generic" remedies established by the EPA that apply to certain frequently encountered types of waste disposal problems. Alternatively, they can formulate designs that meet national cleanup levels that are based on realistic assumptions and practices concerning risks. If the party liable for cleanup believes it can devise an even cheaper remedy that can meet the national health standards, it can perform a site-specific risk analysis to make its case to EPA. This option allows parties to propose remedies based on the ultimate goal of protecting health and the environment, rather than on the "intermediate" targets of reductions in soil or water concentrations, and helps tailor remedies chosen for a site to its particular features.

Most important, a factor in the remedy selection process at individual sites will be a comparison of the reasonableness of costs against several measures of effectiveness. This approach introduces discipline, transparency, and recognition of tradeoffs into the remedy selection process, while retaining consideration of other factors such as community acceptance and meeting the primary criterion of protecting health and the environment. Cost will also be considered in decisions on whether to defer final cleanups for cases where a new technology is on the horizon to replace a current one that has disproportionately high costs.

The Liability System

The transactions costs associated with cleanups, especially litigation expenses, have been massive under current law. One study found that these costs account for 19 to 27 percent of all Superfund costs. Transaction costs are substantial in part because liability under current law is strict, joint and several, and retroactive: A party that contributed waste to a site used by others can be held liable for the entire cost of cleanup, and a party is liable for the results of its dumping even if its action was legal at the time. As a result, potentially responsible parties (PRPs) have strong incentives to contest their liability (resulting in high enforcement costs to the EPA), to sue other PRPs to recover costs, and to sue their insurance companies when the latter refuse to pay related claims.

The Administration's proposal seeks to limit these transactions costs by streamlining the liability allocation process and making it more fair. The new allocation process is based upon nonbinding arbitration, in which PRPs are assigned a share of liability based on factors such as the volume and toxicity of their wastes. PRPs who settle for their assigned shares would surrender their rights to pursue other PRPs for contribution, be protected from suits by other PRPs, and be offered, for a fee, protection from future liability arising from remedy failure or undiscovered harms. As an added incentive to settle, the EPA would pay settling parties for their share of the "orphan shares"—the share of liability attributed to an identified but insolvent party—but nonsettling parties could still be held liable for all or part of the "orphan share."

The Administration proposal also addresses the growing problem of Superfund-related insurance litigation. The problem arises because insurance contracts written before Superfund was enacted did not expressly allocate Superfund liabilities. Subsequently, courts in some States have interpreted those contracts to require insurance companies to assume most Superfund liabilities, but courts in some other States have held the opposite. The scope of insurers' liability in most States is undecided. Building on a proposal originally suggested by the insurance industry, the Administration proposal calls for creation of an Environmental Insurance Resolution Fund financed through fees and assessments on property and casualty insurers. If the PRPs can show sufficient insurance coverage before 1986, the fund would be used to settle their insurance claims for cleanup and restoration costs at pre-1986 NPL sites, as well as some costs at non-NPL sites, at rates determined simultaneously for all of a PRP's sites. The combination of the allocation process and the insurance settlement process should substantially reduce transactions costs and increase fairness.

SUSTAINABLE DEVELOPMENT AND GREEN ACCOUNTING

According to the 1987 report of the World Commission on Environment and Development, sustainable development is that which "meets the needs of the present without compromising the ability of future generations to meet their own needs." In short, future generations must be able to attain a quality of life, in both economic and environmental terms, equal to ours if they desire. To make this possible, the present generation must leave the future with the wherewithal—the "social capital," consisting of human, natural, and physical (manmade) capital—to create our kind of life or a life of at least equal quality to ours. Although this definition is widely accepted, its interpretation remains subject to debate. One controversy concerns the extent to which the three types of capital can substitute for one another, given the underlying scientific principles and economic behavior, while keeping the resulting development sustainable.

However this controversy is resolved, it will be necessary to measure social capital and the value its use brings in order to understand whether a growth path for the economy is sustainable. This is the province of "green accounting," an idea first raised in 1969. Much of the recent research effort to augment the national income and product accounts to incorporate previously unmeasured aspects of social welfare focuses on identifying the net change in the stock of social capital resulting from environmental externalities. This research effort seeks to identify the loss (depreciation) of social capital caused by pollution, the value of the reduction of finite resources (such as fossil fuels and minerals), the loss from overharvesting of renewable resources (such as forests and fisheries), and the value of the environmental services (e.g., clean air) derived from investments in pollution control equipment.

The President has made it a priority of his Administration to augment the national accounts to incorporate these aspects of social capital. In his 1993 Earth Day speech the President directed that "green" gross domestic product (GDP) measures be developed to improve existing national income and wealth accounts that ignore the cost of pollution or the loss of natural resources. In the first phase of fulfilling this mandate, the Commerce Department's Bureau of Economic Analysis will publish modified GDP accounts in 1994 to reflect the depletion of selected natural resources and will continue to explore measures that incorporate additional environmental values. This effort will be aided by the Department of Interior's forthcoming National Biological Survey, an effort to inventory the biological and ecological resources of the Nation.

PROMOTING TECHNOLOGY

Technological progress fuels economic growth. It creates new industries and reinvigorates old ones. It can enable small businesses to do high-quality design and manufacturing work that previously required the resources of big business. It can help big businesses achieve the speed, flexibility, and closeness to customers that once were a defining characteristic of small business. Technology helps to make our work force more productive and, in doing so, improves the Nation's standard of living. Every recent generation has seen its dreams turn into technological marvels, new products from new industries that have transformed the way we live and work: from the telephone, radio, airplanes, and x-rays, to television, xerography, computers, and magnetic resonance imaging equipment. Advances in technical know-how have accounted for at least one-quarter of our Nation's economic growth over the past half-century.

During the past two decades, powerful trends have altered the environment for American technology development. Commercial technology has become increasingly science-based and interdisciplinary. International competition has intensified as other nations have advanced in wealth and technological sophistication. The Nation's defense capability has become increasingly dependent on technologies developed and applied first in commercial markets. A microelectronics-based revolution in production has transformed the organization of office and factory work, increasing the need for a well-trained and flexible work force.

By the end of the 1980s, many analysts believed that these trends required a reexamination of the existing approaches of government and industry for supporting technology development and diffusion. Accordingly, in its first year the Administration has supported tax incentives for investments in research and development (R&D) and new businesses, liberalized export controls, shifted Federal resources toward basic research and civilian technology, invested in worker skills, and promoted defense conversion. In addition, the Administration's technology initiatives, such as the promotion of the National Information Infrastructure discussed above, the Partnership for a New Generation of Vehicles, and the creation of a Manufacturing Extension Partnership, rely on an alliance of government and industry. They also require rigorous attention to the economic rationales for cooperative efforts and then to the details of project design and assessment, to ensure that market failures are corrected, not made worse, by government action.

PRINCIPLES OF TECHNOLOGY POLICY

The Administration's technology initiatives aim to promote the domestic development and diffusion of growth- and productivity-enhancing technologies. They seek to correct market failures that would otherwise generate too little investment in R&D, with programs that avoid "government failure."

The Economics of Appropriability

New technologies often fail to attract sufficient private sector investment because their technical risk is high or because of limited appropriability—that is, the new technologies create economic and social benefits beyond what the investing firms can capture for themselves. Indeed, despite intellectual property protection, the social returns to innovation have been estimated to exceed the private returns by between 35 and 60 percent.

The most important innovations generate spillover benefits for interconnected sectors, creating economic gains well beyond any that eventually accrue to their inventors. These innovations include risky "pathbreaking" technologies that pay off in the creation of new industries (or the transformation of existing industries), and lower risk "infratechnologies" that can enhance the productive performance of a broad spectrum of firms and industries but that receive low levels of investment because of barriers to appropriability and implementation. For example, the development of refrigerated steamships at the end of the nineteenth century increased the availability of perishable agricultural products throughout the world. Most of this benefit ultimately accrued to farmers and consumers rather than to the inventors of refrigerated steamships. Similarly, the principle of interchangeable parts in manufacturing, originally developed for the production of firearms, soon was adopted for use in the fabrication of clocks, hardware, sewing machines, and other manufactured products.

The appropriability problem is not limited to basic research, but frequently extends to so-called precommercial technology development and eventual commercial applications. Indeed, technological progress is full of feedbacks where developments downstream alter the course of behavior upstream, as well as the degree of ultimate market success. A sharp distinction between basic research and precommercial development activities is difficult to draw. Investments that are necessary to the utilization and adoption of research results—investments in information gathering, work force training, or the integration of new production equipment into automated systems—can also create spillover benefits that the investing firm cannot perfectly appropriate. In addition, new manufacturing processes that lower cost or improve quality may not be patentable, and new ideas embodied in computer software can often be imitated rapidly without violating the originator's intellectual property rights. In all of these cases, public actions can offset the effects of underinvestment by the private sector that is caused by limitations on appropriability.

Avoiding "Government Failure"

The goal of technology policy is not to substitute the government's judgment for that of private industry in deciding which potential "winners" to back. Rather, the point is to correct a genuine and significant market failure—underinvestment in basic research and in precommercial R&D resulting from the divergence between private and social returns to those activities. A complementary goal is to design the technology investments that the government itself makes in public goods—national security, public health, education, a clean environment, an efficient transportation system—in ways that maximize the potential external benefits for the Nation's commercial technology base. In both cases, technology policy enhances the Nation's economic and social welfare.

Investments in R&D are risky. Like all risky investments, public or private, government-supported explorations sometimes drill dry holes—such as the efforts during the 1960s and 1970s to develop synthetic fuels, a supersonic transport, and a fast breeder reactor. Yet even research that never delivers an enormous economic payoff for itself often contributes useful technical knowledge and lessons for the future. And when the drilling strikes oil, as with government support of R&D for computers and integrated circuits, jet engines and airframes, and biotechnology and medical equipment, the initial gusher can generate an entire field of newly productive, wealth-enhancing, job-creating economic activity. For this reason, the success of government R&D policy must be measured by the rate of return on the entire portfolio of R&D investments supported by the public.

We can learn from both the gushers and the dry holes about how to design programs to promote investments in basic and precommercial R&D to maximize their prospects for success. Federal R&D investment programs leading to successful commercial products tend to share certain design features: They are insulated from the demands of distributional politics; they subject potential projects to rigorous technical and economic evaluation; and they recognize that product specifications must be developed with an eye toward manufacturability and a balance between product performance and cost that will be acceptable to commercial customers. Accordingly, the Administration's efforts to promote innovative technology contain design features that are meant to limit the possibility of "government failure" in the implementation of technology policy:

- To ensure that R&D funded by the government in cooperative ventures with the private sector has direct market applications, participating firms must bear a significant share of program costs. In most cases, the Administration's technology partnerships require that private firms cover at least 50 percent of the costs.
- To ensure that both the timing and the content of government investments in technology-based infrastructure impart maximum leverage on industry's competitive efforts, research frameworks for collaborative R&D should be initiated and designed by private industry and should be closely coordinated with industry investment patterns.
- To insulate publicly supported R&D efforts from political pressures exerted on behalf of special interests, evaluations of competing R&D proposals should be conducted by independent experts in the relevant scientific, technological, and economic fields. Political considerations should not be allowed to influ-

ence a project's technical objectives, the location of R&D facilities, or the way that management of the project is structured.
- Investments in a broad array of technical fields, including materials sciences, manufacturing product and process technologies, biotechnology and biomedical sciences, and telecommunications and computer-related technologies, should compete for a finite flow of funds. This competition will help to ensure that expanded Federal support for precommercial R&D does not get captured by the champions of any particular technology or by any particular set of firms.
- Government investments in basic and precommercial R&D should be reviewed while in progress to determine whether funding should continue. Such reviews are difficult because the success of an R&D project is often not apparent for many years, but rigorous assessments can nevertheless be made by independent expert panels at regular intervals.

A New Approach

An enduring American approach to promoting technology development and diffusion evolved just after the Second World War. The United States channeled public investment into basic research at universities and government laboratories, then supported the initial application of the results in products and production processes procured by public agencies. New technologies first developed for (and procured by) the Department of Defense, the Department of Energy, or the National Aeronautics and Space Administration (NASA), or supported by the National Science Foundation or the National Institutes of Health (NIH), would then diffuse, or "spin off," into commercial use. In this manner, the Federal Government supported the development and diffusion of jet aircraft and engines, semiconductor microelectronics, computers and computer-controlled machine tools, pharmaceuticals and biotechnology, advanced energy and environmental technologies, advanced materials, and a whole host of other commercially successful technologies.

This system worked well as long as military systems represented the leading-edge applications of new industrial technologies and as long as foreign competitors, with direct support from their own governments, did not pose a significant competitive challenge. In many areas of basic research supported outside the defense establishment, including biomedical research and the development of pharmaceuticals, biotechnology, and medical diagnostic devices, the system continues to work well. But the circumstances that allowed the United States to rely primarily on a defense-led model have changed. With the end of the cold war, demand for new defense systems is now less than it was. Commercial product spinoffs from military research have also diminished from their heyday of the

1950s and 1960s, and American companies face intense international competition from increasingly capable foreign firms. On the other hand, these changes also create exciting new opportunities: Innovative defense technologies are now more likely to emerge first in commercial products and production techniques, and American companies are taking advantage of expanded opportunities in foreign markets. Accordingly, the Administration's technology initiatives are shifting the composition of Federal R&D from military to civilian concerns, and the composition of military R&D toward the development of so-called dual-use technologies—those with applications to both military and commercial products.

THE ADMINISTRATION'S TECHNOLOGY INITIATIVES

The Administration's investments in growth- and productivity-enhancing technologies encompass a wide range of physical and human resource priorities. They finance basic research and leverage private funds for technology development and commercialization. They promote the diffusion and adoption of advanced manufacturing technologies by U.S. industry. They facilitate defense conversion by easing defense suppliers into civilian markets, focusing military R&D on dual-use technologies, and freeing the Pentagon to purchase commercial products and processes. They seek to promote the development of a national telecommunications infrastructure for the information age. Finally, they create partnerships with industry and academia to ensure that the government's investments to solve pressing problems in energy, transportation, and the environment simultaneously work to promote the Nation's economy and overall standard of living.

Basic Research

The Administration worked with the Congress to increase budget authority for basic research in all categories to $13.8 billion in fiscal year 1994. This includes a 7.2-percent increase in the National Science Foundation's budget to a total of $1.9 billion. The National Science Foundation will continue to provide strong support for fundamental research critical to manufacturing, advanced materials, environmental technologies, and biotechnology. It has also doubled its support for modernizing academic research facilities and instrumentation. In addition, basic space science research is continuing at NASA, representing an investment of $1.9 billion in fiscal 1994. The Department of Defense has been appropriated $1.2 billion for basic research in fiscal 1994; the Department of Energy will support an additional $1.7 billion in basic research, in areas including materials science, chemical science, engineering and geoscience, high-energy nuclear physics, and nuclear fusion. Finally, the Administration continues to support basic research conducted through the National Institutes of Health, which account for over 40 percent of federally sponsored basic research. NIH is projected to spend nearly $6 billion for basic research in fiscal 1994, exceeding last year's level by almost $300 million (or 5 percent).

Technology Development and Commercialization

Through the Commerce Department's Advanced Technology Program and through the hundreds of cooperative research and development agreements that have been signed between private firms and researchers at many of America's 726 Federal laboratories, the government is investing in industrial projects to develop and to promote commercialization of technologies with high payoff potential. The Nation's antitrust laws have also been clarified to avoid discouraging beneficial private research collaborations.

The Advanced Technology Program (ATP). The ATP is administered by the Commerce Department's National Institute of Standards and Technology (NIST). In four competitions completed over the past 4 years, the ATP has made 89 awards to 66 companies and 23 joint ventures. The projects receiving awards have included ventures to develop a way to control personal computer programs through "natural language" instructions; a pen-based character-recognition system for the Chinese language, with the goal of enhancing software exports to Chinese-speaking companies; and a technology for preserving patients' bone marrow during chemotherapy.

The ATP is designed to avoid government failure. Government acts as the catalyst, but the ATP relies on industry to define and carry out its R&D projects. Independent expert panels select projects through rigorous competitions based on both technical and business merit. The ATP provides technology development funds under cooperative research agreements. It requires single-company applicants to pay their own indirect costs, and joint ventures to provide matching funds. In general, award recipients may patent inventions or copyright software developed under an ATP award, but the government retains a nonexclusive license.

The total of ATP awards plus private sector funds over the life of the first 89 awards amounts to over $500 million. The Administration has proposed to increase the ATP budget from $68 million in 1993 to $750 million in 1997, and $200 million has been appropriated for the program in 1994. In addition to announcing about 100 new awards to industry in fiscal 1994, the ATP will embark on a set of "strategic" program competitions. These competitions will focus on particular technology areas recommended by industry as having especially significant potential to generate large economic and social payoffs.

Cooperative Research at Government Laboratories. The Nation's 726 Federal laboratories, especially the three large, multiprogram nuclear weapons laboratories (Los Alamos and Sandia in New Mexico and Lawrence Livermore in California), offer a repository of vast technical expertise that can be leveraged to enhance the competitive performance of American industry. As part of its plan to alter the balance between military and civilian objectives in the Federal R&D budget, the Administration has authorized the weapons labs to redirect at least 10 to 20 percent of their defense program budgets to commercial technology-transfer activities with industry. The Department of Energy's 31 laboratories, which employ over 23,000 scientists and engineers and perform $6 billion in civilian and military research annually, already have in place over 650 cooperative research and development agreements (CRADAs) with private firms, totaling $1.4 billion in combined public and private funds. CRADAs are also used to structure public-private partnerships involving laboratories at NIST and the Department of Defense. A similar program is in place at NASA.

Using CRADAS, Federal laboratories have already begun or strengthened jointly financed collaborations with companies and industry consortia in a number of research and production prototyping projects. These have covered semiconductor production equipment, flat panel display technology, new technologies for textile manufacturing, the investigation of new polymer blends, biosensors, new aerospace alloys, and microscopic-sized machines known as microelectromechanical systems. These partnerships may begin a longer term process of redirecting the defense-oriented labs' missions toward civilian needs—ranging from the development of energy-efficient and environmentally sustainable industries to the invention of new medical, manufacturing, and transportation technologies—while utilizing the labs' expertise in such fields as high-performance computing, communications, and new materials.

Collaboration in Research and Development. Competition promotes R&D, but collaboration can also promote both research and the effective commercialization of research results. When firms have complementary skills or information, an R&D joint venture among them may speed the development and commercial adoption of a new technology. And when firms have similar skills or information, an R&D joint venture may avoid costly duplication of effort. Yet allowing collaboration in R&D risks facilitating undesirable cooperation in the firms' other activities. For example, it may make it easier to engage in price fixing or other anticompetitive practices in the sale of the products manufactured by the firms collaborating on research. This risk is small if collaboration is limited to early-phase R&D, however.

The Congress balanced these concerns in 1984 when it passed legislation guaranteeing that collaborative research would violate the antitrust laws only if the collaboration were found unreasonable. That legislation also provided that research joint ventures could register with the government and thereby limit their antitrust exposure to actual damages, rather than face the usual treble damage penalty for antitrust violations. Legislation enacted in 1993 extends these protections to production joint ventures, thereby removing a barrier to collaborative efforts to implement new manufacturing techniques and production processes. Because these aspects of the production process can be understood as research into product commercialization, this extension serves a purpose similar to that of the 1984 legislation.

Development and Diffusion of Advanced Manufacturing Technology

Anecdotal examples abound of technologies developed in the United States, such as numerically controlled machine tools, that were commercially exploited first or more successfully abroad. These anecdotes point to market failures other than imperfect appropriability that also contribute to insufficient adoption and utilization of research results. For example, firms may face unnecessarily high transactions costs for obtaining information, and firms with good ideas but limited sources of collateral or internal finance may find themselves unable to raise funds in the capital markets.

The effort to commercialize a new technology often presents firms with an array of organizational challenges: New manufacturing processes and distribution channels must be developed, workers must be retrained, and new suppliers and perhaps even new customers must be identified. In meeting these challenges, firms develop a great deal of valuable information—from manufacturing know-how to marketing insights—some of which cannot be protected as intellectual property or trade secrets.

On the other hand, firms sometimes have difficulty gaining access to other types of technological know-how developed inside other companies and the ways different firms have met implementation challenges. Adoption of advanced manufacturing technology is typically a "systems" problem. Suppliers must be able to sell components that fit into complex automated production systems. Buyers must be assured of compatibility among machines, robots, transfer lines, and the like, or they will not adopt the technology.

To help remedy these market failures, and so promote more rapid and extensive commercialization and diffusion of important new technologies, the Administration is expanding NIST's Manufacturing Extension Partnership (MEP) program. Manufacturing Technology Centers (MTCs) form the backbone of the program. MTCs offer impartial advice to small and medium-sized manufacturers from people with extensive industrial experience. This advice is backed by hands-on technical assistance. MTCs will be linked among themselves to a set of smaller Manufacturing Outreach Centers (MOCs), geared to areas with smaller concentrations of industry. MOCs will be affiliated with technical colleges, vocational schools, and State technical assistance centers. Together MTCs and MOCs will help firms to identify, evaluate, install, adapt, and then commercially exploit appropriate advanced technology in their manufacturing and business operations. The Administration anticipates that 100 centers will be established nationwide by 1997, up from 7 at the outset of this Administration.

Linkages have also been formed between the MEP and other Federal agencies with roles to play in the delivery of technical assistance, work force training, and small business support services. These agencies include the Department of Energy, NASA, the Small Business Administration, and the Department of Labor. In addition, the Department of Energy dedicated over $400 million to advanced manufacturing-related technologies in fiscal 1993 and has under way or in negotiation more than 115 advanced manufacturing cooperative projects involving over 60 companies. One of these is the AMTEX Partnership, a model collaboration between the Department of Energy's national laboratories and the American textile industry. Finally, the deployment portion of the Administration's defense conversion Technology Reinvestment Project (discussed below) includes an additional $87 million for manufacturing extension programs.

Telecommunications Infrastructure for the Information Age

All Americans have a stake in the construction of the advanced National Information Infrastructure described earlier in this chapter. Private industry is already developing and deploying the NII, and, as explained above, it is the private sector that should build and own the NII of the future. There nevertheless remain essential roles for the government to play in ensuring the growth of an affordable and universally accessible telecommunications infrastructure. Many of the key breakthroughs in telecommunications and computing stemmed from research funded by the Federal Government. For example, the Internet and laser technology both grew out of government-sponsored research.

The Administration will continue the High-Performance Computing and Communications program, which funds R&D into more-powerful computers, faster computer networks, and more-sophisticated software. A key objective of this program is the application of computers to economically important problems. The Department of Energy has funded several collaborations among national laboratories, universities, and industry, applying these computing technologies to materials, chemistry, energy, and environmental problems. Beyond that, the Administration has created a new component of the program, emphasizing information infrastructure technologies and applications. This program will develop and apply high-performance computing and high-speed networking technologies for use in the fields of health care, education, libraries, manufacturing, and provision of government information. Additional research on information technologies and applications will be conducted by the Department of Energy's national laboratories.

Finally, the government is supporting an array of NII pilot and demonstration projects. Federal matching grants will be awarded on a competitive basis to school districts, libraries, State and local governments, health care providers, universities, and other nonprofit entities to connect institutions to existing networks, to enhance those networks, and to permit users to interconnect among different networks. The program is presently funded at $28 million per year and is planned to grow in coming years to $100 million annually. Its goal is to ensure that every school and library in the country is connected. In addition, NASA has launched the Advanced Communications Technology Satellite, an experiment to test pioneering concepts and technologies that promise to advance on-demand, flexible communications services.

Transportation, Energy, and the Environment: New Technologies for Growth

Environmental improvements have traditionally been viewed as something we trade off for increased economic performance. Yet, as noted earlier in this chapter, a strong environmental policy framework can encourage innovation, strengthen key competitive industries, and improve our environment simultaneously. Environmental policy can create new demand for the goods and services of the environmental protection industries, which then increase employment and production to meet this demand. Policies that call for leading-edge environmental solutions can induce U.S. industry to respond with novel, world-class technologies. This response positions U.S. industry to meet the rapidly growing world demand for advanced "green" technologies, providing additional economic and environmental benefits for U.S. consumers and producers.

Accordingly, this Administration is developing an environmental policy framework whose objective is to maintain and strengthen environmental protection while also promoting economic and technological development. The Administration is working with the U.S. business and research communities to promote the development and deployment of new technologies that simultaneously prevent pollution, increase energy efficiency and the efficiency of the Nation's transportation infrastructure, and promote economic growth. Clean technologies—such as energy-efficient light bulbs and motors, alternative fuel vehicles, computerized traffic management systems, and advanced steelmaking—reduce many kinds of pollutants. Such technologies can also reduce the energy needs of U.S. companies, trimming costs and improving international competitiveness. Again, the hoped-for result is both enhanced environmental quality and greater long-term economic growth.

Partnership for a New Generation of Vehicles. This initiative, begun in September 1993, is a joint effort of the Federal Government and the three leading domestic automobile manufacturers. The initiative aims to develop the technologies necessary to create a new type of automobile, one that is both safer and up to three times more fuel efficient than today's cars. In both its goals and its implementation, the program is characteristic of this Administration's technology policy. It focuses on developing technologies that may generate technological progress in two important areas: in making U.S. automobile producers more technologically competitive in the international marketplace and in reducing air pollution. The initiative is structured as a set of public-private partnerships in R&D. One such partnership seeks to develop a "hybrid" vehicle that combines electric propulsion with conventional heat engine systems to increase efficiency and meet tight emission standards.

The Environmental Technologies Initiative. The EPA has launched the Environmental Technologies Initiative to stimulate technological innovation to meet the Nation's environmental objectives. The initiative aims to create a more productive environmental technology marketplace and works toward incorporating environmental considerations into the design of new technologies and into upgrades of existing technologies. This program is also designed to aid the Administration's defense conversion effort by facilitating the use of military bases for demonstrations of environmental remediation or "cleanup" technologies. In addition, the EPA and the Commerce Department are jointly developing environmental technology programs at NIST regional technology centers; and the EPA has undertaken a new collaborative venture with the Small Business Administration to help small businesses access information on pollution prevention. These and other domestic initiatives also support the Administration's strategic framework for environmental technologies exports, which engages U.S. environmental businesses in the design and implementation of market-specific export assistance and export financing strategies.

The NICE[3] program (National Industrial Competitiveness through Energy, Environment, and Economics), jointly administered by the EPA and the Department of Energy, aims to promote innovative technologies that simultaneously improve energy efficiency, reduce waste generation, and increase economic competitiveness and productivity. The program also seeks to improve cooperation between State agencies and industry. In addition, the President has directed the Department of Energy and the EPA to accelerate the commercialization of advanced, energy-efficient technologies through the formation of partnerships with key market players. These partnerships may include contests for new technology introductions; working with government procurement agencies to leverage their purchasing power to acquire qualifying products; and working with utilities to coordinate incentives for markets for new technologies. For instance, the Department of Energy, together with the EPA and utilities, is using such partnerships to create a new market for manufacturers of chlorofluorocarbon-free refrigerators (chlorofluorocarbons have been implicated in degradation of the atmospheric ozone layer).

Finally, the Department of Energy is engaged in developing and deploying innovative environmental remediation and cleanup technologies to deal with the cleanup of military bases slated for closure, as well as of contaminated facilities and sites administered by the Energy Department itself.

Other Transportation Technology Initiatives. The Department of Transportation has begun a series of outreach seminars entitled "Promoting Transportation Applications in Defense Conversion and Other Advanced Technologies." In addition, the department has initiated studies aimed at having a prototype demonstration of an automated intelligent vehicle highway system by 1997. The Defense Department's Advanced Research Projects Agency (ARPA) has selected six regional coalitions—in Hawaii, Sacramento, Los Angeles, Indianapolis, Atlanta, and Boston—to work on electric and hybrid electric vehicle technology and infrastructure. A team of officials from the Departments of Defense and Transportation is also investigating how to augment the existing satellite-based global positioning system for use in improving air navigation and collision avoidance. The Department of Energy's Clean Cities program makes use of the Federal Government's purchasing power to accelerate the introduction of alternative fuel vehicles (and an alternative refueling infrastructure) into urban areas in order to reduce emissions. Finally, the Administration is continuing to fund research into an array of next-generation transportation technologies, including high-speed ground transportation, advanced subsonic planes, and supersonic air transports.

Facilitating Defense Conversion

The share of gross domestic product (GDP) devoted to national defense is expected to shrink from 6.5 percent in 1986 to 3.3 percent in 1997. This decline in defense spending, resulting from the end of the cold war, is smaller relative to the size of the economy than the cutbacks that followed World War II and the Korean and Vietnam wars, and much more gradual. Yet the impact on particular regions, such as southern California, is severe, and three additional factors work to make the economic adjustment this time more difficult. First, the economy's recovery from the recession of 1990–91 was weaker than the average postwar recovery, while efforts to cut the massive Federal budget deficit leave little room for fiscal expansion to stimulate economic growth. Second, many defense firms and workers are more isolated from commercial market practice than during earlier builddowns, because the defense procurement system that has evolved over time has erected a wall between commercial sectors and defense. Third, technological innovation and the economic growth it generates may be hard hit by the defense retrenchment, because nearly 60 percent of Federal support for domestic R&D was defense related and because roughly one-fifth of the Nation's engineers work in defense-related areas.

The end of the cold war was an unanticipated event with serious economic consequences for several domestic economic sectors. Our Nation has long accepted a collective responsibility to ease the transition for those most heavily affected by major economic shocks, for example by providing unemployment insurance and disaster relief. This principle readily extends to transitional assistance when the shock results from a large and unanticipated structural economic change, particularly when government is effectively the agent of that change.

For workers, the problem of large, regionally concentrated economic dislocations is made worse by a capital market imperfection. It is often difficult for workers to borrow for retraining and relocation because their human capital cannot serve as collateral. Such capital market transactions are particularly difficult to arrange for people who have just lost a job or who have incurred a capital loss on their home—a frequent consequence of geographically concentrated defense cuts. Moreover, dislocated workers may have a difficult time learning about job opportunities in other regions or occupations.

Defense conversion is also difficult for firms. Although many defense contractors have access to knowledge, production facilities, and skilled workers that could be valuable if channeled to commercial applications, the many years spent designing their organizations to serve the needs of one customer—the Defense Department—often leave them without crucial skills or the right organizational configuration to serve the commercial marketplace. To the extent that these firms lack internal funds to finance new investment, and to the extent they are unable credibly to demonstrate to lenders and other capital providers their potential to serve other lines of business, these resources will not be able to move to their most efficient uses.

The Administration's 5-year, $22 billion Defense Reinvestment and Conversion Initiative addresses these problems of the post-cold war transition.

Workers. The initiative provides $5 billion over 5 years for worker adjustment, including funding for retraining displaced defense workers and early retirement benefits for military personnel with at least 15 years of service. In addition, the Administration is sponsoring pilot programs to train defense workers and personnel leaving the military for national service as teachers, health care workers, and law enforcement personnel.

Communities. The Administration is also expanding the Defense Department's Office of Economic Adjustment, so that communities affected by scheduled military base closures have the resources and technical assistance necessary to plan a smoother adjustment to new economic activities. More resources are being devoted to the Commerce Department's Economic Development Administration, to target help to communities hardest hit by the defense industry drawdown. Meanwhile the Defense Department is working with the EPA and other public and private bodies to make sure that the process of environmental cleanup and restoration at closed military bases does not hamper local economic recovery.

Technology: The Technology Reinvestment Project. The Administration's Technology Reinvestment Project (TRP) is an effort to promote the development of dual-use (commercial and military) technologies and to help small defense firms make the transition to commercial production. The TRP is jointly implemented by a six-agency council representing the Departments of Commerce, Energy, Transportation, and Defense, NASA, and the National Science Foundation, and is chaired by an official from ARPA. One-hundred and sixty-two projects had been selected for TRP support as of early December 1993, totaling nearly $1 billion in combined public and private funds (the Federal share is about $415 million).

The TRP funds three types of projects: technology development (46 projects), technology deployment (70), and manufacturing education and training (46). Examples include construction of a highway bridge from composite plastics, development of a new jaws-of-life rescue device powered by pyrotechnic cartridges, and the exploration of medical uses for a noninvasive diagnostic device that measures oxygen levels in the blood. The TRP is also funding the development of a new manufacturing engineering curriculum at a State college, a manufacturing technology center to help defense suppliers adapt to other fields, and a project to retrain laidoff defense engineers in pollution-prevention and remediation.

MARITECH. The Defense Department's MARITECH (maritime technology) initiative, a defense conversion program focused on shipbuilding, is structured similarly to the TRP. This 5-year, $220 million program will supply matching funds to help U.S. shipyards shift production from military to commercial markets.

TECHNOLOGY POLICY, GROWTH, AND COMPETITIVENESS

Government must work with American industry to provide a sound communications and transportation infrastructure and a solid science and industrial technology base. These are among the prerequisites for economic growth. Yet to be effective in a market economy, technology policy must leverage private investment, not direct it. It must be sensitive to those reasons why markets by themselves may lead to insufficient investment. The Administration's technology initiatives take their inspiration from a long American history of public-private partnerships, from the Agricultural Extension Service to the Arpanet (now the Internet worldwide computer network). These initiatives seize strategic opportunities inherent in the shifting composition of Federal R&D from military to civilian concerns, help remedy the underinvestment in R&D created by the limitations on private appropriability of its economic returns, and focus Federal R&D funds on facilitating the commercialization and commercial diffusion of technology. Together these technology initiatives are essential to promote U.S. economic competitiveness, meaning not only the ability of American firms to sell high-quality goods and services in the international marketplace, but more importantly, the ability to do so while maintaining high and rising wages and living standards for the American people.

CHAPTER 6

The United States in the World Economy

SOON AFTER TAKING OFFICE, the President described the basic principles and goals of his Administration's international economic policy in a February 1993 speech at American University. He committed the United States to active global engagement to promote world trade and growth, to aid the development of less prosperous nations, to address the emerging problems of global environmental degradation, and to encourage market reform in Russia and other parts of the former Soviet empire. The President affirmed that the United States would continue to champion open markets and expanded trade: In the President's words, "We must compete, not retreat." Acting upon these words, the Administration successfully concluded two of the most important trade agreements in the Nation's history: the North American Free Trade Agreement (NAFTA) and the Uruguay Round Agreement under the General Agreement on Tariffs and Trade (GATT).

Like previous Administrations, Democratic and Republican alike, this Administration recognizes that international trade—the voluntary exchange of goods and services across national borders—is a means of increasing standards of living and economic well-being both at home and abroad. During the last half-century, world trade has grown enormously, largely as a result of American leadership in liberalizing global markets. Trade has been a major engine of growth for the world economy since World War II, in marked contrast to the 1930s, when protectionism worsened and helped spread global economic depression. As economists have long predicted, freer trade has been a win-win strategy for both the United States and its trading partners, allowing all to reap the benefits of enhanced specialization, lower costs, greater choice, and an improved international climate for investment and innovation. American industries—both their workers and their owners—have benefited from increased export markets and from cheaper imported inputs. American consumers have been able to purchase a wider variety of products at lower prices than they could have without the expansion of trade.

Recent changes in the global economy pose new challenges and new opportunities for the United States as we maintain our commitment to an open international trading system. The new opportunities come from the explosion of global markets, while the new challenges come from the development of new global competitors. During much of the last 50 years, the United States was the only global economic superpower. But now there are three: the European Union (EU, the deeper integration of the European Community), Japan, and the United States; and all increasingly interdependent as a result of trade and capital flows, and increasingly competitive. All three superpowers face both intensifying competition from and expanding market opportunities in the rapidly industrializing countries of East Asia, which continue to increase their export competitiveness even as they open their own markets to greater trade and investment. Meanwhile the global trading system is being transformed by the emergence of new democratic and market-oriented regimes in central and eastern Europe, the former Soviet Union, Latin America, and Asia—regimes that have made substantial progress in tearing down their protectionist barriers and are now actively encouraging exports, accepting imports, and seeking foreign capital for development.

This Administration is committed to a high-wage strategy to enable the United States to take advantage of the new opportunities and to meet the new challenges of the changing global marketplace. This strategy consists of two distinct but interrelated parts: trade policies that will promote trade and foster more-open markets both at home and abroad; and domestic policies that will help American companies remain the world's productivity and technological leaders, and American workers remain the most skilled and productive in the world. This two-part strategy reflects the fundamental goal of the Administration's other economic policy initiatives: higher living standards for all Americans. Realizing this goal requires that America compete not on the basis of lower wages, but on the basis of superior productivity, technology, and quality. It also requires that our trade policy be complemented by domestic policies designed to increase labor force skills and facilitate the adjustment of American workers and communities to changing economic circumstances—whatever their source. Other chapters in this *Report* have analyzed the domestic economy. This chapter addresses the international dimension.

TRENDS IN U.S. TRADE

Trade has become increasingly important to the American economy. As shown in Chart 6–1, the share of exports of goods and services in real gross domestic product (GDP) has gradually risen and now stands at a postwar high of 11.6 percent. Between 1985 and 1993, U.S. merchandise exports increased from $222 billion to

$460 billion in current dollars, and by 95 percent in real terms. By 1992, the United States had regained its status as the world's largest exporter, and one in six American manufacturing jobs was directly or indirectly related to exports.

Chart 6-1 **U.S. Trade as Share of Real Gross Domestic Product**
The importance of trade to the U.S. economy has risen more or less steadily for three decades.

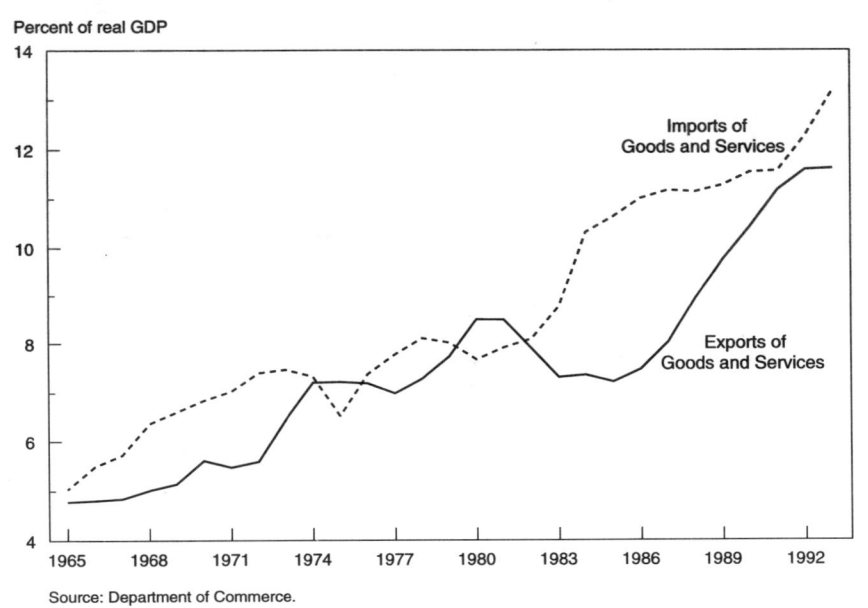

Source: Department of Commerce.

Imports have also grown in significance. As Chart 6–1 shows, the share of imports of goods and services in GDP has increased steadily and is also at a postwar high of 13.2 percent. Perhaps the most striking development has been the increasing role of multinational corporations in U.S. trade and, indeed, the growing importance of intrafirm trade—cross-border trade between the separate operations of a single firm. By 1990, multinational firms accounted for over 75 percent of total U.S. merchandise trade, and around 40 percent of U.S. merchandise trade was intrafirm. And whereas intrafirm trade initially involved mainly U.S.-based multinationals, more recently it has been led by foreign-based firms, especially Japanese firms.

The impact of international trade on the national economy is not restricted to exports and imports. International trade also affects the fortunes of producers who do not directly export or import but interact with producers who do. According to input-output analyses, which take such intersectoral or interproducer relations into account, when the indirect effects of trade are included, exports accounted for nearly four-fifths of the increase in domestic production of manufactures between 1987 and 1992. Moreover, exports have become more dependent on imports. Between 1982 and 1987, the most recent years for which data are available, the import content of exports rose from 10 percent to 14 percent. Thus exports are becoming more important for the economy, and imports are becoming more important for exports. Overall, international trade is increasingly vital to American prosperity.

The growth of U.S. trade has been accompanied by significant changes in both its sectoral and its regional composition. As shown in Chart 6-2, real exports of nonagricultural merchandise and services have grown rapidly during the past quarter-century (Box 6-1), while the contribution of agricultural exports has remained relatively small. At the same time, the relative contributions of particular sectors within nonagricultural merchandise trade have been shifting (Table 6-1).

Chart 6-2 **U.S. Exports of Goods and Services**
Exports of services and nonagricultural goods have grown rapidly since the late 1960s.

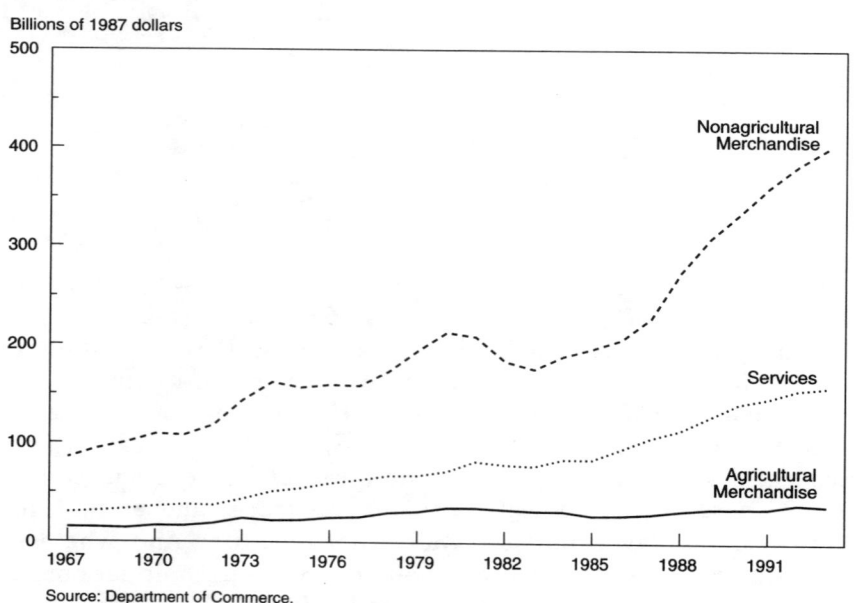

Source: Department of Commerce.

Box 6-1.—U.S. Exports: More Than Peanuts

In 1992, American service firms exported to nonaffiliates abroad:
- over two-thirds as much in passenger fares ($17.4 billion), such as seats on U.S.-flagged air carriers, as the United States exported civilian aircraft ($24.5 billion)
- more educational services ($6.1 billion) than the United States exported corn ($5.7 billion)
- more financial services ($5.4 billion) than the United States exported wheat ($4.6 billion)
- more equipment installation and repair services ($2.8 billion) than the United States exported agricultural machinery ($2.1 billion)
- more information services, including computer and data processing and database services ($2.6 billion), than the United States exported aluminum ($1.2 billion)
- more legal services ($1.4 billion) than the United States exported vegetable oils ($1.0 billion)
- more management consulting services ($0.78 billion) than the United States exported milled rice ($0.72 billion) or peanuts ($0.21 billion).

TABLE 6–1.—*U.S. Merchandise Trade by Industry, 1972 and 1992*
[Percent of total]

Industry	1972 Exports	1972 Imports	1992 Exports	1992 Imports
Agricultural and forest products	18.5	15.4	11.7	6.2
Minerals	3.1	5.8	2.3	2.3
Fuels	3.2	8.5	2.6	11.1
Chemicals	8.4	3.6	10.4	5.4
Textiles, apparel, leather products, and footwear	3.9	8.8	3.4	10.5
Paper	1.5	2.3	1.5	1.6
Nonmetallic minerals products	1.2	2.3	.9	1.8
Iron and steel	1.7	5.3	1.0	1.9
Machinery	27.0	14.0	30.5	24.8
Transportation equipment	16.9	17.5	17.7	15.7
Furniture and fixtures	.3	.7	.9	1.4
Instruments	2.8	1.6	3.6	3.1
Miscellaneous manufactures	3.7	6.5	5.7	7.7
Other industries	7.8	7.5	7.9	6.3

Note.–The classifications are based on the SITC Revision 1 coding system. Import figures have been adjusted to net out reexports.
Detail may not add to 100 percent due to rounding.
Source: United Nations, Commodity Trade Statistics Division.

An important sectoral development in recent years has been the growth of high-technology products and industries in both U.S. exports and imports. In 1992, the United States exported $107 billion in advanced technology products, up in nominal terms from $83 billion in 1989. Imports of these products also increased—from $56 billion in 1989 to $72 billion in 1992. Aerospace, information and communications, and electronics together contributed the predominant share of U.S. high-technology exports. These sectors, along with a few high-technology product lines within other industrial sectors, are considerably more export-intensive than U.S. manufacturing as a whole. Indeed, aircraft and computers and office equipment have the highest ratios of export sales to value added among all manufacturing industries.

Heightened foreign competition and the globalization of production (technology respects no border) have made many high-technology industries relatively import-intensive as well. In fact, the most export-intensive of America's high-technology industries (with the marked exceptions of plastics and aircraft) are now also the most import-intensive. The electronics industries have been the arena of the most dramatic penetration of the U.S. high-technology market, both because Japanese and East Asian electronics producers have become more formidable competitors, and because American electronics multinationals have spread their own production around the world.

Just as the commodity composition of U.S. trade has been changing, so has its geographical composition. As shown in Table 6–2, the shares of U.S. exports going to and imports coming from developing countries have risen, while the shares to and from industrial countries have fallen. These trends reflect the fact that the developing countries as a group have been growing more rapidly than the industrial countries.

TABLE 6–2.—*U.S. Merchandise Trade by World Region, 1972 and 1992*
[Percent of total]

Region	1972 Exports	1972 Imports	1992 Exports	1992 Imports
Industrial countries	66.8	72.4	58.5	57.7
Japan	10.0	16.3	10.7	18.0
European Community [1]	26.8	24.0	23.0	17.6
Other	30.0	32.1	24.9	22.1
Developing countries	33.2	27.6	41.5	42.3
Asia	8.9	9.6	16.6	22.8
Middle East	4.1	1.6	4.5	3.1
Western Hemisphere	14.6	12.6	16.9	13.0
Other	5.6	3.8	3.5	3.4

[1] Membership as of 1992.
Note.—Detail may not add to totals due to rounding.
Source: International Monetary Fund.

The fast-growing countries of Asia have provided a rapidly expanding market for U.S. exports; their share of the total nearly doubled from 9 percent in 1972 to 17 percent in 1992. Indeed, by 1992 our trans-Pacific trade was 50 percent greater than our trans-Atlantic trade. The increasing importance of Asia in U.S. trade appears to contradict the common contention that the world is devolving into three trading blocs centered on Europe, Asia, and North America. Nor is such a conclusion supported by more-sophisticated evidence. When researchers have modeled the pattern of trade flows among different countries, they have found no real evidence that intraregional trade flows in Asia are unusually large once economic fundamentals are taken into account. The observed increases in intraregional flows can be explained largely in terms of differences in economic growth rates and geographical proximity. Likewise, when researchers have looked at financial flows, exchange-rate determination, and the like, there is little evidence that a "yen bloc" is developing in Asia.

In addition to leading the world in trade, the United States leads the world in the stock of foreign direct investment, both as investor and as recipient. In 1992, U.S. firms owned 25 percent, and the United States hosted 22 percent, of the world's foreign direct investment stock. The largest hosts of outward U.S. foreign direct investment (ranked in order of importance) are the United Kingdom, Canada, Germany, Switzerland, and Japan, which together account for nearly half the total (Table 6-3). Similarly, five industrial countries (again ranked in order of importance)—Japan, the United Kingdom, the Netherlands, Canada, and Germany—account for more than three-quarters of existing foreign direct investment in the United States. The predominant role of high-wage industrial countries in *both* inward and outward foreign direct investment in the United States refutes the popular notion that such investment is motivated primarily by the search for lower wages. In fact, many foreign investment decisions are motivated by other considerations, most often the need to have an active presence in large or rapidly expanding markets or the need to overcome trade and other barriers that impede access.

It is sometimes argued that outward foreign direct investment "exports" jobs. However, the parallel expansion of two-way foreign direct investment and intrafirm trade suggests that such investment is more likely to complement rather than substitute for trade, creating high-wage jobs domestically rather than destroying them. Several recent studies have concluded that foreign direct investment is more likely to create trade than reduce it. Another recent study found that inward foreign direct investment brings with it competition, new technologies, and new management techniques,

TABLE 6-3.—*Stock of U.S. Outward and Inward Foreign Direct Investment, 1992*

Country	Billions of dollars
INVESTMENT BY U.S. FIRMS ABROAD (OUTWARD):	
United Kingdom	77.8
Canada	68.4
Germany	35.4
Switzerland	28.7
Japan	26.2
All countries	486.7
INVESTMENT BY FOREIGN FIRMS IN THE UNITED STATES (INWARD):	
Japan	96.7
United Kingdom	94.7
Netherlands	61.3
Canada	39.0
Germany	29.2
All countries	419.5

Note.—All figures are on a historical cost basis.
Source: Department of Commerce, Bureau of Economic Analysis.

each of which has contributed to the resurgence in U.S. productivity, further enhancing national competitiveness.

TRADE, JOBS, AND WAGE INEQUALITY

In the short run, both the level of output and the level of employment in the American economy depend on the level of aggregate demand. One component of aggregate demand is net exports, the difference between exports and imports. Thus, as long as there is slack in the economy, an increase in net exports will stimulate production and create jobs. For example, most scholars estimate that NAFTA will create additional American jobs over the next several years because it will boost U.S. net exports to Mexico. Once the American economy nears full employment, however, additional net exports could create upward pressure on prices as well. Even when the economy is at full employment, however, and even if trade liberalization increases both imports and exports equally, leaving net exports unchanged, the American economy still reaps the benefits of freer trade in the form of greater productive efficiency, lower prices, and higher living standards.

Despite the possible benefits of trade liberalization for the level of employment in the short run, and the certain benefits of trade liberalization for living standards in the long run, some observers worry that expanding trade with developing countries will depress the wages of low-skilled American workers. As explained in Chapter 3, wage inequality has, in fact, increased over the past two decades as the share of trade in the U.S. economy has grown. Not surprisingly, concerns have been voiced that greater international trade may be responsible for greater inequality in the wage distribution.

Such concerns are plausible and are consistent with economic theory. Skilled labor is relatively abundant in the U.S. economy. According to theory, when the United States trades with economies in which unskilled labor is relatively abundant, we will tend to export products requiring skilled labor and import products using unskilled labor. The relative prices of skill-intensive goods will therefore rise in the United States, and U.S. production will expand in export industries and contract in industries that compete with imports. Demand for skilled labor will rise, while demand for unskilled labor falls. These changes in labor demand will raise the wages of skilled workers relative to those of unskilled workers. Thus, on *a priori* grounds, one might expect an expansion of trade with developing countries to lead to greater wage inequality in the United States.

Despite the plausibility of the theoretical argument, however, several studies find that it is difficult to discern any substantial impact of trade on wage inequality. Economists have posited a systematic relationship between the relative prices of goods and the relative returns to factors of production. If increased trade with developing countries were the cause of growing wage inequality, the relative prices of goods that use highly skilled labor would be rising relative to those of goods that use unskilled labor. However, one study has found no evidence that the relative price of skill-intensive goods has risen in the United States. Indeed, it is difficult to find any evidence of the changes in relative prices that would be required for changes in trade patterns to have altered the relative returns to different types of labor.

Similarly, if increased trade were responsible for increased wage inequality, the growth in wage differentials would lead firms in all sectors to substitute unskilled labor for skilled labor. Instead, studies find that virtually all manufacturing industries have increased their relative use of skilled labor despite growing wage differentials. Rising wage differentials along with greater use of skilled labor suggests that demand for skilled labor has been rising broadly in the economy. As expected, these wage differentials have led to an upgrading of skills in the work force, allowing firms to meet their rising demand for skilled labor.

Taken together, this evidence (little change in relative prices, and economy-wide increases in the demand for skilled labor) suggests that growing demand for skilled labor has resulted from widespread changes within industries rather than from changes in the structure of production engendered by greater trade. The preponderance of evidence indicates that the primary sources of growing wage inequality are domestic rather than foreign. As discussed in Chapter 3, the sources of wage inequality are difficult to pinpoint, but to the extent that growing inequality can be explained, technical change has been offered as the leading candidate. Increased trade with developing countries may have reinforced some of the changes in wages caused by technological change, but careful studies have failed to discern a sizable impact of trade on wage inequality.

Two explanations of this finding have been offered. First, although trade with developing countries has been growing, most U.S. trade—about 60 percent—still involves other industrialized countries whose skill levels and wages are similar to those in the United States. Second, while trade is a growing part of the U.S. economy, it remains a relatively small part. Only extremely large changes in the composition of trade could have a discernable impact on wages and wage disparity in the U.S. economy.

Nonetheless, the expansion of trade will inevitably disadvantage some workers in the short run. One goal of Administration policy, as described in Chapter 3, is to facilitate the adjustment of the labor force to changing economic circumstances whatever the putative source of change. It is by recognizing both the opportunities and the challenges presented by the changing global economy that the Administration seeks to achieve a productive and stable basis for U.S. engagement in the world economy.

THE ADMINISTRATION'S TRADE INITIATIVES

The Clinton Administration supports the goal of freer trade on a reciprocal basis. In pursuit of that goal, the Administration is dedicated to working with the private sector and its trading partners to open foreign markets through bilateral, regional, and multilateral trade agreements. At the same time, the Administration believes that trade policy should complement, not substitute for, domestic policies to enhance the global competitiveness of American companies and their workers and to make the United States an attractive production location for both domestic and foreign firms.

DOMESTIC INITIATIVES: THE NATIONAL EXPORT STRATEGY

The Administration's trade policy begins at home with an activist commitment to promote American exports both by reducing domestic barriers to them and by improving the efficiency of our export promotion programs. Working within the interagency Trade Promotion Coordinating Committee, created by the Congress to reduce the fragmentation of our export promotion programs, the Administration unveiled a new National Export Strategy in September 1993. This strategy reflected six underlying themes: streamlining and combining functions across agencies, allocating resources strategically, involving the private sector and State and local governments, effectively advocating the interests of U.S. exporters abroad, measuring performance, and reducing export controls (restrictions on exports to meet national security, antiproliferation, or foreign policy objectives). Among the actions to be undertaken immediately are:

- Revising outmoded export controls on high-technology products. The specific technical revisions are expected to reduce regulation significantly on an estimated $35 billion worth of high-technology exports. For example, export restrictions that previously affected sales of even some personal computers to many foreign markets have been relaxed.
- Consolidating all Federal export promotion services in one location to facilitate "one-stop shopping." Initially, four centers will be created; more will be added until a national network has been created.
- Providing high-level government advocacy on behalf of U.S. firms pursuing major foreign government procurement opportunities through an interagency "Advocacy Network" and an "Advocacy Center" located in the Department of Commerce.
- Improving our export finance programs by combating the "tied aid" practices of other nations, increasing the limits on insurance guarantees by the Overseas Private Investment Corporation, broadening assistance to U.S. companies seeking to participate in activities funded by the multilateral development banks (such as the World Bank), and combining into one agency the infrastructure feasibility funds that are the seed money for U.S. firms' participation in major infrastructure projects abroad.

Taken together, the actions outlined in the National Export Strategy are expected to increase both the responsiveness and the efficiency of export promotion efforts.

BILATERAL NEGOTIATIONS

Along with these unilateral actions, the Administration has engaged numerous foreign countries in bilateral trade talks. The most prominent of these efforts has been with Japan.

The U.S.-Japan Framework Talks

Japan presents a special case for the United States. Japan is the world's second-largest economy, after the United States, and our second-largest trading partner, after Canada. And it is with Japan that the United States maintains its largest bilateral merchandise trade imbalance: a deficit of $49.6 billion in 1992 (Table 6-4). (In the same year, we enjoyed a $13.3 billion surplus with Japan in services trade.) Japan's large surplus with the United States is an important part of its large global current account surplus (the current account is a broader measure of trade that includes both goods and services), which stood at $118 billion in 1992.

TABLE 6–4.—*U.S. Merchandise Trade Balances with Selected Countries, 1987–92*

[Billions of dollars]

Year	European Community	Japan	"Greater China"				Rest of world
			Total	People's Republic of China	Hong Kong	Taiwan	
1987	−20.6	−56.3	−25.9	−2.8	−5.9	−17.2	−49.3
1988	−9.2	−51.8	−20.6	−3.5	−4.6	−12.6	−36.9
1989	1.2	−49.1	−22.6	−6.2	−3.4	−13.0	−38.9
1990	6.3	−41.1	−24.4	−10.4	−2.8	−11.2	−42.5
1991	17.0	−43.4	−23.7	−12.7	−1.1	−9.8	−16.6
1992	9.0	−49.6	−28.4	−18.3	−0.7	−9.3	−15.5

Note.—Exports are f.a.s. and imports are customs value.
China, Hong Kong, and Taiwan have been grouped together as "Greater China" for analytical convenience.
Detail may not add to totals due to rounding.
Source: Department of Commerce, Bureau of the Census.

Moreover, certain of Japan's trade patterns appear to differ from those of other major industrial countries. Japan has an unusually low share of manufactured imports in domestic consumption, an unusually low share of intraindustry trade, an unusually small stock of inward foreign direct investment, an unusually small share of domestic sales accounted for by foreign-owned firms, and an unusually high share of intrafirm trade, which is predominantly controlled, moreover, by Japanese rather than foreign-based firms.

Manufactured imports play a relatively small role in the Japanese economy, with the share of manufactured imports in consumption less than half that of the other major industrialized countries (Table 6–5). And while this measure has risen considerably in the other countries, it has remained relatively unchanged in Japan for 20 years.

TABLE 6–5.—*Selected Trade Indicators for Six Industrialized Countries, 1990*

Indicator	Japan	United States	Germany	United Kingdom	France	Italy
Import share of domestic consumption of manufactures (percent)	5.9	15.3	15.4	17.7	13.7	12.6
Intraindustry trade index	.58	.83	.73	.79	.77	.67
Foreign firms' share of domestic sales (percent)	1.2	16.4	14.0	[1] 24.1	28.4	[2]

[1] Data for 1989.
[2] Not available.

Note.—Intra-European Community trade has been excluded from the intraindustry trade and import share calculations.
Sources: Institute for International Economics; United Nations, Commodity Trade Statistics Division; World Bank; and Department of Commerce.

Another interesting aspect of Japan's trade pattern is its relatively low level of intraindustry trade—trade in differentiated manufactures within a given industry. (One common example is trade in different makes and models of automobiles.) As economies develop and the demands of firms and consumers become more complex, individual firms become less able to produce the vastly broader range of products required to satisfy all demands. Intraindustry trade then increases, as firms penetrate each others' domestic markets to supply those particular products in which they specialize. Intraindustry trade, it is sometimes argued, is of particular importance because the adjustment costs associated with an expansion of intraindustry trade are thought to be lower than for a comparable expansion of interindustry trade—import-competing firms can retool and specialize rather than disappear. If this is so, expansion of intraindustry trade should be more compatible with trade liberalization.

Japan also exhibits an unusually high share of intrafirm trade. Intrafirm trade is important both as a major channel of trade and because intracorporate transactions may be less responsive to normal price and cost determinants than are arm's-length transactions.

This issue is of considerable interest with regard to Japan because of Japan's unusual pattern of intrafirm trade. For most countries, intrafirm trade is dominated by shipments from parent firms to their foreign affiliates. That is to say, intrafirm trade is export-oriented. Japan is unusual in that Japanese parents dominate trade in both exports *and* imports. Some researchers have attributed this dominance to the prominent role of giant trading companies and *keiretsu* relationships in Japanese trade and argue that this pattern of trade is consistent with imperfectly competitive Japanese domestic markets. (*Keiretsu* are large groups of Japanese firms that share financial, production, personnel, and other linkages.)

Table 6–6 reports data on U.S. bilateral trade with Europe and Japan. Intrafirm trade is a more important part of U.S.-Japan trade than of U.S.-Europe trade. Three-quarters of all U.S. imports from Japan are intrafirm (compared with less than 50 percent for trade with Western Europe), and 36 percent of U.S. exports to Japan are intrafirm (compared with 32 percent for Western Europe).

Japanese markets are not completely closed. Indeed, some U.S. firms excel in Japan. On the whole, however, the role of foreign firms and foreign goods is strikingly small (Table 6–5).

Explanations of Japan's apparent distinctiveness fall into two broad groups, one emphasizing direct trade and industrial policy interventions and the other emphasizing structural characteristics

TABLE 6–6.—*Intrafirm Trade as Share of Total U.S. Exports to and Imports from Europe and Japan, 1992*

[Percent of total]

Region	U.S. exports to region	U.S. imports from region
Europe	32.4	46.3
Japan	36.2	75.0
World total	30.6	45.0

Note.—Intrafirm trade is defined as merchandise trade between "related parties" (that is, between affiliates of the same firm).

Source: Department of Commerce, Bureau of the Census.

of the economy. Domestic industrial support policies in Japan have included subsidies to producers and to research and development consortia, preferential tax treatment, preferential access to credit, government procurement preferences, establishment of producer cartels, and lax antitrust enforcement. External policies have included trade protection, restrictions on inward foreign direct investment, and control over high-technology trade. These policies have been applied to both infant and senescent industries.

With a few notable exceptions, including agriculture, Japanese tariffs and import quotas are not significant trade barriers. Yet Japan's market is regarded by many as effectively closed to imports of many foreign manufactures, especially those that directly compete with Japanese goods. Structural barriers alleged to deter imports include reliance on bureaucratic control to ensure product safety; domestic cartels, discriminatory practices by the *keiretsu*, and weak enforcement of competition policies; inadequate intellectual property protection; government procurement procedures that favor domestic suppliers; imperfect capital markets that inhibit inward foreign investment; and impediments in the distribution channels for imported products—to name a few.

Estimating the impact of the mostly overt barriers to trade in primary products is relatively straightforward. One recent study concluded that complete elimination of all agricultural trade barriers in Japan might increase the incomes of U.S. producers by 28 percent of the value of bilateral agricultural exports. This would occur through a combination of higher export volumes to Japan and higher prices on exports to all markets. Comparable figures for potential gains in minerals and, importantly, services, are not available.

What attracts the most attention, however, is the potential gain in manufactures. And here the story is far more controversial because the subtle nature of Japan's trade barriers poses difficult problems for economists trying to assess their impact. In consequence, researchers have eschewed direct measurement of these barriers and focused instead on inferring their impact indirectly by examining differences in predicted and actual trade volumes. These studies have been virtually unanimous in their conclusion that Japan's low volume of manufactured imports cannot be entirely explained by economic fundamentals.

In addition to examining quantities, one can look at prices. If markets were really open, traded goods should sell at "international prices" adjusted for transport costs. A number of studies have concluded that traded-goods prices are far higher in Japan than in other countries. Among these surveys were two involving exact brand and model comparisons conducted by the Department of Commerce and the Japanese Ministry of International Trade and Industry as part of the Structural Impediments Initiative talks. The 1991 survey found that two-thirds of the products covered were on average 37 percent more expensive in Japan than in the United States; the 1989 survey obtained quantitatively similar results. Additional evidence comes from Japanese researchers who used Japan's input-output table to calculate the tariff-equivalents of Japanese nontariff barriers. In some sectors they discovered tariff-equivalents of 500 percent and higher.

The question naturally arises as to why these price differences are not eliminated through arbitrage. Such large price differentials could perhaps be dismissed as the product of exchange-rate misalignment, were they temporary, but their persistence suggests that they are the product of market closure. Indeed, one recent study concluded that Japanese manufactured imports might increase by more than 20 percent if the price differentials were eliminated.

These studies, which extrapolate well beyond the historical experience and are therefore unavoidably imprecise, have reached a variety of conclusions as to the importance of economic policy in determining Japanese trade patterns. The preponderance of evidence, however, points to the closed nature of the Japanese market. According to one recent comprehensive study, if Japan were to eliminate all formal and informal barriers to trade, U.S. exports to Japan would initially increase by somewhere in the range of $9 billion to $18 billion per year.

It should be made clear, however, that even if these barriers were eliminated, the bilateral balance would not change by this full amount: Japanese imports would increase initially, but the resultant depreciation of the yen and reallocation of resources would boost Japanese exports and reduce Japanese imports, at least partly offsetting the initial change in the balance. Moreover, liberalization would occur over an extended period of time, making it potentially difficult to disentangle changes in the balance due to liberalization from those due to macroeconomic developments, even in retrospect but this in no way diminishes the desirability of obtaining greater access to the Japanese market, though. With more-open markets not only will American firms sell more but, because of the exchange-rate adjustments, many American firms will receive more for what they sell. Moreover, Japanese consumers will benefit—for the same reasons that American consumers benefit—from opening trade: Both will have access to a greater variety of goods at lower prices. Open markets are a win-win situation in which both sides gain.

The existence of such a large, technologically dynamic, and distinctive economy as Japan poses special trade problems for the United States. Current U.S. policy centers around the United States-Japan Framework for a New Economic Partnership, announced in July 1993. The Framework is the successor to the 1985–86 Market Oriented Sector Selective (MOSS) talks and the SII talks already mentioned. The Framework document adopted at the time of the 1993 Tokyo economic summit calls for macroeconomic, sectoral, and structural reforms and cooperation on global issues of common interest such as the environment. In particular, Japan committed itself to "actively pursue the medium-run objectives of promoting strong and sustainable domestic demand-led growth...intended to achieve...a highly significant decrease in its current account surplus...." Japan also committed to "promoting a significant increase in global imports of goods and services." For its part, the United States "will...actively pursue the medium-term objectives of substantially reducing the fiscal deficit, promoting domestic saving, and strengthening its international competitiveness."

The sectoral and structural parts of the talks are organized into five baskets: government procurement, regulatory reform and competitiveness, other major sectors (in the first instance, automobiles and auto parts), economic harmonization, and implementation of existing arrangements and measures. Topics under the government procurement basket include Japanese procurement practices in such sectors as computers, supercomputers, satellites, medical technology, and telecommunications, as well as overall government procurement policies in both countries. Regulatory issues include policies and practices relating to financial services, insurance, competition policy, retail and wholesale distribution, and U.S. export competitiveness. Economic harmonization covers foreign direct investment, intellectual property rights, access to technology, and long-term buyer-supplier relationships. The implementation basket is concerned with carrying out existing agreements between the two countries (including SII). The Framework agreement explicitly states that the United States and Japan are committed to the multilateral trading system and that "benefits under this Framework will be on a Most Favored Nation basis."

The Framework represents a departure from previous negotiations in two substantive ways. The first is the use of "objective criteria" to assess progress. The Framework agreement states that "assessment will be based upon sets of objective criteria, either qualitative or quantitative or both as appropriate," on which the two governments will agree. In this sense the negotiation is results-oriented, with both governments agreeing that "tangible progress must be achieved." By establishing objective criteria, progress can be independently verified, allowing negotiators to agree on those areas where problems have successfully been resolved and to focus on those where progress is lacking.

The other innovation of the Framework talks is procedural: By explicitly incorporating biannual meetings between the President of the United States and the Prime Minister of Japan, the Framework dramatically raises the political profile of the negotiations. The hope is that this will significantly increase the pressure on policymakers to make steady progress on resolving outstanding issues.

Trade with China

China is also an important focus of U.S. trade policy because of its size, its reforming economy, and its large trade surplus with the United States, which reached $18.3 billion in 1992.

It is misleading to focus exclusively on China's bilateral balance with the United States. Table 6–4 reports trade balances for China, Taiwan, and Hong Kong and aggregates them as "Greater China." It becomes apparent that the increase in the U.S. deficit with China has been largely offset by declines in the U.S. deficits with Taiwan and Hong Kong. These developments are the result of large realignments in exchange rates since the late 1980s that have encouraged firms to relocate labor-intensive activities, such as the production of shoes, garments, and toys, from Hong Kong and Taiwan to China, where wage rates are lower. In other words, the growing U.S.-China trade imbalance represents in part a geographic reallocation of production, not a fundamental change in U.S. trade relations.

With regard to China, U.S. trade policy centers on prison labor and workers' rights, intellectual property rights, market access, textiles, services, and the issue of China's most-favored-nation (MFN) status. In the area of intellectual property rights, the United States and China signed a memorandum of understanding in January 1992. China agreed to provide product patent protection beginning January 1, 1993, and to adhere to international conventions on the protection of copyrights. A process has been established to enforce the memorandum, although there has been little actual progress on enforcement thus far.

In October 1992 the United States and China signed a market access agreement, under which China committed itself to increase the transparency of its trade regime, to remove import restrictions such as licensing requirements and quotas from hundreds of products, and to liberalize its import administration substantially. The United States agreed to liberalize restrictions that limit Chinese access to technology, providing greater opportunities for U.S. producers. China is largely in compliance with the market access agreement, although some issues remain unresolved with respect to transparency, quotas, and agricultural trade. The Administration is continuing to push for greater access in these areas, as well as for better access to the Chinese market for U.S. providers of financial, maritime, and air transport services.

A memorandum of understanding on exports to the United States produced by prison labor was concluded in 1992 and provides for prison inspections. China has begun to allow U.S. officials access to prisons to investigate allegations, and there has been a decline in such allegations since the memorandum was signed. China continues to be denied coverage under investment guarantees of the Overseas Private Investment Corporation, however. Coverage was suspended in 1990 on the grounds that China was not taking steps to extend internationally recognized workers' rights to its citizens.

In the case of textiles, conflicts have arisen over China's shortcomings in implementing the terms of the Multi-Fiber Arrangement, which regulates trade in textiles and apparel. Chinese producers have at times resorted to fraudulent practices to evade restrictions on Chinese exports of textiles and apparel to the United States. The most common technique has been to ship goods produced in China to third countries, and from there reexport them to the United States under the third countries' quotas. In January 1994 the United States and China reached a new agreement on this issue. In the long run, the transshipment problem can be solved through China's entry into GATT and the tariffication of the U.S. import control system as envisioned in the Uruguay Round agreement (discussed below). In the meantime, however, the United States will continue its two-track policy of negotiations with the Chinese government combined with criminal prosecutions for customs fraud.

The last major remaining U.S.-China issue is the annual renewal of China's MFN status. Under the terms of the Jackson-Vanik Amendment to the Trade Act of 1974, MFN status can be extended to nonmarket economies only if the President grants a waiver certifying that the country does not impede emigration. (The law was originally designed to encourage the Soviet Union to permit the emigration of Soviet Jews.) China first gained MFN status in the U.S. market in 1980, and renewal was routine until the Tiananmen Square incident in 1989. Since then, renewal of China's MFN status has become increasingly controversial, with renewal in 1994 tied explicitly to human rights improvements.

In each trade area, the Administration is carefully monitoring Chinese implementation of the bilateral agreements and will use all means at its disposal to ensure compliance. Successful implementation will lay the foundation for Chinese accession to GATT and a far closer economic relationship between the United States and China.

Trade and the Reform Process in the Former Socialist Bloc

Another crucial focus of the Administration's foreign economic policy is support of the reform process in the countries of central and eastern Europe and the former Soviet Union, especially Russia. Never before has a country of Russia's size and influence (with a population of 150 million, a large conventional military presence, and nuclear weapons) attempted such a rapid metamorphosis. Because of the immediate implications of Russian economic reform for world peace, world economic growth, and the U.S. economy, the President has made support of the reforms one of his top foreign policy objectives. This involves both providing assistance to domestic reforms and facilitating the integration of Russia into the world trading system.

Most of the fundamental issues in economic reform—including liberalization (the freeing of prices), privatization (the transfer of ownership to private entities), and stabilization (the reduction of inflation and the budget deficit)—are essentially Russia's domestic policy decisions. Nevertheless, outside organizations including the International Monetary Fund, the World Bank, the Group of Seven (G–7), and the U.S. Government have important roles to play. Indeed, along with its G–7 partners, the United States has been actively assisting the cause of economic reform in Russia. In April 1993 the G–7 pledged $15 billion of debt rescheduling and $28.4 billion in other assistance. By the end of November over half of this total had been approved.

Economic assistance packages such as the one presented in Tokyo constitute a significant source of finance for reform policies. But Russian exports to the West represent another, perhaps even more important, source of hard-currency revenues. Because the trade patterns of Russia and the other transitional economies were formerly based on arbitrary central planning decisions, not market forces, these countries have encountered difficulties in establishing normal commercial relations with other countries. The transition to a market economy has involved dramatic changes in both the product content and geographical composition of trading patterns. After most of these changes have been effected, Russia may be a substantial participant in world trade. Russia's share of U.S. trade is quite small (0.4 percent of total U.S. trade), but one study found that if the states of the former Soviet Union were like typical industrial economies, their share of world exports would eventually rise to over 10 percent, from around 4 percent in 1988. Through the first 9 months of 1993, Russia's two most important exports to the United States were aluminum ($326 million) and crude oil ($131 million), which together accounted for more than 40 percent of the total.

Expanding trade with economies in transition from socialism raises special problems for the application of U.S. antidumping laws, which divide the world into market and nonmarket economies (NMEs), with separate methodologies for assessing dumping specified for each. (Russia, for example, is classified as an NME.) For market economies, dumping is determined to have occurred when a foreign producer charges lower prices in the U.S. than in its home market (or, alternatively, prices below its costs in the home market). In the case of NMEs, since neither prices nor input costs are market determined, they are not used in dumping investigations. Instead, U.S. law instructs the Commerce Department to construct cost estimates based on costs in a "surrogate" country at a similar stage of development. In practice, the surrogates are often at quite *dis*similar stages of development, thus potentially tilting the calculation toward finding large dumping margins. For example, the Department of Commerce has used Swiss, Canadian, Dutch, French, German, and Japanese producers as surrogates for Chinese firms in antidumping petitions. Perhaps the best known example, however, is that of Polish golf carts, described in Box 6-2.

> **Box 6-2.—The Case of the Polish Golf Carts**
>
> In the mid-1970s an antidumping petition was filed against Polish electric golf carts. Because Poland was an NME that had no golf courses and therefore little domestic demand for golf carts, the U.S. authorities rightly concluded that it was impossible to compare the prices at which the carts were sold in the United States with prices in Poland. Instead, the authorities employed a surrogate-country approach: they attempted to estimate what golf carts cost in a country similar to Poland. Canada was chosen. Unfortunately, Canada didn't produce golf carts either, so the final determination was based on an estimate of what golf carts would have cost in Canada— if Canada had actually produced them.

Reclassification of NMEs such as Russia as market economies would not necessarily solve the problem, however, since they would then become subject to U.S. countervailing duty law at a time when their subsidies to state-owned producers remain sizable. As a result, either the market or the nonmarket methodology may impede imports from economies in transition.

This situation is particularly problematic since allowing Russia and other economies in transition to export the goods in which they have comparative advantage benefits both these economies (which obtain valuable hard-currency revenues as well as experience in world markets) and Western nations (which obtain goods produced relatively more efficiently than they can be produced in the West). Open market access is therefore a positive-sum means of encouraging the reform process.

REGIONAL INITIATIVES

Some issues cannot be handled on a bilateral basis, and the Administration has been deeply engaged in a number of regional efforts. The most prominent of these has been the North American Free Trade Agreement, which will solidify the ongoing reforms in Mexico and help expand U.S.-Mexican trade.

The North American Free Trade Agreement

In November 1993 the Congress ratified the North American Free Trade Agreement, which went into effect on January 1, 1994. NAFTA creates a free-trade area of 370 million consumers and over $6.5 trillion of annual output, linking the United States to Canada and Mexico, our largest and third-largest trading partners. Building on the earlier United States–Canada Free-Trade Agreement, NAFTA will contribute to productive efficiency, enhance the ability of North American producers to compete globally, and raise the standard of living of all three countries. By improving the investment climate in North America, and by providing innovative companies with a larger market, NAFTA will also increase economic growth.

NAFTA will help reinforce the market reforms already under way in Mexico (Box 6–3). Mexico's reforms have raised its rate of economic growth, making it an increasingly important export market for the United States. A stable and prosperous Mexico is important to the United States for both economic and geopolitical reasons. The United States shares a border roughly 2,000 miles long with Mexico; and as economic opportunities in Mexico improve, Mexican workers will have fewer incentives to migrate to the United States. NAFTA will help forge a lasting relationship between the two countries, based on open trade and cooperation.

In addition to dismantling trade barriers in industrial goods, NAFTA includes agreements on services, investment, intellectual property rights, agriculture, and strengthening of trade rules. There are also side agreements on labor adjustment provisions, protection of the environment, and import surges.

> **Box 6–3.—Mexican Economic Reforms**
>
> Mexico is one of the outstanding economic success stories of the last decade. After the debt crisis of 1982, the Mexican government began a broad program of economic reform, which has continued through the early 1990s. Fiscal policy changes, which moved the primary budget (that is, excluding interest payments) from a deficit of about 7 percent of GDP in 1982 to a sustained surplus, were the first step. More-fundamental reform began in December 1987 when the Mexican government implemented a concerted program that combined macroeconomic stabilization with microeconomic liberalization.
>
> Stabilization efforts in 1989–91 were pursued through a fiscal policy of tight spending controls and tax reform that broadened the tax base and lowered tax rates, while maintaining a roughly stable level of revenue. Monetary and exchange-rate policies were combined to reduce inflation while preventing large exchange-rate movements. Finally, incomes policies were used to reduce expectations of inflation and any inflationary inertia.
>
> The microeconomic reforms were sweeping. More than 80 percent of the 1,155 public sector enterprises in existence in 1982 have already been privatized or liquidated. Privatization has enhanced microeconomic efficiency and reduced the fiscal demands imposed by badly run state-owned enterprises. In addition, Mexico joined GATT in 1986. Tariffs were cut sharply and many nontariff barriers to trade, such as quotas and import licenses, were removed. Finally, a renegotiation and restructuring of Mexico's external debt eased its debt burden and greatly reduced the uncertainty associated with debt service.
>
> The results of these reforms have been impressive. Inflation fell from approximately 160 percent in 1987 to 12 percent in 1992. At the same time, real GDP growth rose from –3.8 percent in 1986 to 4.5 percent in 1990 before slowing somewhat to 2.6 percent in 1992. The recent passage of NAFTA should strengthen the reform effort in Mexico and make a positive contribution to its economic performance in the future.

NAFTA and Industrial Trade. As a result of NAFTA, existing duties on most goods from member countries either were eliminated on January 1, 1994, or will be phased out in 5 or 10 years (for certain sensitive items, up to 15 years). Among those industrial goods for which trade is now tariff-free are computers, medical equipment, agricultural equipment, internal combustion engines, and telephone switches, all of which previously faced tariffs of 10 percent or more in the Mexican market. Approximately 65 percent of U.S. industrial and agricultural exports to Mexico will be eligible for duty-free treatment within 5 years. NAFTA will also eliminate quotas and import licenses that are not essential for such purposes as protecting human health.

NAFTA and Services Trade. NAFTA will allow U.S. service firms to provide their services directly from the United States on a nondiscriminatory basis, with any exceptions clearly spelled out. For investors, NAFTA assures nondiscriminatory treatment: Americans will generally be able to establish, acquire, and operate firms on the same basis as Mexicans in Mexico and Canadians in Canada. NAFTA also protects U.S. investors against restrictions on their repatriation of capital, profits, and royalties, and against expropriations without full compensation. Investors can seek monetary relief from an international arbitral panel for violation of their rights.

Virtually all types of inventions, including pharmaceuticals and agricultural chemicals, are protected under NAFTA provisions that require patents to be granted for both products and processes developed by firms in member countries. The agreement also protects copyrights for computer programs and databases, and rental rights for computer programs and sound recordings. Service marks and trade secrets are also covered, along with integrated circuit masks both directly and as components of other products.

NAFTA and Agricultural Trade. NAFTA will virtually eliminate barriers to trade in agricultural commodities between the United States and Mexico over a 15-year period. All restrictions on products representing about 50 percent of U.S.-Mexico agricultural trade were lifted as soon as the agreement took effect. Products such as frozen beef, strawberries, and cut flowers—all of which previously were subject to tariffs of 20 percent or more in the Mexican market—now trade tariff-free. For the remaining products, the phaseout will take between 5 and 15 years. The phaseout for most tariffs imposed by the United States will simply involve an annual reduction in the tariff rate.

In cases where the existing trade barrier is a nontariff barrier, such as an import license or quota, the phaseout process is more complicated. First, the license or quota will be replaced by a "tariff-rate quota," allowing a limited quantity of the good to be imported at a low (or zero) tariff rate, but charging a tariff for quantities above the limit. Second, the tariff-rate quota will be phased out gradually over a 10- to 15-year period by increasing the quantity limit and/or reducing the tariff rate applied to imports above the limit.

With respect to the other bilateral flows, U.S.-Canada trade liberalization will continue as specified under the earlier free-trade agreement, with tariffs on all agricultural goods eliminated by

1998, while nontariff barriers on a few products (poultry, eggs, dairy products, and sugar) are maintained. In a separate agreement under NAFTA, Mexico and Canada will eliminate tariffs on their bilateral trade (except for the four products listed above). All three countries agreed to work for the elimination of agricultural exports subsidies.

As a consequence of these changes under NAFTA, U.S.-Mexico agricultural trade is expected to grow significantly. U.S. corn growers, for example, can expect to export more corn to Mexico, while Mexican farmers can expect to export more fresh vegetables to the Untied States.

NAFTA-Plus: The Side Agreements. The Clinton Administration accepted NAFTA as negotiated by its predecessor, but argued that more was needed. The result was the negotiation of three innovative side agreements.

The North American Agreement on Labor Cooperation represents the first attempt to manage the terms of the potential change in labor markets brought about by an accord between the United States and a trading partner. The agreement involves such issues as restrictions on child labor, health and safety standards, and minimum wages. The supplemental labor agreement was developed around three fundamental principles: (1) enhanced collaboration, cooperation, and information exchange among the three countries; (2) increased efforts to make each country's labor laws and their implementation explicit and highly visible; and (3) increased use of effective mechanisms to encourage the enforcement of national labor laws. The agreement establishes procedural mechanisms for enforcement, including channels of public communication, exchanges of information, discussion of issues, and various levels of consultations. If a solution cannot be reached, the agreement provides for binding arbitration and assessment of penalties. In addition to signing the labor side agreement, the Mexican government has pledged to link increases in the Mexican minimum wage to productivity increases. Moreover, the United States has retained its right to use its domestic trade laws, such as Section 301 of the 1974 trade act, with respect to labor issues not covered under NAFTA.

The North American Agreement on Environmental Cooperation explicitly ensures our right to safeguard the environment. NAFTA maintains all existing U.S. health, safety, and environmental standards. It allows States and cities to enact even tougher standards, while providing mechanisms to encourage all parties to harmonize their standards upward. The environmental side agreement creates a new North American Commission on Environmental Cooperation, with a Council made up of the three countries' top environmental officials. The Commission will have a Secretariat with a permanent staff. There is a "layered" enforcement mechanism to ensure that countries obey their own environmental laws. The mechanism starts with "sunshine" provisions that guarantee public participation in monitoring the enforcement of environmental laws. Trade sanctions are then provided for, if other avenues are not sufficient to resolve disputes. Besides the Commission, two new institutions will be established to fund and implement environmental infrastructure projects along the U.S.-Mexican border.

The side agreement on import surges creates an early warning mechanism to identify those sectors where explosive trade growth may do significant harm to domestic industry. The side agreement also establishes that, in the future, a working group can provide for revisions in the treaty text based on the experience with the existing safeguard mechanisms.

During the transition period, safeguard relief is available in the form of a temporary snapback to pre-NAFTA duties if an import surge threatens serious injury to a domestic industry. And, unless a NAFTA member's exports account for a substantial share of total imports and contribute significantly to the injury or its threat, these exports must be excluded from safeguard actions taken by other members against imports from all countries.

Other NAFTA Issues. NAFTA preserves the right of each member to retain its own contingent protection laws (such as antidumping and countervailing duty laws), but in reviewing determination under these laws, binational panels will replace domestic judicial review (as in the case of the United States–Canada Free-Trade Agreement). The panel will apply to domestic law of the importing country, and its decision is final. Either the importing or the exporting country may request a review of a panel's determination.

In other areas, such as intellectual property rights, dispute resolution is layered. First, a country may request consultations, and should these fail to resolve the dispute, it may call a meeting of the Trade Commission, which will include Ministers from each country. If the Commission is unable to resolve the dispute, it is submitted to an arbitral panel which issues a report. If the panel upholds the complaint, but the disputants are still unable to reach a resolution, the complaining country is authorized to suspend benefits as appropriate.

The North American Development Bank (NADBank) was created to address concerns about the environment and about worker dislocation. It will serve as a major lending institution to finance, coordinate, and implement environmental, infrastructure, and community development projects, both along the border and elsewhere, related to continuing North American integration. NADBank will be organized to invest specifically in the environmental, physical, and social infrastructure that will be needed to bring about an upward convergence in environmental and social standards and practices between Mexico and the United States. In this way it will facilitate the adjustment of workers adversely impacted by NAFTA-related trade liberalization. The bank will be capitalized to provide $2 billion to $3 billion in loans and guarantees and will be able to leverage additional private and public funds, to generate an estimated total of $20 billion in project finance.

The Economic Impact of NAFTA. NAFTA may be the most thoroughly studied trade agreement in history. A review of the major studies of NAFTA's economic impact indicates a broad consensus on key points in the NAFTA debate: (1) All three NAFTA countries gain from the agreement. (2) In the United States, labor will gain from increased employment, increased wages, or both. (3) Increased investment in Mexico will not come at the expense of investment in the United States. The few studies reaching contrary conclusions have been strongly criticized by academic and other professional economists.

In a letter to the President, 286 academic economists, including 13 Nobel Prize winners, expressed their support for NAFTA, stating, "While we may not agree on the precise employment impact of NAFTA, we do concur that the agreement will be a net positive for the United States, both in terms of employment creation and overall economic growth." Nineteen out of twenty studies surveyed found that NAFTA would benefit the United States; the lone negative assessment was based on the unrealistic assumption that factories literally would be dismantled in the United States and moved to Mexico.

It has been estimated that the agreement will increase export employment in the United States by 200,000 jobs; on average Mexican export-related jobs pay wages 12 percent higher than the national average. Moreover, studies of NAFTA have found that gains would occur even among groups sometimes alleged to be adversely affected. For example, it was found that union workers will benefit from NAFTA because the growing sectors of U.S. exports to Mexico are disproportionately unionized. Likewise, African-American workers are more heavily concentrated in industries that export to Mexico than in Mexican import-competing sectors. As a result, African-Americans too may benefit disproportionately from the agreement. Finally, by contributing to the creation of more and better jobs in Mexico, NAFTA will discourage illegal immigration from Mexico to the United States.

In summary, NAFTA is an epochal agreement, and its passage was a triumph of facts over fear. It is the world's first free-trade agreement between industrial and developing countries. Its side agreements embody innovative ideas to deal with environmental and labor issues. The best available evidence shows that NAFTA will create good, high-paying jobs for American workers. It will strengthen the ability of U.S. firms to compete in the global marketplace. It will help the Mexican and Canadian economies as well, providing a disincentive for illegal transborder migration and other illegal activities. The Administration's trade policy can be described as "export activism"—the United States will work actively to open foreign markets, and in return we will keep our market open. NAFTA is a key component of this activist strategy.

Asia-Pacific Economic Cooperation

The Asia-Pacific Economic Cooperation (APEC) was begun in 1989 to encourage economic cooperation among countries of the Pacific region. In the past quarter-century, the United States' APEC partners—Australia, Brunei, Canada, China, Hong Kong, Indonesia, Japan, Malaysia, Mexico, New Zealand, Papua New Guinea, the Philippines, the Republic of Korea, Singapore, Chinese Taipei (Taiwan), and Thailand—have increased their combined share of world income and trade by more than half (Box 6–4). These economies now account for more than half of all U.S. trade, or more than triple U.S. trade with the European Union. Even if Canada and Mexico are excluded from the calculation, U.S. trade with other APEC countries is 76 percent greater than our trade with the EU countries.

One consequence of this rapid growth is striking: as long as the Asian countries grow faster than the United States, they will become more important in our trade while we will become less important in theirs. Therefore past trade strategies based on threats of market closure are liable to become less and less effective.

This analysis suggests that, to achieve its trade policy goals in the region, the United States will increasingly have to act in concert with other countries rather than unilaterally. Thus it may be desirable to begin establishing the appropriate institutional infrastructure for cooperation now, and APEC is the leading candidate. The United States held the rotating chairmanship of APEC in 1993 and hosted the annual Ministerial meeting in Seattle in November, which was attended by economic policymakers from each of its members. The President elevated the importance of APEC by hosting the first-ever meeting of APEC leaders in Seattle.

At the APEC Ministerial meeting, a group of private individuals previously commissioned by the APEC Ministers to serve as an Eminent Persons Group presented its report. The report described the threats to trade and investment in the region and recommended ways to promote regional trade liberalization and cooperation. The Ministers indicated that those recommendations closely linked to ongoing work in APEC should be implemented promptly. These include recommendations to achieve a common set of investment principles, harmonize standards, and create a mecha-

Box 6-4.—The Asian "Miracle"

Per capita gross national product (GNP) in East Asia grew, on average, by over 5 percent per year between 1965 and 1990. During the same period, per capita GNP in the industrialized countries that make up the Organization for Economic Cooperation and Development (OECD) grew by less than 2.5 percent per year. What explains this relatively rapid growth in East Asia? A recent World Bank book argues that a major part of the explanation is that the average OECD member was much more technologically advanced than the average East Asian country in 1965. By adopting and adapting techniques from the industrial countries, the East Asian countries were able to increase both productivity levels and per capita GNP at a rapid pace.

This is undoubtedly true. But other countries that were poor in 1965 did not grow as fast as the successful East Asian nations. Why did East Asia experience faster growth? One key factor is almost certainly the macroeconomic environment: inflation and budget deficits were kept relatively low, and national currencies were kept from becoming overvalued. Macroeconomic policies encouraged, or at least did not discourage, high saving and investment rates as well as strong export growth. Governments also emphasized education. The focus was primarily on the quality of basic education, rather than on higher education. As a result of these policies, East Asian countries accumulated substantial physical and human capital, which spurred relatively rapid growth in GNP per capita.

The impact of other, more interventionist policies on growth in several East Asian countries remains a source of controversy. Some government interventions in the market may have improved economic performance, particularly when they were not excessively distortionary, were administered competently, were aimed at particular market imperfections, and were adapted to meet changing circumstances.

The Asian countries are expected to account for increasing shares of world income and trade. By 2000 it is likely that Asia will have surpassed North America and Europe as the world's largest economic zone. As its share of world income rises, so will its share of world trade—the Asian share of U.S. trade is projected to rise to 40 percent by the end of the decade.

nism for resolving trade and investment disputes. Other recommendations, relating to deepening and broadening the Uruguay Round of GATT, were singled out for additional study. The APEC leaders instructed the Eminent Persons Group to elaborate on their recommendations relating to longer term trade liberalization in a report to be presented to the leaders in 1994 in Indonesia.

MULTILATERAL INITIATIVES: THE URUGUAY ROUND

The most far-reaching of the Administration's market-opening efforts has been on a global scale: the Uruguay Round negotiations of GATT, whose 116 participating countries account for approximately 85 percent of world trade. GATT was created after World War II to reduce tariffs and remove nontariff barriers to international trade. In seven rounds of GATT-sponsored multilateral trade negotiations (the Uruguay Round is the eighth), the member countries have lowered tariffs and agreed on codes of conduct for nontariff barriers.

In the Uruguay Round negotiations, effectively completed on December 15, 1993, the United States and other GATT members agreed not only to lower tariffs on merchandise trade, but also to integrate into GATT certain areas of trade and investment that had not been subject to effective GATT discipline, including agriculture, textiles, trade in services, investment, and intellectual property rights. The Uruguay Round also made progress in reforming multilateral dispute settlement procedures and other multilateral trade rules, including those dealing with nontariff measures. The Congress is expected to ratify this agreement this year.

The stakes in the Uruguay Round negotiations were enormous. In the short run, failure to complete the Round would have significantly undermined business confidence around the globe and might have contributed to the erosion of the open trading system. In the long run, the successful completion of the Round will mean a major boost to the world economy. Preliminary studies suggest that the likely gains to the U.S. economy alone are more than $100 billion but less than $200 billion annually by 2005 (Box 6–5). These efficiency gains will manifest themselves in the form of more and better jobs for American workers.

The Round achieved major reductions in trade barriers facing industrial products. Key provisions of the market access agreement include the following:

- Tariffs imposed by major industrial countries are to be eliminated, and those of many developing countries either eliminated or sharply reduced, in the following areas: construction equipment, agricultural equipment, medical equipment, steel, beer, distilled spirits, pharmaceuticals, paper, toys, and furniture.

> **Box 6-5.—The Economic Impact of the Uruguay Round**
>
> Even before the Uruguay Round was completed, researchers were attempting to quantify its likely effects on the American economy. Studies based on existing formal economic models unanimously conclude that these effects will be beneficial. It is quite likely that new studies incorporating some of the Round's final accomplishments in such areas as intellectual property protection will yield even larger estimates of benefits.
>
> The Uruguay Round will increase American output because the specialization encouraged by more-open markets will raise productivity. As foreign markets open, we will produce more of the goods that make use of the highly skilled, highly productive U.S. work force. Economic models offer a range of estimates of the output gain from greater specialization. A recent OECD study estimates those gains to be 0.4 percent of GDP for the United States. But this is almost certainly a gross underestimate of the impact of the Round, because it ignores a host of important factors, including gains from specialization *within* the manufacturing sector. Another study by World Bank and OECD economists estimates even smaller gains, but focuses on agriculture. Studies that more adequately capture gains from specialization suggest that the benefit to the U.S. economy is likely to be approximately 1 percent of GDP after the Uruguay Round tariff cuts are fully phased in.
>
> Other important sources of benefit are not captured by the existing models, which do not quantify the impact of trade liberalization in services or enhanced protection of intellectual property rights. In addition, higher productivity will result in increased investment and innovation, providing an important additional benefit. These additional gains are difficult to quantify, but they are almost certainly sizable and may even exceed the more easily quantified gains. The total gain 10 years after implementation of the agreement begins is then likely to be more than $100 billion but less than $200 billion annually.

- Major U.S. trading partners agreed to deep tariff cuts, ranging from 50 to 100 percent, on important electronics items including semiconductors, computer parts, and semiconductor manufacturing equipment.
- Tariffs of industrial and major developing countries on chemical products are to be harmonized at very low rates (zero, 5.5, or 6.5 percent, according to product).
- The agreement significantly increased access to markets representing approximately 85 percent of world trade by reducing tariffs on certain specific items of key interest to U.S. export-

ers. Progress in textiles and apparel was particularly significant. For decades, international trade in textiles and apparel products has effectively been exempted from GATT rules. Instead, the Multi-Fiber Arrangement establishes a procedure for limiting textile and apparel exports from developing to industrial countries. Under the final Uruguay Round agreement, products covered by the Multi-Fiber Arrangement will be free of quotas after 10 years, and textiles will be integrated into general GATT rules. Tariffs will be reduced as well.

Throughout the Uruguay Round negotiations, one of the most contentious issues was agricultural trade liberalization. The final agreement on agriculture strengthens the long-term rules for agricultural trade and sharply limits national policies that distort that trade. U.S. agricultural exports will benefit significantly from reductions in foreign export subsidies and from market opening by our trading partners.

The United States was successful in its effort to obtain meaningful rules and explicit commitments to reduce export subsidies, cut domestic subsidies, and increase market access. Agricultural export subsidies and trade-distorting domestic farm subsidies are not only to be reduced, but for the first time will be subject to explicit multilateral disciplines. The United States also prevailed in establishing the principle of comprehensive tariffication, which will lead to the eventual removal of all import quotas and other nontariff import barriers. Nontariff barriers will first be replaced by tariffs, ensuring minimum or current access, and then these tariffs will gradually be reduced.

Progress in creating a more hospitable trading system for high-technology products was achieved on two fronts. First, the United States was able to win greater protection for intellectual property rights, such as patents, copyrights, and trademarks. This is very important for a diverse set of U.S. industries, including the electronics industry (where semiconductor masks will be protected), the pharmaceutical industry (patents), and the communications industry (protection of copyrights).

Second, the Uruguay Round agreement sets forth multilateral rules governing subsidies. Because of the beneficial social spillovers associated with research and development activities, government support cannot and should not be ruled out altogether. The challenge for the multilateral trading system is to find rules that permit governments to support innovations that benefit all nations while precluding rent-shifting subsidies designed to benefit one nation at the expense of others. The Uruguay Round agreement makes progress in this respect by establishing clearer rules and stronger disciplines in the subsidies area. It also makes nonactionable certain subsidies relating to basic research, regional development, and environmental cleanup, provided they are subject to conditions designed to limit their distorting effects.

Negotiators were able to agree on comprehensive GATT rules governing trade and investment in services (the so-called General Agreement on Trade in Services, or GATS), such as telecommunications, professional, and financial services. The agreement contains a strong national-treatment provision: Member countries must accord to service suppliers of other countries treatment no less favorable than that accorded their own suppliers. GATS also includes a market access provision that incorporates disciplines on discriminatory measures that governments frequently impose to limit competition. These measures include restrictions on the number of firms allowed into the market, "economic need" tests, and mandatory local incorporation rules. Because of the breadth and complexity of these issues, not as much progress was made as was desirable. To realize additional progress, GATS establishes a procedural framework for further negotiation.

The Uruguay Round negotiations also yielded systematic prohibitions on trade-related investment measures. For example, the agreement prohibits so-called local content requirements, which force foreign firms to use a set amount of locally produced inputs as a condition for investment. It also prohibits "trade balancing" requirements, under which a foreign affiliate must export as much of its production as it imports for use as inputs. These requirements have bedeviled U.S. firms operating abroad in the past.

Lastly, the Uruguay Round agreement prohibits so-called voluntary export restraints and other, similar measures that are often used as safeguards outside GATT rules. It also provides specific time limits for the formation and operation of dispute settlement panels and requires the automatic adoption of panel reports (except in the case of unanimous veto). Previously, any country, including the country against which the complaint was lodged, could effectively block the implementation of a panel's decision. The new procedures will greatly expedite the resolution of international trade disputes. The members of GATT agreed to establish a new multilateral organization, to be called the World Trade Organization (WTO), to enforce these new agreements.

In summary, the U.S. negotiators in the Uruguay Round were successful in negotiating broad-ranging multilateral trade liberalization. This was accomplished by reducing existing barriers and bringing areas of trade that had been largely outside the GATT system, such as agriculture, textiles, intellectual property, and services, under the GATT rubric. At the same time, GATT procedures have been strengthened to ensure that signatories meet their obligations, without compromising our ability to implement our national trade or other laws (Box 6–6). The liberalization of global trade resulting from these substantive and procedural achievements will raise real incomes in the United States by billions of dollars annually in the coming years.

> **Box 6–6.—The Uruguay Round and U.S. Trade Laws**
>
> The Uruguay Round final agreement contains a number of provisions that will enhance dispute resolution and facilitate better enforcement of U.S. rights. The agreement both moves GATT procedures closer to U.S. laws and complements U.S. laws for dealing with unfair foreign trade practices.
>
> Section 301 of the Trade Act of 1974 provides the basis for actions to enforce U.S. rights under trade agreements and to respond to foreign practices that impede or restrict U.S. exports. When disputes arise in areas covered by GATT, Section 301 requires the United States to use GATT dispute resolution procedures before undertaking unilateral action. The Uruguay Round brings agriculture, textiles, and services under GATT rules for the first time and enhances the speed and effectiveness of GATT dispute resolution procedures. As a result, the United States can now use GATT to accomplish objectives that formerly required unilateral action. When disputes arise in areas outside the GATT framework, the United States can still use Section 301 to combat unfair foreign trade practices.
>
> The Uruguay Round brings GATT closer to U.S. practices in other areas. For example, in dealing with food safety measures, the Uruguay Round agreement allows countries to choose their own levels of safety but requires that each country's standards have a scientific basis and not be used as disguised trade barriers. Because U.S. laws already have a scientific basis, it is unlikely that they will be susceptible to challenge. Other countries, however, have used food safety regulations in an arbitrary manner to block imports. The agreement adopts similar provisions for dealing with technical barriers to trade, such as so-called conformity assessment procedures (registration, inspection, and laboratory accreditation procedures, among others) used to evaluate conformance with technical regulations.
>
> Antidumping is another area in which the post–Uruguay Round GATT will become more like U.S. trade laws. The United States has a transparent process for implementing its antidumping laws. The Uruguay Round agreement will make foreign antidumping actions more transparent, which should help U.S. exporters by improving the fairness of other countries' antidumping procedures.

THE TRADE POLICY AGENDA

By lowering tariffs and providing a framework for cooperation in international trade, GATT has contributed significantly to a more harmonious world trading regime. But new issues in trade policy are coming to the fore as the world economy evolves. Among the important new issues confronting GATT and the new WTO will be issues relating to trade and the environment, competition policies, and regionalism.

TRADE AND THE ENVIRONMENT

Trade and environmental issues have become intertwined in recent years. Some accuse GATT of being hostile to the environment, while others argue that some countries' environmental policies are thinly veiled protectionism. In reality, protectionism often contributes to environmental degradation by encouraging inappropriate patterns of production. An obvious example is agricultural protection, which stimulates agricultural production in poorly suited locations. Farmers in these areas overuse chemicals or exhaust scarce water resources to compensate for their natural disadvantages, thereby contributing to environmental degradation. Freer trade would encourage more-appropriate patterns of production and improve the environment even as it increased living standards.

Standard economic analysis suggests offsetting government action when prices fail to reflect environmental costs (Chapter 5). But trade restraints are rarely the best solution to environmental problems. If the environmental problem is limited to one country, domestic policies, not trade protection, should be employed. If pollution or other environmental problems spill across borders, international rules and cooperation will be necessary. But here again trade protection will seldom be the most effective remedy.

Sometimes trade sanctions are used (or threatened) as a way to enforce environmental agreements. For example, the 1987 Montreal Protocol, which seeks to reverse the depletion of the upper-atmosphere ozone layer caused by the release of chlorofluorocarbons and other chemicals, requires trade actions against countries that do not abide by the environmental standards in the agreement. A second example is the Convention on International Trade in Endangered Species of Wild Fauna and Flora (CITES), which aims to protect endangered species of wildlife by restricting and monitoring their trade.

During 1993, the possibility of using trade sanctions for environmental purposes was raised, pursuant to a recommendation of CITES, in the case of trade by China and Taiwan in rhinoceros and tiger parts, and in regard to Norwegian whaling practices under the Pelly Amendment to enforce the International Whaling Convention moratorium on whaling. In both cases, however, sanctions were deferred.

The founders of GATT could not have foreseen the present importance of environmental problems. Some headway in harmonizing trade and environmental concerns has already been made in the environmental side agreement to NAFTA. And the preamble to the agreement establishing the WTO recognizes the importance of environmental concerns. The WTO negotiators have also agreed to develop a work program on trade and the environment to ensure the responsiveness of the multilateral trading system to environmental objectives.

INTERNATIONAL TRADE AND COMPETITION POLICY

As tariff and nontariff barriers to trade fall and as national economies become more integrated into the world trading system, differences in national business practices and laws become more important determinants of trade outcomes. Currently there are no multilateral rules to redress possibly restrictive practices in the way companies compete—such as price fixing, price discrimination, and the preferential supplier and distributor relationships characteristic of Japan's *keiretsu*. Many nations, including the United States, rely on antitrust laws to prevent anticompetitive business practices by domestic firms in their domestic market.

National antidumping laws are the most commonly used remedy in such circumstances. But unlike domestic antitrust laws, which generally increase competition and lower prices, national antidumping laws sometimes reduce competition and raise prices. Both in the United States and elsewhere, antidumping laws go beyond preventing anticompetitive practices—which *should* be their rationale—and often have the effect of protecting domestic industries from foreign competition. For example, a recent study found that, during the Reagan Administration, nontariff barriers including antidumping actions probably reduced U.S. manufactured imports by around a fifth—largely by discouraging foreign producers from entering the U.S. market or by discouraging those that do export here from lowering their prices.

If sound competition policies were present and effectively enforced in more nations, and if such laws were more easily enforceable against foreign misconduct, they could serve as the first line of defense against restrictive business practices by both domestic and foreign firms. The United States is currently pursuing this goal through such bilateral mechanisms as antitrust cooperation agreements.

Here NAFTA is a step in the right direction. The agreement commits its signatories to cooperate in the area of competition law enforcement, and imposes discipline on certain government-designated monopolies. It also establishes a trilateral committee to consider the relationship between trade and competition policy in the NAFTA countries. Some other free-trade areas have gone further. For example, in the European Union and the Australia-New Zealand Free Trade Area, antidumping laws do not apply to trade among member countries, since this is considered internal trade, subject to organization-wide competition policies.

Until there is greater convergence and international cooperation in the enforcement of antitrust laws against cross-border conduct, international disputes over unfair pricing between corporations of different national origins will often continue to play out in one of two ways: through the application of national competition laws, with the continuing difficulties associated with their international enforcement, or through the application of overly restrictive national trade laws. As part of the Uruguay Round, the WTO Council for Trade in Goods will consider provisions on investment policy and competition policy in the future. The OECD is also pursuing a work program in this area.

REGIONALISM

Although there may be significant benefits to trade liberalization on a regional basis, some nonmember countries could be hurt through trade and investment diversion, as trade and investment are preferentially shifted from them to the member countries. One way to mitigate these concerns is for members of a free-trade area to move toward a customs union whose common external tariff would match the lowest tariff within the region prior to the formation of the customs union. Another possibility would be to open regional arrangements to new members. It has also been suggested that GATT rules be amended to allow compensation for nonmembers hurt by regional liberalization agreements. These and other proposals to deal with regional free-trade associations may need to be discussed in GATT in order to preserve the benefits of regional trade liberalization while addressing the concerns of outsiders.

FOREIGN EXCHANGE MARKET DEVELOPMENTS

The international value of the dollar, as measured by its trade-weighted average exchange rate, rose by an astonishing 50 percent between the end of 1980 and early 1985. By mid-1988, however, the dollar had returned to its 1980 level, and since then it has continued on a slight downward trend, with much narrower fluctuations than earlier in the 1980s. The large appreciation and subsequent depreciation of the dollar had a marked impact on the competitive position of U.S. firms. Had they been offset by differences between the inflation rates of the United States and its trading partners, these large swings in the value of the dollar would have had no impact on our competitiveness. Inflation differentials, however, were much smaller than the exchange-rate swings. As a result, the dollar appreciated and then depreciated in both real and nominal terms by roughly equal amounts.

Chart 6-3 shows indexes of the value of the dollar relative to the currencies of our major trading partners. In addition to the nominal effective exchange rate, which does not adjust for inflation differences, the chart shows two measures of the real effective exchange rate: one in which relative consumer prices are used for the inflation adjustment, and one in which relative unit labor costs are used. The chart clearly demonstrates the high correlation between nominal and real exchange-rate movements since 1980. In addition, the chart shows that relative unit labor costs in manufacturing have declined sharply since their 1985 peak. Partly as a result, U.S. manufacturing firms have become extremely competitive in world markets.

Chart 6-3 **Nominal and Real Effective Dollar Exchange Rates**
The value of the dollar has been more stable in the 1990s than during the 1980s.

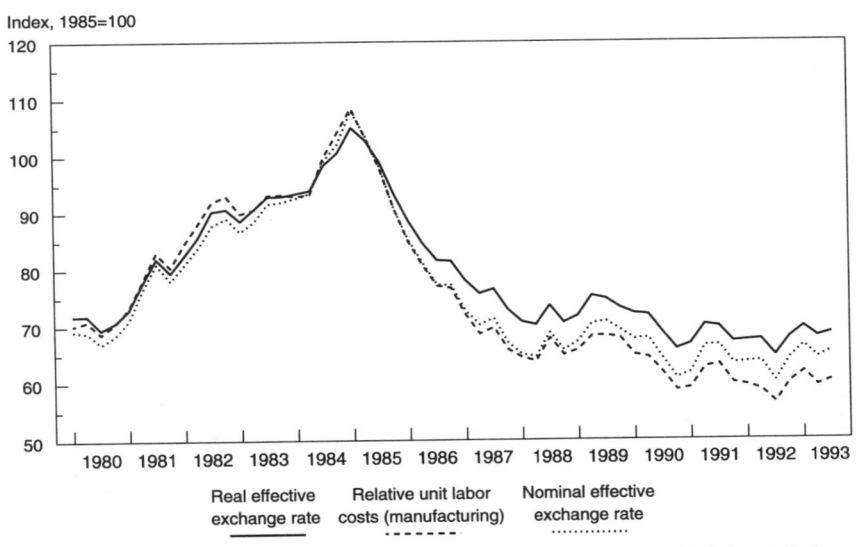

Note: Indexes are based on units of foreign currency per U.S. dollar. A decline in any of the indexes indicates falling relative costs and increasing competitiveness.
Source: International Monetary Fund.

The dollar ended 1993 roughly where it began. After rising sharply in the second half of 1992, it varied in a narrow range in 1993 (Chart 6-4). The relatively small movements in the dollar's effective exchange rate masked considerable changes in the value of the dollar relative to individual currencies, however. The U.S. dollar rose relative to the Canadian dollar and most continental European currencies but declined sharply relative to the yen.

Chart 6-4 **Exchange Rates of the Dollar Against Selected Currencies**
The dollar strengthened against the Canadian and German currencies after mid-1992 but weakened against the yen.

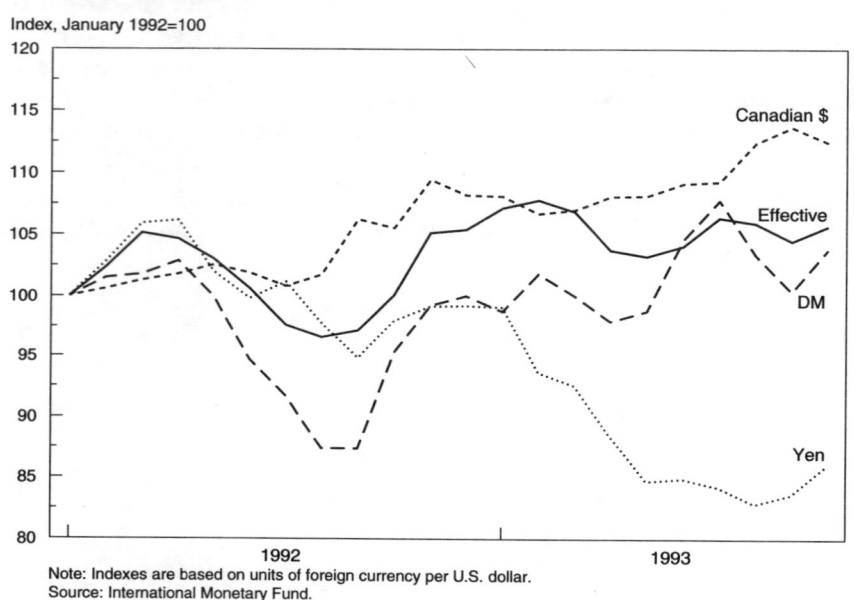

Note: Indexes are based on units of foreign currency per U.S. dollar.
Source: International Monetary Fund.

The appreciation of the dollar relative to the European currencies occurred despite low short-term and falling (until November) long-term interest rates in the United States. Since low and falling interest rates are frequently associated with currency *de*preciations, this may at first appear puzzling. The decline in European interest rates during 1993 explains the apparent puzzle.

The stability of the dollar and the cyclical behavior of the Japanese and European economies are important in understanding the likely impact of the President's deficit reduction package on the U.S. current account. As Chapter 2 points out, deficit reduction is generally associated with an increase in net exports. This expansion in net exports provides a stimulus that partially offsets the impact of spending cuts and tax increases on domestic demand.

The weakness in the economies of our major trading partners has, on the other hand, reduced demand for U.S. exports. Some of the boost to export demand that can be expected to result from the deficit reduction package may therefore be delayed until economic activity picks up in Europe and Japan. But by 1995 export demand should begin to rise.

THE EUROPEAN MONETARY SYSTEM

The European Monetary System (EMS) was created in March 1979 to limit exchange-rate variability among the European currencies (Box 6–7). A majority of countries in the EMS agreed to participate in the system's Exchange Rate Mechanism (ERM), under which most member countries were required to maintain their exchange rates within 2.25 percent of "central rates" between their currency and each of the other members' currencies. When an exchange rate between two members' currencies moves to the limits of the band, both central banks are required to intervene to prevent the exchange rate from moving outside the band. In the event of irresistible pressure on a member country's exchange rate, realignments of the country's central rate are permitted.

Inflation in most European economies declined by the mid-1980s, moving toward the rates of Germany and the Netherlands. Countries concentrated on maintaining their parities with respect to the deutsche mark, since Germany had for historical reasons established an unwavering commitment to price stability. Increasingly, then, the deutsche mark became the monetary anchor for the EMS. By linking their monetary policies to German policy, other ERM members brought their inflation rates down. French inflation, for example, declined from over 10 percent at the start of the 1980s to under 3 percent in 1992.

To some observers, the disinflation achieved within the EMS highlights an important rationale for pegging exchange rates. An alternative view holds that disinflation was not simply a product of the EMS but was worldwide in scope. During the 1980s, for example, inflation also declined in the United Kingdom, which did not join the ERM until 1990, and in the United States and Canada. So perhaps the relative stability of EMS parities in recent years was as much the result as the cause of a convergence in inflation rates.

Realignments took place relatively frequently in the first years of the EMS but not thereafter. Between 1979 and 1987 there were 11 realignments; these tended to be small as well as frequent and thereby occurred without major crises. After January 1987, essentially no realignments took place until September 1992.

> **Box 6-7.—Exchange-Rate Volatility and International Trade**
>
> Proponents of the ERM argue that stabilizing exchange rates is important for expanding trade. Exchange-rate volatility, they argue, is a source of uncertainty to firms engaging in trade because it adds volatility to the domestic currency value of future foreign currency transactions. Firms therefore face greater uncertainty in revenues and profits from foreign sales when exchange rates are more volatile. This added uncertainty, it is claimed, discourages firms from engaging in trade and from making the investments that support trade.
>
> Such claims seem plausible, but they enjoy little empirical support. The volume of U.S. trade did grow slightly faster between 1950 and 1971, when the dollar was fixed, than between 1973 and 1993, when the dollar floated. Relative to GDP, however, trade volumes grew more quickly in the second period. In addition, studies that have examined the extent to which greater exchange-rate volatility inhibits trade flows have generally failed to find a robust relationship. One possible explanation is that financial markets provide firms with risk management tools that can be used to hedge exchange-rate movements. For example, a firm can buy currencies forward to fix the domestic currency value of future payments. Whatever the explanation, it is difficult to find empirical support for an adverse impact of exchange-rate volatility on trade volumes.

THE EUROPEAN CURRENCIES IN TURMOIL

The EMS has experienced a series of crises since the summer of 1992. Germany adopted tight monetary policies in response to inflationary pressures that arose following German reunification in 1990. As a result, German short-term interest rates, which had been rising since 1988, continued to rise, reaching nearly 10 percent by the summer of 1992.

German policy, in turn, created a dilemma for other ERM participants. Maintaining fixed parities with the deutsche mark required them to tighten monetary policy despite stagnating or declining output, rising unemployment, and low rates of inflation.

When investors are free to choose among assets denominated in different currencies, the rates of return they expect to receive for comparable degrees of risk cannot vary too far from one currency to another. Expected exchange-rate changes are important in determining expected rates of return on assets denominated in different currencies. If, for example, investors expect the French franc to depreciate relative to the deutsche mark, they will move funds from French franc deposits into deutsche mark deposits unless they are compensated by a higher franc interest rate. Thus interest rates on franc-denominated assets would have to rise above the interest rate on deutsche mark assets to prevent sustained flows of capital out of franc assets and into deutsche mark assets.

Speculative pressures motivated by the possibility of a change in parities precipitated a crisis in September 1992. In the United Kingdom, where output had declined by more than 4 percent from its previous peak and the unemployment rate had topped 10 percent, pressure increased to realign or to drop out of the EMS so that interest rates could be lowered. Finland and Sweden, although not formal participants in the ERM, had been unilaterally maintaining pegged exchange rates, and so faced similar dilemmas as their economies went through deep and prolonged recessions. In September 1992, Finland, the United Kingdom, and Italy decided to allow their currencies to float, with the last two effectively leaving the ERM. Sweden followed in November. Spain, Portugal, and Ireland all devalued within the ERM between September 1992 and January 1993.

A second crisis erupted in mid-July 1993, following additional signs of growing slack in the European economies. Massive speculative capital flows occurred. Belgium, Denmark, France, and Portugal all raised interest rates and intervened heavily to defend their currencies. Nonetheless, the Belgian franc, the French franc, and the Danish krone dropped through their ERM floors. Selling pressures on these currencies continued, and on August 2, 1993, the countries participating in the ERM decided to widen the bands around the (unchanged) central parities to ±15 percent (Chart 6-5). (A separate agreement maintains bands of ±2.25 percent for the deutsche mark and the Dutch guilder.) Since all currencies were well within the wider bands, central banks were not obliged to intervene and the speculative crisis stopped.

The wider bands allow the participating countries much greater latitude to change interest rates independently. For the most part, however, the authorities have not used this ability to push interest rates down. Instead, they have sought to maintain relatively stable exchange rates with the deutsche mark and have cut interest rates only in parallel with Germany. By the end of 1993 the Belgian, Danish, French, Portuguese, and Spanish currencies were within or near the old ERM limits relative to the deutsche mark. The United Kingdom aggressively cut interest rates after leaving the ERM in September 1992.

THE MAASTRICHT TREATY ON ECONOMIC AND MONETARY UNION

In the Maastricht Treaty of 1991, the members of the European Community agreed to replace the EMS with an Economic and Mon-

Chart 6-5 French Franc-Deutsche Mark Exchange Rates
Last summer's exchange-rate crisis precipitated a widening of the Exchange Rate Mechanism's intervention bands.

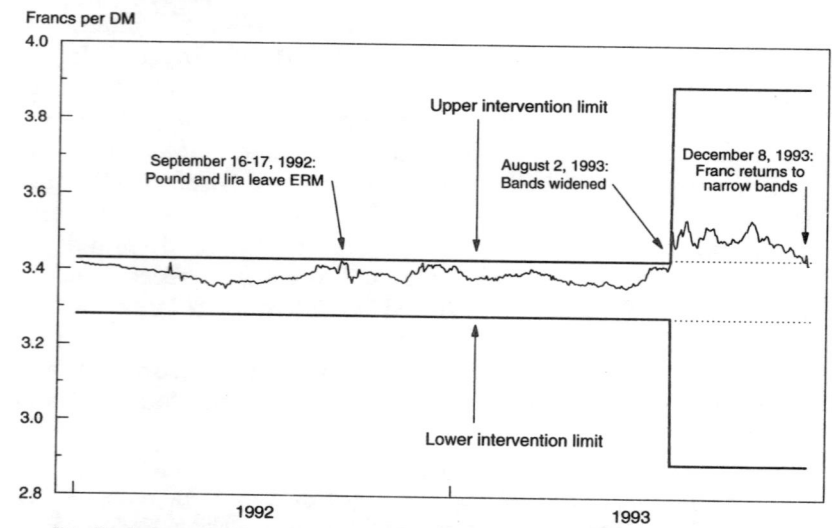

Francs per DM

- September 16-17, 1992: Pound and lira leave ERM
- Upper intervention limit
- August 2, 1993: Bands widened
- December 8, 1993: Franc returns to narrow bands
- Lower intervention limit

Note: The Exchange Rate Mechanism prescribes intervention bands for participating members of the European Monetary System.
Sources: Council of Economic Advisers and Board of Governors of the Federal Reserve System.

etary Union (EMU), a common currency, and a European Central Bank overseeing a single monetary policy. Under the treaty, progress toward EMU would take place in stages, with the final stage—under which exchange rates are fixed irrevocably—coming no later than 1999.

The treaty establishes conditions for implementing a common currency and monetary policy (Box 6-8). As of late 1993, no country in the European Union met these conditions. With reunification swelling its public sector deficit, even Germany failed to meet the criteria.

The process of ratifying the Maastricht Treaty was completed in 1993, although the timing of full implementation will depend in part on the achievement of the agreed conditions. In May 1993, Danish voters reversed the outcome of the previous year's referendum and accepted the treaty. The British House of Commons then approved the treaty in July. The final steps in the ratification process were completed when court challenges to the treaty failed in July in the United Kingdom and in October in Germany. The Maastricht Treaty entered into force on November 1, 1993, creating the European Union.

> **Box 6–8.—Criteria for Joining the Economic and Monetary Union**
>
> Countries acceding to EMU must meet several strict criteria:
>
> - The entering country's inflation rate must not exceed the average of the lowest three members' rates by more than 1.5 percentage points.
> - Its interest rate on long-term government bonds cannot exceed those of the three lowest-inflation members by more than 2 percentage points.
> - The country's general-government budget deficit must not exceed 3 percent of GDP, and outstanding government debt must not exceed 60 percent of GDP.
> - For at least 2 years, the country's currency must have remained within its narrow ERM band without realignment.

Shortly after completing the ratification process, the EU countries selected Frankfurt as the home of the new European Monetary Institute, the forerunner of the European Central Bank. Despite their failure to complete the first stage (bringing all countries within narrow ERM bands), the EU countries are proceeding with the timetable set out in the Maastricht Treaty.

CONCLUSIONS

The year 1993 proved to be the most important year for American trade policy in half a century, thanks to developments that vastly increased the prospects for free and open trade.

During the past year, the Administration completed two landmark negotiations. The first created a North American Free Trade Area encompassing the United States, Canada, and Mexico. In many respects this agreement is historically unprecedented: It is the first free-trade agreement between industrialized and developing countries; it is the first trade agreement to incorporate environmental provisions explicitly; and it contains technical innovations in areas such as dispute settlement that may become models for the global trade regime.

The Administration did not stop there, however. It also led a successful conclusion of the Uruguay Round of GATT, the most far-reaching global trade agreement in history. This agreement will reduce trade barriers, protect the legitimate interests of U.S. producers in areas such as intellectual property rights where none existed before, and bring areas of trade such as agriculture and textiles into the multilateral system for the first time.

Besides bringing these endeavors to fruition, the Administration launched several new trade initiatives and breathed new life into some old ones. The Administration made major progress in establishing APEC as a prominent forum for advancing our interests in the critical Asia-Pacific region. In addition, the United States reached a new bilateral agreement with Japan. Complementing the new international initiatives, the Administration also launched a new National Export Strategy to promote American exports.

This Administration understands that expanding trade relations are not only inevitable but critical to the future health of the U.S. economy. It is determined to ensure that the growing interdependence with our trading partners brings benefits to the United States. To this end the United States Government is committed to act unilaterally, bilaterally, regionally, plurilaterally, and globally to open markets to maintain the ability of U.S. firms to compete around the world. Through increasing integration into the global economy, we can achieve ever-rising living standards for all of our people.

Appendix A
REPORT TO THE PRESIDENT ON THE ACTIVITIES OF THE COUNCIL OF ECONOMIC ADVISERS DURING 1993

LETTER OF TRANSMITTAL

COUNCIL OF ECONOMIC ADVISERS
Washington, D.C., December 31, 1993

MR. PRESIDENT:

The Council of Economic Advisers submits this report on its activities during the calendar year 1993 in accordance with the requirements of the Congress, as set forth in section 10(d) of the Employment Act of 1946 as amended by the Full Employment and Balanced Growth Act of 1978.

Sincerely,

Laura D'Andrea Tyson, *Chair*
Alan S. Blinder, *Member*
Joseph E. Stiglitz, *Member*

Council Members and their Dates of Service

Name	Position	Oath of office date	Separation date
Edwin G. Nourse	Chairman	August 9, 1946	November 1, 1949.
Leon H. Keyserling	Vice Chairman	August 9, 1946	
	Acting Chairman	November 2, 1949	
	Chairman	May 10, 1950	January 20, 1953.
John D. Clark	Member	August 9, 1946	
	Vice Chairman	May 10, 1950	February 11, 1953.
Roy Blough	Member	June 29, 1950	August 20, 1952.
Robert C. Turner	Member	September 8, 1952	January 20, 1953.
Arthur F. Burns	Chairman	March 19, 1953	December 1, 1956.
Neil H. Jacoby	Member	September 15, 1953	February 9, 1955.
Walter W. Stewart	Member	December 2, 1953	April 29, 1955.
Raymond J. Saulnier	Member	April 4, 1955	
	Chairman	December 3, 1956	January 20, 1961.
Joseph S. Davis	Member	May 2, 1955	October 31, 1958.
Paul W. McCracken	Member	December 3, 1956	January 31, 1959.
Karl Brandt	Member	November 1, 1958	January 20, 1961.
Henry C. Wallich	Member	May 7, 1959	January 20, 1961.
Walter W. Heller	Chairman	January 29, 1961	November 15, 1964.
James Tobin	Member	January 29, 1961	July 31, 1962.
Kermit Gordon	Member	January 29, 1961	December 27, 1962.
Gardner Ackley	Member	August 3, 1962	
	Chairman	November 16, 1964	February 15, 1968.
John P. Lewis	Member	May 17, 1963	August 31, 1964.
Otto Eckstein	Member	September 2, 1964	February 1, 1966.
Arthur M. Okun	Member	November 16, 1964	
	Chairman	February 15, 1968	January 20, 1969.
James S. Duesenberry	Member	February 2, 1966	June 30, 1968.
Merton J. Peck	Member	February 15, 1968	January 20, 1969.
Warren L. Smith	Member	July 1, 1968	January 20, 1969.
Paul W. McCracken	Chairman	February 4, 1969	December 31, 1971.
Hendrik S. Houthakker	Member	February 4, 1969	July 15, 1971.
Herbert Stein	Member	February 4, 1969	
	Chairman	January 1, 1972	August 31, 1974.
Ezra Solomon	Member	September 9, 1971	March 26, 1973.
Marina v.N. Whitman	Member	March 13, 1972	August 15, 1973.
Gary L. Seevers	Member	July 23, 1973	April 15, 1975.
William J. Fellner	Member	October 31, 1973	February 25, 1975.
Alan Greenspan	Chairman	September 4, 1974	January 20, 1977.
Paul W. MacAvoy	Member	June 13, 1975	November 15, 1976.
Burton G. Malkiel	Member	July 22, 1975	January 20, 1977.
Charles L. Schultze	Chairman	January 22, 1977	January 20, 1981.
William D. Nordhaus	Member	March 18, 1977	February 4, 1979.
Lyle E. Gramley	Member	March 18, 1977	May 27, 1980.
George C. Eads	Member	June 6, 1979	January 20, 1981.
Stephen M. Goldfeld	Member	August 20, 1980	January 20, 1981.
Murray L. Weidenbaum	Chairman	February 27, 1981	August 25, 1982.
William A. Niskanen	Member	June 12, 1981	March 30, 1985.
Jerry L. Jordan	Member	July 14, 1981	July 31, 1982.
Martin Feldstein	Chairman	October 14, 1982	July 10, 1984.
William Poole	Member	December 10, 1982	January 20, 1985.
Beryl W. Sprinkel	Chairman	April 18, 1985	January 20, 1989.
Thomas Gale Moore	Member	July 1, 1985	May 1, 1989.
Michael L. Mussa	Member	August 18, 1986	September 19, 1988.
Michael J. Boskin	Chairman	February 2, 1989	January 12, 1993.
John B. Taylor	Member	June 9, 1989	August 2, 1991
Richard L. Schmalensee	Member	October 3, 1989	June 21, 1991
David F. Bradford	Member	November 13, 1991	January 20, 1993.
Paul Wonnacott	Member	November 13, 1991	January 20, 1993.
Laura D'Andrea Tyson	Chair	February 5, 1993	
Alan S. Blinder	Member	July 27, 1993	
Joseph E. Stiglitz	Member	July 27, 1993	

Report to the President on the Activities of the Council of Economic Advisers During 1993

The Statutory Mission of the Council

The Council of Economic Advisers was established by the Employment Act of 1946 to provide the President with objective economic analysis and advice on the development and implementation of a wide range of domestic and international economic policy issues.

The Chair of the Council

The inauguration of President Clinton brought changes to the membership of the Council of Economic Advisers. In February 1993, Laura D'Andrea Tyson was appointed Chair of the Council and a Member of the President's Cabinet. Dr. Tyson is on leave from the University of California, Berkeley, where she is Professor of Economics and Business Administration and Research Director of the Berkeley Roundtable on the International Economy. As Chair of the Council, Dr. Tyson is responsible for communicating the Council's views on economic developments to the President through personal discussions and written reports. She is the Council's chief public spokesperson.

Dr. Tyson represents the Council at Cabinet meetings and various other high-level meetings including those of the National Security Council focusing on economic issues, daily White House senior staff meetings, budget team meetings with the President, and many other formal and informal meetings with the President, senior White House staff, and other senior government officials. Dr. Tyson is one of six members of the Principals Committee of the newly established National Economic Council and is a member of the Domestic Policy Council. She guides the work of the Council of Economic Advisers and exercises ultimate responsibility for the work of the professional staff. Dr. Tyson succeeded Michael J. Boskin, who returned to Stanford University, where he is the Friedman Professor of Economics; he is also a Senior Fellow at the Hoover Institution on War, Revolution and Peace.

The Members of the Council

Alan S. Blinder and Joseph E. Stiglitz are the other new Members of the Council of Economic Advisers. They succeeded Paul Wonnacott, who is now a Senior Fellow at the Institute for International Economics, and David F. Bradford, who returned to Princeton University. Dr. Blinder is on leave from Princeton University where he is the Gordon S. Rentschler Memorial Professor of Economics. Dr. Stiglitz is on leave from Stanford University where he is the Joan Kenney Professor of Economics. Members of the Council are involved in the full range of issues within the Council's purview and are responsible for the daily supervision of the work of the professional staff. Members represent the Council at a wide variety of interagency and international meetings and assume major responsibility for selecting issues for the Council's attention.

The small size of the Council permits the Chair and Members to work as a team on most policy issues. The Chair works on the whole range of economic issues under the Council's purview. There continues to be, however, an informal division of subject matter among the Members. Dr. Stiglitz is primarily responsible for microeconomic and sectoral analysis and regulatory issues. Dr. Blinder is primarily responsible for domestic and international macroeconomic analysis and economic projections. All three Members, under Dr. Tyson's lead, are heavily involved in international trade issues and participate in the deliberations of the National Economic Council.

MACROECONOMIC POLICIES

The Council advised the President on all major macroeconomic issues in 1993. The Council prepared for the President, the Vice President, and the White House senior staff a comprehensive series of memoranda on the statistical releases that help monitor U.S. economic activity. It also prepared special analyses of economic policy issues and briefing papers on significant economic events, such as the 1993 floods in the Midwest (and the earthquake in southern California early in 1994).

The Council participated in discussions of macroeconomic policy issues with officials from the Department of the Treasury, the Office of Management and Budget (OMB), and other members of the President's economic policy team. It was a leading participant in the formulation of the Administration's economic policies through various Cabinet and sub-Cabinet working groups. The Council also played an important role in setting priorities within the fiscal 1994 and 1995 budgets.

The Council analyzed the macroeconomic effects of all major Administration policy proposals, including the President's deficit reduction budget package, the North American Free Trade Agreement, and the Uruguay Round of the General Agreement on Tariffs and Trade (GATT). In addition, the Council carefully monitored the response of the interest-sensitive sectors of the economy to the sharp reduction in long-term interest rates that followed the proposal and enactment of the President's deficit reduction plan.

The Council, the Department of the Treasury, and the OMB—the economic "Troika"—produced the economic forecasts that underlie the Administration's budget projections. Dr. Blinder, in collaboration with Dr. Tyson and Council senior economists, led this forecasting effort. Two official forecasts are released each year. The first is published early in the year and is relied upon for the President's budget calculations. An update is then published in the summer as part of the Administration's mid-session budget review. In preparing its forecasts, the Troika took particular care to present economic assumptions that were not unduly optimistic so as to maintain the credibility of the Administration's budget projections and its economic plan. Leading private sector forecasters visited the Council before the forecasting rounds to share their views on the economic outlook.

The Council worked to improve the public's understanding of economic issues and the quality of economic information through regular briefings with the White House financial and general press corps, periodic discussions with distinguished outside economists, and meetings with leading business executives. The Chair and the other Members made numerous presentations to outside organizations to explain the Administration's economic strategy and policies. Dr. Tyson, Dr. Blinder, and Dr. Stiglitz regularly exchanged information and met with the Chairman and Members of the Board of Governors of the Federal Reserve System to discuss the economic outlook and monetary policy.

Finally, the Council worked to improve the quality of government economic statistics. The Council urged increased funding for economic and demographic statistics in interagency discussions and in deliberations over Federal budget priorities.

INTERNATIONAL ECONOMIC POLICIES

International economic issues were a high priority for the Council in 1993. All three Members continued the Council's active role in the Organization of Economic Cooperation and Development (OECD). Dr. Tyson attended the OECD's Economic Policy Committee meeting in Paris in May and served as its Acting Chair in November. Dr. Blinder led the U.S. delegation to the OECD to assess U.S. economic policy and was a member of the U.S. delegation to OECD Working Party 3 on macroeconomic policy coordination. Dr. Stiglitz headed the U.S. delegation to OECD Working Party 1 meetings on microeconomic and structural issues. Senior staff members represented the Council at the semiannual Short-Term Economic Projections meetings at the OECD in Paris, and at the annual Asia-Pacific Economic Experts Meeting in Sydney. The goal of these meetings was to support the coordination of macroeconomic policies to promote economic growth. The Chair and the other Members helped formulate Administration policies that brought to completion two major trade agreements, the North American Free Trade Agreement and the Uruguay Round of GATT, and provided economic analyses of the implications of those agreements for the U.S. economy. The Council also participated in formulating other Administration policies in the international arena, including such important initiatives as the National Export Strategy, and the ongoing evaluation of the economic relationship between the United States and the People's Republic of China.

Dr. Tyson and Dr. Blinder were deeply involved in the negotiations of the United States-Japan Framework for a New Economic Partnership, with Dr. Blinder making two trips to Japan as part of the negotiations. The Council also engaged in discussions with Japan's Economic Planning Agency on the current account imbalances and other macroeconomic issues. The Council was involved throughout the year in Administration policies for advancing economic reform in the former Soviet Union. Dr. Stiglitz traveled to Russia and Ukraine and established an official relationship with the Russian Government's Working Center for Economic Reform.

The Council provided the President with regular briefings on international developments and was particularly active in the preparations for the Asia-Pacific Economic Cooperation (APEC) Ministerial meeting and the first-ever APEC leaders' meeting hosted by the President in Seattle.

MICROECONOMIC POLICIES

The Council was an active participant in a broad range of Administration microeconomic initiatives in 1993. Dr. Tyson and the Secretary of Transportation jointly led the Administration's Working Group on Aviation, which developed the Administration's Civil Aviation Initiative. At the request of the President, Dr. Tyson also served on the National Commission for a Strong, Competitive Airline Industry. The Council also assisted in the development of the Administration's Domestic Natural Gas and Oil Initiative, issued by the Department of Energy.

Dr. Stiglitz played an important role in the development of two Executive Orders—one on regulatory planning and review and another on the Nation's infrastructure. Each order directs executive branch agencies to rely upon cost-benefit analysis when identifying appropriate regulatory approaches and when determining which infrastructure projects should be undertaken. Dr. Stiglitz also serves as co-chair of a committee of the Administration's Regulatory

Working Group studying cost-benefit analysis methodology and he participated in a number of working groups on financial markets and economic development. Dr. Tyson and Dr. Stiglitz are also working closely with the Vice President and other Administration officials in developing legislative proposals for telecommunications regulation. In addition, Dr. Tyson and the other Members are involved in analyzing various proposals for bank regulatory agency consolidation.

Dr. Tyson was a member of the Health Care Task Force headed by the First Lady and the Council was deeply involved with the health care reform effort over the past year, especially in analyzing the economic effects of reform options. The Council also helped develop the tax, empowerment zone, and enterprise communities provisions of the 1993 Omnibus Budget Reconciliation Act (OBRA). Dr. Tyson is a member of the President's Community Enterprise Board. In addition, the Council participated in the development of the Administration's work force security and welfare reform initiatives and in the design of the Administration's defense reinvestment initiative. Dr. Tyson was appointed a member of the President's National Science and Technology Council and was appointed the Administration's representative on the Competitiveness Policy Council. Dr. Tyson and Dr. Stiglitz both served on the Administration's Welfare Reform Task Force.

Dr. Stiglitz was particularly active in the Administration's environmental policymaking efforts. He chaired the Subcommittee on Economics Research on Natural Resources and Environment, created to identify key research areas in economics common to many environmental quality and natural resource management issues. He has also been actively involved in developing the Administration's proposals for Superfund reauthorization, Clean Water Act reauthorization, and the President's Climate Change Action Plan.

WEEKLY ECONOMIC BRIEFINGS

Dr. Tyson conducts a weekly economic briefing for the President, the Vice President, and the President's other senior economic and policy advisers. Dr. Blinder and Dr. Stiglitz also attend. The Council, in cooperation with the Office of the Vice President, prepares a written *Weekly Economic Briefing of the President*, which serves as the basis for the oral briefing. The briefing includes analysis of current economic developments, more extended treatments of a wide range of economic issues and problems, and summaries of news on different regions and sectors of the economy.

The Staff of the Council of Economic Advisers

The professional staff of the Council consists of the Chief of Staff, the Senior Statistician, fourteen senior economists, six staff economists, and two research assistants. The professional staff and their areas of concentration at the end of 1993 were:

Chief of Staff

Thomas P. O'Donnell

Senior Economists

Jonathan B. Baker	Regulation, Industrial Organization, and Law
David M. Cutler	Health
Robert E. Cumby	International Economics
William T. Dickens	Labor, Welfare, and Education
Constance R. Dunham	Financial Markets and Foreign Assistance
Warren E. Farb	Business and Regional Analysis
Sally M. Kane	Climate Change and Natural Resources
Alan J. Krupnick	Environment and Natural Resources
Erik R. Lichtenberg	Agriculture, International Trade, and Natural Resources
Mark J. Mazur	Public Finance
Marcus Noland	International Economics
Matthew D. Shapiro	Macroeconomics and the *Weekly Economic Briefing of the President*
Jay S. Stowsky	Technology, Defense Conversion, and Regional Economic Development
Robert F. Wescott	Macroeconomics and Forecasting

Senior Statistician

Catherine H. Furlong

Staff Economists

Kevin C. Murdock	Technology and Finance
Kimberly J. O'Neill	Health and Public Finance
Peter R. Orszag	International Economics
Jeremy B. Rudd	Macroeconomics and Forecasting
Elizabeth A. Schneirov	Regulation, Industrial Organization, and Environment
Darryl S. Wills	Labor, Welfare, and Agriculture

Research Assistants

D. W. Clark Dees
James C. Hritz

Statistical Office

Mrs. Furlong manages the Statistical Office. The Statistical Office maintains and updates the Council's statistical information, prepares the *Economic Indicators* and the statistical appendix to the *Economic Report*, and verifies statistics in Presidential and Council memoranda, testimony, and speeches.

Susan P. Clements	Statistician
Linda A. Reilly	Statistical Assistant
Brian A. Amorosi	Research Assistant
Margaret L. Snyder	Secretary

The Administrative Office

Elizabeth A. Kaminski	Administrative Officer
Catherine Fibich	Administrative Assistant

Office of the Chair

Alice H. Williams	Executive Assistant to the Chair
Sandra F. Daigle	Executive Assistant to the Chair and Assistant to the Chief of Staff
Lisa D. Branch	Executive Assistant to Dr. Blinder
Francine P. Obermiller	Executive Assistant to Dr. Stiglitz

Staff Secretaries

Mary E. Jones
Rosalind V. Rasin
Mary A. Thomas

Mrs. Thomas also served as Executive Assistant for the *Weekly Economic Briefing of the President*.

Michael Treadway provided editorial assistance in the preparation of the 1994 *Economic Report*.

Sherman Robinson, University of California, Berkeley, served during the summer and early fall of 1993 as a senior economist specializing in the North American Free Trade Agreement. Omri S. Dahan, Michelle R. Dorman, Mark H. Fithian, Ian B. Goldberg, and Jennifer Howard served as student assistants during the year. Suzanne M. Tudor returned to serve as Dr. Blinder's Executive Assistant during Lisa Branch's leave of absence. Volunteers during the year were Diana Billik, William P. Cowin, Matthew T. Henshon, John D. Levin, and Megan R. Sweeney.

DEPARTURES

James D. Foster, who served as Special Assistant to the Chairman, resigned in January 1993 to accept a position with the Tax Foundation. Shelley A. Slomowitz, Staff Assistant to the Chairman, also resigned in January 1993.

The Council's senior economists, in most cases, are on leave of absence from faculty positions at academic institutions or from other government agencies or research institutions. Their tenure with the Council is usually limited to 1 or 2 years. Most of the senior economists who resigned during the year returned to their previous affiliations. They are Kwok-Chiu Fung (University of California, Santa Cruz), Sherry Glied (Columbia University), Andrew S. Joskow (Department of Justice), Steven B. Kamin (Board of Governors of the Federal Reserve System), Michael M. Knetter (Dartmouth College), Howard D. Leathers (University of Maryland), Deborah J. Lucas (Northwestern University), Andrew B. Lyon (University of Maryland), and Raymond L. Squitieri (Department of the Treasury). John H. Kitchen went on to a new position at the Department of the Treasury. Jonathan B. Wiener accepted a position on the faculty of the Duke University Law School.

Kevin Berner, staff economist, accepted a position with McKinsey and Company, Inc., Cleveland, Ohio. Junior staff economists (now designated staff economists) are generally graduate students who spend 1 year with the Council and then return to complete their dissertations. Those who returned to their graduate studies in 1993 are: Christopher J. Acito (University of Chicago), Lucy P. Allen (Yale University), Sherif Lotfi (Columbia University), and Natalie J. Tawil (Massachusetts Institute of Technology). Joshua B. Michael accepted a position with The Eiger Development Corporation, Seattle, Washington. Bret M. Dickey, research assistant, began graduate studies at Stanford University. Janet J. Twyman, staff secretary, resigned in 1993.

Public Information

The Council's *Annual Report* is the principal medium through which the Council informs the public of its work and its views. It is an important vehicle for presenting the Administration's domestic and international economic policies. Annual distribution of the *Report* in recent years has averaged about 45,000 copies. The Council also has primary responsibility for compiling the monthly *Economic Indicators*, which is issued by the Joint Economic Committee of the Congress and has a distribution of approximately 10,000.

Appendix B
**STATISTICAL TABLES RELATING TO INCOME,
EMPLOYMENT, AND PRODUCTION**

CONTENTS

NATIONAL INCOME OR EXPENDITURE:

		Page
B-1.	Gross domestic product, 1959-93	268
B-2.	Gross domestic product in 1987 dollars, 1959-93	270
B-3.	Implicit price deflators for gross domestic product, 1959-93	272
B-4.	Fixed-weighted price indexes for gross domestic product, 1987 weights, 1959-93	274
B-5.	Changes in gross domestic product and personal consumption expenditures, and related implicit price deflators and fixed-weighted price indexes, 1960-93	276
B-6.	Selected per capita product and income series in current and 1987 dollars, 1959-93	277
B-7.	Gross domestic product by major type of product, 1959-93	278
B-8.	Gross domestic product by major type of product in 1987 dollars, 1959-93	279
B-9.	Gross domestic product by sector, 1959-93	280
B-10.	Gross domestic product by sector in 1987 dollars, 1959-93	281
B-11.	Gross domestic product by industry, 1947-91	282
B-12.	Gross domestic product by industry in 1987 dollars, fixed 1987 weights, 1977-91	283
B-13.	Gross domestic product of nonfinancial corporate business, 1959-93	284
B-14.	Output, costs, and profits of nonfinancial corporate business, 1959-93	285
B-15.	Personal consumption expenditures, 1959-93	286
B-16.	Personal consumption expenditures in 1987 dollars, 1959-93	287
B-17.	Gross and net private domestic investment, 1959-93	288
B-18.	Gross and net private domestic investment in 1987 dollars, 1959-93	289
B-19.	Inventories and final sales of domestic business, 1959-93	290
B-20.	Inventories and final sales of domestic business in 1987 dollars, 1959-93	291
B-21.	Foreign transactions in the national income and product accounts, 1959-93	292
B-22.	Exports and imports of goods and services and receipts and payments of factor income in 1987 dollars, 1959-93	293
B-23.	Relation of gross domestic product, gross national product, net national product, and national income, 1959-93	294
B-24.	Relation of national income and personal income, 1959-93	295
B-25.	National income by type of income, 1959-93	296
B-26.	Sources of personal income, 1959-93	298
B-27.	Disposition of personal income, 1959-93	300
B-28.	Total and per capita disposable personal income and personal consumption expenditures in current and 1987 dollars, 1959-93	301
B-29.	Gross saving and investment, 1959-93	302
B-30.	Personal saving, flow of funds accounts, 1946-93	303
B-31.	Median money income (in 1992 dollars) and poverty status of families and persons, by race, selected years, 1971-92	304

POPULATION, EMPLOYMENT, WAGES, AND PRODUCTIVITY:

		Page
B-32.	Population by age group, 1929-93	305
B-33.	Population and the labor force, 1929-93	306
B-34.	Civilian employment and unemployment by sex and age, 1947-93	308
B-35.	Civilian employment by demographic characteristic, 1954-93	309
B-36.	Unemployment by demographic characteristics, 1954-93	310
B-37.	Civilian labor force participation rate and employment/population ratio, 1948-93	311
B-38.	Civilian labor force participation rate by demographic characteristic, 1954-93	312
B-39.	Civilian employment/population ratio by demographic characteristic, 1954-93	313
B-40.	Civilian unemployment rate, 1948-93	314
B-41.	Civilian unemployment rate by demographic characteristic, 1950-93	315
B-42.	Unemployment by duration and reason, 1950-93	316
B-43.	Unemployment insurance programs, selected data, 1962-93	317
B-44.	Employees on nonagricultural payrolls, by major industry, 1946-93	318
B-45.	Hours and earnings in private nonagricultural industries, 1959-93	320
B-46.	Employment cost index, private industry, 1979-93	321
B-47.	Productivity and related data, business sector, 1947-93	322
B-48.	Changes in productivity and related data, business sector, 1948-93	323

PRODUCTION AND BUSINESS ACTIVITY:

B-49.	Industrial production indexes, major industry divisions, 1947-93	324
B-50.	Industrial production indexes, market groupings, 1947-93	325
B-51.	Industrial production indexes, selected manufactures, 1947-93	326
B-52.	Capacity utilization rates, 1948-93	327
B-53.	New construction activity, 1929-93	328
B-54.	New housing units started and authorized, 1959-93	330
B-55.	Business expenditures for new plant and equipment, 1947-94	331
B-56.	Manufacturing and trade sales and inventories, 1950-93	332
B-57.	Manufacturers' shipments and inventories, 1950-93	333
B-58.	Manufacturers' new and unfilled orders, 1950-93	334

PRICES:

B-59.	Consumer price indexes for major expenditure classes, 1950-93	335
B-60.	Consumer price indexes for selected expenditure classes, 1950-93	336
B-61.	Consumer price indexes for commodities, services, and special groups, 1950-93	338
B-62.	Changes in special consumer price indexes, 1958-93	339
B-63.	Changes in consumer price indexes for commodities and services, 1929-93	340
B-64.	Producer price indexes by stage of processing, 1947-93	341
B-65.	Producer price indexes by stage of processing, special groups, 1974-93	343
B-66.	Producer price indexes for major commodity groups, 1950-93	344
B-67.	Changes in producer price indexes for finished goods, 1955-93	346

MONEY STOCK, CREDIT, AND FINANCE:

		Page
B-68.	Money stock, liquid assets, and debt measures, 1959-93	347
B-69.	Components of money stock measures and liquid assets, 1959-93	348
B-70.	Aggregate reserves of depository institutions and monetary base, 1959-93	350
B-71.	Commercial bank loans and securities, 1972-93	351
B-72.	Bond yields and interest rates, 1929-93	352
B-73.	Total funds raised in credit markets by nonfinancial sectors, 1984-93	354
B-74.	Mortgage debt outstanding by type of property and of financing, 1940-93	356
B-75.	Mortgage debt outstanding by holder, 1940-93	357
B-76.	Consumer credit outstanding, 1952-93	358

GOVERNMENT FINANCE:

B-77.	Federal receipts, outlays, surplus or deficit, and debt, selected fiscal years, 1929-95	359
B-78.	Federal receipts, outlays, and debt, fiscal years, 1982-95	360
B-79.	Federal budget receipts, outlays, surplus or deficit, and debt, as percentages of gross domestic product, 1934-95	362
B-80.	Federal and State and local government receipts and expenditures, national income and product accounts, 1959-93	363
B-81.	Federal and State and local government receipts and expenditures, national income and product accounts, by major type, 1959-93	364
B-82.	Federal Government receipts and expenditures, national income and product accounts, 1976-93	365
B-83.	State and local government receipts and expenditures, national income and product accounts, 1959-93	366
B-84.	State and local government revenues and expenditures, selected fiscal years, 1927-91	367
B-85.	Interest-bearing public debt securities by kind of obligation, 1967-93	368
B-86.	Maturity distribution and average length of marketable interest-bearing public debt securities held by private investors, 1967-93	369
B-87.	Estimated ownership of public debt securities by private investors, 1976-93	370

CORPORATE PROFITS AND FINANCE:

B-88.	Corporate profits with inventory valuation and capital consumption adjustments, 1959-93	371
B-89.	Corporate profits by industry, 1959-93	372
B-90.	Corporate profits of manufacturing industries, 1959-93	373
B-91.	Sales, profits, and stockholders' equity, all manufacturing corporations, 1952-93	374
B-92.	Relation of profits after taxes to stockholders' equity and to sales, all manufacturing corporations, 1947-93	375
B-93.	Sources and uses of funds, nonfarm nonfinancial corporate business, 1947-93	376
B-94.	Common stock prices and yields, 1955-93	377
B-95.	Business formation and business failures, 1950-93	378

AGRICULTURE:

		Page
B-96.	Farm income, 1940-93	379
B-97.	Farm output and productivity indexes, 1948-91	380
B-98.	Farm input use, selected inputs, 1948-92	381
B-99.	Indexes of prices received and prices paid by farmers, 1950-93	382
B-100.	U.S. exports and imports of agricultural commodities, 1940-93	383
B-101.	Farm business balance sheet, 1950-92	384

INTERNATIONAL STATISTICS:

B-102.	International investment position of the United States at year-end, 1984-92	385
B-103.	U.S. international transactions, 1946-93	386
B-104.	U.S. merchandise exports and imports by principal end-use category, 1965-93	388
B-105.	U.S. merchandise exports and imports by area, 1984-93	389
B-106.	U.S. merchandise exports, imports, and trade balance, 1972-93	390
B-107.	International reserves, selected years, 1952-93	391
B-108.	Industrial production and consumer prices, major industrial countries, 1967-93	392
B-109.	Civilian unemployment rate, and hourly compensation, major industrial countries, 1967-93	393
B-110.	Foreign exchange rates, 1969-93	394
B-111.	Growth rates in real gross domestic product, 1975-93	395

NATIONAL WEALTH:

B-112.	National wealth, 1946-92	396
B-113.	National wealth in 1987 dollars, 1946-92	397

SUPPLEMENTARY TABLE:

B-114.	Selected historical series on gross domestic product and related series, 1929-58	398

General Notes

Detail in these tables may not add to totals because of rounding.
Unless otherwise noted, all dollar figures are in current dollars.
Symbols used:
    p Preliminary.
    ——Not available (also, not applicable).

Data in these tables reflect revisions made by the source agencies from January 1993 through early February 1994.

NATIONAL INCOME OR EXPENDITURE

TABLE B-1.—*Gross domestic product, 1959–93*

[Billions of dollars, except as noted; quarterly data at seasonally adjusted annual rates]

Year or quarter	Gross domestic product	Personal consumption expenditures				Gross private domestic investment						
		Total	Durable goods	Non-durable goods	Services	Total	Fixed investment					Change in business inventories
							Total	Nonresidential			Residential	
								Total	Structures	Producers' durable equipment		
1959	494.2	318.1	42.8	148.5	126.8	78.8	74.6	46.5	18.1	28.3	28.1	4.2
1960	513.3	332.4	43.5	153.1	135.9	78.7	75.5	49.2	19.6	29.7	26.3	3.2
1961	531.8	343.5	41.9	157.4	144.1	77.9	75.0	48.6	19.7	28.9	26.4	2.9
1962	571.6	364.4	47.0	163.8	153.6	87.9	81.8	52.8	20.8	32.1	29.0	6.1
1963	603.1	384.2	51.8	169.4	163.1	93.4	87.7	55.6	21.2	34.4	32.1	5.7
1964	648.0	412.5	56.8	179.7	175.9	101.7	96.7	62.4	23.7	38.7	34.3	5.0
1965	702.7	444.6	63.5	191.9	189.2	118.0	108.3	74.1	28.3	45.8	34.2	9.7
1966	769.8	481.6	68.5	208.5	204.6	130.4	116.7	84.4	31.3	53.0	32.3	13.8
1967	814.3	509.3	70.6	216.9	221.7	128.0	117.6	85.2	31.5	53.7	32.4	10.5
1968	889.3	559.1	81.0	235.0	243.1	139.9	130.8	92.1	33.6	58.5	38.7	9.1
1969	959.5	603.7	86.2	252.2	265.3	155.2	145.5	102.9	37.7	65.2	42.6	9.7
1970	1,010.7	646.5	85.3	270.4	290.8	150.3	148.1	106.7	40.3	66.4	41.4	2.3
1971	1,097.2	700.3	97.2	283.3	319.8	175.5	167.5	111.7	42.7	69.1	55.8	8.0
1972	1,207.0	767.8	110.7	305.2	351.9	205.6	195.7	126.1	47.2	78.9	69.7	9.9
1973	1,349.6	848.1	124.1	339.6	384.5	243.1	225.4	150.0	55.0	95.1	75.3	17.7
1974	1,458.6	927.7	123.0	380.8	423.9	245.8	231.5	165.6	61.2	104.3	66.0	14.3
1975	1,585.9	1,024.9	134.3	416.0	474.5	226.0	231.7	169.0	61.4	107.6	62.7	−5.7
1976	1,768.4	1,143.1	160.0	451.8	531.2	286.4	269.6	187.2	65.9	121.2	82.5	16.7
1977	1,974.1	1,271.5	182.6	490.4	598.4	358.3	333.5	223.2	74.6	148.7	110.3	24.7
1978	2,232.7	1,421.2	202.3	541.5	677.4	434.0	406.1	274.5	93.9	180.6	131.6	27.9
1979	2,488.6	1,583.7	214.2	613.3	756.2	480.2	467.5	326.4	118.4	208.1	141.0	12.8
1980	2,708.0	1,748.1	212.5	682.9	852.7	467.6	477.1	353.8	137.5	216.4	123.3	−9.5
1981	3,030.6	1,926.2	228.5	744.2	953.5	558.0	532.5	410.0	169.1	240.9	122.5	25.4
1982	3,149.6	2,059.2	236.5	772.3	1,050.4	503.4	519.3	413.7	178.8	234.9	105.7	−15.9
1983	3,405.0	2,257.5	275.0	817.8	1,164.7	546.7	552.2	400.2	153.1	247.1	152.0	−5.5
1984	3,777.2	2,460.3	317.9	873.0	1,269.4	718.9	647.8	468.9	175.6	293.3	178.9	71.1
1985	4,038.7	2,667.4	352.9	919.4	1,395.1	714.5	689.9	504.0	193.4	310.6	185.9	24.6
1986	4,268.6	2,850.6	389.6	952.2	1,508.8	717.6	709.0	492.4	174.0	318.4	216.6	8.6
1987	4,539.9	3,052.2	403.7	1,011.1	1,637.4	749.3	723.0	497.8	171.3	326.5	225.2	26.3
1988	4,900.4	3,296.1	437.1	1,073.8	1,785.2	793.6	777.4	545.4	182.0	363.4	232.0	16.2
1989	5,250.8	3,523.1	459.4	1,149.5	1,914.2	832.3	798.9	568.1	193.3	374.8	230.9	33.3
1990	5,546.1	3,761.2	468.2	1,229.2	2,063.8	808.9	802.0	586.7	201.6	385.1	215.3	6.9
1991	5,722.9	3,906.4	457.8	1,257.9	2,190.7	736.9	745.5	555.9	182.6	373.3	189.6	−8.6
1992	6,038.5	4,139.9	497.3	1,300.9	2,341.6	796.5	789.1	565.5	172.6	392.9	223.6	7.3
1993 ᵖ	6,374.0	4,390.6	537.7	1,350.2	2,502.7	892.0	875.2	622.9	178.6	444.4	252.3	16.8
1982: IV	3,195.1	2,128.7	246.9	787.3	1,094.6	464.2	510.5	397.7	168.9	228.8	112.8	−46.3
1983: IV	3,547.3	2,346.8	297.7	839.8	1,209.3	614.8	594.6	426.9	154.6	272.3	167.7	20.2
1984: IV	3,869.1	2,526.4	328.2	887.8	1,310.4	722.8	671.8	491.5	184.1	307.3	180.4	51.0
1985: IV	4,140.5	2,739.8	354.4	939.5	1,446.0	737.0	704.4	511.3	195.4	315.9	193.1	32.6
1986: IV	4,336.6	2,923.1	406.8	963.7	1,552.6	697.1	715.9	491.7	168.4	323.3	224.2	−18.8
1987: IV	4,683.0	3,124.6	408.8	1,029.4	1,686.4	800.2	740.9	514.3	180.0	334.3	226.5	59.3
1988: IV	5,044.6	3,398.2	452.9	1,105.8	1,839.5	814.8	797.5	560.2	186.8	373.4	237.3	17.3
1989: IV	5,344.8	3,599.1	458.3	1,173.5	1,967.3	825.2	795.0	568.8	198.0	370.8	226.2	30.2
1990: I	5,461.9	3,679.3	479.8	1,201.7	1,997.8	828.9	819.3	586.2	203.6	382.5	233.2	9.6
II	5,540.9	3,727.0	466.0	1,213.6	2,047.5	837.8	804.5	582.1	203.2	378.9	222.4	33.3
III	5,583.8	3,801.7	467.3	1,241.0	2,093.4	812.5	804.1	594.1	203.8	390.3	209.9	8.4
IV	5,597.9	3,836.6	459.5	1,260.7	2,116.4	756.4	780.3	584.4	195.7	388.7	195.8	−23.9
1991: I	5,631.7	3,843.6	448.9	1,252.3	2,142.4	729.1	749.0	566.8	192.2	374.6	182.2	−19.9
II	5,697.7	3,887.8	452.0	1,259.2	2,176.6	721.5	744.5	561.0	188.4	372.6	183.6	−23.0
III	5,758.6	3,929.8	465.1	1,260.0	2,204.8	744.5	745.0	552.6	178.0	374.6	192.4	−.5
IV	5,803.7	3,964.1	465.2	1,260.0	2,239.0	752.4	743.5	543.3	171.7	371.5	200.3	8.9
1992: I	5,908.7	4,046.5	484.0	1,278.2	2,284.4	750.8	755.9	547.0	173.9	373.1	208.9	−5.1
II	5,991.4	4,099.9	487.8	1,288.2	2,323.8	799.7	786.8	566.3	174.5	391.7	220.6	12.9
III	6,059.5	4,157.1	500.9	1,305.7	2,350.5	802.2	792.5	569.2	170.8	398.4	223.3	9.7
IV	6,194.4	4,256.2	516.6	1,331.7	2,407.9	833.3	821.3	579.5	171.1	408.3	241.8	12.0
1993: I	6,261.6	4,296.2	515.3	1,335.3	2,445.5	874.1	839.5	594.7	172.4	422.2	244.9	34.6
II	6,327.6	4,359.9	531.6	1,344.8	2,483.4	874.1	861.0	619.1	177.6	441.6	241.9	13.1
III	6,395.9	4,419.1	541.9	1,352.4	2,524.8	884.0	876.3	624.9	179.1	445.8	251.3	7.7
IV ᵖ	6,510.8	4,487.4	561.9	1,368.4	2,557.2	935.8	924.1	653.0	185.2	467.8	271.1	11.7

See next page for continuation of table.

TABLE B-1.—Gross domestic product, 1959-93—Continued

[Billions of dollars, except as noted; quarterly data at seasonally adjusted annual rates]

Year or quarter	Net exports of goods and services			Government purchases					Final sales of domestic product	Gross domestic purchases [1]	Addendum: Gross national product [2]	Percent change from preceding period	
	Net exports	Exports	Imports	Total	Federal			State and local				Gross domestic product	Gross domestic purchases [1]
					Total	National defense	Non-defense						
1959	-1.7	20.6	22.3	99.0	57.1	46.4	10.8	41.8	490.0	495.8	497.0	8.7	9.1
1960	2.4	25.3	22.8	99.8	55.3	45.3	10.0	44.5	510.1	510.9	516.6	3.9	3.0
1961	3.4	26.0	22.7	107.0	58.6	47.9	10.6	48.4	528.9	528.4	535.4	3.6	3.4
1962	2.4	27.4	25.0	116.8	65.4	52.1	13.3	51.4	565.5	569.1	575.8	7.5	7.7
1963	3.3	29.4	26.1	122.3	66.4	51.5	14.9	55.8	597.5	599.8	607.7	5.5	5.4
1964	5.5	33.6	28.1	128.3	67.5	50.4	17.0	60.9	643.0	642.5	653.0	7.4	7.1
1965	3.9	35.4	31.5	136.3	69.5	51.0	18.5	66.8	693.0	698.8	708.1	8.4	8.8
1966	1.9	38.9	37.1	155.9	81.3	62.0	19.3	74.6	756.0	767.9	774.9	9.5	9.9
1967	1.4	41.4	39.9	175.6	92.8	73.4	19.4	82.7	803.8	812.9	819.8	5.8	5.9
1968	-1.3	45.3	46.6	191.5	99.2	79.1	20.0	92.3	880.2	890.6	895.5	9.2	9.6
1969	-1.2	49.3	50.5	201.8	100.5	78.9	21.6	101.3	949.8	960.7	965.6	7.9	7.9
1970	1.2	57.0	55.8	212.7	100.1	76.8	23.3	112.6	1,008.4	1,009.5	1,017.1	5.3	5.1
1971	-3.0	59.3	62.3	224.3	100.0	74.1	25.9	124.3	1,089.2	1,100.2	1,104.9	8.6	9.0
1972	-8.0	66.2	74.2	241.5	106.9	77.4	29.4	134.7	1,197.1	1,215.0	1,215.7	10.0	10.4
1973	.6	91.8	91.2	257.7	108.5	77.5	31.1	149.2	1,331.9	1,349.0	1,362.3	11.8	11.0
1974	-3.1	124.3	127.5	288.3	117.6	82.6	35.0	170.7	1,444.4	1,461.8	1,474.3	8.1	8.4
1975	13.6	136.3	122.7	321.4	129.4	89.6	39.8	192.0	1,591.5	1,572.3	1,599.1	8.7	7.6
1976	-2.3	148.9	151.1	341.3	135.8	93.4	42.4	205.5	1,751.7	1,770.7	1,785.5	11.5	12.6
1977	-23.7	158.8	182.4	368.0	147.9	100.9	47.0	220.1	1,949.4	1,997.8	1,994.6	11.6	12.8
1978	-26.1	186.1	212.3	403.6	162.2	108.9	53.3	241.4	2,204.8	2,258.8	2,254.5	13.1	13.1
1979	-23.8	228.9	252.7	448.5	179.3	121.9	57.5	269.2	2,475.9	2,512.5	2,520.8	11.5	11.2
1980	-14.7	279.2	293.9	507.1	209.1	142.7	66.4	298.0	2,717.5	2,722.8	2,742.1	8.8	8.4
1981	-14.7	303.0	317.7	561.1	240.8	167.5	73.3	320.3	3,005.2	3,045.3	3,063.8	11.9	11.8
1982	-20.6	282.6	303.2	607.6	266.6	193.8	72.7	341.1	3,165.5	3,170.2	3,179.8	3.9	4.1
1983	-51.4	276.7	328.1	652.3	292.0	214.4	77.5	360.3	3,410.6	3,456.5	3,434.4	8.1	9.0
1984	-102.7	302.4	405.1	700.8	310.9	233.1	77.8	389.9	3,706.1	3,879.9	3,801.5	10.9	12.2
1985	-115.6	302.1	417.6	772.3	344.3	258.6	85.7	428.1	4,014.1	4,154.3	4,053.6	6.9	7.1
1986	-132.5	319.2	451.7	833.0	367.8	276.7	91.1	465.3	4,260.0	4,401.2	4,277.7	5.7	5.9
1987	-143.1	364.0	507.1	881.5	384.9	292.1	92.9	496.6	4,513.7	4,683.0	4,544.5	6.4	6.4
1988	-108.0	444.2	552.2	918.7	387.0	295.6	91.4	531.7	4,884.2	5,008.4	4,908.2	7.9	6.9
1989	-79.7	508.0	587.7	975.2	401.6	299.9	101.7	573.6	5,217.5	5,330.5	5,266.8	7.2	6.4
1990	-71.4	557.1	628.5	1,047.4	426.5	314.0	112.5	620.9	5,539.3	5,617.5	5,567.8	5.6	5.4
1991	-19.6	601.5	621.1	1,099.3	445.9	322.5	123.4	653.4	5,731.6	5,742.5	5,737.1	3.2	2.2
1992	-29.6	640.5	670.1	1,131.8	448.8	313.8	135.0	683.0	6,031.2	6,068.2	6,045.8	5.5	5.7
1993 ᵖ	-65.7	660.1	725.8	1,157.1	443.4	303.6	139.8	713.7	6,357.2	6,439.7	....	5.6	6.1
1982: IV	-29.5	265.6	295.1	631.6	281.4	205.5	75.9	350.3	3,241.4	3,224.6	3,222.6	....	....
1983: IV	-71.8	286.2	358.0	657.6	289.7	222.8	66.9	367.9	3,527.1	3,619.1	3,578.4	....	....
1984: IV	-107.1	308.7	415.7	727.0	324.7	242.9	81.9	402.2	3,818.1	3,976.2	3,890.2	....	....
1985: IV	-135.5	304.7	440.2	799.2	356.9	268.6	88.3	442.4	4,107.9	4,276.0	4,156.2	....	....
1986: IV	-133.2	333.9	467.1	849.7	373.1	278.6	94.5	476.6	4,355.4	4,469.8	4,340.5	....	....
1987: IV	-143.2	392.4	535.6	901.4	392.5	295.8	96.7	509.0	4,623.7	4,826.2	4,690.5	....	....
1988: IV	-106.0	467.0	573.1	937.6	392.0	296.8	95.2	545.7	5,027.3	5,150.7	5,054.3	....	....
1989: IV	-73.9	523.8	597.7	994.5	405.1	302.5	102.6	589.3	5,314.6	5,418.7	5,365.0	....	....
1990: I	-73.9	542.0	615.9	1,027.7	422.7	312.1	110.6	605.0	5,452.4	5,535.9	5,482.1	9.1	8.9
II	-61.3	553.5	614.8	1,037.3	423.6	312.5	111.2	613.7	5,507.6	5,602.2	5,559.3	5.9	4.9
III	-78.7	555.3	634.0	1,048.3	423.2	309.1	114.1	625.1	5,575.3	5,662.4	5,599.9	3.1	4.4
IV	-71.6	577.6	649.2	1,076.5	436.5	322.5	114.0	640.0	5,621.8	5,669.5	5,630.0	1.0	.5
1991: I	-34.0	576.5	610.6	1,093.0	450.2	331.4	118.7	642.9	5,651.6	5,665.8	5,656.1	2.4	-.3
II	-11.5	600.7	612.2	1,099.9	449.4	326.3	123.0	650.5	5,720.8	5,709.2	5,710.6	4.8	3.1
III	-19.8	603.0	622.8	1,104.0	446.8	321.2	125.6	657.3	5,759.1	5,778.4	5,766.2	4.3	4.9
IV	-13.0	625.7	638.8	1,100.2	437.4	311.2	126.2	662.8	5,794.8	5,816.7	5,815.5	3.2	2.7
1992: I	-7.0	633.7	640.7	1,118.5	445.5	312.3	133.1	673.0	5,913.9	5,915.8	5,927.6	7.4	7.0
II	-33.9	632.4	666.3	1,125.8	444.6	310.4	134.2	681.2	5,978.6	6,025.3	5,996.3	5.7	7.6
III	-38.8	641.1	679.9	1,139.1	452.8	316.7	136.1	686.2	6,049.6	6,098.3	6,067.3	4.6	4.9
IV	-38.8	654.7	693.5	1,143.8	452.4	315.7	136.7	691.4	6,182.5	6,233.2	6,191.9	9.2	9.1
1993: I	-48.3	651.3	699.6	1,139.7	442.7	304.8	137.9	697.0	6,227.1	6,309.9	6,262.1	4.4	5.0
II	-65.1	660.0	725.0	1,158.6	447.5	307.6	140.0	711.1	6,314.5	6,392.7	6,327.1	4.3	5.4
III	-71.9	653.2	725.1	1,164.8	443.6	301.9	141.7	721.2	6,388.2	6,467.8	6,402.3	4.4	4.8
IV ᵖ	-77.7	675.8	753.5	1,165.3	439.7	300.0	139.7	725.6	6,499.0	6,588.5	....	7.4	7.7

[1] Gross domestic product (GDP) less exports of goods and services plus imports of goods and services.
[2] GDP plus net receipts of factor income from rest of the world.

Source: Department of Commerce, Bureau of Economic Analysis.

TABLE B-2.—Gross domestic product in 1987 dollars, 1959–93

[Billions of 1987 dollars, except as noted; quarterly data at seasonally adjusted annual rates]

Year or quarter	Gross domestic product	Personal consumption expenditures				Gross private domestic investment					
		Total	Durable goods	Non-durable goods	Services	Total	Fixed investment				Change in business inventories
							Total	Nonresidential			Residential	
								Total	Structures	Producers' durable equipment		

1959	1,928.8	1,178.9	114.4	518.5	546.0	296.4	282.8	165.2	74.4	90.8	117.6	13.6
1960	1,970.8	1,210.8	115.4	526.9	568.5	290.8	282.7	173.3	80.8	92.5	109.4	8.1
1961	2,023.8	1,238.4	109.4	537.7	591.3	289.4	282.2	172.1	82.3	89.8	110.1	7.2
1962	2,128.1	1,293.3	120.2	553.0	620.0	321.2	305.6	185.0	86.1	98.9	120.6	15.6
1963	2,215.6	1,341.9	130.3	563.6	648.0	343.3	327.3	192.3	86.9	105.4	135.0	16.0
1964	2,340.6	1,417.2	140.7	588.2	688.3	371.8	356.2	214.0	95.9	118.1	142.1	15.7
1965	2,470.5	1,497.0	156.2	616.7	724.1	413.0	387.9	250.6	111.5	139.1	137.3	25.1
1966	2,616.2	1,573.8	166.0	647.6	760.2	438.0	401.3	276.7	119.1	157.6	124.5	36.7
1967	2,685.2	1,622.4	167.2	659.0	796.2	418.6	391.0	270.8	116.0	154.8	120.2	27.6
1968	2,796.9	1,707.5	184.5	686.0	837.0	440.1	416.5	280.1	117.4	162.7	136.4	23.6
1969	2,873.0	1,771.2	190.8	703.2	877.2	461.3	436.5	296.4	123.5	172.9	140.1	24.8
1970	2,873.9	1,813.5	183.7	717.2	912.5	429.7	423.8	292.0	123.3	168.7	131.8	5.9
1971	2,955.9	1,873.7	201.4	725.6	946.7	475.7	454.9	286.8	121.2	165.6	168.1	20.8
1972	3,107.1	1,978.4	225.2	755.8	997.4	532.2	509.6	311.6	124.8	186.8	198.0	22.5
1973	3,268.6	2,066.7	246.6	777.9	1,042.2	591.7	554.0	357.4	134.9	222.4	196.6	37.7
1974	3,248.1	2,053.8	227.2	759.8	1,066.8	543.0	512.0	356.5	132.3	224.2	155.6	30.9
1975	3,221.7	2,097.5	226.8	767.1	1,103.6	437.6	451.5	316.8	118.0	198.8	134.7	−13.9
1976	3,380.8	2,207.3	256.4	801.3	1,149.5	520.6	495.1	328.7	120.5	208.2	166.4	25.5
1977	3,533.3	2,296.6	280.0	819.8	1,196.8	600.4	566.2	364.3	126.1	238.2	201.9	34.3
1978	3,703.5	2,391.8	292.9	844.8	1,254.1	664.6	627.4	412.9	144.1	268.8	214.5	37.2
1979	3,796.8	2,448.4	289.0	862.8	1,296.5	669.7	656.1	448.8	163.3	285.5	207.4	13.6
1980	3,776.3	2,447.1	262.7	860.5	1,323.9	594.4	602.7	437.8	170.2	267.6	164.8	−8.3
1981	3,843.1	2,476.9	264.6	867.9	1,344.4	631.1	606.5	455.0	182.9	272.0	151.6	24.6
1982	3,760.3	2,503.7	262.5	872.2	1,368.9	540.5	558.0	433.9	181.3	252.6	124.1	−17.5
1983	3,906.6	2,619.4	297.7	900.3	1,421.4	599.5	595.1	420.8	160.3	260.5	174.2	4.4
1984	4,148.5	2,746.1	338.5	934.6	1,473.0	757.5	689.6	490.2	182.8	307.4	199.3	67.9
1985	4,279.8	2,865.8	370.1	958.7	1,537.0	745.9	723.8	521.8	197.4	324.4	202.0	22.1
1986	4,404.5	2,969.1	402.0	991.0	1,576.1	735.1	726.5	500.3	176.6	323.7	226.2	8.5
1987	4,539.9	3,052.2	403.7	1,011.1	1,637.4	749.3	723.0	497.8	171.3	326.5	225.2	26.3
1988	4,718.6	3,162.4	428.7	1,035.1	1,698.5	773.4	753.4	530.8	174.0	356.8	222.7	19.9
1989	4,838.0	3,223.3	440.7	1,051.6	1,731.0	784.0	754.2	540.0	177.6	362.5	214.2	29.8
1990	4,897.3	3,272.6	443.1	1,060.7	1,768.8	746.8	741.1	546.5	179.5	367.0	194.5	5.7
1991	4,861.4	3,258.6	426.6	1,048.2	1,783.8	675.7	684.1	514.5	160.2	354.3	169.5	−8.4
1992	4,986.3	3,341.8	456.6	1,062.9	1,822.3	732.9	726.4	529.2	150.6	378.6	197.1	6.5
1993 ᵖ	5,132.7	3,452.5	489.7	1,088.1	1,874.7	820.9	805.5	591.3	151.4	439.9	214.2	15.4
1982: IV	3,759.6	2,539.3	272.3	880.7	1,386.2	503.5	548.4	417.2	173.2	244.0	131.2	−44.9
1983: IV	4,012.1	2,678.2	319.1	915.2	1,443.9	669.5	640.2	449.6	162.6	287.0	190.6	29.3
1984: IV	4,194.2	2,784.8	347.7	942.9	1,494.2	756.4	708.4	509.6	189.5	320.1	198.8	47.9
1985: IV	4,333.5	2,895.3	369.6	968.7	1,557.1	763.1	732.9	525.5	198.3	327.2	207.4	30.2
1986: IV	4,427.1	3,012.5	415.7	1,000.9	1,595.8	705.9	725.9	495.5	170.4	325.0	230.5	−20.1
1987: IV	4,625.5	3,074.7	404.7	1,014.6	1,655.5	793.8	733.9	510.6	177.9	332.7	223.3	59.9
1988: IV	4,779.7	3,202.9	439.2	1,046.8	1,716.9	785.0	764.1	538.8	175.7	363.1	225.3	20.9
1989: IV	4,856.7	3,242.0	436.8	1,058.9	1,746.3	769.5	744.6	536.7	179.8	356.9	208.0	24.9
1990: I	4,898.3	3,264.4	454.8	1,059.8	1,749.8	766.5	761.8	550.2	182.9	367.3	211.6	4.7
II	4,917.1	3,271.6	441.8	1,060.6	1,769.2	773.9	745.8	544.5	181.6	363.0	201.2	28.1
III	4,906.5	3,288.4	442.4	1,065.0	1,781.1	751.0	740.1	551.2	180.9	370.3	189.0	10.9
IV	4,867.2	3,265.9	433.2	1,057.5	1,775.2	695.7	716.6	540.2	172.8	367.4	176.3	−20.9
1991: I	4,837.8	3,242.7	420.3	1,048.2	1,774.2	667.8	685.2	521.4	169.0	352.5	163.8	−17.4
II	4,855.6	3,256.9	422.0	1,051.1	1,783.8	659.8	682.1	517.8	165.2	352.6	164.3	−22.3
III	4,872.6	3,267.1	432.6	1,049.3	1,785.2	682.8	683.8	512.8	155.6	357.2	171.0	−.9
IV	4,879.6	3,267.5	431.5	1,044.0	1,792.0	692.3	685.2	506.1	151.0	355.2	179.1	7.1
1992: I	4,922.0	3,302.3	446.6	1,052.0	1,803.7	691.7	696.7	510.5	152.8	357.7	186.2	−5.0
II	4,956.5	3,316.8	447.5	1,055.0	1,814.3	737.0	724.4	528.8	152.9	375.9	195.6	12.6
III	4,998.2	3,350.9	459.0	1,062.9	1,829.0	739.6	730.0	533.8	148.8	385.1	196.2	9.6
IV	5,068.3	3,397.2	473.4	1,081.8	1,842.0	763.0	754.3	543.7	148.0	395.7	210.6	8.7
1993: I	5,078.2	3,403.8	471.9	1,076.0	1,855.9	803.0	773.7	562.3	148.2	414.1	211.4	29.3
II	5,102.1	3,432.7	484.2	1,083.1	1,865.4	803.6	790.6	584.3	151.1	433.2	206.2	13.0
III	5,138.3	3,469.6	493.1	1,093.0	1,883.5	813.4	806.9	594.8	151.2	443.6	212.1	6.5
IV ᵖ	5,212.1	3,503.9	509.9	1,100.4	1,893.9	863.6	851.0	623.8	155.1	468.7	227.2	12.7

See next page for continuation of table.

TABLE B-2.—*Gross domestic product in 1987 dollars, 1959-93*—Continued

[Billions of 1987 dollars, except as noted; quarterly data at seasonally adjusted annual rates]

Year or quarter	Net exports of goods and services				Government purchases						Final sales of domestic product	Gross domestic purchases [1]	Addendum: Gross national product [2]	Percent change from preceding period	
	Net exports	Exports	Imports	Total	Federal				State and local				Gross domestic product	Gross domestic purchases [1]
					Total	National defense	Non-defense							

1959	−21.8	73.8	95.6	475.3	265.7			209.6	1,915.2	1,950.6	1,939.6	5.5	5.8
1960	−7.6	88.4	96.1	476.9	259.0			217.9	1,962.7	1,978.5	1,982.8	2.2	1.4
1961	−5.5	89.9	95.3	501.5	270.1			231.4	2,016.6	2,029.3	2,037.1	2.7	2.6
1962	−10.5	95.0	105.5	524.2	287.3			236.9	2,112.5	2,138.6	2,143.3	5.2	5.4
1963	−5.8	101.8	107.7	536.3	285.7			250.6	2,199.6	2,221.4	2,231.8	4.1	3.9
1964	2.5	115.4	112.9	549.1	281.8			267.3	2,324.9	2,338.1	2,358.1	5.6	5.3
1965	−6.4	118.1	124.5	566.9	282.1			284.8	2,445.4	2,476.9	2,488.9	5.5	5.9
1966	−18.0	125.7	143.7	622.4	319.3			303.1	2,579.5	2,634.2	2,633.2	5.9	6.4
1967	−23.7	130.0	153.7	667.9	350.9			317.0	2,657.5	2,708.9	2,702.6	2.6	2.8
1968	−37.5	140.2	177.7	686.8	353.1			333.7	2,773.2	2,834.4	2,815.6	4.2	4.6
1969	−41.5	147.8	189.2	682.0	340.1			341.9	2,848.2	2,914.5	2,890.9	2.7	2.8
1970	−35.2	161.3	196.4	665.8	315.0			350.9	2,868.0	2,909.1	2,891.5	.0	−.2
1971	−45.9	161.9	207.8	652.4	290.8			361.6	2,935.2	3,001.8	2,975.9	2.9	3.2
1972	−56.5	173.7	230.2	653.0	284.4	209.6	74.8	368.6	3,084.5	3,163.6	3,128.8	5.1	5.4
1973	−34.1	210.3	244.4	644.2	265.3	191.3	74.1	378.9	3,230.9	3,302.7	3,298.6	5.2	4.4
1974	−4.1	234.4	238.4	655.4	262.6	185.8	76.8	392.9	3,217.2	3,252.2	3,282.4	−.6	−1.5
1975	23.1	232.9	209.8	663.5	262.7	184.9	77.8	400.8	3,235.6	3,198.6	3,247.6	−.8	−1.6
1976	−6.4	243.4	249.7	659.2	258.2	179.9	78.3	401.1	3,355.3	3,387.1	3,412.2	4.9	5.9
1977	−27.8	246.9	274.7	664.1	263.1	181.6	81.4	401.0	3,499.0	3,561.1	3,569.0	4.5	5.1
1978	−29.9	270.2	300.1	677.0	268.6	182.1	86.5	408.4	3,666.3	3,733.3	3,739.0	4.8	4.8
1979	−10.6	293.5	304.1	689.3	271.7	185.1	86.6	417.6	3,783.2	3,807.4	3,845.3	2.5	2.0
1980	30.7	320.5	289.9	704.2	284.8	194.2	90.6	419.4	3,784.6	3,745.7	3,823.4	−.5	−1.6
1981	22.0	326.1	304.1	713.2	295.8	206.4	89.4	417.4	3,818.6	3,821.2	3,884.4	1.8	2.0
1982	−7.4	296.7	304.1	723.6	306.0	221.4	84.7	417.6	3,777.8	3,767.7	3,796.1	−2.2	−1.4
1983	−56.1	285.9	342.1	743.8	320.8	234.2	86.6	423.0	3,902.2	3,962.8	3,939.6	3.9	5.2
1984	−122.0	305.7	427.7	766.9	331.0	245.8	85.1	436.0	4,080.6	4,270.5	4,174.5	6.2	7.8
1985	−145.3	309.2	454.6	813.4	355.2	265.6	89.5	458.2	4,257.6	4,425.1	4,295.0	3.2	3.6
1986	−155.1	329.6	484.7	855.4	373.0	280.6	92.4	482.4	4,395.9	4,559.6	4,413.5	2.9	3.0
1987	−143.1	364.0	507.1	881.5	384.9	292.1	92.9	496.6	4,513.7	4,683.0	4,544.5	3.1	2.7
1988	−104.0	421.6	525.7	886.8	377.3	287.0	90.2	509.6	4,698.6	4,822.6	4,726.3	3.9	3.0
1989	−73.7	471.8	545.4	904.4	376.1	281.4	94.8	528.3	4,808.3	4,911.7	4,852.7	2.5	1.8
1990	−54.7	510.5	565.1	932.6	384.1	283.6	100.4	548.5	4,891.6	4,951.9	4,916.5	1.2	.8
1991	−19.1	543.4	562.5	946.3	386.5	281.3	105.3	559.7	4,869.8	4,880.5	4,874.5	−.7	−1.4
1992	−33.6	578.0	611.6	945.2	373.0	261.2	111.8	572.2	4,979.8	5,019.9	4,994.0	2.6	2.9
1993 [p]	−79.3	596.4	675.7	938.6	355.1	242.7	112.5	583.4	5,117.3	5,211.9		2.9	3.8
1982: IV	−19.0	280.4	299.4	735.9	316.0	229.4	86.6	419.9	3,804.5	3,778.6	3,791.7		
1983: IV	−83.7	291.5	375.1	748.1	322.2	242.9	79.3	425.9	3,982.8	4,095.8	4,046.6		
1984: IV	−131.4	312.8	444.2	784.3	341.7	254.3	87.4	442.6	4,146.3	4,325.5	4,216.4		
1985: IV	−155.4	312.0	467.4	830.5	363.7	272.1	91.6	466.7	4,303.3	4,488.9	4,349.5		
1986: IV	−156.0	342.9	498.9	864.8	377.5	282.2	95.3	487.3	4,447.2	4,583.1	4,430.8		
1987: IV	−136.0	386.1	522.1	893.0	391.6	295.0	96.6	501.4	4,565.6	4,761.5	4,633.0		
1988: IV	−102.7	438.2	540.9	894.5	378.4	285.7	92.7	516.1	4,758.7	4,882.4	4,789.0		
1989: IV	−67.4	487.7	555.0	912.6	376.1	281.5	94.7	536.5	4,831.8	4,924.1	4,875.1		
1990: I	−60.8	501.8	562.6	928.1	385.4	285.3	100.1	542.8	4,893.6	4,959.1	4,916.4	3.5	2.9
II	−58.9	511.1	570.0	930.6	384.7	285.0	99.8	545.9	4,889.0	4,976.0	4,933.4	1.5	1.4
III	−62.2	508.6	570.7	929.2	379.6	278.5	101.1	549.6	4,895.6	4,968.6	4,920.9	−.9	−.6
IV	−36.8	520.4	557.2	942.4	386.5	285.7	100.8	555.8	4,888.0	4,904.0	4,895.4	−3.2	−5.1
1991: I	−21.6	519.4	541.0	948.9	393.8	292.0	101.8	555.1	4,855.2	4,859.4	4,859.3	−2.4	−3.6
II	−13.3	542.9	556.2	952.3	393.6	288.7	104.9	558.7	4,878.0	4,869.0	4,867.5	1.5	.8
III	−25.0	546.9	571.9	947.6	386.6	279.4	107.2	561.0	4,873.5	4,897.6	4,880.3	1.4	2.4
IV	−16.4	564.2	580.7	936.2	372.1	264.9	107.2	564.1	4,872.5	4,896.0	4,890.9	.6	−.1
1992: I	−15.2	571.0	586.2	943.1	372.1	261.2	110.9	571.0	4,926.9	4,937.1	4,939.0	3.5	3.4
II	−38.0	570.2	608.2	940.7	369.2	257.9	111.3	571.5	4,943.8	4,994.5	4,962.2	2.8	4.7
III	−42.5	579.3	621.8	950.2	377.0	264.4	112.5	573.2	4,988.6	5,040.7	5,006.4	3.4	3.8
IV	−38.8	591.6	630.3	946.9	373.7	261.3	112.4	573.2	5,059.6	5,107.1	5,068.4	5.7	5.4
1993: I	−59.9	588.0	647.9	931.3	357.6	246.0	111.5	573.7	5,048.9	5,138.1	5,080.7	.8	2.5
II	−75.2	593.2	668.4	941.1	359.4	246.4	113.0	581.6	5,089.1	5,177.4	5,104.1	1.9	3.1
III	−86.3	591.9	678.2	941.7	353.7	240.1	113.7	588.0	5,131.8	5,224.6	5,145.8	2.9	3.7
IV [p]	−95.6	612.5	708.1	940.1	349.8	238.2	111.6	590.4	5,199.4	5,307.7		5.9	6.5

[1] Gross domestic product (GDP) less exports of goods and services plus imports of goods and services.
[2] GDP plus net receipts of factor income from rest of the world.

Source: Department of Commerce, Bureau of Economic Analysis.

TABLE B-3.—*Implicit price deflators for gross domestic product, 1959–93*

[Index numbers, 1987=100, except as noted; quarterly data seasonally adjusted]

Year or quarter	Gross domestic product	Personal consumption expenditures					Gross private domestic investment: Fixed investment				
		Total	Durable goods	Non-durable goods	Services	Total	Nonresidential				Residential
							Total	Structures	Producers' durable equipment		

Year	GDP	Total	Dur	Nondur	Svc	Total	Total	Struct	PDE	Res
1959	25.6	27.0	37.4	28.6	23.2	26.4	28.1	24.4	31.2	23.9
1960	26.0	27.5	37.7	29.1	23.9	26.7	28.4	24.2	32.1	24.0
1961	26.3	27.7	38.3	29.3	24.4	26.6	28.2	24.0	32.2	24.0
1962	26.9	28.2	39.1	29.6	24.8	26.8	28.6	24.1	32.4	24.0
1963	27.2	28.6	39.7	30.1	25.2	26.8	28.9	24.4	32.6	23.8
1964	27.7	29.1	40.4	30.5	25.6	27.1	29.2	24.7	32.8	24.1
1965	28.4	29.7	40.6	31.1	26.1	27.9	29.6	25.4	32.9	24.9
1966	29.4	30.6	41.3	32.2	26.9	29.1	30.5	26.3	33.6	25.9
1967	30.3	31.4	42.3	32.9	27.8	30.1	31.5	27.2	34.7	26.9
1968	31.8	32.7	43.9	34.3	29.0	31.4	32.9	28.6	36.0	28.4
1969	33.4	34.1	45.2	35.9	30.2	33.3	34.7	30.5	37.7	30.4
1970	35.2	35.6	46.4	37.7	31.9	34.9	36.5	32.7	39.4	31.4
1971	37.1	37.4	48.3	39.0	33.8	36.8	39.0	35.2	41.7	33.2
1972	38.8	38.8	49.2	40.4	35.3	38.4	40.5	37.8	42.2	35.2
1973	41.3	41.0	50.3	43.7	36.9	40.7	42.0	40.7	42.7	38.3
1974	44.9	45.2	54.1	50.1	39.7	45.2	46.4	46.3	46.5	42.4
1975	49.2	48.9	59.2	54.2	43.0	51.3	53.3	52.0	54.1	46.6
1976	52.3	51.8	62.4	56.4	46.2	54.5	56.9	54.7	58.2	49.6
1977	55.9	55.4	65.2	59.8	50.0	58.9	61.3	59.2	62.4	54.6
1978	60.3	59.4	69.1	64.1	54.0	64.7	66.5	65.2	67.2	61.3
1979	65.5	64.7	74.1	71.1	58.3	71.2	72.7	72.5	72.9	68.0
1980	71.7	71.4	80.9	79.4	64.4	79.2	80.8	80.8	80.9	74.8
1981	78.9	77.8	86.4	85.7	70.9	87.8	90.1	92.5	88.5	80.9
1982	83.8	82.2	90.1	88.6	76.7	93.1	95.3	98.6	93.0	85.2
1983	87.2	86.2	92.4	90.8	81.9	92.8	95.1	95.5	94.8	87.3
1984	91.0	89.6	93.9	93.4	86.2	93.9	95.7	96.1	95.4	89.7
1985	94.4	93.1	95.4	95.9	90.8	95.3	96.6	98.0	95.7	92.0
1986	96.9	96.0	96.9	96.1	95.7	97.6	98.4	98.5	98.4	95.8
1987	100.0	100.0	100.0	100.0	100.0	100.0	100.0	100.0	100.0	100.0
1988	103.9	104.2	102.0	103.7	105.1	103.2	102.8	104.6	101.9	104.2
1989	108.5	109.3	104.2	109.3	110.6	105.9	105.2	108.9	103.4	107.8
1990	113.3	114.9	105.7	115.9	116.7	108.2	107.3	112.3	104.9	110.7
1991	117.7	119.9	107.3	120.0	122.8	109.0	108.0	114.0	105.4	111.8
1992	121.1	123.9	108.9	122.4	128.5	108.6	106.9	114.6	103.8	113.4
1993 ᵖ	124.2	127.2	109.8	124.1	133.5	108.7	105.3	117.9	101.0	117.8
1982: IV	85.0	83.8	90.6	89.4	79.0	93.1	95.3	97.5	93.8	86.0
1983: IV	88.4	87.6	93.3	91.8	83.7	92.9	95.0	95.1	94.9	88.0
1984: IV	92.3	90.7	94.4	94.2	87.7	94.8	96.4	97.2	96.0	90.7
1985: IV	95.5	94.6	95.9	97.0	92.9	96.1	97.3	98.5	96.5	93.1
1986: IV	98.0	97.0	97.8	96.3	97.3	98.6	99.2	98.8	99.5	97.3
1987: IV	101.2	101.6	101.0	101.5	101.9	101.0	100.7	101.2	100.5	101.5
1988: IV	105.5	106.1	103.1	105.6	107.1	104.4	104.0	106.3	102.8	105.3
1989: IV	110.1	111.0	104.9	110.8	112.7	106.8	106.0	110.1	103.9	108.8
1990: I	111.5	112.7	105.5	113.4	114.2	107.6	106.5	111.3	104.2	110.2
II	112.7	113.9	105.5	114.4	115.7	107.9	106.9	111.9	104.4	110.5
III	113.8	115.6	105.6	116.5	117.5	108.6	107.8	112.7	105.4	111.1
IV	115.0	117.5	106.1	119.2	119.2	108.9	108.2	113.3	105.8	111.1
1991: I	116.4	118.5	106.8	119.5	120.8	109.3	108.7	113.8	106.3	111.3
II	117.3	119.4	107.1	119.8	122.0	109.2	108.3	114.0	105.7	111.7
III	118.2	120.3	107.5	120.1	123.5	109.0	107.8	114.4	104.9	112.5
IV	118.9	121.3	107.8	120.7	124.9	108.5	107.3	113.8	104.6	111.8
1992: I	120.0	122.5	108.4	121.5	126.6	108.5	107.1	113.8	104.3	112.2
II	120.9	123.6	109.0	122.1	128.1	108.6	107.1	114.2	104.2	112.8
III	121.2	124.1	109.1	122.8	128.5	108.6	106.6	114.8	103.5	113.8
IV	122.2	125.3	109.1	123.1	130.7	108.9	106.6	115.7	103.2	114.9
1993: I	123.3	126.2	109.2	124.1	131.8	108.5	105.7	116.3	102.0	115.8
II	124.0	127.0	109.8	124.2	133.1	108.9	106.0	117.5	101.9	117.3
III	124.5	127.4	109.9	123.7	134.0	108.6	105.1	118.5	100.5	118.5
IV ᵖ	124.9	128.1	110.2	124.4	135.0	108.6	104.7	119.4	99.8	119.3

See next page for continuation of table.

TABLE B-3.—*Implicit price deflators for gross domestic product, 1959–93*—Continued

[Index numbers, 1987=100, except as noted; quarterly data seasonally adjusted]

Year or quarter	Exports and imports of goods and services		Government purchases of goods and services				State and local	Final sales of domestic product	Gross domestic purchases [1]	Percent change from preceding period, GDP implicit price deflator [2]
	Exports	Imports	Total	Federal						
				Total	National defense	Non-defense				
1959	28.0	23.4	20.8	21.5			19.9	25.6	25.4	2.8
1960	28.6	23.8	20.9	21.3			20.4	26.0	25.8	1.6
1961	29.0	23.8	21.3	21.7			20.9	26.2	26.0	1.2
1962	28.9	23.7	22.3	22.8			21.7	26.8	26.6	2.3
1963	28.9	24.3	22.8	23.3			22.3	27.2	27.0	1.1
1964	29.1	24.9	23.4	23.9			22.8	27.7	27.5	1.8
1965	30.0	25.3	24.0	24.6			23.5	28.3	28.2	2.5
1966	31.0	25.8	25.0	25.5			24.6	29.3	29.2	3.5
1967	31.8	26.0	26.3	26.5			26.1	30.2	30.0	3.1
1968	32.3	26.2	27.9	28.1			27.7	31.7	31.4	5.0
1969	33.3	26.7	29.6	29.6			29.6	33.3	33.0	5.0
1970	35.3	28.4	31.9	31.8			32.1	35.2	34.7	5.4
1971	36.6	30.0	34.4	34.4			34.4	37.1	36.7	5.4
1972	38.1	32.2	37.0	37.6	36.9	39.3	36.5	38.8	38.4	4.6
1973	43.6	37.3	40.0	40.9	40.5	41.9	39.4	41.2	40.8	6.4
1974	53.0	53.5	44.0	44.8	44.5	45.5	43.5	44.9	44.9	8.7
1975	58.5	58.5	48.4	49.3	48.5	51.2	47.9	49.2	49.2	9.6
1976	61.2	60.5	51.8	52.6	51.9	54.1	51.2	52.2	52.3	6.3
1977	64.3	66.4	55.4	56.2	55.6	57.7	54.9	55.7	56.1	6.9
1978	68.9	70.7	59.6	60.4	59.8	61.7	59.1	60.1	60.5	7.9
1979	78.0	83.1	65.1	66.0	65.8	66.4	64.5	65.4	66.0	8.6
1980	87.1	101.4	72.0	73.4	73.5	73.3	71.1	71.8	72.7	9.5
1981	92.9	104.5	78.7	81.4	81.1	82.1	76.7	78.7	79.7	10.0
1982	95.2	99.7	84.0	87.1	87.6	85.9	81.7	83.8	84.1	6.2
1983	96.8	95.9	87.7	91.0	91.6	89.5	85.2	87.4	87.2	4.1
1984	98.9	94.7	91.4	93.9	94.8	91.3	89.4	90.8	90.9	4.4
1985	97.7	91.9	95.0	96.9	97.3	95.7	93.4	94.3	93.9	3.7
1986	96.9	93.2	97.4	98.6	98.6	98.6	96.4	96.9	96.5	2.6
1987	100.0	100.0	100.0	100.0	100.0	100.0	100.0	100.0	100.0	3.2
1988	105.3	105.1	103.6	102.6	103.0	101.4	104.3	103.9	103.9	3.9
1989	107.7	107.8	107.8	106.8	106.6	107.3	108.6	108.5	108.5	4.4
1990	109.1	111.2	112.3	111.0	110.7	112.0	113.2	113.2	113.4	4.4
1991	110.7	110.4	116.2	115.4	114.7	117.7	116.7	117.7	117.7	3.9
1992	110.8	109.6	119.7	120.3	120.1	120.8	119.4	121.1	120.9	2.9
1993 ᵖ	110.7	107.4	123.3	124.8	125.1	124.3	122.3	124.2	123.6	2.5
1982: IV	94.7	98.5	85.8	89.0	89.6	87.7	83.4	85.2	85.3	....
1983: IV	98.2	95.4	87.9	89.9	91.7	84.3	86.4	88.6	88.4	....
1984: IV	98.7	93.6	92.7	95.0	95.5	93.7	90.9	92.1	91.9	....
1985: IV	97.7	94.2	96.2	98.1	98.7	96.4	94.8	95.5	95.3	....
1986: IV	97.4	93.6	98.3	98.8	98.7	99.2	97.8	97.9	97.5	....
1987: IV	101.6	102.6	100.9	100.2	100.3	100.1	101.5	101.3	101.4	....
1988: IV	106.6	106.0	104.8	103.6	103.9	102.6	105.7	105.6	105.5	....
1989: IV	107.4	107.7	109.0	107.7	107.5	108.4	109.9	110.0	110.0	....
1990: I	108.0	109.5	110.7	109.7	109.4	110.5	111.5	111.4	111.6	5.2
II	108.3	107.9	111.5	110.1	109.6	111.4	112.4	112.7	112.6	4.4
III	109.2	111.1	112.8	111.5	111.0	112.8	113.7	113.9	114.0	4.0
IV	111.0	116.5	114.2	112.9	112.9	113.1	115.2	115.0	115.6	4.3
1991: I	111.0	112.9	115.2	114.3	113.5	116.7	115.8	116.4	116.6	5.0
II	110.6	110.1	115.5	114.2	113.0	117.3	116.4	117.3	117.3	3.1
III	110.2	108.9	116.5	115.6	114.9	117.2	117.2	118.2	118.0	3.1
IV	110.9	110.0	117.5	117.5	117.5	117.8	117.5	118.9	118.8	2.4
1992: I	111.0	109.3	118.6	119.7	119.6	120.0	117.9	120.0	119.8	3.8
II	110.9	109.4	119.7	120.4	120.3	120.6	119.2	120.9	120.6	3.0
III	110.7	109.3	119.9	120.1	119.8	121.0	119.7	121.3	121.0	1.0
IV	110.7	110.0	120.8	121.1	120.8	121.6	120.6	122.2	122.1	3.3
1993: I	110.8	108.0	122.4	123.8	123.9	123.6	121.5	123.3	122.8	3.6
II	111.3	108.5	123.1	124.5	124.8	123.9	122.3	124.1	123.5	2.3
III	110.4	106.9	123.7	125.4	125.7	124.6	122.7	124.5	123.8	1.5
IV ᵖ	110.3	106.4	123.9	125.7	126.0	125.1	122.9	125.0	124.1	1.4

[1] Gross domestic product (GDP) less exports of goods and services plus imports of goods and services.
[2] Quarterly changes are at annual rates.

Note.—Separate deflators are not calculated for gross private domestic investment, change in business inventories, and net exports of goods and services.

Source: Department of Commerce, Bureau of Economic Analysis.

TABLE B-4.—*Fixed-weighted price indexes for gross domestic product, 1987 weights, 1959–93*

[Index numbers, 1987=100, except as noted; quarterly data seasonally adjusted]

Year or quarter	Gross domestic product	Personal consumption expenditures				Gross private domestic investment: Fixed investment				
		Total	Durable goods	Nondurable goods	Services	Total	Nonresidential			Residential
							Total	Structures	Producers' durable equipment	
1959		30.4	54.4	31.4	23.9			24.1		25.0
1960		30.8	54.1	31.8	24.5			24.1		25.1
1961		31.1	53.8	32.0	25.0			24.0		25.1
1962		31.3	53.4	32.1	25.3			24.2		25.0
1963		31.6	53.1	32.5	25.7			24.5		24.7
1964		31.9	53.1	32.8	26.1			24.9		24.9
1965		32.2	52.1	33.3	26.7			25.6		25.5
1966		32.8	51.3	34.3	27.4			26.6		26.4
1967		33.7	51.8	35.1	28.3			27.5		27.2
1968		35.0	53.1	36.5	29.6			28.8		28.6
1969		36.3	54.2	38.1	30.7			30.7		30.6
1970		37.9	55.1	39.9	32.4			32.8		31.7
1971		39.5	56.7	41.1	34.3			35.2		33.5
1972		40.8	57.1	42.4	35.9			37.9		35.5
1973		42.7	57.8	45.3	37.4			40.8		38.6
1974		46.7	61.0	51.3	40.3			46.3		42.7
1975		50.5	66.0	55.3	43.7			51.5		46.7
1976		53.3	69.1	57.5	46.9			53.7		49.7
1977		56.7	71.7	60.8	50.5			57.8		54.7
1978		60.7	75.2	64.7	54.6			63.7		61.4
1979		65.8	80.0	71.3	59.0			71.3		68.2
1980		72.6	84.7	79.6	65.3			78.5		75.3
1981		78.9	89.5	86.0	71.9			87.3		81.3
1982	84.8	83.2	92.4	88.8	77.4	95.6	100.3	92.9	104.2	85.3
1983	88.1	86.7	93.7	91.1	82.4	94.8	98.3	92.5	101.3	87.3
1984	91.1	89.9	94.9	93.7	86.4	94.7	96.8	94.1	98.3	89.8
1985	94.3	93.3	96.0	96.2	90.9	95.7	97.3	96.9	97.5	92.1
1986	97.0	96.1	97.1	96.1	95.8	97.9	98.8	98.5	99.0	95.8
1987	100.0	100.0	100.0	100.0	100.0	100.0	100.0	100.0	100.0	100.0
1988	104.0	104.3	102.0	103.8	105.1	103.2	102.8	104.6	101.9	104.3
1989	108.6	109.5	104.5	109.5	110.7	106.3	105.6	109.0	103.9	107.8
1990	113.6	115.2	106.3	116.2	116.8	109.1	108.4	112.4	106.2	110.7
1991	118.2	120.5	109.1	120.5	123.3	110.8	110.2	113.9	108.3	111.9
1992	122.1	124.9	111.5	123.0	129.5	112.0	111.4	114.6	109.7	113.4
1993 ᵖ	125.9	128.7	113.8	124.9	134.6	114.7	113.3	117.8	110.9	117.7
1982: IV	86.3	84.7	92.6	89.7	79.6	95.4	99.6	93.5	102.8	86.2
1983: IV	89.3	88.2	94.5	92.0	84.2	94.6	97.6	92.4	100.3	88.0
1984: IV	92.3	91.0	95.2	94.4	87.9	95.1	97.0	95.3	97.9	90.8
1985: IV	95.5	94.8	96.3	97.2	92.9	96.4	97.9	97.8	97.9	93.1
1986: IV	98.0	97.1	97.9	96.3	97.3	98.8	99.5	99.0	99.8	97.3
1987: IV	101.3	101.6	101.0	101.5	101.9	101.0	100.7	101.2	100.5	101.5
1988: IV	105.6	106.2	103.3	105.7	107.2	104.5	104.0	106.2	102.9	105.4
1989: IV	110.2	111.2	105.2	111.0	112.8	107.3	106.6	110.3	104.7	108.8
1990: I	111.7	113.0	105.9	113.8	114.3	108.3	107.4	111.4	105.3	110.2
II	112.9	114.2	106.0	114.6	115.9	108.7	107.9	112.0	105.7	110.5
III	114.3	115.9	106.3	116.8	117.8	109.5	108.7	112.8	106.6	111.1
IV	115.3	117.9	106.9	119.7	119.5	110.0	109.4	113.3	107.4	111.1
1991: I	116.8	119.0	108.1	119.9	121.2	110.5	110.1	113.7	108.1	111.4
II	117.8	119.9	108.7	120.3	122.5	110.6	110.1	114.0	108.0	111.8
III	118.7	121.0	109.6	120.5	124.0	111.0	110.3	114.4	108.2	112.6
IV	119.5	122.0	110.0	121.2	125.5	110.9	110.4	113.7	108.7	112.0
1992: I	120.8	123.4	110.7	122.0	127.3	111.2	110.7	113.8	109.1	112.3
II	121.8	124.5	111.5	122.7	128.8	111.7	111.2	114.2	109.6	112.8
III	122.5	125.5	111.8	123.4	130.1	112.4	111.7	114.8	110.1	113.8
IV	123.5	126.5	112.1	123.8	131.6	112.8	112.0	115.6	110.1	114.8
1993: I	124.8	127.5	112.6	124.9	132.8	113.5	112.4	116.3	110.4	115.8
II	125.6	128.4	113.5	125.0	134.2	114.4	113.1	117.4	110.9	117.2
III	126.3	128.9	114.1	124.5	135.2	115.2	113.6	118.4	111.2	118.5
IV ᵖ	127.0	129.7	114.9	125.2	136.2	115.7	114.0	119.3	111.2	119.3

See next page for continuation of table.

TABLE B-4.—*Fixed-weighted price indexes for gross domestic product, 1987 weights, 1959-93*—Continued

[Index numbers, 1987=100, except as noted; quarterly data seasonally adjusted]

Year or quarter	Exports and imports of goods and services		Government purchases of goods and services				State and local	Final sales of domestic product	Gross domestic purchases [1]	Percent change from preceding period, GDP fixed-weighted price index [2]
	Exports	Imports	Total	Federal						
				Total	National defense	Nondefense				
1959			24.6	28.6			21.5			
1960			25.1	29.0			22.1			
1961			25.5	29.3			22.5			
1962			26.3	30.0			23.4			
1963			26.8	30.6			23.8			
1964			27.3	31.3			24.2			
1965			27.9	32.0			24.8			
1966			29.0	32.8			26.0			
1967			30.2	33.9			27.4			
1968			31.8	35.6			28.9			
1969			33.7	37.4			30.8			
1970			36.2	40.2			33.1			
1971			38.6	42.9			35.3			
1972			41.1	46.0	46.2	45.2	37.3			
1973			43.7	48.4	49.0	46.4	40.1			
1974			46.9	50.2	51.2	47.4	44.3			
1975			51.4	54.6	55.1	52.9	48.9			
1976			54.4	57.3	57.8	55.8	52.1			
1977			57.7	60.4	60.7	59.4	55.7			
1978			61.7	64.1	64.5	62.8	59.9			
1979			66.8	68.9	69.6	66.6	65.1			
1980			73.3	75.2	76.3	71.9	71.9			
1981			79.6	82.3	83.3	79.1	77.6			
1982	100.4	101.2	85.0	88.5	89.7	84.7	82.3	84.9	85.4	
1983	99.7	97.7	88.5	92.2	93.5	88.4	85.5	88.2	88.3	3.9
1984	99.9	96.8	92.2	95.6	96.9	91.4	89.6	91.2	91.0	3.4
1985	98.2	94.6	95.4	97.9	98.8	94.9	93.5	94.4	94.0	3.5
1986	97.3	93.8	97.6	99.0	99.5	97.5	96.5	97.0	96.6	2.8
1987	100.0	100.0	100.0	100.0	100.0	100.0	100.0	100.0	100.0	3.1
1988	105.7	105.4	103.7	102.8	103.1	102.0	104.3	104.0	104.0	4.0
1989	108.2	108.5	107.9	107.0	107.1	106.7	108.6	108.6	108.6	4.5
1990	110.0	112.4	112.6	111.8	112.1	110.8	113.2	113.6	113.7	4.6
1991	112.4	113.8	116.7	116.5	116.5	116.6	116.8	118.3	118.2	4.1
1992	113.7	115.1	120.6	121.8	122.3	120.2	119.6	122.2	122.0	3.3
1993 ᵖ	115.5	114.9	124.2	126.1	127.1	122.9	122.8	126.0	125.5	3.1
1982: IV	99.4	99.4	86.7	90.4	91.4	87.1	83.8	86.3	86.7	
1983: IV	100.3	97.3	89.3	92.7	93.9	88.7	86.7	89.4	89.3	
1984: IV	99.3	96.0	93.9	97.7	99.3	92.6	91.1	92.3	92.1	
1985: IV	97.9	96.0	96.9	99.4	100.5	95.9	94.9	95.6	95.4	
1986: IV	97.6	93.7	98.3	99.0	99.3	98.3	97.8	98.0	97.6	
1987: IV	101.7	102.8	101.0	100.2	100.3	100.1	101.5	101.3	101.4	
1988: IV	107.0	106.5	104.8	103.7	103.9	102.9	105.8	105.7	105.6	
1989: IV	108.1	108.6	109.1	108.2	108.3	107.8	109.9	110.2	110.2	
1990: I	108.8	110.3	111.0	110.3	110.6	109.5	111.5	111.8	111.8	5.8
II	109.2	110.8	111.8	111.0	111.3	110.2	112.4	113.0	112.8	4.4
III	110.3	112.0	113.1	112.4	112.7	111.4	113.7	114.3	114.3	4.7
IV	111.9	118.3	114.4	113.5	114.0	112.0	115.1	115.4	115.9	3.8
1991: I	112.4	115.4	115.5	115.2	115.1	115.5	115.8	116.8	117.0	5.1
II	112.2	113.1	116.1	115.6	115.3	116.3	116.4	116.4	117.7	3.4
III	112.1	112.6	117.0	116.7	116.7	116.8	117.2	118.8	118.6	3.4
IV	112.9	114.1	118.0	118.6	118.9	117.5	117.7	119.6	119.5	2.7
1992: I	113.1	113.9	119.3	120.6	121.0	119.6	118.2	120.8	120.6	4.2
II	113.7	114.5	120.3	121.4	121.8	119.9	119.5	121.8	121.6	3.4
III	113.9	116.3	121.0	122.2	122.8	120.3	120.0	122.6	122.5	2.5
IV	114.3	115.9	121.7	122.8	123.5	120.9	120.9	123.6	123.4	3.1
1993: I	114.7	114.5	123.2	125.1	125.9	122.5	121.8	124.9	124.4	4.3
II	115.5	115.6	124.0	125.8	126.8	122.5	122.7	125.7	125.3	2.8
III	115.7	114.8	124.8	126.8	127.9	123.4	123.2	126.4	125.9	2.1
IV ᵖ	116.0	114.9	124.8	126.6	127.7	123.2	123.4	127.1	126.5	2.2

[1] Gross domestic product (GDP) less exports of goods and services plus imports of goods and services.
[2] Quarterly changes are at annual rates.

Note.—Separate deflators are not calculated for gross private domestic investment, change in business inventories, and net exports of goods and services.

Source: Department of Commerce, Bureau of Economic Analysis.

TABLE B-5.—*Changes in gross domestic product and personal consumption expenditures, and related implicit price deflators and fixed-weighted price indexes, 1960–93*

[Percent change from preceding period; quarterly data at seasonally adjusted annual rates]

Year or quarter	Gross domestic product				Personal consumption expenditures			
	Current dollars	Constant (1987) dollars	Implicit price deflator	Fixed-weighted price index (1987 weights)	Current dollars	Constant (1987) dollars	Implicit price deflator	Fixed-weighted price index (1987 weights)
1960	3.9	2.2	1.6		4.5	2.7	1.9	1.3
1961	3.6	2.7	1.2		3.3	2.3	.7	.8
1962	7.5	5.2	2.3		6.1	4.4	1.8	.6
1963	5.5	4.1	1.1		5.4	3.8	1.4	.9
1964	7.4	5.6	1.8		7.4	5.6	1.7	1.1
1965	8.4	5.5	2.5		7.8	5.6	2.1	1.0
1966	9.5	5.9	3.5		8.3	5.1	3.0	1.8
1967	5.8	2.6	3.1		5.8	3.1	2.6	2.6
1968	9.2	4.2	5.0		9.8	5.2	4.1	3.8
1969	7.9	2.7	5.0		8.0	3.7	4.3	3.8
1970	5.3	.0	5.4		7.1	2.4	4.4	4.4
1971	8.6	2.9	5.4		8.3	3.3	5.1	4.4
1972	10.0	5.1	4.6		9.6	5.6	3.7	3.3
1973	11.8	5.2	6.4		10.5	4.5	5.7	4.6
1974	8.1	−.6	8.7		9.4	−.6	10.2	9.3
1975	8.7	−.8	9.6		10.5	2.1	8.2	8.1
1976	11.5	4.9	6.3		11.5	5.2	5.9	5.6
1977	11.6	4.5	6.9		11.2	4.0	6.9	6.4
1978	13.1	4.8	7.9		11.8	4.1	7.2	7.0
1979	11.5	2.5	8.6		11.4	2.4	8.9	8.5
1980	8.8	−.5	9.5		10.4	−.1	10.4	10.3
1981	11.9	1.8	10.0		10.2	1.2	9.0	8.6
1982	3.9	−2.2	6.2		6.9	1.1	5.7	5.4
1983	8.1	3.9	4.1	3.9	9.6	4.6	4.9	4.3
1984	10.9	6.2	4.4	3.4	9.0	4.8	3.9	3.7
1985	6.9	3.2	3.7	3.5	8.4	4.4	3.9	3.8
1986	5.7	2.9	2.6	2.8	6.9	3.6	3.1	3.0
1987	6.4	3.1	3.2	3.1	7.1	2.8	4.2	4.1
1988	7.9	3.9	3.9	4.0	8.0	3.6	4.2	4.3
1989	7.2	2.5	4.4	4.5	6.9	1.9	4.9	5.0
1990	5.6	1.2	4.4	4.6	6.8	1.5	5.1	5.3
1991	3.2	−.7	3.9	4.1	3.9	−.4	4.4	4.5
1992	5.5	2.6	2.9	3.3	6.0	2.6	3.3	3.7
1993 ᵖ	5.6	2.9	2.6	3.1	6.1	3.3	2.7	3.0
1987: I	6.8	3.0	3.3	3.4	5.5	−.1	5.9	5.6
II	8.1	5.1	2.9	2.8	9.4	4.8	4.5	4.4
III	7.2	4.0	3.3	3.3	8.3	3.9	4.1	4.3
IV	9.9	5.9	3.6	3.7	4.4	−.1	4.5	4.5
1988: I	6.1	2.6	3.6	3.7	9.9	7.1	2.8	2.7
II	9.1	4.3	4.4	4.5	7.9	2.5	5.2	5.2
III	7.6	2.5	5.1	5.4	8.4	2.9	5.1	5.3
IV	8.1	3.9	3.9	3.7	8.9	4.1	4.7	4.6
1989: I	8.6	3.2	5.4	5.0	5.1	.1	5.0	5.2
II	6.3	1.8	4.6	4.8	7.0	1.1	5.7	5.9
III	3.8	0	3.8	3.8	6.3	2.9	3.3	3.5
IV	5.1	1.5	3.7	3.7	5.3	.8	4.4	4.4
1990: I	9.1	3.5	5.2	5.8	9.2	2.8	6.3	6.6
II	5.9	1.5	4.4	4.4	5.3	.9	4.3	4.2
III	3.1	−.9	4.0	4.7	8.3	2.1	6.1	6.3
IV	1.0	−3.2	4.3	3.8	3.7	−2.7	6.7	7.0
1991: I	2.4	−2.4	5.0	5.1	.7	−2.8	3.4	3.9
II	4.8	1.5	3.1	3.4	4.7	1.8	3.1	3.2
III	4.3	1.4	3.1	3.4	4.4	1.3	3.0	3.4
IV	3.2	.6	2.4	2.7	3.5	.0	3.4	3.5
1992: I	7.4	3.5	3.8	4.2	8.6	4.3	4.0	4.5
II	5.7	2.8	3.0	3.4	5.4	1.8	3.6	3.6
III	4.6	3.4	1.0	2.5	5.7	4.2	1.6	3.4
IV	9.2	5.7	3.3	3.1	9.9	5.6	3.9	3.1
1993: I	4.4	.8	3.6	4.3	3.8	.8	2.9	3.4
II	4.3	1.9	2.3	2.8	6.1	3.4	2.6	2.9
III	4.4	2.9	1.6	2.1	5.5	4.4	1.3	1.4
IV ᵖ	7.4	5.9	1.3	2.2	6.3	4.0	2.2	2.7

Source: Department of Commerce, Bureau of Economic Analysis.

TABLE B-6.—*Selected per capita product and income series in current and 1987 dollars, 1959–93*

[Quarterly data at seasonally adjusted annual rates, except as noted]

Year or quarter	Current dollars							Constant (1987) dollars							Population (thousands) [1]
	Gross domestic product	Personal income	Disposable personal income	Personal consumption expenditures				Gross domestic product	Disposable personal income	Personal consumption expenditures				
				Total	Durable goods	Non-durable goods	Services			Total	Durable goods	Non-durable goods	Services	
1959	2,791	2,209	1,958	1,796	242	838	716	10,892	7,256	6,658	646	2,928	3,083	177,073
1960	2,840	2,264	1,994	1,839	240	847	752	10,903	7,264	6,698	638	2,915	3,145	180,760
1961	2,894	2,321	2,048	1,869	228	857	784	11,014	7,382	6,740	595	2,926	3,218	183,742
1962	3,063	2,430	2,137	1,953	252	878	823	11,405	7,583	6,931	644	2,964	3,323	186,590
1963	3,186	2,516	2,210	2,030	273	895	861	11,704	7,718	7,089	688	2,977	3,423	189,300
1964	3,376	2,661	2,369	2,149	296	936	917	12,195	8,140	7,384	733	3,065	3,586	191,927
1965	3,616	2,845	2,527	2,287	327	987	974	12,712	8,508	7,703	803	3,173	3,726	194,347
1966	3,915	3,061	2,699	2,450	348	1,060	1,041	13,307	8,822	8,005	844	3,294	3,867	196,599
1967	4,097	3,253	2,861	2,562	355	1,091	1,116	13,510	9,114	8,163	841	3,316	4,006	198,752
1968	4,430	3,536	3,077	2,785	404	1,171	1,211	13,932	9,399	8,506	919	3,417	4,169	200,745
1969	4,733	3,816	3,274	2,978	425	1,244	1,308	14,171	9,606	8,737	941	3,469	4,327	202,736
1970	4,928	4,052	3,521	3,152	416	1,318	1,418	14,013	9,875	8,842	896	3,497	4,449	205,089
1971	5,283	4,302	3,779	3,372	468	1,364	1,540	14,232	10,111	9,022	970	3,494	4,558	207,692
1972	5,750	4,671	4,042	3,658	528	1,454	1,676	14,801	10,414	9,425	1,073	3,601	4,751	209,924
1973	6,368	5,184	4,521	4,002	585	1,602	1,814	15,422	11,013	9,752	1,164	3,670	4,917	211,939
1974	6,819	5,637	4,893	4,337	575	1,780	1,982	15,185	10,832	9,602	1,062	3,552	4,988	213,898
1975	7,343	6,053	5,329	4,745	622	1,926	2,197	14,917	10,906	9,711	1,050	3,552	5,110	215,981
1976	8,109	6,632	5,796	5,241	734	2,072	2,436	15,502	11,192	10,121	1,176	3,674	5,271	218,086
1977	8,961	7,269	6,316	5,772	829	2,226	2,717	16,039	11,406	10,425	1,271	3,722	5,433	220,289
1978	10,029	8,121	7,042	6,384	909	2,432	3,043	16,635	11,851	10,744	1,316	3,795	5,633	222,629
1979	11,055	9,032	7,787	7,035	952	2,725	3,359	16,867	12,039	10,876	1,284	3,833	5,760	225,106
1980	11,892	9,948	8,576	7,677	933	2,999	3,745	16,584	12,005	10,746	1,154	3,779	5,814	227,715
1981	13,177	11,021	9,455	8,375	994	3,236	4,146	16,710	12,156	10,770	1,150	3,774	5,845	229,989
1982	13,564	11,589	9,989	8,868	1,018	3,326	4,523	16,194	12,146	10,782	1,131	3,756	5,895	232,201
1983	14,531	12,216	10,642	9,634	1,173	3,490	4,971	16,672	12,349	11,179	1,270	3,842	6,066	234,326
1984	15,978	13,345	11,673	10,408	1,345	3,693	5,370	17,549	13,029	11,617	1,432	3,953	6,231	236,393
1985	16,933	14,170	12,339	11,184	1,480	3,855	5,849	17,944	13,258	12,015	1,552	4,019	6,444	238,510
1986	17,735	14,917	13,010	11,843	1,619	3,956	6,269	18,299	13,552	12,336	1,670	4,118	6,548	240,691
1987	18,694	15,655	13,545	12,568	1,662	4,163	6,742	18,694	13,545	12,568	1,662	4,163	6,742	242,860
1988	19,994	16,630	14,477	13,448	1,783	4,381	7,284	19,252	13,890	12,903	1,749	4,223	6,930	245,093
1989	21,224	17,706	15,307	14,241	1,857	4,647	7,737	19,556	14,005	13,029	1,781	4,251	6,997	247,397
1990	22,189	18,699	16,205	15,048	1,873	4,918	8,257	19,593	14,101	13,093	1,773	4,244	7,077	249,951
1991	22,647	19,196	16,741	15,459	1,812	4,978	8,669	19,238	13,965	12,895	1,688	4,148	7,059	252,699
1992	23,637	20,139	17,615	16,205	1,947	5,092	9,166	19,518	14,219	13,081	1,787	4,161	7,133	255,472
1993 P	24,681	20,861	18,222	17,001	2,082	5,228	9,691	19,874	14,329	13,369	1,896	4,213	7,259	258,256
1982: IV	13,709	11,786	10,189	9,134	1,059	3,378	4,696	16,132	12,154	10,895	1,169	3,779	5,948	233,060
1983: IV	15,085	12,613	11,033	9,980	1,266	3,572	5,143	17,062	12,591	11,390	1,357	3,892	6,141	235,146
1984: IV	16,310	13,668	11,925	10,649	1,383	3,742	5,524	17,680	13,145	11,739	1,466	3,975	6,298	237,231
1985: IV	17,296	14,440	12,565	11,445	1,480	3,924	6,040	18,102	13,278	12,095	1,544	4,046	6,505	239,387
1986: IV	17,953	15,102	13,121	12,101	1,684	3,990	6,428	18,328	13,522	12,472	1,721	4,144	6,607	241,550
1987: IV	19,213	16,076	13,907	12,819	1,677	4,223	6,919	18,977	13,685	12,615	1,660	4,162	6,792	243,745
1988: IV	20,506	17,053	14,850	13,814	1,841	4,495	7,477	19,429	13,996	13,020	1,785	4,255	6,979	246,004
1989: IV	21,519	17,995	15,558	14,491	1,845	4,725	7,921	19,554	14,015	13,053	1,759	4,263	7,031	248,372
1990: I	21,942	18,421	15,963	14,781	1,928	4,828	8,025	19,678	14,163	13,114	1,827	4,258	7,029	248,927
II	22,203	18,628	16,114	14,935	1,867	4,863	8,205	19,704	14,144	13,110	1,770	4,250	7,089	249,552
III	22,309	18,786	16,275	15,189	1,867	4,958	8,364	19,603	14,078	13,138	1,767	4,255	7,116	250,291
IV	22,299	18,958	16,467	15,283	1,831	5,022	8,431	19,388	14,018	13,010	1,726	4,212	7,072	251,035
1991: I	22,378	19,010	16,560	15,273	1,784	4,976	8,513	19,224	13,971	12,885	1,670	4,165	7,050	251,659
II	22,582	19,156	16,712	15,409	1,792	4,991	8,626	19,245	14,000	12,908	1,672	4,166	7,070	252,312
III	22,757	19,201	16,752	15,530	1,838	4,979	8,713	19,256	13,927	12,911	1,709	4,147	7,055	253,048
IV	22,869	19,417	16,939	15,621	1,833	4,965	8,823	19,228	13,963	12,876	1,700	4,114	7,061	253,776
1992: I	23,227	19,725	17,245	15,906	1,902	5,024	8,980	19,348	14,073	12,981	1,756	4,135	7,090	254,392
II	23,487	19,969	17,481	16,072	1,912	5,050	9,110	19,430	14,142	13,002	1,754	4,136	7,112	255,090
III	23,685	20,090	17,577	16,249	1,958	5,104	9,187	19,537	14,169	13,098	1,794	4,154	7,149	255,836
IV	24,143	20,767	18,153	16,589	2,013	5,190	9,385	19,754	14,490	13,241	1,845	4,216	7,179	256,569
1993: I	24,346	20,430	17,876	16,704	2,004	5,192	9,508	19,744	14,163	13,234	1,835	4,184	7,216	257,197
II	24,538	20,837	18,196	16,907	2,062	5,215	9,631	19,786	14,326	13,312	1,878	4,200	7,234	257,872
III	24,732	20,930	18,265	17,088	2,095	5,229	9,763	19,869	14,341	13,416	1,907	4,226	7,283	258,612
IV P	25,105	21,245	18,549	17,303	2,166	5,276	9,860	20,097	14,484	13,511	1,966	4,242	7,303	259,343

[1] Population of the United States including Armed Forces overseas; includes Alaska and Hawaii beginning 1960. Annual data are averages of quarterly data. Quarterly data are averages for the period.

Source: Department of Commerce (Bureau of Economic Analysis and Bureau of the Census).

TABLE B-7.—*Gross domestic product by major type of product, 1959-93*

[Billions of dollars; quarterly data at seasonally adjusted annual rates]

Year or quarter	Gross domestic product	Final sales of domestic product	Change in business inventories	Goods [1] Total Total	Goods [1] Total Final sales	Goods [1] Total Change in business inventories	Durable goods Final sales	Durable goods Change in business inventories	Nondurable goods Final sales	Nondurable goods Change in business inventories	Services [1]	Structures	Auto output
1959	494.2	490.0	4.2	250.8	246.6	4.2	91.1	3.1	155.5	1.1	181.7	61.7	19.4
1960	513.3	510.1	3.2	257.1	253.9	3.2	93.8	1.6	160.1	1.6	195.1	61.1	21.3
1961	531.8	528.9	2.9	260.4	257.4	2.9	93.1	-.1	164.3	3.0	208.6	62.8	17.8
1962	571.6	565.5	6.1	281.5	275.4	6.1	103.4	3.4	172.0	2.7	223.0	67.0	22.4
1963	603.1	597.5	5.7	293.2	287.5	5.7	110.0	2.7	177.5	3.0	238.1	71.9	25.1
1964	648.0	643.0	5.0	313.5	308.5	5.0	119.6	4.0	188.9	1.0	256.9	77.6	25.9
1965	702.7	693.0	9.7	342.9	333.2	9.7	132.4	6.7	200.8	3.0	276.0	83.8	31.1
1966	769.8	756.0	13.8	380.1	366.3	13.8	147.9	10.2	218.5	3.6	302.8	86.9	30.2
1967	814.3	803.8	10.5	395.1	384.6	10.5	154.5	5.5	230.2	5.0	330.7	88.5	27.8
1968	889.3	880.2	9.1	427.4	418.3	9.1	169.1	4.7	249.1	4.4	363.0	98.9	35.0
1969	959.5	949.8	9.7	456.6	446.8	9.7	180.1	6.4	266.8	3.3	395.8	107.1	34.7
1970	1,010.7	1,008.4	2.3	467.8	465.6	2.3	182.1	-.1	283.5	2.3	434.3	108.6	28.5
1971	1,097.2	1,089.2	8.0	493.0	485.0	8.0	189.4	2.8	295.5	5.2	477.0	127.2	38.9
1972	1,207.0	1,197.1	9.9	537.4	527.5	9.9	209.7	7.2	317.8	2.7	523.6	145.9	41.4
1973	1,349.6	1,331.9	17.7	616.6	598.9	17.7	242.0	15.0	356.9	2.8	571.0	161.9	45.9
1974	1,458.6	1,444.4	14.3	662.8	648.5	14.3	257.1	11.2	391.4	3.1	631.3	164.5	38.8
1975	1,585.9	1,591.5	-5.7	715.1	720.8	-5.7	288.8	-7.0	432.0	1.3	706.9	163.8	40.3
1976	1,768.4	1,751.7	16.7	798.8	782.0	16.7	323.6	10.3	458.4	6.4	782.2	187.5	55.1
1977	1,974.1	1,949.4	24.7	880.4	855.7	24.7	368.3	9.7	487.4	15.0	870.4	223.3	64.2
1978	2,232.7	2,204.8	27.9	989.1	961.2	27.9	416.9	20.3	544.3	7.6	975.5	268.1	67.9
1979	2,488.6	2,475.9	12.8	1,100.2	1,087.5	12.8	474.5	9.6	613.0	3.1	1,079.6	308.8	66.2
1980	2,708.0	2,717.5	-9.5	1,176.2	1,185.7	-9.5	502.1	-2.6	683.6	-6.8	1,215.4	316.4	59.2
1981	3,030.6	3,005.2	25.4	1,324.6	1,299.2	25.4	544.2	6.2	755.0	19.2	1,357.4	348.6	68.3
1982	3,149.6	3,165.5	-15.9	1,315.0	1,330.9	-15.9	541.6	-16.0	789.3	.1	1,494.2	340.4	65.3
1983	3,405.0	3,410.6	-5.5	1,407.3	1,412.8	-5.5	579.4	5.5	833.4	-11.0	1,636.3	361.5	88.3
1984	3,777.2	3,706.1	71.1	1,591.9	1,520.8	71.1	647.0	44.9	873.8	26.2	1,770.7	414.7	104.2
1985	4,038.7	4,014.1	24.6	1,652.6	1,628.0	24.6	704.8	8.6	923.2	16.0	1,939.0	447.1	115.8
1986	4,268.6	4,260.0	8.6	1,705.3	1,696.7	8.6	730.2	1.6	966.5	7.1	2,097.3	466.0	120.4
1987	4,539.9	4,513.7	26.3	1,794.5	1,768.2	26.3	753.5	21.6	1,014.7	4.7	2,267.2	478.2	118.9
1988	4,900.4	4,884.2	16.2	1,942.0	1,925.7	16.2	835.6	24.3	1,090.1	-8.1	2,460.9	497.5	129.1
1989	5,250.8	5,217.5	33.3	2,097.0	2,063.6	33.3	891.2	25.2	1,172.5	8.1	2,642.1	511.7	135.1
1990	5,546.1	5,539.3	6.9	2,185.2	2,178.4	6.9	933.5	-2.1	1,244.8	9.0	2,849.4	511.5	129.2
1991	5,722.9	5,731.6	-8.6	2,218.4	2,227.0	-8.6	934.3	-12.9	1,292.7	4.3	3,032.7	471.9	121.1
1992	6,038.5	6,031.2	7.3	2,312.8	2,305.5	7.3	975.8	2.0	1,329.6	5.3	3,221.1	504.6	133.2
1993 p	6,374.0	6,357.2	16.8	2,419.9	2,403.1	16.8	1,034.6	13.0	1,368.5	3.8	3,409.5	544.6	142.1
1982: IV	3,195.1	3,241.4	-46.3	1,302.2	1,348.5	-46.3	550.6	-41.1	798.0	-5.2	1,553.3	339.5	63.2
1983: IV	3,547.3	3,527.1	20.2	1,483.0	1,462.8	20.2	620.5	25.5	842.3	-5.3	1,686.1	378.2	101.9
1984: IV	3,869.1	3,818.1	51.0	1,617.5	1,566.5	51.0	676.3	38.5	890.2	12.5	1,824.9	426.9	110.4
1985: IV	4,140.5	4,107.9	32.6	1,673.7	1,641.1	32.6	705.7	10.9	935.4	21.7	2,008.9	457.9	115.1
1986: IV	4,336.6	4,355.4	-18.8	1,714.5	1,733.3	-18.8	751.5	-11.9	981.8	-7.0	2,154.1	468.1	122.5
1987: IV	4,683.0	4,623.7	59.3	1,865.4	1,806.1	59.3	769.3	37.1	1,036.9	22.2	2,327.6	490.1	120.9
1988: IV	5,044.6	5,027.3	17.3	2,007.0	1,989.7	17.3	861.0	35.3	1,128.7	-18.0	2,528.5	509.1	136.1
1989: IV	5,344.8	5,314.6	30.2	2,115.9	2,085.7	30.2	893.9	33.0	1,191.8	-2.8	2,715.2	513.7	131.0
1990: I	5,461.9	5,452.4	9.6	2,164.3	2,154.7	9.6	944.6	-4.1	1,210.1	13.7	2,767.7	530.0	128.4
II	5,540.9	5,507.6	33.3	2,193.4	2,160.1	33.3	926.3	10.0	1,233.8	23.3	2,829.0	518.5	132.1
III	5,583.8	5,575.3	8.4	2,194.2	2,185.8	8.4	932.3	9.8	1,253.5	-1.4	2,880.6	509.0	137.6
IV	5,597.9	5,621.8	-23.9	2,189.0	2,212.9	-23.9	931.0	-24.1	1,281.9	.3	2,920.5	488.4	118.8
1991: I	5,631.7	5,651.6	-19.9	2,197.8	2,217.7	-19.9	921.9	-32.1	1,295.9	12.2	2,964.8	469.0	114.2
II	5,697.7	5,720.8	-23.0	2,208.9	2,231.9	-23.0	940.8	-21.0	1,291.1	-2.0	3,018.5	470.4	118.7
III	5,758.6	5,759.1	-.5	2,229.3	2,229.8	-.5	938.8	3.0	1,291.0	-3.5	3,057.0	472.3	127.8
IV	5,803.7	5,794.8	8.9	2,237.6	2,228.7	8.9	935.7	-1.5	1,293.0	10.4	3,090.4	475.7	123.5
1992: I	5,908.7	5,913.9	-5.1	2,264.1	2,269.3	-5.1	953.4	-13.0	1,315.9	7.9	3,152.7	491.9	125.6
II	5,991.4	5,978.6	12.9	2,291.2	2,278.4	12.9	963.2	16.7	1,315.1	-3.8	3,196.2	504.0	137.9
III	6,059.5	6,049.9	9.7	2,318.3	2,308.6	9.7	978.4	5.7	1,330.2	4.0	3,239.3	501.9	133.0
IV	6,194.4	6,182.5	12.0	2,377.6	2,365.6	12.0	1,008.3	-1.2	1,357.3	13.2	3,296.1	520.8	136.4
1993: I	6,261.6	6,227.1	34.6	2,397.4	2,362.9	34.6	1,003.5	15.0	1,359.3	19.5	3,341.8	522.4	142.8
II	6,327.6	6,314.5	13.1	2,408.1	2,395.0	13.1	1,037.8	2.7	1,357.1	10.4	3,388.1	531.5	145.9
III	6,395.9	6,388.2	7.7	2,409.4	2,401.7	7.7	1,032.9	14.8	1,368.8	-7.2	3,437.8	548.7	134.6
IV p	6,510.8	6,499.0	11.7	2,464.7	2,452.9	11.7	1,064.3	19.5	1,388.6	-7.7	3,470.3	575.8	145.1

[1] Exports and imports of certain goods, primarily military equipment purchased and sold by the Federal Government, are included in services.

Source: Department of Commerce, Bureau of Economic Analysis.

TABLE B-8.—*Gross domestic product by major type of product in 1987 dollars, 1959–93*

[Billions of 1987 dollars; quarterly data at seasonally adjusted annual rates]

Year or quarter	Gross domestic product	Final sales of domestic product	Change in business inventories	Goods [1] Total Total	Goods [1] Total Final sales	Goods [1] Total Change in business inventories	Durable goods Final sales	Durable goods Change in business inventories	Nondurable goods Final sales	Nondurable goods Change in business inventories	Services [1]	Structures	Auto output
1959	1,928.8	1,915.2	13.6	825.2	811.6	13.6	273.8	8.6	537.8	5.0	843.7	259.9	59.5
1960	1,970.8	1,962.7	8.1	835.3	827.1	8.1	277.8	4.6	549.3	3.5	877.3	258.2	63.8
1961	2,023.8	2,016.6	7.2	840.9	833.7	7.2	273.5	−.3	560.2	7.5	916.7	266.1	53.1
1962	2,128.1	2,112.5	15.6	889.6	874.0	15.6	296.5	8.6	577.5	7.0	956.8	281.7	63.3
1963	2,215.6	2,199.6	16.0	914.9	898.9	16.0	310.4	7.5	588.5	8.6	999.9	300.8	68.9
1964	2,340.6	2,324.9	15.7	967.6	952.0	15.7	334.3	11.3	617.6	4.4	1,052.6	320.4	69.5
1965	2,470.5	2,445.4	25.1	1,033.0	1,007.9	25.1	364.1	18.3	643.8	6.9	1,102.1	335.4	83.2
1966	2,616.2	2,579.5	36.7	1,113.3	1,076.6	36.7	399.4	27.1	677.2	9.6	1,168.4	334.5	80.4
1967	2,685.2	2,657.5	27.6	1,129.4	1,101.7	27.6	413.7	14.5	688.0	13.1	1,226.6	329.3	72.4
1968	2,796.9	2,773.2	23.6	1,168.9	1,145.3	23.6	430.4	12.8	714.9	10.9	1,277.8	350.1	86.6
1969	2,873.0	2,848.2	24.8	1,193.9	1,169.1	24.8	438.4	15.7	730.7	9.1	1,324.6	354.5	82.9
1970	2,873.9	2,868.0	5.9	1,173.0	1,167.1	5.9	428.0	−.9	739.1	6.9	1,362.0	338.9	65.4
1971	2,955.9	2,935.2	20.8	1,182.0	1,161.3	20.8	419.2	8.9	742.1	11.9	1,401.8	372.1	85.3
1972	3,107.1	3,084.5	22.5	1,251.0	1,228.4	22.5	458.4	16.2	770.0	6.4	1,454.1	401.9	89.9
1973	3,268.6	3,230.9	37.7	1,349.8	1,312.1	37.7	528.0	31.2	784.1	6.5	1,508.3	410.4	98.7
1974	3,248.1	3,217.2	30.9	1,328.2	1,297.3	30.9	524.6	19.6	772.7	11.3	1,553.9	366.1	79.0
1975	3,221.7	3,235.6	−13.9	1,291.8	1,305.7	−13.9	521.6	−11.5	784.1	−2.5	1,602.2	327.7	74.8
1976	3,380.8	3,355.3	25.5	1,372.7	1,347.2	25.5	540.6	17.0	806.6	8.5	1,649.1	359.0	96.8
1977	3,533.3	3,499.0	34.3	1,436.9	1,402.6	34.3	583.6	15.6	819.0	18.7	1,701.2	395.2	106.0
1978	3,703.5	3,666.3	37.2	1,507.3	1,470.1	37.2	623.7	28.7	846.4	8.5	1,770.6	425.6	104.2
1979	3,796.8	3,783.2	13.6	1,537.1	1,523.5	13.6	654.1	11.7	869.3	1.9	1,821.7	438.0	94.8
1980	3,776.3	3,784.6	−8.3	1,509.5	1,517.7	−8.3	626.4	−4.3	891.4	−4.0	1,864.3	402.5	79.1
1981	3,843.1	3,818.6	24.6	1,547.4	1,522.9	24.6	619.4	6.3	903.4	18.3	1,895.7	400.0	86.8
1982	3,760.3	3,777.8	−17.5	1,468.7	1,486.2	−17.5	578.9	−16.0	907.3	−1.5	1,922.8	368.8	79.2
1983	3,906.6	3,902.2	4.4	1,531.7	1,527.3	4.4	601.5	6.3	925.8	−1.8	1,976.8	398.1	101.7
1984	4,148.5	4,080.6	67.9	1,667.7	1,599.8	67.9	655.1	45.7	944.7	22.3	2,033.1	447.7	115.8
1985	4,279.8	4,257.6	22.1	1,695.0	1,672.9	22.1	703.4	9.3	969.5	12.9	2,115.3	469.4	125.0
1986	4,404.5	4,395.9	8.5	1,740.1	1,731.6	8.5	731.5	1.9	1,000.1	6.7	2,185.0	479.3	124.4
1987	4,539.9	4,513.7	26.3	1,794.5	1,768.2	26.3	753.5	21.6	1,014.7	4.7	2,267.2	478.2	118.9
1988	4,718.6	4,698.6	19.9	1,892.5	1,872.6	19.9	833.1	23.3	1,039.5	−3.4	2,349.7	476.4	127.3
1989	4,838.0	4,808.3	29.8	1,961.7	1,932.0	29.8	868.1	23.8	1,063.9	6.0	2,403.9	472.5	128.0
1990	4,897.3	4,891.6	5.7	1,973.2	1,967.5	5.7	893.1	−1.9	1,074.5	7.5	2,464.5	459.6	121.4
1991	4,861.4	4,869.8	−8.4	1,946.5	1,954.9	−8.4	878.9	−12.0	1,076.0	3.6	2,495.9	419.0	109.5
1992	4,986.3	4,979.8	6.5	2,005.7	1,999.2	6.5	911.7	2.4	1,087.6	4.1	2,534.7	445.8	117.4
1993 *p*	5,132.7	5,117.3	15.4	2,081.3	2,065.9	15.4	968.1	12.3	1,097.8	3.1	2,586.2	465.1	120.8
1982: IV	3,759.6	3,804.5	−44.9	1,447.7	1,492.6	−44.9	580.9	−41.9	911.6	−3.0	1,942.1	369.8	75.3
1983: IV	4,012.1	3,982.8	29.3	1,597.8	1,568.5	29.3	639.4	26.7	929.1	2.6	1,998.3	416.0	113.7
1984: IV	4,194.2	4,146.2	47.9	1,680.9	1,633.0	47.9	677.6	39.7	955.3	8.3	2,058.1	455.1	122.4
1985: IV	4,333.5	4,303.3	30.2	1,708.1	1,677.9	30.2	703.1	11.9	974.9	18.3	2,148.8	476.5	122.4
1986: IV	4,427.1	4,447.2	−20.1	1,741.8	1,761.8	−20.1	750.4	−11.9	1,011.4	−8.2	2,208.2	477.2	124.1
1987: IV	4,625.5	4,565.6	59.9	1,850.8	1,790.9	59.9	769.4	36.9	1,021.5	23.0	2,290.9	483.8	120.3
1988: IV	4,779.7	4,758.7	20.9	1,926.0	1,905.0	20.9	852.9	33.5	1,052.2	−12.5	2,372.4	481.3	134.6
1989: IV	4,856.7	4,831.8	24.9	1,956.9	1,932.0	24.9	862.3	31.0	1,069.6	−6.1	2,430.0	469.8	123.8
1990: I	4,898.3	4,893.6	4.7	1,978.0	1,973.3	4.7	907.5	−3.9	1,065.8	8.6	2,441.1	479.2	121.4
II	4,917.1	4,889.0	28.1	1,985.7	1,957.6	28.1	889.9	9.8	1,067.7	18.3	2,464.4	467.1	123.9
III	4,906.5	4,895.6	10.9	1,975.8	1,964.9	10.9	889.2	9.1	1,075.7	1.8	2,475.1	455.6	129.9
IV	4,867.2	4,888.0	−20.9	1,953.5	1,974.3	−20.9	885.7	−22.4	1,088.6	1.5	2,477.3	436.5	110.3
1991: I	4,837.8	4,855.2	−17.4	1,939.1	1,956.5	−17.4	871.8	−28.5	1,084.6	11.1	2,481.2	417.6	104.5
II	4,855.6	4,878.0	−22.3	1,937.5	1,959.8	−22.3	885.6	−19.7	1,074.2	−2.6	2,500.9	417.2	109.0
III	4,872.6	4,873.5	−.9	1,953.3	1,954.2	−.9	881.1	2.3	1,073.1	−3.2	2,502.0	417.3	115.1
IV	4,879.6	4,872.5	7.1	1,956.3	1,949.2	7.1	877.1	−2.0	1,072.1	9.0	2,499.4	423.9	109.5
1992: I	4,922.0	4,926.9	−5.0	1,967.6	1,972.6	−5.0	891.3	−11.6	1,081.3	6.6	2,515.1	439.3	110.9
II	4,956.5	4,943.8	12.6	1,986.6	1,973.9	12.6	897.5	15.6	1,076.3	−2.9	2,522.3	447.7	121.8
III	4,998.2	4,988.6	9.6	2,011.0	2,001.4	9.6	915.2	6.3	1,086.2	3.3	2,544.8	442.3	116.8
IV	5,068.3	5,059.6	8.7	2,057.7	2,049.0	8.7	942.6	−.8	1,106.4	9.6	2,556.5	454.2	120.1
1993: I	5,078.2	5,048.9	29.3	2,060.2	2,030.9	29.3	938.2	13.0	1,092.7	16.3	2,565.3	452.7	122.5
II	5,102.1	5,089.1	13.0	2,069.1	2,056.1	13.0	964.9	3.9	1,091.1	9.1	2,577.5	455.5	123.4
III	5,138.3	5,131.8	6.5	2,074.9	2,068.5	6.5	968.7	13.9	1,099.8	−7.4	2,596.7	466.6	113.5
IV *p*	5,212.1	5,199.4	12.7	2,121.0	2,108.3	12.7	1,000.7	18.3	1,107.6	−5.6	2,605.5	485.6	123.7

[1] Exports and imports of certain goods, primarily military equipment purchased and sold by the Federal Government, are included in services.

Source: Department of Commerce, Bureau of Economic Analysis.

279

TABLE B-9.—*Gross domestic product by sector, 1959–93*

[Billions of dollars; quarterly data at seasonally adjusted annual rates]

Year or quarter	Gross domestic product	Business [1] Total [1]	Business [1] Nonfarm [1]	Business [1] Farm	Business [1] Statistical discrepancy	Households and institutions	General government [2] Total	General government [2] Federal	General government [2] State and local
1959	494.2	436.9	419.8	18.9	−1.8	12.4	44.9	21.7	23.1
1960	513.3	451.4	434.7	19.8	−3.1	13.9	48.1	22.6	25.5
1961	531.8	465.7	447.9	20.1	−2.2	14.5	51.6	23.7	27.9
1962	571.6	500.5	481.4	20.2	−1.0	15.6	55.5	25.2	30.2
1963	603.1	527.1	508.7	20.4	−2.0	16.7	59.3	26.5	32.9
1964	648.0	565.7	547.2	19.3	−.7	17.9	64.4	28.5	35.9
1965	702.7	614.1	592.9	21.9	−.7	19.3	69.3	30.0	39.3
1966	769.8	670.1	644.4	22.9	2.8	21.3	78.4	34.3	44.1
1967	814.3	703.5	680.5	22.2	.8	23.4	87.4	37.9	49.5
1968	889.3	765.4	742.8	22.7	−.1	26.1	97.8	41.9	55.9
1969	959.5	822.5	799.9	25.2	−2.6	29.5	107.5	44.9	62.6
1970	1,010.7	858.7	832.5	26.2	.0	32.4	119.5	48.5	71.1
1971	1,097.2	931.2	900.0	28.1	3.1	35.6	130.4	51.1	79.3
1972	1,207.0	1,025.3	991.7	32.6	1.1	39.0	142.6	54.9	87.7
1973	1,349.6	1,151.5	1,102.2	49.8	−.5	43.0	155.1	57.2	97.9
1974	1,458.6	1,242.7	1,193.9	47.4	1.4	47.2	168.8	61.1	107.6
1975	1,585.9	1,346.1	1,291.4	48.8	6.0	52.0	187.7	66.6	121.1
1976	1,768.4	1,507.4	1,450.6	46.4	10.4	57.1	203.9	71.0	132.9
1977	1,974.1	1,691.1	1,633.0	47.2	10.9	62.4	220.6	75.6	145.0
1978	2,232.7	1,921.1	1,858.4	54.7	7.6	71.0	240.7	81.8	158.9
1979	2,488.6	2,147.9	2,069.7	64.5	13.8	78.9	261.9	87.1	174.8
1980	2,708.0	2,328.9	2,259.2	56.1	13.6	89.3	289.8	96.3	193.5
1981	3,030.6	2,611.7	2,530.9	69.9	10.9	100.5	318.4	107.7	210.7
1982	3,149.6	2,692.1	2,634.4	65.1	−7.4	111.6	345.8	117.3	228.5
1983	3,405.0	2,914.8	2,855.5	49.2	10.2	121.3	368.9	125.0	243.9
1984	3,777.2	3,251.1	3,191.6	68.5	−9.0	132.0	394.1	132.2	261.9
1985	4,038.7	3,473.5	3,420.3	67.1	−13.9	141.7	423.6	140.3	283.2
1986	4,268.6	3,665.7	3,601.5	62.9	1.2	153.3	449.6	143.7	305.9
1987	4,539.9	3,890.8	3,849.5	66.0	−24.8	170.5	478.7	151.4	327.3
1988	4,900.4	4,201.0	4,161.8	67.6	−28.4	187.6	511.7	159.8	351.9
1989	5,250.8	4,495.9	4,413.7	81.1	1.1	206.1	548.8	169.1	379.8
1990	5,546.1	4,725.9	4,633.0	85.1	7.8	227.5	592.8	180.1	412.7
1991	5,722.9	4,848.5	4,760.1	78.8	9.6	245.3	629.1	192.7	436.5
1992	6,038.5	5,114.4	5,006.4	84.4	23.6	267.0	657.1	199.8	457.3
1993 ᵖ	6,374.0	5,400.6	5,301.0	81.3	18.2	286.3	687.1	207.0	480.1
1982: IV	3,195.1	2,724.0	2,674.1	60.0	−10.1	115.5	355.6	121.1	234.5
1983: IV	3,547.3	3,046.6	2,986.9	45.8	13.8	125.1	375.6	126.2	249.4
1984: IV	3,869.1	3,330.3	3,283.2	67.5	−20.5	135.6	403.2	134.1	269.2
1985: IV	4,140.5	3,561.2	3,501.5	65.7	−5.9	145.6	433.6	142.4	291.2
1986: IV	4,336.6	3,718.3	3,656.0	64.3	−2.0	157.8	460.5	144.9	315.6
1987: IV	4,683.0	4,016.6	3,970.9	70.6	−24.9	177.6	488.8	153.2	335.6
1988: IV	5,044.6	4,327.3	4,291.9	60.8	−25.4	194.3	523.0	161.3	361.7
1989: IV	5,344.8	4,569.8	4,476.6	80.4	12.8	213.3	561.7	170.6	391.2
1990: I	5,461.9	4,664.8	4,564.7	86.9	13.1	218.9	578.2	177.9	400.4
II	5,540.9	4,726.2	4,641.0	87.1	−1.8	225.1	589.6	180.4	409.2
III	5,583.8	4,756.1	4,656.4	84.8	14.9	230.9	596.8	179.7	417.1
IV	5,597.9	4,756.5	4,670.1	81.5	4.9	235.0	606.4	182.3	424.1
1991: I	5,631.7	4,770.7	4,691.2	79.2	.2	238.0	623.0	193.2	429.8
II	5,697.7	4,827.3	4,739.9	83.0	4.5	242.7	627.7	192.7	435.1
III	5,758.6	4,880.7	4,774.7	78.7	27.3	247.6	630.2	192.1	438.1
IV	5,803.7	4,915.3	4,834.6	74.5	6.2	252.7	635.6	192.7	442.9
1992: I	5,908.7	5,001.9	4,894.0	84.8	23.1	258.7	648.0	200.0	448.0
II	5,991.4	5,071.2	4,964.2	83.4	23.6	264.0	656.3	200.6	455.7
III	6,059.5	5,130.2	5,028.8	85.8	15.7	269.6	659.8	200.0	459.7
IV	6,194.4	5,254.4	5,138.7	83.6	32.1	275.7	664.3	198.7	465.6
1993: I	6,261.6	5,303.0	5,184.7	83.8	34.4	280.3	678.4	206.2	472.1
II	6,327.6	5,359.0	5,263.7	83.3	12.0	284.7	683.9	206.2	477.7
III	6,395.9	5,416.6	5,330.1	73.2	13.3	288.1	691.2	208.3	483.0
IV ᵖ	6,510.8	5,523.7	5,425.4	85.0	13.3	292.3	694.7	207.1	487.6

[1] Includes compensation of employees in government enterprises.
[2] Compensation of government employees.

Source: Department of Commerce, Bureau of Economic Analysis.

TABLE B-10.—*Gross domestic product by sector in 1987 dollars, 1959–93*

[Billions of 1987 dollars; quarterly data at seasonally adjusted annual rates]

Year or quarter	Gross domestic product	Business [1] Total [1]	Business [1] Nonfarm [1]	Business [1] Farm	Business [1] Statistical discrepancy	Households and institutions	General government [2] Total	General government [2] Federal	General government [2] State and local
1959	1,928.8	1,582.1	1,543.4	45.2	−6.5	80.1	266.5	130.5	136.0
1960	1,970.8	1,609.5	1,574.3	46.4	−11.2	86.5	274.8	132.1	142.7
1961	2,023.8	1,650.7	1,611.6	46.9	−7.8	87.5	285.6	135.3	150.3
1962	2,128.1	1,740.8	1,698.0	46.3	−3.6	91.1	296.2	141.6	154.7
1963	2,215.6	1,818.8	1,778.6	47.1	−6.8	93.6	303.2	140.9	162.3
1964	2,340.6	1,930.4	1,886.8	46.0	−2.4	96.5	313.7	141.7	172.0
1965	2,470.5	2,045.3	2,001.7	46.1	−2.5	100.4	324.8	142.3	182.5
1966	2,616.2	2,162.6	2,109.1	44.5	9.0	104.7	348.9	155.4	193.5
1967	2,685.2	2,208.0	2,158.8	46.5	2.6	108.3	368.9	168.1	200.8
1968	2,796.9	2,303.0	2,258.0	45.1	−.1	111.8	382.1	170.7	211.4
1969	2,873.0	2,366.2	2,326.7	46.8	−7.2	115.5	391.3	171.2	220.1
1970	2,873.9	2,368.4	2,318.9	49.5	.0	114.1	391.4	161.6	229.8
1971	2,955.9	2,447.6	2,388.6	50.5	8.3	116.7	391.8	152.4	239.5
1972	3,107.1	2,594.8	2,541.3	50.7	2.8	120.0	392.2	143.7	248.6
1973	3,268.6	2,749.7	2,702.0	48.6	−1.0	123.2	395.7	138.0	257.7
1974	3,248.1	2,719.6	2,666.0	50.7	3.0	124.3	404.1	137.9	266.2
1975	3,221.7	2,684.6	2,619.6	53.1	11.9	128.0	409.1	137.1	272.0
1976	3,380.8	2,840.1	2,768.1	52.5	19.5	128.6	412.0	137.0	275.0
1977	3,533.3	2,987.8	2,914.6	53.8	19.4	129.8	415.6	137.0	278.6
1978	3,703.5	3,144.2	3,083.8	48.2	12.2	135.1	424.2	138.4	285.8
1979	3,796.8	3,226.0	3,155.0	50.4	20.6	138.3	432.5	137.5	295.0
1980	3,776.3	3,193.4	3,123.4	51.0	19.0	142.6	440.3	139.2	301.1
1981	3,843.1	3,253.6	3,179.2	60.8	13.6	145.6	443.9	140.9	303.0
1982	3,760.3	3,167.3	3,115.8	60.2	−8.7	148.9	444.2	142.4	301.8
1983	3,906.6	3,308.2	3,243.1	53.7	11.5	151.0	447.4	144.8	302.6
1984	4,148.5	3,541.7	3,496.4	55.1	−9.8	154.9	451.9	146.4	305.4
1985	4,279.8	3,658.1	3,608.6	64.2	−14.7	159.9	461.8	148.6	313.2
1986	4,404.5	3,768.3	3,702.8	64.3	1.3	166.3	469.9	149.0	320.8
1987	4,539.9	3,890.8	3,849.5	66.0	−24.8	170.5	478.7	151.4	327.3
1988	4,718.6	4,050.6	4,014.8	63.2	−27.4	180.6	487.4	153.5	333.9
1989	4,838.0	4,150.5	4,083.4	66.2	.9	190.5	497.0	154.2	342.7
1990	4,897.3	4,190.8	4,112.4	71.6	6.9	196.9	509.5	156.2	353.3
1991	4,861.4	4,144.8	4,066.2	70.4	8.1	202.4	514.3	157.3	357.0
1992	4,986.3	4,267.6	4,168.4	79.6	19.7	209.1	509.5	150.5	359.0
1993 ᵖ	5,132.7	4,404.3	4,315.5	73.9	14.9	217.0	511.3	147.4	363.9
1982: IV	3,759.6	3,166.3	3,116.9	61.1	−11.7	149.6	443.8	143.2	300.6
1983: IV	4,012.1	3,411.5	3,349.0	47.0	15.5	151.7	448.9	145.2	303.7
1984: IV	4,194.2	3,583.0	3,548.9	56.1	−22.0	156.8	454.4	147.1	307.3
1985: IV	4,333.5	3,706.1	3,646.8	65.5	−6.2	162.3	465.1	148.7	316.5
1986: IV	4,427.1	3,786.7	3,724.4	64.4	−2.1	166.9	473.5	149.8	323.7
1987: IV	4,625.5	3,969.9	3,925.5	69.0	−24.6	173.2	482.3	152.8	329.5
1988: IV	4,779.7	4,104.2	4,074.5	53.8	−24.1	184.7	490.7	154.0	336.7
1989: IV	4,856.7	4,161.9	4,085.0	65.2	11.7	193.2	501.7	154.8	346.9
1990: I	4,898.3	4,199.4	4,118.7	69.0	11.8	193.8	505.0	155.2	349.9
II	4,917.1	4,211.9	4,141.7	71.8	−1.6	196.2	509.1	156.5	352.6
III	4,906.5	4,197.7	4,112.5	72.1	13.1	198.5	510.2	155.6	354.6
IV	4,867.2	4,154.3	4,076.5	73.5	4.2	199.2	513.6	157.4	356.2
1991: I	4,837.8	4,119.4	4,047.6	71.6	.2	200.0	518.4	161.3	357.1
II	4,855.6	4,137.0	4,062.2	71.0	3.8	201.9	516.7	158.8	357.8
III	4,872.6	4,157.6	4,065.0	69.2	23.3	202.9	512.2	155.6	356.6
IV	4,879.6	4,165.0	4,090.0	69.7	5.3	204.7	509.9	153.3	356.5
1992: I	4,922.0	4,206.7	4,110.0	77.2	19.4	206.5	508.8	152.0	356.8
II	4,956.5	4,239.8	4,141.0	79.1	19.7	207.4	509.3	151.0	358.3
III	4,998.2	4,277.9	4,182.6	82.2	13.1	210.3	510.0	150.1	360.0
IV	5,068.3	4,346.2	4,240.0	79.7	26.5	212.4	509.8	148.8	361.0
1993: I	5,078.2	4,353.9	4,247.4	78.2	28.3	213.5	510.8	148.8	362.0
II	5,102.1	4,374.1	4,288.1	76.2	9.8	216.8	511.3	147.8	363.4
III	5,138.3	4,408.4	4,330.1	67.5	10.8	218.4	511.5	146.9	364.5
IV ᵖ	5,212.1	4,480.8	4,396.4	73.6	10.8	219.5	511.8	146.0	365.8

[1] Includes compensation of employees in government enterprises.
[2] Compensation of government employees.

Source: Department of Commerce, Bureau of Economic Analysis.

TABLE B-11.—*Gross domestic product by industry, 1947-91*

[Billions of dollars]

Year	Gross domestic product	Agriculture, forestry, and fisheries	Mining	Construction	Manufacturing Total	Durable goods	Nondurable goods	Transportation and public utilities	Wholesale trade	Retail trade	Finance, insurance, and real estate	Services	Government	Statistical discrepancy [1]
Based on 1972 SIC:														
1947	234.3	20.8	6.8	9.1	66.2	33.5	32.7	21.0	16.6	27.5	24.0	20.2	20.2	1.8
1948	260.3	24.0	9.4	11.5	74.7	38.2	36.6	23.7	18.3	30.1	27.2	21.9	20.9	-1.2
1949	259.3	19.4	8.1	11.5	72.3	37.2	35.1	23.9	17.6	30.3	29.4	22.6	23.1	1.0
1950	287.0	20.7	9.3	13.2	84.1	45.9	38.2	26.6	19.8	31.7	32.3	24.2	24.2	1.0
1951	331.6	23.8	10.2	15.6	99.1	55.6	43.5	30.1	22.5	34.3	35.8	26.4	30.9	2.9
1952	349.7	23.2	10.2	16.9	103.4	59.0	44.3	32.1	22.7	36.3	39.4	28.2	35.6	1.8
1953	370.0	21.1	10.8	17.5	112.4	66.1	46.4	34.1	23.2	37.2	43.7	30.2	36.8	2.8
1954	370.9	20.7	11.0	17.7	106.8	61.0	45.8	33.7	23.5	38.1	47.5	31.6	37.9	2.4
1955	404.3	19.8	12.5	19.0	121.4	70.8	50.5	36.7	26.6	40.5	51.4	35.2	40.0	1.2
1956	426.2	19.7	13.6	21.2	127.4	74.0	53.5	39.5	29.0	42.4	55.0	38.7	42.5	-2.8
1957	448.6	19.6	13.7	22.1	132.0	78.0	54.0	41.5	30.5	44.6	59.2	41.8	45.4	-1.9
1958	454.7	21.9	12.7	21.8	124.6	70.1	54.5	41.7	31.1	45.3	63.9	44.1	48.9	-1.1
1959	494.2	20.3	12.5	23.7	142.2	81.7	60.5	44.9	34.2	49.1	68.9	48.4	51.7	-1.8
1960	513.3	21.3	12.9	24.2	144.8	82.6	62.2	47.1	35.3	50.4	73.5	51.6	55.4	-3.1
1961	531.8	21.7	13.0	25.2	145.3	81.7	63.6	48.7	36.4	51.7	78.0	55.0	59.1	-2.2
1962	571.6	22.1	13.2	27.0	159.1	92.1	67.1	51.7	38.8	55.4	82.4	59.3	63.5	-1.0
1963	603.1	22.3	13.5	28.9	168.6	98.3	70.4	54.6	40.5	57.9	87.1	63.4	68.4	-2.0
1964	648.0	21.4	13.9	31.5	180.5	105.9	74.6	58.1	43.6	63.5	92.9	69.1	74.1	-.7
1965	702.7	24.2	14.0	34.6	199.1	118.8	80.3	62.2	47.2	68.0	99.9	74.7	79.5	-.7
1966	769.8	25.4	14.7	37.7	218.2	131.1	87.1	67.1	51.5	72.7	108.0	82.6	89.1	2.8
1967	814.3	24.9	15.2	39.5	223.7	134.1	89.6	70.3	54.8	78.2	117.3	90.8	98.8	.8
1968	889.3	25.7	16.3	43.3	244.3	146.4	97.9	76.1	60.2	86.6	126.8	99.4	110.7	-.1
1969	959.5	28.5	17.1	48.4	257.8	154.4	103.4	82.5	65.1	94.2	136.4	110.7	121.4	-2.6
1970	1,010.7	29.8	18.7	51.1	253.1	146.2	106.9	88.0	68.6	100.2	146.3	120.5	134.2	.0
1971	1,097.2	32.1	18.9	56.1	266.7	154.2	112.5	97.1	74.3	109.2	163.1	130.3	146.2	3.1
1972	1,207.0	37.3	19.6	62.5	294.3	172.6	121.7	108.3	83.2	118.9	176.5	144.9	160.4	1.1
1973	1,349.6	55.0	23.8	69.8	327.6	195.8	131.8	119.1	93.5	131.0	193.1	163.2	173.9	-.5
1974	1,458.6	53.2	37.0	73.7	341.2	202.2	139.0	129.9	107.1	136.9	208.9	179.4	189.9	1.4
1975	1,585.9	54.9	42.8	75.2	358.8	207.1	151.7	142.3	117.0	153.0	226.7	199.3	209.8	6.0
1976	1,768.4	53.8	47.5	85.1	409.6	239.9	169.7	161.2	124.8	172.4	250.1	224.1	229.3	10.4
1977	1,974.1	54.4	54.1	93.9	466.8	277.7	189.1	179.2	137.9	190.4	283.6	255.7	247.1	10.9
1978	2,232.7	63.3	61.4	110.7	521.9	317.5	204.5	202.2	157.1	214.9	328.6	294.6	270.5	7.6
1979	2,488.6	74.6	71.2	124.8	575.7	343.8	231.9	219.1	178.6	233.2	370.8	333.0	293.9	13.8
1980	2,708.0	66.7	112.6	128.7	588.3	348.9	239.4	242.2	191.6	244.7	418.4	377.0	324.2	13.6
1981	3,030.6	81.1	148.1	129.4	653.0	385.3	267.7	273.3	212.7	269.3	469.6	425.1	358.1	10.9
1982	3,149.6	77.0	146.1	129.4	647.5	372.9	274.6	292.1	216.5	286.6	503.9	469.8	388.0	-7.4
1983	3,405.0	62.7	127.9	137.9	693.3	396.0	297.3	326.7	223.6	321.1	565.3	521.3	415.0	10.2
1984	3,777.2	83.7	137.1	161.2	773.9	461.2	312.7	358.8	258.4	361.3	619.0	586.9	445.9	-9.0
1985	4,038.7	84.3	130.6	179.2	798.5	471.5	327.0	378.0	276.6	390.9	681.8	650.9	481.8	-13.9
1986	4,268.6	81.7	82.7	201.9	829.3	480.0	349.3	393.8	290.9	418.7	743.5	712.8	512.1	1.2
1987	4,539.9	88.5	83.0	213.0	878.4	503.2	375.2	419.9	302.6	440.1	809.9	784.0	545.3	-24.8
Based on 1987 SIC:														
1987	4,539.9	88.5	83.0	213.0	877.8	501.9	375.9	419.8	303.1	441.8	809.7	782.5	545.3	-24.8
1988	4,900.4	90.8	87.9	227.6	961.0	541.1	419.9	442.1	331.0	471.7	866.3	865.5	584.8	-28.4
1989	5,250.8	104.8	84.2	235.9	1,004.6	562.6	442.0	463.3	351.6	502.5	926.5	948.8	627.6	1.1
1990	5,546.1	112.0	103.1	240.1	1,024.7	563.7	461.0	481.2	363.0	515.7	982.4	1,040.0	676.3	7.8
1991	5,722.9	108.6	91.8	223.4	1,026.2	551.4	474.5	506.0	375.1	532.1	1,039.7	1,089.8	720.6	9.6

[1] Equals gross domestic product (GDP) measured as the sum of expenditures less gross domestic income—that is, GDP measured as the costs incurred and profits earned in domestic production.

Source: Department of Commerce, Bureau of Economic Analysis.

TABLE B-12.—*Gross domestic product by industry in 1987 dollars, fixed 1987 weights, 1977–91*

[Billions of dollars]

Year	Gross domestic product	Agriculture, forestry, and fisheries	Mining	Construction	Manufacturing Total	Durable goods	Non-durable goods	Transportation and public utilities	Wholesale trade	Retail trade	Finance, insurance, and real estate	Services	Government	Statistical discrepancy [1]	Residual [2]
Based on 1972 SIC:															
1977	3,533.3	63.7	83.5	190.8	741.6	440.9	300.7	314.3	170.1	318.0	596.5	538.9	475.7	19.4	20.8
1978	3,703.5	59.2	85.0	198.8	773.1	460.9	312.2	325.1	185.8	338.1	631.0	573.5	488.3	12.2	33.4
1979	3,796.8	62.4	71.9	200.3	777.1	458.0	319.2	335.5	195.8	334.8	667.4	592.8	498.6	20.6	39.6
1980	3,776.3	63.2	79.9	185.4	725.4	424.3	301.1	336.3	190.5	320.1	692.8	609.0	508.9	19.0	45.7
1981	3,843.1	72.7	74.2	174.7	746.7	429.7	317.1	337.1	207.5	330.6	704.7	624.4	511.6	13.6	45.3
1982	3,760.3	73.3	73.1	164.9	711.1	392.4	318.7	331.3	218.2	336.8	708.4	629.2	507.1	−8.7	15.6
1983	3,906.6	68.4	71.3	170.0	733.8	402.5	331.3	351.7	224.2	365.1	727.9	649.5	512.5	11.5	20.8
1984	4,148.5	71.5	82.0	190.9	791.4	458.4	333.0	377.6	259.5	397.7	762.1	687.8	516.9	−9.8	21.0
1985	4,279.8	81.9	83.3	209.0	810.5	468.1	342.4	381.8	273.0	421.4	776.4	722.0	527.5	−14.7	7.7
1986	4,404.5	84.5	83.0	209.1	819.1	471.5	347.7	386.9	307.1	453.2	776.6	751.7	536.4	1.3	−4.4
1987	4,539.9	88.5	83.0	213.0	878.4	503.2	375.2	419.9	302.6	440.1	809.9	784.0	545.3	−24.8	.0
Based on 1987 SIC:															
1987	4,539.9	88.5	83.0	213.0	877.8	501.9	375.9	419.8	303.1	441.8	809.7	782.5	545.3	−24.8	.0
1988	4,718.6	85.1	94.2	211.7	923.5	536.4	387.2	437.1	311.3	469.7	846.5	812.8	555.9	−27.4	−1.8
1989	4,838.0	88.0	83.3	213.1	932.2	543.2	389.1	449.4	324.5	483.9	865.5	845.7	567.0	.9	−15.5
1990	4,897.3	95.8	91.8	210.2	928.5	537.0	391.5	462.6	319.5	478.1	868.3	869.4	581.5	6.9	−15.3
1991	4,861.4	97.4	91.5	194.5	908.0	525.5	382.5	478.1	326.4	474.1	878.4	866.7	586.5	8.1	−48.4

[1] Equals the current-dollar statistical discrepancy deflated by the implicit price deflator for gross domestic business product.
[2] Equals gross domestic product (GDP) in constant dollars measured as the sum of expenditures less the statistical discrepancy in constant dollars and GDP in constant dollars measured as the sum of gross product originating by industry.

Note.—Constant-dollar values are equal to fixed-weighted quantity indexes with 1987 weights divided by 100 and multiplied by the 1987 value of current-dollar GDP.

Source: Department of Commerce, Bureau of Economic Analysis.

TABLE B-13.—*Gross domestic product of nonfinancial corporate business, 1959-93*

[Billions of dollars; quarterly data at seasonally adjusted annual rates]

Year or quarter	Gross domestic product of nonfinancial corporate business	Consumption of fixed capital	Net domestic product Total	Indirect business taxes [1]	Total	Compensation of employees	Corporate profits with inventory valuation and capital consumption adjustments Total	Profits before tax	Profits tax liability	Profits after tax Total	Dividends	Undistributed profits	Inventory valuation adjustment	Capital consumption adjustment	Net interest
1959	267.5	24.2	243.2	26.0	217.2	171.5	42.6	43.6	20.7	22.9	10.0	12.9	-0.3	-0.7	3.1
1960	278.1	25.2	252.9	28.3	224.6	181.2	40.0	40.3	19.2	21.1	10.6	10.6	-.2	-.2	3.5
1961	285.5	26.0	259.6	29.5	230.1	185.3	40.8	40.1	19.5	20.7	10.6	10.1	.3	.3	4.0
1962	311.7	26.9	284.8	32.0	252.8	200.1	48.2	45.0	20.6	24.3	11.4	13.0	.0	3.2	4.5
1963	331.8	28.1	303.7	34.0	269.7	211.1	53.8	49.8	22.8	27.0	12.6	14.4	.1	3.9	4.8
1964	358.1	29.5	328.6	36.6	292.0	226.7	60.0	56.0	24.0	32.1	13.7	18.4	-.5	4.5	5.3
1965	393.5	31.5	362.0	39.2	322.8	246.5	70.3	66.2	27.2	39.0	15.6	23.4	-1.2	5.3	6.1
1966	431.0	34.3	396.7	40.5	356.2	274.0	74.9	71.4	29.5	41.9	16.8	25.1	-2.1	5.6	7.4
1967	453.4	37.5	415.9	43.1	372.8	292.3	71.8	67.5	27.8	39.7	17.5	22.2	-1.6	5.8	8.8
1968	500.5	41.4	459.1	49.7	409.3	323.2	76.0	74.0	33.6	40.4	19.1	21.3	-3.7	5.6	10.1
1969	543.3	45.3	498.0	54.7	443.3	358.8	71.3	70.8	33.3	37.5	19.1	18.4	-5.9	6.3	13.2
1970	561.4	49.7	511.6	58.8	452.8	378.7	57.1	58.1	27.2	31.0	18.5	12.5	-6.6	5.5	17.1
1971	606.4	54.6	551.7	64.5	487.3	402.0	67.2	67.1	29.9	37.1	18.5	18.7	-4.6	4.7	18.1
1972	673.3	61.0	612.4	69.2	543.2	447.1	77.0	78.6	33.8	44.8	20.1	24.7	-6.6	5.0	19.2
1973	754.5	66.2	688.3	76.3	612.0	505.9	83.6	98.6	40.2	58.4	21.1	37.3	-20.0	5.0	22.5
1974	814.6	77.5	737.1	81.4	655.7	556.8	70.6	109.2	42.2	67.0	21.7	45.2	-39.5	.9	28.3
1975	881.2	93.3	788.0	87.4	700.6	580.3	91.5	109.9	41.5	68.4	24.8	43.6	-11.0	-7.4	28.7
1976	994.6	103.8	890.8	95.1	795.7	656.7	111.5	137.3	53.0	84.4	27.8	56.6	-14.9	-10.9	27.5
1977	1,124.7	116.2	1,008.5	104.1	904.4	741.8	132.0	158.6	59.9	98.7	32.0	66.8	-16.6	-10.0	30.6
1978	1,279.4	132.3	1,147.2	114.6	1,032.6	850.2	146.1	183.5	67.1	116.4	37.2	79.1	-25.0	-12.3	36.3
1979	1,423.7	153.0	1,270.7	123.3	1,147.4	964.2	138.1	195.5	69.6	125.9	39.3	86.7	-41.6	-15.9	45.1
1980	1,546.5	174.8	1,371.7	139.4	1,232.4	1,053.5	120.7	181.6	67.0	114.6	45.5	69.1	-43.0	-17.8	58.2
1981	1,748.6	207.0	1,541.5	167.9	1,373.6	1,164.8	136.9	181.0	63.9	117.1	53.4	63.7	-25.7	-18.4	71.9
1982	1,802.8	229.4	1,573.4	169.4	1,404.0	1,209.9	111.5	132.9	46.3	86.7	56.4	30.2	-9.9	-11.5	82.2
1983	1,936.1	242.1	1,694.0	185.8	1,508.2	1,271.6	159.9	155.9	59.4	96.4	66.5	29.9	-8.5	12.5	76.7
1984	2,166.5	248.1	1,918.3	206.9	1,711.4	1,409.2	214.3	189.0	73.7	115.4	69.5	45.9	-4.1	29.4	87.9
1985	2,293.6	258.0	2,035.5	220.3	1,815.3	1,503.2	221.4	165.5	69.9	95.6	74.5	21.1	.2	55.6	90.7
1986	2,386.3	271.4	2,114.9	231.4	1,883.6	1,581.5	203.8	149.1	75.6	73.5	76.3	-2.8	9.7	44.9	98.3
1987	2,547.3	281.4	2,265.9	241.0	2,024.9	1,675.0	244.2	212.0	93.5	118.5	77.9	40.6	-14.5	46.7	105.8
1988	2,764.8	297.5	2,467.3	257.1	2,210.2	1,814.2	274.4	256.6	101.7	154.9	82.0	72.9	-27.3	45.0	121.6
1989	2,913.5	317.4	2,596.2	274.2	2,322.0	1,920.2	255.2	232.9	99.5	133.3	101.9	31.5	-17.5	39.9	146.6
1990	3,045.5	329.3	2,716.2	290.4	2,425.8	2,020.9	256.4	232.1	93.9	138.3	118.1	20.1	-11.0	35.3	148.5
1991	3,082.1	341.5	2,740.6	311.5	2,429.0	2,053.8	233.9	214.8	82.7	132.1	94.0	38.1	4.9	14.2	141.3
1992	3,243.4	352.7	2,890.7	327.7	2,563.1	2,149.5	278.3	255.1	98.2	156.9	105.2	51.7	-5.3	28.5	135.3
1993 ᵖ		362.3		345.5		2,255.4	314.8	286.8	114.9	171.8	125.3	46.5	-7.8	35.9	
1982: IV	1,806.3	238.8	1,567.5	172.6	1,394.9	1,213.9	101.5	116.5	40.6	75.9	59.0	16.9	-8.6	-6.4	79.6
1983: IV	2,037.2	261.5	1,775.7	194.0	1,581.7	1,327.6	175.2	168.1	64.4	103.7	67.4	36.3	-7.6	14.7	78.9
1984: IV	2,228.2	258.9	1,969.4	212.4	1,756.9	1,449.7	211.4	169.0	62.6	106.4	68.7	37.7	3.5	38.9	95.8
1985: IV	2,338.8	263.4	2,075.4	223.8	1,851.6	1,540.1	221.4	168.4	71.1	97.2	74.7	22.5	-3.8	56.9	90.0
1986: IV	2,422.8	275.8	2,147.1	233.6	1,913.5	1,611.4	198.6	168.5	86.5	82.0	75.2	6.8	-10.7	40.8	103.5
1987: IV	2,627.6	286.1	2,341.4	245.4	2,096.0	1,730.1	256.8	224.8	99.6	125.1	84.0	41.2	-17.8	49.8	109.2
1988: IV	2,843.2	304.5	2,538.8	263.1	2,275.7	1,868.8	278.5	271.4	107.9	163.5	84.3	79.2	-31.7	38.8	128.4
1989: IV	2,951.5	326.5	2,625.0	279.0	2,346.0	1,954.6	240.7	215.9	91.1	124.8	102.3	22.5	-13.5	38.3	150.7
1990: I	3,007.7	322.6	2,685.1	285.3	2,399.8	1,987.4	263.9	223.3	89.6	133.7	118.0	15.8	-2.0	42.6	148.5
II	3,064.1	326.6	2,737.5	285.8	2,451.7	2,019.4	282.9	233.8	95.0	138.8	117.4	21.4	8.9	40.1	149.5
III	3,057.8	332.0	2,725.8	294.0	2,431.8	2,037.5	246.5	244.6	98.8	145.8	120.0	25.8	-31.5	33.4	147.9
IV	3,052.5	336.1	2,716.4	296.6	2,419.8	2,039.3	232.4	226.7	92.0	134.8	117.2	17.5	-19.5	25.2	148.2
1991: I	3,048.6	339.4	2,709.2	304.2	2,405.0	2,028.3	232.8	207.8	79.7	128.2	103.1	25.1	8.2	16.8	143.9
II	3,063.4	340.4	2,722.9	307.1	2,415.8	2,040.1	235.5	209.9	81.1	128.8	92.9	35.9	12.7	12.8	140.2
III	3,086.8	342.3	2,744.5	315.3	2,429.2	2,061.6	227.0	218.2	84.3	133.9	89.0	44.9	-3.0	11.8	140.6
IV	3,129.5	343.9	2,785.6	319.5	2,466.1	2,085.3	240.4	223.3	85.9	137.4	90.9	46.5	1.9	15.2	140.5
1992: I	3,159.8	345.1	2,814.6	321.8	2,492.9	2,103.8	252.3	235.1	90.8	144.3	93.9	50.5	-4.6	21.8	136.8
II	3,218.1	347.8	2,870.3	323.9	2,546.4	2,135.4	273.9	260.2	100.8	159.4	100.3	59.1	-13.7	27.4	137.1
III	3,264.2	366.1	2,898.2	329.1	2,569.0	2,162.7	272.7	251.8	95.3	156.5	105.9	50.5	-7.8	28.8	133.6
IV	3,331.6	351.7	2,979.9	336.0	2,643.9	2,195.9	314.1	273.2	105.8	167.4	120.7	46.7	4.9	36.0	133.9
1993: I	3,331.7	356.8	2,975.0	333.0	2,642.0	2,215.0	292.1	268.4	106.4	162.0	127.4	34.6	-12.7	36.4	134.9
II	3,395.9	359.0	3,036.8	344.0	2,692.8	2,244.7	315.0	291.2	117.6	173.6	125.4	48.2	-12.2	36.0	133.1
III	3,432.2	367.0	3,065.1	347.0	2,718.1	2,267.1	318.2	281.8	112.5	169.3	124.0	45.3	1.0	35.4	132.8
IV ᵖ		366.3		357.9		2,294.9							-7.2	35.7	

[1] Indirect business tax and nontax liability plus business transfer payments less subsidies.

Source: Department of Commerce, Bureau of Economic Analysis.

284

TABLE B-14.—*Output, costs, and profits of nonfinancial corporate business, 1959–93*

[Quarterly data at seasonally adjusted annual rates]

Year or quarter	Gross domestic product of nonfinancial corporate business (billions of dollars) Current dollars	Gross domestic product of nonfinancial corporate business (billions of dollars) 1987 dollars	Total cost and profit[2]	Consumption of fixed capital	Indirect business taxes[3]	Compensation of employees	Corporate profits with inventory valuation and capital consumption adjustments Total	Corporate profits with inventory valuation and capital consumption adjustments Profits tax liability	Corporate profits with inventory valuation and capital consumption adjustments Profits after tax[4]	Net interest	Output per hour of all employees (1987 dollars)	Compensation per hour of all employees (dollars)
1959	267.5	928.7	0.288	0.026	0.028	0.185	0.046	0.022	0.024	0.003	15.443	2.851
1960	278.1	955.6	.291	.026	.030	.190	.042	.020	.022	.004	15.661	2.969
1961	285.5	978.2	.292	.027	.030	.189	.042	.020	.022	.004	16.182	3.066
1962	311.7	1,047.5	.298	.026	.031	.191	.046	.020	.026	.004	16.675	3.186
1963	331.8	1,104.8	.300	.025	.031	.191	.049	.021	.028	.004	17.204	3.287
1964	358.1	1,179.3	.304	.025	.031	.192	.051	.020	.031	.005	17.855	3.432
1965	393.5	1,262.2	.312	.025	.031	.195	.056	.022	.034	.005	18.074	3.529
1966	431.0	1,336.0	.323	.026	.030	.205	.056	.022	.034	.006	18.143	3.720
1967	453.4	1,367.4	.332	.027	.032	.214	.052	.020	.032	.006	18.362	3.925
1968	500.5	1,444.3	.347	.029	.034	.224	.053	.023	.029	.007	18.858	4.220
1969	543.3	1,492.5	.364	.030	.037	.240	.048	.022	.025	.009	18.750	4.508
1970	561.4	1,473.4	.381	.034	.040	.257	.039	.018	.020	.012	18.776	4.825
1971	606.4	1,525.9	.397	.036	.042	.263	.044	.020	.024	.012	19.487	5.134
1972	673.3	1,629.5	.413	.037	.042	.274	.047	.021	.027	.012	19.793	5.430
1973	754.5	1,706.9	.442	.039	.045	.296	.049	.024	.025	.013	19.762	5.858
1974	814.6	1,669.7	.488	.046	.049	.333	.042	.025	.017	.017	19.230	6.413
1975	881.2	1,625.6	.542	.057	.054	.357	.056	.026	.031	.018	19.763	7.056
1976	994.6	1,748.5	.569	.059	.054	.376	.064	.030	.033	.016	20.365	7.648
1977	1,124.7	1,866.7	.603	.062	.056	.397	.071	.032	.039	.016	20.766	8.252
1978	1,279.4	1,967.1	.650	.067	.058	.432	.074	.034	.040	.018	20.711	8.951
1979	1,423.7	1,995.7	.713	.077	.062	.483	.069	.035	.034	.023	20.222	9.770
1980	1,546.5	1,980.9	.781	.088	.070	.532	.061	.034	.027	.029	20.265	10.777
1981	1,748.6	2,035.1	.859	.102	.082	.572	.067	.031	.036	.035	20.538	11.755
1982	1,802.8	2,001.3	.901	.115	.085	.605	.056	.023	.033	.041	20.803	12.577
1983	1,936.1	2,112.3	.917	.115	.088	.602	.076	.028	.048	.036	21.596	13.002
1984	2,166.5	2,284.1	.949	.109	.091	.617	.094	.032	.062	.038	21.926	13.527
1985	2,293.6	2,364.3	.970	.109	.093	.636	.094	.030	.064	.038	22.150	14.083
1986	2,386.3	2,439.3	.978	.111	.095	.648	.084	.031	.053	.040	22.735	14.741
1987	2,547.3	2,547.3	1.000	.110	.095	.658	.096	.037	.059	.042	23.129	15.208
1988	2,764.8	2,684.8	1.030	.111	.096	.676	.102	.038	.064	.045	23.572	15.833
1989	2,913.5	2,718.9	1.072	.117	.101	.706	.094	.037	.057	.054	23.189	16.377
1990	3,045.5	2,747.4	1.109	.120	.106	.736	.093	.034	.059	.054	23.446	17.246
1991	3,082.1	2,710.0	1.137	.126	.115	.758	.086	.031	.056	.052	23.865	18.087
1992	3,243.4	2,822.3	1.149	.125	.116	.762	.099	.035	.064	.048	24.836	18.915
1982: IV	1,806.3	1,999.6	.903	.119	.086	.607	.051	.020	.030	.040	21.070	12.791
1983: IV	2,037.2	2,204.2	.924	.119	.088	.602	.079	.029	.050	.036	21.893	13.187
1984: IV	2,228.2	2,328.4	.957	.111	.091	.623	.091	.027	.064	.041	22.054	13.732
1985: IV	2,338.8	2,396.9	.976	.110	.093	.643	.092	.030	.063	.038	22.347	14.359
1986: IV	2,422.8	2,463.3	.984	.112	.095	.654	.081	.035	.045	.042	22.892	14.975
1987: IV	2,627.6	2,604.0	1.009	.110	.094	.664	.099	.038	.060	.042	23.358	15.518
1988: IV	2,843.2	2,719.0	1.046	.112	.097	.687	.102	.040	.063	.047	23.524	16.071
1989: IV	2,951.5	2,722.7	1.084	.120	.102	.718	.088	.033	.055	.055	23.147	16.618
1990: I	3,007.7	2,742.9	1.097	.118	.104	.725	.096	.033	.064	.054	23.231	16.832
II	3,064.1	2,771.4	1.106	.118	.103	.729	.102	.034	.068	.054	23.537	17.150
III	3,057.8	2,750.5	1.112	.121	.107	.741	.090	.036	.054	.054	23.468	17.385
IV	3,052.5	2,725.0	1.120	.123	.109	.748	.085	.034	.052	.054	23.549	17.623
1991: I	3,048.6	2,694.1	1.132	.126	.113	.753	.086	.030	.057	.053	23.634	17.794
II	3,063.4	2,692.4	1.138	.126	.114	.758	.087	.030	.057	.052	23.738	17.988
III	3,086.8	2,708.5	1.140	.126	.116	.761	.084	.031	.053	.052	23.889	18.183
IV	3,129.5	2,745.0	1.140	.125	.116	.760	.088	.031	.056	.051	24.246	18.419
1992: I	3,159.8	2,759.5	1.145	.125	.117	.762	.091	.033	.059	.050	24.394	18.597
II	3,218.1	2,802.6	1.148	.124	.116	.762	.098	.036	.062	.049	24.678	18.803
III	3,264.2	2,839.8	1.149	.129	.116	.762	.096	.034	.062	.047	25.031	19.062
IV	3,331.6	2,887.4	1.154	.122	.116	.761	.109	.037	.072	.046	25.310	19.249
1993: I	3,331.7	2,867.5	1.162	.124	.116	.772	.102	.037	.065	.047	25.053	19.353
II	3,395.9	2,916.6	1.164	.123	.118	.770	.108	.040	.068	.046	25.296	19.468
III	3,432.2	2,948.9	1.164	.124	.118	.769	.108	.038	.070	.045	25.512	19.629

[1] Output is measured by gross domestic product of nonfinancial corporate business in 1987 dollars.
[2] This is equal to the deflator for gross domestic product of nonfinancial corporate business with the decimal point shifted two places to the left.
[3] Indirect business tax and nontax liability plus business transfer payments less subsidies.
[4] With inventory valuation and capital consumption adjustments.

Sources: Department of Commerce (Bureau of Economic Analysis) and Department of Labor (Bureau of Labor Statistics).

TABLE B-15.—*Personal consumption expenditures, 1959–93*

[Billions of dollars; quarterly data at seasonally adjusted annual rates]

Year or quarter	Personal consumption expenditures	Durable goods			Nondurable goods					Services					
		Total [1]	Motor vehicles and parts	Furniture and household equipment	Total [1]	Food	Clothing and shoes	Gasoline and oil	Fuel oil and coal	Total [1]	Housing [2]	Household operation		Transportation	Medical care
												Total [1]	Electricity and gas		
1959	318.1	42.8	18.9	18.1	148.5	80.7	26.4	11.3	4.0	126.8	45.0	18.7	7.6	10.5	16.3
1960	332.4	43.5	19.7	18.0	153.1	82.6	27.0	12.0	3.8	135.9	48.2	20.3	8.3	11.2	17.4
1961	343.5	41.9	17.8	18.3	157.4	84.8	27.6	12.0	3.8	144.1	51.2	21.2	8.8	11.7	18.6
1962	364.4	47.0	21.5	19.3	163.8	87.1	29.0	12.6	3.8	153.6	54.7	22.4	9.4	12.2	20.7
1963	384.2	51.8	24.4	20.7	169.4	89.5	29.8	13.0	4.0	163.1	58.0	23.6	9.9	12.7	22.4
1964	412.5	56.8	26.0	23.2	179.7	94.6	32.4	13.6	4.1	175.9	61.4	25.0	10.4	13.4	25.7
1965	444.6	63.5	29.9	25.1	191.9	101.0	34.1	14.8	4.4	189.2	65.4	26.5	10.9	14.5	27.7
1966	481.6	68.5	30.3	28.2	208.5	109.0	37.4	16.0	4.7	204.6	69.5	28.2	11.5	15.9	30.5
1967	509.3	70.6	30.0	30.0	216.9	112.3	39.2	17.1	4.8	221.7	74.1	30.2	12.2	17.3	33.7
1968	559.1	81.0	36.1	32.9	235.0	121.6	43.2	18.6	4.7	243.1	79.7	32.3	13.0	18.9	39.0
1969	603.7	86.2	38.4	34.7	252.2	130.5	46.5	20.5	4.6	265.3	86.8	35.1	14.0	20.9	44.4
1970	646.5	85.3	35.5	35.7	270.4	142.1	47.8	21.9	4.4	290.8	94.0	37.8	15.2	23.7	50.1
1971	700.3	97.2	44.5	37.8	283.3	147.5	51.7	23.2	4.6	319.8	102.7	41.0	16.6	27.1	56.5
1972	767.8	110.7	51.1	42.4	305.2	158.5	56.4	24.4	5.1	351.9	112.1	45.3	18.4	29.8	63.5
1973	848.1	124.1	56.1	47.9	339.6	176.1	62.5	28.1	6.3	384.5	122.7	49.8	20.0	31.2	71.2
1974	927.7	123.0	49.5	51.5	380.8	198.1	66.0	36.1	7.8	423.9	134.1	55.5	23.3	33.3	80.1
1975	1,024.9	134.3	54.8	54.5	416.0	218.5	70.8	39.7	8.4	474.5	147.0	63.7	28.5	35.7	93.0
1976	1,143.1	160.0	71.3	60.2	451.8	236.0	76.6	43.0	10.1	531.2	161.5	72.4	32.5	41.3	106.2
1977	1,271.5	182.6	83.5	67.1	490.4	255.9	84.1	46.9	11.1	598.4	179.5	81.9	37.6	49.2	122.4
1978	1,421.2	202.3	92.2	74.0	541.5	280.6	94.3	50.1	11.5	677.4	201.7	91.2	42.1	53.6	139.7
1979	1,583.7	214.2	91.5	82.3	613.3	313.0	101.2	66.2	14.4	756.2	226.6	100.0	46.8	59.4	157.8
1980	1,748.1	212.5	84.0	86.0	682.9	341.8	107.3	86.7	15.4	852.7	255.2	113.0	56.3	65.1	181.3
1981	1,926.2	228.5	91.6	91.3	744.2	367.3	117.2	97.9	15.8	953.5	287.1	126.0	63.4	69.4	213.6
1982	2,059.2	236.5	97.7	92.5	772.3	386.0	120.5	94.1	14.5	1,050.4	311.1	141.4	72.6	71.6	240.5
1983	2,257.5	275.0	120.6	104.4	817.8	406.2	130.8	93.3	13.8	1,164.7	334.6	153.6	80.7	78.9	265.7
1984	2,460.3	317.9	144.6	115.3	873.0	430.2	142.5	94.5	14.2	1,269.4	362.3	165.5	84.6	89.1	290.6
1985	2,667.4	352.9	167.4	123.4	919.4	451.1	152.2	96.9	14.1	1,395.1	392.5	176.2	88.7	99.0	319.3
1986	2,850.6	389.6	184.9	135.5	952.2	476.8	163.2	79.7	12.0	1,508.8	421.8	181.1	87.1	105.8	346.4
1987	3,052.2	403.7	183.5	144.0	1,011.1	500.7	174.5	84.7	12.0	1,637.4	452.5	187.8	88.4	116.6	384.7
1988	3,296.1	437.1	197.8	156.7	1,073.8	533.6	186.4	86.9	12.1	1,785.2	484.2	199.5	93.4	128.5	427.7
1989	3,523.1	459.4	205.4	167.9	1,149.5	565.1	200.4	96.2	12.0	1,914.2	514.4	209.8	98.0	135.6	471.9
1990	3,761.2	468.2	202.9	174.2	1,229.2	604.8	207.3	108.4	13.2	2,063.8	547.5	215.6	97.4	142.5	526.2
1991	3,906.4	457.8	185.5	180.6	1,257.9	621.4	213.0	102.9	13.0	2,190.7	574.4	227.1	104.3	146.2	577.1
1992	4,139.9	497.3	204.3	194.5	1,300.9	633.7	228.2	103.4	13.8	2,341.6	600.0	234.4	105.8	155.4	628.4
1993 [P]	4,390.6	537.7	222.4	211.7	1,350.2	658.3	237.1	103.6	15.1	2,502.7	627.7	251.0	113.2	170.2	680.6
1982: IV	2,128.7	246.9	105.1	95.6	787.3	394.9	122.7	93.0	14.0	1,094.6	320.2	145.8	74.9	73.6	250.9
1983: IV	2,346.8	297.7	134.8	109.7	839.8	413.9	136.7	94.9	14.1	1,209.3	344.6	159.3	84.8	82.9	274.8
1984: IV	2,526.4	328.2	149.3	118.7	887.8	436.8	145.7	94.9	13.8	1,310.4	373.8	168.8	85.9	92.5	299.9
1985: IV	2,739.8	354.4	162.9	128.1	939.5	460.7	156.2	97.6	14.3	1,446.0	404.6	180.7	90.1	101.5	333.0
1986: IV	2,923.1	406.8	188.2	140.6	963.7	486.7	165.8	73.0	11.3	1,552.6	432.7	182.5	86.8	109.0	358.4
1987: IV	3,124.6	408.8	186.3	145.9	1,029.4	507.4	177.6	87.8	12.2	1,686.4	466.6	189.7	88.6	121.3	398.5
1988: IV	3,398.2	452.9	203.4	162.5	1,105.8	549.5	194.4	88.5	11.7	1,839.5	496.0	203.8	95.3	132.7	444.4
1989: IV	3,599.1	458.3	198.1	170.8	1,173.5	575.3	205.4	95.9	13.2	1,967.3	526.6	217.7	103.7	137.6	489.2
1990: I	3,679.3	479.8	213.9	175.1	1,201.7	591.0	206.2	102.2	12.3	1,997.8	534.5	208.1	92.4	139.9	504.4
II	3,727.0	466.0	202.2	173.6	1,213.6	601.3	206.8	99.7	12.3	2,047.5	543.2	216.2	98.1	141.7	519.0
III	3,801.7	467.3	202.8	173.5	1,241.0	611.4	208.5	108.7	14.1	2,093.4	553.6	219.1	99.7	143.1	534.8
IV	3,836.6	459.5	192.9	174.5	1,260.7	615.6	207.6	123.0	13.9	2,116.4	558.6	219.1	99.6	145.4	546.6
1991: I	3,843.6	448.9	182.0	176.1	1,252.3	617.1	208.9	107.4	13.5	2,142.4	564.5	220.8	100.5	144.0	558.3
II	3,887.8	452.0	180.0	181.2	1,259.2	623.1	214.3	102.7	12.4	2,176.6	571.4	229.7	107.1	145.0	569.9
III	3,929.8	465.1	190.0	182.9	1,260.0	622.1	215.5	101.1	13.3	2,204.8	577.5	230.3	105.9	147.0	582.4
IV	3,964.1	465.2	190.2	182.4	1,260.0	623.2	213.4	100.3	12.7	2,239.0	584.2	227.8	103.7	148.8	597.6
1992: I	4,046.5	484.0	199.4	188.7	1,278.2	628.8	221.4	99.9	12.8	2,284.4	591.2	228.0	101.3	152.5	609.1
II	4,099.9	487.8	200.6	190.2	1,288.2	626.6	224.5	102.9	14.7	2,323.8	596.9	234.5	104.7	153.7	622.6
III	4,157.1	500.9	203.4	196.5	1,305.7	631.7	230.7	105.8	13.9	2,350.5	602.5	230.3	106.0	153.0	634.9
IV	4,256.2	516.6	213.7	202.7	1,331.7	647.6	236.1	105.2	13.9	2,407.9	609.2	245.0	111.0	162.4	646.9
1993: I	4,296.2	515.3	211.7	203.3	1,335.3	648.2	233.1	106.0	15.1	2,445.5	617.6	245.7	111.1	166.3	662.2
II	4,359.9	531.6	220.8	208.6	1,344.8	654.1	235.2	103.6	14.9	2,483.4	625.1	246.7	109.8	169.1	675.4
III	4,419.1	541.9	221.7	214.0	1,352.4	660.0	238.2	102.4	15.4	2,524.8	631.1	255.2	116.4	170.9	686.9
IV [P]	4,487.4	561.9	235.4	220.9	1,368.4	671.1	241.9	102.5	15.0	2,557.2	636.9	256.3	115.6	174.4	698.0

[1] Includes other items not shown separately.
[2] Includes imputed rental value of owner-occupied housing.

Source: Department of Commerce, Bureau of Economic Analysis.

TABLE B-16.—*Personal consumption expenditures in 1987 dollars, 1959–93*

[Billions of 1987 dollars; quarterly data at seasonally adjusted annual rates]

Year or quarter	Personal consumption expenditures	Durable goods Total [1]	Motor vehicles and parts	Furniture and household equipment	Nondurable goods Total [1]	Food	Clothing and shoes	Gasoline and oil	Fuel oil and coal	Services Total [1]	Housing [2]	Household operation Total [1]	Electricity and gas	Transportation	Medical care
1959	1,178.9	114.4	59.7	38.2	518.5	301.9	58.2	38.1	22.6	546.0	159.8	75.0	34.5	45.4	95.0
1960	1,210.8	115.4	61.3	37.7	526.9	305.8	58.7	39.4	21.7	568.5	168.1	78.5	36.3	46.7	98.4
1961	1,238.4	109.4	54.9	38.1	537.7	312.1	59.8	39.8	20.6	591.3	176.0	81.2	38.3	47.0	102.0
1962	1,293.3	120.2	62.2	40.4	553.0	316.3	62.4	41.5	20.6	620.0	185.8	85.2	40.9	48.7	110.2
1963	1,341.9	130.3	68.4	43.1	563.6	319.2	63.6	42.8	21.6	648.0	194.4	88.4	42.8	50.5	117.1
1964	1,417.2	140.7	71.2	48.3	588.2	331.0	68.5	45.1	22.5	688.3	203.5	92.6	45.1	53.0	129.8
1965	1,497.0	156.2	81.2	52.1	616.7	346.5	71.5	47.3	23.5	724.1	214.6	96.8	47.2	55.4	135.8
1966	1,573.8	166.0	81.8	57.6	647.6	359.1	76.3	50.2	24.2	760.2	224.4	101.4	49.7	58.6	142.3
1967	1,622.4	167.2	80.3	59.5	659.0	364.5	76.9	51.8	24.2	796.2	234.5	106.2	52.4	62.0	148.1
1968	1,707.5	184.5	91.8	62.9	686.0	380.7	80.2	55.5	23.0	837.0	246.0	110.1	55.0	65.4	159.5
1969	1,771.2	190.8	95.1	64.3	703.2	389.7	81.9	59.2	21.8	877.2	259.1	115.3	58.0	68.9	171.3
1970	1,813.5	183.7	85.6	64.4	717.2	397.5	81.0	62.9	20.2	912.5	269.3	118.9	60.4	71.0	180.7
1971	1,873.7	201.4	100.8	66.8	725.6	399.2	84.6	65.9	19.5	946.7	280.9	120.8	61.8	73.6	193.7
1972	1,978.4	225.2	114.3	73.6	755.8	411.9	90.4	68.6	21.5	997.4	295.9	126.8	64.9	77.8	207.0
1973	2,066.7	246.6	123.4	81.5	777.9	412.6	96.9	72.1	23.3	1,042.2	310.8	132.0	66.5	79.6	222.4
1974	2,053.8	227.2	102.2	81.9	759.8	404.7	95.4	68.6	18.4	1,066.8	326.9	132.5	66.9	79.9	231.1
1975	2,097.5	226.8	102.9	79.1	767.1	413.2	98.5	70.6	18.1	1,103.6	336.5	138.1	70.4	81.4	243.8
1976	2,207.3	256.4	124.6	84.2	801.3	431.9	103.2	73.4	20.3	1,149.5	346.7	143.9	72.9	84.4	255.5
1977	2,296.6	280.0	137.3	91.4	819.8	441.5	108.7	75.7	19.6	1,196.8	355.4	151.0	76.0	90.2	267.9
1978	2,391.8	292.9	141.5	96.6	844.8	442.8	119.0	77.4	19.5	1,254.1	372.9	158.0	78.8	92.9	279.2
1979	2,448.4	289.0	130.5	101.3	862.8	448.0	124.1	76.4	18.1	1,296.5	387.9	162.9	79.3	96.1	290.9
1970	2,447.1	262.7	111.4	98.5	860.5	448.8	126.0	72.0	14.0	1,323.9	399.4	167.1	81.6	91.3	302.1
1981	2,476.9	264.6	113.5	97.7	867.9	446.6	132.8	73.2	11.8	1,344.4	407.3	165.6	80.3	88.9	318.3
1982	2,503.7	262.5	115.6	94.2	872.2	451.4	133.7	73.9	10.9	1,368.9	409.6	166.7	81.2	87.4	323.7
1983	2,619.4	297.7	138.1	104.3	900.3	463.4	142.4	75.7	11.1	1,421.4	415.5	169.4	83.7	91.6	332.6
1984	2,746.1	338.5	160.3	115.3	934.6	472.3	153.1	77.9	11.2	1,473.0	426.8	173.7	84.3	100.0	341.9
1985	2,865.8	370.1	180.2	123.8	958.7	483.0	158.8	79.2	11.5	1,537.0	435.9	179.1	86.6	109.2	353.0
1986	2,969.1	402.0	193.3	136.3	991.0	494.1	170.3	82.9	12.1	1,576.8	442.1	180.8	85.6	112.6	366.2
1987	3,052.2	403.7	183.5	144.0	1,011.1	500.7	174.5	84.7	12.0	1,637.4	452.5	187.8	88.4	116.6	384.7
1988	3,162.4	428.7	194.8	155.4	1,035.1	513.4	178.9	86.1	12.0	1,698.5	461.8	196.9	92.7	122.5	399.4
1989	3,223.3	440.7	196.4	165.8	1,051.6	515.0	187.8	87.3	11.4	1,731.0	469.2	202.6	94.3	123.8	408.6
1990	3,272.6	443.1	192.7	171.6	1,060.7	523.9	186.2	86.4	10.5	1,768.8	474.6	204.3	92.2	124.0	424.6
1991	3,258.6	426.6	170.5	180.0	1,048.2	518.7	184.7	83.1	10.7	1,783.8	478.6	208.2	95.8	120.0	437.6
1992	3,341.8	456.6	182.3	194.8	1,062.9	520.5	193.7	83.9	11.9	1,822.3	484.2	211.7	95.3	122.7	449.2
1993 [p]	3,452.5	489.7	191.7	216.3	1,088.1	531.2	199.2	84.9	13.0	1,874.7	492.0	218.7	99.0	126.3	463.2
1982: IV	2,539.3	272.3	123.7	96.4	880.7	458.3	135.7	73.4	10.5	1,386.2	411.0	166.2	80.2	88.2	327.8
1983: IV	2,678.2	319.1	151.6	109.3	915.2	467.1	147.7	76.9	11.4	1,443.9	419.7	173.3	86.8	94.2	334.8
1984: IV	2,784.8	347.7	164.3	118.7	942.9	475.1	154.7	79.0	11.1	1,494.2	431.3	174.8	84.5	103.5	344.9
1985: IV	2,895.3	369.6	173.9	128.6	968.7	488.2	161.7	79.5	11.4	1,557.1	438.1	182.6	88.5	111.2	359.1
1986: IV	3,012.5	415.7	193.6	141.4	1,000.9	496.9	171.9	84.6	12.4	1,595.8	444.8	182.8	86.8	113.4	372.0
1987: IV	3,074.7	404.7	183.6	145.9	1,014.6	502.4	174.5	85.4	11.9	1,655.5	457.0	189.3	88.6	117.9	390.7
1988: IV	3,202.9	439.2	197.7	160.3	1,046.8	518.0	182.8	87.5	12.0	1,716.9	465.6	198.6	93.0	124.2	403.0
1989: IV	3,242.0	436.8	188.3	167.9	1,058.9	515.6	190.9	88.6	12.0	1,746.3	471.3	208.5	98.8	124.3	411.8
1990: I	3,264.4	454.8	203.0	172.0	1,059.8	519.0	188.5	87.9	10.0	1,749.6	473.3	197.9	87.7	124.9	418.0
II	3,271.6	441.8	192.8	171.0	1,060.6	524.1	185.4	86.7	11.0	1,769.2	474.3	205.1	93.2	124.4	423.2
III	3,288.4	442.4	193.0	171.0	1,065.0	526.5	186.4	86.5	11.6	1,781.1	475.0	208.0	94.4	124.0	427.7
IV	3,265.9	433.2	182.1	172.3	1,057.5	525.8	184.5	84.6	9.5	1,775.2	475.9	206.0	93.8	122.7	429.4
1991: I	3,242.7	420.3	169.4	174.3	1,048.2	518.7	182.9	82.7	10.3	1,774.2	476.3	203.8	92.5	120.2	432.6
II	3,256.9	422.0	165.9	180.0	1,051.1	519.0	187.0	83.7	10.6	1,783.8	478.1	211.3	98.9	120.1	435.3
III	3,267.1	432.6	173.7	182.7	1,049.3	518.8	185.9	83.4	11.4	1,785.2	479.4	210.6	97.3	119.7	438.8
IV	3,267.5	431.5	173.0	182.9	1,044.0	518.2	183.1	82.5	10.6	1,792.0	480.6	207.3	94.4	120.2	443.6
1992: I	3,302.3	446.6	180.6	188.2	1,052.0	518.8	188.3	82.7	11.1	1,803.7	481.7	205.9	92.4	120.4	445.3
II	3,316.8	447.5	179.5	189.8	1,055.0	515.7	191.1	83.7	12.8	1,814.3	483.2	210.7	95.1	121.9	447.9
III	3,350.9	459.0	180.6	197.1	1,062.9	518.2	195.4	84.7	11.7	1,829.0	485.1	213.6	95.3	125.0	450.4
IV	3,397.2	473.4	188.6	204.2	1,081.8	529.3	200.0	84.4	11.9	1,842.0	486.7	216.6	98.5	123.7	453.2
1993: I	3,403.8	471.9	185.7	206.5	1,076.0	526.7	194.8	83.9	12.9	1,855.9	488.8	217.9	99.1	124.5	458.0
II	3,432.7	484.2	191.3	212.4	1,083.1	528.5	197.8	84.1	12.6	1,865.4	490.7	215.6	96.2	126.1	461.1
III	3,469.6	493.1	189.9	219.4	1,093.0	532.6	200.6	86.2	13.2	1,883.5	493.3	220.8	100.6	126.5	465.1
IV [p]	3,503.9	509.9	199.9	227.0	1,100.1	536.9	203.7	85.3	13.2	1,893.9	495.0	220.8	100.1	128.3	468.6

[1] Includes other items not shown separately.
[2] Includes imputed rental value of owner-occupied housing.

Source: Department of Commerce, Bureau of Economic Analysis.

TABLE B-17.—Gross and net private domestic investment, 1959-93

[Billions of dollars; quarterly data at seasonally adjusted annual rates]

Year or quarter	Gross private domestic investment	Less: Consumption of fixed capital	Equals: Net private domestic investment							Change in business inventories
			Total	Net fixed investment						
				Total	Nonresidential				Residential	
					Total	Structures	Producers' durable equipment			

Year or quarter	Gross private domestic investment	Less: Consumption of fixed capital	Total	Total	Total	Structures	Producers' durable equipment	Residential	Change in business inventories
1959	78.8	44.6	34.2	30.1	12.3	6.6	5.7	17.8	4.2
1960	78.7	46.3	32.4	29.2	13.8	7.7	6.1	15.4	3.2
1961	77.9	47.7	30.3	27.3	12.2	7.6	4.6	15.1	2.9
1962	87.9	49.3	38.6	32.5	15.3	8.3	7.0	17.2	6.1
1963	93.4	51.3	42.0	36.4	16.4	8.3	8.1	20.0	5.7
1964	101.7	53.9	47.8	42.8	21.3	10.3	11.0	21.5	5.0
1965	118.0	57.3	60.7	51.0	30.3	14.1	16.2	20.7	9.7
1966	130.4	62.1	68.3	54.5	36.7	16.0	20.7	17.8	13.8
1967	128.0	67.4	60.6	50.1	33.2	15.1	18.1	16.9	10.5
1968	139.9	73.9	66.0	56.9	35.0	15.8	19.2	21.9	9.1
1969	155.2	81.5	73.7	64.0	40.5	17.9	22.6	23.5	9.7
1970	150.3	88.8	61.5	59.2	38.4	18.4	20.0	20.8	2.3
1971	175.5	97.6	78.0	69.9	36.8	18.4	18.4	33.1	8.0
1972	205.6	109.9	95.7	85.8	42.5	18.7	23.8	43.2	9.9
1973	243.1	120.4	122.7	105.0	59.0	23.8	35.2	46.0	17.7
1974	245.8	140.2	105.5	91.3	58.9	24.5	34.5	32.3	14.3
1975	226.0	165.2	60.9	66.5	41.5	18.8	22.7	25.1	-5.7
1976	286.4	182.8	103.6	86.8	45.6	19.9	25.6	41.2	16.7
1977	358.3	205.2	153.1	128.3	64.9	23.4	41.5	63.4	24.7
1978	434.0	234.8	199.3	171.3	94.1	35.5	58.6	77.3	27.9
1979	480.2	272.4	207.8	195.1	117.3	49.9	67.4	77.8	12.8
1980	467.6	311.9	155.7	165.2	113.8	59.1	54.7	51.4	-9.5
1981	558.0	362.4	195.6	170.2	127.1	75.5	51.6	43.1	25.4
1982	503.4	399.1	104.3	120.3	99.1	72.4	26.7	21.2	-15.9
1983	546.7	418.4	128.2	133.8	69.1	46.2	22.9	64.6	-5.5
1984	718.9	433.2	285.6	214.6	126.6	65.1	61.5	87.9	71.1
1985	714.5	454.5	260.0	235.4	146.1	75.2	70.9	89.3	24.6
1986	717.6	478.6	239.1	230.4	114.4	51.8	62.6	116.0	8.6
1987	749.3	502.2	247.1	220.9	103.0	46.7	56.3	117.9	26.3
1988	793.6	534.0	259.6	243.4	125.8	47.9	77.9	117.6	16.2
1989	832.3	580.4	251.9	218.6	117.1	48.6	68.5	101.5	33.3
1990	808.9	602.7	206.2	199.3	116.1	51.8	64.3	83.2	6.9
1991	736.9	626.1	110.8	119.5	67.2	27.5	39.7	52.3	-8.6
1992	796.5	657.9	138.6	131.2	60.4	13.9	46.5	70.8	7.3
1993 ᵖ	892.0	671.2	220.8	204.0					16.8
1982: IV	464.2	412.5	51.7	98.0					-46.3
1983: IV	614.8	439.7	175.1	154.9					20.2
1984: IV	722.8	448.0	274.8	223.8					51.0
1985: IV	737.0	465.6	271.4	238.8					32.6
1986: IV	697.1	488.2	208.9	227.8					-18.8
1987: IV	800.2	512.1	288.1	228.8					59.3
1988: IV	814.8	547.2	267.6	250.3					17.3
1989: IV	825.2	600.8	224.4	194.2					30.2
1990: I	828.9	590.2	238.7	229.1					9.6
II	837.8	597.9	239.9	206.6					33.3
III	812.5	607.8	204.7	196.3					8.4
IV	756.4	614.8	141.5	165.4					-23.9
1991: I	729.1	619.9	109.3	129.2					-19.9
II	721.5	622.3	99.2	122.3					-23.0
III	744.5	626.7	117.9	118.4					-.5
IV	752.4	635.4	117.0	108.1					8.9
1992: I	750.8	631.7	119.1	124.2					-5.1
II	799.7	637.2	162.5	149.6					12.9
III	802.2	714.6	87.6	77.9					9.7
IV	833.3	648.0	185.2	173.3					12.0
1993: I	874.1	663.2	210.8	176.3					34.6
II	874.1	663.3	210.8	197.7					13.1
III	884.0	679.7	204.3	196.6					7.7
IV ᵖ	935.8	678.7	257.1	245.4					11.7

Source: Department of Commerce, Bureau of Economic Analysis.

TABLE B-18.—*Gross and net private domestic investment in 1987 dollars, 1959–93*

[Billions of 1987 dollars; quarterly data at seasonally adjusted annual rates]

Year or quarter	Gross private domestic investment	Less: Consumption of fixed capital	Equals: Net private domestic investment						Change in business inventories
			Total	Net fixed investment					
				Total	Nonresidential				Residential	
					Total	Structures	Producers' durable equipment		

1959	296.4	168.8	127.5	114.0	39.2	25.4	13.8	74.8	13.6
1960	290.8	173.7	117.1	109.0	44.1	30.5	13.7	64.8	8.1
1961	289.4	178.6	110.8	103.6	39.9	30.6	9.4	63.7	7.2
1962	321.2	183.6	137.6	122.0	49.5	32.9	16.6	72.5	15.6
1963	343.3	189.6	153.7	137.7	52.8	32.1	20.7	84.9	16.0
1964	371.8	196.4	175.4	159.7	69.7	39.5	30.2	90.0	15.7
1965	413.0	205.0	208.1	182.9	99.9	53.0	46.9	83.0	25.1
1966	438.0	214.9	223.0	186.3	118.1	58.3	59.8	68.2	36.7
1967	418.6	225.2	193.4	165.8	103.9	53.0	50.9	61.9	27.6
1968	440.1	235.3	204.7	181.1	105.1	52.2	52.9	76.0	23.6
1969	461.3	246.7	214.6	189.8	112.2	56.0	56.2	77.6	24.8
1970	429.7	258.0	171.7	165.8	98.7	53.5	45.2	67.1	5.9
1971	475.7	269.1	206.6	185.8	85.0	49.0	36.0	100.8	20.8
1972	532.2	285.0	247.2	224.6	98.9	49.2	49.7	125.7	22.5
1973	591.7	296.4	295.3	257.6	134.6	57.9	76.7	123.0	37.7
1974	543.0	310.3	232.6	201.7	122.3	53.4	68.9	79.4	30.9
1975	437.6	322.8	114.8	128.7	72.0	36.7	35.3	56.8	−13.9
1976	520.6	334.6	186.1	160.6	74.5	36.8	37.7	86.1	25.5
1977	600.4	348.4	252.1	217.8	99.0	39.8	59.2	118.8	34.3
1978	664.6	364.5	300.0	262.8	134.4	55.2	79.2	128.4	37.2
1979	669.7	384.5	285.2	271.6	154.1	70.1	84.0	117.5	13.6
1980	594.4	400.7	193.7	201.9	129.5	73.3	56.1	72.5	−8.3
1981	631.1	417.8	213.2	188.7	131.6	82.0	49.6	57.1	24.6
1982	540.5	429.5	111.0	128.5	101.0	75.3	25.7	27.5	−17.5
1983	599.5	447.4	152.1	147.7	71.6	50.3	21.4	76.0	4.4
1984	757.5	455.5	302.0	234.0	134.3	69.3	65.0	99.8	67.9
1985	745.9	471.5	274.4	252.3	154.0	79.4	74.6	98.3	22.1
1986	735.1	486.7	248.4	239.9	118.3	54.9	63.3	121.6	8.5
1987	749.3	502.2	247.1	220.9	103.0	46.7	56.3	117.9	26.3
1988	773.4	518.5	254.9	235.0	122.6	46.7	75.9	112.4	19.9
1989	784.0	545.5	238.5	208.7	114.8	45.9	68.9	94.0	29.8
1990	746.8	554.8	192.0	186.3	111.1	47.3	63.8	75.2	5.7
1991	675.7	569.2	106.4	114.8	68.2	25.9	42.3	46.6	−8.4
1992	732.9	595.0	137.8	131.3	69.0	13.4	55.5	62.4	6.5
1993 ᵖ	820.9	598.6	222.3	206.9	....	....	....	....	15.4
1982: IV	503.5	439.2	64.3	109.2	....	....	....	....	−44.9
1983: IV	669.5	468.5	201.0	171.7	....	....	....	....	29.3
1984: IV	756.4	467.4	289.0	241.1	....	....	....	....	47.9
1985: IV	763.1	480.1	283.0	252.8	....	....	....	....	30.2
1986: IV	705.9	492.5	213.3	233.4	....	....	....	....	−20.1
1987: IV	793.8	508.1	285.7	225.8	....	....	....	....	59.9
1988: IV	785.0	524.7	260.3	239.3	....	....	....	....	20.9
1989: IV	769.5	559.6	209.9	185.0	....	....	....	....	24.9
1990: I	766.5	549.7	216.8	212.1	....	....	....	....	4.7
II	773.9	553.1	220.7	192.6	....	....	....	....	28.1
III	751.0	556.5	194.5	183.7	....	....	....	....	10.9
IV	695.7	559.9	135.8	156.7	....	....	....	....	−20.9
1991: I	667.8	563.3	104.5	121.9	....	....	....	....	−17.4
II	659.8	566.5	93.2	115.6	....	....	....	....	−22.3
III	682.8	569.5	113.4	114.3	....	....	....	....	−.9
IV	692.3	577.6	114.6	107.6	....	....	....	....	7.1
1992: I	691.7	574.8	116.9	121.9	....	....	....	....	−5.0
II	737.0	577.6	159.5	146.8	....	....	....	....	12.6
III	739.6	643.7	95.9	86.3	....	....	....	....	9.6
IV	763.0	584.0	179.0	170.3	....	....	....	....	8.7
1993: I	803.0	595.0	208.1	178.8	....	....	....	....	29.3
II	803.6	592.5	211.1	198.1	....	....	....	....	13.0
III	813.4	604.4	208.9	202.5	....	....	....	....	6.5
IV ᵖ	863.6	602.6	261.0	248.3	....	....	....	....	12.7

Source: Department of Commerce, Bureau of Economic Analysis.

TABLE B-19.—*Inventories and final sales of domestic business, 1959-93*

[Billions of dollars, except as noted; seasonally adjusted]

Quarter	Inventories [1]							Final sales of domestic business [3]	Ratio of inventories to final sales of domestic business	
	Total [2]	Farm	Nonfarm						Total	Nonfarm
			Total [2]	Manu-facturing	Whole-sale trade	Retail trade	Other			
Fourth quarter:										
1959	141.2	31.6	109.6	55.2	21.0	26.2	7.2	36.5	3.87	3.00
1960	145.2	33.0	112.2	56.2	21.3	27.5	7.2	37.7	3.85	2.97
1961	147.0	33.7	113.4	57.2	21.8	27.0	7.4	39.6	3.71	2.86
1962	153.4	34.8	118.6	60.3	22.4	28.3	7.5	41.9	3.66	2.83
1963	158.7	34.9	123.8	62.2	23.9	29.6	8.0	44.6	3.56	2.78
1964	164.2	33.3	130.9	65.9	25.2	31.0	8.8	47.5	3.46	2.76
1965	178.4	37.4	141.0	70.7	26.9	33.7	9.8	52.5	3.40	2.69
1966	194.0	36.3	157.8	80.9	30.3	36.2	10.4	55.6	3.49	2.84
1967	206.0	36.5	169.5	87.5	32.7	36.9	12.4	59.1	3.48	2.87
1968	221.4	38.7	182.6	94.0	34.6	40.7	13.3	65.0	3.41	2.81
1969	242.5	41.9	200.6	103.4	37.9	44.5	14.9	69.0	3.51	2.91
1970	249.4	40.1	209.2	105.8	41.7	45.8	16.0	72.7	3.43	2.88
1971	267.4	45.0	222.4	107.3	45.2	52.3	17.6	79.2	3.38	2.81
1972	296.6	55.3	241.3	113.6	50.0	57.7	19.9	88.3	3.36	2.73
1973	365.1	78.0	287.1	136.1	59.4	66.4	25.2	97.2	3.76	2.95
1974	435.2	74.3	360.9	177.0	75.6	74.6	33.7	105.2	4.14	3.43
1975	440.1	75.5	364.5	177.8	76.2	74.7	35.8	117.5	3.74	3.10
1976	475.3	72.2	403.1	194.9	86.1	82.7	39.4	129.1	3.68	3.12
1977	521.6	75.2	446.4	210.6	96.2	93.3	46.3	144.3	3.61	3.09
1978	605.3	92.1	513.2	238.0	111.7	107.5	55.9	166.6	3.63	3.08
1979	702.6	97.9	604.7	280.6	141.2	118.9	64.1	185.4	3.79	3.26
1980	784.1	104.9	679.3	309.8	174.2	125.0	70.3	203.5	3.85	3.34
1981	836.2	101.4	734.7	331.9	184.8	137.0	81.1	220.3	3.80	3.34
1982	817.0	103.6	713.5	318.5	174.7	139.5	80.7	230.9	3.54	3.09
1983	827.5	103.2	724.4	319.2	168.9	153.7	82.5	252.2	3.28	2.87
1984	898.9	100.9	797.9	349.0	187.2	173.5	88.3	273.3	3.29	2.92
1985	904.3	96.6	807.7	339.9	184.9	188.6	94.3	294.1	3.08	2.75
1986	887.9	90.5	797.3	328.1	183.4	193.4	92.4	311.4	2.85	2.56
1987	950.6	90.9	859.7	349.3	196.3	216.1	98.0	329.8	2.88	2.61
1988	1,025.1	95.4	929.6	383.2	215.3	229.9	101.2	359.2	2.85	2.59
1989	1,081.6	96.3	985.3	409.7	224.8	250.2	100.6	378.3	2.86	2.60
1990	1,110.4	94.7	1,015.7	423.7	236.9	257.2	98.0	398.4	2.79	2.55
1991	1,083.4	90.7	992.7	407.3	239.7	257.4	88.3	408.9	2.65	2.43
1992	1,099.0	95.1	1,003.9	400.9	247.9	269.5	85.6	436.9	2.52	2.30
1993 [p]	1,133.4	91.9	1,041.5	405.3	255.3	286.9	94.0	459.3	2.47	2.27
1990: I	1,081.8	96.5	985.4	411.5	226.3	246.1	101.5	387.9	2.79	2.54
II	1,090.9	98.2	992.7	412.9	229.5	250.0	100.3	391.1	2.79	2.54
III	1,115.6	97.5	1,018.2	424.7	236.0	258.4	99.0	395.6	2.82	2.57
IV	1,110.4	94.7	1,015.7	423.7	236.9	257.2	98.0	398.4	2.79	2.55
1991: I	1,096.5	98.1	998.4	419.1	236.9	248.6	93.8	399.2	2.75	2.50
II	1,089.6	101.5	988.1	412.1	233.7	249.8	92.4	404.2	2.70	2.44
III	1,085.0	96.6	988.4	409.1	235.3	254.3	89.7	406.8	2.67	2.43
IV	1,083.4	90.7	992.7	407.3	239.7	257.4	88.3	408.9	2.65	2.43
1992: I	1,087.5	94.8	992.7	404.6	239.5	259.8	88.8	417.3	2.61	2.38
II	1,093.9	94.3	999.6	404.6	243.4	264.2	87.5	421.5	2.60	2.37
III	1,098.7	94.9	1,003.8	406.8	244.9	266.4	85.7	426.7	2.57	2.35
IV	1,099.0	95.1	1,003.9	400.9	247.9	269.5	85.6	436.9	2.52	2.30
1993: I	1,119.5	99.1	1,020.4	402.0	249.6	280.1	88.7	439.0	2.55	2.32
II	1,119.6	95.4	1,024.2	402.4	251.3	281.2	89.3	445.5	2.51	2.30
III	1,119.2	95.1	1,024.1	407.0	242.9	282.7	91.5	450.7	2.48	2.27
IV [p]	1,133.4	91.9	1,041.5	405.3	255.3	286.9	94.0	459.3	2.47	2.27

[1] Inventories at end of quarter. Quarter-to-quarter change calculated from this table is not the current-dollar change in business inventories (CBI) component of GDP. The former is the difference between two inventory stocks, each valued at their respective end-of-quarter prices. The latter is the change in the physical volume of inventories valued at average prices of the quarter. In addition, changes calculated from this table are at quarterly rates, whereas CBI is stated at annual rates.
[2] Inventories of construction establishments are included in "other" nonfarm inventories.
[3] Quarterly totals at monthly rates. Final sales of domestic business equals final sales of domestic product less gross product of households and institutions and general government and includes a small amount of final sales by farms.

Note.—The industry classification of inventories is on an establishment basis and is based on the 1987 Standard Industrial Classification (SIC) beginning 1987 and on the 1972 SIC for earlier years shown.

Source: Department of Commerce, Bureau of Economic Analysis.

TABLE B-20.—*Inventories and final sales of domestic business in 1987 dollars, 1959–93*

[Billions of 1987 dollars, except as noted; seasonally adjusted]

Quarter	Inventories [1] Total [2]	Farm	Nonfarm Total [2]	Manu- facturing	Whole- sale trade	Retail trade	Other	Final sales of domestic busi- ness [3]	Ratio of inventories to final sales of domestic business Total	Nonfarm
Fourth quarter:										
1959	388.6	79.6	308.9	152.4	61.2	67.6	27.8	131.5	2.96	2.35
1960	396.7	80.5	316.2	153.9	62.4	71.4	28.5	134.3	2.95	2.35
1961	403.9	82.1	321.8	157.9	63.7	70.2	30.0	139.9	2.89	2.30
1962	419.5	83.9	335.7	166.1	65.9	73.8	29.9	145.3	2.89	2.31
1963	435.6	85.4	350.2	171.6	69.6	76.9	32.0	153.5	2.84	2.28
1964	451.2	83.4	367.8	179.6	73.4	80.3	34.5	161.1	2.80	2.28
1965	476.4	84.6	391.7	190.2	77.6	86.8	37.2	174.2	2.73	2.25
1966	513.1	83.5	429.6	212.1	86.5	92.5	38.4	177.3	2.89	2.42
1967	540.7	84.5	456.3	227.6	92.0	92.1	44.6	183.8	2.94	2.48
1968	564.3	86.9	477.5	237.4	94.7	99.3	46.1	192.6	2.93	2.48
1969	589.2	86.9	502.3	246.7	100.3	105.9	49.4	195.4	3.01	2.57
1970	595.1	86.3	508.8	246.1	106.9	105.8	50.0	197.6	3.01	2.57
1971	615.8	89.2	526.7	243.9	112.3	117.8	52.6	205.1	3.00	2.57
1972	638.4	90.6	547.7	249.6	116.3	125.3	56.5	220.4	2.90	2.49
1973	676.1	92.9	583.3	264.9	121.1	134.5	62.7	225.9	2.99	2.58
1974	707.0	92.5	614.5	283.7	130.8	133.6	66.4	220.9	3.20	2.78
1975	693.1	92.9	600.2	277.2	127.3	127.6	68.0	229.1	3.03	2.62
1976	718.6	90.8	627.8	289.6	135.3	134.8	68.1	238.3	3.02	2.63
1977	752.9	93.6	659.2	297.1	144.4	144.5	73.3	249.4	3.02	2.64
1978	790.1	93.0	697.1	309.2	155.8	153.7	78.3	264.6	2.99	2.63
1979	803.7	95.7	708.0	320.1	157.3	153.5	77.1	270.2	2.97	2.62
1980	795.4	92.3	703.1	319.9	161.9	146.7	74.6	268.5	2.96	2.62
1981	820.0	98.3	721.7	324.0	164.8	152.9	80.0	266.5	3.08	2.71
1982	802.5	101.4	701.0	311.3	159.9	151.7	78.1	267.6	3.00	2.62
1983	806.9	93.1	713.8	311.9	159.3	162.8	79.8	281.8	2.86	2.53
1984	874.8	94.8	780.0	339.4	174.7	181.4	84.5	294.6	2.97	2.65
1985	896.9	97.2	799.8	335.7	178.7	194.1	91.3	306.3	2.93	2.61
1986	905.5	95.1	810.4	333.6	185.7	196.7	94.4	317.2	2.85	2.55
1987	931.8	88.7	843.1	340.2	192.7	213.6	96.6	325.8	2.86	2.59
1988	951.7	81.7	870.0	355.3	199.1	219.7	95.9	340.3	2.80	2.56
1989	981.5	81.6	899.9	373.9	202.5	231.0	92.5	344.7	2.85	2.61
1990	987.2	84.1	903.1	376.9	208.8	229.4	88.0	347.9	2.84	2.60
1991	978.8	84.3	894.5	370.6	212.3	230.5	81.0	346.5	2.82	2.58
1992	985.3	88.1	897.2	365.9	217.7	236.4	77.1	361.5	2.73	2.48
1993 [p]	1,000.6	82.2	918.4	368.0	220.8	247.6	81.9	372.3	2.69	2.47
1990: I	982.6	82.0	900.7	376.0	203.7	227.4	93.6	349.6	2.81	2.58
II	989.7	82.9	906.8	377.5	206.0	230.6	92.8	348.6	2.84	2.60
III	992.4	84.6	907.8	378.8	208.4	231.0	89.5	348.9	2.84	2.60
IV	987.2	84.1	903.1	376.9	208.8	229.4	88.0	347.9	2.84	2.60
1991: I	982.8	84.4	898.4	377.9	209.9	224.8	85.8	344.7	2.85	2.61
II	977.2	85.3	891.9	374.6	207.3	225.3	84.7	346.6	2.82	2.57
III	977.0	85.1	891.9	372.4	208.5	228.5	82.5	346.5	2.82	2.57
IV	978.8	84.3	894.5	370.6	212.3	230.5	81.0	346.5	2.82	2.58
1992: I	977.5	85.5	892.1	368.7	211.3	230.8	81.3	351.0	2.79	2.54
II	980.7	86.9	893.8	367.2	214.2	232.9	79.5	352.3	2.78	2.54
III	983.1	87.8	895.3	369.0	215.1	234.0	77.2	355.7	2.76	2.52
IV	985.3	88.1	897.2	365.9	217.7	236.4	77.1	361.5	2.73	2.48
1993: I	992.6	88.1	904.5	365.7	217.9	242.4	78.5	360.4	2.75	2.51
II	995.9	87.1	908.8	366.9	219.6	243.2	79.1	363.4	2.74	2.50
III	997.5	83.9	913.6	367.7	221.2	244.4	80.3	366.8	2.72	2.49
IV [p]	1,000.6	82.2	918.4	368.0	220.8	247.6	81.9	372.3	2.69	2.47

[1] Inventories at end of quarter. Quarter-to-quarter changes calculated from this table are at quarterly rates, whereas the constant-dollar change in business inventories component of GDP is stated at annual rates.
[2] Inventories of construction establishments are included in "other" nonfarm inventories.
[3] Quarterly totals at monthly rates. Final sales of domestic business equals final sales of domestic product less gross product of households and institutions and general government and includes a small amount of final sales by farms.

Note.—The industry classification of inventories is on an establishment basis and is based on the 1987 Standard Industrial Classification (SIC) beginning 1987 and on the 1972 SIC for earlier years shown.

Source: Department of Commerce, Bureau of Economic Analysis.

TABLE B-21.—*Foreign transactions in the national income and product accounts, 1959–93*

[Billions of dollars; quarterly data at seasonally adjusted annual rates]

Year or quarter	Receipts from rest of the world					Payments to rest of the world									Net foreign invest- ment
	Total [1]	Exports of goods and services			Receipts of factor income [3]	Total	Imports of goods and services			Pay- ments of factor in- come [4]	Transfer payments (net)				
		Total	Mer- chan- dise [2]	Serv- ices [2]			Total	Mer- chan- dise [2]	Serv- ices [2]		Total	From persons (net)	From govern- ment (net)	From business	
1959	25.0	20.6	16.5	4.2	4.3	25.0	22.3	15.3	7.0	1.5	2.4	0.4	1.8	0.1	−1.2
1960	30.2	25.3	20.5	4.8	5.0	30.2	22.8	15.2	7.6	1.8	2.4	.5	1.9	.1	3.2
1961	31.4	26.0	20.9	5.1	5.4	31.4	22.7	15.1	7.6	1.8	2.7	.5	2.1	.1	4.3
1962	33.5	27.4	21.7	5.7	6.1	33.5	25.0	16.9	8.1	1.8	2.8	.5	2.1	.1	3.9
1963	36.1	29.4	23.3	6.1	6.6	36.1	26.1	17.7	8.4	2.1	2.8	.6	2.1	.1	5.0
1964	41.0	33.6	26.7	6.9	7.4	41.0	28.1	19.4	8.7	2.4	3.0	.7	2.1	.2	7.5
1965	43.5	35.4	27.8	7.6	8.1	43.5	31.5	22.2	9.3	2.7	3.0	.8	2.1	.2	6.2
1966	47.2	38.9	30.7	8.2	8.3	47.2	37.1	26.3	10.7	3.1	3.2	.8	2.2	.2	3.9
1967	50.2	41.4	32.2	9.2	8.9	50.2	39.9	27.8	12.2	3.4	3.4	1.0	2.1	.2	3.5
1968	55.6	45.3	35.3	10.0	10.3	55.6	46.6	33.9	12.6	4.1	3.2	1.0	1.9	.3	1.7
1969	61.2	49.3	38.3	11.0	11.9	61.2	50.5	36.8	13.7	5.8	3.2	1.1	1.8	.3	1.8
1970	70.8	57.0	44.5	12.4	13.0	70.8	55.8	40.9	14.9	6.6	3.6	1.2	2.0	.4	4.9
1971	74.2	59.3	45.6	13.8	14.1	74.2	62.3	46.6	15.8	6.4	4.1	1.3	2.4	.4	1.3
1972	83.4	66.2	51.8	14.4	16.4	83.4	74.2	56.9	17.3	7.7	4.3	1.3	2.5	.5	−2.9
1973	115.6	91.8	73.9	17.8	23.8	115.6	91.2	71.8	19.3	11.1	4.6	1.4	2.5	.7	8.7
1974	152.6	124.3	101.0	23.3	30.3	152.6	127.5	104.5	22.9	14.6	5.4	1.2	3.2	1.0	5.1
1975	164.4	136.3	109.6	26.7	28.2	164.4	122.7	99.0	23.7	14.9	5.4	1.2	3.5	.7	21.4
1976	181.6	148.9	117.8	31.1	32.8	181.6	151.1	124.6	26.5	15.7	6.0	1.2	3.7	1.1	8.8
1977	196.5	158.8	123.7	35.1	37.7	196.5	182.4	152.6	29.8	17.2	6.0	1.2	3.4	1.4	−9.2
1978	233.3	186.1	145.4	40.7	47.1	233.3	212.3	177.4	34.8	25.3	6.4	1.3	3.8	1.4	−10.7
1979	299.7	228.9	184.2	44.7	69.7	299.7	252.7	212.8	39.9	37.5	7.5	1.4	4.1	2.0	2.0
1980	360.9	279.2	226.0	53.2	80.6	360.9	293.9	248.6	45.3	46.5	9.0	1.6	5.0	2.4	11.5
1981	398.2	303.0	239.3	63.7	94.1	398.2	317.7	267.7	49.9	60.9	10.0	1.8	5.0	3.2	9.5
1982	379.9	282.6	215.2	67.4	97.3	379.9	303.2	250.6	52.6	67.1	12.1	2.1	6.4	3.6	−2.5
1983	372.5	276.7	207.5	69.2	95.8	372.5	328.1	272.7	55.4	66.5	12.9	1.8	7.3	3.8	−35.0
1984	410.5	302.4	225.8	76.6	108.1	410.5	405.1	336.3	68.8	83.8	15.6	2.3	9.4	3.9	−94.0
1985	399.3	302.1	222.4	79.7	97.3	399.3	417.6	343.3	74.3	82.4	17.4	2.7	11.4	3.2	−118.1
1986	415.2	319.2	226.2	93.0	96.0	415.2	451.7	370.0	81.7	86.9	18.3	2.5	12.3	3.5	−141.7
1987	469.0	364.0	257.7	106.2	105.1	469.0	507.1	414.8	92.3	100.5	16.6	3.0	10.4	3.2	−155.1
1988	572.9	444.2	325.8	118.4	128.7	572.9	552.2	452.1	100.1	120.8	17.8	2.7	10.4	4.8	−118.0
1989	665.5	508.0	371.6	136.4	157.5	665.5	587.7	485.1	102.6	141.5	25.6	8.9	11.3	5.4	−89.3
1990	725.7	557.1	398.7	158.4	168.6	725.7	628.5	509.0	119.5	146.9	28.8	10.1	13.2	5.5	−78.5
1991	747.6	601.5	426.4	175.1	146.1	747.6	621.1	500.7	120.4	131.9	−11.9	10.5	−27.9	5.6	6.4
1992	769.7	640.5	448.7	191.7	129.2	769.7	670.1	544.5	125.6	121.9	32.7	10.4	16.3	6.0	−55.1
1993 *p*		660.1	459.5	200.6			725.8	593.0	132.8		31.4	11.0	14.2	6.1	
1982: IV	357.5	265.6	198.2	67.4	91.9	357.5	295.1	241.6	53.4	64.4	13.8	1.9	8.2	3.7	−15.8
1983: IV	388.3	286.2	218.2	67.9	102.1	388.3	358.0	300.0	58.0	71.0	17.8	2.0	11.0	4.8	−58.5
1984: IV	415.2	308.7	231.4	77.3	106.6	415.2	415.7	344.1	71.6	85.5	20.4	2.5	13.9	4.0	−106.3
1985: IV	402.9	304.7	222.6	82.1	98.1	402.9	440.2	363.0	77.2	82.4	19.4	2.5	13.5	3.4	−139.1
1986: IV	426.7	333.9	235.8	98.1	92.8	426.7	467.1	382.4	84.7	88.9	19.6	2.8	12.8	4.0	−149.0
1987: IV	506.8	392.4	283.3	109.2	114.4	506.8	535.6	437.6	98.0	106.9	21.4	3.1	14.6	3.8	−157.1
1988: IV	606.9	467.0	345.4	121.6	139.9	606.9	573.1	470.1	103.0	130.2	23.8	2.7	15.1	5.9	−120.1
1989: IV	683.1	523.8	380.7	143.1	159.3	683.1	597.7	492.2	105.6	139.1	30.3	9.8	15.1	5.4	−84.0
1990: I	705.9	542.0	391.7	150.2	164.0	705.9	615.9	501.6	114.3	143.8	26.5	9.9	11.6	5.0	−80.3
II	718.9	553.5	399.0	154.6	165.4	718.9	614.8	498.1	116.7	147.0	30.9	10.1	15.3	5.4	−73.8
III	720.5	555.3	395.1	160.1	165.2	720.5	634.0	512.3	121.7	149.0	29.6	10.3	13.4	5.8	−92.1
IV	757.4	577.6	409.0	168.6	179.7	757.4	649.2	523.9	125.4	147.7	28.2	10.2	12.4	5.6	−67.7
1991: I	738.9	576.5	414.3	162.3	162.4	738.9	610.6	489.8	120.8	138.0	−61.1	10.4	−76.9	5.4	51.4
II	747.9	600.7	426.7	174.0	147.2	747.9	612.2	492.3	119.9	134.3	−15.8	10.4	−32.0	5.8	17.2
III	742.1	603.0	424.6	178.3	139.1	742.1	622.8	504.3	118.5	131.5	10.6	10.3	−5.1	5.4	−22.8
IV	761.4	625.7	440.0	185.8	135.7	761.4	638.8	516.3	122.5	123.9	18.9	10.8	2.2	5.9	−20.2
1992: I	768.0	633.7	442.6	191.0	134.4	768.0	640.7	515.4	125.3	115.6	29.6	11.1	12.6	5.9	−17.7
II	765.3	632.4	442.8	189.6	132.9	765.3	666.3	540.6	125.7	127.9	31.6	10.5	15.0	6.1	−60.6
III	768.4	641.1	447.5	193.6	127.3	768.4	679.9	557.3	122.6	119.5	28.5	9.7	12.8	5.9	−59.4
IV	777.0	654.7	462.0	192.8	122.3	777.0	693.5	564.7	128.7	124.8	41.2	10.5	24.6	6.1	−82.4
1993: I	774.1	651.3	453.2	198.0	122.8	774.1	699.6	569.6	130.0	122.4	29.7	11.0	13.1	5.6	−77.6
II	791.8	660.0	458.6	201.3	131.9	791.8	725.0	592.6	132.4	132.3	29.9	11.0	12.9	6.0	−95.4
III	788.3	653.2	452.2	200.9	135.1	788.3	725.1	591.9	133.3	128.7	30.9	10.8	13.7	6.3	−96.4
IV *p*		675.8	473.7	202.1			753.5	618.1	135.3		35.1	11.4	17.2	6.5	

[1] Includes capital grants received by the United States (net), not shown separately. See Table B-29 for data.
[2] Exports and imports of certain goods, primarily military equipment purchased and sold by the Federal Government, are included in services.
[3] Consists largely of receipts by U.S. residents of interest and dividends and reinvested earnings of foreign affiliates of U.S. corporations.
[4] Consists largely of payments to foreign residents of interest and dividends and reinvested earnings of U.S. affiliates of foreign corporations.

Source: Department of Commerce, Bureau of Economic Analysis.

TABLE B–22.—*Exports and imports of goods and services and receipts and payments of factor income in 1987 dollars, 1959–93*

[Billions of 1987 dollars; quarterly data at seasonally adjusted annual rates]

Year or quarter	Exports of goods and services					Receipts of factor income [2]	Imports of goods and services					Payments of factor income [3]
	Total	Merchandise [1]			Services [1]		Total	Merchandise [1]			Services [1]	
		Total	Durable goods	Non-durable goods				Total	Durable goods	Non-durable goods		
1959	73.8	58.0	31.5	26.5	15.8	17.0	95.6	60.2	26.0	34.2	35.4	6.2
1960	88.4	71.2	39.2	32.0	17.2	19.1	96.1	59.1	24.7	34.4	37.0	7.2
1961	89.9	71.5	39.4	32.1	18.4	20.6	95.3	59.2	23.7	35.5	36.1	7.2
1962	95.0	74.8	41.2	33.5	20.3	22.5	105.5	68.0	28.0	40.0	37.5	7.3
1963	101.8	80.3	43.6	36.7	21.5	24.4	107.7	70.9	29.6	41.2	36.8	8.2
1964	115.4	91.4	50.2	41.2	24.0	26.6	112.9	75.6	32.8	42.8	37.3	9.1
1965	118.1	92.1	52.2	39.9	25.9	28.3	124.5	86.5	40.5	46.0	37.9	9.9
1966	125.7	98.4	56.1	42.3	27.3	28.0	143.7	100.2	50.6	49.6	43.5	11.0
1967	130.0	100.1	63.8	36.3	29.9	29.2	153.7	105.2	53.1	52.1	48.6	11.8
1968	140.2	108.8	70.0	38.7	31.5	32.3	177.7	128.1	68.7	59.4	49.6	13.5
1969	147.8	114.4	75.2	39.2	33.3	35.7	189.2	137.0	74.1	62.8	52.3	17.8
1970	161.3	125.2	80.4	44.7	36.1	36.8	196.4	142.1	75.4	66.7	54.4	19.2
1971	161.9	124.1	79.3	44.9	37.8	37.9	207.8	156.1	84.4	71.7	51.7	17.9
1972	173.7	136.5	87.1	49.5	37.2	42.2	230.2	177.5	95.7	81.7	52.8	20.5
1973	210.3	166.9	108.0	58.9	43.4	57.5	244.4	194.7	100.9	93.9	49.7	27.6
1974	234.4	183.4	123.5	59.9	51.0	67.5	238.4	189.3	101.3	87.9	49.2	33.2
1975	232.9	178.5	121.3	57.2	54.4	57.4	209.8	163.3	82.1	81.2	46.5	31.6
1976	243.4	183.9	121.8	62.1	59.5	63.0	249.7	200.4	100.9	99.5	49.3	31.5
1977	246.9	183.9	119.5	64.4	63.0	67.9	274.7	223.2	112.9	110.3	51.5	32.2
1978	270.2	203.0	132.1	70.9	67.2	78.7	300.1	245.2	130.0	115.3	54.8	43.2
1979	293.5	225.7	148.1	77.6	67.8	107.1	304.1	248.7	132.1	116.7	55.3	58.6
1980	320.5	248.2	161.0	87.3	72.3	113.7	289.9	235.6	133.6	102.0	54.2	66.6
1981	326.1	244.0	154.2	89.7	82.2	120.7	304.1	246.1	143.4	102.7	58.0	79.4
1982	296.7	217.7	130.5	87.2	79.0	117.9	304.1	243.1	143.0	100.1	61.1	82.1
1983	285.9	208.3	124.6	83.8	77.6	111.0	342.1	276.5	167.6	108.9	65.6	78.0
1984	305.7	221.3	133.8	87.5	84.4	119.4	427.7	346.1	219.9	126.2	81.6	93.5
1985	309.2	224.8	139.3	85.6	84.4	103.4	454.6	366.5	237.2	129.3	88.1	88.2
1986	329.6	234.3	144.8	89.6	95.3	99.2	484.7	398.0	254.6	143.4	86.7	90.2
1987	364.0	257.7	163.0	94.7	106.2	105.1	507.1	414.8	264.2	150.6	92.3	100.5
1988	421.6	307.4	202.8	104.6	114.2	123.8	525.7	431.3	274.7	156.7	94.3	116.1
1989	471.8	343.8	230.9	112.9	128.0	144.7	545.4	450.4	287.1	163.3	95.0	130.1
1990	510.5	368.9	249.4	119.5	141.6	148.0	565.1	461.4	292.5	168.9	103.7	128.8
1991	543.4	396.7	269.2	127.4	146.7	123.1	562.5	463.9	297.2	166.7	98.5	110.0
1992	578.0	422.7	288.0	134.7	155.4	105.5	611.6	511.9	332.5	179.4	99.7	97.7
1993 ᵖ	596.4	438.2	304.9	133.3	158.2		675.7	572.3	379.9	192.5	103.3	
1982: IV	280.4	202.8	119.0	83.7	77.6	109.7	299.4	236.3	134.6	101.7	63.1	77.6
1983: IV	291.5	215.5	131.0	84.5	75.9	116.5	375.1	306.6	191.1	115.5	68.6	82.0
1984: IV	312.8	229.0	138.5	90.5	83.8	116.1	444.2	357.9	229.3	128.6	86.3	93.9
1985: IV	312.0	226.4	139.6	86.8	85.5	102.9	467.4	380.0	243.5	136.5	87.4	86.8
1986: IV	342.9	243.5	150.0	93.5	99.4	94.8	498.9	409.1	259.8	149.3	89.8	91.2
1987: IV	386.1	278.0	180.1	97.8	108.1	112.9	522.1	427.4	273.8	153.7	94.6	105.4
1988: IV	438.2	322.0	214.7	107.2	116.2	132.3	540.9	444.8	284.0	160.8	96.1	123.0
1989: IV	487.7	354.8	237.8	116.9	132.9	144.3	555.0	458.5	290.4	168.1	96.5	125.9
1990: I	501.8	364.3	245.9	118.4	137.5	146.4	562.6	459.6	285.7	173.8	103.0	128.2
II	511.1	370.4	252.3	118.1	140.7	146.0	570.0	466.5	293.5	173.0	103.5	129.8
III	508.6	366.4	248.6	117.8	142.2	144.4	570.7	466.4	296.2	170.2	104.3	130.0
IV	520.4	374.6	250.9	123.8	145.8	155.4	557.2	453.1	294.4	158.8	104.1	127.1
1991: I	519.4	381.6	254.5	127.2	137.8	138.5	541.0	442.1	284.2	158.0	98.9	117.0
II	542.9	396.1	271.7	124.4	146.8	124.4	556.2	457.2	288.9	168.3	99.1	112.5
III	546.9	398.2	271.7	126.5	148.7	116.7	571.9	474.6	304.7	169.9	97.3	109.0
IV	564.2	410.7	279.0	131.7	153.5	112.9	580.7	481.7	311.2	170.5	98.9	101.6
1992: I	571.0	414.4	280.9	133.5	156.6	110.7	586.2	486.8	315.1	171.7	99.3	93.6
II	570.2	415.9	283.6	132.4	154.2	108.7	608.2	509.0	328.5	180.4	99.2	103.0
III	579.3	423.0	287.4	135.6	156.3	103.7	621.8	521.6	338.4	183.2	100.1	95.5
IV	591.6	437.3	300.0	137.3	154.3	98.9	630.3	530.3	348.0	182.4	100.0	98.8
1993: I	588.0	430.2	296.5	133.7	157.8	98.3	647.9	545.9	360.5	185.5	102.0	95.8
II	593.2	434.5	302.4	132.1	158.6	105.0	668.4	565.7	372.1	193.6	102.7	103.0
III	591.9	434.1	302.2	131.9	157.8	107.1	678.2	574.9	381.0	193.9	103.3	99.6
IV ᵖ	612.5	454.1	318.4	135.6	158.5		708.1	602.8	405.9	196.9	105.3	

[1] Exports and imports of certain goods, primarily military equipment purchased and sold by the Federal Government, are included in services.
[2] Consists largely of receipts by U.S. residents of interest and dividends and reinvested earnings of foreign affiliates of U.S. corporations.
[3] Consists largely of payments to foreign residents of interest and dividends and reinvested earnings of U.S. affiliates of foreign corporations.

Source: Department of Commerce, Bureau of Economic Analysis.

TABLE B-23.—*Relation of gross domestic product, gross national product, net national product, and national income, 1959–93*

[Billions of dollars; quarterly data at seasonally adjusted annual rates]

Year or quarter	Gross domestic product	Plus: Receipts of factor income from rest of the world [1]	Less: Payments of factor income to rest of the world [2]	Equals: Gross national product	Less: Consumption of fixed capital	Equals: Net national product	Less: Indirect business tax and nontax liability	Less: Business transfer payments	Less: Statistical discrepancy	Plus: Subsidies less current surplus of government enterprises	Equals: National income
1959	494.2	4.3	1.5	497.0	44.6	452.5	41.9	1.4	−1.8	−0.9	410.1
1960	513.3	5.0	1.8	516.6	46.3	470.2	45.5	1.4	−3.1	−.8	425.7
1961	531.8	5.4	1.8	535.4	47.7	487.7	48.1	1.5	−2.2	.2	440.5
1962	571.6	6.1	1.8	575.8	49.3	526.5	51.7	1.6	−1.0	.3	474.5
1963	603.1	6.6	2.1	607.7	51.3	556.4	54.7	1.8	−2.0	−.3	501.5
1964	648.0	7.4	2.4	653.0	53.9	599.2	58.8	2.0	−.7	.1	539.1
1965	702.7	8.1	2.7	708.1	57.3	650.7	62.7	2.2	−.7	.3	586.9
1966	769.8	8.3	3.1	774.9	62.1	712.8	65.4	2.3	2.8	1.4	643.7
1967	814.3	8.9	3.4	819.8	67.4	752.4	70.4	2.5	.8	1.2	679.9
1968	889.3	10.3	4.1	895.5	73.9	821.5	79.0	2.8	−.1	1.2	741.0
1969	959.5	11.9	5.8	965.6	81.5	884.2	86.6	3.1	−2.6	1.5	798.6
1970	1,010.7	13.0	6.6	1,017.1	88.8	928.3	94.3	3.2	.0	2.6	833.5
1971	1,097.2	14.1	6.4	1,104.9	97.6	1,007.3	103.6	3.4	3.1	2.4	899.5
1972	1,207.0	16.4	7.7	1,215.7	109.9	1,105.7	111.4	3.9	1.1	3.4	992.9
1973	1,349.6	23.8	11.1	1,362.3	120.4	1,241.9	121.0	4.5	−.5	2.6	1,119.5
1974	1,458.6	30.3	14.6	1,474.3	140.2	1,334.1	129.3	5.0	1.4	.4	1,198.8
1975	1,585.9	28.2	14.9	1,599.1	165.2	1,433.9	140.0	5.2	6.0	2.6	1,285.3
1976	1,768.4	32.8	15.7	1,785.5	182.8	1,602.7	151.6	6.5	10.4	1.4	1,435.5
1977	1,974.1	37.7	17.2	1,994.6	205.2	1,789.4	165.5	7.3	10.9	3.3	1,609.1
1978	2,232.7	47.1	25.3	2,254.5	234.8	2,019.8	177.8	8.2	7.6	3.6	1,829.8
1979	2,488.6	69.7	37.5	2,520.8	272.4	2,248.4	188.7	9.9	13.8	2.9	2,038.9
1980	2,708.0	80.6	46.5	2,742.1	311.9	2,430.2	212.0	11.2	13.6	4.8	2,198.2
1981	3,030.6	94.1	60.9	3,063.8	362.4	2,701.4	249.3	13.4	10.9	4.7	2,432.5
1982	3,149.6	97.3	67.1	3,179.8	399.1	2,780.8	256.4	15.4	−7.4	6.2	2,522.5
1983	3,405.0	95.8	66.5	3,434.4	418.4	3,016.0	280.1	16.6	10.2	11.7	2,720.8
1984	3,777.2	108.1	83.8	3,801.5	433.2	3,368.3	309.5	19.0	−9.0	9.5	3,058.3
1985	4,038.7	97.3	82.4	4,053.6	454.5	3,599.1	329.9	21.0	−13.9	6.4	3,268.4
1986	4,268.6	96.0	86.9	4,277.7	478.6	3,799.2	345.5	24.2	1.2	9.7	3,437.9
1987	4,539.9	105.1	100.5	4,544.5	502.2	4,042.4	365.0	24.0	−24.8	14.1	3,692.3
1988	4,900.4	128.7	120.8	4,908.2	534.0	4,374.2	385.3	25.6	−28.4	10.9	4,002.6
1989	5,250.8	157.5	141.5	5,266.8	580.4	4,686.4	414.7	26.6	1.1	5.4	4,249.5
1990	5,546.1	168.6	146.9	5,567.8	602.7	4,965.1	444.0	26.8	7.8	4.5	4,491.0
1991	5,722.9	146.1	131.9	5,737.1	626.1	5,111.0	476.6	26.3	9.6	−.3	4,598.3
1992	6,038.5	129.2	121.9	6,045.8	657.9	5,387.9	502.8	27.6	23.6	2.7	4,836.6
1993 ᵖ	6,374.0				671.2		530.5	28.0		7.2	
1982: IV	3,195.1	91.9	64.4	3,222.6	412.5	2,810.1	262.3	16.0	−10.1	9.6	2,551.5
1983: IV	3,547.3	102.1	71.0	3,578.4	439.7	3,138.7	291.7	18.1	13.8	19.2	2,834.3
1984: IV	3,869.1	106.6	85.5	3,890.2	448.0	3,442.2	317.7	20.2	−20.5	9.7	3,134.4
1985: IV	4,140.5	98.1	82.4	4,156.2	465.6	3,690.7	335.1	22.2	−5.9	2.6	3,341.9
1986: IV	4,336.6	92.8	88.9	4,340.5	488.2	3,852.3	351.6	24.9	−2.0	8.2	3,486.0
1987: IV	4,683.0	114.4	106.9	4,690.5	512.1	4,178.5	372.3	24.2	−24.9	22.0	3,828.8
1988: IV	5,044.6	139.9	130.2	5,054.3	547.2	4,507.2	394.2	27.2	−25.4	16.5	4,127.6
1989: IV	5,344.8	159.3	139.1	5,365.0	600.8	4,764.2	424.4	26.2	12.8	4.4	4,305.2
1990: I	5,461.9	164.0	143.8	5,482.1	590.2	4,891.9	436.2	26.3	13.1	9.9	4,426.2
II	5,540.9	165.4	147.0	5,559.3	597.9	4,961.4	437.2	27.0	−1.8	3.0	4,502.0
III	5,583.8	165.2	149.0	5,599.9	607.8	4,992.2	448.0	27.1	14.9	−5.6	4,496.6
IV	5,597.9	179.7	147.7	5,630.0	614.8	5,015.1	454.8	26.7	4.9	10.4	4,539.2
1991: I	5,631.7	162.4	138.0	5,656.1	619.9	5,036.2	465.6	26.1	.2	1.8	4,546.0
II	5,697.7	147.2	134.3	5,710.6	622.3	5,088.3	470.5	26.3	4.5	.8	4,587.8
III	5,758.6	139.1	131.5	5,766.2	626.7	5,139.6	481.3	26.0	27.3	−8.0	4,596.9
IV	5,803.7	135.7	123.9	5,815.5	635.4	5,180.0	488.9	26.6	6.2	4.3	4,662.6
1992: I	5,908.7	134.4	115.6	5,927.6	631.7	5,295.9	493.4	27.0	23.1	3.0	4,755.4
II	5,991.4	132.9	127.9	5,996.3	637.2	5,359.1	497.3	27.6	23.6	3.9	4,814.6
III	6,059.5	127.3	119.5	6,067.3	714.6	5,352.8	504.8	27.8	15.7	−3.7	4,800.8
IV	6,194.4	122.3	124.8	6,191.9	648.0	5,543.9	515.7	28.1	32.1	7.7	4,975.8
1993: I	6,261.6	122.8	122.4	6,262.1	663.2	5,598.8	515.6	27.0	34.4	17.1	5,038.9
II	6,327.6	131.9	132.3	6,327.1	663.3	5,663.9	526.2	27.8	12.0	6.1	5,104.0
III	6,395.9	135.1	128.7	6,402.3	679.7	5,722.6	532.4	28.4	13.3	−5.3	5,143.2
IV ᵖ	6,510.8				678.7		547.9	28.8		10.7	

[1] Consists largely of receipts by U.S. residents of interest and dividends and reinvested earnings of foreign affiliates of U.S. corporations.
[2] Consists largely of payments to foreign residents of interest and dividends and reinvested earnings of U.S. affiliates of foreign corporations.

Source: Department of Commerce, Bureau of Economic Analysis.

TABLE B-24.—*Relation of national income and personal income, 1959–93*

[Billions of dollars; quarterly data at seasonally adjusted annual rates]

Year or quarter	National income	Less: Corporate profits with inventory valuation and capital consumption adjustments	Less: Net interest	Less: Contributions for social insurance	Less: Wage accruals less disbursements	Plus: Personal interest income	Plus: Personal dividend income	Plus: Government transfer payments to persons	Plus: Business transfer payments to persons	Equals: Personal income
1959	410.1	52.3	10.2	18.8	0.0	22.7	12.7	25.7	1.3	391.2
1960	425.7	50.7	11.2	21.9	.0	25.0	13.4	27.5	1.3	409.2
1961	440.5	51.6	13.1	22.9	.0	26.9	14.0	31.5	1.4	426.5
1962	474.5	59.6	14.6	25.4	.0	29.3	15.0	32.6	1.5	453.4
1963	501.5	65.1	16.1	28.5	.0	32.4	16.1	34.5	1.7	476.4
1964	539.1	72.1	18.2	30.1	.0	36.1	18.0	36.0	1.8	510.7
1965	586.9	82.9	21.1	31.6	.0	40.3	20.2	39.1	2.0	552.9
1966	643.7	88.6	24.3	40.6	.0	44.9	20.9	43.6	2.1	601.7
1967	679.9	86.0	28.1	45.5	.0	49.5	22.1	52.3	2.3	646.5
1968	741.0	92.6	30.4	50.4	.0	54.6	24.5	60.6	2.5	709.9
1969	798.6	89.6	33.6	57.9	.0	60.8	25.1	67.5	2.8	773.7
1970	833.5	77.5	40.0	62.2	.0	69.2	23.5	81.8	2.8	831.0
1971	899.5	90.3	45.4	68.9	.6	75.7	23.5	97.0	3.0	893.5
1972	992.9	103.2	49.3	79.0	.0	81.8	25.5	108.4	3.4	980.5
1973	1,119.5	116.4	56.5	97.6	−.1	94.1	27.7	124.1	3.8	1,098.7
1974	1,198.8	104.5	71.8	110.5	−.5	112.4	29.6	147.4	4.0	1,205.7
1975	1,285.3	121.9	80.0	118.5	.1	123.0	29.2	185.7	4.5	1,307.3
1976	1,435.5	147.1	85.1	134.5	.1	134.6	34.7	202.8	5.5	1,446.3
1977	1,609.1	175.7	100.7	149.8	.1	155.7	39.4	217.5	5.9	1,601.3
1978	1,829.8	199.7	120.5	171.8	.3	184.5	44.2	234.8	6.8	1,807.9
1979	2,038.9	202.5	149.9	197.8	−.2	223.2	50.4	262.8	7.9	2,033.1
1980	2,198.2	177.7	191.2	216.6	.0	274.0	57.1	312.6	8.8	2,265.4
1981	2,432.5	182.0	233.4	251.3	.1	336.1	66.9	355.7	10.2	2,534.7
1982	2,522.5	151.5	262.4	269.6	.0	376.8	67.1	396.3	11.8	2,690.9
1983	2,720.8	212.7	270.0	290.2	−.4	397.5	77.8	426.1	12.8	2,862.5
1984	3,058.3	264.2	307.9	325.0	.2	461.9	78.8	437.8	15.1	3,154.6
1985	3,268.4	280.8	326.2	353.8	−.2	498.1	87.9	468.1	17.8	3,379.8
1986	3,437.9	271.6	350.2	379.8	.0	531.7	104.7	497.1	20.7	3,590.4
1987	3,692.3	319.8	360.4	400.7	.0	548.1	100.4	521.3	20.8	3,802.0
1988	4,002.6	365.0	387.7	442.3	.0	583.2	108.4	555.9	20.8	4,075.9
1989	4,249.5	362.8	452.7	473.2	.0	668.2	126.5	603.8	21.1	4,380.3
1990	4,491.0	380.6	463.7	503.1	.1	698.2	144.4	666.3	21.3	4,673.8
1991	4,598.3	369.5	462.8	528.4	−.1	715.6	127.9	749.2	20.7	4,850.9
1992	4,836.6	407.2	442.0	555.6	−20.0	694.3	140.4	836.8	21.6	5,144.9
1993 ᵖ	....	....	....	585.3	20.0	695.8	158.3	889.7	21.9	5,387.6
1982: IV	2,551.5	150.3	256.8	272.8	.0	373.6	69.4	419.9	12.3	2,746.8
1983: IV	2,834.3	229.1	281.8	298.3	.0	418.7	80.6	428.0	13.2	2,965.8
1984: IV	3,134.4	261.3	321.1	332.2	.6	485.4	79.3	442.3	16.2	3,242.5
1985: IV	3,341.9	284.9	331.9	362.3	.0	507.5	92.7	474.8	18.8	3,456.7
1986: IV	3,486.0	264.6	349.7	388.7	.0	532.6	105.6	505.8	20.9	3,647.8
1987: IV	3,828.8	343.3	368.6	409.6	−.2	562.3	100.1	528.1	20.4	3,918.5
1988: IV	4,127.6	378.3	408.1	453.5	.0	608.9	113.8	563.5	21.3	4,195.2
1989: IV	4,305.2	354.5	459.8	480.4	.0	681.2	132.9	624.0	20.8	4,469.4
1990: I	4,426.2	382.6	460.5	495.9	.0	686.9	141.2	649.0	21.3	4,585.6
II	4,502.0	409.3	459.5	500.7	.0	692.8	145.6	656.1	21.5	4,648.6
III	4,496.6	367.5	460.6	506.4	.0	702.8	146.6	669.2	21.3	4,701.9
IV	4,539.2	362.8	474.4	509.5	.2	710.3	144.4	690.9	21.1	4,759.1
1991: I	4,546.0	369.3	468.8	520.7	.2	715.4	136.6	724.2	20.8	4,783.9
II	4,587.8	370.8	466.3	525.7	−.4	720.0	126.7	740.9	20.5	4,833.4
III	4,596.9	359.0	464.2	531.5	.0	717.3	123.9	754.8	20.6	4,858.8
IV	4,662.6	378.8	451.9	535.7	.0	709.6	124.3	776.8	20.8	4,927.5
1992: I	4,755.4	409.9	439.5	548.5	.0	694.4	128.2	816.6	21.1	5,017.8
II	4,814.6	411.7	440.8	552.7	.0	696.0	136.0	830.9	21.5	5,093.8
III	4,800.8	367.5	440.1	556.6	.0	692.2	144.9	844.3	21.8	5,139.8
IV	4,975.8	439.5	447.7	564.6	−80.0	694.5	152.3	855.4	22.0	5,328.3
1993: I	5,038.9	432.1	450.1	568.9	80.0	695.4	157.0	873.0	21.4	5,254.7
II	5,104.0	458.1	443.2	585.9	.0	693.1	157.8	883.7	21.8	5,373.2
III	5,143.2	468.5	444.6	590.5	.0	695.7	159.0	896.4	22.1	5,412.7
IV ᵖ	....	....	....	596.0	.0	699.2	159.4	905.6	22.3	5,509.8

Source: Department of Commerce, Bureau of Economic Analysis.

TABLE B-25.—*National income by type of income, 1959-93*

[Billions of dollars; quarterly data at seasonally adjusted annual rates]

Year or quarter	National income [1]	Compensation of employees			Proprietors' income with inventory valuation and capital consumption adjustments							
				Supplements to wages and salaries [2]		Farm			Nonfarm			
		Total	Wages and salaries		Total	Total	Proprietors' income [3]	Capital consumption adjustment	Total	Proprietors' income	Inventory valuation adjustment	Capital consumption adjustment
1959	410.1	281.2	259.8	21.4	51.7	10.7	11.6	−0.9	41.1	40.2	0.0	0.9
1960	425.7	296.7	272.8	23.8	51.9	11.2	12.1	−.8	40.6	39.8	.0	.8
1961	440.5	305.6	280.5	25.1	54.3	11.9	12.7	−.8	42.4	41.8	.0	.6
1962	474.5	327.4	299.3	28.1	56.4	11.9	12.7	−.8	44.5	43.9	.0	.6
1963	501.5	345.5	314.8	30.7	57.7	11.8	12.5	−.7	45.9	45.2	.0	.7
1964	539.1	371.0	337.7	33.2	60.5	10.6	11.3	−.7	49.8	49.2	−.1	.7
1965	586.9	399.8	363.7	36.1	65.0	12.9	13.7	−.7	52.1	51.9	−.2	.4
1966	643.7	443.0	400.3	42.7	69.4	14.0	14.8	−.8	55.3	55.4	−.2	.2
1967	679.9	475.5	428.9	46.6	70.9	12.7	13.5	−.8	58.2	58.3	−.2	.1
1968	741.0	524.7	471.9	52.8	75.1	12.7	13.6	−.9	62.4	63.0	−.4	−.2
1969	798.6	578.4	518.3	60.1	78.9	14.4	15.6	−1.1	64.5	65.0	−.5	.0
1970	833.5	618.3	551.5	66.8	79.9	14.6	15.9	−1.3	65.3	66.0	−.5	−.1
1971	899.5	659.4	584.5	74.9	86.2	15.2	16.6	−1.4	70.9	72.0	−.6	−.5
1972	992.9	726.2	638.7	87.6	97.4	19.1	20.9	−1.8	78.3	79.3	−.7	−.2
1973	1,119.5	812.8	708.6	104.2	116.5	32.2	34.3	−2.0	84.3	86.5	−2.0	−.2
1974	1,198.8	891.3	772.2	119.1	115.3	25.5	28.2	−2.8	89.8	94.2	−3.8	−.6
1975	1,285.3	948.7	814.7	134.0	121.2	23.7	27.5	−3.8	97.5	100.2	−1.2	−1.4
1976	1,435.5	1,058.3	899.6	158.7	132.9	18.3	22.5	−4.2	114.6	117.6	−1.3	−1.7
1977	1,609.1	1,177.3	994.0	183.3	146.4	17.1	21.8	−4.8	129.4	132.5	−1.3	−1.8
1978	1,829.8	1,333.0	1,120.9	212.1	167.7	21.5	27.0	−5.5	146.2	150.2	−2.1	−2.0
1979	2,038.9	1,496.4	1,255.3	241.1	181.8	24.7	31.2	−6.4	157.0	161.8	−2.9	−1.9
1980	2,198.2	1,644.4	1,376.6	267.8	171.8	11.5	19.4	−7.9	160.3	165.8	−3.0	−2.5
1981	2,432.5	1,815.5	1,515.6	299.8	180.8	21.2	30.2	−9.0	159.6	160.9	−1.4	.2
1982	2,522.5	1,916.0	1,593.3	322.7	170.7	13.5	23.1	−9.7	157.3	157.8	−.6	.0
1983	2,720.8	2,029.4	1,684.2	345.2	186.7	2.4	12.1	−9.7	184.3	176.1	−.6	8.7
1984	3,058.3	2,226.9	1,850.0	376.9	236.0	21.3	30.8	−9.4	214.7	197.1	−.5	18.1
1985	3,268.4	2,382.8	1,986.3	396.5	259.9	21.5	30.5	−9.0	238.4	212.4	−.2	26.1
1986	3,437.9	2,523.8	2,105.4	418.4	283.7	22.3	31.0	−8.7	261.5	230.6	−.1	30.9
1987	3,692.3	2,698.7	2,261.2	437.4	310.2	31.3	39.6	−8.3	279.0	252.4	−.8	27.4
1988	4,002.6	2,921.3	2,443.0	478.3	324.3	30.9	38.8	−8.0	293.4	266.8	−1.5	28.1
1989	4,249.5	3,100.2	2,586.4	513.8	347.3	40.2	48.3	−8.1	307.0	281.1	−1.2	27.2
1990	4,491.0	3,297.6	2,745.0	552.5	363.3	41.9	49.8	−7.8	321.4	305.6	−.4	16.2
1991	4,598.3	3,402.4	2,814.9	587.5	376.4	36.8	44.4	−7.6	339.5	327.7	.0	11.8
1992	4,836.2	3,582.0	2,953.1	629.0	414.3	43.7	51.2	−7.5	370.6	358.0	−.5	13.1
1993 ᵖ		3,772.1	3,100.4	671.7	442.1	45.0	52.1	−7.1	397.1	385.2	−1.0	13.0
1982: IV	2,551.5	1,940.4	1,611.8	328.6	179.9	10.2	20.0	−9.8	169.6	168.0	.6	1.1
1983: IV	2,834.3	2,101.2	1,747.3	353.9	200.1	6.3	15.8	−9.5	193.8	182.5	−1.6	12.9
1984: IV	3,134.4	2,288.1	1,903.9	384.2	239.6	21.9	31.2	−9.3	217.7	196.6	.1	21.0
1985: IV	3,341.9	2,442.5	2,039.1	403.3	268.7	17.8	26.7	−8.9	250.9	223.2	−1.4	29.1
1986: IV	3,486.0	2,582.5	2,153.9	428.6	284.4	23.6	32.1	−8.6	260.9	230.0	.7	30.1
1987: IV	3,828.8	2,785.1	2,336.7	448.4	325.0	42.4	50.6	−8.2	282.6	254.2	1.7	26.7
1988: IV	4,127.6	3,004.9	2,510.6	494.3	333.4	30.9	38.8	−7.9	302.5	274.9	−1.4	29.0
1989: IV	4,305.2	3,162.8	2,637.9	524.9	349.7	38.4	46.4	−8.0	311.4	288.7	−.7	23.4
1990: I	4,426.2	3,231.5	2,689.2	542.3	367.5	49.9	57.5	−7.6	317.6	290.4	6.4	20.8
II	4,502.0	3,288.2	2,739.1	549.2	361.4	42.5	50.2	−7.8	318.9	284.0	17.6	17.4
III	4,496.6	3,326.3	2,770.6	555.7	355.5	31.6	39.6	−8.0	323.9	329.5	−19.8	14.3
IV	4,539.2	3,344.2	2,781.3	562.9	368.9	43.8	51.7	−7.9	325.1	318.4	−5.6	12.4
1991: I	4,546.0	3,355.7	2,782.2	573.4	363.8	37.2	45.1	−7.8	326.6	312.8	2.3	11.5
II	4,587.8	3,382.8	2,800.6	582.3	379.7	42.6	50.2	−7.6	337.1	320.6	4.9	11.6
III	4,596.9	3,415.8	2,823.4	592.4	374.2	29.8	37.4	−7.6	344.4	340.1	−7.5	11.7
IV	4,662.6	3,455.4	2,853.6	601.8	387.7	37.6	45.0	−7.4	350.1	337.5	.3	12.3
1992: I	4,755.4	3,507.8	2,892.2	615.7	406.8	45.6	52.9	−7.3	361.2	350.4	−2.1	12.9
II	4,814.6	3,558.1	2,933.6	624.5	411.1	44.9	52.2	−7.2	366.2	360.0	−7.0	13.2
III	4,800.8	3,603.6	2,970.7	632.9	408.1	36.8	44.9	−8.2	371.3	359.4	−.8	12.7
IV	4,975.8	3,658.6	3,015.8	642.8	431.2	47.6	54.8	−7.2	383.6	362.2	7.8	13.7
1993: I	5,038.9	3,705.1	3,054.3	650.7	444.1	55.7	62.8	−7.1	388.4	376.4	−1.6	13.7
II	5,104.0	3,750.6	3,082.7	668.0	439.4	47.0	54.1	−7.1	392.4	380.3	−1.2	13.3
III	5,143.2	3,793.9	3,115.4	678.5	422.5	24.8	32.1	−7.3	397.6	385.4	−.4	12.7
IV ᵖ		3,839.0	3,149.2	689.8	462.4	52.4	59.4	−7.0	410.1	398.7	−.9	12.3

[1] National income is the total net income earned in production. It differs from gross domestic product mainly in that it excludes depreciation charges and other allowances for business and institutional consumption of durable capital goods and indirect business taxes. See Table B-23.

See next page for continuation of table.

TABLE B-25.—*National income by type of income, 1959–93*—Continued

[Billions of dollars; quarterly data at seasonally adjusted annual rates]

Year or quarter	Rental income of persons with capital consumption adjustment			Corporate profits with inventory valuation and capital consumption adjustments										Net interest
	Total	Rental income of persons	Capital consumption adjustment	Total	Profits with inventory valuation adjustment and without capital consumption adjustment							Capital consumption adjustment	
					Total	Profits					Inventory valuation adjustment		
						Profits before tax	Profits tax liability	Profits after tax					
								Total	Dividends	Undistributed profits			
1959	14.7	18.0	-3.4	52.3	53.1	53.4	23.6	29.7	12.7	17.0	-0.3	-0.8	10.2
1960	15.3	18.7	-3.4	50.7	51.0	51.1	22.7	28.4	13.4	15.0	-.2	-.3	11.2
1961	15.8	19.2	-3.3	51.6	51.3	51.0	22.8	28.2	14.0	14.3	.3	.3	13.1
1962	16.5	19.8	-3.3	59.6	56.4	56.4	24.0	32.4	15.0	17.4	.0	3.2	14.6
1963	17.1	20.3	-3.2	65.1	61.2	61.2	26.2	34.9	16.1	18.8	.1	3.9	16.1
1964	17.3	20.5	-3.2	72.1	67.5	68.0	28.0	40.0	18.0	22.0	-.5	4.6	18.2
1965	18.0	21.3	-3.3	82.9	77.6	78.8	30.9	47.9	20.2	27.8	-1.2	5.3	21.1
1966	18.5	22.1	-3.6	88.6	83.0	85.1	33.7	51.4	20.9	30.5	-2.1	5.6	24.3
1967	19.4	23.4	-3.9	86.0	80.3	81.8	32.7	49.2	22.1	27.1	-1.6	5.7	28.1
1968	18.2	22.8	-4.6	92.6	86.9	90.6	39.4	51.2	24.6	26.6	-3.7	5.6	30.4
1969	18.0	23.9	-5.9	89.6	83.2	89.0	39.7	49.4	25.2	24.1	-5.9	6.4	33.6
1970	17.8	24.2	-6.4	77.5	71.8	78.4	34.4	44.0	23.7	20.3	-6.6	5.6	40.0
1971	18.2	25.6	-7.4	90.3	85.5	90.1	37.7	52.4	23.7	28.6	-4.6	4.8	45.4
1972	16.8	26.1	-9.3	103.2	97.9	104.5	41.9	62.6	25.8	36.9	-6.6	5.3	49.3
1973	17.3	28.2	-10.9	116.4	110.9	130.9	49.3	81.6	28.1	53.5	-20.0	5.5	56.5
1974	15.8	29.3	-13.5	104.5	103.4	142.8	51.8	91.0	30.4	60.6	-39.5	1.2	71.8
1975	13.5	29.5	-15.9	121.9	129.4	140.4	50.9	89.5	30.1	59.4	-11.0	-7.6	80.0
1976	12.1	29.9	-17.8	147.1	158.8	173.7	64.2	109.5	35.6	73.9	-14.9	-11.7	85.1
1977	9.0	30.0	-21.0	175.7	186.7	203.3	73.0	130.3	40.7	89.5	-16.6	-11.0	100.7
1978	8.9	34.4	-25.5	199.7	212.8	237.9	83.5	154.4	45.9	108.5	-25.0	-13.1	120.5
1979	8.4	39.1	-30.8	202.5	219.8	261.4	88.0	173.4	52.4	121.0	-41.6	-17.3	149.9
1980	13.2	49.0	-35.8	177.7	197.8	240.9	84.8	156.1	59.0	97.1	-43.0	-20.2	191.2
1981	20.8	61.1	-40.2	182.0	203.2	228.9	81.1	147.8	69.2	78.6	-25.7	-21.2	233.4
1982	21.9	64.4	-42.4	151.5	166.4	176.3	63.1	113.2	70.0	43.2	-9.9	-14.9	262.4
1983	22.1	64.8	-42.8	212.7	202.2	210.7	77.2	133.5	81.2	52.3	-8.5	10.4	270.0
1984	23.3	66.5	-43.2	264.2	236.4	240.5	94.0	146.4	82.7	63.8	-4.1	27.8	307.9
1985	18.7	63.4	-44.6	280.8	225.3	225.0	96.5	128.5	92.4	36.1	.2	55.5	326.2
1986	8.7	53.4	-44.7	271.6	227.6	217.8	106.5	111.3	109.8	1.6	9.7	44.1	350.2
1987	3.2	50.0	-46.8	319.8	273.4	287.9	127.1	160.8	106.2	54.6	-14.5	46.4	360.4
1988	4.3	53.4	-49.1	365.0	320.3	347.5	137.0	210.5	115.3	95.2	-27.3	44.7	387.7
1989	-13.5	44.2	-57.7	362.8	325.4	342.9	141.3	201.6	134.6	67.1	-17.5	37.4	452.7
1990	-14.2	42.7	-56.9	380.6	354.7	365.7	138.7	227.1	153.5	73.6	-11.0	25.9	463.7
1991	-12.8	45.2	-57.9	369.5	367.3	362.3	129.8	232.5	137.4	95.2	4.9	2.2	462.8
1992	-8.9	57.4	-66.3	407.2	390.1	395.4	146.3	249.1	150.5	98.6	-5.3	17.1	442.0
1993 ᵖ	13.0	75.4	-62.5	....	....	....	....	....	169.0	....	....	-7.8	24.3
1982: IV	24.1	66.5	-42.3	150.3	160.0	168.6	58.7	109.9	72.5	37.5	-8.6	-9.6	256.8
1983: IV	22.2	64.5	-42.4	229.1	216.2	223.8	82.2	141.6	84.2	57.4	-7.6	12.9	281.8
1984: IV	24.3	67.6	-43.4	261.3	223.6	220.1	83.8	136.3	83.4	52.9	3.5	37.7	321.1
1985: IV	14.0	60.0	-46.0	284.9	228.0	231.8	97.6	134.2	97.4	36.9	-3.8	56.9	331.9
1986: IV	4.7	50.2	-45.5	264.6	225.0	235.7	116.6	119.2	111.0	8.2	-10.7	39.6	349.7
1987: IV	6.8	54.2	-47.4	343.3	293.4	311.2	135.2	176.0	106.3	69.7	-17.8	49.9	368.6
1988: IV	2.8	52.6	-49.7	378.3	340.5	372.2	146.2	226.0	121.0	105.0	-31.7	37.9	408.1
1989: IV	-21.6	39.8	-61.3	354.5	320.6	334.1	134.2	200.0	141.3	58.7	-13.5	33.9	459.8
1990: I	-15.9	40.1	-56.0	382.6	346.8	348.8	132.0	216.8	149.9	67.0	-2.0	35.8	460.5
II	-16.4	40.2	-56.6	409.3	377.9	369.0	139.8	229.2	154.6	74.6	8.9	31.4	459.5
III	-13.3	44.1	-57.4	367.5	344.7	376.2	145.7	230.5	155.7	74.8	-31.5	22.8	460.6
IV	-11.1	46.4	-57.4	362.8	349.3	368.9	137.0	231.8	153.7	78.1	-19.5	13.5	474.4
1991: I	-11.7	45.1	-56.8	369.3	364.3	356.5	125.4	231.1	145.9	85.2	8.2	4.7	468.8
II	-11.9	44.7	-56.6	370.8	370.1	357.4	128.0	229.4	136.2	93.2	12.7	.7	466.3
III	-16.3	41.0	-57.2	359.0	359.0	362.0	132.5	229.5	133.4	96.1	-3.0	.0	464.2
IV	-11.2	49.8	-61.0	378.8	375.4	373.5	133.4	240.1	133.9	106.1	1.9	3.5	451.9
1992: I	-8.7	47.3	-56.0	409.9	399.7	404.3	147.0	257.3	138.0	119.3	-4.6	10.2	439.5
II	-7.2	49.3	-56.5	411.7	395.7	409.5	153.0	256.5	146.1	110.4	-13.7	16.0	440.8
III	-18.5	75.7	-94.2	367.5	350.1	357.9	130.1	227.8	155.2	72.7	-7.8	17.4	440.1
IV	-1.2	57.4	-58.6	439.5	414.8	409.9	155.0	254.9	162.9	92.0	4.9	24.7	447.7
1993: I	7.5	71.3	-63.8	432.1	407.0	419.8	160.9	258.9	167.5	91.4	-12.7	25.1	450.1
II	12.7	73.2	-60.4	458.1	433.4	445.6	173.3	272.3	168.5	103.9	-12.2	24.7	443.2
III	13.7	77.2	-63.5	468.5	444.8	443.8	169.5	274.3	169.7	104.6	1.0	23.8	444.6
IV ᵖ	17.9	80.0	-62.1	....	....	....	....	....	170.4	....	....	-7.2	23.6

² Consists mainly of employer contributions for social insurance and to private pension, health, and welfare funds.
³ With inventory valuation adjustment.

Source: Department of Commerce, Bureau of Economic Analysis.

TABLE B-26.—*Sources of personal income, 1959–93*

[Billions of dollars; quarterly data at seasonally adjusted annual rates]

| Year or quarter | Personal income | Wage and salary disbursements [1] |||||| Other labor income [1] | Proprietors' income with inventory valuation and capital consumption adjustments ||
| | | Total | Commodity-producing industries || Distributive industries | Service industries | Government | | Farm | Nonfarm |
			Total	Manufacturing						
1959	391.2	259.8	109.9	86.9	65.1	38.8	46.0	10.6	10.7	41.1
1960	409.2	272.8	113.4	89.8	68.6	41.7	49.2	11.2	11.2	40.6
1961	426.5	280.5	114.0	89.9	69.6	44.4	52.4	11.8	11.9	42.4
1962	453.4	299.3	122.2	96.8	73.3	47.6	56.3	13.0	11.9	44.5
1963	476.4	314.8	127.4	100.7	76.8	50.7	60.0	14.0	11.8	45.9
1964	510.7	337.7	136.0	107.3	82.0	54.9	64.9	15.7	10.6	49.8
1965	552.9	363.7	146.6	115.7	87.9	59.4	69.9	17.8	12.9	52.1
1966	601.7	400.3	161.6	128.2	95.1	65.3	78.3	19.9	14.0	55.3
1967	646.5	428.9	169.0	134.3	101.6	72.0	86.4	21.7	12.7	58.2
1968	709.9	471.9	184.1	146.0	110.8	80.4	96.6	25.2	12.7	62.4
1969	773.7	518.3	200.4	157.7	121.7	90.6	105.5	28.5	14.4	64.5
1970	831.0	551.5	203.7	158.4	131.2	99.4	117.1	32.5	14.6	65.3
1971	893.5	583.9	209.1	160.5	140.4	107.9	126.5	36.7	15.2	70.9
1972	980.5	638.7	228.2	175.6	153.3	119.7	137.4	43.0	19.1	78.3
1973	1,098.7	708.7	255.9	196.6	170.3	133.9	148.7	49.2	32.2	84.3
1974	1,205.7	772.6	276.5	211.8	186.8	148.6	160.9	56.5	25.5	89.8
1975	1,307.3	814.6	277.1	211.6	198.1	163.4	176.0	65.9	23.7	97.5
1976	1,446.3	899.5	309.7	238.0	219.5	181.6	188.6	79.7	18.3	114.6
1977	1,601.3	993.9	346.1	266.7	242.7	202.8	202.3	94.7	17.1	129.4
1978	1,807.9	1,120.7	392.6	300.1	274.9	233.7	219.4	110.1	21.5	146.2
1979	2,033.1	1,255.4	442.1	334.9	308.4	267.7	237.3	124.3	24.7	157.0
1980	2,265.4	1,376.6	471.9	355.7	336.4	306.9	261.4	139.8	11.5	160.3
1981	2,534.7	1,515.6	513.7	386.9	368.1	348.1	285.7	153.0	21.2	159.6
1982	2,690.9	1,593.3	513.5	384.3	385.8	386.5	307.5	165.4	13.5	157.3
1983	2,862.5	1,684.7	525.1	397.7	406.2	427.4	325.9	174.6	2.4	184.3
1984	3,154.6	1,849.8	580.8	439.8	445.4	475.8	347.8	184.7	21.3	214.7
1985	3,379.8	1,986.5	612.2	461.3	475.9	524.5	373.9	191.8	21.5	238.4
1986	3,590.4	2,105.4	628.5	473.8	501.7	579.5	395.7	200.7	22.3	261.5
1987	3,802.0	2,261.2	651.8	490.1	536.9	650.7	421.8	210.4	31.3	279.0
1988	4,075.9	2,443.0	699.1	524.5	575.3	719.6	449.0	230.5	30.9	293.4
1989	4,380.3	2,586.4	724.2	542.2	607.0	776.8	478.5	251.9	40.2	307.0
1990	4,673.8	2,745.0	745.7	555.6	635.1	848.3	515.9	274.3	41.9	321.4
1991	4,850.9	2,815.0	738.1	557.2	648.0	883.5	545.4	296.9	36.8	339.5
1992	5,144.9	2,973.1	756.5	577.6	682.0	967.0	567.5	322.7	43.7	370.6
1993 ᵖ	5,387.6	3,080.4	763.6	577.2	706.4	1,020.8	589.7	350.7	45.0	397.1
1982: IV	2,746.8	1,611.7	503.9	378.0	391.2	400.9	315.6	169.2	10.2	169.6
1983: IV	2,965.8	1,747.3	547.6	415.7	422.4	445.8	331.5	179.0	6.3	193.8
1984: IV	3,242.5	1,903.3	594.5	450.5	458.4	494.4	356.1	187.7	21.9	217.7
1985: IV	3,456.7	2,039.1	622.6	469.1	487.6	546.8	382.2	193.9	17.8	250.9
1986: IV	3,647.8	2,153.9	635.3	478.5	512.5	602.1	404.0	205.3	23.6	260.9
1987: IV	3,918.5	2,337.0	668.4	501.6	551.9	685.0	431.7	216.5	42.4	282.6
1988: IV	4,195.2	2,510.6	715.3	537.5	589.9	746.8	458.5	240.3	30.9	302.5
1989: IV	4,469.4	2,637.9	732.1	545.7	616.1	800.0	489.7	259.1	38.4	311.4
1990: I	4,585.6	2,689.1	740.6	549.7	624.7	821.5	502.3	268.0	49.9	317.6
II	4,648.6	2,739.1	748.2	557.5	634.4	843.5	513.0	271.5	42.5	318.9
III	4,701.9	2,770.6	749.1	558.4	640.2	861.4	519.9	276.2	31.6	323.9
IV	4,759.1	2,781.1	744.8	556.9	641.0	866.8	528.5	281.3	43.8	325.1
1991: I	4,783.9	2,782.0	735.3	551.0	639.8	866.1	540.8	287.1	37.2	326.6
II	4,833.4	2,800.9	733.3	552.0	645.8	876.8	545.0	293.3	42.6	337.1
III	4,858.6	2,823.4	739.3	559.3	651.0	886.9	546.2	300.1	29.8	344.4
IV	4,927.5	2,853.6	744.4	566.4	655.4	904.1	549.7	307.0	37.6	350.1
1992: I	5,017.8	2,892.2	741.3	564.0	663.5	928.1	559.3	313.4	45.6	361.2
II	5,093.8	2,933.6	750.0	571.2	672.2	944.6	566.9	319.9	44.9	366.2
III	5,139.8	2,970.7	751.6	573.3	682.5	966.8	569.7	326.0	36.8	371.3
IV	5,328.3	3,095.8	783.3	602.0	709.9	1,028.4	574.2	331.5	47.6	383.6
1993: I	5,254.7	2,974.3	740.7	559.7	682.9	966.6	584.1	338.5	55.7	388.4
II	5,373.2	3,082.7	765.1	580.3	709.1	1,022.2	586.3	346.6	47.0	392.4
III	5,412.7	3,115.4	769.4	581.5	714.4	1,038.8	592.8	354.7	24.8	397.6
IV ᵖ	5,509.8	3,149.2	779.0	587.5	719.2	1,055.5	595.5	362.9	52.4	410.1

[1] The total of wage and salary disbursements and other labor income differs from compensation of employees in Table B-25 in that it excludes employer contributions for social insurance and the excess of wage accruals over wage disbursements.

See next page for continuation of table.

TABLE B-26.—*Sources of personal income, 1959–93*—Continued

[Billions of dollars; quarterly data at seasonally adjusted annual rates]

| Year or quarter | Rental income of persons with capital consumption adjustment | Personal dividend income | Personal interest income | Transfer payments to persons ||||||| Less: Personal contributions for social insurance | Nonfarm personal income [2] |
				Total	Old-age, survivors, disability, and health insurance benefits	Government unemployment insurance benefits	Veterans benefits	Government employees retirement benefits	Aid to families with dependent children (AFDC)	Other		
1959	14.7	12.7	22.7	27.0	10.2	2.8	4.6	2.8	0.9	5.7	7.9	376.7
1960	15.3	13.4	25.0	28.8	11.1	3.0	4.6	3.1	1.0	6.1	9.3	393.7
1961	15.8	14.0	26.9	32.8	12.6	4.3	5.0	3.4	1.1	6.5	9.7	410.4
1962	16.5	15.0	29.3	34.1	14.3	3.1	4.7	3.7	1.3	7.0	10.3	437.0
1963	17.1	16.1	32.4	36.2	15.2	3.0	4.8	4.2	1.4	7.6	11.8	460.0
1964	17.3	18.0	36.1	37.9	16.0	2.7	4.7	4.7	1.5	8.2	12.6	495.3
1965	18.0	20.2	40.3	41.1	18.1	2.3	4.9	5.2	1.7	9.0	13.3	534.9
1966	18.5	20.9	44.9	45.7	20.8	1.9	4.9	6.1	1.9	10.3	17.8	582.4
1967	19.4	22.1	49.5	54.6	25.5	2.2	5.6	6.9	2.3	12.2	20.6	628.3
1968	18.2	24.5	54.6	63.2	30.2	2.1	5.9	7.6	2.8	14.5	22.9	691.4
1969	18.0	25.1	60.8	70.3	32.9	2.2	6.7	8.7	3.5	16.2	26.2	753.1
1970	17.8	23.5	69.2	84.6	38.5	4.0	7.7	10.2	4.8	19.4	27.9	809.8
1971	18.2	23.5	75.7	100.1	44.5	5.8	8.8	11.8	6.2	23.0	30.7	871.5
1972	16.8	25.5	81.8	111.8	49.6	5.7	9.7	13.8	6.9	26.1	34.5	954.2
1973	17.3	27.7	94.1	127.9	60.4	4.4	10.4	16.0	7.2	29.5	42.6	1,058.1
1974	15.8	29.6	112.4	151.3	70.1	6.8	11.8	19.0	7.9	35.7	47.9	1,170.2
1975	13.5	29.2	123.0	190.2	81.4	17.6	14.5	22.7	9.2	44.7	50.4	1,272.5
1976	12.1	34.7	134.6	208.3	92.9	15.8	14.4	26.1	10.1	49.1	55.5	1,415.1
1977	9.0	39.4	155.7	223.3	104.9	12.7	13.8	29.0	10.6	52.4	61.2	1,569.9
1978	8.9	44.2	184.5	241.6	116.2	9.7	13.9	32.7	10.7	58.4	69.8	1,770.3
1979	8.4	50.4	223.2	270.7	131.8	9.8	14.4	36.9	11.0	66.8	81.0	1,989.3
1980	13.2	57.1	274.0	321.5	154.2	16.1	15.0	43.0	12.4	80.8	88.6	2,231.6
1981	20.8	66.9	336.1	365.9	182.0	15.9	16.1	49.4	13.0	89.7	104.5	2,488.5
1982	21.9	67.1	376.8	408.1	204.5	25.2	16.4	54.6	13.3	94.1	112.3	2,649.8
1983	22.1	77.8	397.5	438.9	221.7	26.3	16.6	58.0	14.2	102.1	119.7	2,832.6
1984	23.3	78.8	461.9	452.9	235.7	15.8	16.4	60.9	14.8	109.2	132.8	3,106.1
1985	18.7	87.9	498.1	485.9	253.4	15.7	16.7	66.6	15.4	118.1	149.1	3,333.2
1986	8.7	104.7	531.7	517.8	269.2	16.3	16.7	70.7	16.4	128.5	162.1	3,545.6
1987	3.2	100.4	548.1	542.2	282.9	14.5	16.6	76.0	16.7	135.5	173.6	3,749.4
1988	4.3	108.4	583.2	576.7	300.4	13.4	16.9	82.2	17.3	146.5	194.5	4,023.9
1989	−13.5	126.5	628.9	625.0	325.1	14.4	17.3	87.5	18.0	162.6	211.4	4,318.0
1990	−14.2	144.4	698.2	687.6	352.0	19.0	17.8	94.5	19.8	184.5	224.9	4,608.6
1991	−12.8	127.9	715.6	769.9	382.3	26.7	18.3	102.0	22.0	218.5	237.8	4,792.0
1992	−8.9	140.4	694.3	858.4	413.9	39.2	19.3	108.3	23.3	254.4	249.3	5,080.1
1993 *p*	13.0	158.3	695.8	911.6	438.2	34.0	20.0	115.4	23.9	280.0	264.3	5,320.3
1982: IV	24.1	69.4	373.6	432.2	216.4	31.8	16.6	56.1	13.6	97.6	113.3	2,708.5
1983: IV	22.2	80.6	418.7	441.3	226.7	19.9	16.5	59.5	14.5	104.2	123.4	2,932.0
1984: IV	24.3	79.3	485.4	458.5	241.3	15.6	16.4	58.0	14.8	112.5	135.6	3,193.8
1985: IV	14.0	92.7	507.5	493.6	256.7	15.3	16.5	68.0	15.7	121.3	152.8	3,414.9
1986: IV	4.7	105.6	532.6	526.6	273.3	16.7	16.4	72.4	16.7	131.1	165.4	3,602.3
1987: IV	6.8	100.1	562.3	548.5	285.8	13.4	16.5	77.7	16.7	138.3	177.7	3,854.9
1988: IV	2.8	113.8	608.9	584.8	303.8	13.0	16.8	83.0	17.5	150.6	199.5	4,142.9
1989: IV	−21.6	132.9	681.2	644.8	334.4	15.6	17.3	89.3	18.4	169.9	214.7	4,408.5
1990: I	−15.9	141.2	686.9	670.4	348.1	17.1	18.0	92.8	19.1	175.2	221.6	4,512.7
II	−16.4	145.6	692.8	677.7	348.7	17.7	17.8	93.7	19.6	180.2	223.1	4,582.7
III	−13.3	146.6	702.8	690.4	352.7	19.2	17.7	94.9	20.0	185.9	227.0	4,647.0
IV	−11.1	144.4	710.3	712.0	358.6	22.0	17.8	96.5	20.5	196.6	227.9	4,692.2
1991: I	−11.7	136.6	715.4	745.0	374.5	24.1	18.1	101.6	21.1	205.6	234.4	4,724.0
II	−11.9	126.7	720.0	761.4	379.1	27.1	18.6	101.2	21.8	213.6	236.7	4,768.4
III	−16.3	123.9	717.3	775.4	384.3	26.4	18.3	102.1	22.2	222.0	239.2	4,807.2
IV	−11.2	124.3	709.6	797.6	391.3	29.3	18.3	103.1	22.7	232.9	240.8	4,868.5
1992: I	−8.7	128.2	694.4	837.7	406.3	39.1	20.5	106.7	22.9	242.2	246.2	4,950.8
II	−7.2	136.0	696.0	852.4	412.0	40.4	18.9	107.7	23.2	250.1	248.1	5,027.7
III	−18.5	144.9	692.2	866.1	416.6	39.7	18.8	108.4	23.5	259.2	249.8	5,082.0
IV	−1.2	152.3	694.5	877.4	420.8	37.8	19.0	110.2	23.5	266.2	253.3	5,259.8
1993: I	7.5	157.0	695.4	894.4	433.1	34.5	20.0	112.8	23.6	270.4	256.6	5,177.2
II	12.7	157.8	693.1	905.5	435.0	34.4	20.2	114.6	24.1	277.2	264.5	5,303.8
III	13.7	159.0	695.7	918.5	439.4	35.1	20.1	116.4	24.0	283.5	266.8	5,365.4
IV *p*	17.9	159.4	699.2	927.9	445.4	32.0	19.7	117.9	24.0	289.0	269.2	5,434.7

[2] Personal income exclusive of the farm component of wages and salaries, other labor income, proprietors' income with inventory valuation and capital consumption adjustments, and net interest.

Note.—The industry classification of wage and salary disbursements and proprietors' income is on an establishment basis and is based on the 1987 Standard Industrial Classification (SIC) beginning 1987 and on the 1972 SIC for earlier years shown.

Source: Department of Commerce, Bureau of Economic Analysis.

TABLE B-27.—Disposition of personal income, 1959–93

[Billions of dollars, except as noted; quarterly data at seasonally adjusted annual rates]

Year or quarter	Personal income	Less: Personal tax and nontax payments	Equals: Disposable personal income	Less: Personal outlays Total	Personal consumption expenditures	Interest paid by persons	Personal transfer payments to rest of the world (net)	Equals: Personal saving	Percent of disposable personal income [1] Personal outlays Total	Personal consumption expenditures	Personal saving
1959	391.2	44.5	346.7	324.7	318.1	6.1	0.4	22.0	93.7	91.8	6.3
1960	409.2	48.7	360.5	339.9	332.4	7.0	.5	20.6	94.3	92.2	5.7
1961	426.5	50.3	376.2	351.3	343.5	7.3	.5	24.9	93.4	91.3	6.6
1962	453.4	54.8	398.7	372.8	364.4	7.8	.5	25.9	93.5	91.4	6.5
1963	476.4	58.0	418.4	393.7	384.2	8.9	.6	24.6	94.1	91.8	5.9
1964	510.7	56.0	454.7	423.1	412.5	10.0	.7	31.6	93.1	90.7	6.9
1965	552.9	61.9	491.0	456.4	444.6	11.1	.8	34.6	93.0	90.5	7.0
1966	601.7	71.0	530.7	494.4	481.6	12.0	.8	36.3	93.2	90.7	6.8
1967	646.5	77.9	568.6	522.8	509.3	12.5	1.0	45.8	91.9	89.6	8.1
1968	709.9	92.1	617.8	573.9	559.1	13.8	1.0	43.9	92.9	90.5	7.1
1969	773.7	109.9	663.8	620.5	603.7	15.7	1.1	43.3	93.5	90.9	6.5
1970	831.0	109.0	722.0	664.5	646.5	16.8	1.2	57.5	92.0	89.5	8.0
1971	893.5	108.7	784.9	719.4	700.3	17.8	1.3	65.4	91.7	89.2	8.3
1972	980.5	132.0	848.5	788.7	767.8	19.6	1.3	59.7	93.0	90.5	7.0
1973	1,098.7	140.6	958.1	872.0	848.1	22.4	1.4	86.1	91.0	88.5	9.0
1974	1,205.7	159.1	1,046.5	953.1	927.7	24.2	1.2	93.4	91.1	88.6	8.9
1975	1,307.3	156.4	1,150.9	1,050.6	1,024.9	24.5	1.2	100.3	91.3	89.1	8.7
1976	1,446.3	182.3	1,264.0	1,170.9	1,143.1	26.7	1.2	93.0	92.6	90.4	7.4
1977	1,601.3	210.0	1,391.3	1,303.4	1,271.5	30.7	1.2	87.9	93.7	91.4	6.3
1978	1,807.9	240.1	1,567.8	1,460.0	1,421.2	37.5	1.3	107.8	93.1	90.7	6.9
1979	2,033.1	280.2	1,753.0	1,629.6	1,583.7	44.5	1.4	123.3	93.0	90.3	7.0
1980	2,265.4	312.4	1,952.9	1,799.1	1,748.1	49.4	1.6	153.8	92.1	89.5	7.9
1981	2,534.7	360.2	2,174.5	1,982.6	1,926.2	54.6	1.8	191.8	91.2	88.6	8.8
1982	2,690.9	371.4	2,319.6	2,120.1	2,059.2	58.8	2.1	199.5	91.4	88.8	8.6
1983	2,862.5	368.8	2,493.7	2,325.1	2,257.5	65.7	1.8	168.7	93.2	90.5	6.8
1984	3,154.6	395.1	2,759.5	2,537.5	2,460.3	75.0	2.3	222.0	92.0	89.2	8.0
1985	3,379.8	436.8	2,943.0	2,753.7	2,667.4	83.6	2.7	189.3	93.6	90.6	6.4
1986	3,590.4	459.0	3,131.5	2,944.0	2,850.6	90.9	2.5	187.5	94.0	91.0	6.0
1987	3,802.0	512.5	3,289.5	3,147.5	3,052.2	92.3	3.0	142.0	95.7	92.8	4.3
1988	4,075.9	527.7	3,548.2	3,392.5	3,296.1	93.7	2.7	155.7	95.6	92.9	4.4
1989	4,380.3	593.3	3,787.0	3,634.9	3,523.1	103.0	8.9	152.1	96.0	93.0	4.0
1990	4,673.8	623.3	4,050.5	3,880.6	3,761.2	109.3	10.1	170.0	95.8	92.9	4.2
1991	4,850.9	620.4	4,230.5	4,029.0	3,906.4	112.2	10.5	201.5	95.2	92.3	4.8
1992	5,144.9	644.8	4,500.2	4,261.5	4,139.9	111.1	10.4	238.7	94.7	92.0	5.3
1993 ᵖ	5,387.6	681.6	4,706.0	4,515.7	4,390.6	114.0	11.0	190.3	96.0	93.3	4.0
1982: IV	2,746.8	372.1	2,374.7	2,190.9	2,128.7	60.2	1.9	183.8	92.3	89.6	7.7
1983: IV	2,965.8	371.6	2,594.2	2,417.9	2,346.8	69.2	2.0	176.3	93.2	90.5	6.8
1984: IV	3,242.5	413.4	2,829.1	2,606.5	2,526.4	77.6	2.5	222.6	92.1	89.3	7.9
1985: IV	3,456.7	448.8	3,007.9	2,828.7	2,739.8	86.4	2.5	179.2	94.0	91.1	6.0
1986: IV	3,647.8	478.5	3,169.3	3,018.2	2,923.1	92.3	2.8	151.1	95.2	92.2	4.8
1987: IV	3,918.5	528.6	3,389.9	3,220.1	3,124.6	92.4	3.1	169.8	95.0	92.2	5.0
1988: IV	4,195.2	542.0	3,653.2	3,496.7	3,398.2	95.8	2.7	156.4	95.7	93.0	4.3
1989: IV	4,469.4	605.1	3,864.3	3,715.5	3,599.1	106.7	9.8	148.8	96.2	93.1	3.9
1990: I	4,585.6	611.9	3,973.7	3,797.2	3,679.3	108.0	9.9	176.5	95.6	92.6	4.4
II	4,648.6	627.4	4,021.2	3,845.6	3,727.0	108.4	10.1	175.7	95.6	92.7	4.4
III	4,701.9	628.5	4,073.4	3,921.9	3,801.7	109.8	10.3	151.6	96.3	93.3	3.7
IV	4,759.1	625.2	4,133.9	3,957.7	3,836.6	110.9	10.2	176.2	95.7	92.8	4.3
1991: I	4,783.9	616.4	4,167.5	3,966.0	3,843.6	111.9	10.4	201.5	95.2	92.2	4.8
II	4,833.4	616.6	4,216.8	4,010.7	3,887.8	112.5	10.4	206.0	95.1	92.2	4.9
III	4,858.8	619.7	4,239.1	4,052.3	3,929.8	112.2	10.3	186.8	95.6	92.7	4.4
IV	4,927.5	628.8	4,298.8	4,087.0	3,964.1	112.1	10.8	211.7	95.1	92.2	4.9
1992: I	5,017.8	630.9	4,386.9	4,169.4	4,046.5	111.9	11.1	217.5	95.0	92.2	5.0
II	5,093.8	634.6	4,459.2	4,221.3	4,099.9	110.9	10.5	237.9	94.7	91.9	5.3
III	5,139.8	642.8	4,497.0	4,277.3	4,157.1	110.5	9.7	219.6	95.1	92.4	4.9
IV	5,328.3	670.7	4,657.6	4,377.9	4,256.2	111.3	10.5	279.7	94.0	91.4	6.0
1993: I	5,254.7	657.1	4,597.5	4,419.7	4,296.2	112.5	11.0	177.9	96.1	93.4	3.9
II	5,373.2	681.0	4,692.2	4,483.6	4,359.9	112.7	11.0	208.7	95.6	92.9	4.4
III	5,412.7	689.0	4,723.7	4,544.0	4,419.1	114.1	10.8	179.7	96.2	93.6	3.8
IV ᵖ	5,509.8	699.1	4,810.7	4,615.5	4,487.4	116.7	11.4	195.2	95.9	93.3	4.1

[1] Percents based on data in millions of dollars.

Source: Department of Commerce, Bureau of Economic Analysis.

TABLE B-28.—*Total and per capita disposable personal income and personal consumption expenditures in current and 1987 dollars, 1959–93*

[Quarterly data at seasonally adjusted annual rates, except as noted]

Year or quarter	Disposable personal income				Personal consumption expenditures				Population (thousands)[1]
	Total (billions of dollars)		Per capita (dollars)		Total (billions of dollars)		Per capita (dollars)		
	Current dollars	1987 dollars	Current dollars	1987 dollars	Current dollars	1987 dollars	Current dollars	1987 dollars	
1959	346.7	1,284.9	1,958	7,256	318.1	1,178.9	1,796	6,658	177,073
1960	360.5	1,313.0	1,994	7,264	332.4	1,210.8	1,839	6,698	180,760
1961	376.2	1,356.4	2,048	7,382	343.5	1,238.4	1,869	6,740	183,742
1962	398.7	1,414.8	2,137	7,583	364.4	1,293.3	1,953	6,931	186,590
1963	418.4	1,461.1	2,210	7,718	384.2	1,341.9	2,030	7,089	189,300
1964	454.7	1,562.2	2,369	8,140	412.5	1,417.2	2,149	7,384	191,927
1965	491.0	1,653.5	2,527	8,508	444.6	1,497.0	2,287	7,703	194,347
1966	530.7	1,734.3	2,699	8,822	481.6	1,573.8	2,450	8,005	196,599
1967	568.6	1,811.4	2,861	9,114	509.3	1,622.4	2,562	8,163	198,752
1968	617.8	1,886.8	3,077	9,399	559.1	1,707.5	2,785	8,506	200,745
1969	663.8	1,947.4	3,274	9,606	603.7	1,771.2	2,978	8,737	202,736
1970	722.0	2,025.3	3,521	9,875	646.5	1,813.5	3,152	8,842	205,089
1971	784.9	2,099.9	3,779	10,111	700.3	1,873.7	3,372	9,022	207,692
1972	848.5	2,186.2	4,042	10,414	767.8	1,978.4	3,658	9,425	209,924
1973	958.1	2,334.1	4,521	11,013	848.1	2,066.7	4,002	9,752	211,939
1974	1,046.5	2,317.0	4,893	10,832	927.7	2,053.8	4,337	9,602	213,898
1975	1,150.9	2,355.4	5,329	10,906	1,024.9	2,097.5	4,745	9,711	215,981
1976	1,264.0	2,440.9	5,796	11,192	1,143.1	2,207.3	5,241	10,121	218,086
1977	1,391.3	2,512.6	6,316	11,406	1,271.5	2,296.6	5,772	10,425	220,289
1978	1,567.8	2,638.4	7,042	11,851	1,421.2	2,391.8	6,384	10,744	222,629
1979	1,753.0	2,710.1	7,787	12,039	1,583.7	2,448.4	7,035	10,876	225,106
1980	1,952.9	2,733.6	8,576	12,005	1,748.1	2,447.1	7,677	10,746	227,715
1981	2,174.5	2,795.8	9,455	12,156	1,926.2	2,476.9	8,375	10,770	229,989
1982	2,319.6	2,820.4	9,989	12,146	2,059.2	2,503.7	8,868	10,782	232,201
1983	2,493.7	2,893.6	10,642	12,349	2,257.5	2,619.4	9,634	11,179	234,326
1984	2,759.5	3,080.1	11,673	13,029	2,460.3	2,746.1	10,408	11,617	236,393
1985	2,943.0	3,162.1	12,339	13,258	2,667.4	2,865.8	11,184	12,015	238,510
1986	3,131.5	3,261.9	13,010	13,552	2,850.6	2,969.1	11,843	12,336	240,691
1987	3,289.5	3,289.5	13,545	13,545	3,052.2	3,052.2	12,568	12,568	242,860
1988	3,548.2	3,404.3	14,477	13,890	3,296.1	3,162.4	13,448	12,903	245,093
1989	3,787.0	3,464.9	15,307	14,005	3,523.1	3,223.3	14,241	13,029	247,397
1990	4,050.5	3,524.5	16,205	14,101	3,761.2	3,272.6	15,048	13,093	249,951
1991	4,230.5	3,529.0	16,741	13,965	3,906.4	3,258.6	15,459	12,895	252,699
1992	4,500.2	3,632.5	17,615	14,219	4,139.9	3,341.8	16,205	13,081	255,472
1993 ᵖ	4,706.0	3,700.5	18,222	14,329	4,390.6	3,452.5	17,001	13,369	258,256
1982: IV	2,374.7	2,832.6	10,189	12,154	2,128.7	2,539.3	9,134	10,895	233,060
1983: IV	2,594.3	2,960.6	11,033	12,591	2,346.8	2,678.2	9,980	11,390	235,146
1984: IV	2,829.1	3,118.5	11,925	13,145	2,526.4	2,784.8	10,649	11,739	237,231
1985: IV	3,007.9	3,178.7	12,565	13,278	2,739.8	2,895.3	11,445	12,095	239,387
1986: IV	3,169.3	3,266.2	13,121	13,522	2,923.1	3,012.5	12,101	12,472	241,550
1987: IV	3,389.9	3,335.8	13,907	13,685	3,124.6	3,074.7	12,819	12,615	243,745
1988: IV	3,653.2	3,443.1	14,850	13,996	3,398.2	3,202.9	13,814	13,020	246,004
1989: IV	3,864.3	3,480.9	15,558	14,015	3,599.1	3,242.0	14,491	13,053	248,372
1990: I	3,973.7	3,525.6	15,963	14,163	3,679.3	3,264.4	14,781	13,114	248,927
II	4,021.2	3,529.8	16,114	14,144	3,727.0	3,271.6	14,935	13,110	249,552
III	4,073.4	3,523.5	16,275	14,078	3,801.7	3,288.4	15,189	13,138	250,291
IV	4,133.9	3,519.0	16,467	14,018	3,836.6	3,265.9	15,283	13,010	251,035
1991: I	4,167.5	3,515.9	16,560	13,971	3,843.6	3,242.7	15,273	12,885	251,659
II	4,216.8	3,532.5	16,712	14,000	3,887.8	3,256.9	15,409	12,908	252,312
III	4,239.1	3,524.2	16,752	13,927	3,929.8	3,267.1	15,530	12,911	253,048
IV	4,298.8	3,543.4	16,939	13,963	3,964.1	3,267.5	15,621	12,876	253,776
1992: I	4,386.9	3,580.1	17,245	14,073	4,046.5	3,302.3	15,906	12,981	254,392
II	4,459.2	3,607.5	17,481	14,142	4,099.9	3,316.8	16,072	13,002	255,090
III	4,497.0	3,624.8	17,577	14,169	4,157.1	3,350.9	16,249	13,098	255,836
IV	4,657.6	3,717.6	18,153	14,490	4,256.2	3,397.2	16,589	13,241	256,569
1993: I	4,597.5	3,642.6	17,876	14,163	4,296.2	3,403.8	16,704	13,234	257,197
II	4,692.2	3,694.4	18,196	14,326	4,359.9	3,432.7	16,907	13,312	257,872
III	4,723.7	3,708.7	18,265	14,341	4,419.1	3,469.6	17,088	13,416	258,612
IV ᵖ	4,810.7	3,756.4	18,549	14,484	4,487.4	3,503.9	17,303	13,511	259,343

[1] Population of the United States including Armed Forces overseas; includes Alaska and Hawaii beginning 1960. Annual data are averages of quarterly data. Quarterly data are averages for the period.

Source: Department of Commerce (Bureau of Economic Analysis and Bureau of the Census).

TABLE B-29.—*Gross saving and investment, 1959–93*

[Billions of dollars; quarterly data at seasonally adjusted annual rates]

Year or quarter	Gross saving							Gross investment				Statistical discrepancy
	Total	Gross private saving			Government surplus or deficit (−), national income and product accounts			Capital grants received by the United States (net)[2]	Total	Gross private domestic investment	Net foreign investment[3]	
		Total	Personal saving	Gross business saving[1]	Total	Federal	State and local					
1959	79.4	82.5	22.0	60.5	−3.1	−2.6	−0.5		77.6	78.8	−1.2	−1.8
1960	85.1	81.5	20.6	60.9	3.6	3.5	.0		82.0	78.7	3.2	−3.1
1961	84.4	87.4	24.9	62.5	−3.0	−2.6	−.4		82.2	77.9	4.3	−2.2
1962	92.8	95.8	25.9	69.9	−2.9	−3.4	.5		91.8	87.9	3.9	−1.0
1963	100.4	98.8	24.6	74.1	1.6	1.1	.4		98.4	93.4	5.0	−2.0
1964	110.0	111.5	31.6	80.0	−1.6	−2.6	1.0		109.3	101.7	7.5	−.7
1965	125.0	123.7	34.6	89.2	1.2	1.3	.0		124.2	118.0	6.2	−.7
1966	131.5	132.5	36.3	96.1	−1.0	−1.4	.5		134.3	130.4	3.9	2.8
1967	130.8	144.5	45.8	98.7	−13.7	−12.7	−1.1		131.6	128.0	3.5	.8
1968	141.7	146.4	43.8	102.5	−4.6	−4.7	.1		141.7	139.9	1.7	−.1
1969	159.5	149.5	43.3	106.2	10.0	8.5	1.5		157.0	155.2	1.8	−2.6
1970	155.2	165.8	57.5	108.2	−11.5	−13.3	1.8	0.9	155.2	150.3	4.9	.0
1971	173.7	192.2	65.4	126.8	−19.2	−21.7	2.5	.7	176.8	175.5	1.3	3.1
1972	201.7	204.9	59.7	145.1	−3.9	−17.3	13.4	.7	202.7	205.6	−2.9	1.1
1973	252.3	245.4	86.1	159.3	6.9	−6.6	13.4	0	251.8	243.1	8.7	−.5
1974	249.5	256.0	93.4	162.6	−4.5	−11.6	7.1	[4]−2.0	250.9	245.8	5.1	1.4
1975	241.4	306.3	100.3	206.0	−64.8	−69.4	4.6	0	247.4	226.0	21.4	6.0
1976	284.8	323.1	93.0	230.0	−38.3	−52.9	14.6	0	295.2	286.4	8.8	10.4
1977	338.2	355.0	87.9	267.1	−16.8	−42.4	25.6	0	349.1	358.3	−9.2	10.9
1978	415.7	412.8	107.8	305.0	2.9	−28.1	31.1	0	423.3	434.0	−10.7	7.6
1979	468.5	457.9	123.3	334.5	9.4	−15.7	25.1	1.1	482.2	480.2	2.0	13.8
1980	465.4	499.6	153.8	345.7	−35.3	−60.1	24.8	1.2	479.1	467.6	11.5	13.6
1981	556.6	585.9	191.8	394.1	−30.3	−58.8	28.5	1.1	567.5	558.0	9.5	10.9
1982	508.4	616.9	199.5	417.5	−108.6	−135.5	26.9	0	500.9	503.4	−2.5	−7.4
1983	501.6	641.3	168.7	472.7	−139.8	−180.1	40.3	0	511.7	546.7	−35.0	10.2
1984	633.9	742.7	222.0	520.7	−108.8	−166.9	58.1	0	624.9	718.9	−94.0	−9.0
1985	610.4	735.7	189.3	546.4	−125.3	−181.4	56.1	0	596.5	714.5	−118.1	−13.9
1986	574.6	721.4	187.5	533.9	−146.8	−201.0	54.3	0	575.9	717.6	−141.7	1.2
1987	619.0	730.7	142.0	588.7	−111.7	−151.8	40.1	0	594.2	749.3	−155.1	−24.8
1988	704.0	802.3	155.7	646.6	−98.3	−136.6	38.4	0	675.6	793.6	−118.0	−28.4
1989	741.8	819.4	152.1	667.3	−77.5	−122.3	44.8	0	742.9	832.3	−89.3	1.1
1990	722.7	861.1	170.0	691.2	−138.4	−163.5	25.1	0	730.4	808.9	−78.5	7.8
1991	733.7	929.9	201.5	728.4	−196.2	−203.4	7.3	0	743.3	736.9	6.4	9.6
1992	717.8	986.9	238.7	748.3	−269.1	−276.3	7.2	0	741.4	796.5	−55.1	23.6
1993 *p*			190.3		−223.7	−225.8	2.1	0		892.0		
1982: IV	458.5	615.4	183.8	431.6	−156.9	−183.4	26.5	0	448.4	464.2	−15.8	−10.1
1983: IV	542.4	678.7	176.3	502.4	−136.3	−184.6	48.3	0	556.3	614.8	−58.5	13.8
1984: IV	637.0	764.7	222.6	542.1	−127.8	−186.8	59.0	0	616.5	722.8	−106.3	−20.5
1985: IV	603.8	734.7	179.2	555.5	−130.9	−187.2	56.3	0	597.8	737.0	−139.1	−5.9
1986: IV	550.1	676.3	151.1	525.3	−126.2	−177.5	51.2	0	548.1	697.1	−149.0	−2.0
1987: IV	667.9	783.7	169.8	613.9	−115.8	−152.7	37.0	0	643.0	800.2	−157.1	−24.9
1988: IV	720.1	814.8	156.4	658.3	−94.7	−134.9	40.2	0	694.7	814.8	−120.1	−25.4
1989: IV	728.4	828.6	148.8	679.8	−100.2	−141.5	41.3	0	741.3	825.2	−84.0	12.8
1990: I	735.5	867.4	176.5	690.9	−131.9	−166.4	34.5	0	748.6	828.9	−80.3	13.1
II	765.9	888.5	175.7	712.9	−122.7	−152.0	29.3	0	764.0	837.8	−73.8	−1.8
III	705.5	825.5	151.6	673.9	−119.9	−144.6	24.7	0	720.4	812.5	−92.1	14.9
IV	683.8	863.1	176.2	686.9	−179.3	−191.0	11.7	0	688.7	756.4	−67.7	4.9
1991: I	780.3	919.4	201.5	717.9	−139.1	−145.2	6.1	0	780.5	729.1	51.4	.2
II	734.3	935.0	206.0	728.9	−200.7	−206.2	5.5	0	738.7	721.5	17.2	4.5
III	694.4	906.6	186.8	719.8	−212.2	−217.7	5.5	0	721.8	744.5	−22.8	27.3
IV	726.0	958.7	211.7	746.9	−232.6	−244.7	12.1	0	732.3	752.4	−20.2	6.2
1992: I	709.9	974.1	217.5	756.6	−264.2	−270.2	6.1	0	733.0	750.8	−17.7	23.1
II	715.5	987.7	237.9	749.8	−272.2	−279.9	7.8	0	739.1	799.7	−60.6	23.6
III	727.0	1,016.5	219.6	796.9	−289.5	−290.7	1.2	0	742.7	802.2	−59.4	15.7
IV	718.8	969.4	279.7	689.7	−250.6	−264.2	13.5	0	750.9	833.3	−82.4	32.1
1993: I	762.0	1,024.8	177.9	847.0	−262.8	−263.5	.8	0	796.5	874.1	−77.6	34.4
II	766.7	988.3	208.7	779.6	−221.5	−222.6	1.1	0	778.7	874.1	−95.4	12.0
III	774.3	988.7	179.7	809.0	−214.4	−212.7	−1.7	0	787.6	884.0	−96.4	13.3
IV *p*			195.2					0		935.8		

[1] Undistributed corporate profits with inventory valuation and capital consumption adjustments, corporate and noncorporate consumption of fixed capital, and private wage accruals less disbursements.
[2] Consists mainly of allocations of special drawing rights (SDRs).
[3] Net exports of goods and services plus net receipts of factor income from rest of the world less net transfers plus net capital grants received by the United States. See also Table B-21.
[4] Consists of a U.S. payment to India under the Agricultural Trade Development and Assistance Act. This payment is included in capital grants received by the United States, net.

Source: Department of Commerce, Bureau of Economic Analysis.

TABLE B-30.—*Personal saving, flow of funds accounts, 1946-93* [1]

[Billions of dollars; quarterly data at seasonally adjusted annual rates]

Year or quarter	Personal saving	Total	Checkable deposits and currency	Time and savings deposits	Money market fund shares	Government securities [2]	Corporate equities [3]	Other securities [4]	Insurance and pension reserves [5]	Other financial assets	Owner-occupied homes	Consumer durables	Non-corporate business assets [8]	Mortgage debt on nonfarm homes	Consumer credit	Other debt [8][9]
1946	17.2	19.4	5.6	6.3		-1.5	1.2	-0.8	5.1	3.6	5.8	1.5	0.1	4.1	2.9	2.5
1947	19.0	12.3	.0	3.5		.5	1.2	-.8	5.4	2.5	6.8	9.4	1.5	4.9	3.5	2.6
1948	24.9	8.7	-2.9	2.3		1.0	1.0	.2	5.3	2.0	9.3	10.2	7.0	4.8	3.1	2.6
1949	21.2	8.6	-2.0	2.6		.5	.8	-.3	5.6	1.4	8.5	10.9	2.2	4.2	3.1	1.7
1950	31.1	14.9	2.7	2.4		.9	.7	-.9	6.1	3.0	11.9	14.9	7.4	7.0	6.0	5.1
1951	35.7	19.2	4.6	4.8		-.7	1.9	.7	6.3	1.6	11.9	11.4	4.6	6.4	1.4	3.6
1952	38.7	30.1	1.6	7.4		7.4	1.5	-.1	8.5	3.8	11.6	8.7	2.8	6.4	5.2	2.9
1953	36.2	24.6	.9	8.2		3.7	1.1	.3	8.0	2.4	12.6	10.3	2.3	7.4	4.1	2.0
1954	27.6	20.8	2.1	9.1		.1	.8	-1.4	8.0	2.0	13.0	7.0	1.8	9.0	1.3	4.7
1955	36.0	28.1	1.2	8.5		6.4	1.2	.4	8.7	1.7	17.1	12.7	2.2	12.2	7.0	4.9
1956	38.9	32.0	1.9	9.3		4.5	2.1	1.2	9.7	3.4	16.0	8.8	.7	10.8	3.6	4.3
1957	38.5	29.6	-.4	11.8		3.7	1.6	1.4	9.7	1.9	13.6	7.9	1.8	8.6	2.6	3.2
1958	37.0	32.5	3.7	13.8		-2.7	1.9	.9	10.7	4.3	12.3	3.7	4.2	9.5	.3	6.0
1959	36.0	34.8	1.1	10.5		8.2	.7	.2	12.2	1.9	19.2	7.7	.9	12.9	7.7	6.0
1960	38.5	34.2	.9	12.0		2.0	.3	3.4	11.9	3.7	17.2	7.2	2.2	11.0	4.0	7.2
1961	38.3	36.0	-1.0	18.1		.8	1.1	.0	12.5	4.4	16.3	4.5	2.9	12.2	2.2	7.0
1962	44.8	40.5	-1.2	25.8		1.0	-1.4	.2	13.5	2.5	18.2	8.6	4.3	13.8	5.9	7.2
1963	49.3	45.9	4.2	25.9		-1.1	-1.1	1.2	14.5	2.1	20.5	11.9	4.7	16.2	8.5	9.1
1964	61.5	57.1	6.1	25.9		3.7	.0	1.2	17.1	3.2	22.1	15.1	4.4	16.8	9.5	10.9
1965	68.5	57.3	6.7	27.5		3.8	-1.5	-.1	17.8	3.2	21.6	20.2	8.4	16.8	10.1	12.1
1966	83.0	64.0	2.4	18.8		13.6	.0	4.9	20.2	4.1	19.0	23.2	7.9	12.7	5.9	12.5
1967	84.6	72.4	10.3	34.9		-2.6	-3.0	6.4	19.6	6.8	18.5	21.3	7.3	13.1	5.1	16.6
1968	82.7	69.0	9.5	30.3		1.2	-6.0	7.2	21.1	5.7	19.9	26.9	10.2	16.7	10.8	15.7
1969	82.6	70.6	-1.3	8.6		28.5	-11.1	10.8	23.3	11.8	19.9	26.2	11.7	17.4	9.9	18.6
1970	92.1	79.9	7.4	42.5		-7.5	.2	5.9	25.8	5.5	17.7	19.6	10.1	13.0	4.6	17.6
1971	104.4	107.6	13.5	65.8		-12.7	-11.2	3.7	30.3	18.3	27.8	25.4	15.1	26.3	14.0	31.2
1972	121.9	134.9	13.2	72.6		-2.1	-13.5	-2.8	50.4	17.0	36.7	34.3	18.1	39.3	19.0	43.8
1973	158.3	147.5	13.1	62.8		14.5	-12.2	7.4	41.8	20.1	40.2	40.6	23.2	43.6	22.7	26.9
1974	121.6	152.5	6.3	55.3	2.4	17.0	1.4	17.8	44.6	7.7	30.4	29.1	11.6	34.2	9.4	58.4
1975	150.2	177.2	6.2	79.6	1.3	12.7	2.4	-4.6	71.5	8.0	28.2	27.4	6.1	39.3	8.0	41.4
1976	171.1	211.4	15.6	104.2	.0	2.5	1.1	.5	60.3	27.2	44.8	41.5	4.0	62.0	22.9	45.7
1977	197.4	255.7	19.8	106.3	-.4	7.9	-6.0	16.5	80.3	31.3	65.9	51.5	16.3	93.0	36.7	62.2
1978	206.2	286.5	21.5	103.2	5.7	27.5	-10.2	6.0	94.3	38.5	78.5	56.8	23.1	109.9	45.1	83.7
1979	220.3	329.1	35.8	75.7	30.0	60.6	-20.3	1.8	103.5	42.0	75.2	50.4	32.0	116.2	38.3	111.8
1980	217.6	328.6	9.2	120.8	23.7	29.4	.7	-10.5	126.9	28.5	51.3	26.3	14.2	94.1	4.8	103.9
1981	248.0	324.8	36.2	67.5	87.0	37.4	-38.9	-8.6	126.7	17.5	50.5	27.3	27.5	69.6	16.9	95.7
1982	257.1	379.9	24.6	113.5	31.8	25.4	-16.9	-7.9	178.1	31.3	30.0	22.4	10.1	56.1	16.4	112.7
1983	314.8	496.9	22.5	196.8	-30.1	74.9	4.5	21.7	176.2	30.5	71.3	50.6	-11.8	117.1	48.9	126.3
1984	363.5	532.8	4.7	225.3	43.8	100.3	-44.7	-9.3	162.4	50.4	93.6	81.8	24.3	135.6	81.7	151.8
1985	390.3	625.1	28.6	116.6	3.7	77.8	-37.6	53.1	281.9	101.0	93.6	95.8	26.8	171.7	82.3	197.2
1986	463.7	586.1	97.5	90.3	38.2	-55.2	22.5	33.5	292.0	67.3	119.4	111.4	16.0	203.4	57.5	108.1
1987	363.8	502.4	-1.9	92.8	24.3	112.2	-27.5	31.4	220.9	50.2	123.3	102.9	12.3	240.9	32.9	103.4
1988	361.3	489.9	27.7	134.8	20.2	157.7	-87.1	5.5	165.4	65.6	126.5	112.6	7.4	219.0	50.1	106.1
1989	449.6	556.2	-.5	78.2	85.1	101.2	-94.5	-24.5	338.4	72.8	114.4	109.0	18.4	211.8	49.5	87.1
1990	435.3	483.3	12.3	34.0	44.7	135.1	21.3	26.2	183.8	26.0	98.5	90.0	4.6	176.7	13.4	51.1
1991	384.4	452.0	51.8	-103.9	24.5	-45.6	81.9	5.3	384.5	53.4	75.7	53.1	-23.5	165.5	-13.1	20.5
1992	441.4	499.4	140.2	-123.5	-3.8	9.4	189.1	34.5	243.2	10.3	94.0	67.7	-21.1	175.5	9.3	13.8
1991: I	484.4	543.0	37.3	-44.2	108.6	-55.2	131.5	56.4	433.7	-125.2	68.2	48.2	-18.0	166.7	-16.1	6.5
II	298.1	424.4	39.5	-61.6	-7.2	110.5	5.6	-7.8	195.5	149.9	70.6	49.8	-17.1	159.8	-5.1	74.8
III	410.4	415.9	114.7	-170.3	-17.8	-62.9	69.5	-63.0	470.0	75.6	78.9	60.0	-24.8	159.7	-20.4	-19.6
IV	344.6	424.8	15.7	-139.4	14.6	-174.9	121.0	35.7	438.8	113.3	85.0	54.5	-34.2	176.0	-10.7	20.2
1992: I	432.8	485.1	118.7	-72.6	34.6	116.2	132.4	-13.1	162.8	6.2	86.7	60.3	-13.6	216.0	-9.8	-20.6
II	419.0	446.3	74.7	-160.4	18.6	74.4	171.2	9.7	217.1	41.0	96.5	59.5	-8.7	111.1	-14.7	78.3
III	412.0	524.7	211.8	-142.8	-28.4	-88.1	256.3	16.0	305.8	-6.0	72.0	61.6	-41.6	202.8	13.5	-11.6
IV	501.9	541.7	155.5	-118.0	-40.0	-64.8	196.6	125.5	287.2	-.3	120.9	89.2	-20.2	172.2	48.2	9.3
1993: I	276.3	249.1	6.0	-214.0	-49.7	23.1	172.0	-155.8	392.1	75.4	106.1	78.8	-9.2	127.8	19.2	1.5
II	544.3	562.8	119.8	-36.4	60.7	-70.5	248.3	-87.7	240.8	87.8	103.1	95.0	-7.7	175.6	22.9	10.3
III	390.7	563.4	123.7	-132.6	47.1	-119.7	351.4	-39.5	312.5	20.6	105.5	94.1	-17.1	229.1	60.8	65.2

[1] Saving by households, nonprofit institutions, farms, and other noncorporate business.
[2] Consists of U.S. savings bonds, other U.S. Treasury securities, U.S. Government agency securities and government sponsored enterprise securities, federally-related mortgage pool securities, and State and local obligations.
[3] Includes mutual fund shares.
[4] Corporate and foreign bonds and open-market paper.
[5] Private life insurance reserves, private insured and noninsured pension reserves, and government insurance and pension reserves.
[6] Consists of security credit, mortgages, accident and health insurance reserves, nonlife insurance claims, and investment in bank personal trusts for households, and of consumer credit, equity in government-sponsored enterprises, and nonlife insurance claims for noncorporate business.
[7] Purchases of physical assets less depreciation.
[8] Includes data for corporate farms.
[9] Other debt consists of security credit, U.S. Government and policy loans, and noncorporate business debt.

Source: Board of Governors of the Federal Reserve System.

303

TABLE B-31.—*Median money income (in 1992 dollars) and poverty status of families and persons, by race, selected years, 1971–92*

Year	Families [1]					Persons below poverty level		Median money income (in 1992 dollars) of persons 15 years old and over with income [2][3]			
	Number (millions)	Median money income (in 1992 dollars) [2]	Below poverty level					Males		Females	
			Total		Female householder		Number (millions)	Percent	All persons	Year-round full-time workers	All persons	Year-round full-time workers
			Number (millions)	Percent	Number (millions)	Percent						

ALL RACES

1971	53.3	$33,480	5.3	10.0	2.1	33.9	25.6	12.5	$22,471	$31,351	$7,839	$18,558
1973	55.1	35,821	4.8	8.8	2.2	32.2	23.0	11.1	23,946	34,088	8,311	19,285
1975 [4]	56.2	34,249	5.5	9.7	2.4	32.5	25.9	12.3	22,101	32,289	8,450	19,270
1977	57.2	35,539	5.3	9.3	2.6	31.7	24.7	11.6	22,472	33,454	8,749	19,567
1978	57.8	36,665	5.3	9.1	2.7	31.4	24.5	11.4	22,729	33,385	8,455	20,039
1979 [5]	59.6	37,136	5.5	9.2	2.6	30.4	26.1	11.7	22,332	33,139	8,251	19,966
1980	60.3	35,839	6.2	10.3	3.0	32.7	29.3	13.0	21,360	32,685	8,387	19,760
1981	61.0	34,862	6.9	11.2	3.3	34.6	31.8	14.0	20,980	32,221	8,499	19,398
1982	61.4	34,390	7.5	12.2	3.4	36.3	34.4	15.0	20,473	31,780	8,640	20,051
1983 [4]	62.0	34,757	7.6	12.3	3.6	36.0	35.3	15.2	20,652	31,706	9,022	20,396
1984	62.7	35,693	7.3	11.6	3.5	34.5	33.7	14.4	21,065	32,413	9,274	20,825
1985	63.6	36,164	7.2	11.4	3.5	34.0	33.1	14.0	21,268	32,596	9,410	21,191
1986	64.5	37,709	7.0	10.9	3.6	34.6	32.4	13.6	21,908	33,147	9,742	21,561
1987 [4]	65.2	38,249	7.0	10.7	3.7	34.2	32.2	13.4	21,966	32,952	10,245	21,692
1988	65.8	38,177	6.9	10.4	3.6	33.4	31.7	13.0	22,424	32,427	10,536	21,994
1989	66.1	38,710	6.8	10.3	3.5	32.2	31.5	12.8	22,508	32,155	10,889	22,219
1990	66.3	37,950	7.1	10.7	3.8	33.4	33.6	13.5	21,784	31,108	10,810	22,103
1991	67.2	37,021	7.7	11.5	4.2	35.6	35.7	14.2	21,085	31,244	10,791	21,885
1992	68.1	36,812	8.0	11.7	4.2	34.9	36.9	14.5	20,654	31,012	10,774	22,167

WHITE

1971	47.6	34,740	3.8	7.9	1.2	26.5	17.8	9.9	23,558	32,233	7,969	18,773
1973	48.9	37,438	3.2	6.6	1.2	24.5	15.1	8.4	25,126	35,075	8,391	19,612
1975 [4]	49.9	35,619	3.8	7.7	1.4	25.9	17.8	9.7	23,217	33,035	8,538	19,315
1977	50.5	37,162	3.5	7.0	1.4	24.0	16.4	8.9	23,538	34,138	8,882	19,691
1978	50.9	38,178	3.5	6.9	1.3	23.5	16.3	8.7	23,805	34,005	8,557	20,228
1979 [5]	52.2	38,751	3.6	6.9	1.4	22.3	17.2	9.0	23,330	34,097	8,329	20,141
1980	52.7	37,341	4.2	8.0	1.6	25.7	19.7	10.2	22,721	33,617	8,433	19,951
1981	53.3	36,620	4.7	8.8	1.8	27.4	21.6	11.1	22,261	32,978	8,594	19,721
1982	53.4	36,107	5.1	9.6	1.8	27.9	23.5	12.0	21,644	32,627	8,757	20,321
1983 [4]	53.9	36,395	5.2	9.7	1.9	28.3	24.0	12.1	21,727	32,559	9,180	20,675
1984	54.4	37,385	4.9	9.1	1.9	27.1	23.0	11.5	22,236	33,523	9,383	21,031
1985	55.0	38,011	5.0	9.1	2.0	27.4	22.9	11.4	22,311	33,501	9,593	21,491
1986	55.7	39,439	4.8	8.6	2.0	28.2	22.2	11.0	23,119	34,073	9,934	21,891
1987 [4]	56.1	39,997	4.6	8.1	2.0	26.9	21.2	10.4	23,348	33,720	10,506	22,094
1988	56.5	40,222	4.5	7.9	1.9	26.5	20.7	10.1	23,671	33,518	10,796	22,323
1989	56.6	40,704	4.4	7.8	1.9	25.4	20.8	10.0	23,605	33,572	11,102	22,483
1990	56.8	39,626	4.6	8.1	2.0	26.8	22.3	10.7	22,725	32,290	11,075	22,370
1991	57.2	38,920	5.0	8.8	2.2	28.4	23.7	11.3	22,039	31,885	11,044	22,204
1992	57.9	38,909	5.2	8.9	2.2	28.1	24.5	11.6	21,645	31,737	11,036	22,423

BLACK

1971	5.2	20,964	1.5	28.8	.9	53.5	7.4	32.5	14,050	22,041	6,982	16,576
1973	5.4	21,607	1.5	28.1	1.0	52.7	7.4	31.4	15,198	23,640	7,574	16,631
1975 [4]	5.6	21,916	1.5	27.1	1.0	50.1	7.5	31.3	13,880	24,585	7,756	18,454
1977	5.8	21,229	1.6	28.2	1.2	51.0	7.7	31.3	13,968	23,536	7,670	18,403
1978	5.9	22,612	1.6	27.5	1.2	50.6	7.6	30.6	14,261	26,044	7,705	18,748
1979 [5]	6.2	21,944	1.7	27.8	1.2	49.4	8.1	31.0	14,441	24,573	7,580	18,455
1980	6.3	21,606	1.8	28.9	1.3	49.4	8.6	32.5	13,653	23,653	7,808	18,607
1981	6.4	20,657	2.0	30.8	1.4	52.9	9.2	34.2	13,237	23,332	7,635	17,811
1982	6.5	19,956	2.2	33.0	1.5	56.2	9.7	35.6	12,970	23,173	7,724	18,163
1983 [4]	6.7	20,511	2.2	32.3	1.5	53.7	9.9	35.7	12,706	23,116	7,845	18,312
1984	6.8	20,837	2.1	30.9	1.5	51.7	9.5	33.8	12,758	22,879	8,323	18,953
1985	6.9	21,887	2.0	28.7	1.5	50.5	8.9	31.3	14,040	23,432	8,185	19,024
1986	7.1	22,535	2.0	28.0	1.5	50.1	9.0	31.1	13,853	24,023	8,405	19,156
1987 [4]	7.2	22,732	2.1	29.4	1.6	51.1	9.5	32.4	13,851	24,110	8,582	19,733
1988	7.4	22,924	2.1	28.2	1.6	49.0	9.4	31.3	14,284	24,569	8,716	20,004
1989	7.5	22,866	2.1	27.8	1.5	46.5	9.3	30.7	14,266	23,426	8,910	20,220
1990	7.5	22,997	2.2	29.3	1.6	48.1	9.8	31.9	13,813	23,059	8,940	19,906
1991	7.7	22,197	2.3	30.4	1.8	51.2	10.2	32.7	13,352	23,309	9,081	19,710
1992	7.9	21,161	2.4	30.9	1.8	49.8	10.6	33.3	12,754	22,942	8,857	20,299

[1] The term "family" refers to a group of two or more persons related by birth, marriage, or adoption and residing together; all such persons are considered members of the same family. Beginning 1979, based on householder concept and restricted to primary families.
[2] Current dollar median money income deflated by CPI-U-X1.
[3] Prior to 1979, data are for persons 14 years and over.
[4] Based on revised methodology; comparable with succeeding years.
[5] Based on 1980 census population controls; comparable with succeeding years.

Note.—Poverty rates (percent of persons below poverty level) for all races for years not shown above are: 1959, 22.4; 1960, 22.2; 1961, 21.9; 1962, 21.0; 1963, 19.5; 1964, 19.0; 1965, 17.3; 1966, 14.7; 1967, 14.2; 1968, 12.8; 1969, 12.1; 1970, 12.6; 1972, 11.9; 1974, 11.2; and 1976, 11.8.
Poverty thresholds are updated each year to reflect changes in the consumer price index (CPI-U).
For details see "Current Population Reports," Series P-60, Nos. 184 and 185.

Source: Department of Commerce, Bureau of the Census.

POPULATION, EMPLOYMENT, WAGES, AND PRODUCTIVITY

TABLE B-32.—*Population by age group, 1929–93*

[Thousands of persons]

July 1	Total	Age (years)					
		Under 5	5–15	16–19	20–24	25–44	45–64	65 and over
1929	121,767	11,734	26,800	9,127	10,694	35,862	21,076	6,474
1933	125,579	10,612	26,897	9,302	11,152	37,319	22,933	7,363
1939	130,880	10,418	25,179	9,822	11,519	39,354	25,823	8,764
1940	132,122	10,579	24,811	9,895	11,690	39,868	26,249	9,031
1941	133,402	10,850	24,516	9,840	11,807	40,383	26,718	9,288
1942	134,860	11,301	24,231	9,730	11,955	40,861	27,196	9,584
1943	136,739	12,016	24,093	9,607	12,064	41,420	27,671	9,867
1944	138,397	12,524	23,949	9,561	12,062	42,016	28,138	10,147
1945	139,928	12,979	23,907	9,361	12,036	42,521	28,630	10,494
1946	141,389	13,244	24,103	9,119	12,004	43,027	29,064	10,828
1947	144,126	14,406	24,468	9,097	11,814	43,657	29,498	11,185
1948	146,631	14,919	25,209	8,952	11,794	44,288	29,931	11,538
1949	149,188	15,607	25,852	8,788	11,700	44,916	30,405	11,921
1950	152,271	16,410	26,721	8,542	11,680	45,672	30,849	12,397
1951	154,878	17,333	27,279	8,446	11,552	46,103	31,362	12,803
1952	157,553	17,312	28,894	8,414	11,350	46,495	31,884	13,203
1953	160,184	17,638	30,227	8,460	11,062	46,786	32,394	13,617
1954	163,026	18,057	31,480	8,637	10,832	47,001	32,942	14,076
1955	165,931	18,566	32,682	8,744	10,714	47,194	33,506	14,525
1956	168,903	19,003	33,994	8,916	10,616	47,379	34,057	14,938
1957	171,984	19,494	35,272	9,195	10,603	47,440	34,591	15,388
1958	174,882	19,887	36,445	9,543	10,756	47,337	35,109	15,806
1959	177,830	20,175	37,368	10,215	10,969	47,192	35,663	16,248
1960	180,671	20,341	38,494	10,683	11,134	47,140	36,203	16,675
1961	183,691	20,522	39,765	11,025	11,483	47,084	36,722	17,089
1962	186,538	20,469	41,205	11,180	11,959	47,013	37,255	17,457
1963	189,242	20,342	41,626	12,007	12,714	46,994	37,782	17,778
1964	191,889	20,165	42,297	12,736	13,269	46,958	38,338	18,127
1965	194,303	19,824	42,938	13,516	13,746	46,912	38,916	18,451
1966	196,560	19,208	43,702	14,311	14,050	47,001	39,534	18,755
1967	198,712	18,563	44,244	14,200	15,248	47,194	40,193	19,071
1968	200,706	17,913	44,622	14,452	15,786	47,721	40,846	19,365
1969	202,677	17,376	44,840	14,800	16,480	48,064	41,437	19,680
1970	205,052	17,166	44,816	15,289	17,202	48,473	41,999	20,107
1971	207,661	17,244	44,591	15,688	18,159	48,936	42,482	20,561
1972	209,896	17,101	44,203	16,039	18,153	50,482	42,898	21,020
1973	211,909	16,851	43,582	16,446	18,521	51,749	43,235	21,525
1974	213,854	16,487	42,989	16,769	18,975	53,051	43,522	22,061
1975	215,973	16,121	42,508	17,017	19,527	54,302	43,801	22,696
1976	218,035	15,617	42,099	17,194	19,986	55,852	44,008	23,278
1977	220,239	15,564	41,298	17,276	20,499	57,561	44,150	23,892
1978	222,585	15,735	40,428	17,288	20,946	59,400	44,286	24,502
1979	225,055	16,063	39,552	17,242	21,297	61,379	44,390	25,134
1980	227,726	16,451	38,838	17,167	21,590	63,470	44,504	25,707
1981	229,966	16,893	38,144	16,812	21,869	65,528	44,500	26,221
1982	232,188	17,228	37,784	16,332	21,902	67,692	44,462	26,787
1983	234,307	17,547	37,526	15,823	21,844	69,733	44,474	27,361
1984	236,348	17,695	37,461	15,295	21,737	71,735	44,547	27,878
1985	238,466	17,842	37,450	15,005	21,478	73,673	44,602	28,416
1986	240,651	17,963	37,404	15,024	20,942	75,651	44,660	29,008
1987	242,804	18,052	37,333	15,215	20,385	77,338	44,854	29,626
1988	245,021	18,195	37,593	15,198	19,846	78,595	45,471	30,124
1989	247,342	18,508	37,972	14,913	19,442	79,943	45,882	30,682
1990	249,900	18,850	38,590	14,444	19,302	81,200	46,287	31,228
1991	252,671	19,204	39,201	13,903	19,352	82,488	46,759	31,764
1992	255,462	19,512	39,898	13,644	19,176	82,594	48,352	32,285
1993	258,233							

Note.—Includes Armed Forces overseas beginning 1940. Includes Alaska and Hawaii beginning 1950. All estimates are consistent with decennial census enumerations.

Source: Department of Commerce, Bureau of the Census.

TABLE B-33.—*Population and the labor force, 1929–93*

[Monthly data seasonally adjusted, except as noted]

Year or month	Civilian noninstitutional population [1]	Resident Armed Forces [1]	Labor force including resident Armed Forces	Employment including resident Armed Forces	Civilian labor force Total	Employment Total	Employment Agricultural	Employment Nonagricultural	Unemployment	Unemployment rate All workers [2]	Unemployment rate Civilian workers [3]	Civilian labor force participation rate [4]	Civilian employment/ population ratio [5]
				Thousands of persons 14 years of age and over							Percent		
1929					49,180	47,630	10,450	37,180	1,550		3.2		
1933					51,590	38,760	10,090	28,670	12,830		24.9		
1939					55,230	45,750	9,610	36,140	9,480		17.2		
1940	99,840				55,640	47,520	9,540	37,980	8,120		14.6	55.7	47.6
1941	99,900				55,910	50,350	9,100	41,250	5,560		9.9	56.0	50.4
1942	98,640				56,410	53,750	9,250	44,500	2,660		4.7	57.2	54.5
1943	94,640				55,540	54,470	9,080	45,390	1,070		1.9	58.7	57.6
1944	93,220				54,630	53,960	8,950	45,010	670		1.2	58.6	57.9
1945	94,090				53,860	52,820	8,580	44,240	1,040		1.9	57.2	56.1
1946	103,070				57,520	55,250	8,320	46,930	2,270		3.9	55.8	53.6
1947	106,018				60,168	57,812	8,256	49,557	2,356		3.9	56.8	54.5
				Thousands of persons 16 years of age and over									
1947	101,827				59,350	57,038	7,890	49,148	2,311		3.9	58.3	56.0
1948	103,068				60,621	58,343	7,629	50,714	2,276		3.8	58.8	56.6
1949	103,994				61,286	57,651	7,658	49,993	3,637		5.9	58.9	55.4
1950	104,995	1,169	63,377	60,087	62,208	58,918	7,160	51,758	3,288	5.2	5.3	59.2	56.1
1951	104,621	2,143	64,160	62,104	62,017	59,961	6,726	53,235	2,055	3.2	3.3	59.2	57.3
1952	105,231	2,386	64,524	62,636	62,138	60,250	6,500	53,749	1,883	2.9	3.0	59.0	57.3
1953 [6]	107,056	2,231	65,246	63,410	63,015	61,179	6,260	54,919	1,834	2.8	2.9	58.9	57.1
1954	108,321	2,142	65,785	62,251	63,643	60,109	6,205	53,904	3,532	5.4	5.5	58.8	55.5
1955	109,683	2,064	67,087	64,234	65,023	62,170	6,450	55,722	2,852	4.3	4.4	59.3	56.7
1956	110,954	1,965	68,517	65,764	66,552	63,799	6,283	57,514	2,750	4.0	4.1	60.0	57.5
1957	112,265	1,948	68,877	66,019	66,929	64,071	5,947	58,123	2,859	4.2	4.3	59.6	57.1
1958	113,727	1,847	69,486	64,883	67,639	63,036	5,586	57,450	4,602	6.6	6.8	59.5	55.4
1959	115,329	1,788	70,157	66,418	68,369	64,630	5,565	59,065	3,740	5.3	5.5	59.3	56.0
1960 [6]	117,245	1,861	71,489	67,639	69,628	65,778	5,458	60,318	3,852	5.4	5.5	59.4	56.1
1961	118,771	1,900	72,359	67,646	70,459	65,746	5,200	60,546	4,714	6.5	6.7	59.3	55.4
1962 [6]	120,153	2,061	72,675	68,763	70,614	66,702	4,944	61,759	3,911	5.4	5.5	58.8	55.5
1963	122,416	2,006	73,839	69,768	71,833	67,762	4,687	63,076	4,070	5.5	5.7	58.7	55.4
1964	124,485	2,018	75,109	71,323	73,091	69,305	4,523	64,782	3,786	5.0	5.2	58.7	55.7
1965	126,513	1,946	76,401	73,034	74,455	71,088	4,361	66,726	3,366	4.4	4.5	58.9	56.2
1966	128,058	2,122	77,892	75,017	75,770	72,895	3,979	68,915	2,875	3.7	3.8	59.2	56.9
1967	129,874	2,218	79,565	76,590	77,347	74,372	3,844	70,527	2,975	3.7	3.8	59.6	57.3
1968	132,028	2,253	80,990	78,173	78,737	75,920	3,817	72,103	2,817	3.5	3.6	59.6	57.5
1969	134,335	2,238	82,972	80,140	80,734	77,902	3,606	74,296	2,832	3.4	3.5	60.1	58.0
1970	137,085	2,118	84,889	80,796	82,771	78,678	3,463	75,215	4,093	4.8	4.9	60.4	57.4
1971	140,216	1,973	86,355	81,340	84,382	79,367	3,394	75,972	5,016	5.8	5.9	60.2	56.6
1972 [6]	144,126	1,813	88,847	83,966	87,034	82,153	3,484	78,669	4,882	5.5	5.6	60.4	57.0
1973 [6]	147,096	1,774	91,203	86,838	89,429	85,064	3,470	81,594	4,365	4.8	4.9	60.8	57.8
1974	150,120	1,721	93,670	88,515	91,949	86,794	3,515	83,279	5,156	5.5	5.6	61.3	57.8
1975	153,153	1,678	95,453	87,524	93,775	85,846	3,408	82,438	7,929	8.3	8.5	61.2	56.1
1976	156,150	1,668	97,826	90,420	96,158	88,752	3,331	85,421	7,406	7.6	7.7	61.6	56.8
1977	159,033	1,656	100,665	93,673	99,009	92,017	3,283	88,734	6,991	6.9	7.1	62.3	57.9
1978 [6]	161,910	1,631	103,882	97,679	102,251	96,048	3,387	92,661	6,202	6.0	6.1	63.2	59.3
1979	164,863	1,597	106,559	100,421	104,962	98,824	3,347	95,477	6,137	5.8	5.8	63.7	59.9
1980	167,745	1,604	108,544	100,907	106,940	99,303	3,364	95,938	7,637	7.0	7.1	63.8	59.2
1981	170,130	1,645	110,315	102,042	108,670	100,397	3,368	97,030	8,273	7.5	7.6	63.9	59.0
1982	172,271	1,668	111,872	101,194	110,204	99,526	3,401	96,125	10,678	9.5	9.7	64.0	57.8
1983	174,215	1,676	113,226	102,510	111,550	100,834	3,383	97,450	10,717	9.5	9.6	64.0	57.9
1984	176,383	1,697	115,241	106,702	113,544	105,005	3,321	101,685	8,539	7.4	7.5	64.4	59.5
1985	178,206	1,706	117,167	108,856	115,461	107,150	3,179	103,971	8,312	7.1	7.2	64.8	60.1
1986 [6]	180,587	1,706	119,540	111,303	117,834	109,597	3,163	106,434	8,237	6.9	7.0	65.3	60.7
1987	182,753	1,737	121,602	114,177	119,865	112,440	3,208	109,232	7,425	6.1	6.2	65.6	61.5
1988	184,613	1,709	123,378	116,677	121,669	114,968	3,169	111,800	6,701	5.4	5.5	65.9	62.3
1989	186,393	1,688	125,557	119,030	123,869	117,342	3,199	114,142	6,528	5.2	5.3	66.5	63.0
1990	188,049	1,637	126,424	119,550	124,787	117,914	3,186	114,728	6,874	5.4	5.5	66.4	62.7
1991	189,765	1,564	126,867	118,440	125,303	116,877	3,233	113,644	8,426	6.6	6.7	66.0	61.6
1992	191,576	1,566	128,548	119,164	126,982	117,598	3,207	114,391	9,384	7.3	7.4	66.3	61.4
1993	193,550	1,485	129,525	120,791	128,040	119,306	3,074	116,232	8,734	6.7	6.8	66.2	61.6

[1] Not seasonally adjusted.
[2] Unemployed as percent of labor force including resident Armed Forces.
[3] Unemployed as percent of civilian labor force.
[4] Civilian labor force as percent of civilian noninstitutional population.
[5] Civilian employment as percent of civilian noninstitutional population.

See next page for continuation of table.

TABLE B-33.—*Population and the labor force, 1929-93*—Continued

[Monthly data seasonally adjusted, except as noted]

Year or month	Civilian noninsti- tutional popula- tion [1]	Resi- dent Armed Forces [1]	Labor force includ- ing resident Armed Forces	Employ- ment including resident Armed Forces	Civilian labor force					Unemploy- ment rate		Civil- ian labor force par- tici- pation rate [4]	Civil- ian em- ploy- ment/ pop- ula- tion ratio [5]
					Total	Employment			Un- em- ploy- ment	All work- ers [2]	Civil- ian work- ers [3]		
						Total	Agri- cul- tural	Non- agri- cultural					
	Thousands of persons 16 years of age and over										Percent			

1990: Jan	187,293	1,697	126,298	119,687	124,601	117,990	3,156	114,834	6,611	5.2	5.3	66.5	63.0
Feb	187,412	1,678	126,299	119,714	124,621	118,036	3,123	114,913	6,585	5.2	5.3	66.5	63.0
Mar	187,529	1,669	126,432	119,942	124,763	118,273	3,223	115,050	6,490	5.1	5.2	66.5	63.1
Apr	187,669	1,657	126,470	119,762	124,813	118,105	3,167	114,938	6,708	5.3	5.4	66.5	62.9
May	187,828	1,639	126,554	119,955	124,915	118,316	3,289	115,027	6,599	5.2	5.3	66.5	63.0
June	187,977	1,630	126,282	119,868	124,652	118,238	3,257	114,981	6,414	5.1	5.1	66.3	62.9
July	188,136	1,627	126,284	119,576	124,657	117,949	3,108	114,841	6,708	5.3	5.4	66.3	62.7
Aug	188,261	1,640	126,457	119,446	124,817	117,806	3,149	114,657	7,011	5.5	5.6	66.3	62.6
Sept	188,401	1,601	126,504	119,389	124,903	117,788	3,170	114,618	7,115	5.6	5.7	66.3	62.5
Oct	188,525	1,570	126,480	119,288	124,910	117,718	3,201	114,517	7,192	5.7	5.8	66.3	62.4
Nov	188,697	1,615	126,477	118,974	124,862	117,359	3,149	114,210	7,503	5.9	6.0	66.2	62.2
Dec	188,866	1,617	126,766	119,033	125,149	117,416	3,252	114,164	7,733	6.1	6.2	66.3	62.2
1991: Jan	188,977	1,615	126,402	118,582	124,787	116,967	3,173	113,794	7,820	6.2	6.3	66.0	61.9
Feb	189,115	1,602	126,629	118,471	125,027	116,869	3,228	113,641	8,158	6.4	6.5	66.1	61.8
Mar	189,243	1,460	126,716	118,251	125,256	116,791	3,131	113,660	8,465	6.7	6.8	66.2	61.7
Apr	189,380	1,456	127,177	118,867	125,721	117,411	3,189	114,222	8,310	6.5	6.6	66.4	62.0
May	189,522	1,458	126,643	118,104	125,185	116,646	3,269	113,377	8,539	6.7	6.8	66.1	61.5
June	189,668	1,505	126,872	118,383	125,367	116,878	3,281	113,597	8,489	6.7	6.8	66.1	61.6
July	189,839	1,604	126,706	118,342	125,102	116,738	3,258	113,480	8,364	6.6	6.7	65.9	61.5
Aug	189,973	1,616	126,565	118,121	124,949	116,505	3,273	113,232	8,444	6.7	6.8	65.8	61.3
Sept	190,122	1,624	127,231	118,766	125,607	117,142	3,275	113,867	8,465	6.7	6.7	66.1	61.6
Oct	190,289	1,614	127,192	118,611	125,578	116,997	3,231	113,766	8,581	6.7	6.8	66.0	61.5
Nov	190,452	1,605	127,124	118,453	125,519	116,848	3,255	113,593	8,671	6.8	6.9	65.9	61.4
Dec	190,605	1,604	127,245	118,240	125,641	116,636	3,141	113,495	9,005	7.1	7.2	65.9	61.2
1992: Jan	190,759	1,599	127,748	118,729	126,149	117,130	3,136	113,994	9,019	7.1	7.1	66.1	61.4
Feb	190,884	1,585	127,794	118,504	126,209	116,919	3,218	113,701	9,290	7.3	7.4	66.1	61.3
Mar	191,022	1,585	128,130	118,840	126,545	117,255	3,208	114,047	9,290	7.3	7.3	66.2	61.4
Apr	191,168	1,577	128,494	119,247	126,917	117,670	3,220	114,450	9,247	7.2	7.3	66.4	61.6
May	191,307	1,574	128,610	119,108	127,036	117,534	3,192	114,342	9,502	7.4	7.5	66.4	61.4
June	191,455	1,570	128,839	119,068	127,269	117,498	3,248	114,250	9,771	7.6	7.7	66.5	61.4
July	191,622	1,568	128,926	119,331	127,358	117,763	3,217	114,546	9,595	7.4	7.5	66.5	61.5
Aug	191,790	1,566	128,905	119,315	127,339	117,749	3,237	114,512	9,590	7.4	7.5	66.4	61.4
Sept	191,947	1,566	128,872	119,338	127,306	117,772	3,211	114,561	9,534	7.4	7.5	66.3	61.4
Oct	192,131	1,552	128,485	119,275	126,933	117,723	3,188	114,535	9,210	7.2	7.3	66.1	61.3
Nov	192,316	1,531	128,818	119,505	127,287	117,974	3,170	114,804	9,313	7.2	7.3	66.2	61.3
Dec	192,509	1,517	128,986	119,672	127,469	118,155	3,222	114,933	9,314	7.2	7.3	66.2	61.4
1993: Jan	192,644	1,515	128,739	119,693	127,224	118,178	3,182	114,996	9,046	7.0	7.1	66.0	61.3
Feb	192,786	1,512	128,912	119,954	127,400	118,442	3,116	115,326	8,958	6.9	7.0	66.1	61.4
Mar	192,959	1,497	128,937	120,059	127,440	118,562	3,099	115,463	8,878	6.9	7.0	66.0	61.4
Apr	193,126	1,492	129,031	120,077	127,539	118,585	3,071	115,514	8,954	6.9	7.0	66.0	61.4
May	193,283	1,484	129,559	120,664	128,075	119,180	3,074	116,106	8,895	6.9	6.9	66.3	61.7
June	193,456	1,477	129,533	120,664	128,056	119,187	3,031	116,156	8,869	6.8	6.9	66.2	61.6
July	193,633	1,471	129,573	120,841	128,102	119,370	3,043	116,327	8,732	6.7	6.8	66.2	61.6
Aug	193,793	1,482	129,816	121,174	128,334	119,692	3,005	116,687	8,642	6.7	6.7	66.2	61.8
Sept	193,971	1,482	129,590	121,050	128,108	119,568	3,093	116,475	8,540	6.6	6.7	66.0	61.6
Oct	194,151	1,475	130,055	121,416	128,580	119,941	3,021	116,920	8,639	6.6	6.7	66.2	61.8
Nov	194,321	1,470	130,132	121,802	128,662	120,332	3,114	117,218	8,330	6.4	6.5	66.2	61.9
Dec	194,472	1,461	130,359	122,122	128,898	120,661	3,096	117,565	8,237	6.3	6.4	66.3	62.0

[6] Not strictly comparable with earlier data due to population adjustments as follows: Beginning 1953, introduction of 1950 census data added about 600,000 to population and 350,000 to labor force, total employment, and agricultural employment. Beginning 1960, inclusion of Alaska and Hawaii added about 500,000 to population, 300,000 to labor force, and 240,000 to nonagricultural employment. Beginning 1962, introduction of 1960 census data reduced population by about 50,000 and labor force and employment by 200,000. Beginning 1972, introduction of 1970 census data added about 800,000 to civilian noninstitutional population and 333,000 to labor force and employment. A subsequent adjustment based on 1970 census in March 1973 added 60,000 to labor force and to employment. Beginning 1978, changes in sampling and estimation procedures introduced into the household survey added about 250,000 to labor force and to employment. Unemployment levels and rates were not significantly affected. Beginning 1986, the introduction of revised population controls added about 400,000 to the civilian population and labor force and 350,000 to civilian employment. Unemployment levels and rates were not significantly affected.

Note.—Labor force data in Tables B-33 through B-42 are based on household interviews and relate to the calendar week including the 12th of the month. For definitions of terms, area samples used, historical comparability of the data, comparability with other series, etc., see "Employment and Earnings."

Source: Department of Labor, Bureau of Labor Statistics.

TABLE B-34.—*Civilian employment and unemployment by sex and age, 1947–93*

[Thousands of persons 16 years of age and over; monthly data seasonally adjusted]

Year or month	Total	Civilian employment						Unemployment					
		Males			Females			Total	Males			Females		
		Total	16–19 years	20 years and over	Total	16–19 years	20 years and over		Total	16–19 years	20 years and over	Total	16–19 years	20 years and over
1947	57,038	40,995	2,218	38,776	16,045	1,691	14,354	2,311	1,692	270	1,422	619	144	475
1948	58,343	41,725	2,344	39,382	16,617	1,682	14,936	2,276	1,559	256	1,305	717	153	564
1949	57,651	40,925	2,124	38,803	16,723	1,588	15,137	3,637	2,572	353	2,219	1,065	223	841
1950	58,918	41,578	2,186	39,394	17,340	1,517	15,824	3,288	2,239	318	1,922	1,049	195	854
1951	59,961	41,780	2,156	39,626	18,181	1,611	16,570	2,055	1,221	191	1,029	834	145	689
1952	60,250	41,682	2,107	39,578	18,568	1,612	16,958	1,883	1,185	205	980	698	140	559
1953	61,179	42,430	2,136	40,296	18,749	1,584	17,164	1,834	1,202	184	1,019	632	123	510
1954	60,109	41,619	1,985	39,634	18,490	1,490	17,000	3,532	2,344	310	2,035	1,188	191	997
1955	62,170	42,621	2,095	40,526	19,551	1,547	18,002	2,852	1,854	274	1,580	998	176	823
1956	63,799	43,379	2,164	41,216	20,419	1,654	18,767	2,750	1,711	269	1,442	1,039	209	832
1957	64,071	43,357	2,115	41,239	20,714	1,663	19,052	2,859	1,841	300	1,541	1,018	197	821
1958	63,036	42,423	2,012	40,411	20,613	1,570	19,043	4,602	3,098	416	2,681	1,504	262	1,242
1959	64,630	43,466	2,198	41,267	21,164	1,640	19,524	3,740	2,420	398	2,022	1,320	256	1,063
1960	65,778	43,904	2,361	41,543	21,874	1,768	20,105	3,852	2,486	426	2,060	1,366	286	1,080
1961	65,746	43,656	2,315	41,342	22,090	1,793	20,296	4,714	2,997	479	2,518	1,717	349	1,368
1962	66,702	44,177	2,362	41,815	22,525	1,833	20,693	3,911	2,423	408	2,016	1,488	313	1,175
1963	67,762	44,657	2,406	42,251	23,105	1,849	21,257	4,070	2,472	501	1,971	1,598	383	1,216
1964	69,305	45,474	2,587	42,886	23,831	1,929	21,903	3,786	2,205	487	1,718	1,581	385	1,195
1965	71,088	46,340	2,918	43,422	24,748	2,118	22,630	3,366	1,914	479	1,435	1,452	395	1,056
1966	72,895	46,919	3,253	43,668	25,976	2,468	23,510	2,875	1,551	432	1,120	1,324	405	921
1967	74,372	47,479	3,186	44,294	26,893	2,496	24,397	2,975	1,508	448	1,060	1,468	391	1,078
1968	75,920	48,114	3,255	44,859	27,807	2,526	25,281	2,817	1,419	426	993	1,397	412	985
1969	77,902	48,818	3,430	45,388	29,084	2,687	26,397	2,832	1,403	440	963	1,429	413	1,015
1970	78,678	48,990	3,409	45,581	29,688	2,735	26,952	4,093	2,238	599	1,638	1,855	506	1,349
1971	79,367	49,390	3,478	45,912	29,976	2,730	27,246	5,016	2,789	693	2,097	2,227	568	1,658
1972	82,153	50,896	3,765	47,130	31,257	2,980	28,276	4,882	2,659	711	1,948	2,222	598	1,625
1973	85,064	52,349	4,039	48,310	32,715	3,231	29,484	4,365	2,275	653	1,624	2,089	583	1,507
1974	86,794	53,024	4,103	48,922	33,769	3,345	30,424	5,156	2,714	757	1,957	2,441	665	1,777
1975	85,846	51,857	3,839	48,018	33,989	3,263	30,726	7,929	4,442	966	3,476	3,486	802	2,684
1976	88,752	53,138	3,947	49,190	35,615	3,389	32,226	7,406	4,036	939	3,098	3,369	780	2,588
1977	92,017	54,728	4,174	50,555	37,289	3,514	33,775	6,991	3,667	874	2,794	3,324	789	2,535
1978	96,048	56,479	4,336	52,143	39,569	3,734	35,836	6,202	3,142	813	2,328	3,061	769	2,292
1979	98,824	57,607	4,300	53,308	41,217	3,783	37,434	6,137	3,120	811	2,308	3,018	743	2,276
1980	99,303	57,186	4,085	53,101	42,117	3,625	38,492	7,637	4,267	913	3,353	3,370	755	2,615
1981	100,397	57,397	3,815	53,582	43,000	3,411	39,590	8,273	4,577	962	3,615	3,696	800	2,895
1982	99,526	56,271	3,379	52,891	43,256	3,170	40,086	10,678	6,179	1,090	5,089	4,499	886	3,613
1983	100,834	56,787	3,300	53,487	44,047	3,043	41,004	10,717	6,260	1,003	5,257	4,457	825	3,632
1984	105,005	59,091	3,322	55,769	45,915	3,122	42,793	8,539	4,744	812	3,932	3,794	687	3,107
1985	107,150	59,891	3,328	56,562	47,259	3,105	44,154	8,312	4,521	806	3,715	3,791	661	3,129
1986	109,597	60,892	3,323	57,569	48,706	3,149	45,556	8,237	4,530	779	3,751	3,707	675	3,032
1987	112,440	62,107	3,381	58,726	50,334	3,260	47,074	7,425	4,101	732	3,369	3,324	616	2,709
1988	114,968	63,273	3,492	59,781	51,696	3,313	48,383	6,701	3,655	667	2,987	3,046	558	2,487
1989	117,342	64,315	3,477	60,837	53,027	3,282	49,745	6,528	3,525	658	2,867	3,003	536	2,467
1990	117,914	64,435	3,237	61,198	53,479	3,024	50,455	6,874	3,799	629	3,170	3,075	519	2,555
1991	116,877	63,593	2,879	60,714	53,284	2,749	50,535	8,426	4,817	709	4,109	3,609	581	3,028
1992	117,598	63,805	2,786	61,019	53,793	2,613	51,181	9,384	5,380	761	4,619	4,005	591	3,413
1993	119,306	64,700	2,836	61,865	54,606	2,694	51,912	8,734	4,932	728	4,204	3,801	568	3,234
1992: Jan	117,130	63,499	2,850	60,649	53,631	2,677	50,954	9,019	5,211	724	4,487	3,808	561	3,247
Feb	116,919	63,319	2,740	60,579	53,600	2,676	50,924	9,290	5,379	771	4,608	3,911	579	3,332
Mar	117,255	63,553	2,693	60,860	53,702	2,624	51,078	9,290	5,346	772	4,574	3,944	575	3,369
Apr	117,670	63,853	2,763	61,090	53,817	2,615	51,202	9,247	5,279	703	4,576	3,968	559	3,409
May	117,534	63,821	2,746	61,075	53,713	2,624	51,089	9,502	5,526	742	4,784	3,976	594	3,382
June	117,498	63,732	2,723	61,009	53,766	2,553	51,213	9,771	5,650	865	4,785	4,121	682	3,439
July	117,763	63,830	2,747	61,083	53,933	2,565	51,368	9,595	5,442	768	4,674	4,153	630	3,523
Aug	117,749	63,869	2,765	61,104	53,880	2,642	51,238	9,590	5,476	776	4,700	4,114	577	3,537
Sept	117,772	63,980	2,839	61,141	53,792	2,601	51,191	9,534	5,443	820	4,623	4,091	614	3,477
Oct	117,723	63,920	2,849	61,071	53,803	2,583	51,220	9,210	5,344	683	4,661	3,866	535	3,331
Nov	117,974	64,028	2,828	61,200	53,946	2,579	51,367	9,313	5,330	764	4,566	3,983	615	3,368
Dec	118,155	64,178	2,864	61,314	53,977	2,619	51,358	9,314	5,201	753	4,448	4,113	576	3,537
1993: Jan	118,178	64,237	2,819	61,418	53,941	2,633	51,308	9,046	4,977	737	4,240	4,069	594	3,475
Feb	118,442	64,329	2,852	61,477	54,113	2,634	51,479	8,958	5,067	742	4,325	3,891	596	3,295
Mar	118,562	64,355	2,857	61,498	54,207	2,591	51,616	8,878	5,147	729	4,418	3,731	588	3,143
Apr	118,585	64,416	2,802	61,614	54,169	2,636	51,533	8,954	5,098	810	4,288	3,856	575	3,281
May	119,180	64,687	2,838	61,849	54,493	2,716	51,777	8,895	5,016	731	4,285	3,879	640	3,239
June	119,187	64,642	2,837	61,805	54,545	2,670	51,875	8,869	5,041	759	4,282	3,828	571	3,257
July	119,370	64,728	2,859	61,869	54,642	2,741	51,901	8,732	5,002	731	4,271	3,730	531	3,199
Aug	119,692	64,904	2,898	62,006	54,788	2,704	52,084	8,642	4,943	728	4,215	3,699	534	3,165
Sept	119,568	64,756	2,855	61,901	54,812	2,740	52,072	8,540	4,824	687	4,137	3,716	537	3,179
Oct	119,941	64,971	2,799	62,172	54,970	2,727	52,243	8,639	4,849	715	4,134	3,790	571	3,219
Nov	120,332	65,144	2,829	62,315	55,188	2,765	52,423	8,330	4,586	703	3,883	3,744	546	3,198
Dec	120,661	65,259	2,815	62,444	55,402	2,771	52,631	8,237	4,554	677	3,877	3,683	531	3,152

Note.—See footnote 6 and Note, Table B–33.
Source: Department of Labor, Bureau of Labor Statistics.

TABLE B-35.—*Civilian employment by demographic characteristic, 1954-93*

[Thousands of persons 16 years of age and over; monthly data seasonally adjusted]

Year or month	All civilian workers	White Total	White Males	White Females	White Both sexes 16-19	Black and other Total	Black and other Males	Black and other Females	Black and other Both sexes 16-19	Black Total	Black Males	Black Females	Black Both sexes 16-19
1954	60,109	53,957	37,846	16,111	3,078	6,152	3,773	2,379	396				
1955	62,170	55,833	38,719	17,114	3,225	6,341	3,904	2,437	418				
1956	63,799	57,269	39,368	17,901	3,389	6,534	4,013	2,521	430				
1957	64,071	57,465	39,349	18,116	3,374	6,604	4,006	2,598	407				
1958	63,036	56,613	38,591	18,022	3,216	6,423	3,833	2,590	365				
1959	64,630	58,006	39,494	18,512	3,475	6,623	3,971	2,652	362				
1960	65,778	58,850	39,755	19,095	3,700	6,928	4,149	2,779	430				
1961	65,746	58,913	39,588	19,325	3,693	6,833	4,068	2,765	414				
1962	66,702	59,698	40,016	19,682	3,774	7,003	4,160	2,843	420				
1963	67,762	60,622	40,428	20,194	3,851	7,140	4,229	2,911	404				
1964	69,305	61,922	41,115	20,807	4,076	7,383	4,359	3,024	440				
1965	71,088	63,446	41,844	21,602	4,562	7,643	4,496	3,147	474				
1966	72,895	65,021	42,331	22,690	5,176	7,877	4,588	3,289	545				
1967	74,372	66,361	42,833	23,528	5,114	8,011	4,646	3,365	568				
1968	75,920	67,750	43,411	24,339	5,195	8,169	4,702	3,467	584				
1969	77,902	69,518	44,048	25,470	5,508	8,384	4,770	3,614	609				
1970	78,678	70,217	44,178	26,039	5,571	8,464	4,813	3,650	574				
1971	79,367	70,878	44,595	26,283	5,670	8,488	4,796	3,692	538				
1972	82,153	73,370	45,944	27,426	6,173	8,783	4,952	3,832	573	7,802	4,368	3,433	509
1973	85,064	75,708	47,085	28,623	6,623	9,356	5,265	4,092	647	8,128	4,527	3,601	570
1974	86,794	77,184	47,674	29,511	6,796	9,610	5,352	4,258	652	8,203	4,527	3,677	554
1975	85,846	76,411	46,697	29,714	6,487	9,435	5,161	4,275	615	7,894	4,275	3,618	507
1976	88,752	78,853	47,775	31,078	6,724	9,899	5,363	4,536	611	8,227	4,404	3,823	508
1977	92,017	81,700	49,150	32,550	7,068	10,317	5,579	4,739	619	8,540	4,565	3,975	508
1978	96,048	84,936	50,544	34,392	7,367	11,112	5,936	5,177	703	9,102	4,796	4,307	571
1979	98,824	87,259	51,452	35,807	7,356	11,565	6,156	5,409	727	9,359	4,923	4,436	579
1980	99,303	87,715	51,127	36,587	7,021	11,588	6,059	5,529	689	9,313	4,798	4,515	547
1981	100,397	88,709	51,315	37,394	6,588	11,688	6,083	5,606	637	9,355	4,794	4,561	505
1982	99,526	87,903	50,287	37,615	5,984	11,624	5,983	5,641	565	9,189	4,637	4,552	428
1983	100,834	88,893	50,621	38,272	5,799	11,941	6,166	5,775	543	9,375	4,753	4,622	416
1984	105,005	92,120	52,462	39,659	5,836	12,885	6,629	6,256	607	10,119	5,124	4,995	474
1985	107,150	93,736	53,046	40,690	5,768	13,414	6,845	6,569	666	10,501	5,270	5,231	532
1986	109,597	95,660	53,785	41,876	5,792	13,937	7,107	6,830	681	10,814	5,428	5,386	536
1987	112,440	97,789	54,647	43,142	5,898	14,652	7,459	7,192	742	11,309	5,661	5,648	587
1988	114,968	99,812	55,550	44,262	6,030	15,156	7,722	7,434	774	11,658	5,824	5,834	601
1989	117,342	101,584	56,352	45,232	5,946	15,757	7,963	7,795	813	11,953	5,928	6,025	625
1990	117,914	102,087	56,432	45,654	5,518	15,827	8,003	7,825	743	11,966	5,915	6,051	573
1991	116,877	101,039	55,557	45,482	4,989	15,838	8,036	7,802	639	11,863	5,880	5,983	474
1992	117,598	101,479	55,709	45,770	4,761	16,119	8,096	8,023	637	11,933	5,846	6,087	474
1993	119,306	102,812	56,397	46,415	4,887	16,494	8,303	8,191	642	12,146	5,957	6,189	474
1992: Jan	117,130	101,195	55,485	45,710	4,877	15,928	8,040	7,888	665	11,866	5,876	5,990	519
Feb	116,919	101,051	55,357	45,694	4,782	15,943	8,036	7,907	649	11,799	5,812	5,987	492
Mar	117,255	101,308	55,507	45,801	4,688	15,945	8,041	7,904	609	11,836	5,814	6,022	477
Apr	117,670	101,599	55,745	45,854	4,768	16,029	8,076	7,953	618	11,856	5,823	6,033	461
May	117,534	101,473	55,709	45,764	4,763	16,002	8,038	7,964	597	11,845	5,809	6,036	445
June	117,498	101,277	55,596	45,681	4,601	16,179	8,105	8,074	636	11,982	5,862	6,120	470
July	117,763	101,568	55,768	45,800	4,700	16,168	8,076	8,092	626	11,974	5,826	6,148	462
Aug	117,749	101,479	55,749	45,730	4,756	16,315	8,136	8,179	685	12,079	5,855	6,224	496
Sept	117,772	101,497	55,829	45,668	4,795	16,305	8,157	8,148	639	12,049	5,870	6,179	467
Oct	117,723	101,547	55,823	45,724	4,797	16,210	8,129	8,081	640	11,976	5,850	6,126	451
Nov	117,974	101,793	55,846	45,947	4,764	16,189	8,189	8,000	640	11,958	5,897	6,061	465
Dec	118,155	101,944	56,052	45,892	4,827	16,206	8,118	8,088	648	11,954	5,849	6,105	485
1993: Jan	118,178	102,029	56,086	45,943	4,808	16,126	8,157	7,969	635	11,864	5,895	5,969	485
Feb	118,442	102,076	56,100	45,976	4,824	16,439	8,284	8,155	653	12,157	6,009	6,148	487
Mar	118,562	102,251	56,175	46,076	4,829	16,306	8,162	8,144	593	11,991	5,884	6,107	443
Apr	118,585	102,190	56,166	46,024	4,826	16,354	8,210	8,144	618	11,965	5,846	6,119	436
May	119,180	102,612	56,304	46,308	4,878	16,507	8,307	8,200	675	12,140	5,961	6,179	494
June	119,187	102,721	56,362	46,359	4,835	16,408	8,249	8,159	640	12,076	5,931	6,145	451
July	119,370	102,835	56,336	46,499	4,902	16,459	8,367	8,092	688	12,134	6,008	6,126	513
Aug	119,692	103,179	56,523	46,656	4,930	16,522	8,366	8,156	681	12,225	6,031	6,194	514
Sept	119,568	103,094	56,467	46,627	4,939	16,512	8,302	8,210	652	12,202	5,960	6,242	484
Oct	119,941	103,273	56,627	46,646	4,906	16,697	8,380	8,317	630	12,292	5,991	6,301	463
Nov	120,332	103,662	56,799	46,863	4,991	16,705	8,363	8,342	616	12,297	5,951	6,346	461
Dec	120,661	103,807	56,794	47,013	4,970	16,876	8,476	8,400	628	12,397	6,013	6,384	467

Note.—See footnote 6 and Note, Table B-33.

Source: Department of Labor, Bureau of Labor Statistics.

TABLE B-36.—Unemployment by demographic characteristic, 1954–93

[Thousands of persons 16 years of age and over; monthly data seasonally adjusted]

Year or month	All civilian workers	White Total	White Males	White Females	White Both sexes 16–19	Black and other Total	Black and other Males	Black and other Females	Black and other Both sexes 16–19	Black Total	Black Males	Black Females	Black Both sexes 16–19
1954	3,532	2,859	1,913	946	423	673	431	242	79				
1955	2,852	2,252	1,478	774	373	601	376	225	77				
1956	2,750	2,159	1,366	793	382	591	345	246	95				
1957	2,859	2,289	1,477	812	401	570	364	206	96				
1958	4,602	3,680	2,489	1,191	541	923	610	313	138				
1959	3,740	2,946	1,903	1,043	525	793	517	276	128				
1960	3,852	3,065	1,988	1,077	575	788	498	290	138				
1961	4,714	3,743	2,398	1,345	669	971	599	372	159				
1962	3,911	3,052	1,915	1,137	580	861	509	352	142				
1963	4,070	3,208	1,976	1,232	708	863	496	367	176				
1964	3,786	2,999	1,779	1,220	708	787	426	361	165				
1965	3,366	2,691	1,556	1,135	705	678	360	318	171				
1966	2,875	2,255	1,241	1,014	651	622	310	312	186				
1967	2,975	2,338	1,208	1,130	635	638	300	338	203				
1968	2,817	2,226	1,142	1,084	644	590	277	313	194				
1969	2,832	2,260	1,137	1,123	660	571	267	304	193				
1970	4,093	3,339	1,857	1,482	871	754	380	374	235				
1971	5,016	4,085	2,309	1,777	1,011	930	481	450	249				
1972	4,882	3,906	2,173	1,733	1,021	977	486	491	288	906	448	458	279
1973	4,365	3,442	1,836	1,606	955	924	440	484	280	846	395	451	262
1974	5,156	4,097	2,169	1,927	1,104	1,058	544	514	318	965	494	470	297
1975	7,929	6,421	3,627	2,794	1,413	1,507	815	692	355	1,369	741	629	330
1976	7,406	5,914	3,258	2,656	1,364	1,492	779	713	355	1,334	698	637	330
1977	6,991	5,441	2,883	2,558	1,284	1,550	784	766	379	1,393	698	695	354
1978	6,202	4,698	2,411	2,287	1,189	1,505	731	774	394	1,330	641	690	360
1979	6,137	4,664	2,405	2,260	1,193	1,473	714	759	362	1,319	636	683	333
1980	7,637	5,884	3,345	2,540	1,291	1,752	922	830	377	1,553	815	738	343
1981	8,273	6,343	3,580	2,762	1,374	1,930	997	933	388	1,731	891	840	357
1982	10,678	8,241	4,846	3,395	1,534	2,437	1,334	1,104	443	2,142	1,167	975	396
1983	10,717	8,128	4,859	3,270	1,387	2,588	1,401	1,187	441	2,272	1,213	1,059	392
1984	8,539	6,372	3,600	2,772	1,116	2,167	1,144	1,022	384	1,914	1,003	911	353
1985	8,312	6,191	3,426	2,765	1,074	2,121	1,095	1,026	394	1,864	951	913	357
1986	8,237	6,140	3,433	2,708	1,070	2,097	1,097	999	383	1,840	946	894	347
1987	7,425	5,501	3,132	2,369	995	1,924	969	955	353	1,684	826	858	312
1988	6,701	4,944	2,766	2,177	910	1,757	888	869	316	1,547	771	776	288
1989	6,528	4,770	2,636	2,135	863	1,757	889	868	331	1,544	773	772	300
1990	6,874	5,091	2,866	2,225	856	1,783	933	850	292	1,527	793	734	258
1991	8,426	6,447	3,775	2,672	977	1,979	1,043	936	313	1,679	874	805	270
1992	9,384	7,047	4,121	2,926	983	2,337	1,259	1,079	369	1,958	1,046	912	313
1993	8,734	6,547	3,753	2,793	943	2,187	1,179	1,008	353	1,796	954	842	302
1992: Jan	9,019	6,826	4,053	2,773	939	2,257	1,252	1,005	337	1,871	1,017	854	291
Feb	9,290	6,996	4,132	2,864	999	2,261	1,230	1,031	352	1,924	1,047	877	313
Mar	9,290	7,071	4,136	2,935	1,044	2,242	1,224	1,018	314	1,915	1,040	875	268
Apr	9,247	6,980	4,083	2,897	919	2,245	1,191	1,054	339	1,894	986	908	288
May	9,502	7,040	4,239	2,801	957	2,388	1,264	1,124	372	2,022	1,063	959	322
June	9,771	7,327	4,337	2,990	1,138	2,456	1,298	1,158	398	2,021	1,073	948	328
July	9,595	7,193	4,134	3,059	1,006	2,401	1,293	1,108	386	2,010	1,065	945	321
Aug	9,590	7,166	4,159	3,007	969	2,400	1,296	1,104	375	2,011	1,076	935	316
Sept	9,534	7,214	4,203	3,011	1,032	2,326	1,256	1,070	400	1,927	1,046	881	346
Oct	9,210	6,966	4,055	2,911	864	2,365	1,308	1,057	383	1,982	1,082	900	329
Nov	9,313	6,899	4,029	2,870	992	2,342	1,243	1,099	393	1,944	1,018	926	321
Dec	9,314	6,917	3,933	2,984	948	2,377	1,267	1,110	384	1,979	1,047	932	316
1993: Jan	9,046	6,750	3,847	2,903	951	2,355	1,227	1,128	371	1,953	1,006	947	312
Feb	8,958	6,670	3,849	2,821	963	2,266	1,207	1,059	375	1,857	968	889	311
Mar	8,878	6,671	3,909	2,762	945	2,222	1,248	974	380	1,871	1,034	837	325
Apr	8,954	6,601	3,825	2,776	962	2,318	1,253	1,065	416	1,903	1,034	869	361
May	8,895	6,622	3,781	2,841	983	2,204	1,213	991	379	1,804	970	834	323
June	8,869	6,652	3,818	2,834	945	2,231	1,209	1,022	380	1,846	976	870	321
July	8,732	6,558	3,833	2,725	909	2,169	1,158	1,011	344	1,786	929	857	293
Aug	8,642	6,467	3,756	2,711	934	2,156	1,171	985	319	1,744	931	813	259
Sept	8,540	6,398	3,657	2,741	912	2,132	1,169	963	306	1,750	950	800	275
Oct	8,639	6,736	3,788	2,948	1,003	2,040	1,088	952	314	1,653	863	790	269
Nov	8,330	6,142	3,386	2,756	922	2,133	1,151	982	337	1,760	950	810	301
Dec	8,237	6,209	3,509	2,700	894	2,013	1,046	967	317	1,614	825	789	274

Note.—See footnote 6 and Note, Table B-33.
Source: Department of Labor, Bureau of Labor Statistics.

TABLE B-37.—*Civilian labor force participation rate and employment/population ratio, 1948–93*

[Percent;[1] monthly data seasonally adjusted]

Year or month	Labor force participation rate							Employment/population ratio						
	All civilian workers	Males	Females	Both sexes 16–19 years	White	Black and other	Black	All civilian workers	Males	Females	Both sexes 16–19 years	White	Black and other	Black
1948	58.8	86.6	32.7	52.5				56.6	83.5	31.3	47.7			
1949	58.9	86.4	33.1	52.2				55.4	81.3	31.2	45.2			
1950	59.2	86.4	33.9	51.8				56.1	82.0	32.0	45.5			
1951	59.2	86.3	34.6	52.2				57.3	84.0	33.1	47.9			
1952	59.0	86.3	34.7	51.3				57.3	83.9	33.4	46.9			
1953	58.9	86.0	34.4	50.2				57.1	83.6	33.3	46.4			
1954	58.8	85.5	34.6	48.3	58.2	64.0		55.5	81.0	32.5	42.3	55.2	58.0	
1955	59.3	85.4	35.7	48.9	58.7	64.2		56.7	81.8	34.0	43.5	56.5	58.7	
1956	60.0	85.5	36.9	50.9	59.4	64.9		57.5	82.3	35.1	45.3	57.3	59.5	
1957	59.6	84.8	36.9	49.6	59.1	64.4		57.1	81.3	35.1	43.9	56.8	59.3	
1958	59.5	84.2	37.1	47.4	58.9	64.8		55.4	78.5	34.5	39.9	55.3	56.7	
1959	59.3	83.7	37.1	46.7	58.7	64.3		56.0	79.3	35.0	39.9	55.9	57.5	
1960	59.4	83.3	37.7	47.5	58.8	64.5		56.1	78.9	35.5	40.5	55.9	57.9	
1961	59.3	82.9	38.1	46.9	58.8	64.1		55.4	77.6	35.4	39.1	55.3	56.2	
1962	58.8	82.0	37.9	46.1	58.3	63.2		55.5	77.7	35.6	39.4	55.4	56.3	
1963	58.7	81.4	38.3	45.2	58.2	63.0		55.4	77.1	35.8	37.4	55.3	56.2	
1964	58.7	81.0	38.7	44.5	58.2	63.1		55.7	77.3	36.3	37.3	55.5	57.0	
1965	58.9	80.7	39.3	45.7	58.4	62.9		56.2	77.5	37.1	38.9	56.0	57.8	
1966	59.2	80.4	40.3	48.2	58.7	63.0		56.9	77.9	38.3	42.1	56.8	58.4	
1967	59.6	80.4	41.1	48.4	59.2	62.8		57.3	78.0	39.0	42.2	57.2	58.2	
1968	59.6	80.1	41.6	48.3	59.3	62.2		57.5	77.8	39.6	42.2	57.4	58.0	
1969	60.1	79.8	42.7	49.4	59.9	62.1		58.0	77.6	40.7	43.4	58.0	58.1	
1970	60.4	79.7	43.3	49.9	60.2	61.8		57.4	76.2	40.8	42.3	57.5	56.8	
1971	60.2	79.1	43.4	49.7	60.1	60.9		56.6	74.9	40.4	41.3	56.8	54.9	
1972	60.4	78.9	43.9	51.9	60.4	60.2	59.9	57.0	75.0	41.0	43.5	57.4	54.1	53.7
1973	60.8	78.8	44.7	53.7	60.8	60.5	60.2	57.8	75.5	42.0	45.9	58.2	55.0	54.5
1974	61.3	78.7	45.7	54.8	61.4	60.3	59.8	57.8	74.9	42.6	46.0	58.3	54.3	53.5
1975	61.2	77.9	46.3	54.0	61.5	59.6	58.8	56.1	71.7	42.0	43.3	56.7	51.4	50.1
1976	61.6	77.5	47.3	54.5	61.8	59.8	59.0	56.8	72.0	43.2	44.2	57.5	52.0	50.8
1977	62.3	77.7	48.4	56.0	62.5	60.4	59.8	57.9	72.8	44.5	46.1	58.6	52.5	51.4
1978	63.2	77.9	50.0	57.8	63.3	62.2	61.5	59.3	73.8	46.4	48.3	60.0	54.7	53.6
1979	63.7	77.8	50.9	57.9	63.9	62.2	61.4	59.9	73.8	47.5	48.5	60.6	55.2	53.8
1980	63.8	77.4	51.5	56.7	64.1	61.7	61.0	59.2	72.0	47.7	46.6	60.0	53.6	52.3
1981	63.9	77.0	52.1	55.4	64.3	61.3	60.8	59.0	71.3	48.0	44.6	60.0	52.6	51.3
1982	64.0	76.6	52.6	54.1	64.3	61.6	61.0	57.8	69.0	47.7	41.5	58.8	50.9	49.4
1983	64.0	76.4	52.9	53.5	64.3	62.1	61.5	57.9	68.8	48.0	41.5	58.9	51.0	49.5
1984	64.4	76.4	53.6	53.9	64.6	62.6	62.2	59.5	70.7	49.5	43.7	60.5	53.6	52.3
1985	64.8	76.3	54.5	54.5	65.0	63.3	62.9	60.1	70.9	50.4	44.4	61.0	54.7	53.4
1986	65.3	76.3	55.3	54.7	65.5	63.7	63.3	60.7	71.0	51.4	44.6	61.5	55.4	54.1
1987	65.6	76.2	56.0	54.7	65.8	64.3	63.8	61.5	71.5	52.5	45.5	62.3	56.8	55.6
1988	65.9	76.2	56.6	55.3	66.2	64.0	63.8	62.3	72.0	53.4	46.8	63.1	57.4	56.3
1989	66.5	76.4	57.4	55.9	66.7	64.7	64.2	63.0	72.5	54.3	47.5	63.8	58.2	56.9
1990	66.4	76.1	57.5	53.7	66.8	63.7	63.3	62.7	71.9	54.3	45.4	63.6	57.3	56.2
1991	66.0	75.5	57.3	51.7	66.6	63.1	62.6	61.6	70.2	53.7	42.1	62.6	56.1	54.9
1992	66.3	75.6	57.8	51.3	66.7	63.8	63.3	61.4	69.7	53.8	41.0	62.4	55.7	54.3
1993	66.2	75.2	57.9	51.5	66.7	63.1	62.4	61.6	69.9	54.1	41.7	62.7	55.7	54.4
1992: Jan	66.1	75.4	57.6	51.7	66.6	63.6	63.0	61.4	69.7	53.8	42.0	62.4	55.7	54.4
Feb	66.1	75.4	57.7	51.5	66.6	63.5	62.9	61.3	69.5	53.8	41.3	62.3	55.6	54.1
Mar	66.2	75.5	57.8	50.6	66.8	63.3	62.9	61.4	69.7	53.8	40.4	62.4	55.5	54.2
Apr	66.4	75.7	57.9	50.4	66.9	63.5	62.8	61.6	69.9	53.9	40.8	62.6	55.7	54.2
May	66.4	75.9	57.7	51.1	66.8	63.8	63.3	61.4	69.8	53.8	40.9	62.5	55.5	54.1
June	66.5	75.8	57.9	51.9	66.8	64.5	63.8	61.4	69.7	53.8	40.2	62.3	56.0	54.6
July	66.5	75.7	58.1	51.2	66.9	64.2	63.7	61.5	69.7	53.9	40.5	62.4	55.9	54.5
Aug	66.4	75.7	57.9	51.4	66.7	64.5	64.1	61.4	69.7	53.8	41.1	62.3	56.3	54.9
Sept	66.3	75.7	57.8	52.2	66.7	64.1	63.4	61.4	69.7	53.7	41.3	62.3	56.1	54.7
Oct	66.1	75.4	57.5	50.4	66.6	63.8	63.3	61.3	69.6	53.6	41.2	62.3	55.7	54.3
Nov	66.2	75.7	57.4	51.4	66.6	63.5	62.9	61.3	69.6	53.7	40.9	62.4	55.5	54.1
Dec	66.2	75.4	57.8	51.7	66.7	63.5	63.0	61.4	69.7	53.7	41.6	62.4	55.4	54.0
1993: Jan	66.0	75.1	57.7	51.4	66.6	63.1	62.4	61.3	69.7	53.7	41.3	62.5	55.0	53.5
Feb	66.1	75.3	57.7	51.9	66.5	63.7	63.2	61.4	69.8	53.8	41.7	62.5	56.0	54.8
Mar	66.0	75.3	57.6	51.5	66.6	63.0	62.4	61.4	69.7	53.9	41.4	62.5	55.4	54.0
Apr	66.0	75.2	57.6	51.8	66.5	63.3	62.3	61.4	69.7	53.8	41.3	62.4	55.5	53.8
May	66.3	75.4	57.9	52.5	66.7	63.4	62.6	61.7	69.9	54.1	42.1	62.7	55.9	54.5
June	66.2	75.3	57.9	51.5	66.7	63.0	62.4	61.6	69.8	54.1	41.5	62.7	55.4	54.1
July	66.2	75.2	57.8	51.8	66.7	62.8	62.3	61.6	69.8	54.1	42.2	62.7	55.5	54.3
Aug	66.0	75.3	57.9	51.6	66.8	62.8	62.4	61.8	70.0	54.2	42.1	62.9	55.6	54.6
Sept	66.0	74.9	57.9	51.2	66.7	62.6	62.3	61.6	69.7	54.2	42.0	62.8	55.4	54.5
Oct	66.2	75.1	58.1	51.1	67.0	62.8	62.1	61.8	69.9	54.3	41.4	62.9	56.0	54.8
Nov	66.2	75.0	58.2	51.2	66.8	63.0	62.5	61.9	70.0	54.5	41.8	63.0	55.9	54.7
Dec	66.3	75.0	58.3	50.9	66.9	63.1	62.3	62.0	70.1	54.7	41.9	63.1	56.3	55.1

[1] Civilian labor force or civilian employment as percent of civilian noninstitutional population in group specified.

Note.—Data relate to persons 16 years of age and over.
See footnote 6 and Note, Table B–33.

Source: Department of Labor, Bureau of Labor Statistics.

TABLE B-38.—*Civilian labor force participation rate by demographic characteristic, 1954–93*

[Percent;[1] monthly data seasonally adjusted]

Year or month	All civilian workers	White						Black and other or black					
		Total	Males			Females			Males			Females		
			Total	16–19 years	20 years and over	Total	16–19 years	20 years and over	Total	Total	16–19 years	20 years and over	Total	16–19 years	20 years and over

Black and other

1954	58.8	58.2	85.6	57.6	87.8	33.3	40.6	32.7	64.0	85.2	61.2	87.1	46.1	31.0	47.7
1955	59.3	58.7	85.4	58.6	87.5	34.5	40.7	34.0	64.2	85.1	60.8	87.8	46.1	32.7	47.5
1956	60.0	59.4	85.6	60.4	87.6	35.7	43.1	35.1	64.9	85.1	61.5	87.8	47.3	36.3	48.4
1957	59.6	59.1	84.8	59.2	86.9	35.7	42.2	35.2	64.4	84.2	58.8	87.0	47.1	33.2	48.6
1958	59.5	58.9	84.3	56.5	86.6	35.8	40.1	35.5	64.8	84.1	57.3	87.1	48.0	31.9	49.8
1959	59.3	58.7	83.8	55.9	86.3	36.0	39.6	35.6	64.3	83.4	55.5	86.7	47.7	28.2	49.8
1960	59.4	58.8	83.4	55.9	86.0	36.5	40.3	36.2	64.5	83.0	57.6	86.2	48.2	32.9	49.9
1961	59.3	58.8	83.0	54.5	85.7	36.9	40.6	36.6	64.1	82.2	55.8	85.5	48.3	32.8	50.1
1962	58.8	58.3	82.1	53.8	84.9	36.7	39.8	36.5	63.2	80.8	53.5	84.2	48.0	33.1	49.6
1963	58.7	58.2	81.5	53.1	84.4	37.2	38.7	37.0	63.0	80.2	51.5	83.9	48.1	32.6	49.9
1964	58.7	58.2	81.1	52.7	84.2	37.5	37.8	37.5	63.1	80.1	49.9	84.1	48.6	31.7	50.7
1965	58.9	58.4	80.8	54.1	83.9	38.1	39.2	38.0	62.9	79.6	51.3	83.7	48.6	29.5	51.1
1966	59.2	58.7	80.6	55.9	83.6	39.2	42.6	38.8	63.0	79.0	51.4	83.3	49.4	33.5	51.6
1967	59.6	59.2	80.6	56.3	83.5	40.1	42.5	39.8	62.8	78.5	51.1	82.9	49.5	35.2	51.6
1968	59.6	59.3	80.4	55.9	83.2	40.7	43.0	40.4	62.2	77.7	49.7	82.2	49.3	34.8	51.4
1969	60.1	59.9	80.2	56.8	83.0	41.8	44.6	41.5	62.1	76.9	49.6	81.4	49.8	34.6	52.0
1970	60.4	60.2	80.0	57.5	82.8	42.6	45.6	42.2	61.8	76.5	47.4	81.4	49.5	34.1	51.8
1971	60.2	60.1	79.6	57.9	82.3	42.6	45.4	42.3	60.9	74.9	44.7	80.0	49.2	31.2	51.8
1972	60.4	60.4	79.6	60.1	82.0	43.2	48.1	42.7	60.2	73.9	46.0	78.6	48.8	32.3	51.2

Black

1972	60.4	60.4	79.6	60.1	82.0	43.2	48.1	42.7	59.9	73.6	46.3	78.5	48.7	32.2	51.2
1973	60.8	60.8	79.4	62.0	81.6	44.1	50.1	43.5	60.2	73.4	45.7	78.4	49.3	34.2	51.6
1974	61.3	61.4	79.4	62.9	81.4	45.2	51.7	44.4	59.8	72.9	46.7	77.6	49.0	33.4	51.4
1975	61.2	61.5	78.7	61.9	80.7	45.9	51.5	45.3	58.8	70.9	42.6	76.0	48.8	34.2	51.1
1976	61.6	61.8	78.4	62.3	80.3	46.9	52.8	46.2	59.0	70.0	41.3	75.4	49.8	32.9	52.5
1977	62.3	62.5	78.5	64.0	80.2	48.0	54.5	47.3	59.8	70.6	43.2	75.6	50.8	32.9	53.6
1978	63.2	63.3	78.6	65.0	80.1	49.4	56.7	48.7	61.5	71.5	44.9	76.2	53.1	37.3	55.5
1979	63.7	63.9	78.6	64.8	80.1	50.5	57.4	49.8	61.4	71.3	43.6	76.3	53.1	36.8	55.4
1980	63.8	64.1	78.2	63.7	79.8	51.2	56.2	50.6	61.0	70.3	43.2	75.1	53.1	34.9	55.6
1981	63.9	64.3	77.9	62.4	79.5	51.9	55.4	51.5	60.8	70.0	41.6	74.5	53.5	34.0	56.0
1982	64.0	64.3	77.4	60.0	79.2	52.4	55.0	52.2	61.0	70.1	39.8	74.7	53.7	33.5	56.2
1983	64.0	64.3	77.1	59.4	78.9	52.7	54.5	52.5	61.5	70.6	39.9	75.2	54.2	33.0	56.8
1984	64.4	64.6	77.1	59.0	78.7	53.3	55.4	53.1	62.2	70.8	41.7	74.8	55.2	35.0	57.6
1985	64.8	65.0	77.0	59.7	78.5	54.1	55.2	54.0	62.9	70.8	44.6	74.4	56.5	37.9	58.6
1986	65.3	65.5	76.9	59.3	78.5	55.0	56.3	54.9	63.3	71.2	43.7	74.8	56.9	39.1	58.9
1987	65.6	65.8	76.8	59.0	78.4	55.7	56.5	55.6	63.8	71.1	43.6	74.7	58.0	39.6	60.0
1988	65.9	66.2	76.9	60.0	78.3	56.4	57.2	56.3	63.8	71.0	43.8	74.6	58.0	37.9	60.1
1989	66.5	66.7	77.1	61.0	78.5	57.2	57.1	57.2	64.2	71.0	44.6	74.4	58.7	40.4	60.6
1990	66.4	66.8	76.9	59.4	78.3	57.5	55.4	57.6	63.3	70.1	40.6	73.8	57.8	36.7	60.0
1991	66.0	66.6	76.4	57.2	77.8	57.4	54.3	57.7	62.6	69.5	37.4	73.4	57.0	33.5	59.3
1992	66.3	66.7	76.4	56.7	77.8	57.8	52.6	58.1	63.3	69.7	40.7	73.1	58.0	35.2	60.1
1993	66.2	66.7	76.1	56.5	77.5	58.0	53.7	58.3	62.4	68.6	39.5	72.0	57.4	34.5	59.5
1992: Jan	66.1	66.6	76.3	57.2	77.7	57.7	52.9	58.0	63.0	70.3	44.4	73.3	57.1	33.6	59.3
Feb	66.1	66.6	76.2	56.5	77.6	57.7	53.1	58.0	62.9	69.8	42.9	73.0	57.2	34.8	59.3
Mar	66.2	66.8	76.3	55.9	77.8	57.9	52.9	58.2	62.9	69.7	39.2	73.2	57.4	32.6	59.8
Apr	66.4	66.9	76.5	56.3	78.0	57.9	51.9	58.3	62.8	69.1	37.2	72.8	57.7	35.0	59.8
May	66.4	66.8	76.6	56.4	78.1	57.7	52.6	58.0	63.3	69.7	37.3	73.4	58.1	36.8	60.1
June	66.5	66.8	76.5	57.0	78.0	57.8	52.5	58.1	63.8	70.2	41.4	73.6	58.6	35.8	60.8
July	66.5	66.9	76.4	56.5	77.9	57.9	52.6	58.3	63.7	69.7	40.3	73.1	58.7	35.5	60.9
Aug	66.4	66.7	76.4	56.5	77.8	57.8	52.6	58.1	64.1	70.0	40.6	73.4	59.2	37.8	61.2
Sept	66.3	66.7	76.5	58.6	77.8	57.7	52.4	58.0	63.4	69.7	41.1	73.0	58.3	37.3	60.3
Oct	66.1	66.6	76.2	56.0	77.7	57.6	51.8	58.0	63.3	69.7	41.7	73.0	58.0	33.5	60.3
Nov	66.2	66.6	76.1	56.9	77.5	57.8	52.6	58.1	62.9	69.4	40.9	72.7	57.6	34.7	59.7
Dec	66.2	66.7	76.2	57.1	77.6	57.8	52.7	58.1	63.0	69.1	42.1	72.2	57.9	34.9	60.1
1993: Jan	66.0	66.6	76.1	56.4	77.5	57.7	53.0	58.1	62.4	69.1	41.1	72.3	56.8	35.5	58.9
Feb	66.1	66.5	76.1	56.7	77.5	57.7	53.2	58.1	63.2	69.7	41.7	73.0	57.8	34.9	59.9
Mar	66.0	66.6	76.2	57.0	77.6	57.7	52.5	58.0	62.4	69.0	41.3	72.2	56.9	32.4	59.2
Apr	66.0	66.5	76.0	56.6	77.4	57.6	53.1	57.9	62.3	68.6	44.6	71.3	57.2	31.8	59.6
May	66.3	66.7	76.1	56.1	77.5	58.0	55.0	58.2	62.6	68.9	42.7	72.0	57.4	35.5	59.4
June	66.2	66.7	76.1	56.8	77.5	58.0	52.6	58.4	62.4	68.6	39.8	71.9	57.3	34.0	59.5
July	66.2	66.7	76.1	56.5	77.5	58.0	53.3	58.3	62.3	68.8	41.0	72.0	57.0	36.0	59.8
Aug	66.2	66.8	76.1	57.3	77.5	58.1	53.3	58.5	62.4	68.9	39.2	72.4	57.1	34.5	59.2
Sept	66.0	66.7	75.9	56.1	77.3	58.1	54.1	58.4	62.3	68.3	38.0	71.8	57.3	33.8	59.5
Oct	66.2	67.0	76.2	56.1	77.7	58.3	55.2	58.5	62.1	67.6	34.9	71.5	57.6	34.1	59.8
Nov	66.2	66.8	75.8	56.7	77.2	58.3	54.4	58.6	62.5	68.0	34.9	71.8	58.1	36.9	60.1
Dec	66.3	66.9	75.9	56.0	77.4	58.4	54.2	58.7	62.3	67.3	35.2	70.9	58.1	35.1	60.3

[1] Civilian labor force as percent of civilian noninstitutional population in group specified.
Note.—Data relate to persons 16 years of age and over.
See footnote 6 and Note, Table B-33.
Source: Department of Labor, Bureau of Labor Statistics.

Table B-39.—Civilian employment/population ratio by demographic characteristic, 1954-93

[Percent;[1] monthly data seasonally adjusted]

Year or month	All civilian workers	White Total	White Males Total	White Males 16–19 years	White Males 20 years and over	White Females Total	White Females 16–19 years	White Females 20 years and over	Black and other or black Total	Males Total	Males 16–19 years	Males 20 years and over	Females Total	Females 16–19 years	Females 20 years and over
											Black and other				
1954	55.5	55.2	81.5	49.9	84.0	31.4	36.4	31.1	58.0	76.5	52.4	79.2	41.9	24.7	43.7
1955	56.7	56.5	82.2	52.0	84.7	33.0	37.0	32.7	58.7	77.6	52.7	80.4	42.2	26.4	43.9
1956	57.5	57.3	82.7	54.1	85.0	34.2	38.9	33.8	59.5	78.4	52.2	81.3	43.0	28.0	44.7
1957	57.1	56.8	81.8	52.4	84.1	34.2	38.2	33.9	59.3	77.2	48.0	80.5	43.7	26.5	45.5
1958	55.4	55.3	79.2	47.6	81.8	33.6	35.0	33.5	56.7	72.5	42.0	76.0	42.8	22.8	45.0
1959	56.0	55.9	79.9	48.1	82.8	34.0	34.8	34.0	57.5	73.8	41.4	77.6	43.2	20.3	45.7
1960	56.1	55.9	79.4	48.1	82.4	34.6	35.1	34.5	57.9	74.1	43.8	77.9	43.6	24.8	45.8
1961	55.4	55.3	78.2	45.9	81.4	34.5	34.6	34.5	56.2	71.7	41.0	75.5	42.6	23.2	44.8
1962	55.5	55.4	78.4	46.4	81.5	34.7	34.8	34.7	56.3	72.0	41.7	75.7	42.7	23.1	44.9
1963	55.4	55.3	77.7	44.7	81.1	35.0	32.9	35.2	56.2	71.8	37.4	76.2	42.7	21.3	45.2
1964	55.7	55.5	77.8	45.0	81.3	35.5	32.2	35.8	57.0	72.9	37.8	77.7	43.4	21.8	46.1
1965	56.2	56.0	77.9	47.1	81.5	36.2	33.7	36.5	57.8	73.7	39.4	78.7	44.1	20.2	47.3
1966	56.9	56.8	78.3	50.1	81.7	37.5	37.5	37.5	58.4	74.0	40.5	79.2	45.1	23.1	48.2
1967	57.3	57.2	78.4	50.2	81.7	38.3	37.7	38.3	58.2	73.8	38.8	79.4	45.0	24.8	47.9
1968	57.5	57.4	78.3	50.3	81.6	38.9	37.8	39.1	58.0	73.3	38.7	78.9	45.2	24.7	48.2
1969	58.0	58.0	78.2	51.1	81.4	40.1	39.5	40.1	58.1	72.8	39.0	78.4	45.9	25.1	48.9
1970	57.4	57.5	76.8	49.6	80.1	40.3	39.5	40.4	56.8	70.9	35.5	76.8	44.9	22.4	48.2
1971	56.6	56.8	75.7	49.2	79.0	39.9	38.6	40.1	54.9	68.1	31.8	74.2	43.9	20.2	47.3
1972	57.0	57.4	76.0	51.5	79.0	40.7	41.3	40.6	54.1	67.3	32.4	73.2	43.3	19.9	46.7
											Black				
1972	57.0	57.4	76.0	51.5	79.0	40.7	41.3	40.6	53.7	66.8	31.6	73.0	43.0	19.2	46.5
1973	57.8	58.2	76.5	54.3	79.2	41.8	43.6	41.6	54.5	67.5	32.8	73.7	43.8	22.0	47.2
1974	57.8	58.3	75.9	54.4	78.6	44.3	44.3	42.2	53.5	65.8	31.4	71.9	43.5	20.9	46.9
1975	56.1	56.7	73.0	50.6	75.7	42.0	42.5	41.9	50.1	60.6	26.3	66.5	41.6	20.2	44.9
1976	56.8	57.5	73.4	51.5	76.0	43.2	44.2	43.1	50.8	60.6	25.8	66.8	42.8	19.2	46.4
1977	57.9	58.6	74.1	54.4	76.5	44.5	45.9	44.4	51.4	61.4	26.4	67.5	43.3	18.5	47.0
1978	59.3	60.0	75.0	56.3	77.2	46.3	48.5	46.1	53.6	63.3	28.5	69.1	45.8	22.1	49.3
1979	59.9	60.6	75.1	55.7	77.3	47.5	49.4	47.3	53.8	63.4	28.7	69.1	46.0	22.4	49.3
1980	59.2	60.0	73.4	53.4	75.6	47.8	47.9	47.8	52.3	60.4	27.0	65.8	45.7	21.0	49.1
1981	59.0	60.0	72.8	51.3	75.1	48.3	46.2	48.5	51.3	59.1	24.6	64.5	45.1	19.7	48.5
1982	57.8	58.8	70.6	47.0	73.0	48.1	44.6	48.4	49.4	56.0	20.3	61.4	44.2	17.7	47.5
1983	57.9	58.9	70.4	47.4	72.6	48.5	44.5	48.9	49.5	56.3	20.4	61.6	44.1	17.0	47.4
1984	59.5	60.5	72.1	49.1	74.3	49.8	47.0	50.0	52.3	59.2	23.9	64.1	46.7	20.1	49.8
1985	60.1	61.0	72.3	49.9	74.3	50.7	47.1	51.0	53.4	60.0	26.3	64.6	48.1	23.1	50.9
1986	60.7	61.5	72.3	49.6	74.3	51.7	47.9	52.0	54.1	60.6	26.5	65.1	48.8	23.8	51.6
1987	61.5	62.3	72.7	49.9	74.7	52.8	49.0	53.1	55.6	62.0	28.5	66.4	50.3	25.8	53.0
1988	62.3	63.1	73.2	51.7	75.1	53.8	50.2	54.0	56.3	62.7	29.4	67.1	51.2	25.8	53.9
1989	63.0	63.8	73.7	52.6	75.4	54.6	50.5	54.9	56.9	62.8	30.4	67.0	52.0	27.1	54.6
1990	62.7	63.6	73.2	51.0	75.0	54.8	48.5	55.2	56.2	61.8	27.6	66.1	51.6	25.7	54.2
1991	61.6	62.6	71.5	47.2	73.3	54.3	46.1	54.8	54.9	60.5	23.8	64.9	50.3	21.4	53.1
1992	61.4	62.4	71.1	46.3	72.9	54.3	44.3	54.9	54.3	59.1	23.6	63.3	50.4	22.1	53.1
1993	61.6	62.7	71.3	46.6	73.1	54.7	45.8	55.3	54.4	59.1	23.6	63.2	50.5	21.6	53.2
1992: Jan	61.4	62.4	71.1	47.4	72.8	54.4	44.9	55.0	54.4	59.9	28.1	63.6	50.0	21.9	52.6
Feb	61.3	62.3	70.9	45.7	72.7	54.3	44.9	54.9	54.1	59.2	25.6	63.1	49.9	21.9	52.6
Mar	61.4	62.4	71.0	44.4	73.0	54.4	44.6	55.1	54.2	59.1	24.7	63.1	50.1	21.3	52.9
Apr	61.6	62.6	71.3	46.6	73.1	54.5	44.1	55.1	54.2	59.1	21.5	63.5	50.1	23.0	52.7
May	61.4	62.5	71.2	45.9	73.0	54.3	44.8	55.0	54.1	58.9	21.2	63.3	50.1	21.8	52.8
June	61.4	62.3	71.0	45.1	72.9	54.2	42.7	55.0	54.6	59.3	22.1	63.7	50.7	23.3	53.3
July	61.5	62.4	71.2	46.0	73.0	54.3	43.9	55.0	54.5	58.9	23.0	63.0	50.9	21.7	53.7
Aug	61.4	62.3	71.1	46.1	72.9	54.2	44.7	54.8	54.9	59.1	22.7	63.3	51.5	25.1	54.0
Sept	61.4	62.3	71.1	47.2	72.9	54.1	44.2	54.8	54.7	59.2	23.2	63.3	51.0	21.9	53.8
Oct	61.3	62.3	71.1	47.2	72.8	54.1	44.1	54.8	54.3	58.9	23.7	62.9	50.5	19.7	53.4
Nov	61.3	62.4	71.0	46.9	72.8	54.4	43.7	55.1	54.1	59.2	23.1	63.4	49.9	21.6	52.6
Dec	61.4	62.4	71.2	47.1	73.0	54.3	44.7	54.9	54.0	58.6	24.6	62.6	50.2	22.0	52.9
1993: Jan	61.3	62.5	71.2	46.3	73.0	54.3	45.0	54.9	53.5	59.0	24.8	63.0	49.1	21.8	51.6
Feb	61.4	62.5	71.2	46.6	73.0	54.3	45.0	54.9	54.8	60.1	25.2	64.1	50.5	21.5	53.2
Mar	61.4	62.5	71.2	47.3	73.0	54.4	44.3	55.1	54.0	58.7	23.1	62.8	50.1	19.4	53.0
Apr	61.4	62.4	71.2	46.1	73.0	54.3	45.4	54.9	53.8	58.3	23.7	62.2	50.1	18.0	53.1
May	61.7	62.7	71.3	46.4	73.1	54.6	46.0	55.2	54.5	59.3	25.6	63.2	50.5	21.7	53.2
June	61.6	62.7	71.3	46.3	73.1	54.7	45.2	55.3	54.1	58.9	24.4	62.9	50.2	18.8	53.1
July	61.6	62.7	71.2	46.5	73.0	54.8	46.2	55.4	54.3	59.6	25.5	63.5	50.0	23.5	52.5
Aug	61.8	62.9	71.4	47.2	73.2	54.9	45.9	55.5	54.6	59.7	25.5	63.7	50.5	23.5	53.0
Sept	61.6	62.8	71.3	46.7	73.1	54.9	46.3	55.4	54.5	58.9	22.9	63.1	50.8	22.9	53.4
Oct	61.8	62.9	71.4	46.0	73.3	54.9	46.3	55.4	54.8	59.1	20.8	63.6	51.2	22.9	53.9
Nov	61.9	63.0	71.6	46.7	73.4	55.1	47.2	55.6	54.7	58.6	21.2	63.0	51.5	22.2	54.2
Dec	62.0	63.1	71.5	46.5	73.3	55.2	46.9	55.8	55.1	59.1	21.5	63.5	51.7	22.8	54.5

[1] Civilian employment as percent of civilian noninstitutional population in group specified.

Note.—Data relate to persons 16 years of age and over.
See footnote 6 and Note, Table B-33.

Source: Department of Labor, Bureau of Labor Statistics.

TABLE B-40.—Civilian unemployment rate, 1948-93

[Percent;[1] monthly data seasonally adjusted]

Year or month	All civilian workers	Males Total	Males 16-19 years	Males 20 years and over	Females Total	Females 16-19 years	Females 20 years and over	Both sexes 16-19 years	White	Black and other	Black	Experienced wage and salary workers	Married men, spouse present[2]	Women who maintain families
1948	3.8	3.6	9.8	3.2	4.1	8.3	3.6	9.2	3.5	5.9		4.3		
1949	5.9	5.9	14.3	5.4	6.0	12.3	5.3	13.4	5.6	8.9		6.8	3.5	
1950	5.3	5.1	12.7	4.7	5.7	11.4	5.1	12.2	4.9	9.0		6.0	4.6	
1951	3.3	2.8	8.1	2.5	4.4	8.3	4.0	8.2	3.1	5.3		3.7	1.5	
1952	3.0	2.8	8.9	2.4	3.6	8.0	3.2	8.5	2.8	5.4		3.4	1.4	
1953	2.9	2.8	7.9	2.5	3.3	7.2	2.9	7.6	2.7	4.5		3.2	1.7	
1954	5.5	5.3	13.5	4.9	6.0	11.4	5.5	12.6	5.0	9.9		6.2	4.0	
1955	4.4	4.2	11.6	3.8	4.9	10.2	4.4	11.0	3.9	8.7		4.8	2.6	
1956	4.1	3.8	11.1	3.4	4.8	11.2	4.2	11.1	3.6	8.3		4.4	2.3	
1957	4.3	4.1	12.4	3.6	4.7	10.6	4.1	11.6	3.8	7.9		4.6	2.8	
1958	6.8	6.8	17.1	6.2	6.8	14.3	6.1	15.9	6.1	12.6		7.3	5.1	
1959	5.5	5.2	15.3	4.7	5.9	13.5	5.2	14.6	4.8	10.7		5.7	3.6	
1960	5.5	5.4	15.3	4.7	5.9	13.9	5.1	14.7	5.0	10.2		5.7	3.7	
1961	6.7	6.4	17.1	5.7	7.2	16.3	6.3	16.8	6.0	12.4		6.8	4.6	
1962	5.5	5.2	14.7	4.6	6.2	14.6	5.4	14.7	4.9	10.9		5.6	3.6	
1963	5.7	5.2	17.2	4.5	6.5	17.2	5.4	17.2	5.0	10.8		5.6	3.4	
1964	5.2	4.6	15.8	3.9	6.2	16.6	5.2	16.2	4.6	9.6		5.0	2.8	
1965	4.5	4.0	14.1	3.2	5.5	15.7	4.5	14.8	4.1	8.1		4.3	2.4	
1966	3.8	3.2	11.7	2.5	4.8	14.1	3.8	12.8	3.4	7.3		3.5	1.9	
1967	3.8	3.1	12.3	2.3	5.2	13.5	4.2	12.9	3.4	7.4		3.6	1.8	4.9
1968	3.6	2.9	11.6	2.2	4.8	14.0	3.8	12.7	3.2	6.7		3.4	1.6	4.4
1969	3.5	2.8	11.4	2.1	4.7	13.3	3.7	12.2	3.1	6.4		3.3	1.5	4.4
1970	4.9	4.4	15.0	3.5	5.9	15.6	4.8	15.3	4.5	8.2		4.8	2.6	5.4
1971	5.9	5.3	16.6	4.4	6.9	17.2	5.7	16.9	5.4	9.9		5.7	3.2	7.3
1972	5.6	5.0	15.9	4.0	6.6	16.7	5.4	16.2	5.1	10.0	10.4	5.3	2.8	7.2
1973	4.9	4.2	13.9	3.3	6.0	15.3	4.9	14.5	4.3	9.0	9.4	4.5	2.3	7.1
1974	5.6	4.9	15.6	3.8	6.7	16.6	5.5	16.0	5.0	9.9	10.5	5.3	2.7	7.0
1975	8.5	7.9	20.1	6.8	9.3	19.7	8.0	19.9	7.8	13.8	14.8	8.2	5.1	10.0
1976	7.7	7.1	19.2	5.9	8.6	18.7	7.4	19.0	7.0	13.1	14.0	7.3	4.2	10.1
1977	7.1	6.3	17.3	5.2	8.2	18.3	7.0	17.8	6.2	13.1	14.0	6.6	3.6	9.4
1978	6.1	5.3	15.8	4.3	7.2	17.1	6.0	16.4	5.2	11.9	12.8	5.6	2.8	8.5
1979	5.8	5.1	15.9	4.2	6.8	16.4	5.7	16.1	5.1	11.3	12.3	5.5	2.8	8.3
1980	7.1	6.9	18.3	5.9	7.4	17.2	6.4	17.8	6.3	13.1	14.3	6.9	4.2	9.2
1981	7.6	7.4	20.1	6.3	7.9	19.0	6.8	19.6	6.7	14.2	15.6	7.3	4.3	10.4
1982	9.7	9.9	24.4	8.8	9.4	21.9	8.3	23.2	8.6	17.3	18.9	9.3	6.5	11.7
1983	9.6	9.9	23.3	8.9	9.2	21.3	8.1	22.4	8.4	17.8	19.5	9.2	6.5	12.2
1984	7.5	7.4	19.6	6.6	7.6	18.0	6.8	18.9	6.5	14.4	15.9	7.1	4.6	10.3
1985	7.2	7.0	19.5	6.2	7.4	17.6	6.6	18.6	6.2	13.7	15.1	6.8	4.3	10.4
1986	7.0	6.9	19.0	6.1	7.1	17.6	6.2	18.3	6.0	13.1	14.5	6.6	4.4	9.8
1987	6.2	6.2	17.8	5.4	6.2	15.9	5.4	16.9	5.3	11.6	13.0	5.8	3.9	9.2
1988	5.5	5.5	16.0	4.8	5.6	14.4	4.9	15.3	4.7	10.4	11.7	5.2	3.3	8.1
1989	5.3	5.2	15.9	4.5	5.4	14.0	4.7	15.0	4.5	10.0	11.4	5.0	3.0	8.1
1990	5.5	5.6	16.3	4.9	5.4	14.7	4.8	15.5	4.7	10.1	11.3	5.3	3.4	8.2
1991	6.7	7.0	19.8	6.3	6.3	17.4	5.7	18.6	6.0	11.1	12.4	6.5	4.4	9.1
1992	7.4	7.8	21.5	7.0	6.9	18.5	6.3	20.0	6.5	12.7	14.1	7.1	5.0	9.9
1993	6.8	7.1	20.4	6.4	6.5	17.4	5.9	19.0	6.0	11.7	12.9	6.5	4.4	9.5
1992: Jan	7.1	7.6	20.3	6.9	6.6	17.3	6.0	18.9	6.3	12.4	13.6	6.9	4.8	9.0
Feb	7.4	7.8	22.0	7.1	6.8	17.8	6.1	20.0	6.5	12.4	14.0	7.1	5.1	9.4
Mar	7.3	7.8	22.3	7.0	6.8	18.0	6.2	20.2	6.5	12.3	13.9	7.1	4.8	9.9
Apr	7.3	7.6	20.3	7.0	6.9	17.6	6.2	19.0	6.4	12.3	13.8	7.0	4.9	10.0
May	7.5	8.0	21.3	7.3	6.9	18.5	6.2	19.9	6.5	13.0	14.6	7.2	5.1	9.9
June	7.7	8.1	24.1	7.3	7.1	21.1	6.3	22.7	6.7	13.2	14.4	7.2	5.2	10.0
July	7.5	7.9	21.8	7.1	7.1	19.7	6.4	20.8	6.6	12.9	14.4	7.2	5.2	10.2
Aug	7.5	7.9	21.9	7.1	7.1	17.9	6.5	20.0	6.6	12.8	14.3	7.2	5.2	10.7
Sept	7.5	7.8	22.4	7.0	7.1	19.1	6.4	20.9	6.6	12.5	13.8	7.2	5.2	9.4
Oct	7.3	7.7	19.3	7.1	6.7	17.2	6.1	18.3	6.4	12.7	14.2	7.0	5.1	9.3
Nov	7.3	7.7	21.3	6.9	6.9	19.3	6.2	20.3	6.3	12.6	14.0	7.0	4.9	10.5
Dec	7.3	7.5	20.8	6.8	7.1	18.0	6.4	19.5	6.4	12.8	14.2	7.0	4.8	10.2
1993: Jan	7.1	7.2	20.7	6.5	7.0	18.4	6.3	19.6	6.2	12.7	14.1	6.8	4.5	10.4
Feb	7.0	7.3	20.6	6.6	6.7	18.5	6.0	19.6	6.1	12.1	13.3	6.7	4.6	10.1
Mar	7.0	7.4	20.3	6.7	6.4	18.5	5.7	19.5	6.1	12.0	13.5	6.7	4.7	9.0
Apr	7.0	7.3	22.4	6.5	6.6	17.9	6.0	20.3	6.1	12.4	13.7	6.7	4.5	9.6
May	6.9	7.2	20.5	6.5	6.6	19.1	5.9	19.8	6.1	11.8	12.9	6.6	4.5	9.8
June	6.9	7.2	21.1	6.5	6.6	17.6	5.9	19.5	6.1	12.0	13.3	6.6	4.4	9.7
July	6.8	7.2	20.4	6.5	6.4	16.2	5.8	18.4	6.0	11.6	12.8	6.5	4.5	9.6
Aug	6.7	7.1	20.1	6.4	6.3	16.5	5.7	18.4	5.9	11.5	12.5	6.4	4.4	9.0
Sept	6.7	6.9	19.4	6.3	6.3	16.4	5.8	17.9	5.8	11.4	12.5	6.3	4.2	9.0
Oct	6.7	6.9	20.3	6.2	6.4	17.3	5.8	18.9	6.1	10.9	11.9	6.4	4.4	9.3
Nov	6.5	6.6	19.9	5.9	6.4	16.5	5.7	18.3	5.6	11.3	12.5	6.2	4.0	9.0
Dec	6.4	6.5	19.4	5.8	6.2	16.1	5.7	17.8	5.6	10.7	11.5	6.2	3.9	10.2

[1] Unemployed as percent of civilian labor force in group specified.
[2] Data for 1949 and 1951-54 are for April; 1950, for March.

Note.—Data relate to persons 16 years of age and over.
See footnote 6 and Note, Table B-33.

Source: Department of Labor, Bureau of Labor Statistics.

TABLE B-41.—*Civilian unemployment rate by demographic characteristic, 1950-93*

[Percent;[1] monthly data seasonally adjusted]

Year or month	All civilian workers	White Total	White Males Total	White Males 16-19 years	White Males 20 years and over	White Females Total	White Females 16-19 years	White Females 20 years and over	Black and other or black Total	Black and other or black Males Total	Black and other or black Males 16-19 years	Black and other or black Males 20 years and over	Black and other or black Females Total	Black and other or black Females 16-19 years	Black and other or black Females 20 years and over
											Black and other				
1950	5.3	4.9	4.7			5.3			9.0	9.4			8.4		
1951	3.3	3.1	2.6			4.2			5.3	4.9			6.1		
1952	3.0	2.8	2.5			3.3			5.4	5.2			5.7		
1953	2.9	2.7	2.5			3.1			4.5	4.8			4.1		
1954	5.5	5.0	4.8	13.4	4.4	5.5	10.4	5.1	9.9	10.3	14.4	9.9	9.2	20.6	8.4
1955	4.4	3.9	3.7	11.3	3.3	4.3	9.1	3.9	8.7	8.8	13.4	8.4	8.5	19.2	7.7
1956	4.1	3.6	3.4	10.5	3.0	4.2	9.7	3.7	8.3	7.9	15.0	7.4	8.9	22.8	7.8
1957	4.3	3.8	3.6	11.5	3.2	4.3	9.5	3.8	7.9	8.3	18.4	7.6	7.3	20.2	6.4
1958	6.8	6.1	6.1	15.7	5.5	6.2	12.7	5.6	12.6	13.7	26.8	12.7	10.8	28.4	9.5
1959	5.5	4.8	4.6	14.0	4.1	5.3	12.0	4.7	10.7	11.5	25.2	10.5	9.4	27.7	8.3
1960	5.5	5.0	4.8	14.0	4.2	5.3	12.7	4.6	10.2	10.7	24.0	9.6	9.4	24.8	8.3
1961	6.7	6.0	5.7	15.7	5.1	6.5	14.8	5.7	12.4	12.8	26.8	11.7	11.9	29.2	10.6
1962	5.5	4.9	4.6	13.7	4.0	5.5	12.8	4.7	10.9	10.9	22.0	10.0	11.0	30.2	9.6
1963	5.7	5.0	4.7	15.9	3.9	5.8	15.1	4.8	10.8	10.5	27.3	9.2	11.2	34.7	9.4
1964	5.2	4.6	4.1	14.7	3.4	5.5	14.9	4.6	9.6	8.9	24.3	7.7	10.7	31.6	9.0
1965	4.5	4.1	3.6	12.9	2.9	5.0	14.0	4.0	8.1	7.4	23.3	6.0	9.2	31.7	7.5
1966	3.8	3.4	2.8	10.5	2.2	4.3	12.1	3.3	7.3	6.3	21.3	4.9	8.7	31.3	6.6
1967	3.8	3.4	2.7	10.7	2.1	4.6	11.5	3.8	7.4	6.0	23.9	4.3	9.1	29.6	7.1
1968	3.6	3.2	2.6	10.1	2.0	4.3	12.1	3.4	6.7	5.6	22.1	3.9	8.3	28.7	6.3
1969	3.5	3.1	2.5	10.0	1.9	4.2	11.5	3.4	6.4	5.3	21.4	3.7	7.8	27.6	5.8
1970	4.9	4.5	4.0	13.7	3.2	5.4	13.4	4.4	8.2	7.3	25.0	5.6	9.3	34.5	6.9
1971	5.9	5.4	4.9	15.1	4.0	6.3	15.1	5.3	9.9	9.1	28.8	7.3	10.9	35.4	8.7
1972	5.6	5.1	4.5	14.2	3.6	5.9	14.2	4.9	10.0	8.9	29.7	6.9	11.4	38.4	8.8
											Black				
1972	5.6	5.1	4.5	14.2	3.6	5.9	14.2	4.9	10.4	9.3	31.7	7.0	11.8	40.5	9.0
1973	4.9	4.3	3.8	12.3	3.0	5.3	13.0	4.3	9.4	8.0	27.8	6.0	11.1	36.1	8.6
1974	5.6	5.0	4.4	13.5	3.5	6.1	14.5	5.1	10.5	9.8	33.1	7.4	11.3	37.4	8.8
1975	8.5	7.8	7.2	18.3	6.2	8.6	17.4	7.5	14.8	14.8	38.1	12.5	14.8	41.0	12.2
1976	7.7	7.0	6.4	17.3	5.4	7.9	16.4	6.8	14.0	13.7	37.5	11.4	14.3	41.6	11.7
1977	7.1	6.2	5.5	15.0	4.7	7.3	15.9	6.2	14.0	13.3	39.2	10.7	14.9	43.4	12.3
1978	6.1	5.2	4.6	13.5	3.7	6.2	14.4	5.2	12.8	11.8	36.7	9.3	13.8	40.8	11.2
1979	5.8	5.1	4.5	13.9	3.6	5.9	14.0	5.0	12.3	11.4	34.2	9.3	13.3	39.1	10.9
1980	7.1	6.3	6.1	16.2	5.3	6.5	14.8	5.6	14.3	14.5	37.5	12.4	14.0	39.8	11.9
1981	7.6	6.7	6.5	17.9	5.6	6.9	16.6	5.9	15.6	15.7	40.7	13.5	15.6	42.2	13.4
1982	9.7	8.6	8.8	21.7	7.8	8.3	19.0	7.3	18.9	20.1	48.9	17.8	17.6	47.1	15.4
1983	9.6	8.4	8.8	20.2	7.9	7.9	18.3	6.9	19.5	20.3	48.8	18.1	18.6	48.2	16.5
1984	7.5	6.5	6.4	16.8	5.7	6.5	15.2	5.8	15.9	16.4	42.7	14.3	15.4	42.6	13.5
1985	7.2	6.2	6.1	16.5	5.4	6.4	14.8	5.7	15.1	15.3	41.0	13.2	14.9	39.2	13.1
1986	7.0	6.0	6.0	16.3	5.3	6.1	14.9	5.4	14.5	14.8	39.3	12.9	14.2	39.2	12.4
1987	6.2	5.3	5.4	15.5	4.8	5.2	13.4	4.6	13.0	12.7	34.4	11.1	13.2	34.9	11.6
1988	5.5	4.7	4.7	13.9	4.1	4.7	12.3	4.1	11.7	11.7	32.7	10.1	11.7	32.0	10.4
1989	5.3	4.5	4.5	13.7	3.9	4.5	11.5	4.0	11.4	11.5	31.9	10.0	11.4	33.0	9.8
1990	5.5	4.7	4.8	14.2	4.3	4.6	12.6	4.1	11.3	11.8	32.1	10.4	10.8	30.0	9.6
1991	6.7	6.0	6.4	17.5	5.7	5.5	15.2	4.9	12.4	12.9	36.5	11.5	11.9	36.1	10.5
1992	7.4	6.5	6.9	18.4	6.3	6.0	15.7	5.4	14.1	15.2	42.0	13.4	13.0	37.2	11.7
1993	6.8	6.0	6.2	17.6	5.6	5.7	14.6	5.1	12.9	13.8	40.1	12.1	12.0	37.5	10.6
1992: Jan	7.1	6.3	6.8	17.2	6.2	5.7	15.0	5.2	13.6	14.8	36.7	13.2	12.5	34.9	11.3
Feb	7.4	6.5	6.9	19.0	6.3	5.9	15.4	5.3	14.0	15.3	40.4	13.5	12.8	37.1	11.4
Mar	7.3	6.5	6.9	20.6	6.2	6.0	15.7	5.4	13.9	15.2	37.1	13.8	12.7	34.6	11.5
Apr	7.3	6.4	6.8	17.2	6.3	5.9	15.0	5.4	13.8	14.5	42.3	12.8	13.1	34.4	11.9
May	7.5	6.5	7.1	18.6	6.5	5.8	14.7	5.2	14.6	15.5	43.1	13.8	13.7	40.9	12.1
June	7.7	6.7	7.2	20.8	6.5	6.1	18.7	5.4	14.4	15.5	46.6	13.4	13.4	34.9	12.2
July	7.5	6.6	6.9	18.6	6.3	6.3	16.5	5.7	14.4	15.5	42.9	13.7	13.3	38.9	11.9
Aug	7.5	6.6	6.9	18.5	6.3	6.2	15.1	5.6	14.3	15.5	44.0	13.7	13.1	33.5	11.9
Sept	7.5	6.6	7.0	19.5	6.3	6.2	15.7	5.6	13.8	15.1	43.6	13.3	12.5	41.4	10.8
Oct	7.3	6.4	6.8	15.7	6.3	6.0	14.8	5.5	14.2	15.6	43.0	13.8	12.8	41.1	11.3
Nov	7.3	6.3	6.7	17.6	6.1	5.9	16.8	5.2	14.0	14.7	43.5	12.8	13.3	37.7	11.9
Dec	7.3	6.4	6.6	17.5	6.0	6.1	15.2	5.6	14.2	15.2	41.5	13.4	13.2	37.0	11.9
1993: Jan	7.1	6.2	6.4	17.9	5.8	5.9	15.0	5.4	14.1	14.6	39.7	12.9	13.7	38.5	12.3
Feb	7.0	6.1	6.4	17.8	5.8	5.8	15.3	5.2	13.3	13.9	39.5	12.2	12.6	38.4	11.2
Mar	7.0	6.1	6.5	17.1	5.9	5.7	15.5	5.1	13.5	14.9	44.1	13.0	12.1	40.1	10.6
Apr	7.0	6.1	6.4	18.5	5.7	5.7	14.5	5.2	13.7	15.0	46.8	12.7	12.4	43.2	10.9
May	6.9	6.1	6.3	17.2	5.7	5.8	16.3	5.1	12.9	14.0	40.2	12.2	11.9	38.7	10.4
June	6.9	6.1	6.3	18.4	5.7	5.8	14.0	5.3	13.3	14.1	38.8	12.6	12.4	44.8	10.7
July	6.8	6.0	6.4	17.7	5.8	5.5	13.4	5.1	12.8	13.4	37.9	11.8	12.3	34.7	11.0
Aug	6.7	5.9	6.2	17.7	5.6	5.5	14.0	5.0	12.5	13.4	34.9	12.0	11.6	32.0	10.5
Sept	6.7	5.8	6.1	16.8	5.5	5.6	14.3	5.0	12.5	13.7	39.7	12.1	11.4	32.3	10.2
Oct	6.7	6.1	6.3	17.9	5.7	5.9	16.0	5.3	11.9	12.6	40.6	11.0	11.1	32.8	10.0
Nov	6.5	5.6	5.6	17.7	5.0	5.6	13.3	5.1	12.5	13.8	39.2	12.3	11.3	39.7	9.7
Dec	6.4	5.6	5.8	16.9	5.2	5.4	13.4	4.9	11.5	12.1	38.8	10.5	11.0	35.2	9.7

[1] Unemployed as percent of civilian labor force in group specified.
Note.—See Note, Table B-40.
Source: Department of Labor, Bureau of Labor Statistics.

TABLE B-42.—*Unemployment by duration and reason, 1950–93*

[Thousands of persons, except as noted; monthly data seasonally adjusted [1]]

Year or month	Unem-ploy-ment	Duration of unemployment					Reason for unemployment				
		Less than 5 weeks	5–14 weeks	15–26 weeks	27 weeks and over	Average (mean) dura-tion (weeks)	Median dura-tion (weeks)	Job losers			Job leav-ers	Reen-trants	New en-trants
								Total	On layoff	Other			
1950	3,288	1,450	1,055	425	357	12.1							
1951	2,055	1,177	574	166	137	9.7							
1952	1,883	1,135	516	148	84	8.4							
1953	1,834	1,142	482	132	78	8.0							
1954	3,532	1,605	1,116	495	317	11.8							
1955	2,852	1,335	815	366	336	13.0							
1956	2,750	1,412	805	301	232	11.3							
1957	2,859	1,408	891	321	239	10.5							
1958	4,602	1,753	1,396	785	667	13.9							
1959	3,740	1,585	1,114	469	571	14.4							
1960	3,852	1,719	1,176	503	454	12.8							
1961	4,714	1,806	1,376	728	804	15.6							
1962	3,911	1,663	1,134	534	585	14.7							
1963	4,070	1,751	1,231	535	553	14.0							
1964	3,786	1,697	1,117	491	482	13.3							
1965	3,366	1,628	983	404	351	11.8							
1966	2,875	1,573	779	287	239	10.4							
1967 [2]	2,975	1,634	893	271	177	8.7	2.3	1,229	394	836	438	945	396
1968	2,817	1,594	810	256	156	8.4	4.5	1,070	334	736	431	909	407
1969	2,832	1,629	827	242	133	7.8	4.4	1,017	339	678	436	965	413
1970	4,093	2,139	1,290	428	235	8.6	4.9	1,811	675	1,137	550	1,228	504
1971	5,016	2,245	1,585	668	519	11.3	6.3	2,323	735	1,588	590	1,472	630
1972	4,882	2,242	1,472	601	566	12.0	6.2	2,108	582	1,526	641	1,456	677
1973	4,365	2,224	1,314	483	343	10.0	5.2	1,694	472	1,221	683	1,340	649
1974	5,156	2,604	1,597	574	381	9.8	5.2	2,242	746	1,495	768	1,463	681
1975	7,929	2,940	2,484	1,303	1,203	14.2	8.4	4,386	1,671	2,714	827	1,892	823
1976	7,406	2,844	2,196	1,018	1,348	15.8	8.2	3,679	1,050	2,628	903	1,928	895
1977	6,991	2,919	2,132	913	1,028	14.3	7.0	3,166	865	2,300	909	1,963	953
1978	6,202	2,865	1,923	766	648	11.9	5.9	2,585	712	1,873	874	1,857	885
1979	6,137	2,950	1,946	706	535	10.8	5.4	2,635	851	1,784	880	1,806	817
1980	7,637	3,295	2,470	1,052	820	11.9	6.5	3,947	1,488	2,459	891	1,927	872
1981	8,273	3,449	2,539	1,122	1,162	13.7	6.9	4,267	1,430	2,837	923	2,102	981
1982	10,678	3,883	3,311	1,708	1,776	15.6	8.7	6,268	2,127	4,141	840	2,384	1,185
1983	10,717	3,570	2,937	1,652	2,559	20.0	10.1	6,258	1,780	4,478	830	2,412	1,216
1984	8,539	3,350	2,451	1,104	1,634	18.2	7.9	4,421	1,171	3,250	823	2,184	1,110
1985	8,312	3,498	2,509	1,025	1,280	15.6	6.8	4,139	1,157	2,982	877	2,256	1,039
1986	8,237	3,448	2,557	1,045	1,187	15.0	6.9	4,033	1,090	2,943	1,015	2,160	1,029
1987	7,425	3,246	2,196	943	1,040	14.5	6.5	3,566	943	2,623	965	1,974	920
1988	6,701	3,084	2,007	801	809	13.5	5.9	3,092	851	2,241	983	1,809	816
1989	6,528	3,174	1,978	730	646	11.9	4.8	2,983	850	2,133	1,024	1,843	677
1990	6,874	3,169	2,201	809	695	12.1	5.4	3,322	1,018	2,305	1,014	1,883	654
1991	8,426	3,380	2,724	1,225	1,098	13.8	6.9	4,608	1,279	3,329	979	2,087	753
1992	9,384	3,270	2,760	1,424	1,930	17.9	8.8	5,291	1,246	4,045	975	2,228	890
1993	8,734	3,160	2,522	1,274	1,778	18.1	8.4	4,769	1,104	3,664	946	2,145	874
1992: Jan	9,019	3,326	2,752	1,424	1,600	16.2	8.2	4,948	1,257	3,691	985	2,273	799
Feb	9,290	3,101	2,939	1,489	1,705	16.8	8.3	5,357	1,295	4,062	908	2,158	849
Mar	9,290	3,328	2,707	1,424	1,784	17.2	8.2	5,304	1,249	4,055	914	2,212	824
Apr	9,247	3,232	2,741	1,322	1,784	17.5	8.6	5,254	1,256	3,998	998	2,148	836
May	9,502	3,297	2,705	1,407	1,979	18.1	9.0	5,494	1,201	4,293	987	2,146	848
June	9,771	3,475	2,760	1,512	2,142	18.4	8.8	5,528	1,302	4,226	1,011	2,251	1,028
July	9,595	3,345	2,762	1,446	2,104	18.3	8.7	5,375	1,262	4,113	1,015	2,288	972
Aug	9,590	3,341	2,774	1,472	2,043	18.2	8.9	5,316	1,204	4,112	1,070	2,267	947
Sept	9,534	3,325	2,825	1,353	2,083	18.3	9.1	5,359	1,339	4,020	972	2,297	943
Oct	9,210	3,194	2,605	1,384	2,063	19.1	9.2	5,374	1,218	4,156	894	2,220	765
Nov	9,313	3,182	2,799	1,399	1,925	18.1	9.0	5,183	1,171	4,012	970	2,205	933
Dec	9,314	3,040	2,674	1,538	2,004	19.0	9.3	5,076	1,180	3,896	978	2,270	939
1993: Jan	9,046	3,262	2,543	1,372	1,921	18.5	8.6	4,934	1,072	3,862	834	2,295	950
Feb	8,958	3,232	2,549	1,284	1,890	18.2	8.4	4,799	1,081	3,718	1,020	2,281	899
Mar	8,878	3,148	2,583	1,275	1,835	17.7	8.4	4,856	1,096	3,760	1,061	2,059	922
Apr	8,954	3,309	2,537	1,311	1,675	17.7	8.5	4,862	1,068	3,794	990	2,187	920
May	8,895	3,242	2,526	1,270	1,776	17.8	8.3	4,752	1,144	3,608	960	2,237	890
June	8,869	3,232	2,758	1,257	1,768	17.8	8.3	4,845	1,131	3,714	940	2,201	894
July	8,732	3,223	2,543	1,258	1,749	17.9	8.3	4,872	1,183	3,689	915	2,117	870
Aug	8,642	3,046	2,608	1,259	1,741	18.3	8.4	4,864	1,190	3,674	882	2,081	834
Sept	8,540	3,052	2,457	1,297	1,750	18.4	8.9	4,699	1,112	3,587	926	2,075	843
Oct	8,639	3,156	2,491	1,284	1,746	18.4	8.3	4,779	1,216	3,563	957	2,084	839
Nov	8,330	2,946	2,401	1,216	1,755	18.9	8.5	4,444	963	3,481	960	2,084	833
Dec	8,237	3,063	2,247	1,150	1,714	18.2	8.2	4,442	1,060	3,382	932	2,018	797

[1] Because of independent seasonal adjustment of the various series, detail will not add to totals.
[2] Data for 1967 by reason for unemployment are not strictly comparable with those for later years and the total by reason is not equal to total unemployment.

Note.—Data relate to persons 16 years of age and over.
See footnote 6 and Note, Table B–33.

Source: Department of Labor, Bureau of Labor Statistics.

TABLE B-43.—*Unemployment insurance programs, selected data, 1962-93*

Year or month	All programs						State programs				
	Covered employment [1]	Insured unemployment (weekly average) [2] [3]	Total benefits paid (millions of dollars) [2] [4]	Insured unemployment	Initial claims	Exhaustions [5]	Insured unemployment as percent of covered employment	Benefits paid	
								Total (millions of dollars) [4]	Average weekly check (dollars) [6]
	Thousands			Weekly average; thousands						

1962	47,776	1,946	3,145.1	1,783	302	32	4.4	2,675.4	34.56
1963	48,434	[7] 1,973	3,025.9	[7] 1,806	[7] 298	30	4.3	2,774.7	35.27
1964	49,637	1,753	2,749.2	1,605	268	26	3.8	2,522.1	35.92
1965	51,580	1,450	2,360.4	1,328	232	21	3.0	2,166.0	37.19
1966	54,739	1,129	1,890.9	1,061	203	15	2.3	1,771.3	39.75
1967	56,342	1,270	2,221.5	1,205	226	17	2.5	2,092.3	41.25
1968	57,977	1,187	2,191.0	1,111	201	16	2.2	2,031.6	43.43
1969	59,999	1,177	2,298.6	1,101	200	16	2.1	2,127.9	46.17
1970	59,526	2,070	4,209.3	1,805	296	25	3.4	3,848.5	50.34
1971	59,375	2,608	6,154.0	2,150	295	39	4.1	4,957.0	54.02
1972	66,458	2,192	5,491.1	1,848	261	35	3.5	4,471.0	56.76
1973	69,897	1,793	4,517.3	1,632	247	29	2.7	4,007.6	59.00
1974	72,451	2,558	6,933.9	2,262	363	37	3.5	5,974.9	64.25
1975	71,037	4,937	16,802.4	3,986	478	81	6.0	11,754.7	70.23
1976	73,459	3,846	12,344.8	2,991	386	63	4.6	8,974.5	75.16
1977	76,419	3,308	10,998.9	2,655	375	55	3.9	8,357.2	78.79
1978	88,804	2,645	9,006.9	2,359	346	39	3.3	7,717.2	83.67
1979	92,062	2,592	9,401.3	2,434	388	39	2.9	8,612.9	89.67
1980	92,659	3,837	16,175.4	3,350	488	59	3.9	13,761.1	98.95
1981	93,300	3,410	15,287.1	3,047	460	57	3.5	13,262.1	106.70
1982	91,628	4,592	23,774.8	4,059	583	80	4.6	20,649.5	119.34
1983	91,898	3,774	20,206.2	3,395	438	80	3.9	17,762.8	123.59
1984	96,474	2,560	13,109.6	2,475	377	50	2.8	12,594.7	123.47
1985	99,186	2,699	15,056.3	2,617	397	49	2.9	14,130.8	128.14
1986	101,099	2,739	16,292.5	2,643	378	52	2.8	15,329.3	135.65
1987	103,933	2,369	14,501.0	2,300	328	46	2.4	13,606.8	140.55
1988	107,157	2,135	13,694.4	2,081	310	38	2.0	12,564.7	144.97
1989	109,926	2,205	14,957.0	2,158	330	37	2.1	13,760.3	151.73
1990	111,498	2,575	18,744.6	2,522	388	45	2.4	17,356.0	161.56
1991	109,613	3,406	26,716.7	3,342	447	67	3.2	24,525.7	169.88
1992	[8] 110,167	3,348	[9] 26,487.5	3,245	408	73	3.1	23,893.5	173.64
1993 [p]		2,845	[9] 22,548.3	2,751	340	61	2.6	20,186.1	179.61
				**	**		**		
1992: Jan		4,211	2,807.8	3,350	448	78	3.2	2,723.8	171.65
Feb		4,214	2,555.7	3,326	452	76	3.1	2,476.2	173.39
Mar		4,116	2,750.1	3,337	440	78	3.2	2,664.1	173.87
Apr		3,639	2,477.1	3,340	413	83	3.2	2,397.9	173.88
May		3,202	2,086.0	3,314	408	77	3.2	1,946.0	173.70
June		3,148	2,058.4	3,279	414	76	3.1	1,983.2	173.22
July		3,124	2,129.5	3,304	433	77	3.2	2,049.0	171.51
Aug		3,120	1,978.0	3,178	387	74	3.0	1,899.5	173.95
Sept		2,820	1,861.0	3,168	402	67	3.0	1,778.1	174.09
Oct		2,542	1,682.6	3,035	365	63	2.9	1,601.0	174.86
Nov		2,676	1,681.0	2,937	359	61	2.8	1,598.7	175.55
Dec		3,071	2,131.2	2,783	341	66	2.7	2,035.3	175.49
1993: Jan		3,400	2,162.7	2,715	353	69	2.6	2,075.5	177.36
Feb		3,355	2,109.8	2,640	343	66	2.5	2,024.3	179.47
Mar		3,405	2,456.4	2,701	362	66	2.6	2,361.5	180.70
Apr		2,939	2,034.9	2,764	347	65	2.6	1,958.0	180.50
May		2,604	1,696.8	2,770	341	59	2.6	1,631.5	180.52
June		2,812	1,882.9	2,813	343	61	2.7	1,811.0	179.88
July		2,660	1,750.1	2,832	352	61	2.7	1,684.3	178.29
Aug		2,725	1,814.3	2,796	327	61	2.7	1,746.3	179.71
Sept		2,426	1,616.9	2,810	328	57	2.7	1,552.2	179.61
Oct		2,330	1,472.6	2,806	344	56	2.7	1,402.3	180.45
Nov		2,569	1,709.7	2,780	339	55	2.6	1,609.1	180.07
Dec [p]		2,798	2,014.5	2,710	328	57	2.6	1,904.6	179.17

**Monthly data are seasonally adjusted.
[1] Includes persons under the State, UCFE (Federal employee, effective January 1955), and RRB (Railroad Retirement Board) programs. Beginning October 1958, also includes the UCX program (unemployment compensation for ex-servicemembers).
[2] Includes State, UCFE, RR, UCX, UCV (unemployment compensation for veterans, October 1952–January 1960), and SRA (Servicemen's Readjustment Act, September 1944–September 1951) programs. Also includes Federal and State extended benefit programs. Does not include FSB (Federal supplemental benefits), SUA (special unemployment assistance), Federal Supplemental Compensation, and Emergency Unemployment Compensation programs, except as noted in footnote 9.
[3] Covered workers who have completed at least 1 week of unemployment.
[4] Annual data are net amounts and monthly data are gross amounts.
[5] Individuals receiving final payments in benefit year.
[6] For total unemployment only.
[7] Programs include Puerto Rican sugarcane workers for initial claims and insured unemployment beginning July 1963.
[8] Latest data available for all programs indicated. Workers covered by State programs account for about 97 percent of wage and salary earners.
[9] Including Emergency Unemployment Compensation and Federal Supplemental Compensation, total benefits paid for 1992 and 1993 would be (in millions of dollars): for 1992, 40,275.2 and, for 1993, p34,484.8.

Source: Department of Labor, Employment and Training Administration.

TABLE B-44.—*Employees on nonagricultural payrolls, by major industry, 1946–93*

[Thousands of persons; monthly data seasonally adjusted]

Year or month	Total	Goods-producing industries					
		Total	Mining	Construction	Manufacturing		
					Total	Durable goods	Nondurable goods
1946	41,652	17,248	862	1,683	14,703	7,785	6,918
1947	43,857	18,509	955	2,009	15,545	8,358	7,187
1948	44,866	18,774	994	2,198	15,582	8,298	7,285
1949	43,754	17,565	930	2,194	14,441	7,462	6,979
1950	45,197	18,506	901	2,364	15,241	8,066	7,175
1951	47,819	19,959	929	2,637	16,393	9,059	7,334
1952	48,793	20,198	898	2,668	16,632	9,320	7,313
1953	50,202	21,074	866	2,659	17,549	10,080	7,468
1954	48,990	19,751	791	2,646	16,314	9,101	7,213
1955	50,641	20,513	792	2,839	16,882	9,511	7,370
1956	52,369	21,104	822	3,039	17,243	9,802	7,442
1957	52,853	20,964	828	2,962	17,174	9,825	7,351
1958	51,324	19,513	751	2,817	15,945	8,801	7,144
1959	53,268	20,411	732	3,004	16,675	9,342	7,333
1960	54,189	20,434	712	2,926	16,796	9,429	7,367
1961	53,999	19,857	672	2,859	16,326	9,041	7,285
1962	55,549	20,451	650	2,948	16,853	9,450	7,403
1963	56,653	20,640	635	3,010	16,995	9,586	7,410
1964	58,283	21,005	634	3,097	17,274	9,785	7,489
1965	60,765	21,926	632	3,232	18,062	10,374	7,688
1966	63,901	23,158	627	3,317	19,214	11,250	7,963
1967	65,803	23,308	613	3,248	19,447	11,408	8,039
1968	67,897	23,737	606	3,350	19,781	11,594	8,187
1969	70,384	24,361	619	3,575	20,167	11,862	8,304
1970	70,880	23,578	623	3,588	19,367	11,176	8,190
1971	71,214	22,935	609	3,704	18,623	10,604	8,019
1972	73,675	23,668	628	3,889	19,151	11,022	8,129
1973	76,790	24,893	642	4,097	20,154	11,863	8,291
1974	78,265	24,794	697	4,020	20,077	11,897	8,181
1975	76,945	22,600	752	3,525	18,323	10,662	7,661
1976	79,382	23,352	779	3,576	18,997	11,051	7,946
1977	82,471	24,346	813	3,851	19,682	11,570	8,112
1978	86,697	25,585	851	4,229	20,505	12,245	8,259
1979	89,823	26,461	958	4,463	21,040	12,730	8,310
1980	90,406	25,658	1,027	4,346	20,285	12,159	8,127
1981	91,152	25,497	1,139	4,188	20,170	12,082	8,089
1982	89,544	23,812	1,128	3,904	18,780	11,014	7,766
1983	90,152	23,330	952	3,946	18,432	10,707	7,725
1984	94,408	24,718	966	4,380	19,372	11,476	7,896
1985	97,387	24,842	927	4,668	19,248	11,458	7,790
1986	99,344	24,533	777	4,810	18,947	11,195	7,752
1987	101,958	24,674	717	4,958	18,999	11,154	7,845
1988	105,210	25,125	713	5,098	19,314	11,363	7,951
1989	107,895	25,254	692	5,171	19,391	11,394	7,997
1990	109,419	24,905	709	5,120	19,076	11,109	7,968
1991	108,256	23,745	689	4,650	18,406	10,569	7,837
1992	108,519	23,142	631	4,471	18,040	10,237	7,804
1993 ᵖ	110,171	22,974	599	4,573	17,802	10,047	7,755
1992: Jan	108,310	23,310	653	4,506	18,151	10,328	7,823
Feb	108,045	23,266	649	4,468	18,149	10,336	7,813
Mar	108,164	23,267	645	4,485	18,137	10,324	7,813
Apr	108,347	23,251	642	4,485	18,124	10,304	7,820
May	108,470	23,237	637	4,491	18,109	10,286	7,823
June	108,454	23,172	630	4,469	18,073	10,260	7,813
July	108,605	23,160	628	4,459	18,073	10,236	7,837
Aug	108,615	23,073	623	4,459	17,991	10,192	7,799
Sept	108,674	23,012	616	4,447	17,949	10,164	7,785
Oct	108,789	22,995	618	4,466	17,911	10,135	7,776
Nov	108,921	22,995	616	4,462	17,917	10,142	7,775
Dec	109,079	22,985	613	4,459	17,913	10,136	7,777
1993: Jan	109,235	23,001	611	4,454	17,936	10,152	7,784
Feb	109,539	23,069	600	4,515	17,954	10,163	7,791
Mar	109,565	23,016	600	4,481	17,935	10,144	7,791
Apr	109,820	22,980	600	4,517	17,863	10,090	7,773
May	110,058	23,006	602	4,577	17,827	10,047	7,780
June	110,101	22,941	596	4,574	17,771	10,011	7,760
July	110,338	22,948	595	4,593	17,760	9,996	7,764
Aug	110,305	22,903	592	4,593	17,718	9,974	7,744
Sept	110,502	22,886	596	4,592	17,698	9,974	7,724
Oct	110,664	22,934	596	4,629	17,709	9,988	7,721
Nov ᵖ	110,866	22,992	594	4,663	17,735	10,013	7,722
Dec ᵖ	111,049	23,002	603	4,662	17,737	10,027	7,710

Note.—Data in Tables B-44 and B-45 are based on reports from employing establishments and relate to full- and part-time wage and salary workers in nonagricultural establishments who received pay for any part of the pay period which includes the 12th of the month. Not comparable with labor force data (Tables B-33 through B-42), which include proprietors, self-employed persons, domestic servants,

See next page for continuation of table.

TABLE B-44.—*Employees on nonagricultural payrolls, by major industry, 1946-93*—Continued

[Thousands of persons; monthly data seasonally adjusted]

| Year or month | Service-producing industries ||||||| ||
| | Total | Transportation and public utilities | Wholesale trade | Retail trade | Finance, insurance, and real estate | Services | Government |||
							Total	Federal	State and local
1946	24,404	4,061	2,298	6,077	1,675	4,697	5,595	2,254	3,341
1947	25,348	4,166	2,478	6,477	1,728	5,025	5,474	1,892	3,582
1948	26,092	4,189	2,612	6,659	1,800	5,181	5,650	1,863	3,787
1949	26,189	4,001	2,610	6,654	1,828	5,239	5,856	1,908	3,948
1950	26,691	4,034	2,643	6,743	1,888	5,356	6,026	1,928	4,098
1951	27,860	4,226	2,735	7,007	1,956	5,547	6,389	2,302	4,087
1952	28,595	4,248	2,821	7,184	2,035	5,699	6,609	2,420	4,188
1953	29,128	4,290	2,862	7,385	2,111	5,835	6,645	2,305	4,340
1954	29,239	4,084	2,875	7,360	2,200	5,969	6,751	2,188	4,563
1955	30,128	4,141	2,934	7,601	2,298	6,240	6,914	2,187	4,727
1956	31,266	4,244	3,027	7,831	2,389	6,497	7,278	2,209	5,069
1957	31,889	4,241	3,037	7,848	2,438	6,708	7,616	2,217	5,399
1958	31,811	3,976	2,989	7,761	2,481	6,765	7,839	2,191	5,648
1959	32,857	4,011	3,092	8,035	2,549	7,087	8,083	2,233	5,850
1960	33,755	4,004	3,153	8,238	2,628	7,378	8,353	2,270	6,083
1961	34,142	3,903	3,142	8,195	2,688	7,619	8,594	2,279	6,315
1962	35,098	3,906	3,207	8,359	2,754	7,982	8,890	2,340	6,550
1963	36,013	3,903	3,258	8,520	2,830	8,277	9,225	2,358	6,868
1964	37,278	3,951	3,347	8,812	2,911	8,660	9,596	2,348	7,248
1965	38,839	4,036	3,477	9,239	2,977	9,036	10,074	2,378	7,696
1966	40,743	4,158	3,608	9,637	3,058	9,498	10,784	2,564	8,220
1967	42,495	4,268	3,700	9,906	3,185	10,045	11,391	2,719	8,672
1968	44,160	4,318	3,791	10,308	3,337	10,567	11,839	2,737	9,102
1969	46,023	4,442	3,919	10,785	3,512	11,169	12,195	2,758	9,437
1970	47,302	4,515	4,006	11,034	3,645	11,548	12,554	2,731	9,823
1971	48,278	4,476	4,014	11,338	3,772	11,797	12,881	2,696	10,185
1972	50,007	4,541	4,127	11,822	3,908	12,276	13,334	2,684	10,649
1973	51,897	4,656	4,291	12,315	4,046	12,857	13,732	2,663	11,068
1974	53,471	4,725	4,447	12,539	4,148	13,441	14,170	2,724	11,446
1975	54,345	4,542	4,430	12,630	4,165	13,892	14,686	2,748	11,937
1976	56,030	4,582	4,562	13,193	4,271	14,551	14,871	2,733	12,138
1977	58,125	4,713	4,723	13,792	4,467	15,302	15,127	2,727	12,399
1978	61,113	4,923	4,985	14,556	4,724	16,252	15,672	2,753	12,919
1979	63,363	5,136	5,221	14,972	4,975	17,112	15,947	2,773	13,174
1980	64,748	5,146	5,292	15,018	5,160	17,890	16,241	2,866	13,375
1981	65,655	5,165	5,375	15,171	5,298	18,615	16,031	2,772	13,259
1982	65,732	5,081	5,295	15,158	5,340	19,021	15,837	2,739	13,098
1983	66,821	4,952	5,283	15,587	5,466	19,664	15,869	2,774	13,096
1984	69,690	5,156	5,568	16,512	5,684	20,746	16,024	2,807	13,216
1985	72,544	5,233	5,727	17,315	5,948	21,927	16,394	2,875	13,519
1986	74,811	5,247	5,761	17,880	6,273	22,957	16,693	2,899	13,794
1987	77,284	5,362	5,848	18,422	6,533	24,110	17,010	2,943	14,067
1988	80,086	5,514	6,030	19,023	6,630	25,504	17,386	2,971	14,415
1989	82,642	5,625	6,187	19,475	6,668	26,907	17,779	2,988	14,791
1990	84,514	5,793	6,173	19,601	6,709	27,934	18,304	3,085	15,219
1991	84,511	5,762	6,081	19,284	6,646	28,336	18,402	2,966	15,436
1992	85,377	5,709	6,045	19,346	6,571	29,053	18,653	2,969	15,683
1993 ᵖ	87,197	5,710	6,114	19,734	6,605	30,193	18,841	2,914	15,927
1992: Jan	84,741	5,717	6,044	19,229	6,580	28,645	18,526	2,982	15,544
Feb	84,779	5,719	6,040	19,258	6,581	28,643	18,538	2,982	15,556
Mar	84,897	5,716	6,042	19,268	6,576	28,715	18,580	2,986	15,594
Apr	85,096	5,713	6,041	19,325	6,577	28,833	18,607	2,982	15,625
May	85,233	5,711	6,045	19,357	6,577	28,925	18,618	2,980	15,638
June	85,282	5,711	6,042	19,344	6,569	28,996	18,620	2,973	15,647
July	85,445	5,707	6,037	19,360	6,559	29,111	18,671	2,962	15,709
Aug	85,542	5,701	6,037	19,359	6,558	29,178	18,709	2,961	15,748
Sept	85,662	5,704	6,037	19,380	6,565	29,247	18,729	2,966	15,763
Oct	85,794	5,699	6,052	19,402	6,570	29,361	18,710	2,945	15,765
Nov	85,926	5,699	6,061	19,405	6,569	29,430	18,762	2,943	15,819
Dec	86,094	5,707	6,062	19,460	6,575	29,524	18,766	2,968	15,798
1993: Jan	86,234	5,719	6,086	19,523	6,578	29,573	18,755	2,945	15,810
Feb	86,470	5,725	6,097	19,629	6,577	29,665	18,777	2,944	15,833
Mar	86,549	5,724	6,103	19,604	6,574	29,756	18,788	2,938	15,850
Apr	86,840	5,720	6,110	19,648	6,585	29,977	18,800	2,923	15,877
May	87,052	5,719	6,125	19,702	6,588	30,099	18,819	2,912	15,907
June	87,160	5,711	6,110	19,751	6,590	30,175	18,823	2,901	15,922
July	87,390	5,709	6,126	19,790	6,604	30,320	18,841	2,896	15,945
Aug	87,402	5,690	6,107	19,795	6,602	30,381	18,827	2,906	15,921
Sept	87,616	5,692	6,117	19,836	6,616	30,433	18,922	2,901	16,021
Oct	87,730	5,693	6,122	19,846	6,632	30,534	18,903	2,901	16,002
Nov ᵖ	87,874	5,703	6,128	19,833	6,654	30,651	18,905	2,893	16,012
Dec ᵖ	88,047	5,716	6,138	19,865	6,668	30,719	18,941	2,902	16,039

Note (cont'd).—which count persons as employed when they are not at work because of industrial disputes, bad weather, etc., even if they are not paid for the time off; and which are based on a sample of the working-age population. For description and details of the various establishment data, see "Employment and Earnings."

Source: Department of Labor, Bureau of Labor Statistics.

TABLE B-45.—*Hours and earnings in private nonagricultural industries, 1959-93* [1]

[Monthly data seasonally adjusted, except as noted]

Year or month	Average weekly hours			Average hourly earnings			Average weekly earnings, total private			
	Total private	Manufacturing		Total private		Manu- facturing (current dollars)	Level		Percent change from year earlier [3]	
		Total	Over- time	Current dollars	1982 dol- lars [2]		Current dollars	1982 dollars [2]	Cur- rent dol- lars	1982 dol- lars [2]
1959	39.0	40.3	2.7	$2.02	$6.69	$2.19	$78.78	$260.86	4.9	4.2
1960	38.6	39.7	2.5	2.09	6.79	2.26	80.67	261.92	2.4	.4
1961	38.6	39.8	2.4	2.14	6.88	2.32	82.60	265.59	2.4	1.4
1962	38.7	40.4	2.8	2.22	7.07	2.39	85.91	273.60	4.0	3.0
1963	38.8	40.5	2.8	2.28	7.17	2.45	88.46	278.18	3.0	1.7
1964	38.7	40.7	3.1	2.36	7.33	2.53	91.33	283.63	3.2	2.0
1965	38.8	41.2	3.6	2.46	7.52	2.61	95.45	291.90	4.5	2.9
1966	38.6	41.4	3.9	2.56	7.62	2.71	98.82	294.11	3.5	.8
1967	38.0	40.6	3.4	2.68	7.72	2.82	101.84	293.49	3.1	−.2
1968	37.8	40.7	3.6	2.85	7.89	3.01	107.73	298.42	5.8	1.7
1969	37.7	40.6	3.6	3.04	7.98	3.19	114.61	300.81	6.4	.8
1970	37.1	39.8	3.0	3.23	8.03	3.35	119.83	298.08	4.6	−.9
1971	36.9	39.9	2.9	3.45	8.21	3.57	127.31	303.12	6.2	1.7
1972	37.0	40.5	3.5	3.70	8.53	3.82	136.90	315.44	7.5	4.1
1973	36.9	40.7	3.8	3.94	8.55	4.09	145.39	315.38	6.2	−.0
1974	36.5	40.0	3.3	4.24	8.28	4.42	154.76	302.27	6.4	−4.2
1975	36.1	39.5	2.6	4.53	8.12	4.83	163.53	293.06	5.7	−3.0
1976	36.1	40.1	3.1	4.86	8.24	5.22	175.45	297.37	7.3	1.5
1977	36.0	40.3	3.5	5.25	8.36	5.68	189.00	300.96	7.7	1.2
1978	35.8	40.4	3.6	5.69	8.40	6.17	203.70	300.89	7.8	−.0
1979	35.7	40.2	3.3	6.16	8.17	6.70	219.91	291.66	8.0	−3.1
1980	35.3	39.7	2.8	6.66	7.78	7.27	235.10	274.65	6.9	−5.8
1981	35.2	39.8	2.8	7.25	7.69	7.99	255.20	270.63	8.5	−1.5
1982	34.8	38.9	2.3	7.68	7.68	8.49	267.26	267.26	4.7	−1.2
1983	35.0	40.1	3.0	8.02	7.79	8.83	280.70	272.52	5.0	2.0
1984	35.2	40.7	3.4	8.32	7.80	9.19	292.86	274.73	4.3	.8
1985	34.9	40.5	3.3	8.57	7.77	9.54	299.09	271.16	2.1	−1.3
1986	34.8	40.7	3.4	8.76	7.81	9.73	304.85	271.94	1.9	.3
1987	34.8	41.0	3.7	8.98	7.73	9.91	312.50	269.16	2.5	−1.0
1988	34.7	41.1	3.9	9.28	7.69	10.19	322.02	266.79	3.0	−.9
1989	34.6	41.0	3.8	9.66	7.64	10.48	334.24	264.22	3.8	−1.0
1990	34.5	40.8	3.6	10.01	7.52	10.83	345.35	259.47	3.3	−1.8
1991	34.3	40.7	3.6	10.32	7.45	11.18	353.98	255.40	2.5	−1.6
1992	34.4	41.0	3.8	10.58	7.42	11.46	363.95	255.22	2.8	−.1
1993 [p]	34.5	41.4	4.1	10.83	7.39	11.76	373.64	254.87	2.7	−.1
1992: Jan	34.2	40.8	3.6	10.45	7.43	11.29	357.39	254.01	2.8	.4
Feb	34.5	41.0	3.7	10.49	7.44	11.35	361.91	256.67	3.8	1.0
Mar	34.5	41.1	3.8	10.52	7.43	11.39	362.94	256.49	3.7	.7
Apr	34.3	41.1	3.8	10.51	7.41	11.42	360.49	254.05	2.7	−.2
May	34.5	41.2	4.0	10.54	7.42	11.44	363.63	255.90	3.2	.4
June	34.3	41.1	3.8	10.56	7.42	11.45	362.21	254.36	1.6	−1.3
July	34.3	41.1	3.8	10.57	7.40	11.46	362.55	253.89	2.5	−.5
Aug	34.6	41.1	3.8	10.63	7.43	11.50	367.80	257.02	3.1	.0
Sept	34.2	41.0	3.6	10.62	7.41	11.51	363.20	253.45	1.1	−1.8
Oct	34.4	41.1	3.8	10.65	7.40	11.52	366.36	254.59	2.5	−.6
Nov	34.6	41.2	3.9	10.69	7.41	11.55	369.87	256.50	3.3	.3
Dec	34.3	41.2	3.9	10.68	7.40	11.58	366.32	253.68	1.9	−1.0
1993: Jan	34.5	41.4	4.0	10.73	7.40	11.61	370.19	255.30	3.4	.2
Feb	34.4	41.4	4.2	10.74	7.38	11.64	369.46	253.92	2.2	−.9
Mar	34.2	41.2	4.0	10.78	7.39	11.66	368.68	252.87	2.0	−1.0
Apr	34.4	41.5	4.2	10.77	7.36	11.71	370.49	253.24	2.8	−.3
May	34.7	41.4	4.1	10.82	7.39	11.71	375.45	256.28	3.4	.2
June	34.4	41.2	4.0	10.81	7.38	11.72	371.86	253.83	2.6	−.2
July	34.5	41.4	4.0	10.81	7.37	11.72	372.95	254.40	2.9	.2
Aug	34.7	41.4	4.1	10.86	7.39	11.77	376.84	256.53	2.8	.1
Sept	34.3	41.5	4.1	10.86	7.39	11.84	372.50	253.57	3.0	.5
Oct	34.5	41.6	4.3	10.92	7.40	11.83	376.74	255.24	3.0	.4
Nov [p]	34.6	41.7	4.4	10.93	7.40	11.88	378.18	255.87	2.2	−.3
Dec [p]	34.6	41.7	4.4	10.95	7.40	11.94	378.87	255.99	3.1	.6

[1] For production or nonsupervisory workers; total includes private industry groups shown in Table B-44.
[2] Current dollars divided by the consumer price index for urban wage earners and clerical workers on a 1982=100 base.
[3] Percent changes are based on data that are not seasonally adjusted.

Note.—See Note, Table B-44.

Source: Department of Labor, Bureau of Labor Statistics.

TABLE B-46.—*Employment cost index, private industry, 1979-93*

Year and month	Total private			Goods-producing			Service-producing			Manufacturing			Nonmanufacturing		
	Total compensation	Wages and salaries	Benefits[1]	Total compensation	Wages and salaries	Benefits[1]	Total compensation	Wages and salaries	Benefits[1]	Total compensation	Wages and salaries	Benefits[1]	Total compensation	Wages and salaries	Benefits[1]
Index, June 1989 = 100; not seasonally adjusted															
December:															
1979	59.1	61.5	53.2	60.7	63.7	54.6	57.7	60.0	51.9	60.1	63.0	54.2	58.5	60.8	52.5
1980	64.8	67.1	59.4	66.7	69.7	60.5	63.3	65.3	58.4	66.0	68.9	59.9	64.2	66.2	59.1
1981	71.2	73.0	66.6	73.3	75.7	68.2	69.5	71.1	65.1	72.5	74.9	67.5	70.4	72.1	66.1
1982	75.8	77.6	71.4	77.8	80.0	73.2	74.1	75.9	69.6	76.9	79.1	72.4	75.1	76.8	70.6
1983	80.1	81.4	76.7	81.6	83.2	78.3	78.9	80.2	75.2	80.8	82.5	77.5	79.6	81.0	76.2
1984	84.0	84.8	81.7	85.4	86.4	83.2	82.9	83.7	80.4	85.0	86.1	82.7	83.4	84.2	81.1
1985	87.3	88.3	84.6	88.2	89.4	85.7	86.6	87.7	83.6	87.8	89.2	85.0	87.0	88.0	84.4
1986	90.1	91.1	87.5	91.0	92.3	88.3	89.3	90.3	86.8	90.7	92.1	87.5	89.7	90.6	87.5
1987	93.1	94.1	90.5	93.8	95.2	90.9	92.6	93.4	90.2	93.4	95.2	89.8	92.9	93.7	91.0
1988	97.6	98.0	96.7	97.9	98.2	97.3	97.3	97.8	96.1	97.6	98.1	96.6	97.5	97.8	96.8
1989	102.3	102.0	102.6	102.1	102.0	102.6	102.3	102.2	102.6	102.0	101.9	102.3	102.3	102.2	102.8
1990	107.0	106.1	109.4	107.0	105.8	109.9	107.0	106.3	109.0	107.2	106.2	109.5	106.9	106.1	109.3
1991	111.7	110.0	116.2	111.9	109.7	116.7	111.6	110.2	115.7	112.2	110.3	116.1	111.5	109.8	116.2
1992	115.6	112.9	122.2	116.1	112.8	123.4	115.2	113.0	121.2	116.5	113.7	122.6	115.1	112.6	122.0
1993	119.8	116.4	128.3	120.6	116.1	130.3	119.3	116.6	126.7	121.3	117.3	130.0	119.0	116.0	127.4
1992: Mar	113.1	110.9	118.6	113.5	110.7	119.7	112.8	111.1	117.7	114.0	111.5	119.3	112.7	110.7	118.2
June	113.9	111.6	119.7	114.3	111.4	120.6	113.6	111.7	118.8	114.7	112.2	120.1	113.5	111.3	119.4
Sept	114.8	112.2	121.2	115.3	112.1	122.3	114.4	112.3	120.4	115.7	112.9	121.5	114.4	111.9	121.0
Dec	115.6	112.9	122.2	116.1	112.8	123.4	115.2	113.0	121.2	116.5	113.7	122.6	115.1	112.6	122.0
1993: Mar	117.1	113.9	125.2	118.0	113.8	127.3	116.4	113.9	123.4	118.6	114.7	126.8	116.3	113.4	124.2
June	118.0	114.6	126.7	119.1	114.5	129.0	117.3	114.7	124.6	119.7	115.5	128.6	117.2	114.2	125.5
Sept	119.1	115.7	127.7	119.9	115.3	130.0	118.5	115.9	125.7	120.6	116.3	129.7	118.4	115.4	126.5
Dec	119.8	116.4	128.3	120.6	116.1	130.3	119.3	116.6	126.7	121.3	117.3	130.0	119.0	116.0	127.4
Index, June 1989 = 100; seasonally adjusted															
1992: Mar	112.9	110.9	118.2	113.3	110.7	119.1	112.7	111.1	117.4	113.7	111.5	118.6	112.6	110.7	117.9
June	113.8	111.6	119.5	114.1	111.4	120.4	113.5	111.7	118.7	114.7	112.2	119.8	113.5	111.3	119.2
Sept	114.7	112.1	121.3	115.2	112.1	122.3	114.3	112.1	120.4	115.7	112.9	121.5	114.3	111.8	121.0
Dec	115.7	113.0	122.9	116.3	112.8	124.3	115.3	113.1	121.7	116.9	113.7	123.7	115.3	112.7	122.5
1993: Mar	116.8	113.9	124.7	117.7	113.8	126.7	116.2	113.9	123.1	118.3	114.7	126.0	116.2	113.4	123.9
June	117.9	114.6	126.4	118.8	114.5	128.7	117.2	114.7	124.5	119.6	115.5	128.3	117.2	114.2	125.3
Sept	118.9	115.6	127.7	119.8	115.3	130.0	118.3	115.8	125.7	120.6	116.3	129.7	118.3	115.3	126.5
Dec	119.9	116.5	129.1	120.7	116.1	131.3	119.4	116.7	127.2	121.7	117.3	131.1	119.2	116.1	127.9
Percent change from 12 months earlier, not seasonally adjusted															
December:															
1980	9.6	9.1	11.7	9.9	9.4	10.8	9.7	8.8	12.5	9.8	9.4	10.5	9.7	8.9	12.6
1981	9.9	8.8	12.1	9.9	8.6	12.7	9.8	8.9	11.5	9.8	8.7	12.7	9.7	8.9	11.8
1982	6.5	6.3	7.2	6.1	5.7	7.3	6.6	6.8	6.9	6.1	5.6	7.3	6.7	6.5	6.8
1983	5.7	4.9	7.4	4.9	4.0	7.0	6.5	5.7	8.0	5.1	4.3	7.0	6.0	5.5	7.9
1984	4.9	4.2	6.5	4.7	3.8	6.3	5.1	4.4	6.9	5.2	4.4	6.7	4.8	4.0	6.4
1985	3.9	4.1	3.5	3.3	3.5	3.0	4.5	4.8	4.0	3.3	3.6	2.8	4.3	4.5	4.1
1986	3.2	3.2	3.4	3.2	3.2	3.0	3.1	3.0	3.8	3.3	3.3	2.9	3.1	3.0	3.7
1987	3.3	3.3	3.4	3.1	3.1	2.9	3.7	3.4	3.9	3.0	3.4	2.6	3.6	3.4	4.0
1988	4.8	4.1	6.9	4.4	3.2	7.0	5.1	4.7	6.5	4.5	3.0	7.6	5.0	4.4	6.4
1989	4.8	4.1	6.1	4.3	3.9	5.4	5.1	4.5	6.8	4.5	3.9	5.9	4.9	4.5	6.2
1990	4.6	4.0	6.6	4.8	3.7	7.1	4.6	4.0	6.2	5.1	4.2	7.0	4.5	3.8	6.3
1991	4.4	3.7	6.2	4.6	3.7	6.2	4.3	3.7	6.1	4.7	3.9	6.0	4.3	3.5	6.3
1992	3.5	2.6	5.2	3.8	2.8	5.7	3.2	2.5	4.8	3.8	3.1	5.6	3.2	2.6	5.0
1993	3.6	3.1	5.0	3.9	2.9	5.6	3.6	3.2	4.5	4.1	3.2	6.0	3.4	3.0	4.4
1992: Mar	4.2	3.4	6.3	4.6	3.5	7.0	4.0	3.3	5.7	5.0	3.8	7.3	3.9	3.2	5.6
June	3.7	3.0	5.5	4.1	3.1	5.9	3.5	2.8	5.1	4.3	3.5	6.0	3.5	2.7	5.2
Sept	3.4	2.7	5.2	3.9	3.1	5.6	3.1	2.4	5.1	4.0	3.3	5.4	3.2	2.4	5.1
Dec	3.5	2.6	5.2	3.8	2.8	5.7	3.2	2.5	4.8	3.8	3.1	5.6	3.2	2.6	5.0
1993: Mar	3.5	2.7	5.6	4.0	2.8	6.3	3.2	2.5	4.8	4.0	2.9	6.3	3.2	2.4	5.1
June	3.6	2.7	5.8	4.2	2.8	7.0	3.3	2.7	4.9	4.4	2.9	7.1	3.3	2.6	5.1
Sept	3.7	3.1	5.4	4.0	2.9	6.3	3.6	3.2	4.4	4.2	3.0	6.7	3.5	3.1	4.5
Dec	3.6	3.1	5.0	3.9	2.9	5.6	3.6	3.2	4.5	4.1	3.2	6.0	3.4	3.0	4.4
Percent change from 3 months earlier, seasonally adjusted															
1992: Mar	0.9	0.7	1.2	1.1	0.9	1.4	0.8	0.7	1.1	1.1	1.1	1.3	0.8	0.7	1.0
June	.8	.6	1.1	.7	.6	1.1	.7	.5	1.1	.9	.6	1.0	.8	.5	1.1
Sept	.8	.4	1.5	1.0	.6	1.6	.7	.4	1.4	.9	.6	1.4	.7	.4	1.5
Dec	.9	.8	1.3	1.0	.6	1.6	.9	.9	1.1	1.0	.7	1.8	.9	.8	1.2
1993: Mar	1.0	.8	1.5	1.2	.9	1.9	.8	.7	1.2	1.2	.9	1.9	.8	.6	1.1
June	.9	.6	1.4	.9	.6	1.6	.9	.7	1.1	1.1	.7	1.8	.9	.7	1.1
Sept	.8	.9	1.0	.8	.7	1.0	.9	1.0	1.0	.8	.7	1.1	.9	1.0	1.0
Dec	.8	.8	1.1	.8	.7	1.0	.9	.8	1.2	.9	.9	1.1	.8	.7	1.1

[1] Employer costs for employee benefits.

Note.—The employment cost index is a measure of the change in the cost of labor, free from the influence of employment shifts among occupations and industries.
Data exclude farm and household workers.
Through December 1981, percent changes are based on unrounded data; thereafter changes are based on indexes as published.
Source: Department of Labor, Bureau of Labor Statistics.

TABLE B-47.—*Productivity and related data, business sector, 1947–93*

[1982=100; quarterly data seasonally adjusted]

Year or quarter	Output per hour of all persons		Output [1]		Hours of all persons [2]		Compensation per hour [3]		Real compensation per hour [4]		Unit labor costs		Implicit price deflator [5]	
	Business sector	Nonfarm business sector	Business sector	Nonfarm business sector	Business sector	Nonfarm business sector	Business sector	Nonfarm business sector	Business sector	Nonfarm business sector	Business sector	Nonfarm business sector	Business sector	Nonfarm business sector
1947	43.4	50.6	34.1	33.5	78.7	66.3	10.4	11.3	44.9	49.1	24.0	22.4	23.8	22.5
1948	45.3	52.3	35.9	35.2	79.3	67.4	11.3	12.3	45.2	49.3	24.9	23.6	25.7	24.2
1949	46.0	53.4	35.3	34.6	76.6	64.7	11.5	12.7	46.5	51.5	24.9	23.8	25.4	24.4
1950	49.9	56.8	38.6	37.9	77.4	66.7	12.3	13.5	49.4	54.0	24.7	23.7	25.8	24.8
1951	51.7	58.2	41.1	40.5	79.6	69.7	13.5	14.6	50.2	54.4	26.2	25.2	27.5	26.4
1952	53.6	59.8	42.6	42.1	79.6	70.4	14.4	15.5	52.4	56.3	26.9	25.9	27.8	26.8
1953	55.3	60.7	44.4	43.8	80.3	72.1	15.4	16.3	55.6	59.1	27.8	26.9	28.1	27.5
1954	56.7	62.2	44.0	43.3	77.6	69.6	15.9	16.9	57.0	60.6	28.0	27.1	28.2	27.6
1955	58.6	64.3	47.1	46.5	80.4	72.4	16.3	17.5	58.7	63.1	27.8	27.3	28.9	28.5
1956	59.3	64.5	48.4	47.9	81.6	74.2	17.4	18.6	61.7	65.9	29.3	28.8	29.9	29.5
1957	61.0	65.8	49.0	48.6	80.3	73.8	18.5	19.6	63.6	67.5	30.4	29.8	30.9	30.5
1958	63.0	67.6	48.2	47.8	76.6	70.7	19.4	20.4	64.7	68.2	30.8	30.2	31.3	30.8
1959	64.6	69.2	51.4	51.0	79.6	73.7	20.2	21.3	67.0	70.5	31.3	30.8	32.1	31.8
1960	65.6	69.9	52.2	51.8	79.7	74.2	21.1	22.2	68.8	72.4	32.2	31.8	32.6	32.3
1961	68.1	72.2	53.3	52.9	78.3	73.3	21.9	23.0	70.8	74.1	32.2	31.8	32.8	32.5
1962	70.5	74.5	56.1	55.7	79.6	74.8	23.0	23.9	73.3	76.3	32.6	32.1	33.5	33.1
1963	73.3	77.1	58.7	58.3	80.0	75.7	23.8	24.7	75.1	78.0	32.5	32.1	33.7	33.4
1964	76.5	80.0	62.2	61.9	81.3	77.4	25.1	25.9	78.0	80.5	32.8	32.3	34.1	33.9
1965	78.6	81.8	65.9	65.7	83.9	80.3	26.0	26.7	79.7	81.9	33.1	32.7	35.0	34.6
1966	80.7	83.4	69.3	69.3	85.8	83.1	27.8	28.3	82.9	84.3	34.5	33.9	36.1	35.8
1967	82.8	85.2	70.8	70.8	85.5	83.0	29.4	30.0	85.0	86.6	35.5	35.2	37.2	36.9
1968	85.3	87.7	74.0	74.0	86.7	84.4	31.8	32.3	88.3	89.6	37.3	36.8	38.8	38.6
1969	85.8	87.7	76.2	76.2	88.8	86.9	34.1	34.5	89.8	90.8	39.8	39.4	40.6	40.4
1970	87.0	88.5	75.8	75.7	87.2	85.6	36.7	37.0	91.3	92.0	42.2	41.8	42.4	42.2
1971	89.8	91.3	78.0	77.9	86.8	85.3	39.1	39.4	93.1	93.9	43.5	43.1	44.5	44.3
1972	92.7	94.2	83.0	83.0	89.5	88.1	41.6	41.9	95.9	96.8	44.8	44.5	46.2	45.8
1973	95.0	96.4	88.2	88.4	92.8	91.6	45.1	45.4	98.1	98.7	47.5	47.1	49.0	47.9
1974	93.2	94.5	86.6	86.7	92.9	91.8	49.6	49.9	97.0	97.6	53.1	52.8	53.7	52.8
1975	95.5	96.7	85.0	84.9	89.0	87.9	54.5	54.9	97.8	98.4	57.1	56.8	59.0	58.3
1976	98.3	99.2	89.9	90.0	91.5	90.7	59.5	59.6	100.9	101.1	60.5	60.1	62.4	61.9
1977	99.9	100.7	94.9	95.0	95.0	94.4	64.3	64.4	102.4	102.5	64.3	63.9	66.5	66.1
1978	100.5	101.4	100.1	100.5	99.6	99.2	70.0	70.1	103.6	103.7	69.6	69.1	71.8	71.2
1979	99.4	99.9	102.1	102.5	102.8	102.6	76.8	76.7	102.1	102.0	77.3	76.8	78.3	77.5
1980	98.6	99.9	100.5	100.8	101.9	101.8	85.0	84.9	99.5	99.4	86.2	85.7	85.9	85.6
1981	99.9	99.9	102.4	102.4	102.5	102.5	93.0	93.0	98.7	98.8	93.1	93.1	94.5	94.2
1982	100.0	100.0	100.0	100.0	100.0	100.0	100.0	100.0	100.0	100.0	100.0	100.0	100.0	100.0
1983	102.3	102.5	104.1	104.4	101.8	101.9	103.8	104.0	100.6	100.8	101.5	101.5	103.4	104.0
1984	104.8	104.7	112.6	113.0	107.4	107.9	108.3	108.3	100.6	100.6	103.4	103.4	107.7	107.6
1985	106.3	105.6	116.7	116.8	109.8	110.7	113.2	112.8	101.5	101.2	106.5	106.8	111.2	111.6
1986	108.5	107.7	119.9	120.1	110.5	111.5	118.9	118.4	104.7	104.3	109.5	110.0	113.6	114.2
1987	109.6	108.6	124.8	125.0	113.8	115.1	123.1	122.5	104.6	104.1	112.3	112.8	116.7	117.2
1988	110.7	109.6	130.1	130.6	117.5	119.1	128.5	127.7	104.8	104.2	116.0	116.5	120.8	121.4
1989	109.9	108.6	132.3	132.7	120.4	122.2	133.0	131.9	103.5	102.7	121.0	121.5	126.1	126.5
1990	110.7	109.1	133.3	133.5	120.5	122.4	140.6	139.2	103.8	102.8	127.1	127.6	131.2	131.8
1991	111.8	110.3	131.6	131.8	117.7	119.5	147.4	146.2	104.5	103.6	131.9	132.6	136.1	137.0
1992	115.5	113.7	135.4	135.4	117.3	119.1	154.9	153.7	106.5	105.7	134.1	135.1	139.2	140.3
1982: IV	101.1	101.1	100.0	100.0	98.9	99.0	102.1	102.1	100.6	100.6	101.0	101.0	101.1	101.4
1983: IV	103.1	103.3	107.5	108.1	104.3	104.7	105.3	105.2	100.5	100.4	102.1	101.9	104.8	105.2
1984: IV	105.4	105.3	114.4	114.8	108.5	109.0	109.9	109.9	100.7	100.7	104.3	104.4	109.0	109.0
1985: IV	107.0	106.0	118.0	118.2	110.2	111.4	115.6	115.0	102.4	101.8	108.0	108.5	112.4	112.9
1986: IV	108.3	107.4	120.6	120.8	111.3	112.5	120.9	120.4	105.6	105.2	111.6	112.2	114.6	115.2
1987: IV	110.6	109.5	127.4	127.6	115.1	116.5	125.8	125.1	105.1	104.6	113.7	114.3	117.9	118.5
1988: IV	110.9	110.0	131.7	132.5	118.8	120.5	130.6	129.8	104.7	104.1	117.9	118.0	122.8	123.4
1989: IV	109.7	108.5	132.3	132.7	120.6	122.3	134.9	133.9	103.4	102.6	123.0	123.4	127.8	128.2
1990: IV	110.5	108.9	132.1	132.2	119.6	121.4	143.5	142.1	103.5	102.5	129.8	130.5	133.2	134.0
1991: I	110.9	109.4	131.0	131.2	118.1	119.9	144.9	143.7	103.6	102.7	130.6	131.3	134.8	135.7
II	111.6	110.3	131.5	131.7	117.8	119.5	146.6	145.4	104.2	103.4	131.4	132.0	135.8	136.6
III	111.8	110.4	131.5	131.8	117.6	119.4	148.2	147.1	104.7	103.9	132.6	133.2	136.6	137.5
IV	112.8	111.3	132.4	132.6	117.3	119.2	150.1	148.8	105.2	104.3	133.1	133.7	137.2	138.2
1992: I	114.1	112.4	133.3	133.3	116.8	118.7	152.2	150.9	105.8	104.8	133.4	134.3	138.3	139.3
II	114.8	113.1	134.5	134.4	117.1	118.8	153.7	152.6	106.0	105.2	133.9	134.9	139.1	140.2
III	116.0	114.1	136.0	135.9	117.2	119.0	156.1	154.8	106.9	106.0	134.5	135.6	138.7	139.8
IV	117.1	115.3	137.9	137.9	117.7	119.6	157.8	156.6	107.3	106.4	134.8	135.8	140.6	141.8
1993: I	116.6	114.8	138.0	138.1	118.3	120.3	159.1	157.7	107.1	106.2	136.4	137.4	141.6	142.7
II	116.6	114.7	139.3	139.5	119.5	121.6	160.1	158.4	107.0	105.9	137.3	138.2	142.5	143.5
III	117.6	115.9	140.5	141.0	119.4	121.7	161.6	159.9	107.7	106.6	137.4	138.0	142.9	144.0

[1] Output refers to gross domestic product originating in the sector in 1987 dollars.
[2] Hours at work of all persons engaged in the sector, including hours of proprietors and unpaid family workers. Estimates based primarily on establishment data.
[3] Wages and salaries of employees plus employers' contributions for social insurance and private benefit plans. Also includes an estimate of wages, salaries, and supplemental payments for the self-employed.
[4] Hourly compensation divided by the consumer price index for all urban consumers.
[5] Current dollar gross domestic product divided by constant dollar gross domestic product.

Source: Department of Labor, Bureau of Labor Statistics.

TABLE B-48.—Changes in productivity and related data, business sector, 1948–93

[Percent change from preceding period; quarterly data at seasonally adjusted annual rates]

Year or quarter	Output per hour of all persons — Business sector	Output per hour of all persons — Nonfarm business sector	Output [1] — Business sector	Output [1] — Nonfarm business sector	Hours of all persons [2] — Business sector	Hours of all persons [2] — Nonfarm business sector	Compensation per hour [3] — Business sector	Compensation per hour [3] — Nonfarm business sector	Real compensation per hour [4] — Business sector	Real compensation per hour [4] — Nonfarm business sector	Unit labor costs — Business sector	Unit labor costs — Nonfarm business sector	Implicit price deflator [5] — Business sector	Implicit price deflator [5] — Nonfarm business sector
1948	4.5	3.3	5.2	5.0	0.7	1.7	8.6	8.6	0.5	0.5	4.0	5.2	7.9	7.8
1949	1.6	2.2	−1.8	−1.8	−3.3	−3.9	1.7	3.0	3.0	4.3	.1	.8	−1.2	.8
1950	8.5	6.5	9.5	9.6	.9	3.0	7.4	6.2	6.1	4.8	−.9	−.3	1.6	1.8
1951	3.6	2.3	6.6	7.0	2.8	4.6	9.8	8.7	1.8	.7	6.0	6.2	6.7	6.1
1952	3.7	2.8	3.7	3.8	.0	1.0	6.3	5.6	4.3	3.6	2.6	2.8	1.0	1.6
1953	3.2	1.6	4.1	4.0	.9	2.4	6.8	5.7	6.0	4.9	3.5	4.1	1.3	2.5
1954	2.5	2.5	−.9	−1.0	−3.3	−3.4	3.3	3.3	2.5	2.5	.7	.8	.4	.7
1955	3.4	3.2	7.1	7.3	3.6	3.9	2.6	3.7	3.0	4.1	−.7	.5	2.5	3.2
1956	1.3	.4	2.8	3.0	1.5	2.5	6.7	6.1	5.1	4.5	5.3	5.6	3.3	3.5
1957	2.8	2.0	1.3	1.5	−1.5	−.5	6.6	5.7	3.1	2.3	3.6	3.7	3.2	3.3
1958	3.2	2.7	−1.6	−1.7	−4.6	−4.2	4.6	4.0	1.7	1.2	1.4	1.3	1.4	.9
1959	2.5	2.3	6.5	6.7	3.8	4.3	4.3	4.1	3.6	3.4	1.7	1.7	2.7	3.4
1960	1.6	1.1	1.7	1.7	.1	.6	4.3	4.4	2.6	2.6	2.7	3.3	1.5	1.5
1961	3.8	3.3	2.1	2.1	−1.6	−1.2	4.0	3.4	2.9	2.3	.1	0	.5	.6
1962	3.5	3.1	5.1	5.3	1.6	2.1	4.7	4.1	3.6	3.0	1.2	1.0	2.0	2.1
1963	4.1	3.6	4.6	4.7	.5	1.1	3.8	3.5	2.4	2.2	−.3	−.1	.8	.9
1964	4.3	3.8	6.0	6.2	1.6	2.3	5.2	4.6	3.9	3.3	.9	.8	1.1	1.4
1965	2.7	2.2	6.0	6.1	3.2	3.8	3.8	3.3	2.2	1.7	1.1	1.0	2.5	2.2
1966	2.8	1.9	5.2	5.4	2.3	3.4	7.0	5.9	4.0	2.9	4.1	3.9	3.3	3.3
1967	2.6	2.2	2.2	2.2	−.3	−.1	5.7	5.9	2.6	2.7	3.1	3.5	2.9	3.3
1968	3.0	2.9	4.5	4.6	1.4	1.7	8.1	7.9	3.8	3.5	5.0	4.8	4.4	4.5
1969	.6	−.0	2.9	2.9	2.4	2.9	7.3	6.8	1.7	1.3	6.7	6.9	4.7	4.6
1970	1.4	1.0	−.5	−.6	−1.8	−1.5	7.5	7.2	1.7	1.4	6.1	6.2	4.3	4.5
1971	3.3	3.1	2.9	2.9	−.4	−.3	6.4	6.4	1.9	2.0	3.0	3.2	4.9	5.0
1972	3.2	3.1	6.4	6.5	3.2	3.3	6.4	6.5	3.1	3.2	3.1	3.2	3.8	3.5
1973	2.5	2.4	6.2	6.4	3.6	4.0	8.6	8.2	2.3	1.9	5.9	5.7	6.1	4.5
1974	−1.9	−2.0	−1.8	−1.9	.1	.2	9.8	9.8	−1.1	−1.1	11.9	12.1	9.5	10.2
1975	2.4	2.3	−1.9	−2.0	−4.2	−4.2	10.0	10.0	.8	.8	7.5	7.5	10.0	10.4
1976	3.0	2.6	5.8	5.9	2.8	3.2	9.1	8.7	3.2	2.7	6.0	5.9	5.8	6.3
1977	1.7	1.5	5.6	5.6	3.8	4.1	8.0	8.0	1.4	1.4	6.3	6.4	6.5	6.8
1978	.6	.7	5.5	5.8	4.9	5.0	8.9	8.9	1.2	1.2	8.2	8.1	8.0	7.6
1979	−1.1	−1.4	2.0	2.0	3.2	3.5	9.7	9.5	−1.5	−1.7	11.0	11.0	9.1	8.9
1980	−.8	−.9	−1.6	−1.7	−.9	−.8	10.7	10.7	−2.5	−2.5	11.5	11.7	9.7	10.4
1981	1.3	.9	1.9	1.6	.6	.7	9.4	9.6	−.8	−.7	8.0	8.6	10.1	10.1
1982	.1	.1	−2.3	−2.4	−2.5	−2.4	7.6	7.5	1.3	1.2	7.4	7.4	5.8	6.1
1983	2.3	2.5	4.1	4.4	1.8	1.9	3.8	4.0	.6	.8	1.5	1.5	3.4	4.0
1984	2.4	2.2	8.2	8.2	5.6	5.9	4.3	4.1	.0	−.2	1.9	1.9	4.1	3.5
1985	1.4	.8	3.6	3.4	2.1	2.5	4.5	4.1	.9	.6	3.0	3.3	3.3	3.7
1986	2.1	2.0	2.8	2.8	.6	.8	5.0	5.0	3.1	3.1	2.8	2.9	2.2	2.4
1987	1.0	.8	4.1	4.1	3.0	3.2	3.6	3.5	−.1	−.2	2.5	2.6	2.6	2.6
1988	1.0	.9	4.3	4.4	3.3	3.5	4.4	4.2	.2	.1	3.4	3.2	3.6	3.6
1989	−.7	−.9	1.7	1.7	2.5	2.6	3.5	3.3	−1.3	−1.4	4.3	4.3	4.4	4.2
1990	.7	.4	.7	.6	.1	.2	5.7	5.5	.3	.1	5.0	5.1	4.1	4.2
1991	1.0	1.1	−1.3	−1.3	−2.3	−2.4	4.9	5.0	.6	.8	3.8	3.9	3.7	3.9
1992	3.3	3.1	2.9	2.7	−.4	−.4	5.0	5.1	2.0	2.0	1.7	2.0	2.3	2.4
1991: I	1.5	1.9	−3.3	−3.1	−4.7	−4.9	4.1	4.4	.4	.6	2.5	2.5	4.8	4.9
II	2.5	2.7	1.4	1.5	−1.1	−1.1	4.8	4.9	2.5	2.7	2.2	2.2	3.1	2.7
III	.6	.8	.1	.3	−.5	−.6	4.5	4.6	1.8	1.9	3.8	3.7	2.4	2.6
IV	3.7	3.4	2.7	2.7	−1.0	−.7	5.2	4.9	1.9	1.6	1.4	1.5	1.7	2.2
1992: I	4.7	3.8	2.9	2.1	−1.8	−1.6	5.7	5.6	2.3	2.2	.9	1.7	3.3	3.2
II	2.5	2.8	3.4	3.3	1.0	.5	4.1	4.7	.9	1.5	1.6	1.8	2.4	2.7
III	4.2	3.6	4.6	4.4	.4	.8	6.2	5.9	3.4	3.1	1.9	2.2	−1.2	−1.1
IV	3.8	4.2	5.6	6.0	1.8	1.8	4.6	4.6	1.4	1.4	.7	.4	5.6	5.6
1993: I	−1.6	−1.8	.5	.6	2.1	2.5	3.3	2.9	−.5	−.9	5.0	4.8	2.7	2.5
II	−.0	−.4	3.8	4.0	3.8	4.4	2.5	1.9	−.4	−1.0	2.5	2.3	2.6	2.4
III	3.6	4.3	3.5	4.4	−.1	.1	3.9	3.7	2.7	2.5	.3	−.6	1.2	1.2

[1] Output refers to gross domestic product originating in the sector in 1987 dollars.
[2] Hours at work of all persons engaged in the sector, including hours of proprietors and unpaid family workers. Estimates based primarily on establishment data.
[3] Wages and salaries of employees plus employers' contributions for social insurance and private benefit plans. Also includes an estimate of wages, salaries, and supplemental payments for the self-employed.
[4] Hourly compensation divided by the consumer price index for all urban consumers.
[5] Current dollar gross domestic product divided by constant dollar gross domestic product.

Note.—Percent changes are based on original data and therefore may differ slightly from percent changes based on indexes in Table B–47.

Source: Department of Labor, Bureau of Labor Statistics.

PRODUCTION AND BUSINESS ACTIVITY

TABLE B-49.—*Industrial production indexes, major industry divisions, 1947–93*

[1987=100; monthly data seasonally adjusted]

Year or month	Total industrial production	Manufacturing Total	Manufacturing Durable	Manufacturing Nondurable	Mining	Utilities
1947	22.7	21.2	19.9	22.6	55.5	11.7
1948	23.6	22.0	20.8	23.4	58.3	13.0
1949	22.3	20.8	18.9	23.0	51.7	13.9
1950	25.8	24.2	23.0	25.6	57.7	15.8
1951	28.0	26.1	25.9	26.4	63.4	18.1
1952	29.1	27.2	27.5	26.9	62.8	19.6
1953	31.6	29.6	31.1	28.0	64.5	21.3
1954	29.9	27.7	27.4	28.2	63.2	22.9
1955	33.7	31.3	31.3	31.3	70.5	25.6
1956	35.1	32.5	32.4	32.9	74.2	28.1
1957	35.6	32.9	32.6	33.5	74.3	30.0
1958	33.3	30.6	28.5	33.7	68.1	31.4
1959	37.3	34.5	32.8	37.1	71.3	34.5
1960	38.1	35.2	33.3	38.0	72.7	36.9
1961	38.4	35.3	32.7	39.1	73.1	39.0
1962	41.6	38.4	36.3	41.5	75.2	41.9
1963	44.0	40.7	38.7	43.8	78.2	44.8
1964	47.0	43.5	41.4	46.6	81.4	48.7
1965	51.7	48.2	47.1	49.8	84.4	51.7
1966	56.3	52.6	52.3	52.9	88.9	55.6
1967	57.5	53.6	52.9	54.6	90.6	58.4
1968	60.7	56.6	55.5	58.1	94.1	63.1
1969	63.5	59.1	57.7	61.1	97.8	68.7
1970	61.4	56.4	53.3	61.1	100.4	72.9
1971	62.2	57.3	53.1	63.6	97.8	76.4
1972	68.3	63.3	59.3	69.3	99.9	81.3
1973	73.8	68.9	66.2	72.7	100.8	84.5
1974	72.7	67.9	64.8	72.3	100.3	83.5
1975	66.3	61.1	56.7	67.7	98.0	84.3
1976	72.4	67.4	62.6	74.6	98.9	87.6
1977	78.2	73.3	68.7	80.1	101.5	89.9
1978	82.6	77.8	73.9	83.5	104.6	92.7
1979	85.7	80.9	78.3	84.6	106.6	95.3
1980	84.1	78.8	75.7	83.1	110.0	95.9
1981	85.7	80.3	77.4	84.5	114.3	94.3
1982	81.9	76.6	72.7	82.5	109.3	91.8
1983	84.9	80.9	76.8	87.0	104.8	93.6
1984	92.8	89.3	88.4	90.8	111.9	97.0
1985	94.4	91.6	91.8	91.5	109.0	99.5
1986	95.3	94.3	93.9	94.9	101.0	96.3
1987	100.0	100.0	100.0	100.0	100.0	100.0
1988	104.4	104.7	106.6	102.3	101.3	105.0
1989	106.0	106.4	108.6	103.7	100.0	108.7
1990	106.0	106.1	107.4	104.4	102.0	109.9
1991	104.1	103.7	103.8	103.5	100.4	112.2
1992	106.5	106.9	108.1	105.4	97.6	112.0
1993 ᵖ	111.0	111.9	115.9	106.8	97.0	116.0
1992: Jan	104.5	104.5	104.6	104.4	97.5	110.2
Feb	105.3	105.4	106.2	104.6	96.7	111.0
Mar	105.6	106.1	106.7	105.3	97.2	111.4
Apr	106.3	106.5	107.2	105.5	97.4	112.0
May	106.7	107.1	108.4	105.4	98.8	111.2
June	106.0	106.5	107.6	105.2	97.1	110.0
July	106.8	107.1	108.2	105.7	98.5	111.2
Aug	106.6	107.0	108.5	105.2	97.0	110.4
Sept	106.2	106.8	108.1	105.2	97.1	111.2
Oct	107.5	108.0	109.8	105.8	97.6	112.7
Nov	108.4	108.9	110.9	106.4	97.8	114.7
Dec	108.9	109.2	111.8	106.0	98.2	116.8
1993: Jan	109.3	109.9	112.9	106.4	98.3	112.8
Feb	109.9	110.5	113.8	106.4	95.9	117.5
Mar	110.1	110.8	114.1	106.6	95.3	117.8
Apr	110.4	111.4	115.0	106.9	96.4	114.4
May	110.2	111.3	114.9	106.9	97.3	112.1
June	110.5	111.3	114.6	107.2	98.0	114.9
July	110.8	111.6	115.4	107.0	96.4	116.9
Aug	111.0	111.9	115.7	107.3	95.5	117.7
Sept	111.4	112.3	117.0	106.5	97.7	115.3
Oct ᵖ	112.1	113.2	118.3	107.0	98.2	114.6
Nov ᵖ	113.2	114.5	120.1	107.6	97.4	115.4
Dec ᵖ	114.0	115.3	121.7	107.4	97.9	116.6

Source: Board of Governors of the Federal Reserve System.

TABLE B-50.—Industrial production indexes, market groupings, 1947–93

[1987=100; monthly data seasonally adjusted]

Year or month	Total industrial production	Final products Total	Consumer goods Total	Auto-motive products	Other durable goods	Non-durable goods	Equipment Total [1]	Business	Defense and space	Intermediate products	Materials Total	Durable	Non-durable	Energy
1947	22.7	20.8	25.4	21.7	22.8	27.0	15.0	14.7	7.5	22.4	25.1	21.5		
1948	23.6	21.5	26.2	22.6	23.8	27.7	15.8	15.3	8.8	23.6	26.2	22.1		
1949	22.3	20.9	26.1	22.5	22.0	27.9	14.1	13.4	9.2	22.4	23.9	19.8		
1950	25.8	23.5	29.7	28.3	30.4	30.3	15.3	14.3	10.8	26.1	28.6	24.9		
1951	28.0	25.4	29.4	25.0	26.2	31.3	21.2	17.5	26.5	27.4	31.6	28.3		
1952	29.1	27.3	30.1	22.5	26.2	32.6	25.5	19.8	37.2	27.2	32.1	28.9		
1953	31.6	29.1	31.9	28.4	29.6	33.5	27.6	20.6	44.6	29.1	35.6	33.8		
1954	29.9	27.6	31.7	26.5	27.3	33.9	24.2	18.1	39.3	29.0	32.9	29.2	25.2	52.7
1955	33.7	29.8	35.4	35.2	32.2	36.5	24.7	19.6	35.9	32.9	38.9	35.7	28.9	59.3
1956	35.1	31.6	36.7	28.9	33.9	38.8	27.1	22.7	35.1	34.4	39.9	35.8	30.2	62.7
1957	35.6	32.5	37.6	30.3	33.2	40.1	28.2	23.6	36.7	34.4	39.9	35.8	30.1	63.4
1958	33.3	31.0	37.2	24.1	31.3	41.3	25.2	19.9	36.8	33.6	35.9	30.1	29.9	58.8
1959	37.3	34.0	40.9	30.2	36.0	44.1	27.7	22.4	38.8	37.1	41.4	35.9	34.2	62.3
1960	38.1	35.1	42.4	34.6	36.2	45.5	28.5	23.0	39.9	37.4	42.0	36.3	34.8	63.1
1961	38.4	35.4	43.3	31.6	37.3	47.0	28.1	22.3	40.6	38.1	42.0	35.5	36.2	63.6
1962	41.6	38.4	46.2	38.3	40.5	49.2	31.3	24.3	46.9	40.4	45.8	39.4	39.2	65.8
1963	44.0	40.6	48.8	41.9	43.7	51.4	33.1	25.5	50.6	42.7	48.7	42.1	41.6	69.7
1964	47.0	42.9	51.5	43.9	47.7	54.0	35.0	28.5	49.0	45.5	52.6	45.9	45.2	72.5
1965	51.7	47.1	55.5	54.1	54.1	56.3	39.6	32.6	54.3	48.4	58.7	52.6	49.6	75.8
1966	56.3	51.6	58.4	53.9	59.6	59.0	46.1	37.8	63.7	51.4	63.9	57.9	53.6	80.6
1967	57.5	53.7	59.8	47.4	60.4	62.0	49.0	38.6	72.7	53.5	63.3	55.9	54.5	83.4
1968	60.7	56.3	63.4	56.4	64.7	64.5	50.4	40.3	72.9	56.6	67.5	59.2	59.9	87.2
1969	63.5	58.1	65.8	56.7	69.0	66.7	51.8	42.9	69.4	59.6	71.5	62.3	64.9	91.7
1970	61.4	56.0	65.0	47.7	66.9	67.8	48.1	41.3	58.7	58.7	69.0	56.5	65.2	96.2
1971	62.2	56.5	68.8	60.8	70.8	69.7	45.0	39.3	52.8	60.5	70.0	56.8	68.0	97.1
1972	68.3	61.3	74.3	65.6	81.0	74.2	49.3	44.8	51.3	67.6	77.2	64.2	74.9	100.8
1973	73.8	65.9	77.6	72.4	85.7	76.5	55.0	52.4	50.1	71.9	84.5	73.3	80.4	101.5
1974	72.7	65.7	75.2	62.6	79.3	76.5	56.8	54.7	49.4	69.4	82.8	71.2	80.8	98.9
1975	66.3	61.8	72.3	59.0	69.8	74.9	52.0	48.8	48.5	62.6	72.6	59.3	71.9	96.7
1976	72.4	66.2	79.4	73.2	78.2	80.4	53.8	50.6	49.2	69.0	81.2	68.4	81.4	99.0
1977	78.2	71.6	85.1	84.0	87.4	84.4	58.8	56.7	49.2	74.9	87.3	75.3	86.7	101.1
1978	82.6	76.1	88.4	86.3	91.2	87.8	64.2	63.1	49.5	79.1	91.8	81.4	89.7	102.2
1979	85.7	79.0	87.3	78.5	89.8	87.7	71.0	71.5	51.5	81.2	95.4	85.3	92.9	105.0
1980	84.1	80.0	85.3	59.5	85.1	89.1	74.6	73.5	57.4	77.0	91.3	79.3	88.7	106.2
1981	85.7	82.1	85.8	59.2	86.3	89.6	78.2	76.1	58.5	77.0	92.8	82.1	90.5	104.3
1982	81.9	80.8	84.5	57.5	78.1	89.7	77.0	72.9	65.7	75.1	85.1	73.4	82.1	100.7
1983	84.9	83.0	88.8	71.9	86.2	91.9	76.8	71.9	71.8	80.3	88.3	79.2	89.2	98.9
1984	92.8	91.0	92.8	86.6	94.6	93.4	89.2	85.4	78.9	86.2	96.6	92.1	93.0	103.8
1985	94.4	94.2	93.7	92.7	90.6	94.4	94.8	91.1	89.4	88.3	96.6	92.9	91.7	103.4
1986	95.3	95.7	96.8	95.3	93.9	97.6	94.5	93.1	96.0	91.9	95.9	93.7	94.4	99.5
1987	100.0	100.0	100.0	100.0	100.0	100.0	100.0	100.0	100.0	100.0	100.0	100.0	100.0	100.0
1988	104.4	104.8	102.9	106.4	103.0	102.4	107.6	110.7	99.7	101.8	105.0	106.8	104.4	102.2
1989	106.0	106.8	104.0	108.2	105.2	103.2	110.9	115.5	100.1	102.0	106.7	108.4	107.1	103.1
1990	106.0	107.0	103.4	100.7	103.6	103.8	112.1	116.9	98.8	101.2	106.8	107.6	108.0	104.2
1991	104.1	105.3	102.8	89.8	99.9	105.0	108.9	115.7	91.7	96.5	105.5	105.2	107.1	104.6
1992	106.5	108.2	105.2	99.4	105.2	105.9	112.7	123.2	85.9	97.6	107.9	108.9	110.9	103.4
1993 [p]	111.0	113.5	108.1	110.6	111.9	107.2	121.2	137.0	78.7	100.1	112.2	116.0	114.0	103.5
1992: Jan	104.5	105.3	103.2	90.5	102.5	105.0	108.3	116.3	89.5	97.0	106.2	106.8	108.8	103.1
Feb	105.3	106.5	104.0	95.2	103.6	105.2	110.1	118.8	89.0	97.2	106.8	107.8	109.9	102.5
Mar	105.6	106.9	104.7	96.5	104.7	105.7	110.2	119.0	88.9	97.2	107.3	108.1	110.9	102.7
Apr	106.3	107.7	105.4	99.0	105.8	106.1	111.1	120.6	87.7	97.9	107.9	108.8	111.2	103.5
May	106.7	108.3	105.8	102.9	107.9	105.9	112.0	122.1	87.2	97.9	108.0	109.0	111.5	103.3
June	106.0	107.1	104.0	99.0	104.6	104.6	111.6	121.9	86.5	97.7	107.8	108.7	111.5	103.1
July	106.8	108.1	104.9	98.8	106.3	105.5	112.7	123.7	85.1	98.6	108.5	109.3	111.5	104.4
Aug	106.6	108.9	105.1	99.5	104.0	106.0	114.3	126.1	84.5	97.0	107.6	108.9	110.7	102.5
Sept	106.2	108.1	104.4	97.3	104.1	105.3	113.5	125.0	84.4	96.9	107.4	107.6	111.7	103.6
Oct	107.5	110.1	106.4	103.1	104.9	107.1	115.4	127.5	83.5	97.8	108.1	109.7	111.7	103.0
Nov	108.4	111.0	107.1	104.1	107.1	107.5	116.7	129.0	83.2	98.1	109.3	111.1	112.0	103.9
Dec	108.9	111.5	107.5	108.7	107.2	107.4	117.2	129.6	82.5	98.3	110.0	111.9	111.5	105.1
1993: Jan	109.3	111.9	107.6	112.7	109.3	106.7	118.1	131.2	82.0	98.2	110.4	113.3	112.4	103.4
Feb	109.9	112.4	108.5	111.9	110.7	107.7	118.0	131.7	81.5	99.3	110.9	114.2	112.1	103.8
Mar	110.1	112.7	108.6	111.2	111.7	107.7	118.7	133.4	80.7	99.6	110.9	114.1	112.8	103.5
Apr	110.4	112.8	108.1	112.1	112.3	106.9	119.7	134.8	80.5	100.0	111.5	114.9	113.8	103.4
May	110.2	112.5	107.3	109.7	111.8	106.3	119.9	135.4	79.5	99.7	111.6	114.8	114.1	103.4
June	110.5	112.7	107.3	105.3	110.2	107.2	120.4	136.1	78.6	99.4	112.1	114.9	114.8	104.6
July	110.8	113.2	107.7	103.3	113.2	107.4	121.2	137.1	78.6	100.4	112.0	115.4	114.2	103.7
Aug	111.0	113.5	107.8	103.0	112.2	107.8	121.6	137.6	78.0	100.6	112.2	115.8	115.2	102.8
Sept	111.4	113.8	107.4	105.6	112.5	106.9	122.9	139.4	77.5	100.4	112.7	117.2	113.8	103.3
Oct [p]	112.1	114.8	108.6	113.8	113.8	107.3	123.8	140.8	76.9	101.0	113.2	118.2	114.4	102.9
Nov [p]	113.2	115.9	109.6	119.5	114.9	107.4	125.2	142.9	76.6	101.8	114.3	119.7	115.5	103.0
Dec [p]	114.0	116.6	109.8	123.4	114.4	107.2	126.6	144.9	76.1	101.9	115.5	121.7	115.3	103.9

[1] Two components—oil and gas well drilling and manufactured homes—are included in total equipment, but not in detail shown.

Source: Board of Governors of the Federal Reserve System.

TABLE B-51.—*Industrial production indexes, selected manufactures, 1947–93*

[1987=100; monthly data seasonally adjusted]

Year or month	Durable manufactures								Nondurable manufactures				
	Primary metals		Fabricated metal products	Industrial and commercial machinery and computer equipment	Electrical machinery	Transportation equipment		Lumber and products	Apparel products	Textile mill products	Printing and publishing	Chemicals and products	Foods
	Total	Iron and steel				Total	Motor vehicles and parts						
1947	70.2	102.1	37.5	12.0	8.5	19.6	27.3	38.8	43.1	35.2	22.1	8.7	33.1
1948	73.0	106.8	38.2	12.1	8.8	21.4	29.6	40.4	45.0	37.7	23.2	9.4	32.8
1949	61.4	91.2	34.4	10.3	8.3	21.5	30.4	35.7	44.5	34.8	23.8	9.3	33.1
1950	77.3	112.4	42.2	11.6	11.3	25.7	39.0	43.4	47.9	39.6	24.9	11.6	34.3
1951	84.1	125.7	45.1	14.7	11.4	28.7	35.8	43.2	47.0	39.2	25.4	13.1	35.0
1952	76.8	110.6	44.0	16.0	13.0	33.3	30.7	42.7	49.5	38.9	25.3	13.7	35.7
1953	87.0	127.5	49.6	16.7	14.9	41.8	38.7	45.1	50.1	39.9	26.5	14.8	36.4
1954	70.4	99.1	44.7	14.2	13.3	36.4	33.3	44.8	49.5	37.3	27.6	15.0	37.2
1955	91.5	131.8	51.0	15.6	15.3	41.9	44.6	50.1	54.7	42.5	30.3	17.6	39.3
1956	90.9	129.3	51.8	17.9	16.5	40.6	36.2	49.5	56.0	43.7	32.3	18.9	41.5
1957	87.1	124.6	53.1	17.9	16.4	43.5	38.0	45.4	55.8	41.6	33.4	19.9	42.2
1958	69.0	93.9	47.6	15.0	15.0	34.3	28.0	46.1	54.3	41.1	32.6	20.6	43.2
1959	80.7	108.1	53.4	17.5	18.2	38.9	36.4	52.3	59.7	46.4	34.8	24.0	45.4
1960	80.4	109.9	53.4	17.6	19.8	40.3	41.1	49.3	60.9	45.6	36.2	24.9	46.6
1961	78.9	104.9	52.1	17.1	21.0	37.8	36.0	51.6	61.3	46.9	36.4	26.1	47.9
1962	84.6	109.3	56.7	19.2	24.1	43.7	43.9	54.4	63.8	50.1	37.7	29.0	49.5
1963	91.2	119.1	58.5	20.5	24.8	48.2	48.6	56.9	66.4	51.9	39.7	31.7	51.2
1964	102.9	135.5	62.1	23.3	26.2	49.2	49.9	61.1	68.7	56.0	42.1	34.8	53.6
1965	113.2	148.7	68.3	26.2	31.3	58.5	63.7	63.5	72.6	61.0	44.8	38.7	54.8
1966	120.2	153.1	73.1	30.5	37.5	62.7	62.6	65.9	74.5	64.7	48.3	42.2	56.9
1967	111.1	141.5	76.5	31.1	37.7	61.3	55.1	65.3	74.1	64.8	50.9	44.2	59.4
1968	115.1	146.1	80.6	31.3	39.8	66.6	66.0	67.2	76.0	72.3	51.7	49.6	61.0
1969	123.8	159.2	81.9	33.9	42.3	66.1	66.3	67.1	78.4	76.0	54.2	53.7	63.0
1970	115.2	148.2	75.9	32.8	40.5	55.5	53.3	66.7	75.3	74.4	52.7	55.9	64.0
1971	109.2	135.5	75.6	30.5	40.7	60.1	66.9	68.5	76.2	78.5	53.2	59.5	66.0
1972	122.4	150.6	82.9	35.4	46.5	64.1	73.0	78.4	80.9	86.0	56.7	66.9	69.5
1973	138.9	171.5	92.1	41.4	53.0	73.0	85.0	78.7	81.5	89.6	58.3	73.1	70.9
1974	134.5	166.1	88.4	44.1	52.4	66.4	73.4	71.4	77.9	81.5	57.4	75.8	71.9
1975	107.2	133.5	76.7	38.1	45.1	59.7	62.2	66.5	71.1	77.7	53.7	69.1	71.4
1976	119.9	147.1	84.9	40.0	50.7	68.0	81.9	75.6	83.9	86.3	58.7	77.3	75.5
1977	121.5	145.1	92.7	45.1	58.4	73.7	94.7	82.3	91.6	91.6	64.3	83.3	79.0
1978	130.7	155.3	96.2	50.2	64.0	79.5	99.2	83.6	93.9	92.0	68.1	88.0	81.8
1979	133.0	156.5	99.5	56.9	71.3	81.0	91.0	82.4	89.0	95.0	69.9	91.3	82.6
1980	110.8	126.0	92.5	60.6	73.3	72.3	67.0	76.9	89.2	92.1	70.3	87.8	84.6
1981	117.5	135.1	91.1	65.9	75.4	68.7	64.4	74.7	91.0	89.4	72.1	89.2	86.5
1982	83.2	86.2	83.2	63.9	75.9	64.8	58.8	67.3	90.1	83.0	75.2	81.8	87.7
1983	91.0	96.1	85.5	64.3	80.3	72.7	74.5	79.9	93.8	93.2	79.0	87.5	90.1
1984	102.4	105.9	93.3	80.8	94.1	83.1	90.6	86.0	95.7	93.7	84.5	91.4	92.1
1985	101.8	104.5	94.5	86.8	93.1	91.8	99.0	88.0	92.6	89.7	87.6	91.4	94.9
1986	93.7	90.8	93.8	90.3	94.3	96.9	98.5	95.1	96.3	93.9	90.6	94.6	97.4
1987	100.0	100.0	100.0	100.0	100.0	100.0	100.0	100.0	100.0	100.0	100.0	100.0	100.0
1988	108.7	112.7	104.2	113.0	108.5	105.2	105.7	100.1	98.1	98.6	100.9	106.0	101.5
1989	107.2	111.2	102.8	117.3	111.0	109.6	106.9	99.4	95.0	100.3	101.1	109.2	102.5
1990	106.5	111.5	99.5	117.6	111.4	107.0	101.0	97.1	92.2	97.1	100.8	111.8	103.7
1991	98.4	100.6	94.9	113.7	112.8	101.8	94.3	90.5	91.9	96.8	96.8	111.3	105.3
1992	101.1	104.7	96.7	124.8	119.8	102.6	104.8	96.4	92.3	104.7	95.0	115.0	106.0
1993 ᵖ	105.5	110.5	100.9	146.8	131.7	105.6	120.1	100.0	90.8	106.3	94.1	118.3	106.9
1992: Jan	101.7	105.5	94.9	114.7	114.9	100.6	96.1	95.1	93.4	102.9	96.4	112.8	104.6
Feb	102.4	106.4	95.9	118.1	116.3	102.2	100.3	96.3	93.3	104.3	95.6	113.6	105.8
Mar	102.6	106.5	96.6	120.0	117.2	102.3	101.2	96.5	93.6	104.3	95.1	114.2	106.4
Apr	101.8	105.6	96.8	120.9	118.2	103.2	104.5	95.3	93.4	105.0	95.8	114.6	106.0
May	101.1	104.8	97.2	123.2	119.5	104.5	107.9	96.1	93.5	105.0	94.5	114.8	106.1
June	101.2	103.8	97.1	123.8	119.3	102.7	104.8	93.8	91.7	103.8	95.6	114.9	105.4
July	100.6	104.7	97.0	125.7	120.7	101.4	103.1	96.6	92.7	107.0	95.7	114.6	105.9
Aug	100.5	103.8	97.0	126.9	120.6	102.4	105.0	96.6	91.3	103.5	93.5	114.4	106.3
Sept	98.0	102.0	96.5	127.9	121.5	100.5	102.6	94.7	91.5	105.1	94.1	115.2	105.6
Oct	100.5	104.1	97.5	130.6	122.6	103.0	108.0	97.8	91.7	103.5	94.5	116.2	106.8
Nov	101.6	103.6	97.6	132.8	124.4	103.6	109.9	99.8	92.9	106.0	94.2	117.7	106.4
Dec	102.4	107.4	97.8	133.8	124.8	106.3	116.2	98.0	92.7	106.0	94.7	116.7	106.2
1993: Jan	102.8	107.0	99.8	135.0	125.8	108.4	120.9	99.3	93.1	106.9	94.7	116.8	105.9
Feb	108.0	112.9	99.7	136.7	127.1	107.8	120.7	101.8	92.5	106.2	94.0	116.2	106.9
Mar	104.2	107.6	100.3	139.6	128.5	106.9	120.1	98.0	92.1	105.4	94.7	117.6	106.7
Apr	104.4	108.4	101.4	142.8	129.0	106.9	120.4	98.1	92.0	104.2	95.6	117.8	106.7
May	104.2	108.1	100.6	144.2	129.7	105.5	118.1	97.4	91.2	106.9	94.7	118.1	106.7
June	105.7	110.9	100.1	145.4	130.1	102.6	114.3	96.5	91.1	107.1	94.5	119.1	107.1
July	105.3	111.9	101.2	148.5	132.3	100.8	110.1	99.1	90.7	107.7	93.8	118.7	107.2
Aug	106.2	112.1	101.0	149.9	133.5	100.4	110.0	99.9	90.6	106.3	93.4	119.1	107.8
Sept	106.0	111.4	100.9	152.1	135.2	102.4	115.0	100.7	89.6	105.4	93.8	118.5	107.3
Oct ᵖ	105.0	112.4	101.6	153.7	136.0	106.3	124.1	104.0	89.4	106.6	94.3	118.1	107.8
Nov ᵖ	107.1	111.1	102.7	156.2	137.2	110.0	132.3	104.2	90.0	106.3	94.4	119.6	107.2
Dec ᵖ	109.1	114.6	103.3	158.8	138.7	112.7	138.8	104.6	89.7	106.8	93.3	120.0	107.0

Source: Board of Governors of the Federal Reserve System.

TABLE B-52.—*Capacity utilization rates, 1948–93*

[Percent;[1] monthly data seasonally adjusted]

Year or month	Total industry	Manufacturing					Mining	Utilities
		Total	Durable goods	Non-durable goods	Primary processing	Advanced processing		
1948		82.5			87.3	80.0		
1949		74.2			76.2	73.2		
1950		82.8			88.5	79.8		
1951		85.8			90.2	83.4		
1952		85.4			84.9	85.9		
1953		89.3			89.4	89.3		
1954		80.1			80.6	80.0		
1955		87.0			92.0	84.2		
1956		86.1			89.4	84.4		
1957		83.6			84.7	83.1		
1958		75.0			75.4	74.9		
1959		81.6			83.0	81.1		
1960		80.1			79.8	80.5		
1961		77.3			77.9	77.2		
1962		81.4			81.5	81.6		
1963		83.5			83.8	83.4		
1964		85.6			87.8	84.6		
1965		89.5			91.0	88.8		
1966		91.1			91.4	91.1		
1967	86.4	87.2	87.1	86.3	85.4	88.0	81.2	93.4
1968	86.8	87.2	86.8	86.6	86.3	87.4	83.5	94.1
1969	86.9	86.8	86.3	86.6	86.9	86.5	86.6	95.8
1970	80.8	79.7	76.7	82.9	80.4	79.1	88.9	95.4
1971	79.2	78.2	74.3	82.8	79.3	77.4	87.4	93.9
1972	84.3	83.7	80.9	86.6	86.4	82.5	90.4	94.6
1973	88.4	88.1	87.5	87.5	91.5	86.5	92.5	92.9
1974	84.2	83.8	82.7	84.0	86.0	82.8	92.5	86.8
1975	74.6	73.2	70.2	76.4	72.9	73.5	89.9	84.0
1976	79.3	78.5	75.4	81.8	80.1	77.8	90.0	84.8
1977	83.3	82.8	80.3	85.2	84.0	81.9	90.9	84.6
1978	85.5	85.1	83.5	86.2	86.3	84.3	91.3	84.8
1979	86.2	85.4	84.9	85.1	86.4	84.8	91.9	85.9
1980	82.1	80.2	78.6	81.4	78.0	81.3	94.0	85.5
1981	80.9	78.8	76.6	81.0	78.0	79.1	94.6	82.8
1982	75.0	72.8	69.0	78.0	69.0	74.6	86.5	79.5
1983	75.8	74.9	70.5	81.1	74.8	74.9	79.9	80.3
1984	81.1	80.4	78.3	83.1	80.4	80.3	84.4	82.5
1985	80.3	79.5	77.8	81.9	79.8	79.4	82.9	83.5
1986	79.2	79.1	76.2	83.0	80.9	78.3	78.2	80.2
1987	81.5	81.6	78.6	85.6	84.9	80.1	79.9	82.0
1988	83.7	83.6	81.8	85.9	86.9	82.1	84.4	84.1
1989	83.6	83.1	81.5	85.3	86.2	81.8	85.9	86.0
1990	82.1	81.1	79.0	84.0	84.2	79.8	89.1	86.0
1991	79.2	77.8	74.9	81.7	80.1	76.8	88.6	86.3
1992 ᵖ	79.8	78.8	76.4	82.0	82.4	77.9	86.8	85.3
1993 ᵖ	81.9	81.1	80.4	82.0	84.6	79.6	87.1	87.0
1992: Jan	78.8	77.6	74.6	81.7	82.3	78.7	86.4	84.6
Feb	79.3	78.2	75.6	81.8	82.6	79.1	85.7	85.1
Mar	79.5	78.6	75.8	82.3	83.0	79.2	86.2	85.3
Apr	79.9	78.8	76.1	82.4	82.3	77.3	86.5	85.7
May	80.1	79.1	76.8	82.2	82.6	77.5	87.8	84.9
June	79.5	78.6	76.1	81.9	82.2	77.0	86.3	83.9
July	80.0	78.9	76.4	82.2	82.6	77.3	87.6	84.8
Aug	79.7	78.7	76.5	81.7	81.9	77.3	86.4	84.1
Sept	79.3	78.4	76.1	81.7	81.7	77.0	86.5	84.5
Oct	80.2	79.2	77.1	82.0	82.3	77.9	87.1	85.6
Nov	80.8	79.7	77.8	82.4	83.0	78.4	87.4	87.1
Dec	81.0	79.8	78.2	82.0	82.9	78.6	87.8	88.5
1993: Jan	81.2	80.3	78.9	82.2	83.5	78.9	87.9	85.4
Feb	81.5	80.5	79.4	82.1	84.3	79.0	85.8	88.9
Mar	81.6	80.6	79.5	82.2	83.8	79.3	85.3	89.0
Apr	81.7	80.9	79.9	82.3	84.3	79.5	86.4	86.4
May	81.5	80.7	79.7	82.2	84.2	79.3	87.2	84.6
June	81.5	80.6	79.4	82.3	84.5	78.9	87.9	86.6
July	81.7	80.7	79.8	82.0	84.5	79.2	86.5	88.1
Aug	81.7	80.8	79.9	82.1	84.8	79.2	85.8	88.6
Sept	81.9	81.0	80.6	81.5	84.4	79.6	87.8	86.7
Oct ᵖ	82.3	81.5	81.4	81.7	84.8	80.1	88.4	86.1
Nov ᵖ	83.0	82.3	82.5	82.0	85.7	80.9	87.7	86.6
Dec ᵖ	83.5	82.7	83.4	81.8	86.0	81.4	88.2	87.5

[1] Output as percent of capacity.

Source: Board of Governors of the Federal Reserve System.

TABLE B-53.—*New construction activity, 1929–93*

[Value put in place, billions of dollars; monthly data at seasonally adjusted annual rates]

Year or month	Total new construction	Private construction							Public construction		
		Total	Residential buildings [1]		Nonresidential buildings and other construction [1]				Total	Federal	State and local [5]
			Total [2]	New housing units	Total	Commercial [3]	Industrial	Other [4]			
1929	10.8	8.3	3.6	3.0	4.7	1.1	0.9	2.6	2.5	0.2	2.3
1933	2.9	1.2	.5	.3	.8	.1	.2	.5	1.6	.5	1.1
1939	8.2	4.4	2.7	2.3	1.7	.3	.3	1.2	3.8	.8	3.1
1940	8.7	5.1	3.0	2.6	2.1	.3	.4	1.3	3.6	1.2	2.4
1941	12.0	6.2	3.5	3.0	2.7	.4	.8	1.5	5.8	3.8	2.0
1942	14.1	3.4	1.7	1.4	1.7	.2	.3	1.2	10.7	9.3	1.3
1943	8.3	2.0	.9	.7	1.1	.0	.2	.9	6.3	5.6	.7
1944	5.3	2.2	.8	.6	1.4	.1	.2	1.1	3.1	2.5	.6
1945	5.8	3.4	1.3	.7	2.1	.2	.6	1.3	2.4	1.7	.7
1946	14.3	12.1	6.2	4.8	5.8	1.2	1.7	3.0	2.2	.9	1.4

New series

1947	20.0	16.7	9.9	7.8	6.9	1.0	1.7	4.2	3.3	.8	2.5
1948	26.1	21.4	13.1	10.5	8.2	1.4	1.4	5.5	4.7	1.2	3.5
1949	26.7	20.5	12.4	10.0	8.0	1.2	1.0	5.9	6.3	1.5	4.8
1950	33.6	26.7	18.1	15.6	8.6	1.4	1.1	6.1	6.9	1.6	5.2
1951	35.4	26.2	15.9	13.2	10.3	1.5	2.1	6.7	9.3	3.0	6.3
1952	36.8	26.0	15.8	12.9	10.2	1.1	2.3	6.8	10.8	4.2	6.6
1953	39.1	27.9	16.6	13.4	11.3	1.8	2.2	7.3	11.2	4.1	7.1
1954	41.4	29.7	18.2	14.9	11.5	2.2	2.0	7.2	11.7	3.4	8.3
1955	46.5	34.8	21.9	18.2	12.9	3.2	2.4	7.3	11.7	2.8	8.9
1956	47.6	34.9	20.2	16.1	14.7	3.6	3.1	8.0	12.7	2.7	10.0
1957	49.1	35.1	19.0	14.7	16.1	3.6	3.6	9.0	14.1	3.0	11.1
1958	50.0	34.6	19.8	15.4	14.8	3.6	2.4	8.8	15.5	3.4	12.1
1959	55.4	39.3	24.3	19.2	15.1	3.9	2.1	9.0	16.1	3.7	12.3
1960	54.7	38.9	23.0	17.3	15.9	4.2	2.9	8.9	15.9	3.6	12.2
1961	56.4	39.3	23.1	17.1	16.2	4.7	2.8	8.7	17.1	3.9	13.3
1962	60.2	42.3	25.2	19.4	17.2	5.1	2.8	9.2	17.9	3.9	14.0
1963	64.8	45.5	27.9	21.7	17.6	5.0	2.9	9.7	19.4	4.0	15.4

New series

1964	72.1	51.9	30.5	24.1	21.4	6.8	3.6	11.0	20.2	3.7	16.5
1965	78.0	56.1	30.2	23.8	25.8	8.1	5.1	12.6	21.9	3.9	18.0
1966	81.2	57.4	28.6	21.8	28.8	8.1	6.6	14.1	23.8	3.8	20.0
1967	83.0	57.6	28.7	21.5	28.8	8.0	6.0	14.9	25.4	3.3	22.1
1968	92.4	65.0	34.2	26.7	30.8	9.0	6.0	15.8	27.4	3.2	24.2
1969	99.8	72.0	37.2	29.2	34.8	10.8	6.8	17.2	27.8	3.2	24.6
1970	100.7	72.8	35.9	27.1	37.0	11.2	6.6	19.2	27.9	3.1	24.8
1971	117.3	87.6	48.5	38.7	39.1	13.1	5.5	20.5	29.7	3.8	25.9
1972	133.3	103.3	60.7	50.1	42.6	15.7	4.8	22.1	30.0	4.2	25.8
1973	146.8	114.5	65.1	54.6	49.4	18.1	6.4	24.9	32.3	4.7	27.6
1974	147.5	109.3	56.0	43.4	53.4	18.1	8.1	27.2	38.1	5.1	33.0
1975	145.6	102.3	51.6	36.3	50.7	14.3	8.3	28.2	43.3	6.1	37.2
1976	165.4	121.5	68.3	50.8	53.2	14.1	7.4	31.6	44.0	6.8	37.2
1977	193.1	150.0	92.0	72.2	58.0	16.4	8.0	33.7	43.1	7.1	36.0
1978	230.2	180.0	109.8	85.6	70.2	20.6	11.5	38.2	50.1	8.1	42.0
1979	259.8	203.2	116.4	89.3	86.8	28.3	15.6	42.8	56.6	8.6	48.1
1980	259.7	196.1	100.4	69.6	95.7	34.6	14.6	46.6	63.6	9.6	54.0
1981	272.0	207.3	99.2	69.4	108.0	40.2	18.0	49.8	64.7	10.4	54.3
1982	260.6	197.5	84.7	57.0	112.9	44.1	18.5	50.2	63.1	10.0	53.1
1983	294.9	231.5	125.5	94.6	106.0	43.9	13.8	48.2	63.5	10.6	52.9
1984	348.8	278.6	153.8	113.8	124.8	59.1	14.8	50.8	70.2	11.2	59.0
1985	377.4	299.5	158.5	114.7	141.1	72.6	17.1	51.3	77.8	12.0	65.8
1986	407.7	323.1	187.1	133.2	136.0	69.5	14.9	51.6	84.6	12.4	72.2
1987	419.4	328.7	194.7	139.9	134.1	68.9	15.0	50.1	90.6	14.1	76.6
1988	432.3	337.5	198.1	138.9	139.4	71.5	16.5	51.5	94.8	12.3	82.5
1989	443.6	345.5	196.6	139.2	148.9	73.9	20.4	54.6	98.1	12.2	86.0
1990	442.1	334.7	182.9	128.0	151.8	72.5	23.8	55.4	107.5	12.1	95.4
1991	403.4	293.5	157.8	110.6	135.7	54.8	22.3	58.7	109.9	12.8	97.1
1992	436.0	317.3	187.8	129.6	129.4	45.0	20.7	63.7	118.8	14.3	104.5
1993 ᵖ	470.3	342.7	207.9	144.5	134.8	47.3	20.7	66.8	127.6	14.5	113.1

See next page for continuation of table.

TABLE B-53.—*New construction activity, 1929–93*—Continued

[Value put in place, billions of dollars; monthly data at seasonally adjusted annual rates]

Year or month	Total new construction	Private construction							Public construction		
		Total [2]	Residential buildings [1]		Nonresidential buildings and other construction [1]				Total	Federal	State and local [5]
			Total [2]	New housing units	Total	Commercial [3]	Industrial	Other [4]			
1992: Jan	417.6	300.0	172.1	121.1	127.9	45.8	22.2	59.9	117.7	14.6	103.1
Feb	416.5	297.8	171.7	120.1	126.1	45.7	21.5	58.9	118.7	14.4	104.4
Mar	433.8	312.3	180.3	127.0	131.9	46.2	24.5	61.2	121.5	14.6	106.9
Apr	429.9	313.6	185.4	131.0	128.2	44.7	21.1	62.4	116.3	13.6	102.6
May	436.7	314.8	184.4	128.8	130.5	44.4	21.2	64.9	121.9	14.9	107.0
June	434.9	319.3	186.7	129.4	132.6	47.4	20.5	64.7	115.6	14.0	101.6
July	432.0	314.0	184.6	126.8	129.4	43.8	21.1	64.5	118.0	13.7	104.3
Aug	430.4	312.3	187.3	127.9	125.0	43.0	18.9	63.1	118.1	13.0	105.1
Sept	433.5	317.4	189.2	129.1	128.2	44.1	19.3	64.9	116.1	13.2	102.9
Oct	442.6	324.8	194.6	132.1	130.3	45.6	19.4	65.3	117.7	14.4	103.3
Nov	449.3	328.2	119.3	135.4	128.9	44.8	19.2	64.8	121.1	15.8	105.2
Dec	455.2	335.4	206.4	138.9	128.9	43.6	20.0	65.3	119.9	16.0	103.9
1993: Jan	451.3	335.5	207.2	141.8	128.3	44.8	19.6	63.9	115.8	14.2	101.6
Feb	453.8	334.8	205.7	142.9	129.1	45.9	20.5	62.7	119.0	14.8	104.2
Mar	454.5	337.0	205.5	141.8	131.5	45.3	22.2	64.0	117.5	15.6	101.9
Apr	449.1	328.1	197.3	137.7	130.8	46.2	19.5	65.2	120.9	14.9	106.0
May	453.3	332.2	198.4	138.3	133.9	47.3	20.1	66.4	121.0	12.8	108.2
June	460.7	335.0	200.5	139.3	134.5	47.8	19.3	67.4	125.7	13.4	112.2
July	466.6	337.9	204.6	141.1	133.3	45.8	19.8	67.7	128.7	14.2	114.5
Aug	468.5	341.4	206.6	143.0	134.8	46.8	20.1	67.8	127.2	13.4	113.8
Sept	477.1	345.6	209.5	145.7	136.1	47.0	21.3	67.8	131.6	14.3	117.3
Oct	489.7	354.1	215.2	149.9	138.9	49.1	21.3	68.4	135.6	15.6	120.0
Nov [p]	500.0	364.5	222.3	156.4	142.2	50.5	22.3	69.3	135.6	15.2	120.4
Dec [p]	513.1	371.9	228.6	161.8	143.3	51.3	22.8	69.2	141.2	16.2	125.0

[1] Beginning 1960, farm residential buildings included in residential buildings; prior to 1960, included in nonresidential buildings and other construction.
[2] Includes residential improvements, not shown separately. Prior to 1964, also includes nonhousekeeping units (hotels, motels, etc.).
[3] Office buildings, warehouses, stores, restaurants, garages, etc., and, beginning 1964, hotels and motels; prior to 1964 hotels and motels are included in total residential.
[4] Religious, educational, hospital and institutional, miscellaneous nonresidential, farm (see also footnote 1), public utilities (telecommunications, gas, electric, railroad, and petroleum pipelines), and all other private.
[5] Includes Federal grants-in-aid for State and local projects.

Source: Department of Commerce, Bureau of the Census.

TABLE B-54.—*New housing units started and authorized, 1959-93*

[Thousands of units]

Year or month	New housing units started						New private housing units authorized [2]			
	Private and public [1]		Private (farm and nonfarm) [1]					Type of structure		
	Total (farm and nonfarm)	Nonfarm	Total	Type of structure			Total	1 unit	2 to 4 units	5 units or more
				1 unit	2 to 4 units	5 units or more				
1959	1,553.7	1,531.3	1,517.0	1,234.0	282.9		1,208.3	938.3	77.1	192.9
1960	1,296.1	1,274.0	1,252.2	994.7	257.5		998.0	746.1	64.6	187.4
1961	1,365.0	1,336.8	1,313.0	974.3	338.7		1,064.2	722.8	67.6	273.8
1962	1,492.5	1,468.7	1,462.9	991.4	471.5		1,186.6	716.2	87.1	383.3
1963	1,634.9	1,614.8	1,603.2	1,012.4	590.7		1,334.7	750.2	118.9	465.6
1964	1,561.0	1,534.0	1,528.8	970.5	108.4	450.0	1,285.8	720.1	100.8	464.9
1965	1,509.7	1,487.5	1,472.8	963.7	86.6	422.5	1,239.8	709.9	84.8	445.1
1966	1,195.8	1,172.8	1,164.9	778.6	61.1	325.1	971.9	563.2	61.0	347.7
1967	1,321.9	1,298.8	1,291.6	843.9	71.6	376.1	1,141.0	650.6	73.0	417.5
1968	1,545.4	1,521.4	1,507.6	899.4	80.9	527.3	1,353.4	694.7	84.3	574.4
1969	1,499.5	1,482.3	1,466.8	810.6	85.0	571.2	1,323.7	625.9	85.2	612.7
1970	1,469.0	([3])	1,433.6	812.9	84.8	535.9	1,351.5	646.8	88.1	616.7
1971	2,084.5	([3])	2,052.2	1,151.0	120.3	780.9	1,924.6	906.1	132.9	885.7
1972	2,378.5	([3])	2,356.6	1,309.2	141.3	906.2	2,218.9	1,033.1	148.6	1,037.2
1973	2,057.5	([3])	2,045.3	1,132.0	118.3	795.0	1,819.5	882.1	117.0	820.5
1974	1,352.5	([3])	1,337.7	888.1	68.1	381.6	1,074.4	643.8	64.3	366.2
1975	1,171.4	([3])	1,160.4	892.2	64.0	204.3	939.2	675.5	63.9	199.8
1976	1,547.6	([3])	1,537.5	1,162.4	85.9	289.2	1,296.2	893.6	93.1	309.5
1977	2,001.7	([3])	1,987.1	1,450.9	121.7	414.4	1,690.0	1,126.1	121.3	442.7
1978	2,036.1	([3])	2,020.3	1,433.3	125.0	462.0	1,800.5	1,182.6	130.6	487.3
1979	1,760.0	([3])	1,745.1	1,194.1	122.0	429.0	1,551.8	981.5	125.4	444.8
1980	1,312.6	([3])	1,292.2	852.2	109.5	330.5	1,190.6	710.4	114.5	365.7
1981	1,100.3	([3])	1,084.2	705.4	91.1	287.7	985.5	564.3	101.8	319.4
1982	1,072.1	([3])	1,062.2	662.6	80.0	319.6	1,000.5	546.4	88.3	365.8
1983	1,712.5	([3])	1,703.0	1,067.6	113.5	522.0	1,605.2	901.5	133.6	570.1
1984	1,755.8	([3])	1,749.5	1,084.2	121.4	544.0	1,681.8	922.4	142.6	616.8
1985	1,745.0	([3])	1,741.8	1,072.4	93.4	576.1	1,733.3	956.6	120.1	656.6
1986	1,807.1	([3])	1,805.4	1,179.4	84.0	542.0	1,769.4	1,077.6	108.4	583.5
1987	1,622.7	([3])	1,620.5	1,146.4	65.3	408.7	1,534.8	1,024.4	89.3	421.1
1988	([4])	([3])	1,488.1	1,081.3	58.8	348.0	1,455.6	993.8	75.7	386.1
1989	([4])	([3])	1,376.1	1,003.3	55.2	317.6	1,338.4	931.7	67.0	339.8
1990	([4])	([3])	1,192.7	894.8	37.5	260.4	1,110.8	793.9	54.3	262.6
1991	([4])	([3])	1,013.9	840.4	35.6	137.9	948.8	753.5	43.1	152.1
1992	([4])	([3])	1,199.7	1,029.9	30.7	139.0	1,094.9	910.7	45.8	138.4
1993	([4])	([3])	1,285.1	1,123.4	30.5	131.2	1,214.2	1,004.6	51.2	158.3
			Seasonally adjusted annual rates							
1992: Jan	([4])	([3])	1,164	976	28	160	1,077	893	45	139
Feb	([4])	([3])	1,285	1,137	25	123	1,135	948	41	146
Mar	([4])	([3])	1,318	1,050	51	217	1,082	896	44	142
Apr	([4])	([3])	1,095	939	28	128	1,040	858	42	140
May	([4])	([3])	1,197	1,019	32	146	1,053	877	45	131
June	([4])	([3])	1,141	994	40	107	1,048	878	48	122
July	([4])	([3])	1,106	961	25	120	1,083	882	42	159
Aug	([4])	([3])	1,229	1,038	31	160	1,081	885	52	144
Sept	([4])	([3])	1,218	1,045	28	145	1,120	918	45	157
Oct	([4])	([3])	1,226	1,079	18	129	1,141	954	51	136
Nov	([4])	([3])	1,226	1,089	28	109	1,136	963	49	124
Dec	([4])	([3])	1,286	1,133	32	121	1,196	1,037	45	114
1993: Jan	([4])	([3])	1,171	1,051	26	94	1,157	972	45	140
Feb	([4])	([3])	1,180	1,036	24	120	1,141	957	45	139
Mar	([4])	([3])	1,124	987	32	105	1,034	871	43	120
Apr	([4])	([3])	1,206	1,059	26	121	1,101	925	49	127
May	([4])	([3])	1,248	1,107	26	115	1,121	919	46	156
June	([4])	([3])	1,248	1,079	31	138	1,115	925	47	143
July	([4])	([3])	1,232	1,064	54	114	1,162	977	51	134
Aug	([4])	([3])	1,328	1,183	17	128	1,242	1,015	47	180
Sept	([4])	([3])	1,371	1,166	33	172	1,271	1,047	57	167
Oct	([4])	([3])	1,390	1,211	34	145	1,304	1,097	57	150
Nov [p]	([4])	([3])	1,450	1,285	33	132	1,374	1,145	58	171
Dec [p]	([4])	([3])	1,540	1,330	33	177	1,476	1,198	52	226

[1] Units in structures built by private developers for sale upon completion to local public housing authorities under the Department of Housing and Urban Development "Turnkey" program are classified as private housing. Military housing starts, including those financed with mortgages insured by FHA under Section 803 of the National Housing Act, are included in publicly owned starts and excluded from total private starts.
[2] Authorized by issuance of local building permit: in 17,000 permit-issuing places beginning 1984; in 16,000 places for 1978-83; in 14,000 places for 1972-77; in 13,000 places for 1967-71; in 12,000 places for 1963-66; and in 10,000 places prior to 1963.
[3] Not available separately beginning January 1970.
[4] Series discontinued December 1988.

Source: Department of Commerce, Bureau of the Census.

TABLE B-55.—*Business expenditures for new plant and equipment, 1947–94*

[Billions of dollars; quarterly data at seasonally adjusted annual rates]

Year or quarter	All industries	Manufacturing Total	Durable goods	Nondurable goods	Nonmanufacturing Total [2]	Mining	Transportation	Public utilities	Commercial and other	Total nonfarm business [3]	Manufacturing	Nonmanufacturing Total	Surveyed quarterly	Surveyed annually [4]
1947	20.11	8.73	3.39	5.34	11.38	0.69	2.69	1.64	6.38	22.27	8.73	13.54	11.38	2.16
1948	22.78	9.25	3.54	5.71	13.53	.93	3.17	2.67	6.77	25.97	9.25	16.73	13.53	3.19
1949	20.28	7.32	2.67	4.64	12.96	.88	2.80	3.28	6.01	24.03	7.32	16.72	12.96	3.76
1950	21.56	7.73	3.22	4.51	13.83	.84	2.87	3.42	6.70	25.81	7.73	18.08	13.83	4.25
1951	26.81	11.07	5.12	5.95	15.74	1.11	3.60	3.75	7.29	31.38	11.07	20.31	15.74	4.57
1952	28.16	12.12	5.75	6.37	16.04	1.21	3.56	3.96	7.31	32.16	12.12	20.04	16.04	4.00
1953	29.96	12.43	5.71	6.72	17.53	1.25	3.58	4.61	8.09	34.20	12.43	21.77	17.53	4.23
1954	28.86	12.00	5.49	6.51	16.85	1.29	2.91	4.23	8.42	33.62	12.00	21.62	16.85	4.76
1955	30.94	12.50	5.87	6.62	18.44	1.31	3.10	4.26	9.77	37.08	12.50	24.58	18.44	6.14
1956	37.90	16.33	8.19	8.15	21.57	1.64	3.56	4.78	11.59	45.25	16.33	28.91	21.57	7.35
1957	40.54	17.50	8.59	8.91	23.04	1.69	3.84	5.95	11.56	48.62	17.50	31.11	23.04	8.08
1958	33.84	12.98	6.21	6.77	20.86	1.43	2.72	5.74	10.97	42.55	12.98	29.57	20.86	8.72
1959	35.88	13.76	6.72	7.04	22.12	1.35	3.47	5.46	11.84	45.17	13.76	31.41	22.12	9.29
1960	39.44	16.36	8.28	8.08	23.08	1.29	3.54	5.40	12.86	48.99	16.36	32.63	23.08	9.55
1961	38.34	15.53	7.43	8.10	22.80	1.26	3.14	5.20	13.21	48.14	15.53	32.60	22.80	9.80
1962	40.86	16.03	7.81	8.22	24.83	1.41	3.59	5.12	14.71	51.61	16.03	35.58	24.83	10.75
1963	43.67	17.27	8.64	8.63	26.40	1.26	3.64	5.33	16.17	53.59	17.27	36.33	26.40	9.93
1964	51.26	21.23	10.98	10.25	30.04	1.33	4.71	5.80	18.20	62.02	21.23	40.80	30.04	10.76
1965	59.52	25.41	13.49	11.92	34.12	1.36	5.66	6.49	20.60	70.79	25.41	45.39	34.12	11.27
1966	70.40	31.37	17.23	14.15	39.03	1.42	6.68	7.82	23.11	82.62	31.37	51.25	39.03	12.22
1967	72.75	32.25	17.83	14.42	40.50	1.38	6.57	9.33	23.22	83.82	32.25	51.57	40.50	11.07
1968	76.42	32.34	17.93	14.40	44.08	1.44	6.91	10.52	25.22	88.92	32.34	56.58	44.08	12.50
1969	85.74	36.27	19.97	16.31	49.47	1.77	7.23	11.70	28.77	100.02	36.27	63.74	49.47	14.27
1970	91.91	36.99	19.80	17.19	54.92	2.02	7.17	13.03	32.71	106.15	36.99	69.16	54.92	14.24
1971	92.91	33.60	16.78	16.82	59.31	2.67	6.42	14.70	35.52	109.18	33.60	75.58	59.31	16.26
1972	103.40	35.42	18.22	17.20	67.98	2.88	7.14	16.26	41.69	120.91	35.42	85.49	67.98	17.51
1973	120.03	42.35	22.63	19.72	77.67	3.30	8.00	17.99	48.39	139.26	42.35	96.91	77.67	19.24
1974	139.67	52.48	26.77	25.71	87.19	4.58	9.16	19.96	53.49	159.83	52.48	107.35	87.19	20.16
1975	142.42	53.66	25.37	28.28	88.76	6.12	9.95	20.23	52.47	162.60	53.66	108.95	88.76	20.19
1976	158.44	58.53	27.50	31.03	99.91	7.63	11.10	22.90	58.29	179.91	58.53	121.38	99.91	21.47
1977	184.82	67.48	32.77	34.71	117.34	9.81	12.20	27.83	67.51	208.15	67.48	140.67	117.34	23.33
1978	216.81	78.13	39.02	39.10	138.69	10.55	12.07	32.10	83.96	244.40	78.13	166.27	138.69	27.58
1979	255.26	95.13	47.72	47.41	160.13	11.05	13.91	37.53	97.64	285.24	95.13	190.11	160.13	29.98
1980	286.40	112.60	54.82	57.77	173.80	12.71	13.56	41.32	106.21	318.08	112.60	205.48	173.80	31.68
1981	324.73	128.68	58.93	69.75	196.06	15.81	12.67	47.17	120.41	358.77	128.68	230.09	196.06	34.04
1982	326.19	123.97	54.58	69.39	202.22	14.11	11.75	53.58	122.79	363.08	123.97	239.11	202.22	36.89
1983	321.16	117.35	51.61	65.74	203.82	10.64	10.81	52.95	129.41	359.73	117.35	242.38	203.82	38.56
1984	373.83	139.61	64.57	75.04	234.22	11.86	13.44	57.53	151.39	418.38	139.61	278.77	234.22	44.55
1985	410.12	152.88	70.87	82.01	257.24	12.00	14.57	59.58	171.09	454.93	152.88	302.05	257.24	44.81
1986	399.36	137.95	65.68	72.28	261.40	8.15	15.05	56.61	181.59	447.11	137.95	309.16	261.40	47.75
1987	410.52	141.06	68.03	73.03	269.46	8.28	15.07	56.26	189.84	461.51	141.06	320.45	269.46	50.99
1988	455.49	163.45	77.04	86.41	292.04	9.29	16.63	60.37	205.76	508.22	163.45	344.77	292.04	52.73
1989	507.40	183.80	82.56	101.24	323.60	9.21	18.84	66.28	229.28	563.93	183.80	380.13	323.60	56.53
1990	532.61	192.61	82.58	110.04	339.99	9.88	21.47	67.21	241.43	591.96	192.61	399.34	339.99	59.35
1991	528.39	182.81	77.64	105.17	345.58	10.02	22.66	66.57	246.32	587.93	182.81	405.12	345.58	59.54
1992	546.60	174.02	73.32	100.69	372.58	8.88	22.64	72.21	268.84	607.71	174.02	433.69	372.58	61.11
1993 [5]	584.64	179.46	81.49	97.97	405.18	10.13	22.37	75.00	297.69	....	179.46	....	405.18	....
1994 [5]	616.50	186.27	84.93	101.34	430.22	10.84	20.91	81.42	317.05	....	186.27	....	430.22	....
1992: I	534.85	173.82	73.98	99.85	361.03	8.92	21.83	69.00	261.27	....	173.82	....	361.03	....
II	541.41	171.98	74.07	97.91	369.44	9.20	23.15	72.63	264.46	....	171.98	....	369.44	....
III	547.40	172.86	72.09	100.77	374.54	8.98	23.91	72.18	269.46	....	172.86	....	374.54	....
IV	559.24	176.86	73.30	103.56	382.38	8.47	21.60	74.07	278.24	....	176.86	....	382.38	....
1993: I	564.13	175.05	79.11	95.94	389.08	8.89	22.47	73.51	284.21	....	175.05	....	389.08	....
II	579.79	177.09	80.88	96.21	402.70	9.10	21.58	74.55	297.46	....	177.09	....	402.70	....
III	594.11	182.17	81.99	100.18	411.94	11.14	21.70	75.62	303.47	....	182.17	....	411.94	....
IV [5]	600.53	183.52	83.99	99.53	417.01	11.37	23.73	76.30	305.61	....	183.52	....	417.01	....
1994: I [5]	616.38	186.22	87.50	98.72	430.16	10.83	21.49	77.78	320.06	....	186.22	....	430.16	....
II [5]	624.33	183.44	83.92	99.52	440.89	11.14	21.61	80.80	327.33	....	183.44	....	440.89	....

[1] These industries accounted for 90 percent of total nonfarm spending in 1992.
[2] Excludes forestry, fisheries, and agricultural services; professional services; social services and membership organizations; and real estate, which, effective with the April–May 1984 survey, are no longer surveyed quarterly. See last column ("nonmanufacturing surveyed annually") for data for these industries.
[3] "All industries" plus the part of nonmanufacturing that is surveyed annually.
[4] Consists of forestry, fisheries, and agricultural services; professional services; social services and membership organizations; and real estate.
[5] Planned capital expenditures as reported by business in October and November 1993, corrected for biases.

Source: Department of Commerce, Bureau of the Census.

TABLE B-56.—*Manufacturing and trade sales and inventories, 1950–93*

[Amounts in millions of dollars; monthly data seasonally adjusted]

Year or month	Total manufacturing and trade Sales[1]	Total manufacturing and trade Inventories[2]	Total manufacturing and trade Ratio[3]	Manufacturing Sales[1]	Manufacturing Inventories[2]	Manufacturing Ratio[3]	Merchant wholesalers Sales[1]	Merchant wholesalers Inventories[2]	Merchant wholesalers Ratio[3]	Retail trade Sales[1]	Retail trade Inventories[2]	Retail trade Ratio[3]
1950	38,596	59,822	1.36	18,634	31,078	1.48	7,695	9,284	1.07	12,268	19,460	1.38
1951	43,356	70,242	1.55	21,714	39,306	1.66	8,597	9,886	1.16	13,046	21,050	1.64
1952	44,840	72,377	1.58	22,529	41,136	1.78	8,782	10,210	1.12	13,529	21,031	1.52
1953	47,987	76,122	1.58	24,843	43,948	1.76	9,052	10,686	1.17	14,091	21,488	1.53
1954	46,443	73,175	1.60	23,355	41,612	1.81	8,993	10,637	1.18	14,095	20,926	1.51
1955	51,694	79,516	1.47	26,480	45,069	1.62	9,893	11,678	1.13	15,321	22,769	1.43
1956	54,063	87,304	1.55	27,740	50,642	1.73	10,513	13,260	1.19	15,811	23,402	1.47
1957	55,879	89,052	1.59	28,736	51,871	1.80	10,475	12,730	1.23	16,667	24,451	1.44
1958	54,201	87,055	1.61	27,248	50,203	1.84	10,257	12,739	1.24	16,696	24,113	1.44
1959	59,729	92,097	1.54	30,286	52,913	1.75	11,491	13,879	1.21	17,951	25,305	1.41
1960	60,827	94,719	1.56	30,878	53,786	1.74	11,656	14,120	1.21	18,294	26,813	1.47
1961	61,159	95,580	1.56	30,922	54,871	1.77	11,988	14,488	1.21	18,249	26,221	1.44
1962	65,662	101,049	1.54	33,358	58,172	1.74	12,674	14,936	1.18	19,630	27,941	1.42
1963	68,995	105,463	1.53	35,058	60,029	1.71	13,382	16,048	1.20	20,556	29,386	1.43
1964	73,682	111,504	1.51	37,331	63,410	1.70	14,529	17,000	1.17	21,823	31,094	1.42
1965	80,283	120,929	1.51	40,995	68,207	1.66	15,611	18,317	1.17	23,677	34,405	1.45
1966	87,187	136,824	1.57	44,870	77,986	1.74	16,987	20,765	1.22	25,330	38,073	1.50
1967	90,918	145,681	1.60	46,486	84,646	1.82	19,675	25,786	1.31	24,757	35,249	1.42
1968	98,794	156,611	1.59	50,229	90,560	1.80	21,121	27,166	1.29	27,445	38,885	1.42
1969	105,812	170,400	1.61	53,501	98,145	1.83	22,940	29,800	1.30	29,371	42,455	1.45
1970	108,352	178,594	1.65	52,805	101,599	1.92	24,298	33,354	1.37	31,249	43,641	1.40
1971	117,023	188,991	1.61	55,906	102,567	1.83	26,619	36,568	1.37	34,497	49,856	1.45
1972	131,227	203,227	1.55	63,027	108,121	1.72	30,011	40,297	1.34	38,189	54,809	1.44
1973	153,881	234,406	1.52	72,931	124,499	1.71	38,319	46,918	1.22	42,631	62,989	1.48
1974	178,201	287,144	1.61	84,790	157,625	1.86	48,271	58,667	1.22	45,141	70,852	1.57
1975	182,412	288,992	1.58	86,589	159,708	1.84	46,848	57,774	1.23	48,975	71,510	1.46
1976	204,386	318,345	1.56	98,797	174,636	1.77	50,934	64,622	1.27	54,655	79,087	1.45
1977	229,786	350,706	1.53	113,201	188,378	1.66	56,409	73,179	1.30	60,176	89,149	1.48
1978	260,755	400,931	1.54	126,905	211,691	1.67	66,849	86,934	1.30	67,002	102,306	1.53
1979	298,328	452,640	1.52	143,936	242,157	1.68	79,678	99,679	1.25	74,713	110,804	1.48
1980	328,112	510,126	1.55	154,391	265,215	1.72	93,977	123,833	1.32	79,743	121,078	1.52
1981	356,909	547,181	1.53	168,129	283,413	1.69	102,267	131,049	1.28	86,514	132,719	1.53
1982	348,771	575,504	1.67	163,351	311,852	1.95	96,357	129,024	1.36	89,062	134,628	1.49
1983	370,501	591,875	1.56	172,547	312,379	1.78	100,440	131,663	1.28	97,514	147,833	1.44
1984	411,427	651,551	1.53	190,682	339,516	1.73	113,502	144,223	1.23	107,243	167,812	1.49
1985	423,940	665,835	1.55	194,538	334,799	1.73	114,816	149,155	1.28	114,586	181,881	1.52
1986	431,786	664,624	1.55	194,657	322,669	1.68	116,326	155,445	1.32	120,803	186,510	1.56
1987	459,107	711,725	1.50	206,326	338,075	1.59	124,340	165,814	1.29	128,442	207,836	1.56
1988	497,031	767,538	1.49	223,541	367,422	1.58	135,357	180,519	1.30	138,133	219,597	1.54
1989	523,729	813,793	1.53	232,724	386,911	1.64	144,158	188,539	1.29	146,847	238,343	1.59
1990	543,097	837,445	1.53	239,459	399,068	1.65	149,489	196,901	1.29	154,149	241,476	1.56
1991	538,609	833,518	1.54	235,518	386,348	1.67	147,635	201,285	1.34	155,456	245,885	1.55
1992	560,383	849,117	1.50	244,511	379,238	1.57	152,337	209,232	1.34	163,535	260,647	1.55
1992: Jan	542,949	830,003	1.53	235,239	384,828	1.64	148,745	200,956	1.35	158,965	244,219	1.54
Feb	549,893	830,846	1.51	239,081	383,771	1.61	149,749	201,423	1.35	161,063	245,652	1.53
Mar	553,453	832,300	1.50	242,011	383,508	1.58	151,394	201,463	1.33	160,048	247,329	1.55
Apr	553,683	835,805	1.51	242,706	382,502	1.58	150,726	201,687	1.34	160,251	251,616	1.57
May	551,496	835,685	1.52	241,804	383,404	1.59	148,586	200,997	1.35	161,106	251,284	1.56
June	558,715	839,937	1.50	240,459	382,908	1.55	151,021	204,373	1.35	161,235	252,656	1.57
July	562,128	843,411	1.50	246,259	383,369	1.56	153,762	205,058	1.33	162,107	254,984	1.57
Aug	557,117	844,942	1.52	241,716	385,186	1.59	152,241	205,399	1.35	163,160	254,357	1.56
Sept	564,197	844,032	1.50	246,078	384,013	1.56	153,551	205,264	1.34	164,568	254,755	1.55
Oct	566,536	845,196	1.49	245,459	383,095	1.56	154,211	206,655	1.34	166,866	255,446	1.53
Nov	569,412	846,912	1.49	248,525	381,055	1.53	153,759	208,416	1.36	167,128	257,441	1.54
Dec	580,840	849,117	1.46	256,609	379,238	1.48	155,297	209,232	1.35	168,934	260,647	1.54
1993: Jan	581,584	851,190	1.46	252,845	378,624	1.50	159,507	210,139	1.32	169,232	262,427	1.55
Feb	584,903	854,715	1.46	256,800	379,232	1.48	158,987	209,765	1.32	169,116	265,718	1.57
Mar	583,575	859,094	1.47	258,979	379,539	1.47	157,206	210,503	1.34	167,390	269,052	1.61
Apr	584,943	862,478	1.47	255,114	380,307	1.49	159,291	211,860	1.33	170,538	270,311	1.59
May	587,930	864,198	1.47	254,007	381,591	1.50	162,187	212,190	1.31	171,736	270,417	1.57
June	589,990	864,227	1.46	258,299	381,326	1.48	159,095	212,058	1.33	172,596	270,843	1.57
July	585,626	863,612	1.47	251,680	381,561	1.52	160,531	213,244	1.33	173,415	268,807	1.55
Aug	592,598	865,939	1.46	256,556	381,392	1.49	161,459	215,199	1.33	174,583	269,348	1.54
Sept	595,804	867,395	1.46	260,088	380,689	1.46	160,710	215,103	1.34	175,006	271,603	1.55
Oct	600,304	869,709	1.45	260,471	380,301	1.46	161,284	214,991	1.33	178,549	274,417	1.54
Nov [p]	607,689	874,465	1.44	265,574	380,181	1.43	162,971	216,094	1.33	179,144	278,190	1.55

[1] Annual data are averages of monthly not seasonally adjusted figures.
[2] Seasonally adjusted, end of period. Inventories beginning January 1982 for manufacturing and December 1980 for wholesale and retail trade are not comparable with earlier periods.
[3] Inventory/sales ratio. Annual data are: beginning 1982, averages of monthly ratios; for 1958–81, ratio of December inventories to monthly average sales for the year; and for earlier years, weighted averages. Monthly data are ratio of inventories at end of month to sales for month.

Note.—Earlier data are not strictly comparable with data beginning 1958 for manufacturing and beginning 1967 for wholesale and retail trade.

Source: Department of Commerce, Bureau of the Census.

TABLE B-57.—*Manufacturers' shipments and inventories, 1950–93*

[Millions of dollars; monthly data seasonally adjusted]

Year or month	Shipments[1]			Inventories[2]							
					Durable goods industries				Nondurable goods industries		
	Total	Durable goods industries	Nondurable goods industries	Total	Total	Materials and supplies	Work in process	Finished goods	Total	Materials and supplies	Work in process	Finished goods
1950	18,634	8,845	9,789	31,078	15,539				15,539			
1951	21,714	10,493	11,221	39,306	20,991				18,315			
1952	22,529	11,313	11,216	41,136	23,731				17,405			
1953	24,843	13,349	11,494	43,948	25,878	8,966	10,720	6,206	18,070	8,317	2,472	7,409
1954	23,355	11,828	11,527	41,612	23,710	7,894	9,721	6,040	17,902	8,167	2,440	7,415
1955	26,480	14,071	12,409	45,069	26,405	9,194	10,756	6,348	18,664	8,556	2,571	7,666
1956	27,740	14,715	13,025	50,642	30,447	10,417	12,317	7,565	20,195	8,971	2,721	8,622
1957	28,736	15,237	13,499	51,871	31,728	10,608	12,837	8,125	20,143	8,775	2,864	8,624
1958	27,248	13,553	13,695	50,203	30,194	9,970	12,408	7,816	20,009	8,676	2,827	8,506
1959	30,286	15,597	14,689	52,913	32,012	10,709	13,086	8,217	20,901	9,094	2,942	8,865
1960	30,878	15,870	15,008	53,786	32,337	10,306	12,809	9,222	21,449	9,097	2,947	9,405
1961	30,922	15,601	15,321	54,871	32,496	10,246	13,211	9,039	22,375	9,505	3,108	9,762
1962	33,358	17,247	16,111	58,172	34,565	10,794	14,124	9,647	23,607	9,836	3,304	10,467
1963	35,058	18,255	16,803	60,029	35,776	11,053	14,835	9,888	24,253	10,009	3,420	10,824
1964	37,331	19,611	17,720	63,410	38,421	11,946	16,158	10,317	24,989	10,167	3,531	11,291
1965	40,995	22,193	18,802	68,207	44,198	13,298	18,055	10,836	26,018	10,487	3,825	11,706
1966	44,870	24,617	20,253	77,986	49,852	15,464	21,908	12,480	28,134	11,197	4,226	12,711
1967	46,486	25,233	21,253	84,646	54,896	16,423	24,933	13,540	29,750	11,760	4,431	13,559
1968	50,229	27,624	22,605	90,560	58,732	17,344	27,213	14,175	31,828	12,328	4,852	14,648
1969	53,501	29,403	24,098	98,145	64,598	18,636	30,282	15,680	33,547	12,753	5,120	15,674
1970	52,805	28,156	24,649	101,599	66,651	19,149	29,745	17,757	34,948	13,168	5,271	16,509
1971	55,906	29,924	25,982	102,567	66,136	19,679	28,550	17,907	36,431	13,686	5,678	17,067
1972	63,027	33,987	29,040	108,121	70,067	20,807	30,713	18,547	38,054	14,677	5,998	17,379
1973	72,931	39,635	33,296	124,499	81,192	25,944	35,490	19,758	43,307	18,147	6,729	18,431
1974	84,790	44,173	40,617	157,625	101,493	35,070	42,530	23,893	56,132	23,744	8,189	24,199
1975	86,589	43,598	42,991	159,708	102,590	33,903	43,227	25,460	57,118	23,565	8,834	24,719
1976	98,797	50,623	48,174	174,636	111,988	37,457	46,074	28,457	62,648	25,847	9,929	26,872
1977	113,201	59,168	54,033	188,378	120,877	40,186	50,226	30,465	67,501	27,387	10,961	29,153
1978	126,905	67,731	59,174	211,691	138,181	45,198	58,848	34,135	73,510	29,619	12,085	31,806
1979	143,936	75,927	68,009	242,157	160,734	52,670	69,325	38,739	81,423	32,814	13,910	34,699
1980	154,391	77,419	76,972	265,215	174,788	55,173	76,945	42,670	90,427	36,606	15,884	37,937
1981	168,129	83,727	84,402	283,413	186,443	57,998	80,998	47,447	96,970	38,165	16,194	42,611
1982	163,351	79,212	84,139	311,852	200,444	59,136	86,707	54,601	111,408	44,039	18,612	48,757
1983	172,567	85,481	87,066	312,379	199,854	60,325	86,899	52,630	112,525	44,816	18,691	49,018
1984	190,682	97,940	92,742	339,516	221,330	66,031	98,251	57,048	118,186	45,692	19,328	53,166
1985	194,538	101,279	93,259	334,799	218,212	64,005	98,085	56,122	116,587	44,087	19,445	53,055
1986	194,657	103,238	91,419	322,669	212,006	61,409	96,926	53,671	110,663	42,309	18,124	50,230
1987	206,326	108,128	98,198	338,075	220,776	63,614	102,328	54,834	117,299	45,287	19,279	52,733
1988	223,541	117,993	105,549	367,422	241,402	69,388	112,380	59,634	126,020	49,030	20,446	56,544
1989	232,724	121,703	111,022	386,911	256,065	71,942	121,919	62,204	130,846	49,632	21,261	59,953
1990	239,459	122,387	117,072	399,068	259,988	72,788	122,520	64,680	139,080	51,606	22,447	65,027
1991	235,518	119,151	116,367	386,348	249,117	69,987	115,007	64,023	137,231	51,556	21,886	63,789
1992	244,511	125,553	118,958	379,238	237,717	68,165	107,140	62,412	141,521	52,194	22,887	66,440
1993 p	258,523	135,982	122,542	377,941	236,370	68,388	105,364	62,618	141,571	51,976	23,461	66,134
1992: Jan	235,239	120,173	115,066	384,828	248,183	69,827	114,334	64,022	136,645	51,249	22,103	63,293
Feb	239,081	122,865	116,216	383,771	246,482	69,366	113,342	63,774	137,289	51,362	22,233	63,694
Mar	242,011	124,665	117,346	383,508	245,703	68,872	112,867	63,964	137,805	51,496	22,259	64,050
Apr	242,706	124,249	118,457	382,502	244,355	68,811	111,601	63,943	138,147	51,651	22,480	64,016
May	241,804	123,113	118,691	383,404	244,213	68,909	111,346	63,958	139,191	51,821	22,474	64,896
June	246,459	126,166	120,293	382,908	243,625	69,477	110,257	63,891	139,283	52,188	22,529	64,566
July	246,259	125,083	121,176	383,369	242,976	68,875	109,482	64,619	140,393	52,616	22,506	65,271
Aug	241,716	124,246	117,470	385,186	243,597	69,371	109,507	64,719	141,589	52,471	22,773	66,345
Sept	246,078	125,873	120,205	384,013	242,122	69,399	108,406	64,317	141,891	52,554	22,903	66,434
Oct	245,459	126,425	119,034	383,095	240,909	68,468	108,730	63,737	142,186	52,528	22,817	66,841
Nov	248,525	128,720	119,805	381,055	239,407	68,267	107,472	63,668	141,648	52,137	22,759	66,752
Dec	256,609	134,228	122,381	379,238	237,717	68,165	107,140	62,412	141,521	52,194	22,887	66,440
1993: Jan	252,845	130,805	122,040	378,624	236,332	67,707	106,426	62,199	142,292	52,286	22,962	67,044
Feb	256,800	134,133	122,667	379,232	237,034	67,839	106,552	62,643	142,198	52,121	23,161	66,916
Mar	258,979	135,537	123,442	379,539	236,849	67,864	106,071	62,914	142,690	52,329	23,128	67,233
Apr	255,114	132,763	122,351	380,307	237,043	68,089	105,671	63,283	143,264	52,672	23,099	67,493
May	254,007	132,307	121,700	381,591	237,734	68,401	106,042	63,291	143,857	52,965	22,990	67,902
June	258,299	135,042	123,257	381,326	237,514	68,163	106,306	63,045	143,812	53,055	23,097	67,660
July	251,680	129,257	122,423	381,561	237,937	68,357	106,545	63,035	143,624	52,647	23,202	67,775
Aug	256,556	134,521	122,035	381,392	237,688	68,678	106,463	62,547	143,704	52,594	23,280	67,830
Sept	260,088	137,521	122,567	380,689	237,571	68,441	106,704	62,426	143,118	52,489	23,329	67,300
Oct	260,471	138,153	122,318	380,301	237,632	68,522	106,943	62,167	142,669	52,259	23,437	66,973
Nov p	265,574	142,665	122,909	380,181	237,886	68,670	106,119	63,097	142,295	52,363	23,477	66,455
Dec p	269,227	146,002	123,225	377,941	236,370	68,388	105,364	62,618	141,571	51,976	23,461	66,134

[1] Annual data are averages of monthly not seasonally adjusted figures.
[2] Seasonally adjusted, end of period. Data beginning 1982 are not comparable with data for prior periods.

Note.—Data beginning 1958 are not strictly comparable with earlier data.

Source: Department of Commerce, Bureau of the Census.

Table B-58.—Manufacturers' new and unfilled orders, 1950-93

[Amounts in millions of dollars; monthly data seasonally adjusted]

Year or month	New orders [1] Total	Durable goods industries Total	Capital goods industries, nondefense	Nondurable goods industries	Unfilled orders [2] Total	Durable goods industries	Nondurable goods industries	Unfilled orders—shipments ratio [3] Total	Durable goods industries	Nondurable goods industries
1950	20,110	10,165		9,945	41,456	35,435	6,021			
1951	23,907	12,841		11,066	67,266	63,394	3,872			
1952	23,204	12,061		11,143	75,857	72,680	3,177			
1953	23,586	12,147		11,439	61,178	58,637	2,541			
1954	22,335	10,768		11,566	48,266	45,250	3,016	3.42	4.12	0.96
1955	27,465	14,996		12,469	60,004	56,241	3,763	3.63	4.27	1.12
1956	28,368	15,365		13,003	67,375	63,880	3,495	3.87	4.55	1.04
1957	27,559	14,111		13,448	53,183	50,352	2,831	3.35	4.00	.85
1958	27,193	13,387		13,805	46,609	43,807	2,802	3.02	3.62	.85
1959	30,711	15,979		14,732	51,717	48,369	3,348	2.94	3.47	.92
1960	30,232	15,288		14,944	44,213	41,650	2,563	2.71	3.29	.71
1961	31,112	15,753		15,359	46,624	43,582	3,042	2.58	3.08	.78
1962	33,440	17,363		16,078	47,798	45,170	2,628	2.64	3.18	.68
1963	35,511	18,671		16,840	53,417	50,346	3,071	2.74	3.31	.72
1964	38,240	20,507		17,732	64,518	61,315	3,203	2.99	3.59	.71
1965	42,137	23,286		18,851	78,249	74,459	3,790	3.25	3.86	.79
1966	46,420	26,163		20,258	96,846	93,002	3,844	3.74	4.48	.75
1967	47,067	25,803		21,265	103,711	99,735	3,976	3.66	4.37	.73
1968	50,657	28,051	6,314	22,606	108,377	104,393	3,984	3.79	4.58	.69
1969	53,990	29,876	7,046	24,114	114,341	110,161	4,180	3.71	4.45	.69
1970	52,022	27,340	6,072	24,682	105,008	100,412	4,596	3.61	4.36	.76
1971	55,921	29,905	6,682	26,016	105,247	100,225	5,022	3.32	4.00	.76
1972	64,182	35,038	7,745	29,144	119,349	113,034	6,315	3.26	3.85	.86
1973	76,003	42,627	9,926	33,376	156,561	149,204	7,357	3.80	4.51	.91
1974	87,327	46,862	11,594	40,465	187,043	181,519	5,524	4.09	4.93	.62
1975	85,139	41,957	9,886	43,181	169,546	161,664	7,882	3.69	4.45	.82
1976	99,513	51,307	11,490	48,206	178,128	169,857	8,271	3.24	3.88	.74
1977	115,109	61,035	13,681	54,073	202,024	193,323	8,701	3.24	3.85	.71
1978	131,629	72,278	17,588	59,351	259,169	248,281	10,888	3.57	4.20	.81
1979	147,604	79,483	21,154	68,121	303,593	291,321	12,272	3.89	4.62	.82
1980	156,359	79,392	21,135	76,967	327,416	315,202	12,214	3.85	4.58	.75
1981	168,025	83,654	21,806	84,371	326,547	314,707	11,840	3.87	4.68	.69
1982	162,140	78,064	19,213	84,077	311,887	300,798	11,089	3.84	4.74	.62
1983	175,451	88,140	19,624	87,311	347,273	333,114	14,159	3.53	4.29	.69
1984	192,879	100,164	23,669	92,715	373,529	359,651	13,878	3.60	4.37	.64
1985	195,706	102,356	24,545	93,351	387,095	372,027	15,068	3.67	4.46	.68
1986	195,204	103,647	23,983	91,557	393,412	376,622	16,790	3.59	4.40	.70
1987	209,389	110,809	26,095	98,579	430,288	408,602	21,686	3.63	4.42	.83
1988	227,026	121,445	30,729	105,581	471,951	450,002	21,949	3.64	4.45	.76
1989	235,932	124,933	32,725	110,999	510,459	488,780	21,679	4.00	4.91	.78
1990	240,646	123,556	32,254	117,090	524,846	502,914	21,932	4.14	5.13	.76
1991	234,354	117,878	29,468	116,476	511,122	487,892	23,230	4.08	5.06	.81
1992	241,545	122,614	29,653	118,932	475,304	452,383	22,921	3.46	4.21	.77
1993 ᵖ	255,719	133,300	31,901	122,419	442,111	420,646	21,465	3.04	3.64	.72
1992: Jan	233,924	118,996	29,460	114,928	509,807	486,715	23,092	4.00	4.91	.81
Feb	234,439	118,369	28,897	116,070	505,165	482,219	22,946	3.92	4.81	.80
Mar	239,462	121,882	31,655	117,580	502,616	479,436	23,180	3.84	4.71	.80
Apr	241,747	123,221	29,653	118,526	501,657	478,408	23,249	3.84	4.71	.80
May	238,933	120,522	29,778	118,411	498,786	475,817	22,969	3.86	4.75	.79
June	243,914	123,746	30,168	120,168	496,241	473,397	22,844	3.74	4.58	.78
July	241,079	119,846	28,732	121,233	491,061	468,160	22,901	3.71	4.56	.77
Aug	237,230	120,007	27,486	117,223	486,575	463,921	22,654	3.75	4.59	.79
Sept	240,685	120,608	29,801	120,077	481,182	458,656	22,526	3.65	4.46	.78
Oct	244,882	125,656	30,129	119,226	480,605	457,887	22,718	3.65	4.47	.78
Nov	243,106	123,096	26,804	120,010	475,186	452,263	22,923	3.57	4.35	.78
Dec	256,727	134,348	32,275	122,379	475,304	452,383	22,921	3.46	4.21	.77
1993: Jan	253,626	131,266	28,645	122,360	476,085	452,844	23,241	3.56	4.35	.79
Feb	257,250	134,533	32,748	122,717	476,535	453,244	23,291	3.51	4.27	.79
Mar	253,007	129,903	29,122	123,104	470,563	447,610	22,953	3.42	4.14	.78
Apr	252,369	129,838	30,453	122,531	467,818	444,685	23,133	3.46	4.20	.79
May	248,335	126,783	29,931	121,552	462,146	439,161	22,985	3.42	4.15	.78
June	255,462	132,252	33,850	123,210	459,309	436,371	22,938	3.33	4.02	.78
July	250,566	128,520	30,093	122,046	458,195	435,634	22,561	3.41	4.17	.76
Aug	253,461	131,752	31,992	121,709	455,100	432,865	22,235	3.30	3.99	.76
Sept	255,309	133,176	30,992	122,133	450,321	428,520	21,801	3.22	3.89	.73
Oct	258,270	136,613	32,825	121,657	448,120	426,980	21,140	3.21	3.89	.71
Nov ᵖ	262,773	139,675	34,878	123,098	445,319	423,990	21,329	3.12	3.75	.72
Dec ᵖ	266,019	142,658	35,366	123,361	442,111	420,646	21,465	3.04	3.64	.72

[1] Annual data are averages of monthly not seasonally adjusted figures.
[2] Seasonally adjusted, end of period.
[3] Ratio of unfilled orders at end of period to shipments for period; excludes industries with no unfilled orders. Annual figures relate to seasonally adjusted data for December.

Note.—Data beginning 1958 are not strictly comparable with earlier data.

Source: Department of Commerce, Bureau of the Census.

PRICES

TABLE B-59.—*Consumer price indexes for major expenditure classes, 1950–93*

[For all urban consumers; 1982–84=100]

Year or month	All items (CPI-U)	Food and beverages Total[1]	Food[2]	Housing Total	Shelter[2]	Fuel and other utilities[2]	Household furnishings and operation	Apparel and upkeep	Transportation[2]	Medical care[2]	Entertainment	Other goods and services	Energy[3]
1950	24.1		25.4					40.3	22.7	15.1			
1951	26.0		28.2					43.9	24.1	15.9			
1952	26.5		28.7					43.5	25.7	16.7			
1953	26.7		28.3		22.0	22.5		43.1	26.5	17.3			
1954	26.9		28.2		22.5	22.6		43.1	26.1	17.8			
1955	26.8		27.8		22.7	23.0		42.9	25.8	18.2			
1956	27.2		28.0		23.1	23.6		43.7	26.2	18.9			
1957	28.1		28.9		24.0	24.3		44.5	27.7	19.7			21.5
1958	28.9		30.2		24.5	24.8		44.6	28.6	20.6			21.5
1959	29.1		29.7		24.7	25.4		45.0	29.8	21.5			21.9
1960	29.6		30.0		25.2	26.0		45.7	29.8	22.3			22.4
1961	29.9		30.4		25.4	26.3		46.1	30.1	22.9			22.5
1962	30.2		30.6		25.8	26.3		46.3	30.8	23.5			22.6
1963	30.6		31.1		26.1	26.6		46.9	30.9	24.1			22.6
1964	31.0		31.5		26.5	26.6		47.3	31.4	24.6			22.5
1965	31.5		32.2		27.0	26.6		47.8	31.9	25.2			22.9
1966	32.4		33.8		27.8	26.7		49.0	32.3	26.3			23.3
1967	33.4	35.0	34.1	30.8	28.8	27.1	42.0	51.0	33.3	28.2	40.7	35.1	23.8
1968	34.8	36.2	35.3	32.0	30.1	27.4	43.6	53.7	34.3	29.9	43.0	36.9	24.2
1969	36.7	38.1	37.1	34.0	32.6	28.0	45.2	56.8	35.7	31.9	45.2	38.7	24.8
1970	38.8	40.1	39.2	36.4	35.5	29.1	46.8	59.2	37.5	34.0	47.5	40.9	25.5
1971	40.5	41.4	40.4	38.0	37.0	31.1	48.6	61.1	39.5	36.1	50.0	42.9	26.5
1972	41.8	43.1	42.1	39.4	38.7	32.5	49.7	62.3	39.9	37.3	51.5	44.7	27.2
1973	44.4	48.8	48.2	41.2	40.5	34.3	51.1	64.6	41.2	38.8	52.9	46.4	29.4
1974	49.3	55.5	55.1	45.8	44.4	40.7	56.8	69.4	45.8	42.4	56.9	49.8	38.1
1975	53.8	60.2	59.8	50.7	48.8	45.4	63.4	72.5	50.1	47.5	62.0	53.9	42.1
1976	56.9	62.1	61.6	53.8	51.5	49.4	67.3	75.2	55.1	52.0	65.1	57.0	45.1
1977	60.6	65.8	65.5	57.4	54.9	54.7	70.4	78.6	59.0	57.0	68.3	60.4	49.4
1978	65.2	72.2	72.0	62.4	60.5	58.5	74.7	81.4	61.7	61.8	71.9	64.3	52.5
1979	72.6	79.9	79.9	70.1	68.9	64.8	79.9	84.9	70.5	67.5	76.7	68.9	65.7
1980	82.4	86.7	86.8	81.1	81.0	75.4	86.3	90.9	83.1	74.9	83.6	75.2	86.0
1981	90.9	93.5	93.6	90.4	90.5	86.4	93.0	95.3	93.2	82.9	90.1	82.6	97.7
1982	96.5	97.3	97.4	96.9	96.9	94.9	98.0	97.8	97.0	92.5	96.0	91.1	99.2
1983	99.6	99.5	99.4	99.5	99.1	100.2	100.2	100.2	99.3	100.6	100.1	101.1	99.9
1984	103.9	103.2	103.2	103.6	104.0	104.8	101.9	102.1	103.7	106.8	103.8	107.9	100.9
1985	107.6	105.6	105.6	107.7	109.8	106.5	103.8	105.0	106.4	113.5	107.9	114.5	101.6
1986	109.6	109.1	109.0	110.9	115.8	104.1	105.2	105.9	102.3	122.0	111.6	121.4	88.2
1987	113.6	113.5	113.5	114.2	121.3	103.0	107.1	110.6	105.4	130.1	115.3	128.5	88.6
1988	118.3	118.2	118.2	118.5	127.1	104.4	109.4	115.4	108.7	138.6	120.3	137.0	89.3
1989	124.0	124.9	125.1	123.0	132.8	107.8	111.2	118.6	114.1	149.3	126.5	147.7	94.3
1990	130.7	132.1	132.4	128.5	140.0	111.6	113.3	124.1	120.5	162.8	132.4	159.0	102.1
1991	136.2	136.8	136.3	133.6	146.3	115.3	116.0	128.7	123.8	177.0	138.4	171.6	102.5
1992	140.3	138.7	137.9	137.5	151.2	117.8	118.0	131.9	126.5	190.1	142.3	183.3	103.0
1993	144.5	141.6	140.9	141.2	155.7	121.3	119.3	133.7	130.4	201.4	145.8	192.9	104.2
1992: Jan	138.1	137.9	137.2	135.7	149.2	116.2	116.7	127.9	124.5	184.3	140.1	178.6	100.1
Feb	138.6	138.1	137.5	136.1	149.8	115.9	117.3	130.2	124.1	186.2	140.7	179.4	99.0
Mar	139.3	138.8	138.1	136.6	150.4	115.8	117.7	133.4	124.4	187.3	141.2	179.8	98.9
Apr	139.5	138.8	138.1	136.5	150.2	115.8	118.0	133.3	125.2	188.1	142.0	180.3	99.5
May	139.7	138.3	137.4	136.7	150.2	116.8	117.9	133.1	126.3	188.7	142.0	181.3	102.4
June	140.2	138.3	137.4	137.7	151.1	119.0	118.2	131.0	126.9	189.4	142.0	181.5	105.9
July	140.5	138.1	137.2	138.3	151.8	119.4	118.4	129.2	127.2	190.7	142.4	182.3	106.0
Aug	140.9	138.8	138.0	138.6	152.3	119.4	118.3	130.2	126.9	191.5	142.6	183.9	105.4
Sept	141.3	139.3	138.5	138.4	151.9	119.8	118.3	133.3	126.8	192.3	143.2	187.0	105.9
Oct	141.8	139.2	138.3	138.5	152.5	118.5	118.4	135.0	128.0	193.3	143.5	187.9	104.5
Nov	142.0	139.1	138.3	138.5	152.4	118.3	118.5	134.5	129.2	194.3	143.7	188.0	104.5
Dec	141.9	139.5	138.7	138.5	152.5	118.7	118.2	131.4	129.0	194.7	143.8	189.1	103.9
1993: Jan	142.6	140.5	139.8	139.3	153.7	119.2	118.2	129.7	129.1	196.4	144.3	191.0	103.4
Feb	143.1	140.7	139.9	139.7	154.4	118.4	118.6	133.4	129.2	198.0	144.5	191.5	102.2
Mar	143.6	140.9	140.1	140.2	154.8	119.5	118.7	136.2	129.0	198.6	144.8	192.0	102.5
Apr	144.0	141.4	140.4	140.4	155.0	119.6	119.2	136.9	129.4	199.4	145.3	192.4	103.1
May	144.2	141.8	141.1	140.5	154.9	120.5	119.1	135.0	130.2	200.5	145.0	193.2	104.4
June	144.4	141.1	140.4	141.5	155.7	122.9	119.1	131.9	120.3	201.1	145.5	193.1	106.5
July	144.4	141.1	140.3	141.9	156.3	123.2	118.8	129.4	130.3	202.2	145.3	193.7	105.8
Aug	144.8	141.5	140.8	142.3	156.8	123.3	119.2	131.9	130.2	202.9	145.8	193.4	105.2
Sept	145.1	141.8	141.1	142.3	156.6	123.9	119.6	134.6	130.1	203.3	146.6	193.1	105.2
Oct	145.7	142.3	141.6	142.2	156.8	122.4	120.0	136.1	131.8	204.4	147.3	193.4	105.4
Nov	145.8	142.6	141.9	142.0	156.7	121.2	120.3	136.2	132.6	204.9	147.7	193.8	103.7
Dec	145.8	143.3	142.7	142.3	157.1	121.7	120.3	132.6	132.1	205.2	147.8	194.2	102.4

[1] Includes alcoholic beverages, not shown separately.
[2] See table B-60 for components.
[3] Household fuels—gas (piped), electricity, fuel oil, etc.—and motor fuel. Motor oil, coolant, etc. also included through 1982. See table B-60 for the components.

Note.—Data beginning 1983 incorporate a rental equivalence measure for homeowners' costs.

Source: Department of Labor, Bureau of Labor Statistics.

TABLE B-60.—*Consumer price indexes for selected expenditure classes, 1950-93*

[For all urban consumers; 1982-84=100, except as noted]

Year or month	Food and beverages				Shelter					Fuel and other utilities			
	Total [1]	Food			Total	Renters' costs			Mainte- nance and repairs	Total	Fuels		Other utilities and public services
		Total	At home	Away from home		Total [2]	Rent, resi- dential	Home- owners' costs [2]			Total	Fuel oil and other house- hold fuel com- modities	Gas (piped) and elec- tricity (energy serv- ices)	
---	---	---	---	---	---	---	---	---	---	---	---	---	---	---
1950		25.4	27.3				29.7					11.3	19.2	
1951		28.2	30.3				30.9					11.8	19.3	
1952		28.7	30.8				32.2					12.1	19.5	
1953		28.3	30.3	21.5	22.0		33.9		20.5	22.5		12.6	19.9	
1954		28.2	30.1	21.9	22.5		35.1		20.9	22.6		12.6	20.2	
1955		27.8	29.5	22.1	22.7		35.6		21.4	23.0		12.7	20.7	
1956		28.0	29.6	22.6	23.1		36.3		22.3	23.6		13.3	20.9	
1957		28.9	30.6	23.4	24.0		37.0		23.2	24.3		14.0	21.1	
1958		30.2	32.0	24.1	24.5		37.6		23.6	24.8		13.7	21.9	
1959		29.7	31.2	24.8	24.7		38.2		24.0	25.4		13.9	22.4	
1960		30.0	31.5	25.4	25.2		38.7		24.4	26.0		13.8	23.3	
1961		30.4	31.8	26.0	25.4		39.2		24.8	26.3		14.1	23.5	
1962		30.6	32.0	26.7	25.8		39.7		25.0	26.3		14.2	23.5	
1963		31.1	32.4	27.3	26.1		40.1		25.3	26.6		14.4	23.5	
1964		31.5	32.7	27.8	26.5		40.5		25.8	26.6		14.4	23.5	
1965		32.2	33.5	28.4	27.0		40.9		26.3	26.6		14.6	23.5	
1966		33.8	35.2	29.7	27.8		41.5		27.5	26.7		15.0	23.6	
1967	35.0	34.1	35.1	31.3	28.8		42.2		28.9	27.1	21.4	15.5	23.7	46.6
1968	36.2	35.3	36.3	32.9	30.1		43.3		30.6	27.4	21.7	16.0	23.9	47.1
1969	38.1	37.1	38.0	34.9	32.6		44.7		33.2	28.0	22.1	16.3	24.3	48.4
1970	40.1	39.2	39.9	37.5	35.5		46.5		35.8	29.1	23.1	17.0	25.4	50.0
1971	41.4	40.4	40.9	39.4	37.0		48.7		38.6	31.1	24.7	18.2	27.1	53.4
1972	43.1	42.1	42.7	41.0	38.7		50.4		40.6	32.5	25.7	18.3	28.5	56.2
1973	48.8	48.2	49.7	44.2	40.5		52.5		43.6	34.3	27.5	21.1	29.9	57.8
1974	55.5	55.1	57.1	49.8	44.4		55.2		49.5	40.7	34.4	33.2	34.5	60.7
1975	60.2	59.8	61.8	54.5	48.8		58.0		54.1	45.4	39.4	36.4	40.1	63.9
1976	62.1	61.6	63.1	58.2	51.5		61.1		57.6	49.4	43.3	38.8	44.7	67.7
1977	65.8	65.5	66.8	62.6	54.9		64.8		62.0	54.7	49.0	43.9	50.5	70.8
1978	72.2	72.0	73.8	68.3	60.5		69.3		67.2	58.5	53.0	46.2	55.0	73.7
1979	79.9	79.9	81.8	75.9	68.9		74.3		74.0	64.8	61.3	62.4	61.0	74.3
1980	86.7	86.8	88.4	83.4	81.0		80.9		82.4	75.4	74.8	86.1	71.4	77.0
1981	93.5	93.6	94.8	90.9	90.5		87.9		90.7	86.4	87.2	104.6	81.9	84.3
1982	97.3	97.4	98.1	95.8	96.9		94.6		96.4	94.9	95.6	103.4	93.2	93.3
1983	99.5	99.4	99.1	100.0	99.1	103.0	100.1	102.5	99.9	100.2	100.5	97.2	101.5	99.5
1984	103.2	103.2	102.8	104.2	104.0	108.6	105.3	107.3	103.7	104.8	104.0	99.4	105.4	107.2
1985	105.6	105.6	104.3	108.3	109.8	115.4	111.8	113.1	106.5	106.5	105.5	95.9	107.1	112.1
1986	109.1	109.0	107.3	112.5	115.8	121.9	118.3	119.4	107.9	104.1	99.2	77.6	105.7	117.9
1987	113.5	113.5	111.9	117.0	121.3	128.1	123.1	124.8	111.8	103.0	97.3	77.9	103.8	120.1
1988	118.2	118.2	116.6	121.8	127.1	133.6	127.8	131.1	114.7	104.4	98.0	78.1	104.6	122.9
1989	124.9	125.1	124.2	127.4	132.8	138.9	132.8	137.3	118.0	107.8	100.9	81.7	107.5	127.1
1990	132.1	132.4	132.3	133.4	140.0	146.7	138.4	144.6	122.2	111.6	104.5	99.3	109.3	131.7
1991	136.8	136.3	135.8	137.9	146.3	155.6	143.3	150.2	126.3	115.3	106.7	94.6	112.6	137.9
1992	138.7	137.9	136.8	140.7	151.2	160.9	146.9	155.3	128.6	117.8	108.1	90.7	114.8	142.5
1993	141.6	140.9	140.1	143.2	155.7	165.0	150.3	160.2	130.6	121.3	111.2	90.3	118.5	147.0
1992: Jan	137.9	137.2	136.4	139.7	149.2	158.8	145.4	153.2	128.0	116.2	106.6	92.0	112.8	140.5
Feb	138.1	137.5	136.6	139.9	149.8	160.2	145.6	153.5	128.3	115.9	105.9	91.5	112.0	141.2
Mar	138.8	138.1	137.5	140.1	150.4	161.2	146.4	154.1	128.4	115.8	105.2	90.5	111.5	141.7
Apr	138.8	138.1	137.4	140.2	150.2	160.1	146.2	154.2	128.0	115.8	105.1	89.9	111.3	142.2
May	138.3	137.4	136.2	140.4	150.2	159.5	146.3	154.4	128.1	116.8	106.5	89.8	113.0	142.4
June	138.3	137.4	136.1	140.7	151.1	161.0	146.6	155.0	128.5	119.0	110.2	90.1	117.4	142.2
July	138.1	137.2	135.7	140.8	151.8	162.8	147.0	155.5	128.8	119.4	110.4	90.0	117.6	143.1
Aug	138.8	138.0	136.9	141.0	152.3	163.5	147.0	155.8	128.1	119.4	110.3	89.7	117.5	143.3
Sept	139.3	138.5	137.4	141.2	151.9	161.7	147.2	156.0	128.5	119.8	111.1	89.7	118.5	143.0
Oct	139.2	138.3	137.2	141.3	152.5	161.7	148.0	156.8	129.4	118.5	108.7	91.4	115.4	143.4
Nov	139.1	138.3	137.0	141.5	152.4	160.6	148.6	157.2	129.5	118.3	108.2	92.1	114.8	143.7
Dec	139.5	138.7	137.5	141.6	152.5	160.2	148.6	157.5	129.3	118.7	108.9	91.8	115.6	143.6
1993: Jan	140.5	139.8	139.1	142.0	153.7	162.5	148.9	158.2	129.7	119.2	109.2	92.3	115.9	144.3
Feb	140.7	139.9	139.1	142.2	154.4	164.4	149.1	158.5	130.5	118.4	107.5	92.5	113.8	145.3
Mar	140.9	140.1	139.4	142.4	154.8	165.2	149.1	158.7	131.5	119.5	108.6	92.8	115.1	146.3
Apr	141.4	140.6	140.0	142.7	155.0	164.9	149.7	159.2	131.8	119.6	108.8	92.6	115.3	146.2
May	141.8	141.1	140.7	142.9	154.9	164.2	149.9	159.4	131.6	120.5	110.3	91.3	117.3	146.3
June	141.1	140.4	139.3	143.2	155.7	165.2	150.3	160.1	131.2	122.9	114.1	90.4	122.0	146.5
July	141.1	140.3	139.1	143.4	156.3	166.8	150.4	160.3	131.3	123.2	114.2	89.1	122.2	147.1
Aug	141.5	140.8	139.7	143.6	156.8	167.3	150.8	160.8	131.6	123.3	114.1	87.8	122.2	147.8
Sept	141.8	141.1	140.0	143.8	156.6	165.3	151.0	161.4	131.3	123.9	114.8	87.9	123.1	148.1
Oct	142.3	141.6	140.8	144.0	156.8	165.4	151.4	161.6	130.8	122.4	112.1	89.1	119.7	148.4
Nov	142.6	141.9	141.2	144.2	156.7	164.4	151.6	162.0	127.9	121.2	110.1	89.4	117.3	148.6
Dec	143.3	142.7	142.3	144.3	157.1	164.4	151.9	162.5	127.6	121.7	110.7	88.3	118.1	148.8

[1] Includes alcoholic beverages, not shown separately.
[2] December 1982=100.

See next page for continuation of table.

336

TABLE B-60.—*Consumer price indexes for selected expenditure classes, 1950–93*—Continued

[For all urban consumers; 1982–84=100, except as noted]

Year or month	Transportation								Medical care		
	Total	Private transportation						Public transportation	Total	Medical care commodities	Medical care services
		Total [3]	New cars	Used cars	Motor fuel [4]	Automobile maintenance and repair	Other				
1950	22.7	24.5	41.1	....	19.0	18.9	....	13.4	15.1	39.7	12.8
1951	24.1	25.6	43.1	....	19.5	20.4	....	14.8	15.9	40.8	13.4
1952	25.7	27.3	46.8	....	20.0	20.8	....	15.8	16.7	41.2	14.3
1953	26.5	27.8	47.2	26.7	21.2	22.0	....	16.8	17.3	41.5	14.8
1954	26.1	27.1	46.5	22.7	21.8	22.7	....	18.0	17.8	42.0	15.3
1955	25.8	26.7	44.8	21.5	22.1	23.2	....	18.5	18.2	42.5	15.7
1956	26.2	27.1	46.1	20.7	22.8	24.2	....	19.2	18.9	43.4	16.3
1957	27.7	28.6	48.5	23.2	23.8	25.0	....	19.9	19.7	44.6	17.0
1958	28.6	29.5	50.0	24.0	23.4	25.4	....	20.9	20.6	46.1	17.9
1959	29.8	30.8	52.2	26.8	23.7	26.0	....	21.5	21.5	46.8	18.7
1960	29.8	30.6	51.5	25.0	24.4	26.5	....	22.2	22.3	46.9	19.5
1961	30.1	30.8	51.5	26.0	24.1	27.1	....	23.2	22.9	46.3	20.2
1962	30.8	31.4	51.3	28.4	24.3	27.5	....	24.0	23.5	45.6	20.9
1963	30.9	31.6	51.0	28.7	24.2	27.8	....	24.3	24.1	45.2	21.5
1964	31.4	32.0	50.9	30.0	24.1	28.2	....	24.7	24.6	45.1	22.0
1965	31.9	32.5	49.7	29.8	25.1	28.7	....	25.2	25.2	45.0	22.7
1966	32.3	32.9	48.8	29.0	25.6	29.2	....	26.1	26.3	45.1	23.9
1967	33.3	33.8	49.3	29.9	26.4	30.4	37.9	27.4	28.2	44.9	26.0
1968	34.3	34.8	50.7	([5])	26.8	32.1	39.2	28.7	29.9	45.0	27.9
1969	35.7	36.0	51.5	30.9	27.6	34.1	41.6	30.9	31.9	45.4	30.2
1970	37.5	37.5	53.0	31.2	27.9	36.6	45.2	35.2	34.0	46.5	32.3
1971	39.5	39.4	55.2	33.0	28.1	39.3	48.6	37.8	36.1	47.3	34.7
1972	39.9	39.7	54.7	33.1	28.4	41.1	48.9	39.3	37.3	47.4	35.9
1973	41.2	41.0	54.8	35.2	31.2	43.2	48.4	39.7	38.8	47.5	37.5
1974	45.8	46.2	57.9	36.7	42.2	47.6	50.2	40.6	42.4	49.2	41.4
1975	50.1	50.6	62.9	43.8	45.1	53.7	53.5	43.5	47.5	53.3	46.6
1976	55.1	55.6	66.9	50.3	47.0	57.6	61.8	47.8	52.0	56.5	51.3
1977	59.0	59.7	70.4	54.7	49.7	61.9	67.2	50.0	57.0	60.2	56.4
1978	61.7	62.5	75.8	55.8	51.8	67.0	69.9	51.5	61.8	64.4	61.2
1979	70.5	71.7	81.8	60.2	70.1	73.7	75.2	54.9	67.5	69.0	67.2
1980	83.1	84.2	88.4	62.3	97.4	81.5	84.3	69.0	74.9	75.4	74.8
1981	93.2	93.8	93.7	76.9	108.5	89.2	91.4	85.6	82.9	83.7	82.8
1982	97.0	97.1	97.4	88.8	102.8	96.0	97.7	94.9	92.5	92.3	92.6
1983	99.3	99.3	99.9	98.7	99.4	100.3	98.8	99.5	100.6	100.2	100.7
1984	103.7	103.6	102.8	112.5	97.9	103.8	103.5	105.7	106.8	107.5	106.7
1985	106.4	106.2	106.1	113.7	98.7	106.8	109.0	110.5	113.5	115.2	113.2
1986	102.3	101.2	110.6	108.8	77.1	110.3	115.1	117.0	122.0	122.8	121.9
1987	105.4	104.2	114.6	113.1	80.2	114.8	120.8	121.1	130.1	131.0	130.0
1988	108.7	107.6	116.9	118.0	80.9	119.7	127.9	123.3	138.6	139.9	138.3
1989	114.1	112.9	119.2	120.4	88.5	124.9	135.8	129.5	149.3	150.8	148.9
1990	120.5	118.8	121.0	117.6	101.2	130.1	142.5	142.6	162.8	163.4	162.7
1991	123.8	121.9	125.3	118.1	99.4	136.0	149.1	148.9	177.0	176.8	177.1
1992	126.5	124.6	128.4	123.2	99.0	141.3	153.2	151.4	190.1	188.1	190.5
1993	130.4	127.5	131.5	133.9	98.0	145.9	156.8	167.0	201.4	195.0	202.9
1992: Jan	124.5	122.5	128.0	117.8	94.5	139.0	152.4	151.5	184.3	183.0	184.6
Feb	124.1	122.0	128.1	116.1	92.9	139.7	152.2	150.7	186.2	185.1	186.4
Mar	124.4	122.2	128.2	115.7	93.4	140.3	152.2	153.5	187.3	186.7	187.4
Apr	125.2	122.9	128.2	117.9	95.0	140.5	152.4	154.7	188.1	187.9	188.1
May	126.3	124.3	128.4	120.5	99.4	140.8	152.5	151.6	188.7	187.6	188.9
June	126.9	125.4	128.2	123.1	102.9	141.2	152.6	145.3	189.4	188.0	189.7
July	127.2	125.5	127.8	124.8	102.8	141.4	153.0	148.3	190.7	188.6	191.1
Aug	126.9	125.4	127.6	126.4	101.7	141.6	153.1	146.7	191.5	188.9	192.2
Sept	126.8	125.4	127.4	127.7	101.7	142.2	152.7	145.6	192.3	189.5	192.9
Oct	128.0	126.1	128.2	129.1	101.6	142.5	154.4	152.9	193.3	189.8	194.2
Nov	129.2	127.0	129.7	129.9	102.2	142.8	155.3	157.4	194.3	190.4	195.2
Dec	129.0	126.7	130.5	129.0	100.2	143.2	155.5	158.2	194.7	191.1	195.6
1993: Jan	129.1	126.6	130.9	127.4	98.6	143.4	156.5	161.6	196.4	191.8	197.5
Feb	129.2	126.5	130.9	126.0	98.0	144.3	156.8	164.1	198.0	193.2	199.1
Mar	129.0	126.3	130.9	126.6	97.3	144.7	156.3	163.5	198.6	193.9	199.7
Apr	129.4	126.8	131.1	128.7	98.4	145.2	156.1	162.8	199.4	193.7	200.7
May	130.2	127.5	131.3	131.5	99.7	145.4	156.1	165.5	200.5	194.2	202.0
June	130.3	127.6	131.0	134.3	99.8	145.8	155.8	164.5	201.1	194.7	202.6
July	130.3	127.4	130.9	136.1	98.1	146.2	156.0	167.7	202.2	195.7	203.8
Aug	130.2	127.3	130.8	137.5	97.0	146.2	156.4	168.1	202.9	196.1	204.5
Sept	130.1	127.1	130.6	138.7	96.1	146.8	156.1	168.4	203.2	196.2	205.0
Oct	131.8	129.0	131.9	139.8	99.7	147.1	157.8	168.2	204.4	196.6	206.2
Nov	132.6	129.5	133.4	140.7	98.4	147.4	159.1	173.0	204.9	196.6	206.8
Dec	132.1	128.6	134.2	139.3	94.8	147.7	159.0	176.5	205.2	197.0	207.1

[3] Includes other new vehicles, not shown separately. Includes direct pricing of new trucks and motorcycles beginning September 1982.
[4] Includes direct pricing of diesel fuel and gasohol beginning September 1981.
[5] Not available.

Note.—See Note, Table B-59.

Source: Department of Labor, Bureau of Labor Statistics.

337

TABLE B-61.—*Consumer price indexes for commodities, services, and special groups, 1950–93*

[For all urban consumers; 1982–84=100, except as noted]

Year or month	All items (CPI–U)	Commodities			Services		Services less medical care services	Special indexes				CPI-U-X1 (all items) (Dec. 1982 =97.6)[1]
		All commodities	Food	Commodities less food	All services	Medical care services		All items less food	All items less energy	All items less food and energy	All items less medical care	
1950	24.1	29.0	25.4	31.4	16.9	12.8		23.8				26.2
1951	26.0	31.6	28.2	33.8	17.8	13.4		25.3				28.3
1952	26.5	32.0	28.7	34.1	18.6	14.3		25.9				28.8
1953	26.7	31.9	28.3	34.2	19.4	14.8		26.4				29.0
1954	26.9	31.6	28.2	33.8	20.0	15.3		26.6				29.2
1955	26.8	31.3	27.8	33.6	20.4	15.7		26.6				29.1
1956	27.2	31.6	28.0	33.9	20.9	16.3		27.1				29.6
1957	28.1	32.6	28.9	34.9	21.8	17.0	22.8	28.0	28.9	28.9	28.7	30.5
1958	28.9	33.3	30.2	35.3	22.6	17.9	23.6	28.6	29.7	29.6	29.5	31.4
1959	29.1	33.3	29.7	35.8	23.3	18.7	24.2	29.2	29.9	30.2	29.8	31.6
1960	29.6	33.6	30.0	36.0	24.1	19.5	25.0	29.7	30.4	30.6	30.2	32.2
1961	29.9	33.8	30.4	36.1	24.5	20.2	25.4	30.0	30.7	31.0	30.5	32.5
1962	30.2	34.1	30.6	36.3	25.0	20.9	25.9	30.3	31.1	31.4	30.8	32.8
1963	30.6	34.4	31.1	36.6	25.5	21.5	26.3	30.7	31.5	31.8	31.1	33.3
1964	31.0	34.8	31.5	36.9	26.0	22.0	26.8	31.1	32.0	32.3	31.5	33.7
1965	31.5	35.2	32.2	37.2	26.6	22.7	27.4	31.6	32.5	32.7	32.0	34.2
1966	32.4	36.1	33.8	37.7	27.6	23.9	28.3	32.3	33.5	33.5	33.0	35.2
1967	33.4	36.8	34.1	38.6	28.8	26.0	29.3	33.4	34.4	34.7	33.7	36.3
1968	34.8	38.1	35.3	40.0	30.3	27.9	30.8	34.9	35.9	36.3	35.1	37.7
1969	36.7	39.9	37.1	41.7	32.4	30.2	32.9	36.8	38.0	38.4	37.0	39.4
1970	38.8	41.7	39.2	43.4	35.0	32.3	35.6	39.0	40.3	40.8	39.2	41.3
1971	40.5	43.2	40.4	45.1	37.0	34.7	37.5	40.8	42.0	42.7	40.8	43.1
1972	41.8	44.5	42.1	46.1	38.4	35.9	38.9	42.0	43.4	44.0	42.1	44.4
1973	44.4	47.8	48.2	47.7	40.1	37.5	40.6	43.7	46.1	45.6	44.8	47.2
1974	49.3	53.5	55.1	52.8	43.8	41.4	44.3	48.0	50.6	49.4	49.8	51.9
1975	53.8	58.2	59.8	57.6	48.0	46.6	48.3	52.5	55.1	53.9	54.3	56.2
1976	56.9	60.7	61.6	60.5	52.0	51.3	52.2	56.0	58.2	57.4	57.2	59.4
1977	60.6	64.2	65.5	63.8	56.0	56.4	55.9	59.6	61.9	61.0	60.8	63.2
1978	65.2	68.8	72.0	67.5	60.8	61.2	60.7	63.9	66.7	65.5	65.4	67.5
1979	72.6	76.6	79.9	75.3	67.5	67.2	67.5	71.2	73.4	71.9	72.9	74.0
1980	82.4	86.0	86.8	85.7	77.9	74.8	78.2	81.5	81.9	80.8	82.8	82.3
1981	90.9	93.2	93.6	93.1	88.1	82.8	88.7	90.4	90.1	89.2	91.4	90.1
1982	96.5	97.0	97.4	96.9	96.0	92.6	96.4	96.3	96.1	95.8	96.8	95.6
1983	99.6	99.8	99.4	100.0	99.4	100.7	99.2	99.7	99.6	99.6	99.6	99.6
1984	103.9	103.2	103.2	103.1	104.6	106.7	104.4	104.0	104.3	104.6	103.7	103.9
1985	107.6	105.4	105.6	105.2	109.9	113.2	109.6	108.0	108.4	109.1	107.2	107.6
1986	109.6	104.4	109.0	101.7	115.4	121.9	114.6	109.8	112.6	113.5	108.8	109.6
1987	113.6	107.7	113.5	104.3	120.2	130.0	119.1	113.6	117.2	118.2	112.6	113.6
1988	118.3	111.5	118.2	107.7	125.7	138.3	124.3	118.3	122.3	123.4	117.0	118.3
1989	124.0	116.7	125.1	112.0	131.9	148.9	130.1	123.7	128.1	129.0	122.4	124.0
1990	130.7	122.8	132.4	117.4	139.2	162.7	136.8	130.3	134.7	135.5	128.8	130.7
1991	136.2	126.6	136.3	121.3	146.3	177.1	143.3	136.1	140.9	142.1	133.8	136.2
1992	140.3	129.1	137.9	124.2	152.0	190.5	148.4	140.8	145.4	147.3	137.5	140.3
1993	144.5	131.5	140.9	126.3	157.9	202.9	153.6	145.1	150.0	152.2	141.2	144.5
1992: Jan	138.1	127.2	137.2	121.6	149.6	184.6	146.3	138.3	143.3	144.9	135.5	
Feb	138.6	127.6	137.5	122.1	150.1	186.4	146.6	138.8	144.0	145.6	135.9	
Mar	139.3	128.4	138.1	123.0	150.7	187.4	147.1	139.5	144.7	146.4	136.5	
Apr	139.5	128.8	138.1	123.5	150.8	188.1	147.2	139.7	144.9	146.6	136.7	
May	139.7	129.1	137.4	124.4	150.9	188.9	147.3	140.1	144.9	146.7	136.9	
June	140.2	129.2	137.4	124.5	151.7	189.7	148.1	140.7	145.0	146.9	137.4	
July	140.5	129.0	137.2	124.3	152.5	191.1	148.8	141.1	145.3	147.3	137.6	
Aug	140.9	129.3	138.0	124.3	153.0	192.2	149.2	141.4	145.8	147.7	138.0	
Sept	141.3	129.9	138.5	125.1	153.2	192.9	149.4	141.8	146.2	148.1	138.4	
Oct	141.8	130.3	138.3	125.7	153.7	194.2	149.9	142.4	146.9	149.0	138.8	
Nov	142.0	130.5	138.3	126.1	154.0	195.2	150.1	142.7	147.1	149.3	139.0	
Dec	141.9	130.1	138.7	125.3	154.2	195.6	150.3	142.5	147.1	149.2	138.9	
1993: Jan	142.6	130.4	139.8	125.1	155.2	197.5	151.2	143.1	147.9	149.9	139.5	
Feb	143.1	130.9	139.9	125.8	155.8	199.1	151.7	143.7	148.7	150.8	140.0	
Mar	143.6	131.4	140.1	126.4	156.2	199.7	152.1	144.2	149.1	151.4	140.4	
Apr	144.0	131.9	140.6	127.0	156.5	200.7	152.3	144.6	149.5	151.7	140.8	
May	144.2	132.0	141.1	126.9	156.9	202.0	152.6	144.8	149.6	151.7	141.0	
June	144.4	131.4	140.4	126.3	157.8	202.6	153.6	145.1	149.6	151.8	141.1	
July	144.4	130.9	140.3	125.5	158.4	203.8	154.1	145.2	149.7	152.0	141.1	
Aug	144.8	131.1	140.8	125.7	159.0	204.5	154.7	145.6	150.3	152.6	141.6	
Sept	145.1	131.3	141.1	125.9	159.3	205.0	155.0	145.9	150.6	152.9	141.8	
Oct	145.7	132.3	141.6	127.1	159.5	206.2	155.1	146.4	151.2	153.5	142.3	
Nov	145.8	132.5	141.9	127.3	159.6	206.8	155.2	146.6	151.5	153.9	142.5	
Dec	145.8	132.0	142.7	126.1	160.0	207.1	155.6	146.4	151.7	154.0	142.5	

[1] CPI-U-X1 is a rental equivalence approach to homeowners' costs for the consumer price index for years prior to 1983, the first year for which the official index (CPI-U) incorporates such a measure. CPI-U-X1 is rebased to the December 1982 value of the CPI-U (1982–84=100); thus it is identical with CPI-U data for December 1982 and all subsequent periods. Data prior to 1967 estimated by moving the series at the same rate as the CPI-U for each year.

Note.—See Note, Table B-59.

Source: Department of Labor, Bureau of Labor Statistics.

TABLE B-62.—*Changes in special consumer price indexes, 1958–93*

[For all urban consumers; percent change]

Year or month	All items (CPI–U) Dec. to Dec.[1]	All items (CPI–U) Year to year	All items less food Dec. to Dec.[1]	All items less food Year to year	All items less energy Dec. to Dec.[1]	All items less energy Year to year	All items less food and energy Dec. to Dec.[1]	All items less food and energy Year to year	All items less medical care Dec. to Dec.[1]	All items less medical care Year to year
1958	1.8	2.8	1.8	2.1	2.1	2.8	1.7	2.4	1.7	2.8
1959	1.7	.7	2.1	2.1	1.3	.7	2.0	2.0	1.4	1.0
1960	1.4	1.7	1.0	1.7	1.3	1.7	1.0	1.3	1.3	1.3
1961	.7	1.0	1.3	1.0	.7	1.0	1.3	1.3	.3	1.0
1962	1.3	1.0	1.0	1.0	1.3	1.3	1.3	1.3	1.3	1.0
1963	1.6	1.3	1.6	1.3	1.9	1.3	1.6	1.3	1.6	1.0
1964	1.0	1.3	1.0	1.3	1.3	1.6	1.2	1.6	1.0	1.3
1965	1.9	1.6	1.6	1.6	1.9	1.6	1.5	1.2	1.9	1.6
1966	3.5	2.9	3.5	2.2	3.4	3.1	3.3	2.4	3.4	3.1
1967	3.0	3.1	3.3	3.4	3.2	2.7	3.8	3.6	2.7	2.1
1968	4.7	4.2	5.0	4.5	4.9	4.4	5.1	4.6	4.7	4.2
1969	6.2	5.5	5.6	5.4	6.5	5.8	6.2	5.8	6.1	5.4
1970	5.6	5.7	6.6	6.0	5.4	6.1	6.6	6.3	5.2	5.9
1971	3.3	4.4	3.0	4.6	3.4	4.2	3.1	4.7	3.2	4.1
1972	3.4	3.2	2.9	2.9	3.5	3.3	3.0	3.0	3.4	3.2
1973	8.7	6.2	5.6	4.0	8.2	6.2	4.7	3.6	9.1	6.4
1974	12.3	11.0	12.2	9.8	11.7	9.8	11.1	8.3	12.2	11.2
1975	6.9	9.1	7.3	9.4	6.6	8.9	6.7	9.1	6.7	9.0
1976	4.9	5.8	6.1	6.7	4.8	5.6	6.1	6.5	4.5	5.3
1977	6.7	6.5	6.4	6.4	6.7	6.4	6.5	6.3	6.7	6.3
1978	9.0	7.6	8.3	7.2	9.1	7.8	8.5	7.4	9.1	7.6
1979	13.3	11.3	14.0	11.4	11.1	10.0	11.3	9.8	13.4	11.5
1980	12.5	13.5	13.0	14.5	11.7	11.6	12.2	12.4	12.5	13.6
1981	8.9	10.3	9.8	10.9	8.5	10.0	9.5	10.4	8.8	10.4
1982	3.8	6.2	4.1	6.5	4.2	6.7	4.5	7.4	3.6	5.9
1983	3.8	3.2	4.1	3.5	4.5	3.6	4.8	4.0	3.6	2.9
1984	3.9	4.3	3.9	4.3	4.4	4.7	4.7	5.0	3.9	4.1
1985	3.8	3.6	4.1	3.8	4.0	3.9	4.3	4.3	3.5	3.4
1986	1.1	1.9	.5	1.7	3.8	3.9	3.8	4.0	.7	1.5
1987	4.4	3.6	4.6	3.5	4.1	4.1	4.2	4.1	4.3	3.5
1988	4.4	4.1	4.2	4.1	4.7	4.4	4.7	4.4	4.2	3.9
1989	4.6	4.8	4.5	4.6	4.6	4.7	4.4	4.5	4.5	4.6
1990	6.1	5.4	6.3	5.3	5.2	5.2	5.2	5.0	5.9	5.2
1991	3.1	4.2	3.3	4.5	3.9	4.6	4.4	4.9	2.7	3.9
1992	2.9	3.0	3.2	3.5	3.0	3.2	3.3	3.7	2.7	2.8
1993	2.7	3.0	2.7	3.1	3.1	3.2	3.2	3.3	2.6	2.7

Percent change from preceding period

	Unadjusted	Seasonally adjusted	Unadjusted	Seasonally adjusted	Unadjusted	Seasonally adjusted	Unadjusted	Seasonally adjusted	Unadjusted	Seasonally adjusted
1992: Jan	0.1	0.3	0.1	0.3	0.4	0.3	0.3	0.4	0.1	0.2
Feb	.4	.2	.4	.2	.5	.3	.5	.3	.3	.2
Mar	.5	.4	.5	.4	.5	.3	.5	.3	.4	.4
Apr	.1	.3	.1	.3	.1	.2	.1	.1	.1	.2
May	.1	.1	.3	.3	0	.1	.1	.3	.1	.1
June	.4	.2	.4	.3	.1	.2	.1	.1	.4	.2
July	.2	.3	.3	.3	.2	.2	.3	.3	.1	.2
Aug	.3	.2	.2	.2	.3	.3	.3	.2	.3	.2
Sept	.3	.1	.3	.1	.3	.1	.3	.1	.3	.1
Oct	.4	.4	.4	.4	.5	.5	.4	.6	.5	.4
Nov	.1	.2	.2	.2	.3	.1	.2	.3	.1	.2
Dec	−.1	.1	−.1	.1	0	.2	−.1	.2	−.1	.1
1993: Jan	.5	.5	.4	.4	.5	.5	.5	.5	.4	.4
Feb	.4	.3	.4	.4	.5	.5	.4	.6	.4	.4
Mar	.3	.1	.3	.3	.2	.3	.1	.4	.3	.1
Apr	.3	.4	.3	.3	.3	.3	.4	.2	.3	.4
May	.1	.1	.1	.1	.1	.1	.2	0	.1	.1
June	.1	0	.2	.1	0	.1	.1	.1	.1	−.1
July	0	.1	.1	.1	.1	.1	.1	.1	0	.1
Aug	.3	.3	.3	.3	.4	.3	.4	.3	.4	.2
Sept	.2	0	.2	0	.2	0	.2	.1	.1	0
Oct	.4	.4	.3	.4	.4	.3	.4	.3	.4	.4
Nov	.1	.2	.1	.1	.2	.3	.3	.3	.1	.2
Dec	0	.2	−.1	.1	.1	.3	0	.3	0	.1

[1] Changes from December to December are based on unadjusted indexes.

Note.—See Note, Table B–59.

Source: Department of Labor, Bureau of Labor Statistics.

TABLE B-63.—*Changes in consumer price indexes for commodities and services, 1929–93*

[For all urban consumers; percent change]

Year	All items (CPI–U) Dec. to Dec.[1]	All items (CPI–U) Year to year	Commodities Total Dec. to Dec.[1]	Commodities Total Year to year	Commodities Food Dec. to Dec.[1]	Commodities Food Year to year	Services Total Dec. to Dec.[1]	Services Total Year to year	Services Medical care Dec. to Dec.[1]	Services Medical care Year to year	Medical care[2] Dec. to Dec.[1]	Medical care[2] Year to year	Energy[3] Dec. to Dec.[1]	Energy[3] Year to year
1929	0.6	0			2.5	1.2								
1933	.8	−5.1			6.9	−2.8								
1939	0	−1.4	−0.7	−2.0	−2.5	−2.5	0	0	1.2	1.2	1.0	0		
1940	.7	.7	1.4	.7	2.5	1.7	.8	.8	0	0	0	1.0		
1941	9.9	5.0	13.3	6.7	15.7	9.2	2.4	.8	1.2	0	1.0	0		
1942	9.0	10.9	12.9	14.5	17.9	17.6	2.3	3.1	3.5	3.5	3.8	2.9		
1943	3.0	6.1	4.2	9.3	3.0	11.0	2.3	2.3	5.6	4.5	4.6	4.7		
1944	2.3	1.7	2.0	1.0	0	−1.2	2.2	2.2	3.2	4.3	2.6	3.6		
1945	2.2	2.3	2.9	3.0	3.5	2.4	.7	1.5	3.1	3.1	2.6	2.6		
1946	18.1	8.3	24.8	10.6	31.3	14.5	3.6	1.4	9.0	5.1	8.3	5.0		
1947	8.8	14.4	10.3	20.5	11.3	21.7	5.6	4.3	6.4	8.7	6.9	8.0		
1948	3.0	8.1	1.7	7.2	−.8	8.3	5.9	6.1	6.9	7.1	5.8	6.7		
1949	−2.1	−1.2	−4.1	−2.7	−3.9	−4.2	3.7	5.1	1.6	3.3	1.4	2.8		
1950	5.9	1.3	7.8	.7	9.8	1.6	3.6	3.0	4.0	2.4	3.4	2.0		
1951	6.0	7.9	5.9	9.0	7.1	11.0	5.2	5.3	5.3	4.7	5.8	5.3		
1952	.8	1.9	−.9	1.3	−1.0	1.8	4.4	4.5	5.8	6.7	4.3	5.0		
1953	.7	.8	−.3	−.3	−1.1	−1.4	4.2	4.3	3.4	3.5	3.5	3.6		
1954	−.7	.7	−1.6	−.9	−1.8	−.4	2.0	3.1	2.6	3.4	2.3	2.9		
1955	.4	−.4	−.3	−.9	−.7	−1.4	2.0	2.0	3.2	2.6	3.3	2.2		
1956	3.0	1.5	2.6	1.0	2.9	.7	3.4	2.5	3.8	3.8	3.2	3.8		
1957	2.9	3.3	2.8	3.2	2.8	3.2	4.2	4.3	4.8	4.3	4.7	4.2		
1958	1.8	2.8	1.2	2.1	2.4	4.5	2.7	3.7	4.6	5.3	4.5	4.6	−0.9	0
1959	1.7	.7	.6	0	−1.0	−1.7	3.9	3.1	4.9	4.5	3.8	4.4	4.7	1.9
1960	1.4	1.7	1.2	.9	3.1	1.0	2.5	3.4	3.7	4.3	3.2	3.7	1.3	2.3
1961	.7	1.0	0	.6	−.7	1.3	2.1	1.7	3.5	3.6	3.1	2.7	−1.3	.4
1962	1.3	1.0	.9	.9	1.3	.7	1.6	2.0	2.9	3.5	2.2	2.6	2.2	.4
1963	1.6	1.3	1.5	.9	2.0	1.6	2.4	2.0	2.8	2.9	2.5	2.6	−.9	0
1964	1.0	1.3	.9	1.2	1.3	1.3	1.6	2.0	2.3	2.3	2.1	2.1	0	−.4
1965	1.9	1.6	1.4	1.1	3.5	2.2	2.7	2.3	3.6	3.2	2.8	2.4	1.8	1.8
1966	3.5	2.9	2.5	2.6	4.0	5.0	4.8	3.8	8.3	5.3	6.7	4.4	1.7	1.7
1967	3.0	3.1	2.5	1.9	1.2	.9	4.3	4.3	8.0	8.8	6.3	7.2	1.7	2.1
1968	4.7	4.2	4.0	3.5	4.4	3.5	5.8	5.2	7.1	7.3	6.2	6.0	1.7	1.7
1969	6.2	5.5	5.4	4.7	7.0	5.1	7.7	6.9	7.3	8.2	6.2	6.7	2.9	2.5
1970	5.6	5.7	3.9	4.5	2.3	5.7	8.1	8.0	8.1	7.0	7.4	6.6	4.8	2.8
1971	3.3	4.4	2.8	3.6	4.3	3.1	4.1	5.7	5.4	7.4	4.6	6.2	3.1	3.9
1972	3.4	3.2	3.4	3.0	4.6	4.2	3.4	3.8	3.7	3.5	3.3	3.3	2.6	2.6
1973	8.7	6.2	10.4	7.4	20.3	14.5	6.2	4.4	6.0	4.5	5.3	4.0	17.0	8.1
1974	12.3	11.0	12.8	11.9	12.0	14.3	11.4	9.2	13.2	10.4	12.6	9.3	21.6	29.6
1975	6.9	9.1	6.2	8.8	6.6	8.5	8.2	9.6	10.3	12.6	9.8	12.0	11.4	10.5
1976	4.9	5.8	3.3	4.3	.5	3.0	7.2	8.3	10.8	10.1	10.0	9.5	7.1	7.1
1977	6.7	6.5	6.1	5.8	8.1	6.3	8.0	7.7	9.0	9.9	8.9	9.6	7.2	9.5
1978	9.0	7.6	8.8	7.2	11.8	9.9	9.3	8.6	9.3	8.5	8.8	8.4	7.9	6.3
1979	13.3	11.3	13.0	11.3	10.2	11.0	13.6	11.0	10.5	9.8	10.1	9.2	37.5	25.1
1980	12.5	13.5	11.0	12.3	10.2	8.6	14.2	15.4	10.1	11.3	9.9	11.0	18.0	30.9
1981	8.9	10.3	6.0	8.4	4.3	7.8	13.0	13.1	12.6	10.7	12.5	10.7	11.9	13.6
1982	3.8	6.2	3.6	4.1	3.1	4.1	4.3	9.0	11.2	11.8	11.0	11.6	1.3	1.5
1983	3.8	3.2	2.9	2.9	2.7	2.1	4.8	3.5	6.2	8.7	6.4	8.8	−.5	.7
1984	3.9	4.3	2.7	3.4	3.8	3.8	5.4	5.2	5.8	6.0	6.1	6.2	.2	1.0
1985	3.8	3.6	2.5	2.1	2.6	2.3	5.1	5.1	6.8	6.1	6.8	6.3	1.8	.7
1986	1.1	1.9	−2.0	−.9	3.8	3.2	4.5	5.0	7.9	7.7	7.7	7.5	−19.7	−13.2
1987	4.4	3.6	4.6	3.2	3.5	4.1	4.3	4.2	5.6	6.6	5.8	6.6	8.2	.5
1988	4.4	4.1	3.8	3.5	5.2	4.1	4.8	4.6	6.9	6.4	6.9	6.5	.5	.8
1989	4.6	4.8	4.1	4.7	5.6	5.8	5.1	4.9	8.6	7.7	8.5	7.7	5.1	5.6
1990	6.1	5.4	6.6	5.2	5.3	5.8	5.7	5.5	9.9	9.3	9.6	9.0	18.1	8.3
1991	3.1	4.2	1.2	3.1	1.9	2.9	4.6	5.1	8.0	8.9	7.9	8.7	−7.4	.4
1992	2.9	3.0	2.0	2.0	1.5	1.2	3.6	3.9	7.0	7.6	6.6	7.4	2.0	.5
1993	2.7	3.0	1.5	1.9	2.9	2.2	3.8	3.9	5.7	6.5	5.4	5.9	−1.4	1.2

[1] Changes from December to December are based on unadjusted indexes.
[2] Commodities and services.
[3] Household fuels—gas (piped), electricity, fuel oil, etc.—and motor fuel. Motor oil, coolant, etc. also included through 1982.

Note.—See Note, Table B–59.

Source: Department of Labor, Bureau of Labor Statistics.

TABLE B-64.—*Producer price indexes by stage of processing, 1947-93*

[1982 = 100]

Year or month	Total finished goods	Consumer foods			Finished goods excluding consumer foods					Total finished consumer goods
		Total	Crude	Processed	Total	Consumer goods			Capital equipment	
						Total	Durable	Non-durable		
1947	26.4	31.9	39.3	31.1	....	27.4	32.9	24.2	19.8	28.6
1948	28.5	34.9	42.4	34.0	....	29.2	35.2	25.7	21.6	30.8
1949	27.7	32.1	40.1	31.1	....	28.6	36.1	24.7	22.7	29.4
1950	28.2	32.7	36.5	32.4	....	29.0	36.5	25.1	23.2	29.9
1951	30.8	36.7	41.9	36.2	....	31.1	38.9	27.0	25.5	32.7
1952	30.6	36.4	44.6	35.4	....	30.7	39.2	26.3	25.9	32.3
1953	30.3	34.5	41.6	33.6	....	31.0	39.5	26.6	26.3	31.7
1954	30.4	34.2	37.5	34.0	....	31.1	39.8	26.7	26.7	31.7
1955	30.5	33.4	39.1	32.7	....	31.3	40.2	26.8	27.4	31.5
1956	31.3	33.3	39.1	32.7	....	32.1	41.6	27.3	29.5	32.0
1957	32.5	34.4	38.5	34.1	....	32.9	42.8	27.9	31.3	32.9
1958	33.2	36.5	41.0	36.1	....	32.9	43.4	27.8	32.1	33.6
1959	33.1	34.8	37.3	34.7	....	33.3	43.9	28.2	32.7	33.3
1960	33.4	35.5	39.8	35.2	....	33.5	43.8	28.4	32.8	33.6
1961	33.4	35.4	38.0	35.3	....	33.4	43.6	28.4	32.9	33.6
1962	33.5	35.7	38.4	35.6	....	33.4	43.4	28.4	33.0	33.7
1963	33.4	35.3	37.8	35.2	....	33.4	43.1	28.5	33.1	33.5
1964	33.5	35.4	38.9	35.2	....	33.3	43.3	28.4	33.4	33.6
1965	34.1	36.8	39.0	36.8	....	33.6	43.2	28.8	33.8	34.2
1966	35.2	39.2	41.5	39.2	....	34.1	43.4	29.3	34.6	35.4
1967	35.6	38.5	39.6	38.8	35.0	34.7	44.1	30.0	35.8	35.6
1968	36.6	40.0	42.5	40.0	35.9	35.5	45.1	30.6	37.0	36.5
1969	38.0	42.4	45.9	42.3	36.9	36.3	45.9	31.5	38.3	37.9
1970	39.3	43.8	46.0	43.9	38.2	37.4	47.2	32.5	40.1	39.1
1971	40.5	44.5	45.8	44.7	39.6	38.7	48.9	33.5	41.7	40.2
1972	41.8	46.9	48.0	47.2	40.4	39.4	50.0	34.1	42.8	41.5
1973	45.6	56.5	63.6	55.8	42.0	41.2	50.9	36.1	44.2	46.0
1974	52.6	64.4	71.6	63.9	48.8	48.2	55.5	44.0	50.5	53.1
1975	58.2	69.8	71.7	70.3	54.7	53.2	61.0	48.9	58.2	58.2
1976	60.8	69.6	76.7	69.0	58.1	56.5	63.7	52.4	62.1	60.4
1977	64.7	73.3	79.5	72.7	62.2	60.6	67.4	56.8	66.1	64.3
1978	69.8	79.9	85.8	79.4	66.7	64.9	73.6	60.0	71.3	69.4
1979	77.6	87.3	92.3	86.8	74.6	73.5	80.8	69.3	77.5	77.5
1980	88.0	92.4	93.9	92.3	86.7	87.1	91.0	85.1	85.8	88.6
1981	96.1	97.8	104.4	97.2	95.6	96.1	96.4	95.8	94.6	96.6
1982	100.0	100.0	100.0	100.0	100.0	100.0	100.0	100.0	100.0	100.0
1983	101.6	101.0	102.4	100.9	101.8	101.2	102.8	100.5	102.8	101.3
1984	103.7	105.4	111.4	104.9	103.2	102.2	104.5	101.1	105.2	103.3
1985	104.7	104.6	102.9	104.8	104.6	103.3	106.5	101.7	107.5	103.8
1986	103.2	107.3	105.6	107.4	101.9	98.5	108.9	93.3	109.7	101.4
1987	105.4	109.5	107.1	109.6	104.0	100.7	111.5	94.9	111.7	103.6
1988	108.0	112.6	109.8	112.7	106.5	103.1	113.8	97.3	114.3	106.2
1989	113.6	118.7	119.6	118.6	111.8	108.9	117.6	103.8	118.8	112.1
1990	119.2	124.4	123.0	124.4	117.4	115.3	120.4	111.5	122.9	118.2
1991	121.7	124.1	119.3	124.4	120.9	118.7	123.9	115.0	126.7	120.5
1992	123.2	123.3	107.6	124.4	123.1	120.8	125.7	117.3	129.1	121.7
1993	124.7	125.7	114.3	126.5	124.4	121.7	128.1	117.6	131.4	123.0
1992: Jan	121.8	122.5	109.7	123.4	121.5	118.8	125.8	114.4	128.6	120.0
Feb	122.1	123.4	118.7	123.7	121.6	118.8	125.5	114.6	128.7	120.3
Mar	122.2	123.3	115.8	123.8	121.8	119.0	125.8	114.8	128.9	120.4
Apr	122.4	122.8	105.2	124.0	122.3	119.6	125.6	115.7	129.1	120.7
May	123.2	123.1	98.6	124.8	123.1	120.9	125.6	117.5	129.0	121.7
June	123.9	123.1	96.3	125.1	124.0	122.1	125.2	119.5	128.9	122.6
July	123.7	122.8	97.3	124.7	123.8	122.0	125.4	119.2	128.8	122.4
Aug	123.6	123.4	104.5	124.8	123.5	121.5	125.1	118.6	128.9	122.2
Sept	123.3	123.3	104.6	124.7	123.2	121.4	123.4	119.3	128.1	122.2
Oct	124.4	123.8	113.0	124.6	124.5	122.3	127.1	118.9	130.2	122.9
Nov	124.0	123.4	110.4	124.3	124.1	121.7	127.1	118.1	130.2	122.4
Dec	123.8	124.2	117.4	124.7	123.6	121.1	126.9	117.2	130.2	122.2
1993: Jan	124.2	124.3	114.8	125.0	124.0	121.4	127.2	117.6	130.8	122.5
Feb	124.5	124.6	114.5	125.2	124.4	121.8	127.6	117.9	131.1	122.8
Mar	124.7	124.8	113.8	125.6	124.6	122.1	127.6	118.4	131.2	123.1
Apr	125.5	126.5	126.5	126.5	125.1	122.7	127.9	119.1	131.2	124.0
May	125.8	126.9	125.2	127.0	125.4	123.3	127.8	119.9	131.2	124.5
June	125.5	125.4	102.3	127.1	125.5	123.4	127.7	120.1	131.0	124.1
July	125.3	125.0	100.7	126.8	125.3	123.0	127.9	119.5	131.3	123.8
Aug [1]	124.2	125.4	107.4	126.7	123.8	120.9	127.9	116.6	131.2	122.4
Sept	123.9	125.5	107.9	126.9	123.3	120.6	126.4	116.8	133.3	122.2
Oct	124.7	125.5	105.6	126.9	124.3	121.2	129.2	116.5	132.4	122.6
Nov	124.4	126.7	123.0	127.0	123.7	120.3	129.7	114.9	132.5	122.3
Dec	124.1	127.2	129.7	126.9	123.1	119.4	129.7	113.6	132.7	121.8

[1] Data have been revised through August 1993 to reflect the availability of late reports and corrections by respondents. All data are subject to revision 4 months after original publication.

See next page for continuation of table.

TABLE B-64.—*Producer price indexes by stage of processing, 1947-93*—Continued

[1982=100]

Year or month	Intermediate materials, supplies, and components							Crude materials for further processing				
	Total	Foods and feeds[2]	Other	Materials and components		Processed fuels and lubricants	Containers	Supplies	Total	Foodstuffs and feedstuffs	Other		
				For manufacturing	For construction						Total	Fuel	Other
1947	23.3	....	22.2	24.9	22.5	14.4	23.4	28.5	31.7	45.1	....	7.5	24.0
1948	25.2	....	24.1	26.8	24.9	16.4	24.4	29.8	34.7	48.8	....	8.9	26.7
1949	24.2	....	23.5	25.7	24.9	14.9	24.5	28.0	30.1	40.5	....	8.8	24.3
1950	25.3	....	24.6	26.9	26.2	15.2	25.2	29.0	32.7	43.4	....	8.8	27.8
1951	28.4	....	27.6	30.5	28.7	15.9	29.6	32.6	37.6	50.2	....	9.0	32.0
1952	27.5	....	26.7	29.3	28.5	15.7	28.0	32.6	34.5	47.3	....	9.0	27.8
1953	27.7	....	27.0	29.7	29.0	15.8	28.0	31.0	31.9	42.3	....	9.3	26.6
1954	27.9	....	27.2	29.8	29.1	15.8	28.5	31.7	31.6	42.3	....	8.9	26.1
1955	28.4	....	28.0	30.5	30.3	15.8	28.9	31.2	30.4	38.4	....	8.9	27.5
1956	29.6	....	29.3	32.0	31.8	16.3	31.0	32.0	30.6	37.6	....	9.5	28.6
1957	30.3	....	30.1	32.7	32.0	17.2	32.4	32.3	31.2	39.2	....	10.1	28.2
1958	30.4	....	30.1	32.8	32.0	16.2	33.2	33.1	31.9	41.6	....	10.2	27.1
1959	30.8	....	30.5	33.3	32.9	16.2	33.0	33.5	31.1	38.8	....	10.4	28.1
1960	30.8	....	30.7	33.3	32.7	16.6	33.4	33.3	30.4	38.4	....	10.5	26.9
1961	30.6	....	30.3	32.9	32.2	16.8	33.2	33.7	30.2	37.9	....	10.5	27.2
1962	30.6	....	30.2	32.7	32.1	16.7	33.6	34.5	30.5	38.6	....	10.4	27.1
1963	30.7	....	30.1	32.7	32.2	16.6	33.2	35.0	29.9	37.5	....	10.5	26.7
1964	30.8	....	30.3	33.1	32.5	16.2	32.9	34.7	29.6	36.6	....	10.5	27.2
1965	31.2	....	30.7	33.6	32.8	16.5	33.5	35.0	31.1	39.2	....	10.6	27.7
1966	32.0	....	31.3	34.3	33.6	16.8	34.5	36.5	33.1	42.7	....	10.9	28.3
1967	32.2	41.8	31.7	34.5	34.0	16.9	35.0	36.8	31.3	40.3	21.1	11.3	26.5
1968	33.0	41.5	32.5	35.3	35.7	16.5	35.9	37.1	31.8	40.9	21.6	11.5	27.1
1969	34.1	42.9	33.6	36.5	37.7	16.6	37.2	37.8	33.9	44.1	22.5	12.0	28.4
1970	35.4	45.6	34.8	38.0	38.3	17.7	39.0	39.7	35.2	45.2	23.8	13.8	29.1
1971	36.8	46.7	36.2	38.9	40.8	19.5	40.8	40.8	36.0	46.1	24.7	15.7	29.4
1972	38.2	49.5	37.7	40.4	43.0	20.1	42.7	42.5	39.9	51.5	27.0	16.8	32.3
1973	42.4	70.3	40.6	44.1	46.5	22.2	45.2	51.7	54.5	72.6	34.3	18.6	42.9
1974	52.5	83.6	50.5	56.0	55.0	33.6	53.3	56.8	61.4	76.4	44.1	24.8	54.5
1975	58.0	81.6	56.6	61.7	60.1	39.4	60.0	61.8	61.6	77.4	43.7	30.6	50.0
1976	60.9	77.4	60.0	64.0	64.1	42.3	63.1	65.8	63.4	76.8	48.2	34.5	54.9
1977	64.9	79.6	64.1	67.4	69.3	47.7	65.9	69.3	65.5	77.5	51.7	42.0	56.3
1978	69.5	84.8	68.6	72.0	76.5	49.9	71.0	72.9	73.4	87.3	57.5	48.2	61.9
1979	78.4	94.5	77.4	80.9	84.2	61.6	79.4	80.2	85.9	100.0	69.6	57.3	75.5
1980	90.3	105.5	89.4	91.7	91.3	85.0	89.1	89.9	95.3	104.6	84.6	69.4	91.8
1981	98.6	104.6	98.2	98.7	97.9	100.6	96.7	96.9	103.0	103.9	101.8	84.8	109.8
1982	100.0	100.0	100.0	100.0	100.0	100.0	100.0	100.0	100.0	100.0	100.0	100.0	100.0
1983	100.6	103.6	100.5	101.2	102.8	95.4	100.4	101.8	101.3	101.8	100.7	105.1	98.8
1984	103.1	105.7	103.0	104.1	105.6	95.7	105.9	104.1	103.5	104.7	102.2	105.1	101.0
1985	102.7	97.3	103.0	103.3	107.3	92.8	109.0	104.4	95.8	94.8	96.9	102.7	94.3
1986	99.1	96.2	99.3	102.2	108.1	72.7	110.3	105.6	87.7	93.2	81.6	92.2	76.0
1987	101.5	99.2	101.7	105.3	109.8	73.3	114.5	107.7	93.7	96.2	87.9	84.1	88.5
1988	107.1	109.5	106.9	113.2	116.1	71.2	120.1	113.7	96.0	106.1	85.5	82.1	85.9
1989	112.0	113.8	111.9	118.1	121.3	76.4	125.4	118.1	103.1	111.2	93.4	85.3	95.8
1990	114.5	113.3	114.5	118.7	122.9	85.9	127.7	119.4	108.9	113.1	101.5	84.8	107.3
1991	114.4	111.1	114.6	118.1	124.5	85.3	128.1	121.4	101.2	105.5	94.6	82.9	97.5
1992	114.7	110.7	114.9	117.9	126.5	84.5	127.7	122.7	100.4	105.1	93.5	84.0	94.2
1993	116.2	112.7	116.4	118.9	132.0	84.7	126.4	125.0	102.4	108.3	94.7	87.0	94.1
1992: Jan	113.2	110.7	113.3	117.2	124.9	80.2	127.6	122.0	96.9	103.7	88.8	83.5	87.2
Feb	113.5	110.7	113.6	117.4	125.9	80.6	127.7	122.1	98.6	106.0	90.1	82.6	89.7
Mar	113.6	110.7	113.7	117.5	126.6	80.0	127.7	122.4	97.9	107.2	88.2	79.1	88.8
Apr	113.8	110.4	114.0	117.6	126.8	80.7	127.8	122.4	98.8	105.5	90.7	78.5	93.0
May	114.5	111.5	114.7	117.9	126.8	83.6	127.7	122.7	101.2	108.4	92.8	79.8	95.3
June	115.4	112.3	115.6	118.2	126.5	88.1	127.6	122.7	102.1	107.4	94.8	78.5	99.1
July	115.5	111.2	115.7	118.3	126.3	88.2	127.7	122.7	101.7	105.0	95.7	83.7	97.6
Aug	115.5	110.3	115.8	118.3	126.4	88.0	127.6	122.7	100.6	103.7	94.8	82.8	96.8
Sept	115.8	111.0	116.1	118.4	126.8	89.0	127.7	123.0	102.4	102.9	98.0	88.3	98.6
Oct	115.4	109.7	115.7	118.1	126.7	87.2	127.8	123.2	101.9	103.7	96.8	85.8	98.1
Nov	115.0	109.6	115.2	118.0	126.9	85.0	127.8	123.3	101.8	102.8	97.2	94.1	94.0
Dec	114.8	110.7	115.1	118.0	127.8	83.5	127.7	123.6	100.9	104.6	94.6	90.7	92.0
1993: Jan	115.2	110.9	115.4	118.4	129.1	83.2	126.7	124.2	101.4	105.6	94.8	90.6	92.4
Feb	115.6	109.8	115.9	118.7	130.9	83.3	126.8	124.3	101.4	106.0	94.6	83.4	96.1
Mar	116.0	109.9	116.3	118.8	132.5	83.8	126.7	124.3	102.6	108.3	95.0	81.4	97.9
Apr	116.3	111.2	116.6	119.1	132.8	84.3	126.5	124.8	103.9	110.4	95.8	82.4	98.5
May	116.2	111.8	116.5	118.9	132.0	85.2	126.5	124.7	106.5	112.2	98.8	89.4	99.1
June	116.7	111.1	117.0	118.8	131.3	88.1	126.5	124.7	104.2	107.2	98.3	94.9	95.3
July	116.6	114.0	116.7	118.9	131.1	87.1	126.4	125.2	101.5	107.5	93.9	85.5	93.8
Aug [1]	116.6	114.3	116.7	119.0	131.6	86.3	126.1	125.5	100.6	108.0	92.1	84.4	91.7
Sept	116.8	113.9	117.0	119.0	132.4	87.1	126.0	125.4	101.0	107.5	92.9	88.1	90.9
Oct	116.6	113.8	116.8	119.0	132.7	85.7	126.1	125.5	102.2	105.6	96.1	89.8	94.7
Nov	116.2	115.0	116.3	119.1	133.4	82.8	126.1	125.7	102.5	109.5	94.1	89.5	91.9
Dec	115.9	117.0	115.8	119.2	134.1	79.5	126.5	126.1	100.4	111.5	89.5	85.2	87.4

[2] Intermediate materials for food manufacturing and feeds.

Source: Department of Labor, Bureau of Labor Statistics.

342

TABLE B-65.—*Producer price indexes by stage of processing, special groups, 1974–93*

[1982=100]

Year or month	Finished goods			Excluding foods and energy			Intermediate materials, supplies, and components				Crude materials for further processing			
	Total	Foods	Energy	Total	Capital equipment	Consumer goods excluding foods and energy	Total	Foods and feeds[1]	Energy	Other	Total	Foodstuffs and feedstuffs	Energy	Other
1974	52.6	64.4	26.2	53.6	50.5	55.5	52.5	83.6	33.1	54.0	61.4	76.4	27.8	83.3
1975	58.2	69.8	30.7	59.7	58.2	60.6	58.0	81.6	38.7	60.2	61.6	77.4	33.3	69.3
1976	60.8	69.6	34.3	63.1	62.1	63.7	60.9	77.4	41.5	63.8	63.4	76.8	35.3	80.2
1977	64.7	73.3	39.7	66.9	66.1	67.3	64.9	79.6	46.8	67.6	65.5	77.5	40.4	79.8
1978	69.8	79.9	42.3	71.9	71.3	72.2	69.5	84.8	49.1	72.5	73.4	87.3	45.2	87.8
1979	77.6	87.3	57.1	78.3	77.5	78.8	78.4	94.5	61.1	80.7	85.9	100.0	54.9	106.2
1980	88.0	92.4	85.2	87.1	85.8	87.8	90.3	105.5	84.9	90.3	95.3	104.6	73.1	113.1
1981	96.1	97.8	101.5	94.6	94.6	94.6	98.6	104.6	100.5	97.7	103.0	103.9	97.7	111.7
1982	100.0	100.0	100.0	100.0	100.0	100.0	100.0	100.0	100.0	100.0	100.0	100.0	100.0	100.0
1983	101.6	101.0	95.2	103.0	102.8	103.1	100.6	103.6	95.3	101.6	101.3	101.8	98.7	105.3
1984	103.7	105.4	91.2	105.5	105.2	105.7	103.1	105.7	95.5	104.7	103.5	104.7	98.0	111.7
1985	104.7	104.6	87.6	108.1	107.5	108.4	102.7	97.3	92.6	105.2	95.8	94.8	93.3	104.9
1986	103.2	107.3	63.0	110.6	109.7	111.1	99.1	96.2	72.6	104.9	87.7	93.2	71.8	103.1
1987	105.4	109.5	61.8	113.3	111.7	114.2	101.5	99.2	73.0	107.8	93.7	96.2	75.0	115.7
1988	108.0	112.6	59.8	117.0	114.3	118.5	107.1	109.5	70.9	115.2	96.0	106.1	67.7	133.0
1989	113.6	118.7	65.7	122.1	118.8	124.0	112.0	113.8	76.1	120.2	103.1	111.2	75.9	137.9
1990	119.2	124.4	75.0	126.6	122.9	128.8	114.5	113.3	85.5	120.9	108.9	113.1	85.9	136.3
1991	121.7	124.1	78.1	131.1	126.7	133.7	114.4	111.1	85.1	121.4	101.2	105.5	80.4	128.2
1992	123.2	123.3	77.8	134.2	129.1	137.3	114.7	110.7	84.3	122.0	100.4	105.1	78.8	128.4
1993	124.7	125.7	78.0	135.8	131.4	138.5	116.2	112.7	84.6	123.8	102.4	108.3	76.7	140.1
1992: Jan	121.8	122.5	74.3	133.4	128.6	136.4	113.2	110.7	80.1	121.1	96.9	103.7	74.4	123.0
Feb	122.1	123.4	74.3	133.5	128.7	136.4	113.5	110.7	80.4	121.4	98.6	106.0	75.5	125.2
Mar	122.2	123.3	74.4	133.7	128.9	136.6	113.6	110.7	79.9	121.6	97.9	107.2	72.2	128.1
Apr	122.4	122.8	75.4	134.0	129.1	137.0	113.8	110.4	80.6	121.8	98.8	105.5	75.0	129.1
May	123.2	123.1	77.8	134.2	129.0	137.5	114.5	111.5	83.4	121.9	101.2	108.4	77.4	129.7
June	123.9	123.1	81.0	134.1	128.9	137.3	115.4	112.3	87.8	122.0	102.1	107.4	80.1	129.2
July	123.7	122.8	80.4	134.2	128.8	137.5	115.5	111.2	88.0	122.1	101.7	105.0	81.0	130.0
Aug	123.6	123.4	80.2	133.8	128.9	136.8	115.5	110.3	87.8	122.2	100.6	103.7	79.7	130.8
Sept	123.3	123.3	80.8	133.2	128.1	136.4	115.8	111.0	88.7	122.4	102.4	102.9	83.8	130.4
Oct	124.4	123.8	80.0	135.2	130.2	138.2	115.4	109.7	87.0	122.3	101.9	103.7	82.9	128.2
Nov	124.0	123.4	78.4	135.2	130.2	138.3	115.0	109.6	84.9	122.3	101.8	102.8	83.8	127.1
Dec	123.8	124.2	76.4	135.4	130.2	138.6	114.8	110.7	83.4	122.4	100.9	104.6	79.8	129.7
1993: Jan	124.2	124.3	76.6	135.9	130.8	139.0	115.2	110.7	83.1	122.9	101.4	106.6	78.6	134.3
Feb	124.5	124.5	76.9	136.2	131.1	139.4	115.6	109.8	83.2	123.5	101.4	106.0	77.5	137.4
Mar	124.7	124.8	77.5	136.3	131.2	139.5	116.0	109.9	83.7	123.9	102.6	108.3	77.7	138.2
Apr	125.5	126.5	78.3	136.7	131.2	140.0	116.3	111.2	84.2	124.1	103.9	110.4	78.0	140.7
May	125.8	126.9	79.6	136.6	131.2	140.0	116.2	111.8	85.1	123.8	106.5	112.2	81.3	142.2
June	125.5	125.4	80.5	136.3	131.0	139.5	116.7	111.1	87.9	123.7	104.2	107.2	80.9	141.7
July	125.3	125.0	79.6	136.4	131.3	139.5	116.6	114.0	87.0	123.6	101.5	107.5	75.0	142.6
Aug[2]	124.2	125.4	79.1	134.6	131.2	136.7	116.6	114.3	86.1	123.8	100.6	108.0	73.6	139.8
Sept	123.9	125.6	79.5	133.8	130.3	136.0	116.8	113.9	86.9	124.0	101.0	107.5	74.9	138.9
Oct	124.7	125.5	78.9	135.4	132.4	137.3	116.6	113.8	85.6	124.0	102.2	105.6	78.6	139.6
Nov	124.4	126.7	76.2	135.6	132.5	137.5	116.2	115.0	82.7	124.1	102.5	109.5	75.6	141.4
Dec	124.1	127.2	73.5	135.9	132.7	137.8	115.9	117.0	79.4	124.4	100.4	111.5	68.9	144.8

[1] Intermediate materials for food manufacturing and feeds.
[2] Data have been revised through August 1993 to reflect the availability of late reports and corrections by respondents. All data are subject to revision 4 months after original publication.

Source: Department of Labor, Bureau of Labor Statistics.

TABLE B-66.—*Producer price indexes for major commodity groups, 1950–93*

[1982=100]

Year or month	Farm products and processed foods and feeds			Industrial commodities				
	Total	Farm products	Processed foods and feeds	Total	Textile products and apparel	Hides, skins, leather, and related products	Fuels and related products and power [1]	Chemicals and allied products [1]
1950	37.7	44.0	33.2	25.0	50.2	32.9	12.6	30.4
1951	43.0	51.2	36.9	27.6	56.0	37.7	13.0	34.8
1952	41.3	48.4	36.4	26.9	50.5	30.5	13.0	33.0
1953	38.6	43.8	34.8	27.2	49.3	31.0	13.4	33.4
1954	38.5	43.2	35.4	27.2	48.2	29.5	13.2	33.8
1955	36.6	40.5	33.8	27.8	48.2	29.4	13.2	33.7
1956	36.4	40.0	33.8	29.1	48.2	31.2	13.6	33.9
1957	37.7	41.1	34.8	29.9	48.3	31.2	14.3	34.6
1958	39.4	42.9	36.5	30.0	47.4	31.6	13.7	34.9
1959	37.6	40.2	35.6	30.5	48.1	35.9	13.7	34.8
1960	37.7	40.1	35.6	30.5	48.6	34.6	13.9	34.8
1961	37.7	39.7	36.2	30.4	47.8	34.9	14.0	34.5
1962	38.1	40.4	36.5	30.4	48.2	35.3	14.0	33.9
1963	37.7	39.6	36.8	30.3	48.2	34.3	13.9	33.5
1964	37.5	39.0	36.7	30.5	48.5	34.4	13.5	33.6
1965	39.0	40.7	38.0	30.9	48.8	35.9	13.8	33.9
1966	41.6	43.7	40.2	31.5	48.9	39.4	14.1	34.0
1967	40.2	41.3	39.8	32.0	48.9	38.1	14.4	34.2
1968	41.1	42.3	40.6	32.8	50.7	39.3	14.3	34.1
1969	43.4	45.0	42.7	33.9	51.8	41.5	14.6	34.2
1970	44.9	45.8	44.6	35.2	52.4	42.0	15.3	35.0
1971	45.8	46.6	45.5	36.5	53.3	43.4	16.6	35.6
1972	49.2	51.6	48.0	37.8	55.5	50.0	17.1	35.6
1973	63.9	72.7	58.9	40.3	60.5	54.5	19.4	37.6
1974	71.3	77.4	68.0	49.2	68.0	55.2	30.1	50.2
1975	74.0	77.0	72.6	54.9	67.4	56.5	35.4	62.0
1976	73.6	78.8	70.8	58.4	72.4	63.9	38.3	64.0
1977	75.9	79.4	74.0	62.5	75.3	68.3	43.6	65.9
1978	83.0	87.7	80.6	67.0	78.1	76.1	46.5	68.0
1979	92.3	99.6	88.5	75.7	82.5	96.1	58.9	76.0
1980	98.3	102.9	95.9	88.0	89.7	94.7	82.8	89.0
1981	101.1	105.2	98.9	97.4	97.6	99.3	100.2	98.4
1982	100.0	100.0	100.0	100.0	100.0	100.0	100.0	100.0
1983	102.0	102.4	101.8	101.1	100.3	103.2	95.9	100.3
1984	105.5	105.5	105.4	103.3	102.7	109.0	94.8	102.9
1985	100.7	95.1	103.5	103.7	102.9	108.9	91.4	103.7
1986	101.2	92.9	105.4	100.0	103.2	113.0	69.8	102.6
1987	103.7	95.5	107.9	102.6	105.1	120.4	70.2	106.4
1988	110.0	104.9	112.7	106.3	109.2	131.4	66.7	116.3
1989	115.4	110.9	117.8	111.6	112.3	136.3	72.9	123.0
1990	118.6	112.2	121.9	115.8	115.0	141.7	82.3	123.6
1991	116.4	105.7	121.9	116.5	116.3	138.9	81.2	125.6
1992	115.9	103.6	122.1	117.4	117.8	140.4	80.4	125.9
1993	118.4	107.0	124.0	119.0	118.1	143.6	80.0	128.2
1992: Jan	115.2	102.8	121.3	115.7	117.4	138.6	76.3	124.6
Feb	116.3	105.5	121.7	116.0	117.6	139.0	76.8	124.5
Mar	116.7	106.4	121.8	115.9	117.7	139.8	75.8	124.4
Apr	115.8	103.2	122.0	116.4	117.8	139.9	77.1	124.8
May	117.0	105.8	122.5	117.3	117.7	140.7	79.7	125.2
June	116.9	104.7	123.0	118.2	117.9	140.8	83.2	126.0
July	115.8	102.5	122.4	118.3	117.8	140.1	83.3	126.4
Aug	115.4	102.2	122.1	118.1	117.8	140.8	82.8	126.7
Sept	115.3	101.6	122.1	118.5	118.0	140.9	84.4	127.0
Oct	115.4	102.7	121.8	118.6	118.1	141.0	82.2	127.1
Nov	115.0	101.8	121.6	118.3	118.0	140.6	82.1	127.5
Dec	116.2	103.7	122.4	117.9	118.0	142.0	79.7	127.0
1993: Jan	116.6	104.3	122.7	118.3	118.0	143.6	79.4	127.6
Feb	116.6	104.4	122.7	118.7	117.9	142.5	79.2	128.1
Mar	117.5	106.4	122.9	119.0	117.9	142.9	79.7	127.8
Apr	119.1	109.7	123.7	119.4	118.1	143.6	80.3	128.6
May	119.8	111.0	124.2	119.7	118.0	143.8	81.9	128.2
June	117.5	104.3	124.0	119.9	118.0	143.7	83.2	128.5
July	118.0	105.4	124.3	119.4	118.2	143.5	81.0	128.2
Aug [2]	118.4	106.6	124.3	118.8	118.3	143.9	80.2	128.3
Sept	118.3	106.1	124.3	118.8	118.2	144.1	80.9	128.2
Oct	117.8	104.1	124.6	119.4	118.2	143.7	81.2	128.3
Nov	119.8	109.3	125.0	118.8	118.1	143.9	78.3	128.5
Dec	121.2	112.4	125.5	117.9	117.8	144.3	74.4	128.0

[1] Prices for some items in this grouping are lagged and refer to 1 month earlier than the index month.
[2] Data have been revised through August 1993 to reflect the availability of late reports and corrections by respondents. All data are subject to revision 4 months after original publication.

See next page for continuation of table.

TABLE B-66.—*Producer price indexes for major commodity groups, 1950-93*—Continued

[1982=100]

Year or month	Industrial commodities—Continued									
	Rubber and plastic products	Lumber and wood products	Pulp, paper, and allied products	Metals and metal products	Machinery and equipment	Furniture and household durables	Non-metallic mineral products	Transportation equipment		Miscellaneous products
								Total	Motor vehicles and equipment	
1950	35.6	31.4	25.7	22.0	22.6	40.9	23.5	....	30.0	28.6
1951	43.7	34.1	30.5	24.5	25.3	44.4	25.0	....	31.6	30.3
1952	39.6	33.2	29.7	24.5	25.3	43.5	25.0	....	33.4	30.2
1953	36.9	33.1	29.6	25.3	25.9	44.4	26.0	....	33.3	31.0
1954	37.5	32.5	29.6	25.5	26.3	44.9	26.6	....	33.4	31.3
1955	42.4	34.1	30.4	27.2	27.2	45.1	27.3	....	34.3	31.3
1956	43.0	34.6	32.4	29.6	29.3	46.3	28.5	....	36.3	31.7
1957	42.8	32.8	33.0	30.2	31.4	47.5	29.6	....	37.9	32.6
1958	42.8	32.5	33.4	30.0	32.1	47.9	29.9	....	39.0	33.3
1959	42.6	34.7	33.7	30.6	32.8	48.0	30.3	....	39.9	33.4
1960	42.7	33.5	34.0	30.6	33.0	47.8	30.4	....	39.3	33.6
1961	41.1	32.0	33.0	30.5	33.0	47.5	30.5	....	39.2	33.7
1962	39.9	32.2	33.4	30.2	33.0	47.2	30.5	....	39.2	33.9
1963	40.1	32.8	33.1	30.3	33.1	46.9	30.3	....	38.9	34.2
1964	39.6	33.5	33.0	31.1	33.3	47.1	30.4	....	39.1	34.4
1965	39.7	33.7	33.3	32.0	33.7	46.8	30.4	....	39.2	34.7
1966	40.5	35.2	34.2	32.8	34.7	47.4	30.7	....	39.2	35.3
1967	41.4	35.1	34.6	33.2	35.9	48.3	31.2	....	39.8	36.2
1968	42.8	39.8	35.0	34.0	37.0	49.7	32.4	40.4	40.9	37.0
1969	43.6	44.0	36.0	36.0	38.2	50.7	33.6	40.4	41.7	38.1
1970	44.9	39.9	37.5	38.7	40.0	51.9	35.3	41.9	43.3	39.8
1971	45.2	44.7	38.1	39.4	41.4	53.1	38.2	44.2	45.7	40.8
1972	45.3	50.7	39.3	40.9	42.3	53.8	39.4	45.5	47.0	41.5
1973	46.6	62.2	42.3	44.0	43.7	55.7	40.7	46.1	47.4	43.3
1974	56.4	64.5	52.5	57.0	50.0	61.8	47.8	50.3	51.4	48.1
1975	62.2	62.1	59.0	61.5	57.9	67.5	54.4	56.7	57.6	53.4
1976	66.0	72.2	62.1	65.0	61.3	70.3	58.2	60.5	61.2	55.6
1977	69.4	83.0	64.6	69.3	65.2	73.2	62.6	64.6	65.2	59.4
1978	72.4	96.9	67.7	75.3	70.3	77.5	69.6	69.5	70.0	66.7
1979	80.5	105.5	75.9	86.0	76.7	82.8	77.6	75.3	75.8	75.5
1980	90.1	101.5	86.3	95.0	86.0	90.7	88.4	82.9	83.1	93.6
1981	96.4	102.8	94.8	99.6	94.4	95.9	96.7	94.3	94.6	96.1
1982	100.0	100.0	100.0	100.0	100.0	100.0	100.0	100.0	100.0	100.0
1983	100.8	107.9	103.3	101.8	102.7	103.4	101.6	102.8	102.2	104.8
1984	102.3	108.0	110.3	104.8	105.1	105.7	105.4	105.2	104.1	107.0
1985	101.9	106.6	113.3	104.4	107.2	107.1	108.6	107.9	106.4	109.4
1986	101.9	107.2	116.1	103.2	108.8	108.2	110.0	110.5	109.1	111.6
1987	103.0	112.8	121.8	107.1	110.4	109.9	110.0	112.5	111.7	114.9
1988	109.3	118.9	130.4	118.7	113.2	113.1	111.2	114.3	113.1	120.2
1989	112.6	126.7	137.8	124.1	117.4	116.9	112.6	117.7	116.2	126.5
1990	113.6	129.7	141.2	122.9	120.7	119.2	114.7	121.5	118.2	134.2
1991	115.1	132.1	142.9	120.2	123.0	121.2	117.2	126.4	122.1	140.8
1992	115.1	146.6	145.2	119.2	123.4	122.2	117.3	130.4	124.9	145.3
1993	116.0	174.0	147.3	119.2	124.0	123.6	120.0	133.7	128.0	145.5
1992: Jan	114.7	137.6	144.1	118.2	123.3	121.8	117.2	129.8	124.8	143.9
Feb	114.3	142.9	144.2	118.9	123.5	121.8	117.1	129.7	124.6	143.9
Mar	114.3	145.7	144.4	119.4	123.6	121.9	117.3	130.0	124.9	144.0
Apr	114.6	147.5	144.9	119.6	123.4	122.0	116.9	130.2	124.8	144.8
May	114.9	147.6	145.2	119.5	123.4	122.1	116.9	130.2	124.7	146.4
June	115.0	146.3	145.1	119.6	123.2	122.2	117.0	130.1	124.3	146.2
July	115.2	145.3	145.2	120.0	123.1	122.2	117.1	130.2	124.4	146.3
Aug	115.3	145.4	145.4	120.2	123.2	122.2	117.4	130.0	123.9	143.8
Sept	115.5	148.7	145.8	119.6	123.2	122.4	117.4	128.5	121.3	145.3
Oct	115.7	148.7	146.1	118.8	123.3	122.3	117.4	132.3	127.1	145.5
Nov	115.8	149.5	145.9	118.2	123.4	122.6	117.7	132.2	127.1	145.8
Dec	115.7	154.4	145.9	118.5	123.5	122.6	117.8	132.1	126.9	147.3
1993: Jan	115.7	160.2	147.0	118.9	123.9	122.6	118.4	132.7	127.1	148.6
Feb	115.7	169.3	147.1	119.2	123.9	122.9	118.6	133.1	127.8	149.4
Mar	115.6	176.9	147.3	119.0	123.9	123.0	118.9	133.3	127.8	149.4
Apr	116.0	181.2	147.7	118.7	124.0	123.2	119.6	133.4	127.7	150.4
May	115.8	179.8	147.7	118.4	123.9	123.4	119.7	133.3	127.6	150.7
June	115.9	174.1	147.1	118.9	124.0	123.6	120.0	133.3	127.7	149.6
July	115.9	171.7	147.1	119.5	124.0	123.8	120.2	133.6	127.8	149.6
Aug [2]	116.0	171.1	147.1	119.5	124.0	124.0	120.5	133.5	127.7	138.9
Sept	116.5	173.0	147.2	119.5	124.1	124.0	120.7	131.6	125.0	139.3
Oct	116.5	173.1	147.4	119.4	124.1	124.2	121.3	135.3	129.7	139.2
Nov	116.4	177.0	147.4	119.5	124.1	124.4	121.4	135.3	129.9	139.5
Dec	116.5	180.9	147.6	120.2	124.2	124.5	121.3	135.5	130.0	141.0

Source: Department of Labor, Bureau of Labor Statistics.

TABLE B-67.—Changes in producer price indexes for finished goods, 1955–93

[Percent change]

Year or month	Total finished goods Dec. to Dec.[1]	Total finished goods Year to year	Finished consumer foods Dec. to Dec.[1]	Finished consumer foods Year to year	Finished goods excluding consumer foods – Total Dec. to Dec.[1]	Total Year to year	Consumer goods Dec. to Dec.[1]	Consumer goods Year to year	Capital equipment Dec. to Dec.[1]	Capital equipment Year to year	Finished energy goods Dec. to Dec.[1]	Finished energy goods Year to year	Finished goods excluding foods and energy Dec. to Dec.[1]	Finished goods excluding foods and energy Year to year
1955	1.0	0.3	-3.0	-2.3			1.6	0.6	5.6	2.6				
1956	4.2	2.6	3.7	-.3			2.5	2.6	8.1	7.7				
1957	3.4	3.8	5.1	3.3			1.5	2.5	4.6	6.1				
1958	.3	2.2	.6	6.1			.3	0	1.2	2.6				
1959	-.3	-.3	-3.7	-4.7			.9	1.2	.9	1.9				
1960	1.8	.9	5.3	2.0			.3	.6	.3	.3				
1961	-.6	0	-1.9	-.3			-.3	-.3	0	.3				
1962	.3	.3	.6	.8			0	0	.3	.3				
1963	-.3	-.3	-1.4	-1.1			0	0	.6	.3				
1964	.6	.3	.6	.3			.3	-.3	.9	.9				
1965	3.3	1.8	9.1	4.0			.9	.9	1.5	1.2				
1966	2.0	3.2	1.3	6.5			1.8	1.5	3.8	2.4				
1967	1.7	1.1	-.3	-1.8			2.0	1.8	3.1	3.5				
1968	3.1	2.8	4.6	3.9	2.5	2.6	2.0	2.3	3.0	3.4				
1969	4.9	3.8	8.1	6.0	3.3	2.8	2.8	2.3	4.8	3.5				
1970	2.1	3.4	-2.3	3.3	4.3	3.5	3.8	3.0	4.8	4.7				
1971	3.3	3.1	5.8	1.6	2.0	3.7	2.1	3.5	2.4	4.0				
1972	3.9	3.2	7.9	5.4	2.3	2.0	2.1	1.8	2.1	2.6				
1973	11.7	9.1	22.7	20.5	6.6	4.0	7.5	4.6	5.1	3.3				
1974	18.3	15.4	12.8	14.0	21.1	16.2	20.3	17.0	22.7	14.3			17.7	11.4
1975	6.6	10.6	5.6	8.4	7.2	12.1	6.8	10.4	8.1	15.2	16.3	17.2	6.0	11.4
1976	3.8	4.5	-2.5	-.3	6.2	6.2	6.0	6.2	6.5	6.7	11.6	11.7	5.7	5.7
1977	6.7	6.4	6.9	5.3	6.8	7.1	6.7	7.3	7.2	6.4	12.0	15.7	6.2	6.0
1978	9.3	7.9	11.7	9.0	8.3	7.2	8.5	7.1	8.0	7.9	8.5	6.5	8.4	7.5
1979	12.8	11.2	7.4	9.3	14.8	11.8	17.6	13.3	8.8	8.7	58.1	35.0	9.4	8.9
1980	11.8	13.4	7.5	5.8	13.4	16.2	14.1	18.5	11.4	10.7	27.9	49.2	10.8	11.2
1981	7.1	9.2	1.5	5.8	8.7	10.3	8.6	10.3	9.2	10.3	14.1	19.1	7.7	8.6
1982	3.6	4.1	2.0	2.2	4.2	4.6	4.2	4.1	3.9	5.7	-.1	-1.5	4.9	5.7
1983	.6	1.6	2.3	1.0	0	1.8	-.9	1.2	2.0	2.8	-9.2	-4.8	1.9	3.0
1984	1.7	2.1	3.5	4.4	1.1	1.4	.8	1.0	1.8	2.3	-4.2	-4.2	2.0	2.4
1985	1.8	1.0	.6	-.8	2.2	1.4	2.1	1.1	2.7	2.2	-.2	-3.9	2.7	2.5
1986	-2.3	-1.4	2.8	2.6	-4.0	-2.6	-6.6	-4.6	2.1	2.0	-38.1	-28.1	2.7	2.3
1987	2.2	2.1	-.2	2.1	3.2	2.1	4.1	2.2	1.3	1.8	11.2	-1.9	2.1	2.4
1988	4.0	2.5	5.7	2.8	3.2	2.4	3.1	2.4	3.6	2.3	-3.6	-3.2	4.3	3.3
1989	4.9	5.2	5.2	5.4	4.8	5.0	5.3	5.6	3.8	3.9	9.5	9.9	4.2	4.4
1990	5.7	4.9	2.6	4.8	6.9	5.0	8.7	5.9	3.4	3.5	30.7	14.2	3.5	3.7
1991	-.1	2.1	-1.5	-.2	.3	3.0	-.7	2.9	2.5	3.1	-9.6	4.1	3.1	3.6
1992	1.6	1.2	1.6	-.6	1.6	1.8	1.6	1.8	1.7	1.9	-.3	-.4	2.0	2.4
1993	.2	1.2	2.4	1.9	-.4	1.1	-1.4	.7	1.9	1.8	-3.8	.2	.4	1.2

Percent change from preceding month

	Unadjusted	Seasonally adjusted	Unadjusted	Seasonally adjusted	Unadjusted	Seasonally adjusted	Unadjusted	Seasonally adjusted	Unadjusted	Seasonally adjusted	Unadjusted	Seasonally adjusted	Unadjusted	Seasonally adjusted
1992: Jan	-0.1	0	0.2	-0.4	-0.2	0.1	-0.3	-0.1	0.5	0.5	-3.0	-2.0	0.5	0.5
Feb	.2	.2	.7	.4	.1	.2	0	.3	.1	.1	0	1.3	.1	.1
Mar	.1	.2	-.1	-.1	.2	.3	.2	.3	.2	.3	.1	.4	.1	.3
Apr	.2	.2	-.4	-.3	.4	.3	.5	.4	.2	.2	1.3	.7	.2	.3
May	.7	.3	.2	-.1	.7	.4	1.1	.6	-.1	.1	3.2	.8	.1	.4
June	.6	.2	0	.2	.7	.3	1.0	.4	-.1	-.1	4.1	2.4	-.1	-.2
July	-.2	0	-.2	-.1	-.2	.1	-.1	-.1	-.1	.1	-.7	-.4	.1	.1
Aug	-.1	.1	.5	.7	-.2	-.1	-.4	-.3	-.1	.2	-.2	-.6	-.3	0
Sept	-.2	.2	-.1	.4	-.2	.2	-.1	.2	-.6	0	.7	.1	-.4	.1
Oct	.9	.1	.4	.1	1.1	.1	.7	.2	1.6	-.2	-1.0	1.0	1.5	-.1
Nov	-.3	-.2	-.3	-.6	-.3	-.1	-.5	-.2	0	.2	-2.0	-1.3	0	.2
Dec	-.2	0	.6	1.3	-.4	-.3	-.5	-.6	0	.2	-2.6	-2.4	.1	.1
1993: Jan	.3	.3	.1	-.6	.3	.6	.2	.6	.5	.5	.3	1.0	.4	.4
Feb	.2	.4	.2	0	.3	.5	.3	.6	.2	.3	.4	1.7	.2	.2
Mar	.2	.3	.2	.2	.3	.3	.2	.5	.1	.2	.8	1.1	.1	.2
Apr	.6	.6	1.4	1.4	.4	.4	.5	.4	0	.2	1.0	.3	.1	.4
May	.2	0	.3	0	.2	0	.5	0	0	.1	1.7	-.5	-.1	.1
June	-.2	-.6	-1.2	-1.0	.1	-.4	.1	-.6	-.2	-.2	1.1	-.5	-.2	-.4
July	-.2	0	-.3	-.2	-.2	0	-.3	-.1	.2	.4	-1.1	-.9	.1	.2
Aug[2]	-.9	-.6	.3	.5	-1.2	-1.0	-1.7	-1.5	-.1	.2	-.6	-1.0	-1.3	-1.0
Sept	-.2	.2	.2	.7	-.4	.1	-.2	.1	-.7	0	.5	.1	-.6	.1
Oct	.6	-.2	-.1	-.5	.8	-.2	.5	-.1	1.6	-.4	-.8	1.3	1.2	-.5
Nov	-.2	0	1.0	.8	-.5	-.7	-.7	-.4	.1	.2	-3.4	-2.7	.1	.4
Dec	-.2	-.1	.4	1.1	-.5	-.4	-.7	-.7	.2	.3	-3.5	-3.5	.2	.2

[1] Changes from December to December are based on unadjusted indexes.
[2] Data have been revised through August 1993 to reflect the availability of late reports and corrections by respondents. All data are subject to revision 4 months after original publication.

Source: Department of Labor, Bureau of Labor Statistics.

MONEY STOCK, CREDIT, AND FINANCE

TABLE B-68.—*Money stock, liquid assets, and debt measures, 1959-93*

[Averages of daily figures; billions of dollars, seasonally adjusted]

Year and month	M1 Sum of currency, demand deposits, travelers checks, and other checkable deposits (OCDs)	M2 M1 plus overnight RPs and Eurodollars, MMMF balances (general purpose and broker/dealer), MMDAs, and savings and small time deposits	M3 M2 plus large time deposits, term RPs, term Eurodollars, and institution-only MMMF balances	L M3 plus other liquid assets	Debt [1] Debt of domestic nonfinancial sectors (monthly average)	M1	M2	M3	Debt
December:									
1959	140.0	297.8	299.8	388.6	687.2	....	4.9	5.2	7.5
1960	140.7	312.3	315.3	403.6	723.6	0.5	4.9	5.2	5.3
1961	145.2	335.5	341.0	430.8	766.5	3.2	7.4	8.2	5.9
1962	147.8	362.7	371.4	466.1	819.4	1.8	8.1	8.9	6.9
1963	153.3	393.2	406.0	503.8	874.5	3.7	8.4	9.3	6.7
1964	160.3	424.8	442.5	540.4	938.1	4.6	8.0	9.0	7.3
1965	167.9	459.3	482.2	584.4	1,005.1	4.7	8.1	9.0	7.1
1966	172.0	480.0	505.1	614.7	1,072.3	2.4	4.5	4.7	6.7
1967	183.3	524.3	557.1	666.5	1,146.6	6.6	9.2	10.3	6.9
1968	197.4	566.3	606.2	728.9	1,238.1	7.7	8.0	8.8	8.0
1969	203.9	589.5	615.0	763.5	1,329.3	3.3	4.1	1.5	7.4
1970	214.4	628.0	677.3	816.2	1,419.6	5.1	6.5	10.1	6.8
1971	228.3	712.6	776.1	902.9	1,552.0	6.5	13.5	14.6	9.3
1972	249.2	805.1	886.0	1,022.9	1,707.5	9.2	13.0	14.2	10.0
1973	262.8	860.9	984.9	1,142.5	1,894.1	5.5	6.9	11.2	10.9
1974	274.3	908.4	1,070.3	1,250.2	2,067.0	4.4	5.5	8.7	9.1
1975	287.5	1,023.1	1,172.1	1,366.9	2,251.4	4.8	12.6	9.5	8.9
1976	306.3	1,163.5	1,311.6	1,516.4	2,496.3	6.5	13.7	11.9	10.9
1977	331.1	1,286.4	1,472.3	1,705.0	2,813.7	8.1	10.6	12.3	12.7
1978	358.2	1,388.5	1,646.2	1,910.3	3,192.2	8.2	7.9	11.8	13.5
1979	382.5	1,496.4	1,802.6	2,115.6	3,568.2	6.8	7.8	9.5	11.8
1980	408.5	1,629.2	1,986.8	2,323.5	3,896.8	6.8	8.9	10.2	9.2
1981	436.3	1,792.6	2,233.4	2,596.0	4,278.7	6.8	10.0	12.4	9.8
1982	474.4	1,952.7	2,440.6	2,850.3	4,691.6	8.7	8.9	9.3	9.7
1983	521.2	2,186.5	2,693.1	3,154.4	5,257.5	9.9	12.0	10.3	12.1
1984	552.4	2,376.0	2,988.2	3,529.5	6,006.1	6.0	8.7	11.0	14.2
1985	620.1	2,572.4	3,203.6	3,830.9	6,901.1	12.3	8.3	7.2	14.9
1986	724.5	2,816.1	3,491.7	4,131.9	7,778.6	16.8	9.5	9.0	12.7
1987	750.0	2,917.2	3,674.8	4,333.5	8,543.3	3.5	3.6	5.2	9.8
1988	787.1	3,078.2	3,915.4	4,669.4	9,306.1	4.9	5.5	6.5	8.9
1989	794.6	3,233.3	4,056.1	4,886.1	10,030.7	1.0	5.0	3.6	7.8
1990	827.2	3,345.5	4,116.7	4,966.6	10,670.1	4.1	3.5	1.5	6.4
1991	899.3	3,445.8	4,168.1	4,982.3	11,145.5	8.7	3.0	1.2	4.5
1992	1,026.6	3,494.8	4,163.4	5,040.4	11,721.1	14.2	1.4	−.1	5.2
1993	1,131.2	3,551.7	4,207.7	....	....	10.2	1.6	1.1	....
1992: Jan	911.5	3,451.0	4,172.2	4,978.3	11,189.9	11.5	2.1	.6	4.2
Feb	926.2	3,467.7	4,189.0	4,999.1	11,235.0	13.4	3.0	1.6	4.2
Mar	935.1	3,467.8	4,184.8	5,010.0	11,284.9	14.4	2.9	1.7	4.5
Apr	941.2	3,464.8	4,177.9	5,009.0	11,335.6	14.0	2.5	1.1	4.5
May	952.2	3,467.8	4,180.1	5,011.4	11,381.7	13.7	1.9	.8	4.8
June	952.5	3,464.2	4,172.5	5,017.2	11,434.8	11.8	1.1	.2	5.2
July	963.2	3,465.4	4,171.2	5,014.7	11,494.1	11.3	.8	−.0	5.4
Aug	975.5	3,473.6	4,180.6	5,027.8	11,553.4	10.6	.3	−.4	5.7
Sept	990.1	3,481.0	4,184.5	5,038.9	11,597.8	11.8	.8	−.0	5.5
Oct	1,006.0	3,491.5	4,180.6	5,041.3	11,625.7	13.8	1.5	.1	5.1
Nov	1,019.1	3,496.2	4,176.6	5,049.0	11,665.6	14.1	1.6	−.2	5.0
Dec	1,026.6	3,494.8	4,163.4	5,040.4	11,721.1	15.6	1.8	−.4	5.0
1993: Jan	1,033.2	3,485.7	4,138.1	5,015.8	11,757.8	14.5	1.2	−1.6	4.6
Feb	1,033.0	3,474.1	4,131.8	5,011.8	11,781.6	11.8	.0	−2.3	4.0
Mar	1,035.2	3,471.6	4,127.2	5,011.0	11,821.3	9.1	−.5	−2.7	3.9
Apr	1,043.0	3,473.8	4,137.7	5,027.0	11,867.4	7.4	−1.0	−2.1	4.2
May	1,066.9	3,503.0	4,165.4	5,065.2	11,912.7	9.4	.4	−.5	4.2
June	1,073.3	3,509.6	4,164.1	5,066.7	11,976.1	9.1	.8	.0	4.4
July	1,085.3	3,515.7	4,162.2	5,064.1	12,033.4	10.1	1.7	1.2	4.7
Aug	1,094.4	3,518.9	4,164.3	5,075.5	12,088.3	11.9	2.6	1.6	5.2
Sept	1,106.8	3,531.0	4,177.7	5,066.2	12,141.9	13.8	3.4	2.4	5.4
Oct	1,116.4	3,533.2	4,184.8	5,076.5	12,179.2	14.1	3.4	2.3	5.3
Nov	1,125.9	3,545.0	4,197.8	5,093.4	12,241.8	11.1	2.4	1.6	5.5
Dec	1,131.2	3,551.7	4,207.7	....	....	10.8	2.4	2.1	....

[1] Consists of outstanding credit market debt of the U.S. Government, State and local governments, and private nonfinancial sectors; data derived from flow of funds accounts.
[2] Annual changes are from December to December; monthly changes are from 6 months earlier at a simple annual rate.

Note.—See Table B-69 for components.
Data do not reflect revisions of February 3, 1994.

Source: Board of Governors of the Federal Reserve System.

TABLE B-69.—*Components of money stock measures and liquid assets, 1959–93*

[Averages of daily figures; billions of dollars, seasonally adjusted, except as noted]

Year and month	Currency	Travelers checks	Demand deposits	Other checkable deposits (OCDs)	Overnight repurchase agreements (RPs) net, plus overnight Eurodollars [1] NSA	Money market mutual fund (MMMF) balances — General purpose and broker/dealer [2]	Money market mutual fund (MMMF) balances — Institution only [2]	Savings deposits, including money market deposit accounts (MMDAs) [3]
December:								
1959	28.8	0.3	110.8	0.0	0.0	0.0	0.0	146.5
1960	28.7	.3	111.6	.0	.0	.0	.0	159.1
1961	29.3	.4	115.5	.0	.0	.0	.0	175.5
1962	30.3	.4	117.1	.0	.0	.0	.0	194.7
1963	32.2	.4	120.6	.1	.0	.0	.0	214.4
1964	33.9	.5	125.8	.1	.0	.0	.0	235.3
1965	36.0	.5	131.3	.1	.0	.0	.0	256.9
1966	38.0	.6	133.4	.1	.0	.0	.0	253.2
1967	40.0	.6	142.5	.1	.0	.0	.0	263.7
1968	43.0	.7	153.6	.1	.0	.0	.0	268.9
1969	45.7	.8	157.3	.2	2.2	.0	.0	263.6
1970	48.6	.9	164.7	.1	1.3	.0	.0	260.9
1971	52.0	1.0	175.1	.2	2.3	.0	.0	292.2
1972	56.2	1.2	191.6	.2	2.8	.0	.0	321.4
1973	60.8	1.4	200.3	.3	5.3	.0	.0	326.8
1974	67.0	1.7	205.1	.4	5.7	1.7	.2	338.4
1975	72.8	2.1	211.6	.9	5.9	2.7	.4	388.8
1976	79.5	2.6	221.5	2.7	10.7	2.4	.6	453.0
1977	87.4	2.9	236.7	4.2	14.9	2.4	.9	492.1
1978	96.0	3.3	250.4	8.4	20.7	6.4	3.1	481.7
1979	104.8	3.6	257.4	16.8	21.7	33.4	9.5	423.6
1980	115.4	3.9	261.2	28.0	28.8	61.6	15.2	400.1
1981	122.6	4.1	231.2	78.4	36.6	150.6	38.0	343.9
1982	132.5	4.1	234.0	103.8	39.9	185.6	50.0	400.0
1983	146.2	4.7	238.5	131.9	55.6	139.1	41.9	685.0
1984	156.1	5.0	244.0	147.3	60.6	168.0	63.2	704.7
1985	167.9	5.6	266.9	179.7	73.5	177.2	65.5	815.1
1986	180.8	6.1	302.3	235.3	82.3	209.0	86.1	940.9
1987	196.9	6.6	287.1	259.3	84.1	222.6	92.7	937.6
1988	212.3	7.0	287.1	280.7	83.2	242.9	92.0	926.6
1989	222.7	6.9	279.8	285.3	77.6	317.4	108.8	891.0
1990	246.7	7.8	278.2	294.5	74.7	350.5	135.9	920.8
1991	267.2	7.8	290.5	333.8	76.3	363.9	182.1	1,042.5
1992	292.3	8.1	340.8	385.2	74.7	342.3	202.3	1,186.0
1993	321.5	8.0	386.1	415.7	84.7	336.4	198.8	1,218.6
1992: Jan	269.0	7.7	296.3	338.6	77.9	360.3	186.1	1,060.3
Feb	270.8	7.7	303.3	344.3	77.9	362.3	192.0	1,080.7
Mar	271.9	7.7	308.0	347.5	74.7	358.0	192.2	1,094.3
Apr	273.6	7.7	310.8	349.0	72.8	354.5	195.9	1,107.5
May	275.1	7.7	314.6	354.7	69.8	354.9	202.2	1,119.6
June	276.6	7.7	312.3	355.9	74.6	353.5	206.3	1,126.0
July	279.5	7.7	317.5	358.6	75.2	350.4	212.5	1,134.5
Aug	282.4	7.8	322.5	362.8	78.7	348.9	220.9	1,145.7
Sept	286.3	8.1	329.0	366.7	76.2	343.9	220.7	1,158.9
Oct	288.0	8.3	336.0	373.7	77.1	346.3	210.9	1,170.5
Nov	289.8	8.2	339.5	381.6	75.8	343.7	209.2	1,180.4
Dec	292.3	8.1	340.8	385.2	74.7	342.3	202.3	1,186.0
1993: Jan	294.8	8.0	341.9	388.6	73.3	340.0	197.7	1,184.4
Feb	296.9	8.0	341.8	386.4	74.0	333.2	201.9	1,182.4
Mar	299.0	8.0	341.9	386.3	74.5	332.7	200.9	1,178.8
Apr	301.4	8.1	347.3	386.2	72.8	331.7	200.4	1,181.6
May	304.0	8.2	359.2	395.5	70.0	335.5	202.8	1,193.7
June	306.8	8.0	360.7	397.8	73.6	334.3	198.1	1,198.8
July	309.6	7.9	365.9	401.9	77.2	333.2	195.0	1,200.1
Aug	312.6	7.8	370.9	403.1	78.3	331.5	193.3	1,205.1
Sept	316.4	7.8	376.6	406.0	81.9	329.4	194.1	1,208.7
Oct	318.2	7.9	380.2	410.1	84.3	330.0	196.6	1,209.6
Nov	320.0	8.0	385.5	412.5	84.8	333.5	196.7	1,214.5
Dec	321.5	8.0	386.1	415.7	84.7	336.4	198.8	1,218.6

[1] Includes continuing contract RPs.
[2] Data prior to 1983 are not seasonally adjusted.
[3] Data prior to 1982 are savings deposits only; MMDA data begin December 1982.

See next page for continuation of table.

TABLE B-69.—*Components of money stock measures and liquid assets, 1959–93*—Continued

[Averages of daily figures; billions of dollars, seasonally adjusted, except as noted]

Year and month	Small denomination time deposits [4]	Large denomination time deposits [4]	Term repurchase agreements (RPs) NSA	Term Eurodollars NSA	Savings bonds	Short-term Treasury securities	Bankers acceptances	Commercial paper
December:								
1959	11.4	1.2	0.0	0.7	46.1	38.6	0.6	3.6
1960	12.5	2.0	.0	.8	45.7	36.7	.9	5.1
1961	14.8	3.9	.0	1.5	46.5	37.0	1.1	5.2
1962	20.1	7.0	.0	1.6	46.9	39.8	1.1	6.8
1963	25.6	10.8	.0	1.9	48.1	40.7	1.2	7.7
1964	29.2	15.2	.0	2.4	49.0	38.5	1.3	9.1
1965	34.5	21.2	.0	1.8	49.6	40.7	1.6	10.2
1966	55.0	23.1	.0	2.2	50.2	43.2	1.8	14.4
1967	77.8	30.9	.0	2.2	51.2	38.7	1.8	17.8
1968	100.6	37.4	.0	2.9	51.8	46.1	2.3	22.5
1969	120.4	20.4	2.7	2.7	51.7	59.5	3.3	34.0
1970	151.1	45.2	1.6	2.2	52.0	48.8	3.5	34.5
1971	189.7	57.7	2.7	2.7	54.3	36.0	3.8	32.7
1972	231.6	73.4	3.5	3.6	57.6	40.7	3.5	35.2
1973	265.8	111.1	6.7	5.5	60.4	49.3	5.0	42.8
1974	287.9	144.8	7.8	8.1	63.3	52.8	12.6	51.2
1975	337.9	129.7	8.1	9.8	67.2	68.4	10.7	48.5
1976	390.8	118.1	13.9	14.8	71.8	69.8	10.8	52.5
1977	445.5	145.2	18.9	20.2	76.4	78.1	14.1	64.1
1978	521.0	195.7	26.2	31.8	80.3	81.1	22.0	80.7
1979	634.4	223.3	29.1	44.7	79.6	107.8	27.2	98.4
1980	728.7	260.5	33.5	50.3	72.3	133.5	32.1	98.8
1981	823.2	303.1	35.3	67.5	67.8	149.4	40.0	105.3
1982	851.0	327.2	33.4	81.7	68.0	183.6	44.5	113.7
1983	784.1	327.6	49.9	91.5	71.1	211.9	45.0	133.2
1984	888.9	416.5	57.6	82.9	74.2	260.9	45.4	160.8
1985	885.5	434.1	62.4	76.5	79.5	298.2	42.0	207.6
1986	858.9	431.3	80.6	83.8	91.8	280.0	37.0	231.4
1987	922.8	475.4	106.0	91.0	100.6	253.1	44.3	260.7
1988	1,038.3	525.4	121.8	105.7	109.4	269.2	39.9	335.5
1989	1,152.7	548.8	99.0	79.5	117.6	324.9	40.2	347.3
1990	1,172.3	489.6	89.6	68.7	126.1	331.1	35.5	357.1
1991	1,064.7	424.7	72.5	57.6	138.0	315.0	23.4	337.7
1992	867.3	356.1	81.1	45.6	156.8	331.4	20.4	368.4
1993	783.5	331.5	95.3	47.8	....	....	....	....
1992: Jan	1,043.0	418.9	71.0	55.7	139.0	311.9	22.9	332.3
Feb	1,021.5	413.6	72.6	56.1	140.2	320.0	22.6	327.3
Mar	1,004.0	407.4	74.3	58.0	141.3	325.1	22.2	336.7
Apr	986.1	402.2	74.1	54.9	142.4	326.0	21.8	341.0
May	969.6	396.0	76.4	52.8	143.5	329.4	22.0	336.4
June	955.7	389.4	76.4	51.9	144.6	330.1	22.0	348.1
July	941.0	382.7	75.2	51.1	145.8	324.9	21.7	351.2
Aug	925.7	378.5	76.0	51.4	147.4	322.9	21.1	355.7
Sept	911.0	374.3	77.8	49.4	149.3	321.0	20.7	363.4
Oct	894.4	367.3	79.9	48.1	151.9	320.2	20.5	368.0
Nov	879.3	360.8	81.8	47.2	154.7	325.1	20.3	372.4
Dec	867.3	356.1	81.1	45.6	156.8	331.4	20.4	368.4
1993: Jan	858.3	348.8	80.1	43.5	158.9	337.5	20.6	360.7
Feb	853.1	344.3	82.3	46.7	161.1	342.9	20.1	355.9
Mar	848.1	338.4	86.0	49.8	162.7	341.6	19.2	360.3
Apr	841.2	343.5	88.9	48.7	163.9	340.7	19.2	365.5
May	834.4	343.4	89.8	48.7	164.8	347.1	19.4	368.4
June	826.9	340.0	92.8	45.5	165.7	349.1	18.7	369.1
July	817.8	335.6	96.5	41.9	166.8	348.5	17.5	369.1
Aug	810.3	336.1	96.5	44.1	167.8	345.7	16.4	381.3
Sept	803.7	334.8	96.4	45.2	168.8	323.8	16.3	379.6
Oct	796.1	335.6	95.1	45.4	169.8	317.6	16.3	388.0
Nov	788.8	333.0	94.5	50.0	170.9	322.3	16.2	386.2
Dec	783.5	331.5	95.3	47.8	....	....	....	....

[4] Small denomination and large denomination deposits are those issued in amounts of less than $100,000 and more than $100,000, respectively.

Note.—NSA indicates data are not seasonally adjusted.
See also Table B-68.
Data do not reflect revisions of February 3, 1994.
Source: Board of Governors of the Federal Reserve System.

TABLE B-70.—*Aggregate reserves of depository institutions and monetary base, 1959–93*

[Averages of daily figures [1]; millions of dollars; seasonally adjusted, except as noted]

| Year and month | Adjusted for changes in reserve requirements [2] ||||| Borrowings of depository institutions from the Federal Reserve, NSA |||
| | Reserves of depository institutions |||| Monetary base | Total | Seasonal | Extended credit |
	Total	Nonborrowed	Nonborrowed plus extended credit	Required				
December:								
1959	11,109	10,168	10,168	10,603	40,880	941		
1960	11,247	11,172	11,172	10,503	40,977	74		
1961	11,499	11,366	11,366	10,915	41,853	133		
1962	11,604	11,344	11,344	11,033	42,957	260		
1963	11,730	11,397	11,397	11,239	45,003	332		
1964	12,011	11,747	11,747	11,605	47,161	264		
1965	12,316	11,872	11,872	11,892	49,620	444		
1966	12,223	11,690	11,690	11,884	51,565	532		
1967	13,180	12,952	12,952	12,805	54,579	228		
1968	13,767	13,021	13,021	13,341	58,357	746		
1969	14,168	13,049	13,049	13,882	61,569	1,119		
1970	14,558	14,225	14,225	14,309	65,013	332		
1971	15,230	15,104	15,104	15,049	69,108	126		
1972	16,645	15,595	15,595	16,361	75,167	1,050		
1973	17,021	15,723	15,723	16,717	81,073	1,298	41	
1974	17,550	16,823	16,970	17,292	87,535	727	32	147
1975	17,822	17,692	17,704	17,556	93,887	130	14	12
1976	18,388	18,335	18,335	18,115	101,515	53	13	
1977	18,990	18,420	18,420	18,800	110,323	569	55	
1978	19,753	18,885	18,885	19,521	120,445	868	135	
1979	20,720	19,248	19,248	20,279	131,143	1,473	82	
1980	22,015	20,325	20,328	21,501	142,004	1,690	116	3
1981	22,443	21,807	21,956	22,124	149,021	636	54	148
1982	23,600	22,966	23,152	23,100	160,127	634	33	186
1983	25,367	24,593	24,595	24,806	175,467	774	96	2
1984	26,845	23,659	26,263	25,990	187,237	3,186	113	2,604
1985	31,448	30,129	30,628	30,411	203,585	1,318	56	499
1986	38,943	38,116	38,419	37,573	223,667	827	38	303
1987	38,862	38,085	38,568	37,816	239,872	777	93	483
1988	40,398	38,683	39,927	39,351	256,922	1,716	130	1,244
1989	40,492	40,227	40,247	39,570	267,734	265	84	20
1990	41,767	41,441	41,464	40,102	293,185	326	76	23
1991	45,533	45,341	45,342	44,555	317,169	192	38	1
1992	54,351	54,228	54,228	53,196	350,798	124	18	1
1993	60,536	60,454	60,454	59,474	386,072	82	31	0
1992: Jan	46,227	45,994	45,995	45,224	319,385	233	17	1
Feb	47,795	47,717	47,719	46,730	322,849	77	22	2
Mar	48,509	48,418	48,420	47,481	324,655	91	32	2
Apr	48,992	48,902	48,904	47,855	326,691	90	47	2
May	49,496	49,341	49,341	48,495	328,863	155	98	0
June	49,316	49,087	49,087	48,403	330,228	229	149	0
July	49,629	49,345	49,345	48,664	333,177	284	203	0
Aug	50,341	50,091	50,091	49,407	336,844	251	223	0
Sept	51,274	50,987	50,987	50,280	341,585	287	193	0
Oct	52,836	52,693	52,693	51,763	344,849	143	114	0
Nov	53,815	53,711	53,711	52,772	347,832	104	40	0
Dec	54,351	54,228	54,228	53,196	350,798	124	18	1
1993: Jan	54,665	54,500	54,501	53,405	353,224	165	11	1
Feb	54,922	54,876	54,877	53,818	355,734	45	18	0
Mar	55,166	55,074	55,074	53,953	358,374	91	26	0
Apr	55,197	55,124	55,124	54,101	360,634	73	41	0
May	56,877	56,756	56,756	55,881	364,769	121	84	0
June	57,119	56,938	56,938	56,209	368,069	181	142	0
July	57,567	57,323	57,323	56,478	370,978	244	210	0
Aug	58,033	57,680	57,680	57,080	374,532	352	234	0
Sept	58,837	58,410	58,410	57,747	379,261	428	236	0
Oct	59,819	59,534	59,534	58,730	381,765	285	192	0
Nov	60,459	60,370	60,370	59,359	384,580	89	75	0
Dec	60,536	60,454	60,454	59,474	386,072	82	31	0

[1] Data are prorated averages of biweekly (maintenance period) averages of daily figures.
[2] Aggregate reserves incorporate adjustments for discontinuities associated with regulatory changes to reserve requirements. For details on aggregate reserves series see *Federal Reserve Bulletin*.

Note.—NSA indicates data are not seasonally adjusted.
Monetary base data do not reflect revisions released on February 3, 1994.
Source: Board of Governors of the Federal Reserve System.

TABLE B-71.—*Commercial bank loans and securities, 1972–93*

[Monthly average; billions of dollars, seasonally adjusted [1]]

Year and month	Total loans and securities [2]	U.S. Government securities	Other securities	Loans and leases										
				Total [2]	Commercial and industrial	Real estate	Individual	Security	Nonbank financial institutions	Agricultural	State and political subdivisions	Foreign banks	Foreign official institutions	Lease financing receivables	Other

Year and month	Total loans and securities [2]	U.S. Govt securities	Other securities	Total [2]	Commercial and industrial	Real estate	Individual	Security	Nonbank financial institutions	Agricultural	State and political subdivisions	Foreign banks	Foreign official institutions	Lease financing receivables	Other
December:															
1972	572.5	89.0	93.4	390.1	137.1	98.1	86.3	15.6	21.7	14.3		3.9	1.6	1.4	10.1
1973	647.8	88.2	99.4	460.2	165.0	117.3	98.6	12.9	28.5	17.2		6.2	2.1	2.1	10.2
1974	713.7	86.3	107.5	519.9	196.6	130.1	102.4	12.7	34.5	18.3		8.3	2.2	3.2	11.5
1975	745.1	116.7	111.2	517.2	189.3	134.4	104.9	13.5	28.9	20.1		9.0	2.4	4.0	10.7
1976	804.6	136.3	113.5	554.8	190.9	148.8	116.3	17.7	26.4	23.2		11.7	2.8	5.1	11.9
1977	891.5	136.6	122.7	632.3	211.0	175.2	138.3	21.0	25.8	25.8		13.7	2.7	5.7	13.0
1978	1,013.9	137.6	129.2	747.1	246.2	210.5	164.7	19.7	26.2	28.2		21.5	4.9	7.4	17.8
1979	1,135.6	144.3	141.9	849.4	291.4	241.9	184.5	18.7	29.3	31.1		18.6	6.9	9.3	17.8
1980	1,238.6	170.6	154.4	913.5	325.7	262.6	179.2	18.0	29.3	31.6		23.8	11.5	10.9	21.1
1981	1,307.0	179.3	160.5	967.3	355.4	284.1	182.5	21.4	29.9	33.1		18.1	7.2	12.7	22.9
1982	1,400.4	201.7	164.8	1,033.9	392.5	299.9	188.2	25.3	31.2	36.2		14.7	5.9	13.3	26.8
1983	1,552.2	259.2	169.1	1,123.9	414.2	331.0	212.9	28.0	30.4	39.2		13.4	9.4	13.7	31.8
1984	1,722.9	259.8	140.9	1,322.2	473.2	376.3	254.2	35.0	31.6	40.1	46.1	11.4	8.4	16.1	29.9
1985	1,910.4	270.8	179.0	1,460.6	500.2	425.8	295.0	43.3	32.8	36.1	56.8	9.7	6.3	19.1	35.5
1986	2,093.7	310.1	193.9	1,589.7	536.7	494.1	315.4	40.3	35.3	31.6	58.4	10.1	6.3	22.5	39.0
1987	2,241.2	335.8	195.8	1,709.6	566.4	587.2	328.2	34.5	32.1	29.4	52.5	7.7	5.1	24.7	41.7
1988	2,422.9	362.7	193.7	1,866.5	605.3	670.1	354.8	40.9	32.5	29.0	45.3	7.6	5.0	29.4	46.5
1989	2,590.8	397.0	182.4	2,011.4	638.4	760.1	375.2	41.3	34.4	30.1	40.0	8.2	3.5	31.9	48.1
1990	2,732.4	452.1	178.8	2,101.4	642.6	843.4	380.3	44.7	35.9	32.3	34.0	7.7	2.9	32.9	44.9
1991	2,836.9	559.3	179.9	2,097.8	617.0	871.8	363.9	54.3	41.4	34.2	29.0	7.3	2.4	31.7	44.7
1992	2,937.6	657.1	176.0	2,104.6	597.6	892.4	355.5	64.8	43.6	35.0	24.8	7.7	2.8	30.9	49.5
1993	3,087.2	727.2	181.9	2,178.2	584.2	927.2	385.6	86.0	43.2	35.4	21.6	7.7	3.3	32.8	51.1
1992:															
Jan	2,846.0	564.2	179.6	2,102.2	615.4	873.2	363.4	58.0	42.1	34.1	28.6	7.1	2.3	31.4	46.5
Feb	2,855.4	570.9	180.3	2,104.3	613.5	876.7	363.8	58.9	43.0	34.1	28.3	6.9	2.2	31.5	45.5
Mar	2,862.7	579.6	178.5	2,104.5	610.8	879.1	362.3	60.7	43.6	34.3	28.0	6.6	2.1	31.4	45.5
Apr	2,874.3	590.8	178.5	2,104.9	609.0	881.8	360.8	63.4	43.2	34.3	27.6	6.7	2.0	31.1	45.1
May	2,875.3	600.2	176.9	2,098.2	607.6	883.3	359.2	60.9	43.3	34.3	27.3	7.0	2.0	30.9	42.4
June	2,882.8	610.7	175.8	2,096.2	604.6	881.8	359.0	63.3	42.4	34.6	26.8	7.5	2.0	31.0	43.3
July	2,886.9	619.2	177.9	2,089.8	602.5	881.5	358.6	60.5	41.5	34.9	26.2	7.7	2.2	30.8	43.2
Aug	2,902.2	632.6	178.2	2,091.4	601.4	883.1	357.4	61.6	42.0	35.3	25.9	7.2	2.3	30.8	44.3
Sept	2,917.4	640.6	178.2	2,098.6	601.2	886.8	357.0	64.0	44.0	35.2	25.8	7.9	2.5	31.0	43.2
Oct	2,926.0	647.3	178.8	2,099.8	600.8	890.7	355.8	64.7	43.9	35.1	25.4	7.6	2.4	30.8	42.6
Nov	2,932.4	651.4	177.3	2,103.8	600.5	892.5	355.4	64.2	44.7	35.2	25.1	7.5	2.8	30.9	45.0
Dec	2,937.6	657.1	176.0	2,104.6	597.6	892.4	355.5	64.8	43.6	35.0	24.8	7.7	2.8	30.9	49.5
1993:															
Jan	2,935.3	656.5	174.5	2,104.4	598.0	890.8	358.4	63.5	45.1	34.5	24.2	7.7	2.9	30.4	48.8
Feb	2,943.9	666.2	176.4	2,101.3	596.7	890.1	361.9	62.8	44.6	34.3	23.8	8.8	3.2	30.6	44.5
Mar	2,960.2	680.2	179.0	2,101.0	593.1	891.9	362.3	64.2	44.2	34.0	23.6	8.5	3.2	30.6	45.3
Apr	2,970.9	691.0	181.0	2,098.9	587.5	892.2	364.4	62.3	45.0	34.1	23.1	8.4	3.2	30.7	48.0
May	2,991.2	693.5	181.2	2,116.5	589.9	898.0	367.5	68.6	45.9	34.3	23.0	8.4	3.1	30.9	46.8
June	3,014.1	704.3	179.6	2,130.3	590.9	904.0	368.8	71.4	46.0	34.3	22.8	8.6	3.2	31.3	49.0
July	3,037.4	708.2	181.5	2,147.8	590.2	907.7	372.5	81.6	46.5	34.7	22.8	9.0	3.2	31.6	47.9
Aug	3,046.6	714.8	182.4	2,149.4	589.6	910.8	374.7	79.9	46.8	34.8	22.7	9.5	3.1	31.7	46.0
Sept	3,057.2	720.6	182.6	2,153.9	586.2	914.6	376.0	82.7	46.1	34.8	22.4	8.7	3.4	31.8	47.3
Oct	3,056.6	718.4	180.7	2,157.5	585.7	918.1	380.3	79.5	44.9	35.0	22.2	8.9	3.5	32.1	47.3
Nov	3,072.6	720.0	180.9	2,171.7	585.4	921.8	383.2	87.0	44.2	35.5	21.8	8.1	3.3	32.5	49.1
Dec	3,087.2	727.2	181.9	2,178.2	584.2	927.2	385.6	86.0	43.2	35.4	21.6	7.7	3.3	32.8	51.1

[1] Data are prorated averages of Wednesday figures for domestically chartered banks and for foreign-related institutions beginning July 1981. Prior to July 1981, data for foreign-related institutions are averages of current and previous month-end data.
[2] Excludes loans to commercial banks in the United States.

Note.—Data are not strictly comparable because of breaks in the series.

Source: Board of Governors of the Federal Reserve System.

TABLE B-72.—*Bond yields and interest rates, 1929-93*

[Percent per annum]

Year and month	U.S. Treasury securities					Corporate bonds (Moody's)		High-grade municipal bonds (Standard & Poor's)	New-home mortgage yields [3]	Commercial paper, 6 months [4]	Prime rate charged by banks [5]	Discount rate, Federal Reserve Bank of New York [5]	Federal funds rate [6]
	Bills (new issues) [1]		Constant maturities [2]										
	3-month	6-month	3-year	10-year	30-year	Aaa	Baa						
1929						4.73	5.90	4.27		5.85	5.50-6.00	5.16	
1933	0.515					4.49	7.76	4.71		1.73	1.50-4.00	2.56	
1939	.023					3.01	4.96	2.76		.59	1.50	1.00	
1940	.014					2.84	4.75	2.50		.56	1.50	1.00	
1941	.103					2.77	4.33	2.10		.53	1.50	1.00	
1942	.326					2.83	4.28	2.36		.66	1.50	[7]1.00	
1943	.373					2.73	3.91	2.06		.69	1.50	[7]1.00	
1944	.375					2.72	3.61	1.86		.73	1.50	[7]1.00	
1945	.375					2.62	3.29	1.67		.75	1.50	[7]1.00	
1946	.375					2.53	3.05	1.64		.81	1.50	[7]1.00	
1947	.594					2.61	3.24	2.01		1.03	1.50-1.75	1.00	
1948	1.040					2.82	3.47	2.40		1.44	1.75-2.00	1.34	
1949	1.102					2.66	3.42	2.21		1.49	2.00	1.50	
1950	1.218					2.62	3.24	1.98		1.45	2.07	1.59	
1951	1.552					2.86	3.41	2.00		2.16	2.56	1.75	
1952	1.766					2.96	3.52	2.19		2.33	3.00	1.75	
1953	1.931		2.47	2.85		3.20	3.74	2.72		2.52	3.17	1.99	
1954	.953		1.63	2.40		2.90	3.51	2.37		1.58	3.05	1.60	
1955	1.753		2.47	2.82		3.06	3.53	2.53		2.18	3.16	1.89	1.78
1956	2.658		3.19	3.18		3.36	3.88	2.93		3.31	3.77	2.77	2.73
1957	3.267		3.98	3.65		3.89	4.71	3.60		3.81	4.20	3.12	3.11
1958	1.839		2.84	3.32		3.79	4.73	3.56		2.46	3.83	2.15	1.57
1959	3.405	3.832	4.46	4.33		4.38	5.05	3.95		3.97	4.48	3.36	3.30
1960	2.928	3.247	3.98	4.12		4.41	5.19	3.73		3.85	4.82	3.53	3.22
1961	2.378	2.605	3.54	3.88		4.35	5.08	3.46		2.97	4.50	3.00	1.96
1962	2.778	2.908	3.47	3.95		4.33	5.02	3.18		3.26	4.50	3.00	2.68
1963	3.157	3.253	3.67	4.00		4.26	4.86	3.23	5.89	3.55	4.50	3.23	3.18
1964	3.549	3.686	4.03	4.19		4.40	4.83	3.22	5.83	3.97	4.50	3.55	3.50
1965	3.954	4.055	4.22	4.28		4.49	4.87	3.27	5.81	4.38	4.54	4.04	4.07
1966	4.881	5.082	5.23	4.92		5.13	5.67	3.82	6.25	5.55	5.63	4.50	5.11
1967	4.321	4.630	5.03	5.07		5.51	6.23	3.98	6.46	5.10	5.61	4.19	4.22
1968	5.339	5.470	5.68	5.65		6.18	6.94	4.51	6.97	5.90	6.30	5.16	5.66
1969	6.677	6.853	7.02	6.67		7.03	7.81	5.81	7.81	7.83	7.96	5.87	8.20
1970	6.458	6.562	7.29	7.35		8.04	9.11	6.51	8.45	7.71	7.91	5.95	7.18
1971	4.348	4.511	5.65	6.16		7.39	8.56	5.70	7.74	5.11	5.72	4.88	4.66
1972	4.071	4.466	5.72	6.21		7.21	8.16	5.27	7.60	4.73	5.25	4.50	4.43
1973	7.041	7.178	6.95	6.84		7.44	8.24	5.18	7.96	8.15	8.03	6.44	8.73
1974	7.886	7.926	7.82	7.56		8.57	9.50	6.09	8.92	9.84	10.81	7.83	10.50
1975	5.838	6.122	7.49	7.99		8.83	10.61	6.89	9.00	6.32	7.86	6.25	5.82
1976	4.989	5.266	6.77	7.61		8.43	9.75	6.49	9.00	5.34	6.84	5.50	5.04
1977	5.265	5.510	6.69	7.42	7.75	8.02	8.97	5.56	9.02	5.61	6.83	5.46	5.54
1978	7.221	7.572	8.29	8.41	8.49	8.73	9.49	5.90	9.56	7.99	9.06	7.46	7.93
1979	10.041	10.017	9.71	9.44	9.28	9.63	10.69	6.39	10.78	10.91	12.67	10.28	11.19
1980	11.506	11.374	11.55	11.46	11.27	11.94	13.67	8.51	12.66	12.29	15.27	11.77	13.36
1981	14.029	13.776	14.44	13.91	13.45	14.17	16.04	11.23	14.70	14.76	18.87	13.42	16.38
1982	10.686	11.084	12.92	13.00	12.76	13.79	16.11	11.57	15.14	11.89	14.86	11.02	12.26
1983	8.63	8.75	10.45	11.10	11.18	12.04	13.55	9.47	12.57	8.89	10.79	8.50	9.09
1984	9.58	9.80	11.89	12.44	12.41	12.71	14.19	10.15	12.38	10.16	12.04	8.80	10.23
1985	7.48	7.66	9.64	10.62	10.79	11.37	12.72	9.18	11.55	8.01	9.93	7.69	8.10
1986	5.98	6.03	7.06	7.68	7.78	9.02	10.39	7.38	10.17	6.39	8.33	6.33	6.81
1987	5.82	6.05	7.68	8.39	8.59	9.38	10.58	7.73	9.31	6.85	8.21	5.66	6.66
1988	6.69	6.92	8.26	8.85	8.96	9.71	10.83	7.76	9.19	7.68	9.32	6.20	7.57
1989	8.12	8.04	8.55	8.49	8.45	9.26	10.18	7.24	10.13	8.80	10.87	6.93	9.21
1990	7.51	7.47	8.26	8.55	8.61	9.32	10.36	7.25	10.05	7.95	10.01	6.98	8.10
1991	5.42	5.49	6.82	7.86	8.14	8.77	9.80	6.89	9.32	5.85	8.46	5.45	5.69
1992	3.45	3.57	5.30	7.01	7.67	8.14	8.98	6.41	8.24	3.80	6.25	3.25	3.52
1993	3.02	3.14	4.44	5.87	6.59	7.22	7.93	5.63	7.20	3.30	6.00	3.00	3.02

[1] Rate on new issues within period; bank-discount basis.
[2] Yields on the more actively traded issues adjusted to constant maturities by the Treasury Department.
[3] Effective rate (in the primary market) on conventional mortgages, reflecting fees and charges as well as contract rate and assuming, on the average, repayment at end of 10 years. Rates beginning January 1973 not strictly comparable with prior rates.
[4] Bank-discount basis; prior to November 1979, data are for 4-6 months paper.
[5] For monthly data, high and low for the period. Prime rate for 1929-33 and 1947-48 are ranges of the rate in effect during the period.
[6] Since July 19, 1975, the daily effective rate is an average of the rates on a given day weighted by the volume of transactions at these rates. Prior to that date, the daily effective rate was the rate considered most representative of the day's transactions, usually the one at which most transactions occurred.
[7] From October 30, 1942, to April 24, 1946, a preferential rate of 0.50 percent was in effect for advances secured by Government securities maturing in 1 year or less.

See next page for continuation of table.

TABLE B-72.—*Bond yields and interest rates, 1929-93*—Continued

[Percent per annum]

Year and month	U.S. Treasury securities					Corporate bonds (Moody's)		High-grade municipal bonds (Standard & Poor's)	New-home mortgage yields [3]	Commercial paper, 6 months [4]	Prime rate charged by banks [5]	Discount rate, Federal Reserve Bank of New York [5]	Federal funds rate [6]
	Bills (new issues) [1]		Constant maturities [2]										
	3-month	6-month	3-year	10-year	30-year	Aaa	Baa						
											High-low	High-low	
1989:													
Jan	8.29	8.38	9.20	9.09	8.93	9.62	10.65	7.41	9.52	9.02	10.50-10.50	6.50-6.50	9.12
Feb	8.48	8.49	9.32	9.17	9.01	9.64	10.61	7.47	9.82	9.35	11.50-10.50	7.00-6.50	9.36
Mar	8.83	8.87	9.61	9.36	9.17	9.80	10.67	7.61	9.99	9.97	11.50-11.50	7.00-7.00	9.85
Apr	8.70	8.73	9.40	9.18	9.03	9.79	10.61	7.49	10.17	9.78	11.50-11.50	7.00-7.00	9.84
May	8.40	8.39	8.98	8.86	8.83	9.57	10.46	7.25	10.18	9.29	11.50-11.50	7.00-7.00	9.81
June	8.22	8.00	8.37	8.28	8.27	9.10	10.03	6.97	10.42	8.80	11.50-11.00	7.00-7.00	9.53
July	7.92	7.63	7.83	8.02	8.08	8.93	9.87	6.97	10.48	8.35	11.00-10.50	7.00-7.00	9.24
Aug	7.91	7.72	8.13	8.11	8.12	8.96	9.88	7.08	10.22	8.32	10.50-10.50	7.00-7.00	8.99
Sept	7.72	7.74	8.26	8.19	8.15	9.01	9.91	7.27	10.24	8.50	10.50-10.50	7.00-7.00	9.02
Oct	7.63	7.61	8.02	8.01	8.00	8.92	9.81	7.22	10.11	8.24	10.50-10.50	7.00-7.00	8.84
Nov	7.65	7.46	7.80	7.87	7.90	8.89	9.81	7.13	10.09	8.00	10.50-10.50	7.00-7.00	8.55
Dec	7.64	7.45	7.77	7.84	7.90	8.86	9.82	7.01	10.07	7.93	10.50-10.50	7.00-7.00	8.45
1990:													
Jan	7.64	7.52	8.13	8.21	8.26	8.99	9.94	7.13	9.91	7.96	10.50-10.00	7.00-7.00	8.23
Feb	7.76	7.72	8.39	8.47	8.50	9.22	10.14	7.21	9.88	8.04	10.00-10.00	7.00-7.00	8.24
Mar	7.87	7.83	8.63	8.59	8.56	9.37	10.21	7.29	10.03	8.23	10.00-10.00	7.00-7.00	8.28
Apr	7.78	7.82	8.78	8.79	8.76	9.46	10.30	7.36	10.17	8.29	10.00-10.00	7.00-7.00	8.26
May	7.78	7.82	8.69	8.76	8.73	9.47	10.41	7.34	10.28	8.23	10.00-10.00	7.00-7.00	8.18
June	7.74	7.64	8.40	8.48	8.46	9.26	10.22	7.22	10.13	8.06	10.00-10.00	7.00-7.00	8.29
July	7.66	7.57	8.26	8.47	8.50	9.24	10.20	7.15	10.08	7.90	10.00-10.00	7.00-7.00	8.15
Aug	7.44	7.36	8.22	8.75	8.86	9.41	10.41	7.31	10.11	7.77	10.00-10.00	7.00-7.00	8.13
Sept	7.38	7.33	8.27	8.89	9.03	9.56	10.64	7.40	9.90	7.83	10.00-10.00	7.00-7.00	8.20
Oct	7.19	7.20	8.07	8.72	8.86	9.53	10.74	7.40	9.98	7.81	10.00-10.00	7.00-7.00	8.11
Nov	7.07	7.04	7.74	8.39	8.54	9.30	10.62	7.10	9.90	7.74	10.00-10.00	7.00-7.00	7.81
Dec	6.81	6.76	7.47	8.08	8.24	9.05	10.43	7.04	9.76	7.49	10.00-10.00	7.00-6.50	7.31
1991:													
Jan	6.30	6.34	7.38	8.09	8.27	9.04	10.45	7.05	9.65	7.02	10.00- 9.50	6.50-6.50	6.91
Feb	5.95	5.93	7.08	7.85	8.03	8.83	10.07	6.90	9.57	6.41	9.50- 9.00	6.50-6.00	6.25
Mar	5.91	5.91	7.35	8.11	8.29	8.93	10.09	7.07	9.43	6.36	9.00- 9.00	6.00-6.00	6.12
Apr	5.67	5.73	7.23	8.04	8.21	8.86	9.94	7.05	9.60	6.07	9.00- 9.00	6.00-5.50	5.91
May	5.51	5.65	7.12	8.07	8.27	8.86	9.86	6.95	9.52	5.94	9.00- 8.50	5.50-5.50	5.78
June	5.60	5.76	7.39	8.28	8.47	9.01	9.96	7.09	9.46	6.16	8.50- 8.50	5.50-5.50	5.90
July	5.58	5.71	7.38	8.27	8.45	9.00	9.89	7.03	9.43	6.14	8.50- 8.50	5.50-5.50	5.82
Aug	5.39	5.47	6.80	7.90	8.14	8.75	9.65	6.89	9.48	5.76	8.50- 8.50	5.50-5.50	5.66
Sept	5.25	5.29	6.50	7.65	7.95	8.61	9.51	6.80	9.30	5.59	8.50- 8.00	5.50-5.00	5.45
Oct	5.03	5.08	6.23	7.53	7.93	8.55	9.49	6.59	9.04	5.33	8.00- 8.00	5.00-5.00	5.21
Nov	4.60	4.66	5.90	7.42	7.92	8.48	9.45	6.64	8.64	4.93	8.00- 7.50	5.00-4.50	4.81
Dec	4.12	4.16	5.39	7.09	7.70	8.31	9.26	6.63	8.53	4.49	7.50- 6.50	4.50-3.50	4.43
1992:													
Jan	3.84	3.88	5.40	7.03	7.58	8.20	9.13	6.41	8.49	4.06	6.50-6.50	3.50-3.50	4.03
Feb	3.84	3.94	5.72	7.34	7.85	8.29	9.23	6.67	8.65	4.13	6.50-6.50	3.50-3.50	4.06
Mar	4.05	4.19	6.18	7.54	7.97	8.35	9.25	6.69	8.51	4.38	6.50-6.50	3.50-3.50	3.98
Apr	3.81	3.93	5.93	7.48	7.96	8.33	9.21	6.64	8.58	4.13	6.50-6.50	3.50-3.50	3.73
May	3.66	3.78	5.81	7.39	7.89	8.28	9.13	6.57	8.59	3.97	6.50-6.50	3.50-3.50	3.82
June	3.70	3.81	5.60	7.26	7.84	8.22	9.05	6.50	8.43	3.99	6.50-6.50	3.50-3.50	3.76
July	3.28	3.36	4.91	6.84	7.60	8.07	8.84	6.12	8.00	3.53	6.50-6.00	3.50-3.00	3.25
Aug	3.14	3.23	4.72	6.59	7.39	7.95	8.65	6.08	8.00	3.44	6.00-6.00	3.00-3.00	3.30
Sept	2.97	3.01	4.42	6.42	7.34	7.92	8.62	6.24	7.93	3.26	6.00-6.00	3.00-3.00	3.22
Oct	2.84	2.98	4.64	6.59	7.53	7.99	8.84	6.38	7.90	3.33	6.00-6.00	3.00-3.00	3.10
Nov	3.14	3.35	5.14	6.87	7.61	8.10	8.96	6.35	8.07	3.67	6.00-6.00	3.00-3.00	3.09
Dec	3.25	3.39	5.21	6.77	7.44	7.98	8.81	6.24	7.88	3.70	6.00-6.00	3.00-3.00	2.92
1993:													
Jan	3.06	3.17	4.93	6.60	7.34	7.91	8.67	6.18	7.82	3.35	6.00-6.00	3.00-3.00	3.02
Feb	2.95	3.08	4.58	6.26	7.09	7.71	8.39	5.87	7.77	3.27	6.00-6.00	3.00-3.00	3.03
Mar	2.97	3.08	4.40	5.98	6.82	7.58	8.15	5.65	7.46	3.24	6.00-6.00	3.00-3.00	3.07
Apr	2.89	3.00	4.30	5.97	6.85	7.46	8.14	5.78	7.46	3.19	6.00-6.00	3.00-3.00	2.96
May	2.96	3.07	4.40	6.04	6.92	7.43	8.21	5.81	7.37	3.20	6.00-6.00	3.00-3.00	3.00
Jun	3.10	3.23	4.53	5.96	6.81	7.33	8.07	5.73	7.23	3.38	6.00-6.00	3.00-3.00	3.04
Jul	3.05	3.15	4.43	5.81	6.63	7.17	7.93	5.60	7.20	3.35	6.00-6.00	3.00-3.00	3.06
Aug	3.05	3.17	4.36	5.68	6.32	6.85	7.60	5.50	7.05	3.33	6.00-6.00	3.00-3.00	3.03
Sep	2.96	3.06	4.17	5.36	6.00	6.66	7.34	5.31	6.95	3.25	6.00-6.00	3.00-3.00	3.09
Oct	3.04	3.13	4.18	5.33	5.94	6.67	7.31	5.29	6.80	3.27	6.00-6.00	3.00-3.00	2.99
Nov	3.12	3.27	4.50	5.72	6.21	6.93	7.66	5.47	6.80	3.43	6.00-6.00	3.00-3.00	3.02
Dec	3.08	3.25	4.54	5.77	6.25	6.93	7.69	5.35	6.92	3.40	6.00-6.00	3.00-3.00	2.96

Sources: Department of the Treasury, Board of Governors of the Federal Reserve System, Federal Housing Finance Board, Moody's Investors Service, and Standard & Poor's Corporation.

TABLE B-73.—*Total funds raised in credit markets by nonfinancial sectors, 1984–93*

[Billions of dollars; quarterly data at seasonally adjusted annual rates]

Item	1984	1985	1986	1987	1988	1989	1990	1991	1992
	\multicolumn{9}{c}{Net credit market borrowing by nonfinancial sectors}
Total net borrowing by domestic nonfinancial sectors	764.6	934.6	855.8	739.9	752.6	723.0	631.0	475.5	582.4
U.S. Government	197.2	225.7	216.0	143.9	155.1	146.4	246.9	278.2	304.0
Treasury issues	197.4	225.8	215.6	142.4	137.7	144.7	238.7	292.0	303.8
Agency issues and mortgages	−.2	−.1	.4	1.5	17.4	1.6	8.2	−13.8	.2
Private domestic nonfinancial sectors	567.4	708.9	639.9	596.0	597.5	576.6	384.1	197.3	278.4
Debt capital instruments	329.2	523.4	478.4	497.9	436.4	408.3	293.1	313.4	254.0
Tax-exempt obligations	58.7	178.6	45.7	83.5	53.7	65.3	57.3	69.6	65.7
Corporate bonds	48.1	83.2	127.1	78.8	103.1	73.8	47.1	78.8	67.3
Mortgages	222.4	261.7	305.6	335.7	279.6	269.1	188.7	165.1	121.1
Home mortgages	136.2	172.3	204.2	241.6	219.6	212.5	177.2	166.0	176.0
Multi-family residential	25.1	30.3	36.4	24.9	16.1	12.0	3.4	−2.5	−11.1
Commercial	62.3	65.6	75.1	76.2	48.5	47.3	8.9	.9	−45.5
Farm	−1.2	−6.6	−10.1	−6.9	−4.6	−2.7	−.8	.7	1.6
Other debt instruments	238.3	185.5	161.5	98.1	161.0	168.3	91.0	−116.1	24.4
Consumer credit	81.7	82.3	57.5	32.9	50.1	49.5	13.4	−13.1	9.3
Bank loans n.e.c	64.0	43.8	58.9	14.7	44.7	36.4	4.2	−46.8	−5.6
Open-market paper	21.7	14.6	−9.3	1.6	11.9	21.4	9.7	−18.4	8.6
Other	70.9	44.8	54.3	48.9	54.3	61.0	63.6	−37.8	12.0
By borrowing sector:	567.4	708.9	639.9	596.0	597.5	576.6	384.1	197.3	278.4
State and local governments	35.7	134.0	59.2	83.0	48.9	63.5	54.5	62.3	59.4
Households	221.2	295.6	266.2	307.5	300.1	276.7	207.7	168.4	215.0
Nonfinancial business	310.5	279.3	314.5	205.5	248.4	236.3	121.9	−33.4	4.0
Farm	−.4	−14.5	−16.9	−11.1	−10.0	.5	1.8	2.4	1.5
Nonfarm noncorporate	123.3	133.2	106.1	76.0	57.2	49.4	19.4	−24.5	−39.4
Corporate	187.6	160.6	225.3	140.7	201.3	186.5	100.7	−11.3	41.8
Foreign net borrowing in United States	8.4	1.2	9.7	6.2	6.4	10.2	23.9	13.9	24.2
Bonds	3.8	3.8	3.1	7.4	6.9	4.9	21.4	14.1	17.3
Bank loans n.e.c	−6.6	−2.8	−1.0	−3.6	−1.8	−.1	−2.9	3.1	2.3
Open-market paper	6.2	6.2	11.5	3.8	8.7	13.1	12.3	6.4	5.2
U.S. Government and other loans	5.0	−6.0	−3.9	−1.4	−7.5	−7.6	−7.0	−9.8	−.6
Total domestic plus foreign	773.0	935.8	865.6	746.2	758.9	733.1	654.9	489.4	606.6
	\multicolumn{9}{c}{Direct and indirect supply of funds to credit markets}
Total funds supplied to domestic nonfinancial sectors	764.6	934.6	855.8	739.9	752.6	723.0	631.0	475.5	582.4
Private domestic nonfinancial sectors	446.7	487.2	329.9	405.0	421.8	285.4	259.7	−38.4	67.8
Deposits and currency	310.1	204.0	273.0	163.3	225.7	162.8	96.9	−22.3	−11.2
Checkable deposits and currency	37.0	56.9	114.1	18.1	29.1	9.6	21.9	70.1	131.0
Time and savings deposits	221.2	122.6	86.2	99.4	139.7	70.1	28.4	−104.9	−133.4
Money market fund shares	48.7	2.1	41.8	25.2	16.9	85.6	54.9	29.8	.8
Security repurchase agreements	9.8	17.7	20.0	21.5	32.9	−2.1	−22.1	−14.5	−.5
Foreign deposits	−6.5	4.7	10.8	−1.0	7.1	−.3	13.9	−2.8	−9.1
Credit market instruments	136.6	283.2	56.9	241.7	196.1	122.6	162.8	−16.1	79.0
Foreign funds	76.0	86.1	115.7	107.9	117.9	74.8	105.9	2.8	149.6
At banks	9.0	19.6	12.9	43.7	9.3	−9.5	23.8	−22.8	48.9
Credit market instruments	67.1	66.5	102.8	64.2	108.6	84.4	82.1	25.6	100.7
U.S. Government and related loans, net	16.0	37.4	17.0	5.6	−18.2	−49.9	17.3	32.8	20.5
U.S. Government cash balances	4.0	10.3	1.7	−5.8	7.3	−3.4	5.3	5.5	−5.9
Private insurance and pension reserves	139.9	215.7	233.7	184.8	127.7	293.7	146.8	297.9	167.3
Other sources	81.9	98.0	157.8	42.4	96.1	122.3	96.0	175.0	183.0

See next page for continuation of table.

TABLE B-73.—*Total funds raised in credit markets by nonfinancial sectors, 1984-93*—Continued

[Billions of dollars; quarterly data at seasonally adjusted annual rates]

Item	1991 I	1991 II	1991 III	1991 IV	1992 I	1992 II	1992 III	1992 IV	1993 I	1993 II	1993 III
	Net credit market borrowing by nonfinancial sectors											
Total net borrowing by domestic nonfinancial sectors	425.5	565.4	500.0	411.4	603.3	586.2	610.8	529.1	399.3	667.5	579.7
U.S. Government	191.7	269.3	379.5	272.5	323.8	352.9	299.1	240.1	229.6	348.2	177.2
Treasury issues	215.7	275.5	408.2	268.7	335.0	352.5	290.1	237.4	226.4	344.1	160.9
Agency issues and mortgages	−24.0	−6.2	−28.8	3.8	−11.2	.4	9.0	2.7	3.2	4.1	16.2
Private domestic nonfinancial sectors	233.8	296.1	120.5	138.9	279.5	233.4	311.7	289.0	169.7	319.2	402.5
Debt capital instruments	371.1	376.6	222.8	283.1	329.7	224.1	272.2	190.1	237.5	266.7	317.3
Tax-exempt obligations	62.3	69.6	68.8	77.6	68.0	76.6	75.8	42.4	62.4	67.2	38.9
Corporate bonds	76.7	96.5	81.6	60.2	76.3	77.8	61.3	53.7	75.0	64.9	55.2
Mortgages	232.2	210.5	72.3	145.2	185.4	69.8	135.1	93.9	100.2	134.5	223.2
Home mortgages	167.1	160.2	160.1	176.5	216.5	111.6	203.3	172.8	128.4	176.2	229.7
Multi-family residential	12.1	11.7	−34.2	.2	11.6	−16.9	−11.2	−27.9	−6.6	−12.8	.2
Commercial	47.7	40.1	−55.6	−28.6	−46.9	−25.7	−57.7	−51.6	−21.7	−29.1	−6.9
Farm	5.2	−1.5	2.1	−2.9	4.2	.8	.8	.6	.1	.2	.2
Other debt instruments	−137.3	−80.5	−102.2	−144.2	−50.2	9.3	39.4	99.0	−67.7	52.5	85.2
Consumer credit	−16.1	−5.1	−20.4	−10.7	−9.8	−14.7	13.5	48.2	19.2	22.9	60.8
Bank loans n.e.c	−59.5	−30.2	−44.0	−53.7	−47.3	27.7	−24.1	21.4	−39.7	31.8	8.1
Open-market paper	−25.1	−16.5	−26.9	−5.0	2.5	−2.6	9.3	25.4	−24.2	34.8	24.2
Other	−36.7	−28.8	−10.9	−74.9	4.5	−1.1	40.8	3.9	−23.0	−37.0	−8.0
By borrowing sector:	233.8	296.1	120.5	138.9	279.5	233.4	311.7	289.0	169.7	319.2	402.5
State and local governments	62.6	59.7	52.8	74.0	62.1	66.9	73.5	35.1	71.2	68.9	43.7
Households	130.1	195.1	154.5	193.8	199.2	176.5	217.7	266.6	137.4	215.8	322.4
Nonfinancial business	41.0	41.3	−86.8	−129.0	18.2	−10.1	20.5	−12.7	−38.9	34.5	36.4
Farm	9.8	.2	4.3	−4.6	4.3	3.6	−.1	−1.6	−2.5	3.4	4.6
Nonfarm noncorporate	21.2	20.2	−81.5	−57.9	−21.8	−47.4	−37.3	−51.0	−36.7	−31.4	−14.1
Corporate	10.0	20.9	−9.6	−66.5	35.7	33.7	57.9	39.9	.3	62.5	46.0
Foreign net borrowing in United States	57.8	−60.4	23.8	34.3	1.9	57.7	37.8	−.6	50.3	26.8	78.5
Bonds	11.3	10.9	15.6	18.5	4.9	21.9	20.3	22.2	75.6	30.4	85.5
Bank loans n.e.c	8.1	−3.5	1.4	6.5	1.5	14.1	3.9	−10.3	1.6	6.5	1.0
Open-market paper	46.7	−51.9	16.0	14.9	−8.0	27.8	13.1	−12.1	−21.7	−.6	−1.6
U.S. Government and other loans	−8.4	−15.9	−9.2	−5.6	3.6	−6.1	.5	−.4	−5.3	−9.5	−6.4
Total domestic plus foreign	483.3	504.9	523.7	445.6	605.3	644.0	648.7	528.5	449.5	694.2	658.2
	Direct and indirect supply of funds to credit markets											
Total funds supplied to domestic nonfinancial sectors	425.5	565.4	500.0	411.4	603.3	586.2	610.8	529.1	399.3	667.5	579.7
Private domestic nonfinancial sectors	38.5	133.1	−157.0	−168.2	206.6	59.4	−54.1	59.4	−382.1	35.4	−101.5
Deposits and currency	60.8	5.4	−57.9	−97.5	71.2	−91.5	8.2	−32.7	−241.3	153.5	53.7
Checkable deposits and currency	70.9	37.2	135.5	37.0	147.9	76.6	163.9	135.5	15.7	122.7	126.7
Time and savings deposits	−34.3	−50.3	−174.3	−160.8	−86.1	−175.3	−143.8	−128.6	−202.7	−30.7	−127.0
Money market fund shares	115.4	−2.2	−13.5	19.2	39.3	23.1	−23.7	−35.4	−45.1	65.2	51.7
Security repurchase agreements	−47.4	.7	−17.1	5.9	−8.7	12.9	−12.4	6.2	2.7	−4.7	−2.2
Foreign deposits	−43.9	19.9	11.6	1.2	−21.3	−28.8	24.1	−10.3	−11.9	.9	4.4
Credit market instruments	−22.3	127.8	−99.1	−70.7	135.5	150.9	−62.3	92.1	−140.8	−118.1	−155.2
Foreign funds	.9	−64.2	40.5	33.9	90.8	219.1	158.9	129.7	54.4	158.1	141.6
At banks	1.5	−98.3	13.1	−7.3	−5.7	78.4	80.7	42.2	−18.8	68.6	−2.3
Credit market instruments	−.5	34.2	27.4	41.3	96.5	140.7	78.1	87.5	73.2	89.5	144.0
U.S. Government and related loans, net	46.3	96.6	33.1	−44.9	122.9	−71.5	−43.5	74.0	−47.5	53.4	−70.8
U.S. Government cash balances	31.3	−23.2	5.2	8.7	−30.1	15.7	4.4	−13.5	1.3	9.0	3.6
Private insurance and pension reserves	396.7	117.9	371.3	305.5	49.8	170.8	225.8	222.9	359.9	180.6	286.6
Other sources	−88.3	305.1	206.9	276.4	163.2	192.7	319.4	56.6	413.3	231.0	320.3

Source: Board of Governors of the Federal Reserve System.

TABLE B-74.—*Mortgage debt outstanding by type of property and of financing, 1940-93*

[Billions of dollars]

End of year or quarter	All properties	Farm properties	Nonfarm properties				Nonfarm properties by type of mortgage					
							Government underwritten				Conventional [2]	
								1- to 4-family houses				
			Total	1- to 4-family houses	Multi-family properties	Commercial properties	Total [1]	Total	FHA insured	VA guaranteed	Total	1- to 4-family houses
1940	36.5	6.5	30.0	17.4	5.7	6.9	2.3	2.3	2.3		27.7	15.1
1941	37.6	6.4	31.2	18.4	5.9	7.0	3.0	3.0	3.0		28.2	15.4
1942	36.7	6.0	30.8	18.2	5.8	6.7	3.7	3.7	3.7		27.1	14.5
1943	35.3	5.4	29.9	17.8	5.8	6.3	4.1	4.1	4.1		25.8	13.7
1944	34.7	4.9	29.7	17.9	5.6	6.2	4.2	4.2	4.2		25.5	13.7
1945	35.5	4.8	30.8	18.6	5.7	6.4	4.3	4.3	4.1	0.2	26.5	14.3
1946	41.8	4.9	36.9	23.0	6.1	7.7	6.3	6.1	3.7	2.4	30.6	16.9
1947	48.9	5.1	43.9	28.2	6.6	9.1	9.8	9.3	3.8	5.5	34.1	18.9
1948	56.2	5.3	50.9	33.3	7.5	10.2	13.6	12.5	5.3	7.2	37.3	20.8
1949	62.7	5.6	57.1	37.6	8.6	10.8	17.1	15.0	6.9	8.1	40.0	22.6
1950	72.8	6.1	66.7	45.2	10.1	11.5	22.1	18.8	8.5	10.3	44.7	26.3
1951	82.3	6.7	75.6	51.7	11.5	12.5	26.6	22.9	9.7	13.2	49.1	28.9
1952	91.4	7.2	84.2	58.5	12.3	13.4	29.3	25.4	10.8	14.6	54.9	33.2
1953	101.3	7.7	93.6	66.1	12.9	14.5	32.1	28.1	12.0	16.1	61.5	38.0
1954	113.7	8.2	105.4	75.7	13.5	16.3	36.2	32.1	12.8	19.3	69.3	43.6
1955	129.9	9.0	120.9	88.2	14.3	18.3	42.9	38.9	14.3	24.6	78.0	49.3
1956	144.5	9.8	134.6	99.0	14.9	20.7	47.8	43.9	15.5	28.4	86.8	55.1
1957	156.5	10.4	146.1	107.6	15.3	23.2	51.6	47.2	16.5	30.7	94.6	60.4
1958	171.8	11.1	160.7	117.7	16.8	26.1	55.2	50.1	19.7	30.4	105.5	67.6
1959	190.8	12.1	178.7	130.9	18.7	29.2	59.3	53.8	23.8	30.0	119.4	77.0
1960	207.5	12.8	194.7	141.9	20.3	32.4	62.3	56.4	26.7	29.7	132.3	85.5
1961	228.0	13.9	214.1	154.6	23.0	36.5	65.6	59.1	29.5	29.6	148.5	95.5
1962	251.4	15.2	236.2	169.3	25.8	41.1	69.4	62.2	32.3	29.9	166.9	107.1
1963	278.5	16.8	261.7	186.4	29.0	46.2	73.4	65.9	35.0	30.9	188.2	120.5
1964	305.9	18.9	287.0	203.4	33.6	50.0	77.2	69.2	38.3	30.9	209.8	134.1
1965	333.3	21.2	312.1	220.5	37.2	54.5	81.2	73.1	42.0	31.1	231.0	147.4
1966	356.5	23.1	333.4	232.9	40.3	60.1	84.1	76.1	44.8	31.3	249.3	156.9
1967	381.2	25.1	356.1	247.3	43.9	64.8	88.2	79.9	47.4	32.5	267.9	167.4
1968	411.1	27.5	383.5	264.8	47.3	71.4	93.4	84.4	50.6	33.8	290.1	180.4
1969	441.6	29.4	412.2	283.2	52.2	76.9	100.2	90.2	54.5	35.7	312.0	193.0
1970	473.7	30.5	443.2	297.4	60.1	85.6	109.2	97.3	59.9	37.3	333.9	200.2
1971	524.2	32.4	491.8	325.9	70.1	95.9	120.7	105.2	65.7	39.5	371.1	220.7
1972	597.4	35.4	562.0	366.5	82.8	112.7	131.1	113.0	68.2	44.7	430.9	253.5
1973	672.6	39.8	632.8	407.9	93.1	131.7	135.0	116.2	66.2	50.0	497.7	291.7
1974	732.5	44.9	687.5	440.7	100.0	146.9	140.2	121.3	65.1	56.2	547.3	319.4
1975	791.9	49.9	742.0	482.1	100.6	159.3	147.0	127.7	66.1	61.6	595.0	354.3
1976	878.6	55.4	823.2	546.3	105.7	171.2	154.1	133.5	66.5	67.0	669.0	412.8
1977	1,010.3	63.9	946.4	642.7	114.0	189.7	161.7	141.6	68.0	73.6	784.6	501.0
1978	1,163.0	72.8	1,090.2	753.5	124.9	211.8	176.4	153.4	71.4	82.0	913.9	600.2
1979	1,328.4	86.8	1,241.7	870.5	134.9	236.3	199.0	172.9	81.0	92.0	1,042.7	697.6
1980	1,460.4	97.5	1,362.9	965.1	142.3	255.5	225.1	195.2	93.6	101.6	1,137.8	769.9
1981	1,566.7	107.2	1,459.5	1,039.8	142.1	277.5	238.9	207.6	101.3	106.2	1,220.6	832.2
1982	1,641.1	111.3	1,529.8	1,081.7	145.8	302.2	248.9	217.9	108.0	109.9	1,280.9	863.9
1983	1,828.8	113.7	1,715.1	1,199.4	160.9	354.8	279.8	248.8	127.4	121.4	1,435.3	950.6
1984	2,054.6	112.4	1,942.2	1,335.1	185.7	421.4	294.8	265.9	136.7	129.1	1,647.3	1,069.2
1985	2,312.8	105.9	2,206.9	1,504.7	215.6	486.6	328.3	288.8	153.0	135.8	1,878.6	1,215.9
1986	2,615.4	95.2	2,520.2	1,707.1	251.8	561.3	370.5	328.6	185.5	143.1	2,149.7	1,378.5
1987	2,963.2	87.7	2,875.5	1,936.1	276.0	663.4	431.4	387.9	235.5	152.4	2,444.1	1,548.2
1988	3,248.6	83.0	3,165.7	2,169.3	293.7	702.7	459.7	414.2	258.8	155.4	2,706.0	1,755.1
1989	3,549.6	80.5	3,469.1	2,408.4	306.5	754.2	486.8	440.1	282.8	157.3	2,982.2	1,968.3
1990	3,761.5	78.4	3,683.1	2,615.4	309.4	758.3	517.9	470.9	310.9	160.0	3,165.2	2,144.5
1991	3,923.4	79.3	3,844.2	2,778.8	306.4	759.0	537.2	493.3	330.6	162.7	3,307.0	2,285.5
1992	4,042.9	80.7	3,962.2	2,953.5	295.0	713.7	533.3	489.8	326.0	163.8	3,428.9	2,463.8
1991: I	3,812.0	79.7	3,732.3	2,649.9	312.3	770.1	525.3	478.0	317.0	161.0	3,206.9	2,171.9
II	3,874.2	79.3	3,794.9	2,700.1	314.8	779.9	545.7	497.3	334.1	163.2	3,249.2	2,202.8
III	3,874.6	79.9	3,794.8	2,722.8	305.9	766.0	535.3	491.4	329.1	162.2	3,259.4	2,231.5
IV	3,923.4	79.1	3,844.2	2,778.8	306.4	759.0	537.2	493.3	330.6	162.7	3,307.0	2,285.5
1992: I	3,959.7	80.2	3,879.5	2,823.1	309.0	747.4	538.1	494.3	330.6	163.7	3,341.5	2,328.7
II	3,982.9	80.4	3,902.5	2,856.7	304.8	741.0	536.1	492.4	328.8	163.6	3,366.4	2,364.3
III	4,020.6	80.6	3,940.0	2,911.4	302.0	726.6	537.5	493.9	329.5	164.4	3,402.5	2,417.6
IV	4,042.9	80.7	3,962.2	2,953.5	295.0	713.7	533.3	489.8	326.0	163.8	3,428.9	2,463.8
1993: I	4,059.2	80.8	3,978.4	2,976.8	293.6	708.1	530.5	487.0	323.4	163.6	3,447.9	2,489.8
II	4,099.6	80.8	4,018.8	3,026.9	290.6	701.3	522.6	479.0	315.2	163.8	3,496.2	2,548.0
III	4,160.2	80.9	4,079.3	3,088.5	290.9	699.5	517.9	474.2	310.5	163.7	3,561.4	2,614.3

[1] Includes FHA insured multifamily properties, not shown separately.
[2] Derived figures. Total includes multifamily and commercial properties, not shown separately.

Source: Board of Governors of the Federal Reserve System, based on data from various Government and private organizations.

TABLE B-75.—*Mortgage debt outstanding by holder, 1940–93*

[Billions of dollars]

End of year or quarter	Total	Major financial institutions				Other holders	
		Total	Savings institutions [1]	Commercial banks [2]	Life insurance companies	Federal and related agencies [3]	Individuals and others [4]
1940	36.5	19.5	9.0	4.6	6.0	4.9	12.0
1941	37.6	20.7	9.4	4.9	6.4	4.7	12.2
1942	36.7	20.7	9.2	4.7	6.7	4.3	11.7
1943	35.3	20.2	9.0	4.5	6.7	3.6	11.5
1944	34.7	20.2	9.1	4.4	6.7	3.0	11.5
1945	35.5	21.0	9.6	4.8	6.6	2.4	12.1
1946	41.8	26.0	11.5	7.2	7.2	2.0	13.8
1947	48.9	31.8	13.8	9.4	8.7	1.8	15.3
1948	56.2	37.8	16.1	10.9	10.8	1.8	16.6
1949	62.7	42.9	18.3	11.6	12.9	2.3	17.5
1950	72.8	51.7	21.9	13.7	16.1	2.8	18.4
1951	82.3	59.5	25.5	14.7	19.3	3.5	19.3
1952	91.4	66.9	29.8	15.9	21.3	4.1	20.4
1953	101.3	75.1	34.9	16.9	23.3	4.6	21.7
1954	113.7	85.7	41.1	18.6	26.0	4.8	23.2
1955	129.9	99.3	48.9	21.0	29.4	5.3	25.3
1956	144.5	111.2	55.5	22.7	33.0	6.2	27.1
1957	156.5	119.7	61.2	23.3	35.2	7.7	29.1
1958	171.8	131.5	68.9	25.5	37.1	8.0	32.3
1959	190.8	145.5	78.1	28.1	39.2	10.2	35.1
1960	207.5	157.6	87.0	28.8	41.8	11.5	38.4
1961	228.0	172.6	98.0	30.4	44.2	12.2	43.1
1962	251.4	192.5	111.1	34.5	46.9	12.6	46.3
1963	278.5	217.1	127.2	39.4	50.5	11.8	49.5
1964	305.9	241.0	141.9	44.0	55.2	12.2	52.7
1965	333.3	264.6	154.9	49.7	60.0	13.5	55.2
1966	356.5	280.8	161.8	54.4	64.6	17.5	58.2
1967	381.2	298.8	172.3	59.0	67.5	20.9	61.4
1968	411.1	319.9	184.3	65.7	70.0	25.1	66.1
1969	441.6	339.1	196.4	70.7	72.0	31.1	71.4
1970	473.7	355.9	208.3	73.3	74.4	38.3	79.4
1971	524.2	394.2	236.2	82.5	75.5	46.4	83.6
1972	597.4	450.0	273.7	99.3	76.9	54.6	92.8
1973	672.6	505.4	305.0	119.1	81.4	64.8	102.4
1974	732.5	542.6	324.2	132.1	86.2	82.2	107.7
1975	791.9	581.2	355.8	136.2	89.2	101.1	109.6
1976	878.6	647.5	404.6	151.3	91.6	116.7	114.4
1977	1,010.3	745.2	469.4	179.0	96.8	140.5	124.6
1978	1,163.0	848.2	528.0	214.0	106.2	170.6	144.3
1979	1,328.4	938.2	574.6	245.2	118.4	216.0	174.3
1980	1,460.4	996.8	603.1	262.7	131.1	256.8	206.8
1981	1,566.7	1,040.5	618.5	284.2	137.7	289.4	236.8
1982	1,641.0	1,021.3	578.1	301.3	142.0	355.4	264.4
1983	1,828.8	1,108.2	626.7	330.5	151.0	433.4	287.2
1984	2,054.6	1,245.9	709.7	379.5	156.7	490.6	318.1
1985	2,312.8	1,361.5	760.5	429.2	171.8	581.9	369.4
1986	2,615.4	1,474.3	778.0	502.5	193.8	733.7	407.3
1987	2,963.2	1,665.3	860.5	592.4	212.4	858.9	439.0
1988	3,248.6	1,831.5	924.6	674.0	232.9	937.8	479.4
1989	3,549.6	1,931.5	910.3	767.1	254.2	1,067.3	550.7
1990	3,761.5	1,914.3	801.6	844.8	267.9	1,258.9	588.3
1991	3,923.4	1,846.7	705.4	876.1	265.3	1,422.6	654.0
1992	4,042.9	1,769.2	628.0	894.5	246.7	1,558.3	715.4
1991: I	3,812.0	1,902.9	776.5	857.4	269.0	1,302.3	606.8
II	3,874.2	1,899.4	755.4	872.4	271.7	1,351.7	623.0
III	3,874.6	1,860.8	719.7	871.0	270.1	1,389.5	624.3
IV	3,923.4	1,846.7	705.4	876.1	265.3	1,422.6	654.0
1992: I	3,959.7	1,826.7	682.3	881.0	263.3	1,458.1	674.9
II	3,982.9	1,803.8	659.6	885.0	259.3	1,497.1	681.9
III	4,020.6	1,793.5	648.2	891.4	253.9	1,521.5	705.6
IV	4,042.9	1,769.2	628.0	894.5	246.7	1,558.3	715.4
1993: I	4,059.2	1,753.0	617.2	891.8	244.1	1,587.0	719.2
II	4,099.6	1,765.1	612.4	910.9	241.7	1,600.5	734.0
III	4,160.2	1,770.3	610.1	922.4	237.8	1,637.9	752.0

[1] Includes savings banks and savings and loan associations. Data reported by Federal Savings and Loan Insurance Corporation-insured institutions include loans in process for 1987 and exclude loans in process beginning 1988.
[2] Includes loans held by nondeposit trust companies, but not by bank trust departments.
[3] Includes Government National Mortgage Association (GNMA), Federal Housing Administration, Veterans Administration, Farmers Home Administration (FmHA), and in earlier years Reconstruction Finance Corporation, Homeowners Loan Corporation, Federal Farm Mortgage Corporation, and Public Housing Administration. Also includes U.S.-sponsored agencies such as Federal National Mortgage Association (FNMA), Federal Land Banks, Federal Home Loan Mortgage Corporation (FHLMC), and mortgage pass-through securities issued or guaranteed by GNMA, FHLMC, FNMA or FmHA. Other U.S. agencies (amounts small or current separate data not readily available) included with "individuals and others."
[4] Includes private mortgage pools.

Source: Board of Governors of the Federal Reserve System, based on data from various Government and private organizations.

TABLE B-76.—*Consumer credit outstanding, 1952-93*

[Amount outstanding (end of month); millions of dollars, seasonally adjusted]

Year and month	Total consumer credit	Installment credit [1]				Noninstallment credit [4]
		Total	Automobile	Revolving [2]	Other [3]	
December:						
1952	29,766	20,121	7,651		12,470	9,645
1953	33,769	23,870	9,702		14,168	9,899
1954	35,027	24,470	9,755		14,715	10,557
1955	41,885	29,809	13,485		16,324	12,076
1956	45,503	32,660	14,499		18,161	12,843
1957	48,132	34,914	15,493		19,421	13,218
1958	48,356	34,736	14,267		20,469	13,620
1959	55,878	40,421	16,641		23,780	15,457
1960	60,035	44,335	18,108		26,227	15,700
1961	62,340	45,438	17,656		27,782	16,902
1962	68,231	50,375	20,001		30,374	17,856
1963	76,606	57,056	22,891		34,165	19,550
1964	85,989	64,674	25,865		38,809	21,315
1965	95,948	72,814	29,378		43,436	23,134
1966	101,839	78,162	31,024		47,138	23,677
1967	106,716	81,783	31,136		50,647	24,933
1968	117,231	90,112	34,352	2,022	53,738	27,119
1969	126,928	99,381	36,946	3,563	58,872	27,547
1970	131,600	103,905	36,348	4,900	62,657	27,695
1971	147,058	116,434	40,522	8,252	67,660	30,624
1972	166,009	131,258	47,835	9,391	74,032	34,751
1973	190,601	152,910	53,740	11,318	87,852	37,691
1974	199,365	162,203	54,241	13,232	94,730	37,162
1975	204,963	167,043	56,989	14,507	95,547	37,920
1976	228,162	187,782	66,821	16,595	104,366	40,380
1977	263,808	221,475	80,948	36,689	103,838	42,333
1978	308,272	261,976	98,739	45,202	118,035	46,296
1979	347,507	296,483	112,475	53,357	130,651	51,024
1980	350,269	298,154	111,991	55,111	131,053	52,115
1981	366,369	311,259	119,008	61,070	131,182	55,610
1982	383,132	325,805	125,945	66,454	133,406	57,327
1983	431,170	368,966	143,560	79,088	146,318	62,204
1984	511,314	442,602	173,564	100,280	168,758	68,713
1985	591,291	517,660	210,238	121,758	185,664	73,631
1986	647,982	572,006	247,772	135,825	188,408	75,976
1987	680,036	608,675	266,295	153,064	189,316	71,362
1988 [5]	729,121	662,553	285,364	174,269	202,921	66,568
1989	786,732	724,353	292,536	198,544	233,273	62,379
1990	798,274	738,765	284,739	222,552	231,474	59,509
1991	784,061	733,510	260,898	243,564	229,048	50,551
1992	793,175	741,093	259,627	254,299	227,167	52,082
1992: Jan	786,081	735,406	261,553	245,609	228,243	50,676
Feb	784,884	734,225	260,666	246,474	227,085	50,659
Mar	784,676	734,434	262,087	246,324	226,023	50,242
Apr	780,983	731,736	260,746	246,987	224,002	49,247
May	780,283	730,612	259,844	247,205	223,562	49,671
June	780,163	730,866	257,989	248,795	224,081	49,297
July	779,563	730,496	258,259	248,980	223,257	49,067
Aug	781,043	731,023	258,827	249,384	222,812	50,020
Sept	782,778	733,023	259,433	250,456	223,135	49,755
Oct	784,113	734,195	258,208	251,806	224,181	49,919
Nov	787,521	736,023	258,860	252,086	225,077	51,497
Dec	793,175	741,093	259,627	254,299	227,167	52,082
1993: Jan	797,126	743,583	258,737	255,984	228,862	53,543
Feb	799,251	747,228	261,434	258,384	227,410	52,023
Mar	800,930	750,131	262,313	259,661	228,157	50,799
Apr	804,514	752,193	262,463	261,450	228,280	52,321
May	804,406	750,293	264,007	262,690	223,596	54,113
June	805,691	752,428	265,388	263,338	223,701	53,263
July	810,546	757,465	267,468	266,938	223,058	53,081
Aug	813,472	762,503	268,784	270,753	222,967	50,969
Sept	820,017	768,573	270,650	273,703	224,220	51,444
Oct	827,318	776,234	274,600	277,125	224,509	51,084
Nov ᵖ	833,437	783,115	277,576	279,273	226,266	50,322

[1] Installment credit covers most short- and intermediate-term credit extended to individuals through regular business channels, usually to finance the purchase of consumer goods and services or to refinance debts incurred for such purposes, and scheduled to be repaid (or with the option of repayment) in two or more installments. Credit secured by real estate is excluded.
[2] Consists of credit cards at retailers, gasoline companies, and commercial banks, and check credit at commercial banks. Excludes 30-day charge credit held by travel and entertainment companies. Prior to 1968, included in "other," except gasoline companies included in noninstallment credit prior to 1971. Beginning 1977, includes open-end credit at retailers, previously included in "other." Also beginning 1977, some retail credit was reclassified from commercial into consumer credit.
[3] Includes mobile home loans and all other installment loans not included in automobile or revolving credit, such as loans for education, boats, trailers, or vacations. These loans may be secured or unsecured.
[4] Noninstallment credit is credit scheduled to be repaid in a lump sum, including single-payment loans, charge accounts, and service credit. Because of inconsistencies in the data and infrequent benchmarking, series is no longer published by the Federal Reserve Board on a regular basis. Data are shown here as a general indication of trends.
[5] Data newly available in January 1989 result in breaks in many series between December 1988 and subsequent months.

Source: Board of Governors of the Federal Reserve System.

GOVERNMENT FINANCE

TABLE B-77.—*Federal receipts, outlays, surplus or deficit, and debt, selected fiscal years, 1929–95*

[Billions of dollars; fiscal years]

Fiscal year or period	Total Receipts	Total Outlays	Total Surplus or deficit (−)	On-budget Receipts	On-budget Outlays	On-budget Surplus or deficit (−)	Off-budget Receipts	Off-budget Outlays	Off-budget Surplus or deficit (−)	Gross Federal debt Total	Gross Federal debt Held by the public	Addendum: Gross domestic product
1929	3.9	3.1	0.7							[1] 16.9		
1933	2.0	4.6	−2.6							[1] 22.5		
1939	6.3	9.1	−2.8	5.8	9.2	−3.4	0.5	−0.0	0.5	48.2	41.4	87.8
1940	6.5	9.5	−2.9	6.0	9.5	−3.5	.6	−.0	.6	50.7	42.8	95.4
1941	8.7	13.7	−4.9	8.0	13.6	−5.6	.7	.0	.7	57.5	48.2	112.5
1942	14.6	35.1	−20.5	13.7	35.1	−21.3	.9	.1	.8	79.2	67.8	141.8
1943	24.0	78.6	−54.6	22.9	78.5	−55.6	1.1	.1	1.0	142.6	127.8	175.4
1944	43.7	91.3	−47.6	42.5	91.2	−48.7	1.3	.1	1.2	204.1	184.8	201.7
1945	45.2	92.7	−47.6	43.8	92.6	−48.7	1.3	.1	1.2	260.1	235.2	212.0
1946	39.3	55.2	−15.9	38.1	55.0	−17.0	1.2	.2	1.0	271.0	241.9	212.5
1947	38.5	34.5	4.0	37.1	34.2	2.9	1.5	.3	1.2	257.1	224.3	222.9
1948	41.6	29.8	11.8	39.9	29.4	10.5	1.6	.4	1.2	252.0	216.3	246.7
1949	39.4	38.8	.6	37.7	38.4	−.7	1.7	.4	1.3	252.6	214.3	262.7
1950	39.4	42.6	−3.1	37.3	42.0	−4.7	2.1	.5	1.6	256.9	219.0	265.8
1951	51.6	45.5	6.1	48.5	44.2	4.3	3.1	1.3	1.8	255.3	214.3	313.5
1952	66.2	67.7	−1.5	62.6	66.0	−3.4	3.6	1.7	1.9	259.1	214.8	340.5
1953	69.6	76.1	−6.5	65.5	73.8	−8.3	4.1	2.3	1.8	266.0	218.4	363.8
1954	69.7	70.9	−1.2	65.1	67.9	−2.8	4.6	2.9	1.7	270.8	224.5	368.0
1955	65.5	68.4	−3.0	60.4	64.5	−4.1	5.1	4.0	1.1	274.4	226.6	384.7
1956	74.6	70.6	3.9	68.2	65.7	2.5	6.4	5.0	1.5	272.7	222.2	416.3
1957	80.0	76.6	3.4	73.2	70.6	2.6	6.8	6.0	.8	272.3	219.3	438.3
1958	79.6	82.4	−2.8	71.6	74.9	−3.3	8.0	7.5	.5	279.7	226.3	448.1
1959	79.2	92.1	−12.8	71.0	83.1	−12.1	8.3	9.0	−.7	287.5	234.7	480.2
1960	92.5	92.2	.3	81.9	81.3	.5	10.6	10.9	−.2	290.5	236.8	504.6
1961	94.4	97.7	−3.3	82.3	86.0	−3.8	12.1	11.7	.4	292.6	238.4	517.0
1962	99.7	106.8	−7.1	87.4	93.3	−5.9	12.3	13.5	−1.3	302.9	248.0	555.2
1963	106.6	111.3	−4.8	92.4	96.4	−4.0	14.2	15.0	−.8	310.3	254.0	584.5
1964	112.6	118.5	−5.9	96.2	102.8	−6.5	16.4	15.7	.6	316.1	256.8	625.3
1965	116.8	118.2	−1.4	100.1	101.7	−1.6	16.7	16.5	.2	322.3	260.8	671.0
1966	130.8	134.5	−3.7	111.7	114.8	−3.1	19.1	19.7	−.6	328.5	263.7	735.4
1967	148.8	157.5	−8.6	124.4	137.0	−12.6	24.4	20.4	4.0	340.4	266.6	793.3
1968	153.0	178.1	−25.2	128.1	155.8	−27.7	24.9	22.3	2.6	368.7	289.5	847.2
1969	186.9	183.6	3.2	157.9	158.4	−.5	29.0	25.2	3.7	365.8	278.1	925.7
1970	192.8	195.6	−2.8	159.3	168.0	−8.7	33.5	27.6	5.9	380.9	283.2	985.4
1971	187.1	210.2	−23.0	151.3	177.3	−26.1	35.8	32.8	3.0	408.2	303.0	1,050.9
1972	207.3	230.7	−23.4	167.4	193.8	−26.4	39.9	36.9	3.1	435.9	322.4	1,147.8
1973	230.8	245.7	−14.9	184.7	200.1	−15.4	46.1	45.6	.5	466.3	340.9	1,274.0
1974	263.2	269.4	−6.1	209.3	217.3	−8.0	53.9	52.1	1.8	483.9	343.7	1,403.6
1975	279.1	332.3	−53.2	216.6	271.9	−55.3	62.5	60.4	2.0	541.9	394.7	1,509.8
1976	298.1	371.8	−73.7	231.7	302.2	−70.5	66.4	69.6	−3.2	629.0	477.4	1,684.2
Transition quarter	81.2	96.0	−14.7	63.2	76.6	−13.3	18.0	19.4	−1.4	643.6	495.5	445.0
1977	355.6	409.2	−53.7	278.7	328.5	−49.8	76.8	80.7	−3.9	706.4	549.1	1,917.2
1978	399.6	458.7	−59.2	314.2	369.1	−54.9	85.4	89.7	−4.3	776.6	607.1	2,155.0
1979	463.3	503.5	−40.2	365.3	403.5	−38.2	98.0	100.0	−2.0	828.9	639.8	2,429.5
1980	517.1	590.9	−73.8	403.9	476.6	−72.7	113.2	114.3	−1.1	908.5	709.3	2,644.1
1981	599.3	678.2	−79.0	469.1	543.1	−74.0	130.2	135.2	−5.0	994.3	784.8	2,964.4
1982	617.8	745.8	−128.0	474.3	594.4	−120.1	143.5	151.4	−7.9	1,136.8	919.2	3,122.2
1983	600.6	808.4	−207.8	453.2	661.3	−208.0	147.3	147.1	.2	1,371.2	1,131.0	3,316.5
1984	666.5	851.8	−185.4	500.4	686.0	−185.7	166.1	165.8	.3	1,564.1	1,300.0	3,695.0
1985	734.1	946.4	−212.3	547.9	769.6	−221.7	186.2	176.8	9.4	1,817.0	1,499.4	3,967.7
1986	769.1	990.3	−221.2	568.9	806.8	−238.0	200.2	183.5	16.7	2,120.1	1,736.2	4,219.0
1987	854.1	1,003.9	−149.8	640.7	810.1	−169.3	213.4	193.8	19.6	2,345.6	1,888.1	4,452.4
1988	909.0	1,064.1	−155.2	667.5	861.4	−194.0	241.5	202.7	38.8	2,600.8	2,050.3	4,808.4
1989	990.7	1,143.2	−152.5	727.0	932.3	−205.2	263.7	210.9	52.8	2,867.5	2,189.3	5,173.3
1990	1,031.3	1,252.7	−221.4	749.7	1,027.6	−278.0	281.7	225.1	56.6	3,206.2	2,410.4	5,481.5
1991	1,054.3	1,323.8	−269.5	760.4	1,082.1	−321.7	293.9	241.7	52.2	3,598.3	2,687.9	5,673.3
1992	1,090.5	1,380.9	−290.4	788.0	1,128.5	−340.5	302.4	252.3	50.1	4,001.9	2,998.6	5,937.2
1993	1,153.5	1,408.2	−254.7	841.6	1,141.6	−300.0	311.9	266.6	45.3	4,351.2	3,247.2	6,294.8
1994 [2]	1,249.1	1,483.8	−234.8	912.9	1,203.0	−290.1	336.2	280.9	55.3	4,676.0	3,472.4	6,641.2
1995 [2]	1,353.8	1,518.9	−165.1	998.6	1,223.6	−225.0	355.2	295.4	59.9	4,960.1	3,646.1	7,022.0

[1] Not strictly comparable with later data.
[2] Estimates.

Note.—Through fiscal year 1976, the fiscal year was on a July 1–June 30 basis; beginning October 1976 (fiscal year 1977), the fiscal year is on an October 1–September 30 basis. The 3-month period from July 1, 1976 through September 30, 1976 is a separate fiscal period known as the transition quarter.
Refunds of receipts are excluded from receipts and outlays.
See *Budget of the United States Government, Fiscal Year 1995*, February 1994, for additional information.
Sources: Department of Commerce (Bureau of Economic Analysis), Department of the Treasury, and Office of Management and Budget.

TABLE B-78.—*Federal receipts, outlays, and debt, fiscal years 1982–95*

[Millions of dollars; fiscal years]

Description	Actual						
	1982	1983	1984	1985	1986	1987	1988
RECEIPTS AND OUTLAYS:							
Total receipts	617,766	600,562	666,457	734,057	769,091	854,143	908,954
Total outlays	745,755	808,380	851,846	946,391	990,336	1,003,911	1,064,140
Total surplus or deficit (−)	−127,989	−207,818	−185,388	−212,334	−221,245	−149,769	−155,187
On-budget receipts	474,299	453,242	500,382	547,886	568,862	640,741	667,463
On-budget outlays	594,351	661,272	686,032	769,584	806,838	810,079	861,449
On-budget surplus or deficit (−)	−120,052	−208,030	−185,650	−221,698	−237,976	−169,339	−193,986
Off-budget receipts	143,467	147,320	166,075	186,171	200,228	213,402	241,491
Off-budget outlays	151,404	147,108	165,813	176,807	183,498	193,832	202,691
Off-budget surplus or deficit (−)	−7,937	212	262	9,363	16,731	19,570	38,800
OUTSTANDING DEBT, END OF PERIOD:							
Gross Federal debt	1,136,798	1,371,164	1,564,110	1,816,974	2,120,082	2,345,578	2,600,760
Held by Government accounts	217,560	240,114	264,159	317,612	383,919	457,444	550,507
Held by the public	919,238	1,131,049	1,299,951	1,499,362	1,736,163	1,888,134	2,050,252
Federal Reserve System	134,497	155,527	155,122	169,806	190,855	212,040	229,218
Other	784,741	975,522	1,144,829	1,329,556	1,545,308	1,676,094	1,821,034
RECEIPTS: ON-BUDGET AND OFF-BUDGET	617,766	600,562	666,457	734,057	769,091	854,143	908,954
Individual income taxes	297,744	288,938	298,415	334,531	348,959	392,557	401,181
Corporation income taxes	49,207	37,022	56,893	61,331	63,143	83,926	94,508
Social insurance taxes and contributions	201,498	208,994	239,376	265,163	283,901	303,318	334,335
On-budget	58,031	61,674	73,301	78,992	83,673	89,916	92,845
Off-budget	143,467	147,320	166,075	186,171	200,228	213,402	241,491
Excise taxes	36,311	35,300	37,361	35,992	32,919	32,457	35,227
Estate and gift taxes	7,991	6,053	6,010	6,422	6,958	7,493	7,594
Customs duties and fees	8,854	8,655	11,370	12,079	13,327	15,085	16,198
Miscellaneous receipts:							
Deposits of earnings by Federal Reserve System	15,186	14,492	15,684	17,059	18,374	16,817	17,163
All other	975	1,108	1,347	1,480	1,510	2,490	2,747
OUTLAYS: ON-BUDGET AND OFF-BUDGET	745,755	808,380	851,846	946,391	990,336	1,003,911	1,064,140
National defense	185,309	209,903	227,413	252,748	273,375	281,999	290,361
International affairs	12,300	11,848	15,876	16,176	14,152	11,649	10,471
General science, space, and technology	7,200	7,935	8,317	8,627	8,976	9,216	10,841
Energy	13,527	9,353	7,086	5,685	4,735	4,115	2,297
Natural resources and environment	12,998	12,672	12,593	13,357	13,639	13,363	14,606
Agriculture	15,944	22,901	13,613	25,565	31,449	26,606	17,210
Commerce and housing credit	6,256	6,681	6,917	4,229	4,890	6,182	18,815
On-budget	6,256	6,681	6,917	4,229	4,890	6,182	18,815
Off-budget							
Transportation	20,625	21,334	23,669	25,838	28,117	26,222	27,272
Community and regional development	8,347	7,560	7,673	7,680	7,233	5,051	5,294
Education, training, employment, and social services	27,029	26,606	27,579	29,342	30,585	29,724	31,938
Health	27,445	28,641	30,417	33,542	35,936	39,967	44,487
Medicare	46,567	52,588	57,540	65,822	70,164	75,120	78,878
Income security	107,717	122,598	112,668	128,200	119,796	123,250	129,332
Social security	155,964	170,724	178,223	188,623	198,757	207,353	219,341
On-budget	844	19,993	7,056	5,189	8,072	4,930	4,852
Off-budget	155,120	150,731	171,167	183,434	190,684	202,422	214,489
Veterans benefits and services	23,958	24,846	25,614	26,292	26,356	26,782	29,428
Administration of justice	4,712	5,105	5,663	6,270	6,572	7,553	9,236
General government	10,914	11,235	11,817	11,588	12,564	7,565	9,464
Net interest	85,044	89,828	111,123	129,504	136,047	138,652	151,838
On-budget	87,114	91,673	114,432	133,622	140,377	143,942	159,253
Off-budget	−2,071	−1,845	−3,310	−4,118	−4,329	−5,290	−7,416
Allowances							
Undistributed offsetting receipts	−26,099	−33,976	−31,957	−32,698	−33,007	−36,455	−36,967
On-budget	−24,453	−32,198	−29,913	−30,189	−30,150	−33,155	−32,585
Off-budget	−1,646	−1,778	−2,044	−2,509	−2,857	−3,300	−4,382

Note.—Through fiscal year 1976, the fiscal year was on a July 1–June 30 basis; beginning October 1976 (fiscal year 1977), the fiscal year is on an October 1–September 30 basis. The 3-month period from July 1, 1976 through September 30, 1976 is a separate fiscal period known as the transition quarter.

Refunds of receipts are excluded from receipts and outlays.

See next page for continuation of table.

TABLE B-78.—*Federal receipts, outlays, and debt, fiscal years 1982-95*—Continued

[Millions of dollars; fiscal years]

Description	Actual					Estimates	
	1989	1990	1991	1992	1993	1994	1995
RECEIPTS AND OUTLAYS:							
Total receipts	990,691	1,031,321	1,054,272	1,090,453	1,153,535	1,249,071	1,353,815
Total outlays	1,143,172	1,252,705	1,323,793	1,380,856	1,408,205	1,483,829	1,518,945
Total surplus or deficit (−)	−152,481	−221,384	−269,521	−290,403	−254,670	−234,758	−165,130
On-budget receipts	727,026	749,666	760,388	788,027	841,601	912,892	998,594
On-budget outlays	932,261	1,027,640	1,082,106	1,128,518	1,141,618	1,202,953	1,223,582
On-budget surplus or deficit (−)	−205,235	−277,974	−321,719	−340,490	−300,017	−290,061	−224,987
Off-budget receipts	263,666	281,656	293,885	302,426	311,934	336,179	355,221
Off-budget outlays	210,911	225,065	241,687	252,339	266,587	280,876	295,364
Off-budget surplus or deficit (−)	52,754	56,590	52,198	50,087	45,347	55,303	59,857
OUTSTANDING DEBT, END OF PERIOD:							
Gross Federal debt	2,867,493	3,206,207	3,598,303	4,001,941	4,351,223	4,676,029	4,960,128
Held by Government accounts	678,157	795,841	910,362	1,003,302	1,104,045	1,203,617	1,314,001
Held by the public	2,189,336	2,410,366	2,687,942	2,998,639	3,247,178	3,472,412	3,646,127
Federal Reserve System	220,088	234,410	258,591	296,397	325,653		
Other	1,969,248	2,175,956	2,429,351	2,702,243	2,921,526		
RECEIPTS: ON-BUDGET AND OFF-BUDGET	990,691	1,031,321	1,054,272	1,090,453	1,153,535	1,249,071	1,353,815
Individual income taxes	445,690	466,884	467,827	475,964	509,680	549,901	595,048
Corporation income taxes	103,291	93,507	98,086	100,270	117,520	130,719	140,437
Social insurance taxes and contributions	359,416	380,047	396,016	413,689	428,300	461,923	490,393
On-budget	95,751	98,392	102,131	111,263	116,366	125,744	135,172
Off-budget	263,666	281,656	293,885	302,426	311,934	336,179	355,221
Excise taxes	34,386	35,345	42,402	45,569	48,057	54,550	71,888
Estate and gift taxes	8,745	11,500	11,138	11,143	12,577	12,749	13,885
Customs duties and fees	16,334	16,707	15,949	17,359	18,802	19,198	20,856
Miscellaneous receipts:							
Deposits of earnings by Federal Reserve System	19,604	24,319	19,158	22,920	14,908	15,847	16,604
All other	3,225	3,011	3,696	3,538	3,691	4,184	4,705
OUTLAYS: ON-BUDGET AND OFF-BUDGET	1,143,172	1,252,705	1,323,793	1,380,856	1,408,205	1,483,829	1,518,945
National defense	303,559	299,331	273,292	298,350	291,086	279,824	270,725
International affairs	9,573	13,764	15,851	16,107	16,826	18,968	17,798
General science, space, and technology	12,838	14,444	16,111	16,409	17,030	17,279	16,941
Energy	2,706	3,341	2,436	4,500	4,319	4,988	4,564
Natural resources and environment	16,182	17,080	18,559	20,025	20,239	22,285	21,817
Agriculture	16,919	11,958	15,183	15,205	20,443	16,868	12,795
Commerce and housing credit	29,211	67,142	75,639	10,083	−22,725	504	−5,482
On-budget	29,520	65,516	74,321	9,424	−24,166	−1,245	−8,741
Off-budget	−310	1,626	1,317	659	1,441	1,748	3,259
Transportation	27,608	29,485	31,099	33,333	35,004	37,582	38,368
Community and regional development	5,362	8,498	6,811	6,838	9,051	9,282	9,154
Education, training, employment, and social services	36,674	38,755	43,354	45,248	50,012	50,793	53,524
Health	48,390	57,716	71,183	89,497	99,415	112,252	123,077
Medicare	84,964	98,102	104,489	119,024	130,552	143,651	156,228
Income security	136,031	147,019	170,301	196,958	207,257	214,626	221,440
Social security	232,542	248,623	269,015	287,585	304,585	320,460	337,168
On-budget	5,069	3,625	2,619	6,166	6,236	5,796	6,639
Off-budget	227,473	244,998	266,395	281,418	298,349	314,663	330,529
Veterans benefits and services	30,066	29,112	31,349	34,138	35,720	38,129	39,247
Administration of justice	9,474	9,995	12,276	14,426	14,955	16,479	17,331
General government	9,017	10,734	11,661	12,990	13,009	14,299	13,807
Net interest	169,266	184,221	194,541	199,421	198,811	203,448	212,835
On-budget	180,661	200,212	214,763	223,059	225,599	232,521	244,504
Off-budget	−11,395	−15,991	−20,222	−23,637	−26,788	−29,073	−31,669
Allowances							205
Undistributed offsetting receipts	−37,212	−36,615	−39,356	−39,280	−37,386	−37,887	−42,597
On-budget	−32,354	−31,048	−33,553	−33,179	−30,970	−31,425	−35,841
Off-budget	−4,858	−5,567	−5,804	−6,101	−6,416	−6,463	−6,756

See *Budget of the United States Government, Fiscal Year 1995*, February 1994, for additional information.

Sources: Department of the Treasury and Office of Management and Budget.

TABLE B-79.—*Federal budget receipts, outlays, surplus or deficit, and debt, as percentages of gross domestic product, 1934-95*

[Percent; fiscal years]

Fiscal year	Receipts	Outlays Total	Outlays National defense	Surplus or deficit (−)	Gross Federal debt (end of period) Total	Gross Federal debt (end of period) Held by public
1934	4.9	10.8		−5.9		
1935	5.3	9.3		−4.1		
1936	5.1	10.6		−5.6		
1937	6.2	8.7		−2.5		
1938	7.7	7.8		−.1		
1939	7.2	10.4		−3.2		
1940	6.9	9.9	1.7	−3.1	53.1	44.8
1941	7.7	12.1	5.7	−4.4	51.1	42.9
1942	10.3	24.8	18.1	−14.5	55.9	47.8
1943	13.7	44.8	38.0	−31.1	81.3	72.8
1944	21.7	45.3	39.2	−23.6	101.2	91.6
1945	21.3	43.7	39.1	−22.4	122.7	110.9
1946	18.5	26.0	20.1	−7.5	127.5	113.8
1947	17.3	15.5	5.7	1.8	115.4	100.6
1948	16.8	12.1	3.7	4.8	102.2	87.7
1949	15.0	14.8	5.0	.2	96.2	81.6
1950	14.8	16.0	5.2	−1.2	96.6	82.4
1951	16.5	14.5	7.5	1.9	81.4	68.4
1952	19.4	19.9	13.5	−.4	76.1	63.1
1953	19.1	20.9	14.5	−1.8	73.1	60.0
1954	18.9	19.3	13.4	−.3	73.6	61.0
1955	17.0	17.8	11.1	−.8	71.3	58.9
1956	17.9	17.0	10.2	.9	65.5	53.4
1957	18.3	17.5	10.4	.8	62.1	50.0
1958	17.8	18.4	10.4	−.6	62.4	50.5
1959	16.5	19.2	10.2	−2.7	59.9	48.9
1960	18.3	18.3	9.5	.1	57.6	46.9
1961	18.3	18.9	9.6	−.6	56.6	46.1
1962	18.0	19.2	9.4	−1.3	54.6	44.7
1963	18.2	19.0	9.1	−.8	53.1	43.5
1964	18.0	19.0	8.8	−.9	50.5	41.1
1965	17.4	17.6	7.5	−.2	48.0	38.9
1966	17.8	18.3	7.9	−.5	44.7	35.9
1967	18.8	19.8	9.0	−1.1	42.9	33.6
1968	18.1	21.0	9.7	−3.0	43.5	34.2
1969	20.2	19.8	8.9	.4	39.5	30.0
1970	19.6	19.9	8.3	−.3	38.7	28.7
1971	17.8	20.0	7.5	−2.2	38.8	28.8
1972	18.1	20.1	6.9	−2.0	38.0	28.1
1973	18.1	19.3	6.0	−1.2	36.6	26.8
1974	18.8	19.2	5.7	−.4	34.5	24.5
1975	18.5	22.0	5.7	−3.5	35.9	26.1
1976	17.7	22.1	5.3	−4.4	37.3	28.3
Transition quarter	18.3	21.6	5.0	−3.3	36.2	27.8
1977	18.5	21.3	5.1	−2.8	36.8	28.6
1978	18.5	21.3	4.8	−2.7	36.0	28.2
1979	19.1	20.7	4.8	−1.7	34.1	26.3
1980	19.6	22.3	5.1	−2.8	34.4	26.8
1981	20.2	22.9	5.3	−2.7	33.5	26.5
1982	19.8	23.9	5.9	−4.1	36.4	29.4
1983	18.1	24.4	6.3	−6.3	41.3	34.1
1984	18.0	23.1	6.2	−5.0	42.3	35.2
1985	18.5	23.9	6.4	−5.4	45.8	37.8
1986	18.2	23.5	6.5	−5.2	50.3	41.2
1987	19.2	22.5	6.3	−3.4	52.7	42.4
1988	18.9	22.1	6.0	−3.2	54.1	42.6
1989	19.2	22.1	5.9	−2.9	55.4	42.3
1990	18.8	22.9	5.5	−4.0	58.5	44.0
1991	18.6	23.3	4.8	−4.8	63.4	47.4
1992	18.4	23.3	5.0	−4.9	67.4	50.5
1993	18.3	22.4	4.6	−4.0	69.1	51.6
1994 [1]	18.8	22.3	4.2	−3.5	70.4	52.3
1995 [1]	19.3	21.6	3.9	−2.4	70.6	51.9

[1] Estimates.

Note.—Through fiscal year 1976, the fiscal year was on a July 1–June 30 basis; beginning October 1976 (fiscal year 1977), the fiscal year is on an October 1–September 30 basis. The 3-month period from July 1, 1976 through September 30, 1976 is a separate fiscal period known as the transition quarter.

See *Budget of the United States Government, Fiscal Year 1995,* February 1994, for additional information.

Sources: Department of the Treasury and Office of Management and Budget.

TABLE B-80.—*Federal and State and local government receipts and expenditures, national income and product accounts, 1959–93*

[Billions of dollars; quarterly data at seasonally adjusted annual rates]

Year or quarter	Total government Receipts	Total government Expenditures	Total government Surplus or deficit (−), national income and product accounts	Federal Government Receipts	Federal Government Expenditures	Federal Government Surplus or deficit (−), national income and product accounts	State and local government Receipts	State and local government Expenditures	State and local government Surplus or deficit (−), national income and product accounts
1959	128.8	131.9	−3.1	90.6	93.2	−2.6	45.0	45.5	−0.5
1960	138.8	135.2	3.6	97.0	93.4	3.5	48.3	48.3	.0
1961	144.1	147.1	−3.0	99.0	101.7	−2.6	52.4	52.7	−.4
1962	155.8	158.7	−2.9	107.2	110.6	−3.4	56.6	56.1	.5
1963	167.5	165.9	1.6	115.5	114.4	1.1	61.1	60.6	.4
1964	172.9	174.5	−1.6	116.2	118.8	−2.6	67.1	66.1	1.0
1965	187.0	185.8	1.2	125.8	124.6	1.3	72.3	72.3	.0
1966	210.7	211.6	−1.0	143.5	144.9	−1.4	81.5	81.1	.5
1967	226.4	240.2	−13.7	152.6	165.2	−12.7	89.8	90.9	−1.1
1968	260.9	265.5	−4.6	176.8	181.5	−4.7	102.7	102.6	.1
1969	294.0	284.0	10.0	199.6	191.0	8.5	114.8	113.3	1.5
1970	299.8	311.2	−11.5	195.2	208.5	−13.3	129.0	127.2	1.8
1971	318.9	338.1	−19.2	202.6	224.3	−21.7	145.3	142.8	2.5
1972	364.2	368.1	−3.9	232.0	249.3	−17.3	169.7	156.3	13.4
1973	408.5	401.6	6.9	263.7	270.3	−6.6	185.3	171.9	13.4
1974	450.7	455.2	−4.5	294.0	305.6	−11.6	200.6	193.5	7.1
1975	465.8	530.6	−64.8	294.8	364.2	−69.4	225.6	221.0	4.6
1976	532.6	570.9	−38.3	339.9	392.7	−52.9	253.9	239.3	14.6
1977	598.4	615.2	−16.8	384.0	426.4	−42.4	281.9	256.3	25.6
1978	673.2	670.3	2.9	441.2	469.3	−28.1	309.3	278.2	31.1
1979	754.7	745.3	9.4	504.7	520.3	−15.7	330.6	305.4	25.1
1980	825.7	861.0	−35.3	553.0	613.1	−60.1	361.4	336.6	24.8
1981	941.9	972.3	−30.3	639.0	697.8	−58.8	390.8	362.3	28.5
1982	960.5	1,069.1	−108.6	635.4	770.9	−135.5	409.0	382.1	26.9
1983	1,016.4	1,156.2	−139.8	660.0	840.0	−180.1	443.4	403.2	40.3
1984	1,123.6	1,232.4	−108.8	725.8	892.7	−166.9	492.2	434.1	58.1
1985	1,217.0	1,342.2	−125.3	788.6	969.9	−181.4	528.7	472.6	56.1
1986	1,290.5	1,437.5	−146.8	827.2	1,028.2	−201.0	571.2	517.0	54.3
1987	1,405.2	1,516.9	−111.7	913.8	1,065.6	−151.8	594.3	554.2	40.1
1988	1,492.4	1,590.7	−98.3	972.3	1,109.0	−136.6	631.3	593.0	38.4
1989	1,622.6	1,700.1	−77.5	1,059.3	1,181.6	−122.3	681.5	636.7	44.8
1990	1,709.1	1,847.5	−138.4	1,111.4	1,274.9	−163.5	730.0	704.9	25.1
1991	1,755.2	1,951.3	−196.2	1,127.8	1,331.2	−203.4	780.5	773.2	7.3
1992	1,849.4	2,118.5	−269.1	1,183.0	1,459.3	−276.3	837.8	830.6	7.2
1993 ᵖ	1,969.1	2,192.7	−223.7	1,267.6	1,493.4	−225.8	887.3	885.2	2.1
1982: IV	965.9	1,122.8	−156.9	632.3	815.7	−183.4	417.9	391.4	26.5
1983: IV	1,043.7	1,180.0	−136.3	671.1	855.7	−184.6	459.5	411.1	48.3
1984: IV	1,147.1	1,274.9	−127.8	739.8	926.6	−186.8	505.1	446.1	59.0
1985: IV	1,243.8	1,374.7	−130.9	803.6	990.8	−187.2	544.8	488.4	56.3
1986: IV	1,335.4	1,461.6	−126.2	856.8	1,034.3	−177.5	582.4	531.1	51.2
1987: IV	1,445.7	1,561.5	−115.8	943.5	1,096.3	−152.7	605.1	568.1	37.0
1988: IV	1,535.8	1,630.5	−94.7	1,000.6	1,135.5	−134.9	648.2	607.9	40.2
1989: IV	1,644.1	1,744.3	−100.2	1,068.3	1,209.8	−141.5	697.7	656.4	41.3
1990: I	1,676.1	1,808.0	−131.9	1,091.3	1,257.8	−166.4	712.5	677.9	34.5
II	1,705.1	1,827.7	−122.7	1,114.5	1,266.5	−152.0	722.4	693.1	29.3
III	1,728.7	1,848.6	−119.9	1,123.7	1,268.3	−144.6	736.9	712.2	24.7
IV	1,726.5	1,905.8	−179.3	1,115.8	1,306.9	−191.0	748.3	736.5	11.7
1991: I	1,728.1	1,867.2	−139.1	1,115.8	1,261.0	−145.2	756.2	750.1	6.1
II	1,740.9	1,941.6	−200.7	1,120.3	1,326.5	−206.2	772.0	766.5	5.5
III	1,765.0	1,977.2	−212.2	1,132.6	1,350.2	−217.7	787.0	781.5	5.5
IV	1,786.8	2,019.4	−232.6	1,142.5	1,387.2	−244.7	806.6	794.5	12.1
1992: I	1,819.7	2,083.9	−264.2	1,165.9	1,436.1	−270.2	817.2	811.2	6.1
II	1,837.6	2,109.7	−272.2	1,176.1	1,456.0	−279.9	833.2	825.5	7.8
III	1,834.4	2,123.8	−289.5	1,169.1	1,459.8	−290.7	839.0	837.8	1.2
IV	1,906.0	2,156.6	−250.6	1,221.1	1,485.3	−264.2	861.6	848.0	13.5
1993: I	1,902.5	2,165.3	−262.8	1,218.4	1,481.9	−263.5	860.2	859.4	.8
II	1,966.3	2,187.9	−221.5	1,268.0	1,490.6	−222.6	881.0	880.0	1.1
III	1,981.4	2,195.8	−214.4	1,275.9	1,488.5	−212.7	894.2	895.9	−1.7
IV ᵖ		2,222.1			1,512.5			905.5	

Note.—Federal grants-in-aid to State and local governments are reflected in Federal expenditures and State and local receipts. Total government receipts and expenditures have been adjusted to eliminate this duplication.

Source: Department of Commerce, Bureau of Economic Analysis.

TABLE B-81.—*Federal and State and local government receipts and expenditures, national income and product accounts, by major type, 1959–93*

[Billions of dollars; quarterly data at seasonally adjusted annual rates]

Year or quarter	Receipts					Expenditures							Subsidies less current surplus of government enterprises	Surplus or deficit (−), national income and product accounts	Addendum: Grants-in-aid to State and local governments
	Total	Personal tax and nontax receipts	Corporate profits tax accruals	Indirect business tax and nontax accruals	Contributions for social insurance	Total [1]	Purchases	Transfer payments	Net interest paid			Less: Dividends received by government [2]			
									Total	Interest paid	Less: Interest received by government [2]				
1959	128.8	44.5	23.6	41.9	18.8	131.9	99.0	27.5	6.3				−0.9	−3.1	6.8
1960	138.8	48.7	22.7	45.5	21.9	135.2	99.8	29.3	6.9	10.1	3.3		−.8	3.6	6.5
1961	144.1	50.3	22.8	48.1	22.9	147.1	107.0	33.6	6.4	9.9	3.5		.2	−3.0	7.2
1962	155.8	54.8	24.0	51.7	25.4	158.7	116.8	34.7	6.9	10.8	3.9		.3	−2.9	8.0
1963	167.5	58.0	26.2	54.7	28.5	165.9	122.3	36.6	7.4	11.6	4.2		−.3	1.6	9.1
1964	172.9	56.0	28.0	58.8	30.1	174.5	128.3	38.1	7.9	12.5	4.6		.1	−1.6	10.4
1965	187.0	61.9	30.9	62.7	31.6	185.8	136.3	41.1	8.1	13.2	5.1		.3	1.2	11.1
1966	210.7	71.0	33.7	65.4	40.6	211.6	155.9	45.8	8.5	14.5	6.0		1.4	−1.0	14.4
1967	226.4	77.9	32.7	70.4	45.5	240.2	175.6	54.5	8.9	15.7	6.8		1.2	−13.7	15.9
1968	260.9	92.1	39.4	79.0	50.4	265.5	191.5	62.6	10.3	18.1	7.7	0.1	1.2	−4.6	18.6
1969	294.0	109.9	39.7	86.6	57.9	284.0	201.8	69.3	11.5	19.8	8.3	.2	1.5	10.0	20.3
1970	299.8	109.0	34.4	94.3	62.2	311.2	212.7	83.8	12.4	22.3	9.9	.2	2.6	−11.5	24.4
1971	318.9	108.7	37.7	103.6	68.9	338.1	224.3	99.4	12.5	23.1	10.6	.3	2.4	−19.2	29.0
1972	364.2	132.0	41.9	111.4	79.0	368.1	241.5	110.9	12.9	24.8	11.9	.3	3.4	−3.9	37.5
1973	408.5	140.6	49.3	121.0	97.6	401.6	257.7	126.6	15.2	29.6	14.4	.5	2.6	6.9	40.6
1974	450.7	159.1	51.8	129.3	110.5	455.2	288.3	150.5	16.3	33.6	17.3	.9	.4	−4.5	43.9
1975	465.8	156.4	50.9	140.0	118.5	530.6	321.4	189.2	18.5	37.7	19.2	.9	2.6	−64.8	54.6
1976	532.6	182.3	64.2	151.6	134.5	570.9	341.3	206.5	22.8	43.6	20.9	.9	1.4	−38.3	61.1
1977	598.4	210.0	73.0	165.5	149.8	615.2	368.0	220.9	24.4	47.9	23.5	1.3	3.3	−16.8	67.5
1978	673.2	240.1	83.5	177.8	171.8	670.3	403.6	238.6	26.5	56.8	30.3	1.7	3.6	2.9	77.3
1979	754.7	280.2	88.0	188.7	197.8	745.3	448.5	266.9	28.7	68.6	39.9	2.0	2.9	9.4	80.5
1980	825.7	312.4	84.8	212.0	216.6	861.0	507.1	317.6	33.4	83.9	50.5	1.9	4.8	−35.3	88.7
1981	941.9	360.2	81.1	249.3	251.3	972.3	561.1	360.7	48.1	110.2	62.1	2.3	4.7	−30.3	87.9
1982	960.5	371.4	63.1	256.4	269.6	1,069.1	607.6	402.7	55.5	130.6	75.0	2.9	6.2	−108.6	83.9
1983	1,016.4	368.8	77.2	280.1	290.2	1,156.2	652.3	433.4	61.8	146.6	84.8	3.4	11.7	−139.8	87.0
1984	1,123.6	395.1	94.0	309.5	325.0	1,232.4	700.8	447.2	79.1	174.6	95.6	3.9	9.5	−108.8	94.4
1985	1,217.0	436.8	96.5	329.9	353.8	1,342.2	772.3	479.5	88.3	195.9	107.6	4.5	6.4	−125.3	100.3
1986	1,290.8	459.0	106.5	345.5	379.8	1,437.5	833.0	509.4	90.6	207.9	117.3	5.1	9.7	−146.8	107.6
1987	1,405.2	512.5	127.1	365.0	400.7	1,516.9	881.5	531.8	95.4	215.9	120.5	5.9	14.1	−111.7	102.8
1988	1,492.4	527.7	137.0	385.3	442.3	1,590.7	918.7	566.2	101.8	229.9	128.1	6.9	10.9	−98.3	111.3
1989	1,622.6	593.3	141.3	414.7	473.2	1,700.1	975.2	615.1	112.4	251.0	138.6	8.1	5.4	−77.5	118.2
1990	1,709.1	623.3	138.7	444.0	503.1	1,847.5	1,047.4	679.5	125.2	269.6	144.5	9.0	4.5	−138.4	132.3
1991	1,755.2	620.4	129.8	476.6	528.4	1,951.3	1,099.3	721.3	140.5	284.4	143.9	9.5	−.3	−196.2	153.0
1992	1,849.4	644.8	146.3	502.8	555.6	2,118.5	1,131.8	853.1	141.1	286.1	144.9	10.2	2.7	−269.1	171.4
1993 [p]	1,969.1	681.6	171.7	530.5	585.3	2,192.7	1,157.1	903.9	135.3	286.2	150.9	10.7	7.2	−223.7	185.8
1982: IV	965.9	372.1	58.7	262.3	272.8	1,122.8	631.6	428.1	56.6	135.6	79.0	3.1	9.6	−156.9	84.3
1983: IV	1,043.7	371.6	82.2	291.7	298.3	1,180.0	657.6	439.1	67.7	156.1	88.4	3.5	19.2	−136.3	86.9
1984: IV	1,147.1	413.4	83.8	317.7	332.2	1,274.9	727.0	456.2	86.7	186.5	99.8	4.1	9.7	−127.8	97.7
1985: IV	1,243.8	448.8	97.6	335.1	362.3	1,374.7	799.2	488.3	89.2	201.6	112.3	4.7	2.6	−130.9	104.5
1986: IV	1,335.4	478.5	116.6	351.6	388.7	1,461.6	849.7	518.6	90.5	208.7	118.2	5.4	8.2	−126.2	103.8
1987: IV	1,445.7	528.6	135.2	372.3	409.6	1,561.5	901.4	542.6	101.3	222.9	121.6	6.1	22.0	−115.8	102.9
1988: IV	1,535.8	542.0	146.2	394.2	453.5	1,630.5	937.6	578.6	105.0	236.0	131.0	7.2	16.5	−94.7	113.0
1989: IV	1,644.1	605.1	134.2	424.4	480.4	1,744.3	994.5	639.0	114.8	256.0	141.2	8.5	4.4	−100.2	121.9
1990: I	1,676.1	611.9	132.0	436.2	495.9	1,808.0	1,027.7	660.5	118.4	260.0	141.6	8.7	9.9	−131.9	127.7
II	1,705.1	627.4	139.8	437.2	500.7	1,827.7	1,037.3	671.4	124.9	266.1	141.2	9.0	3.0	−122.7	131.9
III	1,728.7	628.5	145.7	448.0	506.4	1,848.6	1,048.3	682.6	132.4	274.1	141.7	9.0	−5.6	−119.9	131.9
IV	1,726.5	625.2	137.0	454.8	509.5	1,905.8	1,076.5	703.3	125.1	278.3	153.2	9.3	10.4	−179.3	137.6
1991: I	1,728.1	616.4	125.4	465.6	520.7	1,867.2	1,093.0	647.4	134.6	280.3	145.7	9.3	1.8	−139.1	143.8
II	1,740.9	616.6	128.0	470.5	525.7	1,941.6	1,099.9	708.9	141.1	284.2	143.1	9.5	.8	−200.7	151.5
III	1,765.0	619.7	132.5	481.3	531.5	1,977.2	1,104.0	749.8	140.9	285.2	144.3	9.5	−8.0	−212.2	154.6
IV	1,786.8	628.8	133.4	488.9	535.7	2,019.4	1,100.2	779.0	145.5	287.8	142.3	9.7	4.3	−232.6	162.3
1992: I	1,819.7	630.9	147.0	493.4	548.5	2,083.9	1,118.5	829.2	143.0	285.4	142.4	9.8	3.0	−264.2	163.4
II	1,837.6	634.6	153.0	497.3	552.7	2,109.7	1,125.8	845.9	144.4	287.8	143.4	10.2	3.9	−272.2	171.8
III	1,834.4	642.8	130.1	504.8	556.6	2,123.8	1,139.1	857.1	141.6	287.6	146.0	10.3	−3.7	−289.5	173.7
IV	1,906.0	670.7	155.0	515.7	564.6	2,156.6	1,143.8	880.1	135.6	283.5	147.9	10.5	7.7	−250.6	176.7
1993: I	1,902.5	657.1	160.9	515.6	568.9	2,165.3	1,139.7	886.2	132.8	281.8	149.0	10.5	17.1	−262.8	176.1
II	1,966.3	681.0	173.3	526.2	585.9	2,187.9	1,158.6	896.6	137.2	287.4	150.2	10.7	6.1	−221.5	182.8
III	1,981.4	689.0	169.5	532.4	590.5	2,195.8	1,164.8	910.1	137.0	288.9	151.9	10.8	−5.3	−214.4	188.6
IV [p]		699.1		547.9	596.0	2,222.1	1,165.7	922.8	134.3	286.8	152.5	10.9	10.7		195.8

[1] Includes an item for the difference between wage accruals and disbursements, not shown separately.
[2] Prior to 1968, dividends received is included in interest received.

Source: Department of Commerce, Bureau of Economic Analysis.

364

TABLE B-82.—*Federal Government receipts and expenditures, national income and product accounts, 1976–93*

[Billions of dollars; quarterly data at seasonally adjusted annual rates]

Year or quarter	Receipts					Expenditures								Surplus or deficit (−), national income and product accounts
	Total	Personal tax and nontax receipts	Corporate profits tax accruals	Indirect business tax and nontax accruals	Contributions for social insurance	Total [1]	Purchases		Transfer payments		Grants-in-aid to State and local governments	Net interest paid	Subsidies less current surplus of government enterprises	
							Total	National defense	To persons	To rest of the world (net)				
Fiscal: [2]														
1976	322.0	136.5	51.7	24.6	109.2	379.0	132.6	91.5	154.3	3.1	57.5	25.1	6.5	−57.0
1977	375.4	165.2	59.8	25.0	125.4	417.1	144.7	99.2	167.1	3.4	66.3	28.5	7.2	−41.7
1978	423.8	185.5	67.4	27.9	143.0	458.0	158.1	106.3	179.3	3.5	74.7	33.1	9.4	−34.1
1979	490.5	221.6	75.3	29.9	163.7	505.4	174.5	117.7	198.5	4.0	79.1	40.2	9.1	−14.9
1980	538.1	249.1	70.4	36.2	182.3	587.1	201.0	136.9	235.4	4.3	86.7	50.1	9.6	−49.0
1981	623.0	287.9	69.3	54.3	211.5	679.9	232.9	160.9	274.6	5.2	90.1	66.1	11.0	−56.9
1982	642.7	308.4	51.6	51.5	231.2	747.6	259.5	187.3	305.6	5.8	83.4	81.8	11.5	−105.0
1983	646.4	290.7	56.4	52.0	247.3	829.2	289.8	210.2	339.8	6.5	86.2	89.6	16.8	−182.8
1984	711.7	300.4	75.1	57.0	279.3	875.3	302.2	228.2	342.4	8.7	91.5	107.5	23.0	−163.6
1985	777.0	337.0	75.0	59.1	305.9	952.9	335.2	251.7	360.7	11.5	98.6	125.2	21.6	−175.9
1986	813.8	353.1	80.4	53.8	326.5	1,017.6	363.7	274.3	380.6	12.5	108.3	130.5	22.1	−203.9
1987	899.1	396.3	99.4	57.8	345.5	1,051.0	379.9	287.6	399.4	9.9	103.4	133.6	24.9	−151.9
1988	955.1	403.8	107.6	59.6	384.1	1,098.5	386.3	295.1	420.7	10.2	108.4	143.8	28.9	−143.3
1989	1,050.1	456.9	119.2	62.2	411.8	1,164.5	399.4	295.5	449.6	11.6	115.8	160.5	27.6	−114.3
1990	1,092.0	475.2	115.4	63.1	438.3	1,250.0	418.1	309.0	491.3	14.4	128.3	175.1	22.8	−157.9
1991	1,121.4	475.7	108.4	76.7	460.6	1,309.2	446.0	325.8	535.9	−26.1	147.0	183.2	23.3	−187.8
1992	1,165.6	484.0	116.3	80.8	484.5	1,436.0	444.9	311.7	595.8	11.5	167.4	189.7	26.7	−270.4
1993	1,249.3	511.7	135.6	86.0	516.0	1,484.5	445.0	306.8	630.2	16.2	182.1	181.3	29.7	−235.2
Calendar:														
1976	339.9	146.6	54.6	23.8	115.0	392.7	135.8	93.4	159.3	3.7	61.1	26.8	6.2	−52.9
1977	384.0	169.1	61.6	25.6	127.7	426.4	147.9	100.9	170.1	3.4	67.5	29.1	8.4	−42.4
1978	441.2	193.8	71.4	28.9	147.1	469.3	162.2	108.9	182.4	3.8	77.3	34.6	9.2	−28.1
1979	504.7	229.7	74.4	30.1	170.4	520.3	179.3	121.9	205.7	4.1	80.5	42.1	8.7	−15.7
1980	553.0	256.2	70.3	39.6	186.8	613.1	209.1	142.7	247.0	5.0	88.7	52.7	10.6	−60.1
1981	639.0	297.2	65.7	57.3	218.8	697.8	240.8	167.5	282.1	5.0	87.9	71.7	10.3	−58.8
1982	635.4	302.9	49.0	49.7	233.8	770.9	266.6	193.8	316.4	6.4	83.9	84.4	13.3	−135.5
1983	660.0	292.6	61.3	53.5	252.6	840.0	292.0	214.4	340.2	7.3	87.0	92.7	20.4	−180.1
1984	725.8	308.0	75.2	57.8	284.8	892.7	310.9	233.1	344.3	9.4	94.4	113.1	20.8	−166.9
1985	788.6	342.8	76.3	58.6	310.9	969.9	344.3	258.6	366.8	11.4	100.3	127.0	19.9	−181.4
1986	827.2	357.4	83.8	53.5	332.5	1,028.2	367.8	276.7	386.2	12.3	107.6	131.0	23.4	−201.0
1987	913.8	400.6	103.2	58.4	351.5	1,065.6	384.9	292.1	401.8	10.4	102.8	136.6	29.1	−151.8
1988	972.3	410.1	111.0	60.9	390.4	1,109.0	387.0	295.6	425.9	10.4	111.3	146.0	28.4	−136.6
1989	1,059.3	461.9	117.1	61.9	418.5	1,181.6	401.6	299.9	460.2	11.3	118.2	164.8	25.5	−122.3
1990	1,111.4	484.3	116.4	65.8	444.8	1,274.9	426.5	314.0	500.9	13.2	132.3	176.5	25.6	−163.5
1991	1,127.8	474.9	107.1	79.1	466.7	1,331.2	445.9	322.5	550.0	−27.9	153.0	187.6	22.6	−203.4
1992	1,183.0	490.8	120.2	81.3	490.7	1,459.3	448.8	313.8	608.2	16.3	171.4	187.1	27.5	−276.3
1993 [P]	1,267.6	521.2	141.1	87.4	517.9	1,493.4	443.4	303.6	635.8	14.2	185.8	180.6	33.6	−225.8
1982: IV	632.3	301.6	45.5	49.2	235.9	815.7	281.4	205.5	337.8	8.2	84.3	86.8	17.3	−183.4
1983: IV	671.1	290.5	65.4	55.4	259.8	855.7	289.7	222.8	340.0	11.0	86.9	99.2	28.8	−184.6
1984: IV	739.8	323.5	67.0	58.2	291.1	926.6	324.7	242.9	346.2	13.9	97.7	122.3	22.2	−186.8
1985: IV	803.6	351.8	77.0	56.8	318.0	990.8	356.9	268.6	370.3	13.5	104.5	129.2	16.4	−187.2
1986: IV	856.8	371.7	91.4	54.8	338.8	1,034.3	373.1	278.6	391.4	12.8	103.8	131.1	22.1	−177.5
1987: IV	943.5	414.8	109.7	59.5	359.4	1,096.3	392.5	295.8	405.1	14.6	102.9	143.1	37.8	−152.7
1988: IV	1,000.6	420.0	118.5	61.4	400.7	1,135.5	392.0	296.8	429.4	15.1	113.0	151.2	34.9	−134.9
1989: IV	1,068.3	470.1	111.3	62.2	424.7	1,209.8	405.1	302.5	473.7	15.1	121.9	168.9	25.0	−141.5
1990: I	1,091.3	476.0	110.8	65.3	439.2	1,257.8	422.7	312.1	493.6	11.6	127.7	171.5	30.7	−166.4
II	1,114.5	489.5	117.2	64.9	442.9	1,266.5	423.6	312.5	494.9	15.3	131.9	176.9	23.9	−152.0
III	1,123.7	487.9	122.3	65.9	447.6	1,268.3	423.2	309.1	501.1	13.4	131.9	183.1	15.7	−144.6
IV	1,115.8	483.9	115.1	67.1	449.7	1,306.9	436.5	322.5	514.1	12.4	137.6	174.4	32.0	−191.0
1991: I	1,115.8	474.1	103.7	77.7	460.3	1,261.0	450.2	331.4	537.5	−76.9	143.8	182.6	23.9	−145.2
II	1,120.3	472.4	105.7	77.9	464.2	1,326.5	449.4	326.3	545.6	−32.0	151.5	188.3	23.4	−206.2
III	1,132.6	474.5	109.2	79.5	469.4	1,350.2	446.8	321.2	551.3	−5.1	154.6	187.6	15.1	−217.7
IV	1,142.5	478.5	109.8	81.3	472.8	1,387.2	437.4	311.2	565.4	2.2	162.3	191.9	27.9	−244.7
1992: I	1,165.9	479.7	121.1	80.4	484.7	1,436.1	445.5	312.3	598.4	12.6	163.4	189.3	27.0	−270.2
II	1,176.1	482.0	125.8	80.2	488.1	1,456.0	444.6	310.4	605.8	15.0	171.8	190.4	28.5	−279.9
III	1,169.1	489.5	107.0	81.1	491.4	1,459.8	452.8	316.7	611.6	12.8	173.7	187.4	21.4	−290.7
IV	1,221.1	511.8	127.1	83.5	498.7	1,485.3	452.4	315.7	617.1	24.6	176.7	181.3	33.2	−264.2
1993: I	1,218.4	502.1	132.4	81.5	502.3	1,481.9	442.2	304.8	628.9	13.1	176.1	178.3	42.9	−263.5
II	1,268.0	520.7	142.4	86.2	518.7	1,490.6	447.5	307.6	632.7	12.9	182.8	182.5	32.3	−222.6
III	1,275.9	527.1	139.3	86.7	522.8	1,488.5	443.6	301.9	635.3	13.7	188.6	182.2	21.4	−212.7
IV [P]		535.0			95.2	527.6	1,512.5	439.7	300.0	642.5	17.2	195.8	179.3	38.0	

[1] Includes an item for the difference between wage accruals and disbursements, not shown separately.
[2] Through fiscal year 1976, the fiscal year was on a July 1–June 30 basis; beginning October 1976 (fiscal year 1977), the fiscal year is on an October 1–September 30 basis. The 3-month period from July 1, 1976 through September 30, 1976 is a separate fiscal period known as the transition quarter. Data are not seasonally adjusted.

Sources: Department of Commerce (Bureau of Economic Analysis) and Office of Management and Budget.

TABLE B-83.—*State and local government receipts and expenditures, national income and product accounts, 1959–93*

[Billions of dollars; quarterly data at seasonally adjusted annual rates]

Year or quarter	Receipts Total	Personal tax and nontax receipts	Corporate profits tax accruals	Indirect business tax and nontax accruals	Contributions for social insurance	Federal grants-in-aid	Expenditures Total[1]	Purchases	Transfer payments to persons	Net interest paid less dividends received	Subsidies less current surplus of government enterprises	Surplus or deficit (−), national income and product accounts
1959	45.0	4.6	1.2	29.3	3.1	6.8	45.5	41.8	5.6	0.1	−2.0	−0.5
1960	48.3	5.2	1.2	32.0	3.4	6.5	48.3	44.5	5.9	.1	−2.2	.0
1961	52.4	5.7	1.3	34.4	3.7	7.2	52.7	48.4	6.5	.1	−2.3	−.4
1962	56.6	6.3	1.5	37.0	3.9	8.0	56.1	51.4	7.0	.2	−2.5	.5
1963	61.1	6.7	1.7	39.4	4.2	9.1	60.6	55.8	7.5	.1	−2.8	.4
1964	67.1	7.5	1.8	42.6	4.7	10.4	66.1	60.9	8.2	−.1	−2.8	1.0
1965	72.3	8.1	2.0	46.1	5.0	11.1	72.3	66.8	8.8	−.3	−3.0	.0
1966	81.5	9.5	2.2	49.7	5.7	14.4	81.1	74.6	10.1	−.6	−3.0	.5
1967	89.8	10.6	2.6	53.9	6.7	15.9	90.9	82.7	12.1	−.9	−3.1	−1.1
1968	102.7	12.7	3.3	60.8	7.2	18.6	102.6	92.3	14.5	−1.1	−3.2	.1
1969	114.8	15.2	3.6	67.4	8.3	20.3	113.3	101.3	16.7	−1.3	−3.3	1.5
1970	129.0	16.7	3.7	74.8	9.2	24.4	127.2	112.6	20.1	−2.0	−3.6	1.8
1971	145.3	18.7	4.3	83.1	10.2	29.0	142.8	124.3	24.0	−1.6	−3.7	2.5
1972	169.7	24.2	5.3	91.2	11.5	37.5	156.3	134.7	27.5	−1.8	−4.2	13.4
1973	185.3	26.3	6.0	99.5	13.0	40.6	171.9	149.2	30.4	−3.3	−4.3	13.4
1974	200.6	28.2	6.7	107.2	14.6	43.9	193.5	170.7	32.3	−5.2	−4.4	7.1
1975	225.6	31.0	7.3	115.8	16.8	54.6	221.0	192.0	38.9	−5.4	−4.5	4.6
1976	253.9	35.8	9.6	127.8	19.5	61.1	239.3	205.5	43.6	−5.0	−4.8	14.6
1977	281.9	41.0	11.4	139.9	22.1	67.5	256.3	220.1	47.4	−6.0	−5.1	25.6
1978	309.3	46.3	12.1	148.9	24.7	77.3	278.2	241.4	52.4	−9.8	−5.6	31.1
1979	330.6	50.5	13.6	158.6	27.4	80.5	305.4	269.2	57.2	−15.3	−5.7	25.1
1980	361.4	56.2	14.5	172.3	29.7	88.7	336.6	298.0	65.7	−21.2	−5.8	24.8
1981	390.8	63.0	15.4	192.0	32.5	87.9	362.3	320.3	73.6	−25.9	−5.6	28.5
1982	409.0	68.5	14.0	206.8	35.8	83.9	382.1	341.1	79.9	−31.8	−7.1	26.9
1983	443.4	76.2	15.9	226.6	37.7	87.0	403.2	360.3	85.9	−34.3	−8.7	40.3
1984	492.2	87.1	18.8	251.7	40.2	94.4	434.1	389.9	93.5	−37.9	−11.4	58.1
1985	528.7	94.0	20.2	271.4	42.8	100.3	472.6	428.1	101.2	−43.2	−13.5	56.1
1986	571.2	101.6	22.7	292.0	47.3	107.6	517.0	465.3	110.9	−45.6	−13.7	54.3
1987	594.3	111.8	23.9	306.5	49.2	102.8	554.2	496.6	119.6	−47.0	−14.9	40.1
1988	631.3	117.6	26.0	324.9	51.9	111.3	593.0	531.7	130.0	−51.1	−17.5	38.4
1989	681.5	131.4	24.2	352.8	54.8	118.2	636.7	573.6	143.6	−60.4	−20.1	44.8
1990	730.0	138.9	22.3	378.2	58.3	132.3	704.9	620.9	165.4	−60.3	−21.1	25.1
1991	780.5	145.5	22.7	397.5	61.7	153.0	773.2	653.4	199.2	−56.5	−22.9	7.3
1992	837.8	154.0	26.0	421.5	64.9	171.4	830.6	683.0	228.6	−56.2	−24.8	7.2
1993 ᵖ	887.3	160.3	30.5	443.1	67.4	185.8	885.2	713.7	253.9	−56.0	−26.5	2.1
1982: IV	417.9	70.5	13.1	213.1	36.8	84.3	391.4	350.3	82.1	−33.2	−7.7	26.5
1983: IV	459.5	81.1	16.8	236.3	38.4	86.9	411.1	367.9	88.0	−35.1	−9.6	48.3
1984: IV	505.1	89.9	16.8	259.6	41.1	97.7	446.1	402.2	96.1	−39.7	−12.5	59.0
1985: IV	544.8	97.0	20.6	278.3	44.3	104.5	488.4	442.4	104.5	−44.7	−13.8	56.3
1986: IV	582.4	106.8	25.2	296.8	49.8	103.8	531.1	476.6	114.4	−45.9	−13.9	51.2
1987: IV	605.1	113.8	25.5	312.8	50.2	102.9	568.1	509.0	122.9	−48.0	−15.8	37.0
1988: IV	648.2	122.0	27.7	332.7	52.8	113.0	607.9	545.7	134.2	−53.4	−18.5	40.2
1989: IV	697.7	135.0	22.8	362.2	55.8	121.9	656.4	589.3	150.2	−62.6	−20.6	41.3
1990: I	712.5	135.9	21.2	370.9	56.7	127.7	677.9	605.0	155.4	−61.8	−20.7	34.5
II	722.4	137.8	22.6	372.3	57.8	131.9	693.1	613.7	161.3	−61.0	−20.9	29.3
III	736.9	140.6	23.4	382.1	58.9	131.9	712.2	625.1	168.1	−59.7	−21.2	24.7
IV	748.3	141.3	21.9	387.7	59.7	137.6	736.5	640.0	176.8	−58.7	−21.6	11.7
1991: I	756.2	142.3	21.7	387.9	60.5	143.8	750.1	642.9	186.7	−57.3	−22.1	6.1
II	772.0	144.2	22.4	392.6	61.4	151.5	766.5	650.5	195.3	−56.6	−22.6	5.5
III	787.0	145.2	23.3	401.8	62.1	154.6	781.5	657.3	203.5	−56.2	−23.1	5.5
IV	806.6	150.2	23.6	407.5	62.9	162.3	794.5	662.8	211.4	−56.0	−23.6	12.1
1992: I	817.2	151.2	25.9	413.0	63.8	163.4	811.2	673.0	218.3	−56.1	−24.0	6.1
II	833.2	152.6	27.2	417.1	64.6	171.8	825.5	681.2	225.1	−56.2	−24.6	7.8
III	839.0	153.3	23.1	423.7	65.2	173.7	837.8	686.2	232.8	−56.1	−25.1	1.2
IV	861.6	158.8	27.9	432.2	65.9	176.7	848.0	691.4	238.4	−56.2	−25.5	13.5
1993: I	860.2	155.0	28.5	434.1	66.5	176.1	859.4	697.0	244.1	−56.0	−25.8	.8
II	881.0	160.3	30.8	440.0	67.2	182.8	880.0	711.1	251.0	−56.0	−26.2	1.1
III	894.2	162.0	30.1	445.7	67.7	188.6	895.9	721.2	257.2	−55.9	−26.7	−1.7
IV ᵖ		164.1		452.6	68.3	195.8	905.5	725.6	263.1	−56.0	−27.3	

[1] Includes an item for the difference between wage accruals and disbursements, not shown separately.

Source: Department of Commerce, Bureau of Economic Analysis.

TABLE B-84.—*State and local government revenues and expenditures, selected fiscal years, 1927–91*

[Millions of dollars]

Fiscal year [1]	General revenues by source [2]							General expenditures by function [2]				
	Total	Property taxes	Sales and gross receipts taxes	Individual income taxes	Corporation net income taxes	Revenue from Federal Government	All other [3]	Total	Education	Highways	Public welfare	All other [4]
1927	7,271	4,730	470	70	92	116	1,793	7,210	2,235	1,809	151	3,015
1932	7,267	4,487	752	74	79	232	1,643	7,765	2,311	1,741	444	3,269
1934	7,678	4,076	1,008	80	49	1,016	1,449	7,181	1,831	1,509	889	2,952
1936	8,395	4,093	1,484	153	113	948	1,604	7,644	2,177	1,425	827	3,215
1938	9,228	4,440	1,794	218	165	800	1,811	8,757	2,491	1,650	1,069	3,547
1940	9,609	4,430	1,982	224	156	945	1,872	9,229	2,638	1,573	1,156	3,862
1942	10,418	4,537	2,351	276	272	858	2,123	9,190	2,586	1,490	1,225	3,889
1944	10,908	4,604	2,289	342	451	954	2,269	8,863	2,793	1,200	1,133	3,737
1946	12,356	4,986	2,986	422	447	855	2,661	11,028	3,356	1,672	1,409	4,591
1948	17,250	6,126	4,442	543	592	1,861	3,685	17,684	5,379	3,036	2,099	7,170
1950	20,911	7,349	5,154	788	593	2,486	4,541	22,787	7,177	3,803	2,940	8,867
1952	25,181	8,652	6,357	998	846	2,566	5,763	26,098	8,318	4,650	2,788	10,342
1953	27,307	9,375	6,927	1,065	817	2,870	6,252	27,910	9,390	4,987	2,914	10,619
1954	29,012	9,967	7,276	1,127	778	2,966	6,897	30,701	10,557	5,527	3,060	11,557
1955	31,073	10,735	7,643	1,237	744	3,131	7,584	33,724	11,907	6,452	3,168	12,197
1956	34,667	11,749	8,691	1,538	890	3,335	8,465	36,711	13,220	6,953	3,139	13,399
1957	38,164	12,864	9,467	1,754	984	3,843	9,252	40,375	14,134	7,816	3,485	14,940
1958	41,219	14,047	9,829	1,759	1,018	4,865	9,699	44,851	15,919	8,567	3,818	16,547
1959	45,306	14,983	10,437	1,994	1,001	6,377	10,516	48,887	17,283	9,592	4,136	17,876
1960	50,505	16,405	11,849	2,463	1,180	6,974	11,634	51,876	18,719	9,428	4,404	19,325
1961	54,037	18,002	12,463	2,613	1,266	7,131	12,563	56,201	20,574	9,844	4,720	21,063
1962	58,252	19,054	13,494	3,037	1,308	7,871	13,489	60,206	22,216	10,357	5,084	22,549
1963	62,890	20,089	14,456	3,269	1,505	8,722	14,850	64,816	23,776	11,136	5,481	24,423
1962–63	62,269	19,833	14,446	3,267	1,505	8,663	14,556	63,977	23,729	11,150	5,420	23,678
1963–64	68,443	21,241	15,762	3,791	1,695	10,002	15,951	69,302	26,286	11,664	5,766	25,586
1964–65	74,000	22,583	17,118	4,090	1,929	11,029	17,250	74,678	28,563	12,221	6,315	27,579
1965–66	83,036	24,670	19,085	4,760	2,038	13,214	19,269	82,843	33,287	12,770	6,757	30,029
1966–67	91,197	26,047	20,530	5,825	2,227	15,370	21,197	93,350	37,919	13,932	8,218	33,281
1967–68	101,264	27,747	22,911	7,308	2,518	17,181	23,598	102,411	41,158	14,481	9,857	36,915
1968–69	114,550	30,673	26,519	8,908	3,180	19,153	26,118	116,728	47,238	15,417	12,110	41,963
1969–70	130,756	34,054	30,322	10,812	3,738	21,857	29,971	131,332	52,718	16,427	14,679	47,508
1970–71	144,927	37,852	33,233	11,900	3,424	26,146	32,374	150,674	59,413	18,095	18,226	54,940
1971–72	167,541	42,877	37,518	15,227	4,416	31,342	36,162	168,549	65,814	19,021	21,117	62,597
1972–73	190,222	45,283	42,047	17,994	5,425	39,264	40,210	181,357	69,714	18,615	23,582	69,446
1973–74	207,670	47,705	46,098	19,491	6,015	41,820	46,541	198,959	75,833	19,946	25,085	78,096
1974–75	228,171	51,491	49,815	21,454	6,642	47,034	51,735	230,721	87,858	22,528	28,155	92,180
1975–76	256,176	57,001	54,547	24,575	7,273	55,589	57,191	256,731	97,216	23,907	32,604	103,004
1976–77	285,157	62,527	60,641	29,246	9,174	62,444	61,124	274,215	102,780	23,058	35,906	112,472
1977–78	315,960	66,422	67,596	33,176	10,738	69,592	68,436	296,984	110,758	24,609	39,140	122,477
1978–79	343,236	64,944	74,247	36,932	12,128	75,164	79,821	327,517	119,448	28,440	41,898	137,731
1979–80	382,322	68,499	79,927	42,080	13,321	83,029	95,466	369,086	133,211	33,311	47,288	155,277
1980–81	423,404	74,969	85,971	46,426	14,143	90,294	111,599	407,449	145,784	34,603	54,105	172,957
1981–82	457,654	82,067	93,613	50,738	15,028	87,282	128,926	436,733	154,282	34,520	57,996	189,935
1982–83	486,753	89,105	100,247	55,129	14,258	90,007	138,008	466,516	163,876	36,655	60,906	205,079
1983–84	542,730	96,457	114,097	64,529	17,141	96,935	153,570	505,008	176,108	39,419	66,414	223,068
1984–85	598,121	103,757	126,376	70,361	19,152	106,158	172,317	553,899	192,686	44,989	71,479	244,745
1985–86	641,486	111,709	135,005	74,365	19,994	113,099	187,314	605,623	210,819	49,368	75,868	269,568
1986–87	686,860	121,203	144,091	83,935	22,425	114,857	200,350	657,134	226,619	52,355	82,650	295,510
1987–88	726,762	132,212	156,452	88,350	23,663	117,602	208,482	704,921	242,683	55,621	89,090	317,528
1988–89	786,129	142,400	166,336	97,806	25,926	125,824	227,838	762,360	263,898	58,105	97,879	342,479
1989–90	849,502	155,613	177,885	105,640	23,566	136,802	249,996	834,818	288,148	61,057	110,518	375,095
1990–91	902,207	167,999	185,570	109,341	22,242	154,099	262,956	908,108	309,302	64,937	130,402	403,467

[1] Fiscal years not the same for all governments. See Note.
[2] Excludes revenues or expenditures of publicly owned utilities and liquor stores, and of insurance-trust activities. Intergovernmental receipts and payments between State and local governments are also excluded.
[3] Includes other taxes and charges and miscellaneous revenues.
[4] Includes expenditures for libraries, hospitals, health, employment security administration, veterans' services, air transportation, water transport and terminals, parking facilities, and transit subsidies, police protection, fire protection, correction, protective inspection and regulation, sewerage, natural resources, parks and recreation, housing and community development, solid waste management, financial administration, judicial and legal, general public buildings, other government administration, interest on general debt, and general expenditures, n.e.c.

Note.—Data for fiscal years listed from 1962–63 to 1990–91 are the aggregations of data for government fiscal years that ended in the 12-month period from July 1 to June 30 of those years. Data for 1963 and earlier years include data for government fiscal years ending during that particular calendar year.
Data are not available for intervening years.

Source: Department of Commerce, Bureau of the Census.

TABLE B-85.—*Interest-bearing public debt securities by kind of obligation, 1967-93*

[Millions of dollars]

End of year or month	Total interest-bearing public debt securities	Marketable				Nonmarketable				
		Total [1]	Treasury bills	Treasury notes	Treasury bonds	Total	U.S. savings bonds	Foreign government and public series [2]	Government account series	Other [3]
Fiscal year:										
1967	322,286	[4] 210,672	58,535	49,108	97,418	111,614	51,213	1,514	56,155	2,731
1968	344,401	226,592	64,440	71,073	91,079	117,808	51,712	3,741	59,526	2,828
1969	351,729	226,107	68,356	78,946	78,805	125,623	51,711	4,070	66,790	3,051
1970	369,026	232,599	76,154	93,489	62,956	136,426	51,281	4,755	76,323	4,068
1971	396,289	245,473	86,677	104,807	53,989	150,816	53,003	9,270	82,784	5,759
1972	425,360	257,202	94,648	113,419	49,135	168,158	55,921	18,985	89,598	3,654
1973	456,353	262,971	100,061	117,840	45,071	193,382	59,418	28,524	101,738	3,701
1974	473,238	266,575	105,019	128,419	33,137	206,663	61,921	25,011	115,442	4,289
1975	532,122	315,606	128,569	150,257	36,779	216,516	65,482	23,216	124,173	3,644
1976	619,254	392,581	161,198	191,758	39,626	226,673	69,733	21,500	130,557	4,883
1977	697,629	443,508	156,091	241,692	45,724	254,121	75,411	21,799	140,113	16,797
1978	766,971	485,155	160,936	267,865	56,355	281,816	79,798	21,680	153,271	27,067
1979	819,007	506,693	161,378	274,242	71,073	312,314	80,440	28,115	176,360	27,400
1980	906,402	594,506	199,832	310,903	83,772	311,896	72,727	25,158	189,848	24,164
1981	996,495	683,209	223,388	363,643	96,178	313,286	68,017	20,499	201,052	23,718
1982	1,140,883	824,422	277,900	442,890	103,631	316,461	67,274	14,641	210,462	24,085
1983	1,375,751	1,024,000	340,733	557,525	125,742	351,751	70,024	11,450	234,684	35,593
1984	1,559,570	1,176,556	356,798	661,687	158,070	383,015	72,832	8,806	259,534	41,843
1985	1,821,010	1,360,179	384,220	776,449	199,510	460,831	77,011	6,638	313,928	63,255
1986	2,122,684	[1] 1,564,329	410,730	896,884	241,716	558,355	85,551	4,128	365,872	102,804
1987	2,347,750	[1] 1,675,980	378,263	1,005,127	277,590	671,769	97,004	4,350	440,658	129,758
1988	2,599,877	[1] 1,802,905	398,451	1,089,578	299,875	796,972	106,176	6,320	536,455	148,023
1989	2,836,309	[1] 1,892,763	406,597	1,133,193	337,974	943,546	114,025	6,818	663,677	159,025
1990	3,210,943	[1] 2,092,759	482,454	1,218,081	377,224	1,118,184	122,152	36,041	779,412	180,581
1991	3,662,759	[1] 2,390,660	564,589	1,387,717	423,354	1,272,099	133,512	41,639	908,406	188,541
1992	4,061,801	[1] 2,677,476	634,287	1,566,349	461,840	1,384,325	148,266	37,039	1,011,020	188,000
1993	4,408,567	[1] 2,904,910	658,381	1,734,161	497,367	1,503,657	167,024	42,459	1,114,289	179,886
1992: Jan	3,806,526	[1] 2,486,097	586,759	1,448,869	435,470	1,320,429	137,293	42,025	954,823	186,287
Feb	3,814,147	[1] 2,493,416	591,223	1,443,400	443,793	1,320,731	138,656	41,971	952,963	187,140
Mar	3,878,494	[1] 2,552,261	615,818	1,477,653	443,791	1,326,233	139,924	41,966	956,123	188,219
Apr	3,889,211	[1] 2,554,175	598,383	1,497,003	443,789	1,335,036	141,320	42,164	961,491	190,060
May	3,919,096	[1] 2,572,961	620,107	1,483,559	454,295	1,346,135	142,217	42,259	970,957	190,702
June	3,981,791	[1] 2,605,058	618,218	1,517,548	454,292	1,376,733	143,215	38,698	1,002,534	192,285
July	4,007,778	[1] 2,637,918	632,322	1,536,306	454,289	1,369,861	144,503	38,456	999,957	186,945
Aug	4,046,065	[1] 2,672,225	637,025	1,558,359	461,841	1,373,840	146,083	37,023	1,002,969	187,765
Sept	4,061,801	[1] 2,677,476	634,287	1,566,349	461,840	1,384,325	148,266	37,039	1,011,020	188,000
Oct	4,050,814	[1] 2,661,374	627,762	1,556,785	461,827	1,389,441	151,147	36,526	1,016,380	185,388
Nov	4,130,034	[1] 2,734,642	644,964	1,602,153	472,525	1,395,392	153,528	37,370	1,019,979	184,516
Dec	4,173,885	[1] 2,754,113	657,661	1,608,929	472,524	1,419,772	154,955	37,348	1,043,508	183,960
1993: Jan	4,150,059	[1] 2,732,962	647,041	1,598,398	472,523	1,417,098	157,647	37,167	1,043,062	179,222
Feb	4,180,254	[1] 2,760,533	648,459	1,616,923	480,151	1,419,722	159,888	37,006	1,042,760	180,066
Mar	4,227,628	[1] 2,807,092	659,877	1,652,068	480,148	1,420,536	161,441	37,038	1,039,995	182,062
Apr	4,251,164	[1] 2,808,859	642,189	1,671,522	480,147	1,442,306	162,644	43,791	1,053,080	182,791
May	4,279,221	[1] 2,821,933	657,491	1,661,834	487,608	1,457,288	163,550	43,221	1,066,394	184,123
June	4,349,011	[1] 2,860,622	659,280	1,698,736	487,606	1,488,389	164,424	42,964	1,097,751	183,251
July	4,333,507	[1] 2,852,073	671,190	1,678,277	487,606	1,481,434	165,319	43,007	1,094,815	178,293
Aug	4,400,313	[1] 2,917,196	677,030	1,727,799	497,368	1,483,116	166,181	42,496	1,095,548	178,892
Sept	4,408,567	[1] 2,904,910	658,381	1,734,161	497,367	1,503,657	167,024	42,459	1,114,289	179,886
Oct	4,403,759	[1] 2,892,521	668,723	1,711,432	497,366	1,511,239	168,155	43,777	1,120,822	178,485
Nov	4,490,639	[1] 2,977,823	709,212	1,757,755	495,856	1,512,817	168,993	43,596	1,120,345	179,883
Dec	4,532,325	[1] 2,989,475	714,631	1,763,989	495,855	1,542,850	169,425	43,480	1,150,041	179,904

[1] Includes Federal Financing Bank securities, not shown separately, in the amount of 15,000 million dollars.
[2] Nonmarketable certificates of indebtedness, notes, bonds, and bills in the Treasury foreign series of dollar-denominated and foreign-currency denominated issues.
[3] Includes depository bonds, retirement plan bonds, Rural Electrification Administration bonds, State and local bonds, and special issues held only by U.S. Government agencies and trust funds and the Federal home loan banks.
[4] Includes $5,610 million in certificates not shown separately.

Note.—Through fiscal year 1976, the fiscal year was on a July 1–June 30 basis; beginning October 1976 (fiscal year 1977), the fiscal year is on an October 1–September 30 basis.

Source: Department of the Treasury.

TABLE B-86.—*Maturity distribution and average length of marketable interest-bearing public debt securities held by private investors, 1967–93*

End of year or month	Amount outstanding, privately held	Within 1 year	1 to 5 years	5 to 10 years	10 to 20 years	20 years and over	Average length Years	Months
			Maturity class					
		Millions of dollars					Years	Months
Fiscal year:								
1967	150,321	56,561	53,584	21,057	6,153	12,968	5	1
1968	159,671	66,746	52,295	21,850	6,110	12,670	4	5
1969	156,008	69,311	50,182	18,078	6,097	12,337	4	2
1970	157,910	76,443	57,035	8,286	7,876	8,272	3	8
1971	161,863	74,803	58,557	14,503	6,357	7,645	3	6
1972	165,978	79,509	57,157	16,033	6,358	6,922	3	3
1973	167,869	84,041	54,139	16,385	8,741	4,564	3	1
1974	164,862	87,150	50,103	14,197	9,930	3,481	2	11
1975	210,382	115,677	65,852	15,385	8,857	4,611	2	8
1976	279,782	150,296	90,578	24,169	8,087	6,652	2	7
1977	326,674	161,329	113,319	33,067	8,428	10,531	2	11
1978	356,501	163,819	132,993	33,500	11,383	14,805	3	3
1979	380,530	181,883	127,574	32,279	18,489	20,304	3	7
1980	463,717	220,084	156,244	38,809	25,901	22,679	3	9
1981	549,863	256,187	182,237	48,743	32,569	30,127	4	0
1982	682,043	314,436	221,783	75,749	33,017	37,058	3	11
1983	862,631	379,579	294,955	99,174	40,826	48,097	4	1
1984	1,017,488	437,941	332,808	130,417	49,664	66,658	4	6
1985	1,185,675	472,661	402,766	159,383	62,853	88,012	4	11
1986	1,354,275	506,903	467,348	189,995	70,664	119,365	5	3
1987	1,445,366	483,582	526,746	209,160	72,862	153,016	5	9
1988	1,555,208	524,201	552,993	232,453	74,186	171,375	5	9
1989	1,654,660	546,751	578,333	247,428	80,616	201,532	6	0
1990	1,841,903	626,297	630,144	267,573	82,713	235,176	6	1
1991	2,113,799	713,778	761,243	280,574	84,900	273,304	6	0
1992	2,363,802	808,705	866,329	295,921	84,706	308,141	5	11
1993	2,562,336	858,135	978,714	306,663	94,346	324,479	5	10
1992: Jan	2,201,642	749,495	806,162	278,275	87,297	280,413	5	11
Feb	2,211,963	758,592	785,152	291,657	85,798	290,764	6	1
Mar	2,266,806	786,988	812,043	291,507	85,708	290,559	5	11
Apr	2,268,375	769,874	828,118	293,819	85,798	290,766	5	11
May	2,284,866	786,584	816,200	295,318	85,788	300,976	6	0
June	2,310,321	784,194	845,264	294,745	85,793	300,326	5	11
July	2,344,094	800,084	861,247	296,644	85,793	300,326	5	10
Aug	2,372,764	811,729	868,080	297,830	85,572	309,553	5	11
Sept	2,363,802	808,705	866,329	295,921	84,706	308,141	5	11
Oct	2,362,075	806,345	860,918	299,422	85,529	309,861	5	11
Nov	2,425,550	825,445	893,133	303,863	92,798	310,312	5	11
Dec	2,434,333	843,416	890,778	301,395	91,441	307,304	5	10
1993: Jan	2,419,561	832,988	881,132	303,279	92,356	309,807	5	10
Feb	2,443,020	833,583	894,130	308,058	89,376	317,874	5	11
Mar	2,484,628	849,766	922,468	306,175	88,626	317,593	5	10
Apr	2,486,231	833,935	937,347	308,094	88,834	318,022	5	10
May	2,496,615	854,658	919,114	313,037	85,273	324,532	5	10
June	2,515,501	849,639	949,127	309,295	84,237	323,204	5	10
July	2,521,249	864,355	940,460	304,447	85,708	326,279	5	10
Aug	2,578,501	874,599	976,547	308,413	94,487	324,455	5	10
Sept	2,562,336	858,135	978,714	306,663	94,346	324,479	5	10
Oct	2,552,880	866,988	968,794	298,460	94,436	324,203	5	10
Nov	2,626,085	898,241	1,008,468	308,219	87,131	324,025	5	9
Dec	2,628,352	905,311	1,011,213	304,863	86,143	320,822	5	8

Note.—All issues classified to final maturity.
Through fiscal year 1976, the fiscal year was on a July 1–June 30 basis; beginning October 1976 (fiscal year 1977), the fiscal year is on an October 1–September 30 basis.

Source: Department of the Treasury.

TABLE B-87.—*Estimated ownership of public debt securities by private investors, 1976–93*

[Par values;[1] billions of dollars]

End of month	Total	Commercial banks [2]	Held by private investors								
			Nonbank investors									
			Total	Individuals [3]			Insurance companies	Money market funds	Corporations [5]	State and local governments [6]	Foreign and international [7]	Other investors [8]
				Total	Savings bonds [4]	Other securities						
1976: June	376.4	92.5	283.9	96.1	69.6	26.5	10.7	0.8	23.3	32.7	69.8	50.5
Dec	409.5	103.8	305.7	101.6	72.0	29.6	12.7	1.1	23.5	39.3	78.1	49.4
1977: June	421.0	102.9	318.1	104.9	74.4	30.5	13.0	.8	22.1	49.6	87.9	39.8
Dec	461.3	102.0	359.3	107.8	76.7	31.1	15.1	.9	18.2	59.1	109.6	48.6
1978: June	477.8	99.6	378.2	109.0	79.1	29.9	14.2	1.3	17.3	69.6	119.5	47.3
Dec	508.6	95.3	413.3	114.0	80.7	33.3	15.3	1.5	17.3	81.1	133.1	51.0
1979: June	516.6	94.6	422.0	115.5	80.6	34.9	16.0	3.8	18.6	86.2	114.9	67.0
Dec	540.5	95.6	444.9	118.0	79.9	38.1	15.6	5.6	17.0	86.2	119.0	83.5
1980: June	558.2	98.5	459.7	116.5	73.4	43.1	15.3	5.3	14.0	85.1	118.2	105.3
Dec	616.4	111.5	504.9	117.1	72.5	44.6	18.1	3.5	19.3	90.3	129.7	126.9
1981: June	651.2	115.0	536.2	107.4	69.2	38.2	19.9	9.0	19.9	95.9	136.6	147.5
Dec	694.5	113.8	580.7	110.8	68.1	42.7	21.6	21.5	17.9	99.9	136.6	172.4
1982: June	740.9	114.7	626.2	114.1	67.4	46.7	24.4	22.4	17.6	106.0	137.2	204.5
Dec	848.4	134.0	714.4	116.5	68.3	48.2	30.6	42.6	24.5	118.6	149.5	232.1
1983: June	948.6	167.4	781.2	121.3	69.7	51.6	37.8	28.3	32.8	138.1	160.1	262.8
Dec	1,022.6	179.5	843.1	133.4	71.5	61.9	46.0	22.8	39.7	153.0	166.3	281.9
1984: June	1,102.2	180.6	921.6	142.2	72.9	69.3	51.2	14.9	45.3	168.5	171.6	327.9
Dec	1,212.5	181.5	1,031.0	143.8	74.5	69.3	64.5	25.9	50.1	188.4	205.9	352.4
1985: June	1,292.0	195.6	1,096.4	148.7	76.7	72.0	69.1	24.8	54.9	213.4	213.8	371.7
Dec	1,417.2	189.4	1,227.8	154.8	79.8	75.0	80.5	25.1	59.0	303.6	224.8	380.0
1986: June	1,502.7	194.3	1,308.4	159.5	83.8	75.7	87.9	22.8	61.2	319.5	250.9	406.6
Dec	1,602.0	197.5	1,404.5	162.7	92.3	70.4	101.6	28.6	68.8	346.6	263.4	432.8
1987: June	1,658.1	192.3	1,465.8	165.6	96.8	68.8	104.7	20.6	79.7	383.9	281.1	430.2
Dec	1,731.4	194.2	1,537.2	172.4	101.1	71.3	108.1	14.6	84.6	418.4	299.7	439.4
1988: Mar	1,779.6	195.6	1,584.0	178.1	104.0	74.1	110.2	15.2	86.3	432.5	332.5	429.2
June	1,786.7	190.7	1,596.0	182.0	106.2	75.8	111.0	13.4	87.6	446.9	345.4	409.7
Sept	1,821.2	191.2	1,630.0	186.8	107.8	79.0	115.9	11.1	85.9	457.7	345.9	426.7
Dec	1,858.5	184.9	1,673.6	190.4	109.6	80.8	118.6	11.8	86.0	471.6	362.2	433.0
1989: Mar	1,903.4	192.0	1,711.4	204.2	112.2	92.0	119.7	13.0	89.4	477.9	376.6	430.6
June	1,909.1	178.0	1,731.1	211.7	114.0	97.7	120.3	11.3	91.0	483.5	369.1	444.2
Sept	1,958.3	166.6	1,791.7	213.5	115.7	97.8	121.4	12.9	90.9	487.1	394.9	471.0
Dec	2,015.8	164.9	1,850.9	216.4	117.7	98.7	125.1	14.9	93.4	487.5	429.6	484.0
1990: Mar	2,115.1	178.4	1,936.7	222.8	119.9	102.9	134.9	31.3	94.9	493.8	421.8	537.2
June	2,141.8	176.9	1,964.9	229.6	121.9	107.7	137.6	28.0	96.9	494.5	427.3	551.0
Sept	2,207.3	179.5	2,027.8	232.5	123.9	108.6	141.2	34.0	102.0	492.1	440.3	585.7
Dec	2,288.3	171.5	2,116.8	233.8	126.2	107.6	142.0	45.5	108.9	490.4	458.4	637.7
1991: Mar	2,360.6	188.5	2,172.1	238.3	129.7	108.6	147.2	65.4	114.9	510.4	464.3	631.6
June	2,397.9	197.3	2,200.6	243.5	133.2	110.3	156.7	55.4	130.8	510.8	473.6	629.8
Sept	2,489.4	218.6	2,270.8	257.5	135.4	122.1	171.2	64.5	142.0	512.9	477.3	645.5
Dec	2,563.2	233.4	2,329.8	263.9	138.1	125.8	181.8	80.0	150.8	520.3	491.7	641.3
1992: Mar	2,664.0	256.6	2,407.4	268.1	142.0	126.1	187.4	84.8	166.0	521.8	507.9	671.5
June	2,712.4	267.3	2,445.1	275.1	145.4	129.7	190.9	79.4	175.0	528.5	529.6	666.7
Sept	2,765.5	287.4	2,478.1	281.2	150.3	130.9	194.9	79.4	180.8	529.5	535.2	677.0
Dec	2,839.9	294.0	2,545.9	289.2	157.3	131.9	197.5	79.7	192.5	534.8	549.7	702.4
1993: Mar	2,895.0	310.0	2,585.0	297.7	163.6	134.1	205.0	77.7	199.3	541.0	565.5	698.8
June	2,938.4	305.9	2,632.5	303.0	166.5	136.4	208.1	76.2	206.1	553.9	568.2	717.0
Sept	2,983.0	306.0	2,677.0	305.8	169.1	136.7	210.0	75.2	215.6	558.0	592.3	720.0

[1] U.S. savings bonds, series A–F and J, are included at current redemption value.
[2] Includes domestically chartered banks, U.S. branches and agencies of foreign banks, New York investment companies majority owned by foreign banks, and Edge Act corporations owned by domestically chartered and foreign banks.
[3] Includes partnerships and personal trust accounts.
[4] Includes U.S. savings notes. Sales began May 1, 1967, and were discontinued June 30, 1970.
[5] Exclusive of banks and insurance companies.
[6] Includes State and local government series (SLGs) as well as State and local pension funds.
[7] Consists of the investments of foreign and international accounts (both official and private) in U.S. public debt issues. Reflects 1978 benchmark through December 1984 and 1984 benchmark to date.
[8] Includes savings and loan associations, credit unions, nonprofit institutions, mutual savings banks, corporate pension trust funds, dealers and brokers, certain Government deposit accounts, and Government-sponsored enterprises.

Source: Department of the Treasury.

CORPORATE PROFITS AND FINANCE

Table B-88.—*Corporate profits with inventory valuation and capital consumption adjustments, 1959–93*

[Billions of dollars; quarterly data at seasonally adjusted annual rates]

Year or quarter	Corporate profits with inventory valuation and capital consumption adjustments	Corporate profits tax liability	Corporate profits after tax with inventory valuation and capital consumption adjustments			Undistributed profits with inventory valuation and capital consumption adjustments
			Total	Dividends	
1959	52.3	23.6	28.6	12.7	15.9
1960	50.7	22.7	28.0	13.4	14.6
1961	51.6	22.8	28.8	14.0	14.8
1962	59.6	24.0	35.6	15.0	20.6
1963	65.1	26.2	38.9	16.1	22.8
1964	72.1	28.0	44.1	18.0	26.1
1965	82.9	30.9	52.0	20.2	31.8
1966	88.6	33.7	54.9	20.9	34.0
1967	86.0	32.7	53.3	22.1	31.2
1968	92.6	39.4	53.2	24.6	28.6
1969	89.6	39.7	49.9	25.2	24.7
1970	77.5	34.4	43.1	23.7	19.4
1971	90.3	37.7	52.6	23.7	28.8
1972	103.2	41.9	61.3	25.8	35.5
1973	116.4	49.3	67.1	28.1	39.0
1974	104.5	51.8	52.7	30.4	22.3
1975	121.9	50.9	71.0	30.1	40.9
1976	147.1	64.2	82.8	35.6	47.2
1977	175.7	73.0	102.6	40.7	61.9
1978	199.7	83.5	116.2	45.9	70.3
1979	202.5	88.0	114.5	52.4	62.1
1980	177.7	84.8	92.9	59.0	33.9
1981	182.0	81.1	100.9	69.2	31.7
1982	151.5	63.1	88.4	70.0	18.4
1983	212.7	77.2	135.4	81.2	54.2
1984	264.2	94.0	170.2	82.7	87.5
1985	280.8	96.5	184.2	92.4	91.9
1986	271.6	106.5	165.1	109.8	55.4
1987	319.8	127.1	192.8	106.2	86.5
1988	365.0	137.0	228.0	115.3	112.6
1989	362.8	141.3	221.5	134.6	86.9
1990	380.6	138.7	241.9	153.5	88.5
1991	369.5	129.8	239.7	137.4	102.3
1992	407.2	146.3	260.9	150.5	110.4
1993 *p*				169.0	
1982: IV	150.3	58.7	91.7	72.5	19.2
1983: IV	229.1	82.2	146.9	84.2	62.7
1984: IV	261.3	83.8	177.5	83.4	94.1
1985: IV	284.9	97.6	187.2	97.4	89.9
1986: IV	264.6	116.6	148.1	111.0	37.1
1987: IV	343.3	135.2	208.1	106.3	101.8
1988: IV	378.3	146.2	232.2	121.0	111.2
1989: IV	354.5	134.2	220.3	141.3	79.0
1990: I	382.6	132.0	250.6	149.9	100.7
II	409.3	139.8	269.5	154.6	115.0
III	367.5	145.7	221.8	155.7	66.1
IV	362.8	137.0	225.8	153.7	72.1
1991: I	369.3	125.4	243.9	145.9	98.0
II	370.8	128.0	242.8	136.2	106.6
III	359.0	132.5	226.5	133.4	93.1
IV	378.8	133.4	245.4	133.9	111.5
1992: I	409.9	147.0	262.9	138.0	124.9
II	411.7	153.0	258.7	146.1	112.6
III	367.5	130.1	237.4	155.2	82.3
IV	439.5	155.0	284.5	162.9	121.7
1993: I	432.1	160.9	271.2	167.5	103.7
II	458.1	173.3	284.8	168.5	116.3
III	468.5	169.5	299.1	169.7	129.3
IV *p*				170.4	

Source: Department of Commerce, Bureau of Economic Analysis.

TABLE B-89.—*Corporate profits by industry, 1959-93*

[Billions of dollars; quarterly data at seasonally adjusted annual rates]

Year or quarter	Total	Corporate profits with inventory valuation adjustment and without capital consumption adjustment										Rest of the world
		Domestic industries										
		Total	Financial [1]			Nonfinancial					
			Total	Federal Reserve banks	Other	Total	Manu- fac- turing [2]	Trans- portation and public utilities	Wholesale and retail trade	Other	
1959	53.1	50.4	7.0	0.7	6.3	43.4	26.5	7.1	6.2	3.6	2.7
1960	51.0	47.8	7.7	.9	6.7	40.2	23.8	7.5	5.2	3.6	3.1
1961	51.3	48.0	7.5	.8	6.8	40.4	23.4	7.9	5.5	3.6	3.3
1962	56.4	52.6	7.6	.9	6.8	45.0	26.3	8.5	6.3	3.9	3.8
1963	61.2	57.1	7.3	1.0	6.4	49.8	29.6	9.5	6.4	4.4	4.1
1964	67.5	63.0	7.5	1.1	6.4	55.5	32.4	10.2	7.9	5.1	4.5
1965	77.6	72.9	7.9	1.3	6.5	65.0	39.7	11.0	8.6	5.6	4.7
1966	83.0	78.5	9.2	1.7	7.5	69.3	42.4	11.9	8.8	6.2	4.5
1967	80.3	75.5	9.5	2.0	7.6	66.0	39.0	10.9	9.7	6.4	4.8
1968	86.9	81.3	10.9	2.5	8.4	70.4	41.7	11.0	10.9	6.8	5.6
1969	83.2	76.6	11.6	3.1	8.5	65.0	37.0	10.6	11.2	6.2	6.6
1970	71.8	64.7	13.1	3.5	9.6	51.6	27.1	8.2	10.3	5.9	7.1
1971	85.5	77.7	15.2	3.3	11.9	62.5	34.8	8.9	12.3	6.6	7.9
1972	97.9	88.4	16.4	3.3	13.1	72.0	41.4	9.4	14.1	7.1	9.5
1973	110.9	96.0	17.5	4.5	13.0	78.5	46.7	9.0	14.6	8.2	14.9
1974	103.4	85.9	16.2	5.7	10.5	69.7	40.7	7.6	13.7	7.7	17.5
1975	129.4	114.8	15.9	5.6	10.3	98.9	54.5	10.9	21.9	11.6	14.6
1976	158.8	142.3	19.9	5.9	14.0	122.4	70.7	15.3	23.1	13.3	16.5
1977	186.7	167.7	25.7	6.1	19.6	142.0	78.5	18.5	27.8	17.1	18.9
1978	212.8	190.2	31.8	7.6	24.1	158.4	89.6	21.7	27.7	19.4	22.6
1979	219.8	185.6	31.6	9.4	22.2	153.9	88.3	16.9	28.3	20.5	34.3
1980	197.8	162.9	24.3	11.8	12.6	138.5	75.8	18.3	22.8	21.6	35.0
1981	203.2	174.0	18.7	14.4	4.3	155.3	87.4	20.1	31.6	16.2	29.2
1982	166.4	138.6	15.6	15.2	.4	123.0	63.1	20.8	31.9	7.2	27.8
1983	202.2	171.9	24.5	14.6	9.9	147.4	71.4	28.9	38.7	8.4	30.4
1984	236.4	205.2	20.3	16.4	3.9	185.0	86.7	39.9	49.7	8.7	31.2
1985	225.3	194.5	28.7	16.3	12.4	165.8	80.1	34.1	43.1	8.5	30.8
1986	227.6	194.6	35.8	15.5	20.3	158.9	59.0	36.5	46.3	17.1	32.9
1987	273.4	233.9	36.4	15.7	20.7	197.5	87.0	43.4	39.9	27.2	39.5
1988	320.3	271.2	41.8	17.6	24.2	229.4	117.5	47.5	37.1	27.3	49.1
1989	325.4	266.0	50.6	20.1	30.5	215.3	108.0	42.1	39.7	25.5	59.4
1990	354.7	286.7	65.7	21.4	44.3	221.1	109.1	44.0	37.2	30.8	67.9
1991	367.3	300.4	80.7	20.2	60.4	219.7	89.8	54.4	47.4	28.2	66.9
1992	390.1	327.8	78.1	17.8	60.3	249.8	115.5	52.0	46.3	36.0	62.3
1993 ᵖ		377.7	98.7	16.1	82.5	279.0	128.5	57.3	53.4	39.8	
1982: IV	160.0	130.8	23.0	14.6	8.3	107.8	50.1	18.2	33.8	5.7	29.2
1983: IV	216.2	182.6	22.1	15.2	6.9	160.5	90.5	19.1	40.7	10.2	33.6
1984: IV	223.6	192.9	20.3	17.2	3.2	172.6	79.2	33.5	50.8	9.0	30.7
1985: IV	228.0	193.5	29.0	16.0	13.0	164.5	83.3	31.3	39.0	11.0	34.5
1986: IV	225.0	192.5	34.7	15.2	19.5	157.8	63.9	34.2	43.1	16.6	32.6
1987: IV	293.4	246.3	39.4	16.1	23.3	207.0	98.7	43.1	39.3	25.8	47.0
1988: IV	340.5	285.9	46.1	18.9	27.2	239.7	129.3	47.6	39.3	23.5	54.6
1989: IV	320.6	254.8	52.5	20.4	32.1	202.3	94.5	38.8	39.2	29.8	65.8
1990: I	346.8	282.2	60.9	20.7	40.2	221.3	108.3	45.0	38.4	29.7	64.6
II	377.9	310.1	67.3	21.3	46.1	242.8	117.4	49.7	44.9	30.8	67.8
III	344.7	280.9	67.8	22.2	45.6	213.1	112.3	42.5	29.4	28.8	63.8
IV	349.3	273.8	66.6	21.4	45.2	207.2	98.5	38.7	36.2	33.8	75.5
1991: I	364.6	291.9	75.9	21.0	54.8	216.0	91.5	50.0	46.5	28.0	72.8
II	370.1	303.6	81.0	20.2	60.8	222.6	89.6	57.1	49.6	26.3	66.5
III	359.0	299.3	84.2	20.0	64.2	215.1	89.3	53.1	45.6	27.2	59.7
IV	375.4	306.8	81.6	19.7	61.9	225.2	88.9	57.4	47.8	31.1	68.5
1992: I	399.7	328.5	97.9	18.8	79.1	230.5	98.9	57.6	40.0	34.0	71.2
II	395.7	334.2	87.7	18.3	69.4	246.5	115.7	51.3	46.0	33.4	61.5
III	350.1	288.6	44.6	17.1	27.5	244.0	119.3	48.7	41.3	34.6	61.5
IV	414.8	360.1	82.0	16.7	65.3	278.1	128.0	50.4	57.7	42.0	54.7
1993: I	407.0	348.0	92.3	16.6	75.7	255.7	118.9	53.3	46.0	37.5	59.0
II	433.4	375.3	96.4	16.2	80.2	278.9	132.5	53.9	55.4	37.2	58.1
III	444.8	382.1	99.3	16.0	83.3	282.8	126.7	59.0	55.1	42.1	62.7

[1] Consists of the following industries: Depository institutions; nondepository credit institutions; security and commodity brokers; insurance carriers; regulated investment companies; small business investment companies; and real estate investment trusts.
[2] See Table B-90 for industry detail.

Note.—The industry classification is on a company basis and is based on the 1987 Standard Industrial Classification (SIC) beginning 1987, and on the 1972 SIC for earlier years shown.

Source: Department of Commerce, Bureau of Economic Analysis.

TABLE B-90.—*Corporate profits of manufacturing industries, 1959–93*

[Billions of dollars; quarterly data at seasonally adjusted annual rates]

Year or quarter	Total manufacturing	Durable goods							Nondurable goods				
		Total	Primary metal industries	Fabricated metal products	Industrial machinery and equipment	Electronic and other electric equipment	Motor vehicles and equipment	Other	Total	Food and kindred products	Chemicals and allied products	Petroleum and coal products	Other
1959	26.5	13.7	2.3	1.1	2.2	1.7	3.0	3.5	12.8	2.5	3.5	2.6	4.3
1960	23.8	11.7	2.0	.8	1.8	1.3	3.0	2.8	12.1	2.2	3.1	2.6	4.2
1961	23.4	11.4	1.6	1.0	1.9	1.3	2.5	3.1	12.0	2.4	3.3	2.2	4.2
1962	26.3	14.1	1.6	1.2	2.4	1.5	4.0	3.5	12.2	2.4	3.2	2.2	4.4
1963	29.6	16.4	2.0	1.3	2.5	1.6	4.9	4.0	13.2	2.7	3.7	2.2	4.7
1964	32.4	18.0	2.5	1.4	3.3	1.7	4.6	4.5	14.4	2.7	4.1	2.3	5.3
1965	39.7	23.2	3.1	2.1	4.0	2.7	6.2	5.2	16.4	2.8	4.6	2.9	6.1
1966	42.4	23.9	3.6	2.4	4.5	3.0	5.1	5.3	18.4	3.3	4.9	3.4	6.8
1967	39.0	21.2	2.7	2.5	4.1	3.0	4.0	5.0	17.8	3.2	4.3	3.9	6.4
1968	41.7	22.4	1.9	2.3	4.1	2.9	5.5	5.7	19.2	3.2	5.2	3.7	7.0
1969	37.0	19.0	1.4	2.0	3.7	2.3	4.8	4.9	18.0	3.0	4.6	3.3	7.0
1970	27.1	10.4	.8	1.1	3.0	1.3	1.3	3.0	16.8	3.2	3.9	3.6	6.1
1971	34.8	16.6	.8	1.5	3.0	1.9	5.1	4.2	18.2	3.5	4.5	3.7	6.5
1972	41.4	22.6	1.6	2.2	4.3	2.8	5.9	5.7	18.8	2.9	5.2	3.2	7.5
1973	46.7	25.0	2.3	2.6	4.7	3.2	5.9	6.3	21.7	2.5	6.1	5.2	7.9
1974	40.7	15.1	5.0	1.8	3.1	.5	.7	4.1	25.7	2.6	5.2	10.7	7.2
1975	54.5	20.3	2.7	3.2	4.8	2.6	2.2	4.8	34.1	8.6	6.3	9.8	9.4
1976	70.7	31.2	2.1	3.9	6.7	3.8	7.4	7.4	39.5	7.1	8.2	13.3	11.0
1977	78.5	37.6	1.0	4.5	8.3	5.8	9.3	8.6	41.0	6.8	7.7	12.9	13.6
1978	89.6	45.0	3.6	5.0	10.4	6.6	8.9	10.5	44.6	6.1	8.2	15.5	14.8
1979	88.3	36.5	3.5	5.2	9.1	5.4	4.6	8.6	51.8	5.8	7.1	24.5	14.6
1980	75.8	17.9	2.6	4.3	7.5	5.0	−4.3	2.8	57.8	6.0	5.5	33.6	12.9
1981	87.4	18.1	3.0	4.4	8.2	4.9	.2	−2.7	69.3	9.0	7.6	38.6	14.2
1982	63.1	4.8	−4.7	2.6	3.4	1.3	−.4	2.6	58.3	7.2	4.7	31.6	14.8
1983	71.4	18.4	−4.9	3.1	4.4	3.4	5.2	7.2	53.0	5.8	6.8	22.1	18.3
1984	86.7	37.2	−.4	4.5	6.3	4.8	8.9	13.1	49.5	7.3	7.3	15.9	19.1
1985	80.1	29.0	−.9	4.7	5.3	2.4	7.3	10.1	51.1	8.4	6.0	17.1	19.7
1986	59.0	30.0	.9	5.3	3.2	2.6	4.4	13.7	29.0	7.5	8.0	−8.5	21.9
1987	87.0	42.2	2.6	5.2	7.3	6.2	3.7	17.3	44.8	11.4	15.1	−3.6	21.9
1988	117.5	52.2	5.9	6.4	10.5	7.6	5.7	16.1	65.3	11.8	19.3	10.4	23.8
1989	108.0	49.3	6.1	6.6	10.3	9.3	2.3	14.6	58.8	10.7	18.5	5.7	23.9
1990	109.1	39.2	3.3	6.1	9.6	7.9	−2.2	14.6	69.9	14.0	16.2	17.3	22.5
1991	89.8	30.9	1.2	5.6	5.2	8.6	−5.6	15.9	59.0	16.6	14.5	5.8	22.1
1992	115.5	48.3	.6	7.4	6.6	12.1	3.5	18.1	67.2	17.0	15.7	6.1	28.5
1993 ᵖ	128.5	58.0	1.2	6.4	7.5	14.3	7.6	21.1	70.5	15.6	16.2	11.1	27.6
1982: IV	50.1	−5.3	−5.2	1.1	1.0	−1.0	−2.9	1.7	55.5	6.7	3.1	29.0	16.6
1983: IV	90.5	33.4	−3.7	4.9	6.5	6.6	9.4	9.7	57.1	6.1	7.7	24.1	19.2
1984: IV	79.2	34.2	−1.0	5.2	5.0	4.1	8.5	12.4	45.0	7.3	6.0	13.0	18.6
1985: IV	83.3	28.8	−1.3	4.0	7.0	2.0	7.3	9.7	54.5	7.8	3.5	24.1	19.2
1986: IV	63.9	34.2	1.7	4.7	2.6	3.3	4.5	17.4	29.7	8.2	9.5	−13.3	25.3
1987: IV	98.7	35.2	3.3	6.0	6.3	2.9	.6	16.2	63.4	13.4	18.5	7.4	24.1
1988: IV	129.3	56.4	6.5	6.4	8.0	9.7	9.6	16.2	72.9	12.3	24.0	14.2	22.4
1989: IV	94.5	43.0	4.1	5.3	12.6	10.9	−3.1	13.2	51.6	9.8	15.0	4.6	22.2
1990: I	108.3	44.3	4.7	7.6	11.2	9.6	−4.1	15.3	64.0	9.1	17.3	13.7	23.9
II	117.4	42.4	3.4	6.3	9.7	8.7	−.3	14.6	74.9	14.9	19.9	16.2	23.9
III	112.3	40.5	2.1	5.4	9.8	7.8	.7	14.5	71.9	15.7	15.6	17.3	23.2
IV	98.5	29.5	3.0	5.0	7.6	5.4	−5.3	13.8	69.1	16.2	12.0	22.0	18.9
1991: I	91.5	24.8	1.5	3.9	7.1	7.5	−9.6	14.4	66.7	16.8	12.8	17.1	19.9
II	89.6	32.4	1.1	6.0	5.8	8.5	−6.4	17.4	57.2	16.5	12.5	5.9	22.3
III	89.3	31.5	.2	6.0	2.0	7.8	−2.8	18.3	57.8	18.8	14.8	−.2	24.4
IV	88.9	34.7	1.9	6.5	6.0	10.4	−3.7	13.5	54.2	14.4	17.8	.4	21.7
1992: I	98.9	39.4	.9	6.8	5.5	10.0	1.9	14.4	59.6	14.5	15.3	4.9	24.9
II	115.7	45.8	1.0	8.1	6.6	8.7	4.8	16.6	69.9	19.6	14.8	7.7	27.8
III	119.3	49.9	.3	8.0	6.5	12.2	2.4	20.5	69.4	18.5	15.0	6.7	29.2
IV	128.0	58.0	.0	6.6	7.8	17.6	4.9	21.0	70.0	15.2	17.7	5.0	32.1
1993: I	118.9	48.0	−.5	5.5	5.7	14.9	3.1	19.4	70.9	18.0	18.4	7.2	27.3
II	132.5	58.4	2.5	6.9	6.2	12.1	10.0	20.7	74.2	14.8	16.3	13.5	29.5
III	126.7	59.9	1.1	6.3	8.8	14.4	8.1	21.3	66.8	14.6	14.6	12.0	25.6

Note.—The industry classification is on a company basis and is based on the 1987 Standard Industrial Classification (SIC) beginning 1987 and on the 1972 SIC for earlier years shown. In the 1972 SIC, the categories shown here as "industrial machinery and equipment" and "electronic and other electric equipment" were identified as "machinery, except electrical" and "electric and electronic equipment," respectively.

Source: Department of Commerce, Bureau of Economic Analysis.

TABLE B–91.—*Sales, profits, and stockholders' equity, all manufacturing corporations, 1952–93*

[Billions of dollars]

Year or quarter	All manufacturing corporations				Durable goods industries				Nondurable goods industries			
	Sales (net)	Profits Before income taxes [1]	Profits After income taxes	Stock- holders' equity [2]	Sales (net)	Profits Before income taxes [1]	Profits After income taxes	Stock- holders' equity [2]	Sales (net)	Profits Before income taxes [1]	Profits After income taxes	Stock- holders' equity [2]
1952	250.2	22.9	10.7	103.7	122.0	12.9	5.5	49.8	128.0	10.0	5.2	53.9
1953	265.9	24.4	11.3	108.2	137.9	14.0	5.8	52.4	128.0	10.4	5.5	55.7
1954	248.5	20.9	11.2	113.1	122.8	11.4	5.6	54.9	125.7	9.6	5.6	58.2
1955	278.4	28.6	15.1	120.1	142.1	16.5	8.1	58.8	136.3	12.1	7.0	61.3
1956	307.3	29.8	16.2	131.6	159.5	16.5	8.3	65.2	147.8	13.2	7.8	66.4
1957	320.0	28.2	15.4	141.1	166.0	15.8	7.9	70.5	154.1	12.4	7.5	70.6
1958	305.3	22.7	12.7	147.4	148.6	11.4	5.8	72.8	156.7	11.3	6.9	74.6
1959	338.0	29.7	16.3	157.1	169.4	15.8	8.1	77.9	168.5	13.9	8.3	79.2
1960	345.7	27.5	15.2	165.4	173.9	14.0	7.0	82.3	171.8	13.5	8.2	83.1
1961	356.4	27.5	15.3	172.6	175.2	13.6	6.9	84.9	181.2	13.9	8.5	87.7
1962	389.4	31.9	17.7	181.4	195.3	16.8	8.6	89.1	194.1	15.1	9.2	92.3
1963	412.7	34.9	19.5	189.7	209.0	18.5	9.5	93.3	203.6	16.4	10.0	96.3
1964	443.1	39.6	23.2	199.8	226.3	21.2	11.6	98.5	216.8	18.3	11.6	101.3
1965	492.2	46.5	27.5	211.7	257.0	26.2	14.5	105.4	235.2	20.3	13.0	106.3
1966	554.2	51.8	30.9	230.3	291.7	29.2	16.4	115.2	262.4	22.6	14.6	115.1
1967	575.4	47.8	29.0	247.6	300.6	25.7	14.6	125.0	274.8	22.0	14.4	122.6
1968	631.9	55.4	32.1	265.9	335.5	30.6	16.5	135.6	296.4	24.8	15.5	130.3
1969	694.6	58.1	33.2	289.9	366.5	31.5	16.9	147.6	328.1	26.6	16.4	142.3
1970	708.8	48.1	28.6	306.8	363.1	23.0	12.9	155.1	345.7	25.2	15.7	151.7
1971	751.1	52.9	31.0	320.8	381.8	26.5	14.5	160.4	369.3	26.5	16.5	160.5
1972	849.5	63.2	36.5	343.4	435.8	33.6	18.4	171.4	413.7	29.6	18.0	172.0
1973	1,017.2	81.4	48.1	374.1	527.3	43.6	24.8	188.7	489.9	37.8	23.3	185.4
1973: IV	275.1	21.4	13.0	386.4	140.1	10.8	6.3	194.7	135.0	10.6	6.7	191.7
New series:												
1973: IV	236.6	20.6	13.2	368.0	122.7	10.1	6.2	185.8	113.9	10.5	7.0	182.1
1974	1,060.6	92.1	58.7	395.0	529.0	41.1	24.7	196.0	531.6	51.0	34.1	199.0
1975	1,065.2	79.9	49.1	423.4	521.1	35.3	21.4	208.1	544.1	44.6	27.7	215.3
1976	1,203.2	104.9	64.5	462.7	589.6	50.7	30.8	224.3	613.7	54.3	33.7	238.4
1977	1,328.1	115.1	70.4	496.7	657.3	57.9	34.8	239.9	670.8	57.2	35.5	256.8
1978	1,496.4	132.5	81.1	540.5	760.7	69.6	41.8	262.6	735.7	62.9	39.3	277.9
1979	1,741.8	154.2	98.7	600.5	865.7	72.4	45.2	292.5	876.1	81.8	53.5	308.0
1980	1,912.8	145.8	92.6	668.1	889.1	57.4	35.6	317.7	1,023.7	88.4	56.9	350.4
1981	2,144.7	158.6	101.3	743.4	979.5	67.2	41.6	350.4	1,165.2	91.3	59.6	393.0
1982	2,039.4	108.2	70.9	770.2	913.1	34.7	21.7	355.5	1,126.4	73.6	49.3	414.7
1983	2,114.3	133.1	85.8	812.8	973.5	48.7	30.0	372.4	1,140.8	84.4	55.8	440.4
1984	2,335.0	165.6	107.6	864.2	1,107.6	75.5	48.9	395.6	1,227.5	90.0	58.8	468.5
1985	2,331.4	137.0	87.6	866.2	1,142.6	61.5	38.6	420.9	1,188.8	75.6	49.1	445.3
1986	2,220.9	129.3	83.1	874.7	1,125.5	52.1	32.6	436.3	1,095.4	77.2	50.5	438.4
1987	2,378.2	173.0	115.6	900.9	1,178.0	78.0	53.0	444.3	1,200.3	95.1	62.6	456.6
1988	2,596.2	216.1	154.6	957.6	1,284.7	91.7	67.1	468.7	1,311.5	124.4	87.5	488.9
1989	2,745.1	188.8	136.3	999.0	1,356.6	75.2	55.7	501.3	1,388.5	113.5	80.6	497.7
1990	2,810.7	159.6	111.6	1,043.8	1,357.2	57.6	40.9	515.0	1,453.5	102.0	70.6	528.9
1991	2,761.1	99.8	67.5	1,064.1	1,304.0	14.1	7.4	506.8	1,457.1	85.7	60.1	557.4
1992	2,890.3	33.4	24.0	1,036.8	1,389.9	-33.2	-23.5	473.9	1,500.4	66.6	47.5	562.8
1991: I	655.1	27.0	18.3	1,050.4	303.9	3.4	1.4	503.5	351.2	23.6	16.8	546.8
II	698.8	32.8	23.1	1,057.6	335.3	10.7	7.6	507.8	363.5	22.1	15.4	549.8
III	698.7	27.8	17.6	1,069.1	328.0	3.2	1.1	505.9	370.7	24.6	16.5	563.2
IV	708.4	12.2	8.5	1,079.4	336.7	-3.2	-2.8	509.8	371.7	15.3	11.3	569.6
1992: I [3]	679.6	-65.1	-44.2	1,015.0	325.4	-59.0	-40.2	462.0	354.2	-6.1	-4.0	553.0
II	733.6	42.2	30.0	1,035.4	355.9	15.3	11.2	475.5	377.7	26.9	18.9	560.0
III	729.9	37.3	27.7	1,056.8	346.2	10.9	8.9	487.4	383.7	26.5	18.8	569.4
IV	747.2	18.9	10.4	1,039.8	362.4	-.5	-3.4	470.9	384.8	19.4	13.8	568.9
1993: I	717.7	16.6	14.0	1,031.5	349.5	-1.9	.3	467.7	368.3	18.5	13.7	563.7
II	766.5	37.7	25.3	1,047.6	380.8	15.7	9.3	483.1	385.8	22.0	15.9	564.5
III	752.5	37.7	25.1	1,056.1	368.3	16.1	11.5	492.9	384.2	21.6	13.6	563.1
Addendum: Impact of Accounting Change [3]—First quarter 1992												
1992: I		-99.2	-68.9	-69.2		-69.9	-48.0	-48.1		-29.3	-21.0	-21.1

[1] In the old series, "income taxes" refers to Federal income taxes only, as State and local income taxes had already been deducted. In the new series, no income taxes have been deducted.
[2] Annual data are average equity for the year (using four end-of-quarter figures).
[3] Data for the first quarter of 1992 were revised significantly as a result of the early adoption of Financial Accounting Standards Board Statement 106 (Employer's Accounting for Post-Retirement Benefits Other Than Pensions) by a large number of companies during the fourth quarter of 1992. Corporations must show the cumulative effect of a change in accounting principle in the first quarter of the year in which the change is adopted.

Note.—Data are not necessarily comparable from one period to another due to changes in accounting principles, industry classifications, sampling procedures, etc. For explanatory notes concerning compilation of the series, see "Quarterly Financial Report for Manufacturing, Mining, and Trade Corporations," Department of Commerce, Bureau of the Census.

Source: Department of Commerce, Bureau of the Census.

TABLE B-92.—*Relation of profits after taxes to stockholders' equity and to sales, all manufacturing corporations, 1947–93*

Year or quarter	Ratio of profits after income taxes (annual rate) to stockholders' equity—percent [1]			Profits after income taxes per dollar of sales—cents		
	All manufacturing corporations	Durable goods industries	Nondurable goods industries	All manufacturing corporations	Durable goods industries	Nondurable goods industries
1947	15.6	14.4	16.6	6.7	6.7	6.7
1948	16.0	15.7	16.2	7.0	7.1	6.8
1949	11.6	12.1	11.2	5.8	6.4	5.4
1950	15.4	16.9	14.1	7.1	7.7	6.5
1951	12.1	13.0	11.2	4.9	5.3	4.5
1952	10.3	11.1	9.7	4.3	4.5	4.1
1953	10.5	11.1	9.9	4.3	4.2	4.3
1954	9.9	10.3	9.6	4.5	4.6	4.4
1955	12.6	13.8	11.4	5.4	5.7	5.1
1956	12.3	12.8	11.8	5.3	5.2	5.3
1957	10.9	11.3	10.6	4.8	4.8	4.9
1958	8.6	8.0	9.2	4.2	3.9	4.4
1959	10.4	10.4	10.4	4.8	4.8	4.9
1960	9.2	8.5	9.8	4.4	4.0	4.8
1961	8.9	8.1	9.6	4.3	3.9	4.7
1962	9.8	9.6	9.9	4.5	4.4	4.7
1963	10.3	10.1	10.4	4.7	4.5	4.9
1964	11.6	11.7	11.5	5.2	5.1	5.4
1965	13.0	13.8	12.2	5.6	5.7	5.5
1966	13.4	14.2	12.7	5.6	5.6	5.6
1967	11.7	11.7	11.8	5.0	4.8	5.3
1968	12.1	12.2	11.9	5.1	4.9	5.2
1969	11.5	11.4	11.5	4.8	4.6	5.0
1970	9.3	8.3	10.3	4.0	3.5	4.5
1971	9.7	9.0	10.3	4.1	3.8	4.5
1972	10.6	10.8	10.5	4.3	4.2	4.4
1973	12.8	13.1	12.6	4.7	4.7	4.8
1973: IV	13.4	12.9	14.0	4.7	4.5	5.0
New series:						
1973: IV	14.3	13.3	15.3	5.6	5.0	6.1
1974	14.9	12.6	17.1	5.5	4.7	6.4
1975	11.6	10.3	12.9	4.6	4.1	5.1
1976	13.9	13.7	14.2	5.4	5.2	5.5
1977	14.2	14.5	13.8	5.3	5.3	5.3
1978	15.0	16.0	14.2	5.4	5.5	5.3
1979	16.4	15.4	17.4	5.7	5.2	6.1
1980	13.9	11.2	16.3	4.8	4.0	5.6
1981	13.6	11.9	15.2	4.7	4.2	5.1
1982	9.2	6.1	11.9	3.5	2.4	4.4
1983	10.6	8.1	12.7	4.1	3.1	4.9
1984	12.5	12.4	12.5	4.6	4.4	4.8
1985	10.1	9.2	11.0	3.8	3.4	4.1
1986	9.5	7.5	11.5	3.7	2.9	4.6
1987	12.8	11.9	13.7	4.9	4.5	5.2
1988	16.1	14.3	17.9	6.0	5.2	6.7
1989	13.6	11.1	16.2	5.0	4.1	5.8
1990	10.7	8.0	13.4	4.0	3.0	4.9
1991	6.3	1.5	10.8	2.4	.6	4.1
1992	2.3	−5.0	8.4	.8	−1.7	3.2
1991: I	7.0	1.2	12.3	2.8	.5	4.8
II	8.7	6.0	11.2	3.3	2.3	4.2
III	6.6	.9	11.7	2.5	.3	4.4
IV	3.2	−2.2	8.0	1.2	−.8	3.0
1992: I [2]	−17.4	−34.8	−2.9	−6.5	−12.4	−1.1
II	11.6	9.4	13.5	4.1	3.1	5.0
III	10.5	7.3	13.2	3.8	2.6	4.9
IV	4.0	−2.9	9.7	1.4	−.9	3.6
1993: I	5.4	.3	9.7	2.0	.1	3.7
II	9.7	7.7	11.3	3.3	2.5	4.1
III	9.5	9.3	9.6	3.3	3.1	3.5

[1] Annual ratios based on average equity for the year (using four end-of-quarter figures). Quarterly ratios based on equity at end of quarter only.

[2] See footnote 3, Table B-91.

Note.—Based on data in millions of dollars.
See Note, Table B-91.

Source: Department of Commerce, Bureau of the Census.

TABLE B-93.—*Sources and uses of funds, nonfarm nonfinancial corporate business, 1947–93*

[Billions of dollars; quarterly data at seasonally adjusted annual rates]

Year or quarter	Sources Total	Internal Total	U.S. undistributed profits	Inventory valuation and capital consumption adjustments	Capital consumption allowances	Foreign earnings retained abroad [1]	External Total	Credit market funds Total	Securities and mortgages	Loans and short-term paper	Other [2]	Uses Total	Capital expenditures [3]	Increase in financial assets	Discrepancy (sources less uses)
1947....	27.3	13.3	12.7	−8.7	9.0	0.3	14.0	8.6	5.6	3.0	5.4	26.4	18.1	8.3	0.9
1948....	29.7	19.7	14.0	−5.2	10.4	.4	10.1	7.7	7.0	.7	2.4	25.6	20.7	4.9	4.1
1949....	21.3	20.0	9.6	−1.0	11.2	.3	1.3	3.8	5.6	−1.9	−2.5	18.4	14.9	3.5	2.9
1950....	42.9	18.5	14.1	−7.9	12.0	.3	24.4	8.7	4.8	3.9	15.7	40.3	24.0	16.3	2.5
1951....	37.3	20.8	10.8	−4.4	13.8	.6	16.6	11.5	7.1	4.4	5.1	37.9	30.6	7.3	−.6
1952....	31.1	22.7	9.1	−2.0	14.8	.8	8.4	9.3	8.2	1.1	−.9	29.8	25.3	4.5	1.3
1953....	29.3	22.6	9.4	−3.3	15.8	.7	6.8	6.3	6.7	−.4	.5	28.3	26.1	2.2	1.0
1954....	30.3	24.7	9.3	−1.9	16.7	.5	5.6	6.4	6.9	−.5	−.8	27.8	23.0	4.8	2.5
1955....	53.7	30.3	13.7	−2.0	17.8	.8	23.4	10.6	6.9	3.7	12.8	49.0	32.6	16.4	4.6
1956....	46.7	30.5	13.1	−3.7	20.0	1.0	16.2	13.4	8.1	5.3	2.8	40.9	37.0	3.9	5.8
1957....	44.8	32.4	11.9	−2.7	22.0	1.2	12.4	12.8	10.8	1.9	−.4	39.8	35.7	4.1	4.9
1958....	43.5	31.2	8.8	−1.4	23.0	.8	12.3	11.0	11.1	−.1	1.3	38.7	28.0	10.7	4.8
1959....	57.2	37.0	13.0	−1.0	24.1	.9	20.2	12.4	8.4	4.0	7.8	51.8	37.8	14.1	5.4
1960....	50.4	36.4	10.5	−.4	25.1	1.2	14.0	12.2	8.3	3.9	1.7	41.5	37.7	3.8	8.9
1961....	56.2	37.5	10.2	.6	25.8	1.0	18.7	12.4	10.9	1.5	6.3	50.6	36.5	14.1	5.6
1962....	62.2	44.0	13.0	3.2	26.8	1.1	18.2	13.4	9.5	4.0	4.8	54.6	42.2	12.3	7.7
1963....	70.4	47.8	14.5	4.0	27.9	1.4	22.6	12.8	9.1	3.7	9.8	59.9	44.4	15.5	10.5
1964....	76.3	53.0	18.4	4.0	29.3	1.3	23.3	15.0	9.0	6.0	8.3	64.5	49.8	14.7	11.8
1965....	94.8	60.1	23.4	4.0	31.3	1.4	34.8	19.7	7.8	11.9	15.1	82.4	60.8	21.6	12.4
1966....	101.1	64.3	25.0	3.5	34.1	1.7	36.8	26.5	16.0	10.5	10.3	91.0	74.5	16.5	10.1
1967....	97.0	65.3	22.2	4.2	37.3	1.6	31.6	27.2	19.0	8.2	4.4	87.3	71.2	16.2	9.6
1968....	115.6	66.7	21.3	1.9	41.1	2.3	49.0	29.4	16.8	12.6	19.6	107.3	76.8	30.5	8.3
1969....	122.9	66.5	18.4	.4	45.0	2.8	56.3	35.7	17.8	17.9	20.7	116.8	85.5	31.3	6.1
1970....	107.5	64.0	12.6	−1.1	49.4	3.2	43.5	36.8	28.8	8.0	6.7	100.2	82.0	18.3	7.2
1971....	131.8	76.1	18.7	.0	54.2	3.2	55.7	39.4	34.7	4.7	16.3	124.3	88.2	36.1	7.5
1972....	160.2	88.1	24.6	−1.6	60.5	4.7	72.0	45.2	29.3	15.9	26.8	149.8	100.4	49.4	10.4
1973....	222.8	95.5	36.9	−15.2	65.6	8.1	127.3	81.3	49.4	31.9	46.0	195.0	125.2	69.8	27.7
1974....	190.6	91.0	45.3	−38.8	76.8	7.7	99.5	58.6	25.0	33.5	41.0	195.0	143.7	51.3	−4.5
1975....	157.3	125.0	43.4	−18.6	92.2	8.1	32.4	24.4	40.6	−16.3	8.0	157.2	117.5	39.7	.1
1976....	210.8	140.5	56.5	−26.1	102.5	7.6	70.3	50.2	41.7	8.5	20.2	210.7	159.0	51.7	.1
1977....	260.1	162.7	66.9	−27.0	114.8	8.1	97.4	68.9	44.1	24.8	28.5	245.8	185.5	60.3	14.3
1978....	319.3	183.6	78.7	−37.8	131.1	11.7	135.7	73.1	39.7	33.3	62.6	328.7	223.1	105.7	−9.4
1979....	336.5	198.5	86.4	−58.0	151.6	18.6	138.0	67.8	16.0	51.8	70.2	373.2	245.6	127.6	−36.8
1980....	334.7	199.7	69.2	−61.4	173.2	18.7	135.0	77.0	35.9	41.1	58.0	337.8	255.7	82.1	−3.1
1981....	390.7	238.9	64.2	−44.8	205.3	14.2	151.8	102.0	32.7	69.3	49.8	421.4	313.0	108.4	−30.7
1982....	330.8	247.5	30.6	−22.4	227.5	11.8	83.3	69.2	11.8	57.5	14.1	349.9	285.3	64.6	−19.1
1983....	439.8	292.3	30.5	2.9	240.1	18.8	147.5	96.2	56.2	40.0	51.3	416.5	300.1	116.4	23.3
1984....	501.0	336.3	46.4	24.1	246.1	19.7	164.7	108.6	−5.5	114.1	56.1	515.3	398.5	116.8	−14.3
1985....	486.3	351.9	21.7	54.4	256.0	19.8	134.4	76.1	13.0	63.1	58.3	465.8	374.9	91.0	20.4
1986....	531.9	336.7	−2.1	53.4	269.2	16.2	195.2	140.3	65.5	74.7	54.9	503.3	351.9	151.5	28.5
1987....	540.5	375.9	41.3	30.6	279.2	24.8	164.6	65.2	27.8	37.4	99.4	489.9	365.0	124.9	50.7
1988....	610.9	404.3	73.6	15.7	295.1	19.9	206.6	71.8	−14.6	86.4	134.9	558.2	394.4	163.8	52.7
1989....	562.3	399.9	32.2	19.8	314.8	32.8	162.6	62.4	−32.9	95.2	100.2	523.6	403.8	119.8	38.7
1990....	522.8	409.4	20.5	21.8	326.6	40.6	113.4	37.7	−18.9	56.6	75.7	502.0	407.3	94.7	20.8
1991....	473.2	437.8	38.2	17.5	338.6	43.6	35.4	6.9	95.9	−89.0	28.4	451.2	381.6	69.6	22.0
1992....	586.6	462.7	52.2	21.9	349.5	39.0	124.0	68.6	68.3	.3	55.4	537.8	397.2	140.6	48.8
1991:															
I......	450.9	433.0	24.9	23.1	336.1	48.8	17.9	4.0	92.5	−88.5	13.9	403.5	377.2	26.2	47.4
II......	473.4	440.9	36.0	23.9	337.6	43.3	32.5	32.9	123.7	−90.8	−.4	455.1	367.4	87.7	18.3
III......	480.9	426.9	45.0	7.2	339.5	35.2	54.0	9.4	72.2	−62.8	44.6	461.4	388.3	73.0	19.5
IV......	487.4	450.5	46.8	15.6	341.2	46.8	37.0	−18.5	95.3	−113.8	55.6	484.8	393.6	91.2	2.6
1992:															
I......	560.4	454.6	50.9	15.8	341.6	46.3	105.8	81.7	95.6	−13.9	24.1	520.8	369.9	150.9	39.6
II......	600.8	452.2	59.6	12.4	344.4	35.7	148.6	69.7	96.9	−27.2	78.9	567.4	401.2	166.1	33.4
III......	588.2	468.5	51.2	19.8	362.7	34.8	119.7	68.9	37.8	31.1	50.8	520.0	402.7	117.3	68.2
IV......	597.0	475.4	47.2	39.7	349.2	39.2	121.7	53.9	42.8	11.1	67.7	543.0	415.2	127.8	54.0
1993:															
I......	468.3	460.6	35.3	22.6	354.5	48.2	7.7	9.3	69.9	−60.6	−1.6	456.7	446.4	10.3	11.6
II......	593.6	471.4	48.7	22.7	357.5	42.5	122.2	88.5	76.9	11.6	33.6	563.7	449.2	114.4	29.9
III......	611.4	485.8	44.9	34.1	364.8	42.0	125.5	76.0	83.3	−7.4	49.6	585.7	457.7	128.0	25.6

[1] Foreign branch profits, dividends, and subsidiaries' earnings retained abroad.
[2] Consists of tax liabilities, trade debt, and direct foreign investment in the United States.
[3] Plant and equipment, residential structures, inventory investment, and mineral rights from U.S. Government.

Source: Board of Governors of the Federal Reserve System.

TABLE B-94.—*Common stock prices and yields, 1955–93*

| Year or month | Common stock prices [1] |||||| Standard & Poor's composite index (1941-43=10) [2] | Common stock yields (S&P) (percent) [4] ||
| | New York Stock Exchange indexes (Dec. 31, 1965=50) [2] ||||| Dow Jones industrial average [2] | | Dividend-price ratio [5] | Earnings-price ratio [6] |
	Composite	Industrial	Transportation	Utility [3]	Finance				
1955	21.54					442.72	40.49	4.08	7.95
1956	24.40					493.01	46.62	4.09	7.55
1957	23.67					475.71	44.38	4.35	7.89
1958	24.56					491.66	46.24	3.97	6.23
1959	30.73					632.12	57.38	3.23	5.78
1960	30.01					618.04	55.85	3.47	5.90
1961	35.37					691.55	66.27	2.98	4.62
1962	33.49					639.76	62.38	3.37	5.82
1963	37.51					714.81	69.87	3.17	5.50
1964	43.76					834.05	81.37	3.01	5.32
1965	47.39					910.88	88.17	3.00	5.59
1966	46.15	46.18	50.26	90.81	44.45	873.60	85.26	3.40	6.63
1967	50.77	51.97	53.51	90.86	49.82	879.12	91.93	3.20	5.73
1968	55.37	58.00	50.58	88.38	65.85	906.00	98.70	3.07	5.67
1969	54.67	57.44	46.96	85.60	70.49	876.72	97.84	3.24	6.08
1970	45.72	48.03	32.14	74.47	60.00	753.19	83.22	3.83	6.45
1971	54.22	57.92	44.35	79.05	70.38	884.76	98.29	3.14	5.41
1972	60.29	65.73	50.17	76.95	78.35	950.71	109.20	2.84	5.50
1973	57.42	63.08	37.74	75.38	70.12	923.88	107.43	3.06	7.12
1974	43.84	48.08	31.89	59.58	49.67	759.37	82.85	4.47	11.59
1975	45.73	50.52	31.10	63.00	47.14	802.49	86.16	4.31	9.15
1976	54.46	60.44	39.57	73.94	52.94	974.92	102.01	3.77	8.90
1977	53.69	57.86	41.09	81.84	55.25	894.63	98.20	4.62	10.79
1978	53.70	58.23	43.50	78.44	56.65	820.23	96.02	5.28	12.03
1979	58.32	64.76	47.34	76.41	61.42	844.40	103.01	5.47	13.46
1980	68.10	78.70	60.61	74.69	64.25	891.41	118.78	5.26	12.66
1981	74.02	85.44	72.61	77.81	73.52	932.92	128.05	5.20	11.96
1982	68.93	78.18	60.41	79.49	71.99	884.36	119.71	5.81	11.60
1983	92.63	107.45	89.36	93.99	95.34	1,190.34	160.41	4.40	8.03
1984	92.46	108.01	85.63	92.89	89.28	1,178.48	160.46	4.64	10.02
1985	108.09	123.79	104.11	113.49	114.21	1,328.23	186.84	4.25	8.12
1986	136.00	155.85	119.87	142.72	147.20	1,792.76	236.34	3.49	6.09
1987	161.70	195.31	140.39	148.57	146.48	2,275.99	286.83	3.08	5.48
1988	149.91	180.95	134.12	143.53	127.26	2,060.82	265.79	3.64	8.01
1989	180.02	216.23	175.28	174.87	151.88	2,508.91	322.84	3.45	7.41
1990	183.46	225.78	158.62	181.20	133.26	2,678.94	334.59	3.61	6.47
1991	206.33	258.14	173.99	185.32	150.82	2,929.33	376.18	3.24	4.81
1992	229.01	284.62	201.09	198.91	179.26	3,284.29	415.74	2.99	4.22
1993	249.58	299.99	242.49	228.90	216.42	3,522.06	451.41	2.78	
1992: Jan	229.34	286.62	201.55	198.61	174.50	3,227.06	416.08	2.90	
Feb	228.12	286.09	205.53	192.35	174.08	3,257.27	412.56	2.94	
Mar	225.21	282.36	204.07	188.31	173.49	3,247.42	407.36	3.01	4.01
Apr	224.55	281.60	201.28	189.83	171.10	3,294.08	407.41	3.02	
May	228.61	285.25	207.93	196.52	175.90	3,376.79	414.81	2.99	
June	224.68	279.54	202.02	194.46	174.82	3,337.79	408.27	3.06	4.18
July	228.17	281.90	198.36	202.35	181.00	3,329.41	415.05	3.00	
Aug	230.07	284.44	191.31	206.83	180.47	3,307.45	417.93	2.97	
Sept	230.13	285.76	191.61	204.52	178.27	3,293.92	418.48	3.00	4.32
Oct	226.97	279.70	192.30	203.24	181.36	3,198.70	412.50	3.07	
Nov	232.84	287.30	204.78	202.26	189.27	3,238.49	422.84	2.98	
Dec	239.47	294.86	212.35	207.69	196.87	3,303.15	435.64	2.90	4.38
1993: Jan	239.67	292.11	221.00	211.04	203.38	3,277.72	435.23	2.88	
Feb	243.41	294.40	226.96	218.89	209.93	3,367.26	441.70	2.81	
Mar	248.12	298.75	229.42	225.07	217.01	3,440.74	450.16	2.76	4.39
Apr	244.72	292.19	237.97	227.56	216.02	3,423.63	443.08	2.82	
May	246.02	297.83	237.80	222.41	209.40	3,478.17	445.25	2.80	
June	247.16	298.78	234.30	226.53	209.75	3,513.81	448.06	2.81	4.29
July	247.85	295.34	238.30	232.55	218.94	3,529.43	447.29	2.81	
Aug	251.93	298.83	250.82	237.44	224.96	3,597.01	454.13	2.76	
Sept	254.86	300.92	248.15	244.21	229.35	3,592.29	459.24	2.73	4.46
Oct	257.53	306.61	254.04	240.97	228.18	3,625.81	463.90	2.72	
Nov	255.93	310.84	262.96	230.12	214.08	3,674.70	462.89	2.72	
Dec	257.73	313.22	268.11	229.95	216.00	3,744.10	465.95	2.72	

[1] Averages of daily closing prices, except NYSE data through May 1964 are averages of weekly closing prices.
[2] Includes stocks as follows: for NYSE, all stocks listed (more than 2,000); for Dow-Jones industrial average, 30 stocks; and for S&P composite index, 500 stocks.
[3] Effective April 1993, the NYSE doubled the value of the utility index to facilitate trading of options and futures on the index. All indexes shown here reflect the doubling.
[4] Based on 500 stocks in the S&P composite index.
[5] Aggregate cash dividends (based on latest known annual rate) divided by aggregate market value based on Wednesday closing prices. Monthly data are averages of weekly figures; annual data are averages of monthly figures.
[6] Quarterly data are ratio of earnings (after taxes) for 4 quarters ending with particular quarter to price index for last day of that quarter. Annual data are averages of quarterly ratios.

Note.—All data relate to stocks listed on the New York Stock Exchange.

Sources: New York Stock Exchange (NYSE), Dow Jones & Co., Inc., and Standard & Poor's Corporation (S&P).

TABLE B-95.—*Business formation and business failures, 1950-93*

Year or month	Index of net business formation (1967=100)	New business incorporations (number)	Business failure rate [2]	Business failures [1]					
				Number of failures			Amount of current liabilities (millions of dollars)		
				Total	Liability size class		Total	Liability size class	
					Under $100,000	$100,000 and over		Under $100,000	$100,000 and over
1950	87.7	93,092	34.3	9,162	8,746	416	248.3	151.2	97.1
1951	86.7	83,778	30.7	8,058	7,626	432	259.5	131.6	128.0
1952	90.8	92,946	28.7	7,611	7,081	530	283.3	131.9	151.4
1953	89.7	102,706	33.2	8,862	8,075	787	394.2	167.5	226.6
1954	88.8	117,411	42.0	11,086	10,226	860	462.6	211.4	251.2
1955	96.6	139,915	41.6	10,969	10,113	856	449.4	206.4	243.0
1956	94.6	141,163	48.0	12,686	11,615	1,071	562.7	239.8	322.9
1957	90.3	137,112	51.7	13,739	12,547	1,192	615.3	267.1	348.2
1958	90.2	150,781	55.9	14,964	13,499	1,465	728.3	297.6	430.7
1959	97.9	193,067	51.8	14,053	12,707	1,346	692.8	278.9	413.9
1960	94.5	182,713	57.0	15,445	13,650	1,795	938.6	327.2	611.4
1961	90.8	181,535	64.4	17,075	15,006	2,069	1,090.1	370.1	720.0
1962	92.6	182,057	60.8	15,782	13,772	2,010	1,213.6	346.5	867.1
1963	94.4	186,404	56.3	14,374	12,192	2,182	1,352.6	321.0	1,031.6
1964	98.2	197,724	53.2	13,501	11,346	2,155	1,329.2	313.6	1,015.6
1965	99.8	203,897	53.3	13,514	11,340	2,174	1,321.7	321.7	1,000.0
1966	99.3	200,010	51.6	13,061	10,833	2,228	1,385.7	321.5	1,064.1
1967	100.0	206,569	49.0	12,364	10,144	2,220	1,265.2	297.9	967.3
1968	108.3	233,635	38.6	9,636	7,829	1,807	941.0	241.1	699.9
1969	115.8	274,267	37.3	9,154	7,192	1,962	1,142.1	231.3	910.8
1970	108.8	264,209	43.8	10,748	8,019	2,729	1,887.8	269.3	1,618.4
1971	111.1	287,577	41.7	10,326	7,611	2,715	1,916.9	271.3	1,645.6
1972	119.3	316,601	38.3	9,566	7,040	2,526	2,000.2	258.8	1,741.5
1973	119.1	329,358	36.4	9,345	6,627	2,718	2,298.6	235.6	2,063.0
1974	113.2	319,149	38.4	9,915	6,733	3,182	3,053.1	256.9	2,796.3
1975	109.9	326,345	42.6	11,432	7,504	3,928	4,380.2	298.6	4,081.6
1976	120.4	375,766	34.8	9,628	6,176	3,452	3,011.3	257.8	2,753.4
1977	130.8	436,170	28.4	7,919	4,861	3,058	3,095.3	208.3	2,887.0
1978	138.1	478,019	23.9	6,619	3,712	2,907	2,656.0	164.7	2,491.3
1979	138.3	524,565	27.8	7,564	3,930	3,634	2,667.4	179.9	2,487.5
1980	129.9	533,520	42.1	11,742	5,682	6,060	4,635.1	272.5	4,362.6
1981	124.8	581,242	61.3	16,794	8,233	8,561	6,955.2	405.8	6,549.3
1982	116.4	566,942	88.4	24,908	11,509	13,399	15,610.8	541.7	15,069.1
1983	117.5	600,400	109.7	31,334	15,572	15,762	16,072.9	635.1	15,437.8
1984	121.3	634,991	107.0	52,078	33,527	18,551	29,268.6	409.8	28,858.8
1985	120.9	662,047	115.0	57,253	36,551	20,702	36,937.4	423.9	36,513.5
1986	120.4	702,738	120.0	61,616	38,908	22,708	44,724.0	838.3	43,885.7
1987	121.2	685,572	102.0	61,111	38,949	22,162	34,723.8	746.0	33,977.8
1988	124.1	685,095	98.0	57,097	38,300	18,797	39,573.0	686.9	38,886.1
1989	124.8	676,565	65.0	50,361	33,312	17,049	42,328.8	670.5	41,658.2
1990	120.7	647,366	74.0	60,747	40,833	19,914	56,130.1	735.6	55,394.5
1991	115.2	628,604	107.0	88,140	60,612	27,528	96,825.3	1,044.9	95,780.4
1992	116.3	666,800	110.0	97,069	68,264	28,805	94,317.5	1,096.7	93,220.8
1993				85,565	61,091	24,474	48,914.1	941.6	47,972.5
Seasonally adjusted								
1992: Jan	117.2	58,141		8,588	6,040	2,548	6,356.0	93.1	6,263.0
Feb	116.0	55,092		8,093	5,697	2,396	9,857.8	94.7	9,763.1
Mar	116.4	57,449		9,143	6,365	2,778	6,322.2	106.6	6,215.6
Apr	115.4	54,474		8,704	6,059	2,645	7,907.0	97.2	7,809.7
May	113.2	48,688		7,803	5,419	2,384	13,842.4	88.6	13,753.8
June	117.4	58,730		8,462	6,050	2,412	13,665.1	97.2	13,567.8
July	116.6	56,942		8,637	6,137	2,500	3,272.0	97.2	3,174.8
Aug	114.1	51,245		7,981	5,587	2,394	9,056.2	89.4	8,966.8
Sept	118.5	59,179		7,598	5,392	2,206	3,220.7	87.7	3,132.9
Oct	116.4	52,492		8,014	5,621	2,393	8,383.6	87.9	8,295.7
Nov	115.3	55,392		7,167	5,092	2,075	3,984.1	84.1	3,900.0
Dec	119.0	61,695		6,879	4,805	2,074	8,450.5	73.0	8,377.5
1993: Jan	119.3	55,689		7,654	5,398	2,256	6,174.9	80.3	6,094.6
Feb	121.1	59,691		7,062	5,103	1,959	2,406.7	76.8	2,329.9
Mar	121.8	61,002		8,422	5,955	2,467	4,343.0	90.9	4,252.1
Apr	120.8	59,648		7,827	5,504	2,323	2,973.4	94.5	2,878.9
May	117.5	51,765		7,530	5,292	2,238	6,634.4	84.3	6,550.1
June	120.6	60,422		7,131	5,085	2,046	2,675.4	79.6	2,595.8
July	122.5	58,341		6,766	4,831	1,935	5,496.4	76.4	5,420.0
Aug	123.1	57,909		7,109	5,173	1,936	7,382.0	78.8	7,303.2
Sept	120.9			7,510	5,555	1,955	3,062.6	74.9	2,987.6
Oct	121.4			6,570	4,719	1,851	2,222.1	72.4	2,149.8
Nov	123.7			6,200	4,428	1,772	2,991.0	67.8	2,923.2
Dec				5,784	4,048	1,736	2,552.3	64.9	2,487.4

[1] Commercial and industrial failures only through 1983, excluding failures of banks, railroads, real estate, insurance, holding, and financial companies, steamship lines, travel agencies, etc.
  Data beginning 1984 are based on expanded coverage and new methodology and are therefore not generally comparable with earlier data. Data for 1992 and 1993 are subject to revision due to amended court filings.
[2] Failure rate per 10,000 listed enterprises.

Sources: Department of Commerce (Bureau of Economic Analysis) and The Dun & Bradstreet Corporation.

AGRICULTURE

TABLE B-96.—*Farm income, 1940–93*

[Billions of dollars; quarterly data at seasonally adjusted annual rates]

Year or quarter	Gross farm income				Value of inventory changes [2]	Production expenses	Net farm income	
	Total [1]	Cash marketing receipts					Current dollars	1987 dollars [3]
		Total	Livestock and products	Crops				
1940	11.3	8.4	4.9	3.5	0.3	6.9	4.5	40.7
1941	14.3	11.1	6.5	4.6	.4	7.8	6.5	55.5
1942	19.9	15.6	9.0	6.5	1.1	10.0	9.9	80.1
1943	23.3	19.6	11.5	8.1	−.1	11.6	11.7	93.9
1944	24.0	20.5	11.4	9.2	−.4	12.3	11.7	92.9
1945	25.4	21.7	12.0	9.7	−.4	13.1	12.3	92.6
1946	29.6	24.8	13.8	11.0	.0	14.5	15.1	90.2
1947	32.4	29.6	16.5	13.1	−1.8	17.0	15.4	82.1
1948	36.5	30.2	17.1	13.1	1.7	18.8	17.7	88.3
1949	30.8	27.8	15.4	12.4	−.9	18.0	12.8	64.2
1950	33.1	28.5	16.1	12.4	.8	19.5	13.6	67.6
1951	38.3	32.9	19.6	13.2	1.2	22.3	15.9	74.8
1952	37.8	32.5	18.2	14.3	.9	22.8	15.0	69.6
1953	34.4	31.0	16.9	14.1	−.6	21.5	13.0	59.0
1954	34.2	29.8	16.3	13.6	.5	21.8	12.4	55.7
1955	33.5	29.5	16.0	13.5	.2	22.2	11.3	49.4
1956	34.0	30.4	16.4	14.0	−.5	22.7	11.3	47.7
1957	34.8	29.7	17.4	12.3	.6	23.7	11.1	45.4
1958	39.0	33.5	19.2	14.2	.8	25.8	13.2	52.9
1959	37.9	33.6	18.9	14.7	.0	27.2	10.7	41.9
1960	38.6	34.0	19.0	15.0	.4	27.4	11.2	43.1
1961	40.5	35.2	19.5	15.7	.3	28.6	12.0	45.5
1962	42.3	36.5	20.2	16.3	.6	30.3	12.1	44.8
1963	43.4	37.5	20.0	17.4	.6	31.6	11.8	43.3
1964	42.3	37.3	19.9	17.4	−.8	31.8	10.5	37.9
1965	46.5	39.4	21.9	17.5	1.0	33.6	12.9	45.4
1966	50.5	43.4	25.0	18.4	−.1	36.5	14.0	47.5
1967	50.5	42.8	24.4	18.4	.7	38.2	12.3	40.7
1968	51.8	44.2	25.5	18.7	.1	39.5	12.3	38.8
1969	56.4	48.2	28.6	19.6	.1	42.1	14.3	42.8
1970	58.8	50.5	29.5	21.0	.0	44.5	14.4	40.8
1971	62.1	52.7	30.5	22.3	1.4	47.1	15.0	40.5
1972	71.1	61.1	35.6	25.5	.9	51.7	19.5	50.1
1973	98.9	86.9	45.8	41.1	3.4	64.6	34.4	83.2
1974	98.2	92.4	41.3	51.1	−1.6	71.0	27.3	60.7
1975	100.6	88.9	43.1	45.8	3.4	75.0	25.5	51.9
1976	102.9	95.4	46.3	49.0	−1.5	82.7	20.2	38.6
1977	108.8	96.2	47.6	48.6	1.1	88.9	19.9	35.6
1978	128.4	112.4	59.2	53.2	1.9	103.3	25.2	41.8
1979	150.7	131.5	69.2	62.3	5.0	123.3	27.4	41.9
1980	149.3	139.7	68.0	71.7	−6.3	133.1	16.1	22.5
1981	166.3	141.6	69.2	72.5	6.5	139.4	26.9	34.1
1982	164.1	142.6	70.3	72.3	−1.4	140.3	23.8	28.4
1983	153.9	136.8	69.6	67.2	−10.9	139.6	14.2	16.3
1984	168.0	142.8	72.9	69.9	6.0	141.9	26.1	28.7
1985	161.2	144.1	69.8	74.3	−2.3	132.4	28.8	30.5
1986	156.1	135.4	71.6	63.8	−2.2	125.1	31.1	32.0
1987	168.5	141.8	76.0	65.9	−2.3	128.8	39.7	39.7
1988	175.8	151.2	79.4	71.7	−3.4	137.0	38.8	37.3
1989	190.9	161.2	84.1	77.0	4.8	144.0	46.9	43.2
1990	196.4	170.0	89.8	80.1	3.4	149.9	46.5	41.0
1991	190.3	168.7	86.8	81.9	−.3	150.3	40.0	34.0
1992	197.7	171.2	86.4	84.8	3.8	149.1	48.6	40.2
1991: I	190.5	166.5	89.6	76.9	1.2	147.5	43.0	37.0
II	191.2	166.8	87.6	79.2	.6	149.8	41.4	35.3
III	186.8	172.2	84.9	87.3	.1	151.7	35.2	29.8
IV	192.7	169.4	85.0	84.4	−3.1	152.2	40.5	34.1
1992: I	199.6	167.1	84.2	82.9	4.7	146.3	53.3	44.4
II	202.8	174.2	86.0	88.1	4.3	148.6	54.2	44.8
III	197.3	178.9	85.3	93.6	3.5	150.4	46.8	38.6
IV	191.3	164.5	89.9	74.6	2.5	151.0	40.3	33.0
1993: I	197.0	169.9	86.2	83.7	−3.6	148.2	48.8	39.5
II	203.7	180.5	92.2	88.2	−3.4	150.5	53.2	42.9
III *p*	188.1	175.4	90.7	84.7	−2.7	152.4	35.7	28.7

[1] Cash marketing receipts and inventory changes plus Government payments, other farm cash income, and nonmoney income furnished by farms.
[2] Physical changes in end-of-period inventory of crop and livestock commodities valued at average prices during the period.
[3] Income in current dollars divided by the GDP implicit price deflator (Department of Commerce).

Note.—Data include net Commodity Credit Corporation loans and operator households.

Source: Department of Agriculture, except as noted.

TABLE B-97.—*Farm output and productivity indexes, 1948-91*

[1982=100]

Year	Farm output Total [1]	Livestock and products [2][3]	Crops [2] Total [4]	Feed crops	Food grains	Oil crops	Productivity indicators [5] Farm output per unit of total factor input	Farm output per unit of farm labor
1948	48	54	46	33	40	15	52	19
1949	47	57	40	17	34	14	51	19
1950	47	60	39	22	32	17	50	20
1951	49	63	39	20	32	15	51	21
1952	51	64	42	22	42	15	53	23
1953	51	65	42	22	36	14	53	23
1954	51	68	39	28	34	16	54	24
1955	54	70	43	30	34	19	54	26
1956	54	71	42	28	35	22	55	27
1957	52	70	40	37	30	21	54	29
1958	55	72	44	36	46	27	59	32
1959	58	76	46	34	38	24	59	33
1960	59	75	48	44	46	25	60	36
1961	60	78	47	37	42	29	63	37
1962	62	79	50	38	40	30	65	38
1963	63	81	51	42	40	31	67	41
1964	63	83	49	34	47	32	67	43
1965	66	82	56	52	46	36	71	47
1966	65	83	52	44	48	40	71	50
1967	69	86	57	60	54	43	74	55
1968	69	86	57	54	57	48	75	55
1969	71	86	61	57	54	50	77	58
1970	71	90	58	49	50	53	77	60
1971	76	91	65	77	58	52	81	64
1972	76	92	64	67	57	56	83	65
1973	79	93	70	71	63	67	86	68
1974	75	92	65	53	66	54	78	66
1975	80	87	76	78	79	67	84	70
1976	82	91	75	75	77	58	84	74
1977	86	93	82	89	74	78	90	80
1978	86	93	81	91	67	86	85	80
1979	92	93	91	95	79	104	88	86
1980	87	99	78	64	86	80	82	81
1981	98	101	96	102	102	89	95	93
1982	100	100	100	100	100	100	100	100
1983	82	102	67	31	84	75	86	86
1984	98	100	95	108	93	87	100	101
1985	104	103	104	125	87	96	110	117
1986	100	103	95	119	77	88	109	115
1987	102	105	97	101	77	88	114	121
1988	95	108	83	63	70	71	109	111
1989	105	110	99	117	77	87	120	127
1990	112	112	111	114	99	87	126	128
1991	110	114	106	114	76	92	124	125

[1] Farm output measures the annual volume of net farm production available for eventual human use through sales from farms or consumption in farm households.
[2] Gross production.
[3] Horses and mules excluded.
[4] Includes items not included in groups shown.
[5] See Table B-98 for farm inputs.

Source: Department of Agriculture.

TABLE B-98.—*Farm input use, selected inputs, 1948–92*

Year	Farm population, April [1] Number (thousands)	As percent of total population [2]	Farm employment (thousands) [3] Total	Family workers	Hired workers	Crops harvested (millions of acres) [4]	Selected indexes of input use (1982=100) Total	Farm labor	Farm real estate	Durable equipment	Energy	Agricultural chemicals [5]	Feed, seed, and livestock purchases [6]	Other purchased inputs
1948	24,383	16.6	10,363	8,026	2,337	356	93	251	83	38	65	34	45	74
1949	24,194	16.2	9,964	7,712	2,252	360	91	241	86	45	72	36	40	77
1950	23,048	15.2	9,926	7,597	2,329	345	94	237	88	52	73	43	44	78
1951	21,890	14.2	9,546	7,310	2,236	344	96	228	90	58	76	42	49	80
1952	21,748	13.9	9,149	7,005	2,144	349	96	222	92	63	79	43	47	83
1953	19,874	12.5	8,864	6,775	2,089	348	97	220	95	66	81	42	50	82
1954	19,019	11.7	8,651	6,570	2,081	346	95	216	96	69	81	43	46	81
1955	19,078	11.5	8,381	6,345	2,036	340	99	211	98	70	83	45	59	83
1956	18,712	11.1	7,852	5,900	1,952	324	98	197	99	71	83	50	62	81
1957	17,656	10.3	7,600	5,660	1,940	324	97	183	99	69	82	49	68	85
1958	17,128	9.8	7,503	5,521	1,982	324	95	176	99	68	80	49	67	81
1959	16,592	9.3	7,342	5,390	1,952	324	98	173	99	68	81	56	69	99
1960	15,635	8.7	7,057	5,172	1,885	324	97	163	99	69	82	58	74	99
1961	14,803	8.1	6,919	5,029	1,890	302	96	161	97	68	84	61	68	98
1962	14,313	7.7	6,700	4,873	1,827	295	94	159	95	67	85	55	66	100
1963	13,367	7.1	6,518	4,738	1,780	298	94	153	96	67	86	61	67	100
1964	12,954	6.7	6,110	4,506	1,604	298	93	145	95	67	88	68	68	97
1965	12,363	6.4	5,610	4,128	1,482	298	93	141	95	69	89	73	69	96
1966	11,595	5.9	5,214	3,854	1,360	294	92	128	94	71	90	83	70	96
1967	10,875	5.5	4,903	3,650	1,253	306	93	124	97	73	90	80	76	97
1968	10,454	5.2	4,749	3,535	1,213	300	92	125	95	76	90	68	75	97
1969	10,307	5.1	4,596	3,419	1,176	290	93	123	94	78	92	73	84	93
1970	9,712	4.7	4,523	3,348	1,175	293	93	119	94	78	92	76	87	90
1971	9,425	4.5	4,436	3,275	1,161	305	93	118	96	79	90	80	87	87
1972	9,610	4.6	4,373	3,228	1,146	294	91	117	94	79	89	85	81	85
1973	9,472	4.5	4,337	3,169	1,168	321	92	117	98	81	90	94	71	91
1974	9,264	4.3	4,389	3,075	1,314	328	97	115	99	85	86	99	87	97
1975	8,864	4.1	4,331	3,021	1,310	336	96	114	98	89	101	91	86	94
1976	8,253	3.8	4,363	2,992	1,371	337	97	111	99	91	113	100	84	99
1977	[7] 6,194	[7] 2.8	4,143	2,852	1,291	345	96	107	99	94	119	98	77	100
1978	[7] 6,501	[7] 2.9	3,937	2,680	1,256	338	101	107	98	96	125	108	91	118
1979	[7] 6,241	[7] 2.8	3,765	2,495	1,270	348	104	107	99	99	113	118	97	127
1980	[7] 6,051	[7] 2.7	3,699	2,401	1,298	352	106	108	101	102	110	131	102	116
1981	[7] 5,850	[7] 2.5	[8] 3,582	[8] 2,324	[8] 1,258	366	103	105	101	102	106	122	98	111
1982	[7] 5,628	[7] 2.4	[8] 3,466	[8] 2,248	[8] 1,218	362	100	100	100	100	100	100	100	100
1983	[7] 5,787	[7] 2.5	[8] 3,349	[8] 2,171	[8] 1,178	306	96	95	92	95	97	93	99	107
1984	5,754	2.4	[8] 3,233	[8] 2,095	[8] 1,138	348	98	97	98	91	100	106	101	108
1985	5,355	2.2	3,116	2,018	1,098	342	95	89	97	86	90	101	106	99
1986	5,226	2.2	2,912	1,873	1,039	325	92	87	94	80	84	111	105	89
1987	4,986	2.1	2,897	1,846	1,051	302	89	84	91	74	93	100	101	92
1988	4,951	2.1	2,954	1,967	1,037	297	87	86	90	70	93	90	98	90
1989	4,801	2.0	2,863	1,935	928	318	87	82	91	66	91	93	99	96
1990	4,591	1.9	2,891	2,000	892	322	89	87	90	64	90	90	105	97
1991	4,632	1.9	2,875	1,964	911	318	89	88	89	63	89	94	104	100
1992			2,810	1,944	866	320								

[1] Farm population as defined by Department of Agriculture and Department of Commerce, i.e., civilian population living on farms in rural areas, regardless of occupation. See also footnote 7. Series discontinued in 1992.
[2] Total population of United States including Armed Forces overseas, as of July 1.
[3] Includes persons doing farmwork on all farms. These data, published by the Department of Agriculture, differ from those on agricultural employment by the Department of Labor (see Table B-33) because of differences in the method of approach, in concepts of employment, and in time of month for which the data are collected.
[4] Acreage harvested plus acreages in fruits, tree nuts, and farm gardens.
[5] Fertilizer, lime, and pesticides.
[6] Nonfarm constant dollar value of feed, seed, and livestock purchases.
[7] Based on new definition of a farm. Under old definition of a farm, farm population (in thousands and as percent of total population) for 1977, 1978, 1979, 1980, 1981, 1982, and 1983 is 7,806 and 3.6; 8,005 and 3.6; 7,553 and 3.4; 7,241 and 3.2; 7,014 and 3.1; 6,880 and 3.0; 7,029 and 3.0, respectively.
[8] Basis for farm employment series was discontinued for 1981 through 1984. Employment is estimated for these years.
Note.—Population includes Alaska and Hawaii beginning 1960.

Sources: Department of Agriculture and Department of Commerce (Bureau of the Census).

TABLE B-99.—*Indexes of prices received and prices paid by farmers, 1950–93*

[1977 = 100]

Year or month	Prices received by farmers			Prices paid by farmers						Addendum: Average farm real estate value per acre [3]
	All farm products	Crops	Livestock and products	All commodities, services, interest, taxes, and wage rates [1]	Production items				
					Total [2]	Tractors and self-propelled machinery	Fertilizer	Fuels and energy	Wage rates	
1950	56	54	58	37	42		54		22	14
1951	66	61	70	41	47		57		25	16
1952	63	62	64	42	47		59		26	18
1953	56	55	56	40	44		59		27	18
1954	54	56	52	40	44		59		27	18
1955	51	53	49	40	43		58		27	19
1956	50	54	47	40	43		57		28	19
1957	51	52	51	42	44		58		29	21
1958	55	52	57	43	46		58		30	22
1959	53	51	53	43	46		57		32	23
1960	52	51	53	44	46		57		33	24
1961	53	52	52	44	46		58		33	25
1962	53	54	53	45	47		58		34	26
1963	53	55	51	45	47		57		35	27
1964	52	55	49	45	47		57		36	29
1965	54	53	54	47	48	39	57	49	38	31
1966	58	55	60	49	50	40	56	49	41	33
1967	55	52	57	49	50	42	55	50	44	35
1968	56	52	60	51	50	44	52	50	48	38
1969	59	50	67	53	52	47	48	51	53	40
1970	60	52	67	55	54	49	48	52	57	42
1971	62	56	67	58	57	51	51	53	60	43
1972	69	60	77	62	61	54	52	53	63	47
1973	98	91	104	71	73	58	56	57	69	53
1974	105	117	94	81	83	68	92	79	79	66
1975	101	105	98	89	91	82	120	88	85	75
1976	102	102	101	95	97	91	102	93	93	86
1977	100	100	100	100	100	100	100	100	100	100
1978	115	105	124	108	108	109	100	105	107	109
1979	132	116	147	123	125	122	108	137	118	125
1980	134	125	144	138	138	136	134	188	127	145
1981	139	134	143	150	148	152	144	213	138	158
1982	133	121	145	159	153	165	144	210	144	157
1983	135	128	141	161	152	174	137	202	148	148
1984	142	138	146	164	155	181	143	201	152	146
1985	128	120	136	162	151	178	135	201	154	128
1986	123	107	138	159	144	174	124	162	160	112
1987	127	106	146	162	148	174	118	164	166	103
1988	138	126	150	169	157	181	130	167	171	106
1989	147	134	160	177	165	193	136	180	186	111
1990	149	127	170	183	171	202	131	204	192	112
1991	146	129	161	187	173	211	134	203	201	115
1992	139	121	157	189	174	219	131	199	210	115
1993 [p]	143	123	162	195	179	227	128	201	217	117
1992: Jan	138	124	152	188	171	216	132	192	216	115
Feb	143	129	156							
Mar	144	132	155							
Apr	141	126	156	189	174	217	132	194	212	
May	141	123	158							
June	140	121	157							
July	138	117	158	190	175	217	132	206	212	
Aug	138	116	160							
Sept	138	116	158							
Oct	138	116	158	190	175	224	128	205	201	
Nov	136	115	156							
Dec	137	117	156							
1993: Jan	138	117	159	192	176	224	128	199	217	117
Feb	140	118	162							
Mar	141	116	166							
Apr	146	125	167	196	180	223	129	201	223	
May	144	120	168							
June	140	113	166							
July	141	121	161	195	179	223	129	199	221	
Aug	144	125	162							
Sept	145	128	160							
Oct	145	130	159	196	181	237	127	204	206	
Nov	144	128	158							
Dec	145	133	156							

[1] Includes items used for family living, not shown separately.
[2] Includes other production items not shown separately.
[3] Average for 48 States. Annual data are for March 1 of each year through 1975, February 1 for 1976–81, April 1 for 1982–85, February 1 for 1986–89, and January 1 for 1990–93.

Source: Department of Agriculture.

TABLE B-100.—*U.S. exports and imports of agricultural commodities, 1940-93*

[Billions of dollars]

Year	Exports Total [1]	Feed grains	Food grains [2]	Oilseeds and products	Cotton	Tobacco	Animals and products	Imports Total [1]	Crops, fruits, and vegetables [3]	Animals and products	Coffee	Cocoa beans and products	Agricultural trade balance
1940	0.5	([4])	([4])	([4])	0.2	([4])	0.1	1.3	([4])	0.2	0.1	([4])	−0.8
1941	.7	([4])	0.1	([4])	.1	0.1	.3	1.7	0.1	.3	.2	([4])	−1.0
1942	1.2	([4])	([4])	([4])	.1	.1	.8	1.3	([4])	.5	.2	([4])	−.1
1943	2.1	([4])	.1	0.1	.2	.2	1.2	1.5	.1	.4	.3	([4])	.6
1944	2.1	([4])	.1	.1	.1	.1	1.3	1.8	.1	.3	.3	([4])	.3
1945	2.3	([4])	.4	([4])	.3	.2	.9	1.7	.1	.4	.3	([4])	.5
1946	3.1	0.1	.7	([4])	.5	.4	.9	2.3	.2	.4	.5	0.1	.8
1947	4.0	.4	1.4	.1	.3	.7	.7	2.8	.1	.4	.6	.2	1.2
1948	3.5	.1	1.5	.2	.5	.2	.5	3.1	.2	.6	.7	.2	.3
1949	3.6	.3	1.1	.3	.9	.3	.4	2.9	.2	.4	.8	.1	.7
1950	2.9	.2	.6	.2	1.0	.3	.3	4.0	.2	.2	1.1	.2	−1.1
1951	4.0	.3	1.1	.3	1.1	.3	.5	5.2	.2	1.1	1.4	.2	−1.1
1952	3.4	.3	1.1	.2	.9	.2	.3	4.5	.2	.7	1.4	.2	−1.1
1953	2.8	.3	.7	.2	.5	.3	.4	4.2	.2	.6	1.5	.2	−1.3
1954	3.1	.2	.5	.3	.8	.3	.5	4.0	.2	.5	1.5	.3	−.9
1955	3.2	.3	.6	.4	.5	.4	.6	4.0	.2	.5	1.4	.2	−.8
1956	4.2	.4	1.0	.5	.7	.3	.7	4.0	.2	.4	1.4	.2	.2
1957	4.5	.3	1.0	.5	1.0	.4	.7	4.0	.2	.5	1.4	.2	.6
1958	3.9	.5	.8	.4	.7	.4	.5	3.9	.2	.7	1.2	.2	([4])
1959	4.0	.6	.9	.6	.4	.3	.6	4.1	.2	.8	1.1	.2	−.1
1960	4.8	.5	1.2	.6	1.0	.4	.6	3.8	.2	.6	1.0	.2	1.0
1961	5.0	.5	1.4	.6	.9	.4	.6	3.7	.2	.7	1.0	.2	1.3
1962	5.0	.8	1.3	.7	.5	.4	.6	3.9	.2	.9	1.0	.2	1.2
1963	5.6	.8	1.5	.8	.6	.4	.7	4.0	.3	.9	1.0	.2	1.6
1964	6.3	.9	1.7	1.0	.7	.4	.8	4.1	.3	.8	1.2	.2	2.3
1965	6.2	1.1	1.4	1.2	.5	.4	.8	4.1	.3	.9	1.1	.1	2.1
1966	6.9	1.3	1.8	1.2	.4	.5	.7	4.5	.4	1.2	1.1	.1	2.4
1967	6.4	1.1	1.5	1.3	.5	.5	.7	4.5	.4	1.1	1.0	.2	1.9
1968	6.3	.9	1.4	1.3	.5	.5	.7	5.0	.5	1.3	1.2	.2	1.3
1969	6.0	.9	1.2	1.3	.3	.6	.8	5.0	.5	1.4	.9	.2	1.1
1970	7.3	1.1	1.4	1.9	.4	.5	.9	5.8	.5	1.6	1.2	.3	1.5
1971	7.7	1.0	1.3	2.2	.6	.5	1.0	5.8	.6	1.5	1.2	.2	1.9
1972	9.4	1.5	1.8	2.4	.5	.7	1.1	6.5	.7	1.8	1.3	.2	2.9
1973	17.7	3.5	4.7	4.3	.9	.7	1.6	8.4	.8	2.6	1.7	.3	9.3
1974	21.9	4.6	5.4	5.7	1.3	.8	1.8	10.2	.8	2.2	1.6	.5	11.7
1975	21.9	5.2	6.2	4.5	1.0	.9	1.7	9.3	.8	1.8	1.7	.5	12.6
1976	23.0	6.0	4.7	5.1	1.0	.9	2.4	11.0	.9	2.3	2.9	.6	12.0
1977	23.6	4.9	3.6	6.6	1.5	1.1	2.7	13.4	1.2	2.3	4.2	1.0	10.2
1978	29.4	5.9	5.5	8.2	1.7	1.4	3.0	14.8	1.5	3.1	4.0	1.4	14.6
1979	34.7	7.7	6.3	8.9	2.2	1.2	3.8	16.7	1.7	3.9	4.2	1.2	18.0
1980	41.2	9.8	7.9	9.4	2.9	1.3	3.8	17.4	1.7	3.8	4.2	.9	23.8
1981	43.3	9.4	9.6	9.6	2.3	1.5	4.2	16.9	2.0	3.5	2.9	.9	26.4
1982	36.6	6.4	7.9	9.1	2.0	1.5	3.9	15.3	2.3	3.7	2.9	.7	21.3
1983	36.1	7.3	7.4	8.7	1.8	1.5	3.8	16.5	2.3	3.8	2.8	.8	19.6
1984	37.8	8.1	7.5	8.4	2.4	1.5	4.2	19.3	3.1	4.1	3.3	1.1	18.5
1985	29.0	6.0	4.5	5.8	1.6	1.5	4.1	20.0	3.5	4.2	3.3	1.4	9.1
1986	26.2	3.1	3.8	6.5	.8	1.2	4.5	21.5	3.6	4.5	4.6	1.1	4.7
1987	28.7	3.8	3.8	6.4	1.6	1.1	5.2	20.4	3.6	4.9	2.9	1.2	8.3
1988	37.1	5.9	5.9	7.7	2.0	1.3	6.4	21.0	3.8	5.2	2.5	1.0	16.1
1989	39.9	7.7	7.1	6.3	2.3	1.3	6.4	21.7	4.2	5.1	2.4	1.0	18.2
1990	39.4	7.0	4.8	5.7	2.8	1.4	6.7	22.8	4.9	5.6	1.9	1.1	16.6
1991	39.2	5.7	4.2	6.4	2.5	1.4	7.0	22.7	4.8	5.5	1.9	1.1	16.5
1992	42.9	5.7	5.4	7.2	2.0	1.7	7.9	24.6	4.9	5.7	1.7	1.1	18.3
Jan-Nov:													
1992	39.1	5.2	4.9	6.5	1.8	1.5	7.3	22.6	4.4	5.2	1.5	1.0	16.5
1993	38.5	4.5	5.1	6.5	1.4	1.2	7.2	22.6	4.5	5.4	1.4	.9	15.9

[1] Total includes items not shown separately.
[2] Rice, wheat, and wheat flour.
[3] Includes nuts, fruits, and vegetable preparations.
[4] Less than $50 million.

Note.—Data derived from official estimates released by the Bureau of the Census, Department of Commerce. Agricultural commodities are defined as (1) nonmarine food products and (2) other products of agriculture which have not passed through complex processes of manufacture. Export value, at U.S. port of exportation, is based on the selling price and includes inland freight, insurance, and other charges to the port. Import value, defined generally as the market value in the foreign country, excludes import duties, ocean freight, and marine insurance.

Source: Department of Agriculture.

TABLE B-101.—*Farm business balance sheet, 1950–92*

[Billions of dollars]

| End of year | Total assets | Physical assets ||||| Financial assets || Total claims | Real estate debt [5] | Nonreal estate debt [6] | Proprietors' equity |
		Real estate	Livestock and poultry [1]	Machinery and motor vehicles	Crops [2]	Purchased inputs [3]	Investments in cooperatives	Other [4]				
1950	121.6	75.4	17.1	12.3	7.1		2.7	7.0	121.6	5.2	5.7	110.7
1951	136.1	83.8	19.5	14.3	8.2		2.9	7.3	136.1	5.7	6.9	123.7
1952	133.0	85.1	14.8	15.0	7.9		3.2	7.1	133.0	6.2	7.1	119.7
1953	128.7	84.3	11.7	15.6	6.8		3.3	7.0	128.7	6.6	6.3	115.7
1954	132.6	87.8	11.2	15.7	7.5		3.5	6.9	132.6	7.1	6.7	118.9
1955	137.0	93.0	10.6	16.3	6.5		3.7	6.9	137.0	7.8	7.3	121.9
1956	145.7	100.3	11.0	16.9	6.8		4.0	6.7	145.7	8.5	7.4	129.8
1957	154.5	106.4	13.9	17.0	6.4		4.2	6.6	154.5	9.0	8.2	137.3
1958	168.7	114.6	17.7	18.1	6.9		4.5	6.9	168.7	9.7	9.4	149.7
1959	173.0	121.2	15.2	19.3	6.2		4.8	6.2	173.0	10.6	10.7	151.7
1960	174.2	123.3	15.6	19.1	6.2		4.2	5.8	174.2	11.3	11.1	151.7
1961	181.4	129.1	16.4	19.3	6.3		4.5	5.9	181.4	12.3	11.8	157.3
1962	188.7	134.6	17.3	19.9	6.3		4.6	5.9	188.7	13.5	13.2	162.0
1963	196.5	142.4	15.9	20.4	7.2		5.0	5.7	196.5	15.0	14.6	166.9
1964	204.0	150.5	14.4	21.2	6.8		5.2	5.8	204.0	16.9	15.3	171.8
1965	220.6	161.5	17.6	22.4	7.7		5.4	6.0	220.6	18.9	16.9	184.8
1966	233.8	171.2	19.0	24.1	7.9		5.7	6.0	233.8	20.7	18.5	194.6
1967	245.8	180.9	18.8	26.3	7.7		5.8	6.1	245.8	22.6	19.6	203.6
1968	257.0	189.4	20.2	27.7	7.2		6.1	6.3	257.0	24.7	19.2	213.0
1969	267.3	195.3	22.5	28.6	8.1		6.4	6.4	267.3	26.4	20.0	220.8
1970	278.7	202.4	23.7	30.4	8.5		7.2	6.5	278.7	27.5	21.2	229.9
1971	301.5	217.6	27.3	32.4	9.7		7.9	6.7	301.5	29.3	24.0	248.3
1972	339.7	243.0	33.7	34.6	12.7		8.7	6.9	339.7	32.0	26.7	281.0
1973	418.3	298.3	42.4	39.7	21.2		9.7	7.1	418.3	36.1	31.6	350.7
1974 [7]	449.2	335.6	24.6	48.5	22.5		11.2	6.9	449.2	40.8	35.1	373.3
1975	510.7	383.6	29.4	57.4	20.5		13.0	6.9	510.7	45.3	39.7	425.7
1976	590.7	456.5	29.0	63.3	20.6		14.3	6.9	590.7	50.5	45.6	494.7
1977	651.5	509.3	31.9	69.3	20.5		13.5	7.0	651.5	58.4	52.4	540.7
1978	767.3	601.8	50.1	68.5	23.8		16.1	7.1	767.3	66.7	60.7	639.9
1979	898.1	706.1	61.4	75.4	29.9		18.1	7.3	898.1	79.7	71.8	746.6
1980	983.2	782.8	60.6	80.3	32.7		19.3	7.4	983.2	89.7	77.1	816.4
1981	982.3	785.6	53.5	85.5	29.5		20.6	7.6	982.3	98.8	83.6	799.9
1982	944.5	750.0	53.0	86.0	25.8		21.9	7.8	944.5	101.8	87.0	755.7
1983	943.3	753.4	49.5	85.8	23.6		22.8	8.1	943.3	103.2	87.9	752.2
1984	857.0	661.8	49.5	85.0	26.1	2.0	24.3	8.3	857.0	106.7	87.1	663.3
1985	772.7	586.2	46.3	82.9	22.9	1.2	24.3	9.0	772.7	100.1	77.5	595.1
1986	724.4	542.3	47.8	81.5	16.3	2.1	24.4	10.0	724.4	90.4	66.6	567.5
1987	772.6	578.9	58.0	80.0	17.5	3.2	25.3	9.9	772.6	82.4	62.0	628.2
1988	801.1	595.5	62.2	81.2	23.3	3.5	25.1	10.3	801.1	77.6	61.7	661.7
1989	829.7	615.7	66.2	85.1	23.4	2.6	26.3	10.5	829.7	75.4	61.9	692.4
1990	848.3	628.2	70.9	85.4	22.8	2.8	27.5	10.9	848.3	74.1	63.2	710.9
1991	842.2	623.2	68.1	85.8	22.0	2.6	28.7	11.8	842.2	74.5	64.3	703.5
1992	861.5	633.1	71.3	85.6	24.1	3.9	29.7	13.6	861.5	75.0	63.6	722.9

[1] Excludes commercial broilers; excludes horses and mules beginning 1959; excludes turkeys beginning 1986.
[2] Non-Commodity Credit Corporation (CCC) crops held on farms plus value above loan rate for crops held under CCC.
[3] Includes fertilizer, chemicals, fuels, parts, feed, seed, and other supplies.
[4] Sum of currency, demand deposits, time deposits, and U.S. savings bonds.
[5] Includes CCC storage and drying facilities loans.
[6] Does not include CCC crop loans.
[7] Beginning 1974, data are for farms included in the new farm definition, that is, places with sales of $1,000 or more annually.

Note.—Data exclude operator households.
Beginning 1959, data include Alaska and Hawaii.

Source: Department of Agriculture.

INTERNATIONAL STATISTICS

TABLE B-102.—*International investment position of the United States at year-end, 1984-92*

[Billions of dollars]

Type of investment	1984	1985	1986	1987	1988	1989	1990	1991	1992
NET INTERNATIONAL INVESTMENT POSITION OF THE UNITED STATES:									
With direct investment at current cost	234.2	139.1	19.2	−34.0	−140.3	−288.5	−291.9	−364.9	−521.3
With direct investment at market value	177.3	142.3	109.7	46.8	5.4	−128.9	−269.7	−396.4	−611.5
U.S. ASSETS ABROAD:									
With direct investment at current cost	1,178.9	1,252.6	1,410.7	1,557.3	1,698.0	1,857.0	1,924.8	1,998.4	2,003.4
With direct investment at market value	1,083.1	1,244.6	1,508.2	1,641.0	1,860.9	2,114.7	2,018.4	2,152.6	2,113.3
U.S. official reserve assets	105.0	117.9	139.9	162.4	144.2	168.7	174.7	159.2	150.3
Gold [1]	81.2	85.8	102.4	127.6	107.4	105.2	102.4	92.6	90.0
Special drawing rights	5.6	7.3	8.4	10.3	9.6	10.0	11.0	11.2	8.5
Reserve position in the International Monetary Fund	11.5	11.9	11.7	11.3	9.7	9.0	9.1	9.5	11.8
Foreign currencies	6.7	12.9	17.3	13.1	17.4	44.6	52.2	45.9	40.0
U.S. Government assets other than official reserves	85.0	87.8	89.6	88.9	86.1	84.5	82.2	79.1	80.8
U.S. credits and other long-term assets	82.9	85.8	88.7	88.1	85.4	83.9	81.5	77.5	79.1
Repayable in dollars	81.1	84.1	87.1	86.5	83.9	82.4	80.1	76.3	77.7
Other	1.8	1.7	1.6	1.6	1.5	1.5	1.3	1.2	1.4
U.S. foreign currency holdings and U.S. short-term assets	2.1	1.9	.9	.8	.7	.6	.7	1.6	1.7
U.S. private assets:									
With direct investment at current cost	988.9	1,047.0	1,181.2	1,306.1	1,467.7	1,603.8	1,668.0	1,760.0	1,772.3
With direct investment at market value	893.1	1,038.9	1,278.7	1,389.7	1,630.6	1,861.5	1,761.6	1,914.2	1,882.3
Direct investment abroad:									
At current cost	361.6	387.2	421.2	493.3	515.7	560.0	622.7	655.3	666.3
At market value	265.8	379.1	518.7	577.0	678.6	817.8	716.3	809.6	776.3
Foreign securities	88.8	112.8	142.0	153.7	176.6	216.0	229.3	294.2	327.4
Bonds	62.8	71.8	79.0	84.1	90.6	96.2	119.2	135.4	149.5
Corporate stocks	26.0	41.0	63.0	69.6	86.0	119.9	110.0	158.8	178.0
U.S. claims on unaffiliated foreigners reported by U.S. nonbanking concerns	92.9	99.6	110.7	109.6	122.2	113.9	120.3	118.6	111.7
U.S. claims reported by U.S. banks, not included elsewhere	445.6	447.4	507.3	549.5	653.2	713.8	695.7	691.9	666.9
FOREIGN ASSETS IN THE UNITED STATES:									
With direct investment at current cost	944.7	1,113.6	1,391.5	1,591.4	1,838.3	2,145.5	2,216.7	2,363.2	2,524.7
With direct investment at market value	905.9	1,102.3	1,398.6	1,594.1	1,855.5	2,243.6	2,288.0	2,549.0	2,724.8
Foreign official assets in the United States	199.7	202.5	241.2	283.1	322.0	341.9	375.6	402.1	443.4
U.S. Government securities	144.7	145.1	178.9	220.5	260.9	263.7	295.0	315.9	335.7
U.S. Treasury securities	138.2	138.4	173.3	213.7	253.0	257.3	287.9	307.1	323.0
Other	6.5	6.6	5.6	6.8	8.0	6.4	7.1	8.8	12.7
Other U.S. Government liabilities	15.0	15.8	18.0	15.7	15.2	15.4	17.5	19.1	21.6
U.S. liabilities reported by U.S. banks, not included elsewhere	26.1	26.7	27.9	31.8	31.5	36.5	39.9	38.4	54.8
Other foreign official assets	14.0	14.9	16.4	15.0	14.4	26.3	23.2	28.7	31.3
Other foreign assets in the United States:									
With direct investment at current cost	745.0	911.1	1,150.2	1,308.3	1,516.3	1,803.6	1,841.1	1,961.1	2,081.4
With direct investment at market value	706.2	899.8	1,157.4	1,311.1	1,533.4	1,901.8	1,912.4	2,146.9	2,281.5
Direct investment in the United States:									
At current cost	211.2	231.3	265.8	313.5	374.3	436.6	468.2	487.2	492.3
At market value	172.4	220.0	273.0	316.2	391.5	534.7	539.6	673.0	692.3
U.S. Treasury securities	62.1	88.0	96.1	82.6	100.9	166.5	162.4	189.5	224.9
U.S. securities other than U.S. Treasury securities	128.5	207.9	309.8	341.7	392.3	482.9	469.0	556.3	617.3
Corporate and other bonds	32.4	82.3	140.9	166.1	191.3	231.7	247.2	284.4	317.2
Corporate stocks	96.1	125.6	168.9	175.6	201.0	251.2	221.7	271.9	300.2
U.S. liabilities to unaffiliated foreigners reported by U.S. nonbanking concerns	31.0	29.5	26.9	29.8	35.0	40.5	48.0	46.1	46.3
U.S. liabilities reported by U.S. banks, not included elsewhere	312.2	354.5	451.6	540.7	613.7	677.1	693.4	682.1	700.7

[1] Valued at market price.

Note.—For details regarding these data, see *Survey of Current Business*, June 1991, June 1992, and June 1993.

Source: Department of Commerce, Bureau of Economic Analysis.

TABLE B-103.—U.S. international transactions, 1946–93

[Millions of dollars; quarterly data seasonally adjusted, except as noted. Credits (+), debits (−)]

Year or quarter	Merchandise [1] [2] Exports	Imports	Net	Net military transactions [3] [4]	Net travel and transportation receipts	Other services, net	Receipts on U.S. assets abroad	Payments on foreign assets in U.S.	Net	Balance on goods, services, and income	Unilateral transfers, net [4]	Balance on current account
1946	11,764	−5,067	6,697	−424	733	310	772	−212	560	7,876	−2,991	4,885
1947	16,097	−5,973	10,124	−358	946	145	1,102	−245	857	11,714	−2,722	8,992
1948	13,265	−7,557	5,708	−351	374	175	1,921	−437	1,484	7,390	−4,973	2,417
1949	12,213	−6,874	5,339	−410	230	208	1,831	−476	1,355	6,722	−5,849	873
1950	10,203	−9,081	1,122	−56	−120	242	2,068	−559	1,509	2,697	−4,537	−1,840
1951	14,243	−11,176	3,067	169	298	254	2,633	−583	2,050	5,838	−4,954	884
1952	13,449	−10,838	2,611	528	83	309	2,751	−555	2,196	5,727	−5,113	614
1953	12,412	−10,975	1,437	1,753	−238	307	2,736	−624	2,112	5,371	−6,657	−1,286
1954	12,929	−10,353	2,576	902	−269	305	2,929	−582	2,347	5,861	−5,642	219
1955	14,424	−11,527	2,897	−113	−297	299	3,406	−676	2,730	5,516	−5,086	430
1956	17,556	−12,803	4,753	−221	−361	447	3,837	−735	3,102	7,720	−4,990	2,730
1957	19,562	−13,291	6,271	−423	−189	482	4,180	−796	3,384	9,525	−4,763	4,762
1958	16,414	−12,952	3,462	−849	−633	486	3,790	−825	2,965	5,431	−4,647	784
1959	16,458	−15,310	1,148	−831	−821	573	4,132	−1,061	3,071	3,140	−4,422	−1,282
1960	19,650	−14,758	4,892	−1,057	−964	639	4,616	−1,238	3,379	6,886	−4,062	2,824
1961	20,108	−14,537	5,571	−1,131	−978	732	4,999	−1,245	3,755	7,949	−4,127	3,822
1962	20,781	−16,260	4,521	−912	−1,152	912	5,618	−1,324	4,294	7,664	−4,277	3,387
1963	22,272	−17,048	5,224	−742	−1,309	1,036	6,157	−1,560	4,596	8,806	−4,392	4,414
1964	25,501	−18,700	6,801	−794	−1,146	1,161	6,824	−1,783	5,041	11,063	−4,240	6,823
1965	26,461	−21,510	4,951	−487	−1,280	1,480	7,437	−2,088	5,350	10,014	−4,583	5,431
1966	29,310	−25,493	3,817	−1,043	−1,331	1,497	7,528	−2,481	5,047	7,987	−4,955	3,031
1967	30,666	−26,866	3,800	−1,187	−1,750	1,742	8,021	−2,747	5,274	7,878	−5,294	2,583
1968	33,626	−32,991	635	−596	−1,548	1,759	9,367	−3,378	5,990	6,240	−5,629	611
1969	36,414	−35,807	607	−718	−1,763	1,964	10,913	−4,869	6,044	6,135	−5,735	399
1970	42,469	−39,866	2,603	−641	−2,038	2,330	11,748	−5,515	6,233	8,486	−6,156	2,331
1971	43,319	−45,579	−2,260	653	−2,345	2,649	12,707	−5,435	7,272	5,969	−7,402	−1,433
1972	49,381	−55,797	−6,416	1,072	−3,063	2,965	14,765	−6,572	8,192	2,749	−8,544	−5,795
1973	71,410	−70,499	911	740	−3,158	3,406	21,808	−9,655	12,153	14,053	−6,913	7,140
1974	98,306	−103,811	−5,505	165	−3,184	4,231	27,587	−12,084	15,503	11,210	[5] −9,249	1,962
1975	107,088	−98,185	8,903	1,461	−2,812	4,854	25,351	−12,564	12,787	25,191	−7,075	18,116
1976	114,745	−124,228	−9,483	931	−2,558	5,027	29,375	−13,311	16,063	9,982	−5,686	4,295
1977	120,816	−151,907	−31,091	1,731	−3,565	5,680	32,354	−14,217	18,137	−9,109	−5,226	−14,335
1978	142,075	−176,002	−33,927	857	−3,573	6,879	42,088	−21,680	20,408	−9,355	−5,788	−15,143
1979	184,439	−212,007	−27,568	−1,313	−2,935	7,251	63,834	−32,961	30,873	6,308	−6,593	−285
1980	224,250	−249,750	−25,500	−1,822	−997	8,912	72,606	−42,532	30,073	10,666	−8,349	2,317
1981	237,044	−265,067	−28,023	−844	144	12,552	86,529	−53,626	32,903	16,732	−11,702	5,030
1982	211,157	−247,642	−36,485	112	−992	13,209	86,200	−56,412	29,788	5,632	−17,075	−11,443
1983	201,799	−268,901	−67,102	−563	−4,227	14,095	84,778	−53,700	31,078	−26,719	−17,741	−44,460
1984	219,926	−332,418	−112,492	−2,547	−8,438	14,277	99,056	−69,572	29,483	−79,716	−20,612	−100,328
1985	215,915	−338,088	−122,173	−4,390	−9,798	14,266	89,489	−68,314	21,175	−100,920	−22,950	−123,870
1986	223,344	−368,425	−145,081	−5,181	−7,382	18,855	87,497	−74,736	12,761	−126,028	−24,176	−150,203
1987	250,208	−409,765	−159,557	−3,844	−6,481	17,900	95,129	−87,403	7,726	−144,256	−23,052	−167,308
1988	320,230	−447,189	−126,959	−6,315	−1,511	19,961	122,275	−109,653	12,621	−102,203	−24,965	−127,168
1989	362,116	−477,365	−115,249	−6,726	5,071	26,558	144,904	−130,091	14,813	−75,532	−26,092	−101,624
1990	389,303	−498,336	−109,033	−7,833	8,979	29,505	151,201	−130,853	20,348	−58,034	−33,827	−91,861
1991	416,937	−490,739	−73,802	−5,851	17,933	33,799	127,292	−114,272	13,020	−14,899	6,575	−8,324
1992	440,138	−536,276	−96,138	−2,751	19,718	39,444	110,612	−104,391	6,222	−33,505	−32,895	−66,400
1991:												
I	101,333	−120,123	−18,790	−2,532	2,926	7,935	36,018	−30,247	5,771	−4,690	14,096	9,406
II	104,206	−120,525	−16,319	−1,402	4,299	8,397	32,057	−29,147	2,910	−2,115	3,884	1,769
III	103,764	−123,404	−19,640	−1,164	5,228	8,660	30,074	−28,447	1,627	−5,289	−6,564	−11,853
IV	107,634	−126,687	−19,053	−755	5,481	8,809	29,144	−26,431	2,713	−2,805	−4,839	−7,644
1992:												
I	108,347	−126,110	−17,763	−571	5,011	9,608	29,028	−24,609	4,419	704	−7,389	−6,685
II	108,306	−133,107	−24,801	−727	5,201	9,177	28,641	−27,734	907	−10,243	−8,010	−18,253
III	109,493	−137,105	−27,612	−617	4,882	11,016	27,195	−25,492	1,703	−10,628	−7,147	−17,775
IV	113,992	−139,954	−25,962	−836	4,624	9,641	25,749	−26,555	−806	−13,339	−10,348	−23,687
1993:												
I	111,530	−140,839	−29,309	−145	5,014	9,755	26,078	−26,115	−37	−14,722	−7,586	−22,308
II	113,118	−147,502	−34,384	−226	5,372	9,313	27,876	−27,829	47	−19,878	−7,294	−27,172
III [p]	111,912	−148,191	−36,279	−341	5,279	9,169	28,695	−26,947	1,748	−20,424	−7,562	−27,986

[1] Excludes military.
[2] Adjusted from Census data for differences in valuation, coverage, and timing.
[3] Quarterly data are not seasonally adjusted.
[4] Includes transfers of goods and services under U.S. military grant programs.

See next page for continuation of table.

TABLE B-103.—*U.S. international transactions, 1946-93*—Continued

[Millions of dollars; quarterly data seasonally adjusted, except as noted]

Year or quarter	U.S. assets abroad, net [increase/capital outflow (−)]				Foreign assets in the U.S., net [increase/capital inflow (+)]			Allocations of special drawing rights (SDRs)	Statistical discrepancy	
	Total	U.S. official reserve assets [3] [6]	Other U.S. Government assets	U.S. private assets	Total	Foreign official assets [3]	Other foreign assets		Total (sum of the items with sign reversed)	Of which: Seasonal adjustment discrepancy
1946		−623								
1947		−3,315								
1948		−1,736								
1949		−266								
1950		1,758								
1951		−33								
1952		−415								
1953		1,256								
1954		480								
1955		182								
1956		−869								
1957		−1,165								
1958		2,292								
1959		1,035								
1960	−4,099	2,145	−1,100	−5,144	2,294	1,473	821		−1,019	
1961	−5,538	607	−910	−5,235	2,705	765	1,939		−989	
1962	−4,174	1,535	−1,085	−4,623	1,911	1,270	641		−1,124	
1963	−7,270	378	−1,662	−5,986	3,217	1,986	1,231		−360	
1964	−9,560	171	−1,680	−8,050	3,643	1,660	1,983		−907	
1965	−5,716	1,225	−1,605	−5,336	742	134	607		−457	
1966	−7,321	570	−1,543	−6,347	3,661	−672	4,333		629	
1967	−9,757	53	−2,423	−7,386	7,379	3,451	3,928		−205	
1968	−10,977	−870	−2,274	−7,833	9,928	−774	10,703		438	
1969	−11,585	−1,179	−2,200	−8,206	12,702	−1,301	14,002		−1,516	
1970	−9,337	2,481	−1,589	−10,229	6,359	6,908	−550	867	−219	
1971	−12,475	2,349	−1,884	−12,940	22,970	26,879	−3,909	717	9,779	
1972	−14,497	−4	−1,568	−12,925	21,461	10,475	10,986	710	−1,879	
1973	−22,874	158	−2,644	−20,388	18,388	6,026	12,362		−2,654	
1974	−34,745	−1,467	[5] −366	−33,643	34,241	10,546	23,696		−1,458	
1975	−39,703	−849	−3,474	−35,380	15,670	7,027	8,643		5,917	
1976	−51,269	−2,558	−4,214	−44,498	36,518	17,693	18,826		10,455	
1977	−34,785	−375	−3,693	−30,717	51,319	36,816	14,503		−2,199	
1978	−61,130	732	−4,660	−57,202	64,036	33,678	30,358		12,236	
1979	−66,054	−1,133	−3,746	−61,176	38,752	−13,665	52,416	1,139	26,449	
1980	−86,967	−8,155	−5,162	−73,651	58,112	15,497	42,615	1,152	25,386	
1981	−114,147	−5,175	−5,097	−103,875	83,032	4,960	78,072	1,093	24,992	
1982	−122,335	−4,965	−6,131	−111,239	92,418	3,593	88,826		41,359	
1983	−58,735	−1,196	−5,006	−52,533	83,380	5,845	77,534		19,815	
1984	−29,654	−3,131	−5,489	−21,035	102,010	3,140	98,870		27,972	
1985	−34,687	−3,858	−2,821	−28,009	130,966	−1,119	132,084		27,592	
1986	−91,260	312	−2,022	−89,551	223,191	35,648	187,543		18,272	
1987	−61,254	9,149	1,006	−71,408	229,972	45,387	184,585		−1,410	
1988	−91,423	−3,912	2,967	−90,477	219,489	39,758	179,731		−899	
1989	−129,331	−25,293	1,259	−105,297	213,571	8,503	205,068		17,384	
1990	−44,132	−2,158	2,307	−44,280	105,173	34,198	70,975		30,820	
1991	−59,974	5,763	2,905	−68,643	83,439	17,564	65,875		−15,140	
1992	−50,961	3,901	−1,609	−53,253	129,579	40,684	88,895		−12,218	
1991:										
I	−5,555	−353	559	−5,761	−20	5,604	−5,624		−3,831	4,710
II	−875	1,014	−419	−1,470	7,120	−4,924	12,044		−8,014	−120
III	−15,672	3,877	3,224	−22,774	23,514	3,855	19,659		4,011	−6,506
IV	−37,870	1,225	−459	−38,637	52,826	13,029	39,798		−7,312	1,911
1992:										
I	−1,029	−1,057	−275	303	19,834	21,124	−1,290		−12,120	4,878
II	−8,695	1,464	−293	−9,866	44,450	21,008	23,442		17,502	653
III	−10,798	1,952	−305	−12,445	26,450	−7,378	33,828		2,123	−6,754
IV	−30,438	1,542	−737	−31,243	38,845	5,931	32,914		15,280	1,222
1993:										
I	−12,358	−983	535	−11,910	25,718	10,929	14,789		8,948	5,814
II	−29,341	822	−275	−29,888	42,380	17,699	24,681		14,133	681
III ᵖ	−43,961	−545	−86	−43,331	66,452	19,646	46,806		5,495	−7,605

[5] Includes extraordinary U.S. Government transactions with India.
[6] Consists of gold, special drawing rights, foreign currencies, and the U.S. reserve position in the International Monetary Fund (IMF).

Source: Department of Commerce, Bureau of Economic Analysis.

TABLE B-104.—*U.S. merchandise exports and imports by principal end-use category, 1965–93*

[Billions of dollars; quarterly data seasonally adjusted]

Year or quarter	Exports Total	Agricultural products	Nonagricultural Total	Industrial supplies and materials	Capital goods except automotive	Automotive	Other	Imports Total	Petroleum and products	Nonpetroleum Total	Industrial supplies and materials	Capital goods except automotive	Automotive	Other
1965	26.5	6.3	20.2	7.6	8.1	1.9	2.6	21.5	2.0	19.5	9.1	1.5	0.9	8.0
1966	29.3	6.9	22.4	8.2	8.9	2.4	2.9	25.5	2.1	23.4	10.2	2.2	1.8	9.2
1967	30.7	6.5	24.2	8.5	9.9	2.8	3.0	26.9	2.1	24.8	10.0	2.5	2.4	9.9
1968	33.6	6.3	27.3	9.6	11.1	3.5	3.2	33.0	2.4	30.6	12.0	2.8	4.0	11.8
1969	36.4	6.1	30.3	10.3	12.4	3.9	3.7	35.8	2.6	33.2	11.8	3.4	4.9	13.0
1970	42.5	7.4	35.1	12.3	14.7	3.9	4.3	39.9	2.9	36.9	12.4	4.0	5.5	15.0
1971	43.3	7.8	35.5	10.9	15.4	4.7	4.5	45.6	3.7	41.9	13.8	4.3	7.4	16.4
1972	49.4	9.5	39.9	11.9	16.9	5.5	5.6	55.8	4.7	51.1	16.3	5.9	8.7	20.2
1973	71.4	18.0	53.4	17.0	22.0	6.9	7.6	70.5	8.4	62.1	19.6	8.3	10.3	23.9
1974	98.3	22.4	75.9	26.3	30.9	8.6	10.0	103.8	26.6	77.2	27.8	9.8	12.0	27.5
1975	107.1	22.2	84.8	26.8	36.6	10.6	10.8	98.2	27.0	71.2	24.0	10.2	11.7	25.3
1976	114.7	23.4	91.4	28.4	39.1	12.1	11.7	124.2	34.6	89.7	29.8	12.3	16.2	31.4
1977	120.8	24.3	96.5	29.8	39.8	13.4	13.5	151.9	45.0	106.9	35.7	14.0	18.6	38.6
1978 [1]	142.1	29.9	112.2	34.2	47.5	15.2	15.3	176.0	42.6	133.4	40.7	19.3	25.0	48.4
1979	184.4	35.5	149.0	52.2	60.2	17.9	18.7	212.0	60.4	151.6	47.5	24.6	26.6	52.8
1980	224.3	42.0	182.2	65.1	76.3	17.4	23.4	249.8	79.5	170.2	53.0	31.6	28.3	57.4
1981	237.0	44.1	193.0	63.6	84.2	19.7	25.5	265.1	78.4	186.7	56.1	37.1	31.0	62.4
1982	211.2	37.3	173.9	57.7	76.5	17.2	22.4	247.6	62.0	185.7	48.6	38.4	34.3	64.3
1983	201.8	37.1	164.7	52.7	71.7	18.5	21.8	268.9	55.1	213.8	53.7	43.7	43.0	73.3
1984	219.9	38.4	181.5	56.8	77.0	22.4	25.3	332.4	58.1	274.4	66.1	60.4	56.5	91.4
1985	215.9	29.6	186.3	54.8	79.3	24.9	27.2	338.1	51.4	286.7	62.6	61.3	64.9	97.9
1986	223.3	27.2	196.2	59.4	82.8	25.1	28.9	368.4	34.3	334.1	69.9	72.0	78.1	114.2
1987	250.2	29.8	220.4	63.7	92.7	27.6	36.4	409.8	42.9	366.8	70.8	85.1	85.2	125.7
1988	320.2	38.8	281.4	82.6	119.1	33.4	46.3	447.2	39.6	407.6	83.1	102.2	87.9	134.4
1989	362.1	42.2	319.9	91.9	139.6	34.9	53.5	477.4	50.9	426.4	84.2	112.5	87.4	142.4
1990	389.3	40.2	349.1	97.1	153.3	36.5	62.3	498.3	62.3	436.0	82.5	116.0	88.5	149.0
1991	416.9	40.1	376.8	101.8	167.0	40.0	67.9	490.7	51.8	439.0	80.9	120.7	85.7	151.7
1992	440.1	44.0	396.1	101.8	176.9	47.1	70.3	536.3	51.6	484.7	88.6	134.2	91.8	170.1
1991: I	101.3	9.9	91.5	26.3	39.1	9.0	17.0	120.1	13.1	107.0	20.1	29.9	20.7	36.4
II	104.2	9.6	94.6	25.4	42.5	9.9	16.7	120.5	13.1	107.5	20.0	30.1	20.2	37.1
III	103.8	9.9	93.8	25.1	41.7	10.6	16.5	123.4	13.2	110.2	19.9	30.2	22.3	37.7
IV	107.6	10.7	96.9	25.0	43.8	10.5	17.7	126.7	12.3	114.3	20.8	30.5	22.4	40.6
1992: I	108.3	10.8	97.5	24.9	44.3	10.8	17.5	126.1	10.5	115.6	21.2	31.4	22.3	40.8
II	108.3	10.7	97.7	25.2	43.7	11.6	17.1	133.1	13.1	120.0	22.0	32.9	22.8	42.3
III	109.5	11.2	98.3	25.6	43.3	12.0	17.5	137.1	14.3	122.8	22.1	34.5	22.9	43.3
IV	114.0	11.4	102.6	26.1	45.5	12.7	18.3	140.0	13.7	126.2	23.4	35.4	23.8	43.7
1993: I	111.5	10.8	100.7	25.6	44.5	12.8	17.8	140.8	12.8	128.1	23.5	35.7	25.1	43.8
II	113.1	10.8	102.3	25.9	45.8	12.8	17.8	147.5	14.3	133.2	24.7	37.7	25.5	45.3
III	111.9	10.6	101.3	26.1	44.7	12.1	18.4	148.2	12.6	135.6	25.9	38.2	25.0	46.5

[1] End-use categories beginning 1978 are not strictly comparable with data for earlier periods. See *Survey of Current Business*, June 1988.

Note.—Data are on an international transactions basis and exclude military.

In June 1990, end-use categories for merchandise exports were redefined to include reexports; beginning with data for 1978, reexports (exports of foreign merchandise) are assigned to detailed end-use categories in the same manner as exports of domestic merchandise.

Source: Department of Commerce, Bureau of Economic Analysis.

TABLE B-105.—*U.S. merchandise exports and imports by area, 1984-93*

[Billions of dollars]

Item	1984	1985	1986	1987	1988	1989	1990	1991	1992	1993 first 3 quarters at annual rate [1]
Exports	219.9	215.9	223.3	250.2	320.2	362.1	389.3	416.9	440.1	448.7
Industrial countries	141.0	140.5	150.3	165.6	207.3	234.2	253.8	261.3	264.9	267.2
Canada	53.0	55.4	56.5	62.0	74.3	81.1	83.5	85.9	91.1	99.4
Japan	23.2	22.1	26.4	27.6	37.2	43.9	47.8	47.2	46.9	47.2
Western Europe [2]	56.9	56.0	60.4	68.6	86.4	98.4	111.4	116.8	114.5	109.2
Australia, New Zealand, and South Africa	7.8	7.0	7.1	7.4	9.4	10.9	11.2	11.4	12.4	11.4
Australia	4.9	5.1	5.1	5.3	6.8	8.1	8.3	8.3	8.7	8.0
Other countries, except Eastern Europe	74.6	71.9	71.0	82.3	109.1	122.2	130.6	150.4	169.5	175.8
OPEC [3]	13.8	11.4	10.4	10.7	13.8	13.3	13.4	18.5	20.7	18.7
Other [4]	60.8	60.5	60.6	71.6	95.3	108.9	117.2	131.9	148.8	157.1
Eastern Europe [2]	4.3	3.2	2.1	2.3	3.8	5.5	4.3	4.8	5.6	5.7
International organizations and unallocated	.0	.2			.1	.2	.6	.4	.1	
Imports	332.4	338.1	368.4	409.8	447.2	477.4	498.3	490.7	536.3	582.0
Industrial countries	205.5	219.0	245.4	259.7	283.2	292.5	299.9	294.2	316.2	342.2
Canada	67.6	70.2	69.7	73.6	84.6	89.9	93.1	93.0	100.9	112.5
Japan	60.2	65.7	80.8	84.6	89.8	93.5	90.4	92.3	97.4	105.2
Western Europe [2]	72.1	77.5	89.0	96.1	102.6	102.4	109.2	101.9	111.3	118.0
Australia, New Zealand, and South Africa	5.6	5.6	5.9	5.4	6.2	6.6	7.3	7.0	6.6	6.5
Australia	2.8	2.7	2.6	3.0	3.5	3.9	4.4	4.1	3.7	3.3
Other countries, except Eastern Europe	124.7	117.3	121.1	148.2	161.8	182.8	196.1	194.8	218.1	236.6
OPEC [3]	26.9	22.8	18.9	24.4	23.0	30.7	38.2	33.4	33.7	35.0
Other [4]	97.8	94.5	102.2	123.8	138.8	152.1	157.9	161.4	184.4	201.7
Eastern Europe [2]	2.2	1.8	2.0	1.9	2.2	2.1	2.3	1.8	2.0	3.2
International organizations and unallocated										
Balance (excess of exports +)	−112.5	−122.2	−145.1	−159.6	−127.0	−115.2	−109.0	−73.8	−96.1	−133.3
Industrial countries	−64.5	−78.4	−95.1	−94.1	−75.9	−58.3	−46.1	−32.8	−51.3	−75.0
Canada	−14.6	−14.8	−13.2	−11.6	−10.3	−8.9	−9.6	−7.1	−9.7	−13.0
Japan	−37.0	−43.5	−54.4	−56.9	−52.6	−49.7	−42.6	−45.0	−50.5	−58.0
Western Europe [2]	−15.2	−21.4	−28.6	−27.5	−16.2	−4.0	2.2	14.9	3.2	−8.9
Australia, New Zealand, and South Africa	2.2	1.4	1.1	2.0	3.2	4.2	3.9	4.4	5.8	4.9
Australia	2.1	2.4	2.5	2.3	3.3	4.2	3.9	4.2	5.0	4.7
Other countries, except Eastern Europe	−50.1	−45.3	−50.1	−65.8	−52.7	−60.6	−65.6	−44.4	−48.6	−60.9
OPEC [3]	−13.1	−11.4	−8.5	−13.7	−9.2	−17.4	−24.8	−15.0	−13.0	−16.3
Other [4]	−37.0	−33.9	−41.6	−52.1	−43.5	−43.2	−40.7	−29.4	−35.6	−44.5
Eastern Europe [2]	2.1	1.4	.1	.3	1.6	3.5	2.1	3.0	3.7	2.6
International organizations and unallocated	.0	.2			.1	.2	.6	.4	.1	

[1] Preliminary; seasonally adjusted.
[2] The former German Democratic Republic (East Germany) included in Western Europe beginning fourth quarter 1990 and in Eastern Europe prior to that time.
[3] Organization of Petroleum Exporting Countries, consisting of Algeria, Ecuador (through 1992), Gabon, Indonesia, Iran, Iraq, Kuwait, Libya, Nigeria, Qatar, Saudi Arabia, United Arab Emirates, and Venezuela.
[4] Latin America, other Western Hemisphere, and other countries in Asia and Africa, less members of OPEC.

Note.—Data are on an international transactions basis and exclude military.

Source: Department of Commerce, Bureau of Economic Analysis.

TABLE B-106.—*U.S. merchandise exports, imports, and trade balance, 1972–93*

[Billions of dollars; monthly data seasonally adjusted]

Year or month	Merchandise exports (f.a.s. value)[1] Total[2]	Foods, feeds, and beverages	Industrial supplies and materials	Capital goods except automotive	Automotive vehicles, parts, and engines	Consumer goods (nonfood) except automotive	Other[2]	General merchandise imports (customs value)[3] Total	Foods, feeds, and beverages	Industrial supplies and materials	Capital goods except automotive	Automotive vehicles, parts, and engines	Consumer goods (nonfood) except automotive	Other	General merchandise imports (c.i.f. value)[4]	Exports (f.a.s.) less imports (customs value)	Exports (f.a.s.) less imports (c.i.f.)
	F.a.s. value[5]							Customs value									
1972	49.9							55.6							58.9	-5.7	-9.0
1973	71.9							69.5							73.2	2.4	-1.3
								F.a.s. value[5]									
1974	99.4							103.3							110.9	-3.9	-11.4
1975	108.9							99.3							105.9	9.6	3.0
1976	116.8							124.6							132.5	-7.8	-15.7
1977	123.2							151.5							160.4	-28.4	-37.2
1978	145.8							176.1							186.0	-30.2	-40.2
1979	186.4							210.3							222.2	-23.9	-35.9
1980	225.6							245.3							257.0	-19.7	-31.4
								Customs value									
1981	238.7							261.0							273.4	-22.3	-34.6
1982	216.4	31.3	61.7	72.7	15.7	14.3	20.7	244.0	17.1	112.0	35.4	33.3	39.7	6.5	254.9	-27.5	-38.4
1983	205.6	30.9	56.7	67.2	16.8	13.4	20.5	258.0	18.2	107.0	40.9	40.8	44.9	6.3	269.9	-52.4	-64.2
1984	224.0	31.5	61.7	72.0	20.6	13.3	24.0	[6]330.7	21.0	123.7	59.8	53.5	60.0	7.8	346.4	-106.7	-122.4
1985	[7]218.8	24.0	58.5	73.9	22.9	12.6	27.3	[6]336.5	21.9	113.9	65.1	66.8	68.3	9.4	352.5	-117.7	-133.6
1986	[7]227.2	22.3	57.3	75.8	21.7	14.2	35.9	365.4	24.4	101.3	71.8	78.2	79.4	10.4	382.3	-138.3	-155.1
1987	254.1	24.3	66.7	86.2	24.6	17.7	34.6	406.2	24.8	111.0	84.5	85.2	88.7	12.1	424.4	-152.1	-170.3
1988	322.4	32.3	85.1	109.2	29.3	23.1	43.4	441.0	24.8	118.3	101.4	87.7	95.9	12.8	459.5	-118.5	-137.1
1989	363.8	37.2	99.3	138.8	34.8	36.4	17.2	473.2	25.1	132.3	113.3	86.1	102.9	13.6	493.2	-109.4	-129.4
1990	393.6	35.1	104.4	152.7	37.4	43.3	20.7	495.3	26.6	143.2	116.4	87.3	105.7	16.1	517.0	-101.7	-123.4
1991	421.7	35.7	109.7	166.7	40.0	45.9	23.7	488.5	26.5	131.6	120.7	85.7	108.0	15.9	508.4	-66.7	-86.6
1992	448.2	40.2	109.3	176.7	47.1	50.4	24.5	532.7	27.9	138.3	134.2	91.8	123.0	17.6	554.0	-84.5	-105.9
1992:																	
Jan	35.6	3.1	9.2	14.0	3.4	3.9	2.0	41.6	2.3	10.6	10.3	7.5	9.5	1.3	43.4	-6.0	-7.8
Feb	37.6	3.6	8.9	15.2	3.8	4.1	2.1	41.0	2.2	10.3	10.3	7.1	9.7	1.5	42.7	-3.4	-5.1
Mar	37.2	3.3	8.8	15.1	3.7	4.1	2.2	42.7	2.3	10.6	10.6	7.6	10.0	1.5	44.5	-5.5	-7.3
Apr	36.4	3.4	8.8	14.4	3.9	3.9	2.0	43.4	2.4	11.2	10.9	7.6	9.9	1.4	45.2	-7.0	-8.8
May	36.0	3.0	9.1	13.9	3.9	4.1	2.1	43.6	2.3	11.5	10.9	7.6	10.1	1.4	45.4	-7.7	-9.4
June	38.0	3.1	9.4	15.4	3.8	4.2	2.2	44.9	2.5	12.0	11.1	7.6	10.1	1.5	46.6	-6.8	-8.6
July	37.4	3.4	9.6	14.4	3.9	4.2	2.0	44.9	2.5	12.0	11.3	7.4	10.3	1.5	46.7	-7.5	-9.3
Aug	36.4	3.3	8.9	14.0	4.1	4.1	2.0	45.1	2.3	11.9	11.4	7.7	10.3	1.3	46.8	-8.7	-10.5
Sept	37.7	3.5	9.0	14.8	4.0	4.4	2.0	46.0	2.2	12.0	11.6	7.8	10.9	1.4	47.8	-8.3	-10.1
Oct	38.9	3.6	9.6	15.3	3.8	4.5	2.1	46.1	2.3	12.5	11.8	7.5	10.5	1.5	47.9	-7.2	-9.1
Nov	37.8	3.4	9.0	14.5	4.4	4.5	2.0	45.6	2.2	11.8	11.6	8.0	10.3	1.7	47.4	-7.8	-9.6
Dec	39.2	3.4	9.2	15.8	4.6	4.3	1.9	46.1	2.3	11.5	11.9	8.2	10.7	1.5	47.9	-7.0	-8.8
1993:																	
Jan	37.5	3.3	9.4	14.5	4.1	4.3	2.0	45.2	2.3	11.6	11.7	7.9	10.3	1.4	47.0	-7.7	-9.5
Feb	36.9	3.4	8.7	14.3	4.4	4.2	1.9	44.8	2.2	11.1	11.7	8.3	10.3	1.3	46.6	-7.9	-9.6
Mar	38.9	3.5	9.2	15.6	4.3	4.4	2.0	49.3	2.4	12.6	12.4	8.8	11.5	1.6	51.3	-10.5	-12.4
Apr	38.5	3.4	9.1	15.2	4.4	4.2	2.1	48.7	2.2	12.6	12.4	8.8	11.1	1.5	50.6	-10.2	-12.1
May	38.9	3.3	9.7	15.3	4.3	4.5	1.9	47.3	2.3	12.3	12.3	8.2	10.7	1.6	49.1	-8.4	-10.2
June	37.6	3.2	8.8	15.3	4.1	4.3	2.0	49.7	2.3	12.8	13.1	8.6	11.3	1.6	51.6	-12.1	-14.0
July	37.1	3.2	9.3	14.3	3.8	4.4	2.0	47.5	2.3	12.1	12.8	7.8	11.0	1.5	49.4	-10.4	-12.3
Aug	38.1	3.1	9.0	15.3	4.2	4.5	2.1	48.1	2.3	11.7	12.5	8.5	11.7	1.4	50.0	-10.0	-11.9
Sept	38.9	3.4	9.6	15.0	4.1	4.6	2.2	49.5	2.4	12.2	13.0	8.7	11.6	1.5	51.5	-10.6	-12.6
Oct	40.1	3.5	9.9	15.6	4.5	4.6	2.0	51.0	2.6	12.5	13.7	9.0	11.7	1.5	53.0	-10.9	-12.9
Nov	40.1	3.4	9.6	15.5	4.7	4.8	2.0	50.2	2.3	12.2	13.7	8.8	11.5	1.7	52.2	-10.2	-12.2

[1] Department of Defense shipments of grant-aid military supplies and equipment under the Military Assistance Program are excluded from total exports through 1985 and included beginning 1986.
[2] Includes undocumented exports to Canada through 1988. Beginning 1989, undocumented exports to Canada are included in the appropriate end-use category.
[3] Total arrivals of imported goods other than intransit shipments.
[4] C.i.f. (cost, insurance, and freight) import value at first port of entry into United States. Data for 1967–73 are estimates.
[5] F.a.s. (free alongside ship) value basis at U.S. port of exportation for exports and at foreign port of exportation for imports.
[6] Total includes revisions not reflected in detail.
[7] Total exports are on a revised statistical month basis; end-use categories are on a statistical month basis.

Note.—Data are as reported by the Bureau of the Census adjusted to include silver ore and bullion reported separately prior to 1969. Trade in gold is included beginning 1974. Export statistics cover all merchandise shipped from the U.S. customs area, except supplies for the U.S. Armed Forces. Exports include shipments under Agency for International Development and Food for Peace programs as well as other private relief shipments.
Data beginning 1974 include trade of the U.S. Virgin Islands.

Source: Department of Commerce, Bureau of the Census.

TABLE B-107.—*International reserves, selected years, 1952-93*

[Millions of SDRs; end of period]

Area and country	1952	1962	1972	1982	1990	1991	1992	1993 Oct	1993 Nov
All countries	49,388	62,851	146,658	361,253	670,678	704,672	725,652	760,728	765,608
Industrial countries [1]	39,280	53,502	113,362	214,014	441,946	428,438	424,229	439,197	442,458
United States	24,714	17,220	12,112	29,918	59,958	55,769	52,995	54,747	54,679
Canada	1,944	2,561	5,572	3,428	13,060	11,816	8,662	9,256	8,729
Australia	920	1,168	5,656	6,053	11,710	11,837	8,429	8,318	8,341
Japan	1,101	2,021	16,916	22,001	56,027	51,224	52,937	71,346	
New Zealand	183	251	767	577	2,902	2,062	2,239	2,525	
Austria	116	1,081	2,505	5,544	7,305	7,924	9,703	10,066	10,381
Belgium	1,133	1,753	3,564	4,757	9,599	9,573	10,914	8,843	9,005
Denmark	150	256	787	2,111	7,502	5,234	8,090	6,448	6,456
Finland	132	237	664	1,420	6,849	5,389	3,862	3,472	3,650
France	686	4,049	9,224	17,850	28,716	24,735	22,522		
Germany	960	6,958	21,908	43,909	51,060	47,375	69,489	59,011	60,110
Greece	94	287	950	916	2,517	3,747	3,369	4,476	
Iceland	8	32	78	133	308	316	364	321	288
Ireland	318	359	1,038	2,390	3,684	4,026	2,514	4,685	4,693
Italy	722	4,068	5,605	15,108	46,565	36,365	22,438	23,001	23,735
Netherlands	953	1,943	4,407	10,723	13,827	13,980	17,492	24,089	24,072
Norway	164	304	1,220	6,272	10,819	9,292	8,725	14,284	14,448
Portugal	603	680	2,129	1,179	10,736	14,977	14,474		
Spain	134	1,045	4,618	7,450	36,555	46,562	33,640	30,142	30,225
Sweden	504	802	1,453	3,397	12,856	13,028	16,667	14,399	
Switzerland	1,667	2,919	6,961	16,930	23,456	23,191	27,100	25,186	25,463
United Kingdom	1,956	3,308	5,201	11,904	25,864	29,948	27,300		
Developing countries: Total [2]	9,648	9,349	33,295	147,239	228,732	276,234	301,423	321,531	323,149
By area:									
Africa	1,786	2,110	3,962	7,734	12,053	14,587	13,095	13,452	13,230
Asia [2]	3,793	2,772	8,129	44,490	128,826	157,535	164,417	175,191	176,557
Europe	269	381	2,680	5,359	15,535	15,823	15,171	16,321	16,371
Middle East	1,183	1,805	9,436	64,094	37,956	41,777	43,877	45,155	45,296
Western Hemisphere	2,616	2,282	9,089	25,563	34,361	46,512	64,861	71,412	71,696
Memo:									
Oil-exporting countries	1,699	2,030	9,956	67,163	43,875	48,883	45,871	45,534	45,280
Non-oil developing countries [2]	7,949	7,319	23,339	80,076	184,857	227,351	255,552	275,997	277,869

[1] Includes data for Luxembourg.
[2] Includes data for Taiwan Province of China.

Note.—International reserves is comprised of monetary authorities' holdings of gold (at SDR 35 per ounce), special drawing rights (SDRs), reserve positions in the International Monetary Fund, and foreign exchange. Data exclude U.S.S.R., other Eastern European countries, and Cuba (after 1960).

U.S. dollars per SDR (end of period) are: 1952 and 1962—1.00000; 1972—1.08571; 1982—1.10311; 1990—1.42266; 1991—1.43043; 1992—1.37500; October 1993—1.39293; and November 1993—1.38389.

Source: International Monetary Fund, *International Financial Statistics*.

TABLE B-108.—*Industrial production and consumer prices, major industrial countries, 1967-93*

Year or quarter	United States	Canada	Japan	European Community [1]	France	Germany [2]	Italy	United Kingdom
Industrial production (1987=100) [3]									
1967	57.5	51.1	36.2	59.3	61	57.6	58.5	70.5
1968	60.7	54.3	41.7	63.7	62	62.9	61.9	75.9
1969	63.5	58.1	48.3	69.6	69	70.9	64.2	78.5
1970	61.4	58.8	55.0	73.1	72	75.5	68.3	78.9
1971	62.2	62.0	56.5	74.7	77	77.0	68.0	78.5
1972	68.3	66.7	59.6	78.0	81	79.9	70.8	79.9
1973	73.8	73.8	67.9	83.7	87	85.0	77.7	87.0
1974	72.7	76.1	66.4	84.3	90	84.8	81.2	85.4
1975	66.3	71.6	59.4	78.7	83	79.6	73.7	80.8
1976	72.4	76.0	66.0	84.5	90	86.8	82.9	83.4
1977	78.2	79.3	68.6	86.6	92	88.0	83.8	87.6
1978	82.6	82.1	73.0	95.4	94	90.4	85.4	90.1
1979	85.7	86.1	78.1	93.1	99	94.7	91.1	93.6
1980	84.1	82.8	81.7	92.8	98.9	95.0	96.2	86.9
1981	85.7	84.5	82.6	91.1	98.3	93.2	94.7	84.1
1982	81.9	76.2	82.9	89.9	97.3	90.3	91.7	85.7
1983	84.9	81.2	85.5	90.8	96.5	90.9	88.9	88.9
1984	92.8	91.0	93.4	92.8	97.1	93.5	91.8	89.0
1985	94.4	96.1	96.8	95.8	97.2	97.7	92.9	93.9
1986	95.3	95.4	96.6	98.0	98.0	99.6	96.2	96.2
1987	100.0	100.0	100.0	100.0	100.0	100.0	100.0	100.0
1988	104.4	105.3	109.3	104.2	104.6	103.9	105.9	104.8
1989	106.0	105.2	115.9	108.2	108.9	108.8	109.2	107.0
1990	106.0	101.8	121.4	110.3	111.0	114.1	109.4	106.7
1991	104.1	98.1	123.7	110.2	110.9	117.4	107.1	102.5
1992	106.5	98.5	116.5	108.9	109.8	116.0	106.5	102.0
1993 *p*	111.0							
1992: I	105.1	97.5	119.7	106.8	110.4	119.2	110.3	101.4
II	106.3	98.0	116.9	109.5	110.4	117.3	107.2	101.3
III	106.5	98.5	116.5	108.6	110.3	115.7	104.7	102.5
IV	108.3	100.0	113.5	106.6	107.3	110.3	104.0	103.1
1993: I	109.7	101.8	114.1	105.1	104.8	106.9	105.2	103.2
II	110.4	102.6	112.2		104.9	106.9	102.0	104.3
III	111.1	103.6	112.0			106.9	103.0	105.3
IV *p*	113.1							
Consumer prices (1982-84=100)									
1967	33.4	31.3	32.2	23.5	24.6	49.3	16.0	18.5
1968	34.8	32.5	34.0	24.3	25.7	50.1	16.2	19.4
1969	36.7	34.0	35.8	25.3	27.4	51.0	16.6	20.4
1970	38.8	35.1	38.5	26.6	28.7	52.9	16.8	21.8
1971	40.5	36.1	40.9	28.3	30.3	55.6	17.6	23.8
1972	41.8	37.9	42.9	30.1	32.2	58.7	18.7	25.5
1973	44.4	40.7	47.9	32.7	34.5	62.8	20.6	27.9
1974	49.3	45.2	59.0	37.4	39.3	67.2	24.6	32.3
1975	53.8	50.1	65.9	42.8	43.9	71.2	28.8	40.2
1976	56.9	53.8	72.2	47.9	48.1	74.2	33.6	46.8
1977	60.6	58.1	78.1	53.8	52.7	76.9	40.1	54.2
1978	65.2	63.3	81.4	58.7	57.5	79.0	45.1	58.7
1979	72.6	69.1	84.4	65.1	63.6	82.3	52.1	66.6
1980	82.4	76.1	91.0	74.0	72.3	86.8	63.2	78.5
1981	90.9	85.6	95.3	83.2	82.0	92.2	75.4	87.9
1982	96.5	94.9	98.0	92.2	91.6	97.0	87.7	95.4
1983	99.6	100.4	99.8	100.2	100.5	100.3	100.8	99.8
1984	103.9	104.8	102.1	107.4	107.9	102.7	111.5	104.8
1985	107.6	108.9	104.1	114.0	114.2	104.8	121.1	111.1
1986	109.6	113.4	104.8	118.2	117.2	104.7	128.5	114.9
1987	113.6	118.4	104.9	122.2	120.9	104.9	134.4	119.7
1988	118.3	123.2	105.7	126.7	124.2	106.3	141.1	125.6
1989	124.0	129.3	108.0	133.3	128.6	109.2	150.4	135.4
1990	130.7	135.5	111.4	140.8	133.0	112.1	159.6	148.2
1991	136.2	143.1	115.0	147.9	137.2	116.0	169.8	156.9
1992	140.3	145.2	116.9	154.3	140.6	120.6	178.9	162.7
1993	144.5	147.9				125.5	186.4	165.3
1992: I	138.7	144.2	115.9	152.1	139.5	119.1	175.9	160.0
II	139.8	144.9	117.5	154.0	140.6	120.4	178.2	163.5
III	140.9	145.6	117.0	154.8	140.6	121.0	179.4	163.4
IV	141.9	146.1	117.4	156.2	141.3	122.1	181.7	164.0
1993: I	143.1	147.2	117.4	157.5	142.5	124.2	183.5	162.9
II	144.2	147.5	118.5	159.2	143.4	125.5	185.5	165.6
III	144.8	148.1	119.1	160.1	143.7	126.0	187.3	166.0
IV	145.8	148.8				126.6	189.2	166.6

[1] Consists of Belgium-Luxembourg, Denmark, France, Greece, Ireland, Italy, Netherlands, United Kingdom, Germany, Portugal, and Spain. Industrial production prior to July 1981 excludes data for Greece, which joined the EC in 1981. Data for Portugal and Spain, which became members on January 1, 1986 are excluded prior to 1982.
[2] Former West Germany.
[3] All data exclude construction. Quarterly data are seasonally adjusted.

Sources: National sources as reported by Department of Commerce (International Trade Administration, Office of Trade and Economic Analysis, Trade and Industry Statistics Division), Department of Labor (Bureau of Labor Statistics), and Board of Governors of the Federal Reserve System.

TABLE B-109.—*Civilian unemployment rate, and hourly compensation, major industrial countries, 1967-93*

[Quarterly data seasonally adjusted]

Year or quarter	United States	Canada	Japan	France	Germany [1]	Italy	United Kingdom
			Civilian unemployment rate (percent) [2]				
1967	3.8	3.8	1.3	2.1	1.3	3.4	3.3
1968	3.6	4.5	1.2	2.7	1.1	3.5	3.2
1969	3.5	4.4	1.1	2.3	.6	3.5	3.1
1970	4.9	5.7	1.2	2.5	.5	3.2	3.1
1971	5.9	6.2	1.3	2.8	.6	3.3	3.9
1972	5.6	6.2	1.4	2.9	.7	3.8	4.2
1973	4.9	5.5	1.3	2.8	.7	3.7	3.2
1974	5.6	5.3	1.4	2.9	1.6	3.1	3.1
1975	8.5	6.9	1.9	4.2	3.4	3.4	4.6
1976	7.7	7.1	2.0	4.6	3.4	3.9	5.9
1977	7.1	8.1	2.0	5.2	3.4	4.1	6.4
1978	6.1	8.3	2.3	5.4	3.3	4.1	6.3
1979	5.8	7.4	2.1	6.1	2.9	4.4	5.4
1980	7.1	7.5	2.0	6.5	2.8	4.4	7.0
1981	7.6	7.5	2.2	7.6	4.0	4.9	10.5
1982	9.7	11.0	2.4	8.3	5.6	5.4	11.3
1983	9.6	11.8	2.7	8.6	[3] 6.9	5.9	11.8
1984	7.5	11.2	2.8	10.0	7.1	5.9	11.8
1985	7.2	10.5	2.6	10.5	7.2	6.0	11.2
1986	7.0	9.5	2.8	10.6	6.6	[3] 7.5	11.2
1987	6.2	8.8	2.9	10.8	6.3	7.9	10.3
1988	5.5	7.8	2.5	10.3	6.3	7.9	8.6
1989	5.3	7.5	2.3	9.6	5.7	7.8	7.3
1990	5.5	8.1	2.1	9.1	p 5.0	p 7.0	6.9
1991	6.7	10.3	2.1	9.6	p 4.4	[3] p 6.9	p 8.8
1992	7.4	11.3	2.2	p 10.4	p 4.7	p 7.3	p 10.0
1993	6.8	11.2	....	....	....	....	p 10.4
1992: I	7.3	10.7	2.1	10.2	4.4	6.9	9.6
II	7.5	11.3	2.1	10.2	4.6	7.0	9.8
III	7.5	11.5	2.2	10.3	4.8	7.0	10.2
IV	7.3	11.5	2.3	10.6	5.0	8.3	10.5
1993: I	7.0	11.0	2.3	10.8	5.4	[3] 9.4	10.6
II	7.0	11.4	2.4	11.2	5.8	10.8	10.4
III	6.7	11.4	2.6	11.5	6.1	10.6	10.4
IV	6.5	11.1	....	....	....	....	10.1
		Manufacturing hourly compensation in U.S. dollars (1982=100) [4]					
1967	....	26.1	10.5	17.9	15.2	17.7	16.9
1968	....	28.2	12.2	20.2	16.3	18.9	15.8
1969	....	30.4	14.6	20.5	18.1	20.6	17.2
1970	....	33.9	17.4	21.6	22.9	25.1	19.9
1971	....	37.7	20.7	24.4	27.0	29.4	23.5
1972	....	41.3	27.3	29.4	32.5	34.9	27.7
1973	....	44.3	37.4	38.4	44.2	41.2	31.0
1974	....	52.2	45.6	42.1	51.6	48.1	35.6
1975	....	57.3	52.1	58.2	59.7	60.5	44.9
1976	....	67.7	56.2	59.9	62.9	59.0	42.3
1977	62.8	69.5	68.6	66.1	74.5	65.7	46.2
1978	67.9	69.8	94.0	81.4	92.8	78.8	59.2
1979	74.4	74.8	95.5	97.5	109.1	97.4	77.9
1980	83.3	83.0	98.3	113.3	119.3	111.1	103.7
1981	91.5	93.1	107.6	101.8	102.2	100.9	104.8
1982	100.0	100.0	100.0	100.0	100.0	100.0	100.0
1983	102.7	106.2	107.7	95.3	99.9	104.3	93.2
1984	105.9	105.9	111.0	90.2	93.9	103.5	88.8
1985	111.2	105.6	115.0	95.0	96.0	107.0	94.7
1986	115.8	107.8	171.2	128.4	135.6	142.7	113.7
1987	118.4	116.3	204.2	153.4	171.4	173.3	138.9
1988	123.0	130.9	234.4	160.6	182.1	179.9	158.6
1989	127.9	143.2	231.2	158.1	178.4	188.5	167.3
1990	134.7	155.5	237.5	192.4	222.2	241.0	191.4
1991	141.9	167.8	270.8	193.5	230.6	257.5	210.8
1992	148.1	165.7	300.6	213.5	260.0	277.1	228.4

[1] Former West Germany.
[2] Civilian unemployment rates, approximating U.S. concepts. Quarterly data for France, Germany, and United Kingdom should be viewed as less precise indicators of unemployment under U.S. concepts than the annual data. Many Italians reported as unemployed did not actively seek work in the past 30 days, and they have been excluded for comparability with U.S. concepts. Inclusion of such persons would about double the unemployment rate for Italy through 1985, and increase it to 11-12 percent for 1986-92 and 13 percent in 1993.
[3] There are breaks in the series for Germany (1983) and Italy (1986, 1991, and 1993). Based on the prior series, the rate for Germany was 7.2 percent in 1983, and the rate for Italy was 6.3 percent in 1986 and 6.6 in 1991. The break in 1993 raised Italy's rate by approximately 1.1 percentage points.
[4] Hourly compensation in manufacturing, U.S. dollar basis. Data relate to all employed persons (wage and salary earners and the self-employed) in the United States and Canada, and to all employees (wage and salary earners) in the other countries. For France and United Kingdom, compensation adjusted to include changes in employment taxes that are not compensation to employees, but are labor costs to employers.

Source: Department of Labor, Bureau of Labor Statistics.

TABLE B-110.—*Foreign exchange rates, 1969-93*

[Currency units per U.S. dollar, except as noted]

Period	Belgium (franc)	Canada (dollar)	France (franc)	Germany (mark)	Italy (lira)	Japan (yen)
March 1973	39.408	0.9967	4.5156	2.8132	568.17	261.90
1969	50.142	1.0769	5.1999	3.9251	627.32	358.36
1970	49.656	1.0444	5.5288	3.6465	627.12	358.16
1971	48.598	1.0099	5.5100	3.4830	618.34	347.79
1972	44.020	.9907	5.0444	3.1886	583.70	303.13
1973	38.955	1.0002	4.4535	2.6715	582.41	271.31
1974	38.959	.9780	4.8107	2.5868	650.81	291.84
1975	36.800	1.0175	4.2877	2.4614	653.10	296.78
1976	38.609	.9863	4.7825	2.5185	833.58	296.45
1977	35.849	1.0633	4.9161	2.3236	882.78	268.62
1978	31.495	1.1405	4.5091	2.0097	849.13	210.39
1979	29.342	1.1713	4.2567	1.8343	831.11	219.02
1980	29.238	1.1693	4.2251	1.8175	856.21	226.63
1981	37.195	1.1990	5.4397	2.2632	1138.58	220.63
1982	45.781	1.2344	6.5794	2.4281	1354.00	249.06
1983	51.123	1.2325	7.6204	2.5539	1519.32	237.55
1984	57.752	1.2952	8.7356	2.8455	1756.11	237.46
1985	59.337	1.3659	8.9800	2.9420	1908.88	238.47
1986	44.664	1.3896	6.9257	2.1705	1491.16	168.35
1987	37.358	1.3259	6.0122	1.7981	1297.03	144.60
1988	36.785	1.2306	5.9595	1.7570	1302.39	128.17
1989	39.409	1.1842	6.3802	1.8808	1372.28	138.07
1990	33.424	1.1668	5.4467	1.6166	1198.27	145.00
1991	34.195	1.1460	5.6468	1.6610	1241.28	134.59
1992	32.148	1.2085	5.2935	1.5618	1232.17	126.78
1993	34.581	1.2902	5.6669	1.6545	1573.41	111.08
1992: I	33.347	1.1775	5.5137	1.6204	1218.54	128.77
II	33.220	1.1940	5.4416	1.6146	1217.23	130.37
III	30.170	1.2016	4.9628	1.4643	1135.18	124.93
IV	31.915	1.2617	5.2671	1.5509	1362.89	123.02
1993: I	33.686	1.2608	5.5463	1.6349	1547.37	120.67
II	33.311	1.2703	5.4635	1.6198	1506.55	110.05
III	35.447	1.3039	5.8180	1.6776	1586.56	105.65
IV	35.857	1.3251	5.8368	1.6851	1653.17	108.35

	Netherlands (guilder)	Sweden (krona)	Switzerland (franc)	United Kingdom (pound) [1]	Multilateral trade-weighted value of the U.S. dollar (March 1973=100)	
					Nominal	Real [2]
March 1973	2.8714	4.4294	3.2171	2.4724	100.0	100.0
1969	3.6240	5.1701	4.3131	2.3901	122.4	
1970	3.6166	5.1862	4.3106	2.3959	121.1	
1971	3.4953	5.1051	4.1171	2.4442	117.8	
1972	3.2098	4.7571	3.8186	2.5034	109.1	
1973	2.7946	4.3619	3.1688	2.4525	99.1	98.9
1974	2.6879	4.4387	2.9805	2.3403	101.4	99.4
1975	2.5293	4.1531	2.5839	2.2217	98.5	94.1
1976	2.6449	4.3580	2.5002	1.8048	105.7	97.6
1977	2.4548	4.4802	2.4065	1.7449	103.4	93.3
1978	2.1643	4.5207	1.7907	1.9184	92.4	84.4
1979	2.0073	4.2893	1.6644	2.1224	88.1	83.2
1980	1.9875	4.2310	1.6772	2.3246	87.4	84.9
1981	2.4999	5.0660	1.9675	2.0243	103.4	100.9
1982	2.6719	6.2839	2.0327	1.7480	116.6	111.8
1983	2.8544	7.6718	2.1007	1.5159	125.3	117.3
1984	3.2085	8.2708	2.3500	1.3368	138.2	128.8
1985	3.3185	8.6032	2.4552	1.2974	143.0	132.4
1986	2.4485	7.1273	1.7979	1.4677	112.2	103.6
1987	2.0264	6.3469	1.4918	1.6398	96.9	90.9
1988	1.9778	6.1370	1.4643	1.7813	92.7	88.2
1989	2.1219	6.4559	1.6369	1.6382	98.6	94.4
1990	1.8215	5.9231	1.3901	1.7841	89.1	86.0
1991	1.8720	6.0521	1.4356	1.7674	89.8	86.5
1992	1.7587	5.8258	1.4064	1.7663	86.6	83.4
1993	1.8585	7.7956	1.4781	1.5016	93.2	89.9
1992: I	1.8243	5.8854	1.4573	1.7692	88.2	84.8
II	1.8182	5.8302	1.4780	1.8070	88.0	84.4
III	1.6506	5.3523	1.3041	1.9030	81.9	78.9
IV	1.7448	6.2581	1.3888	1.5781	88.5	85.4
1993: I	1.8387	7.5299	1.5063	1.4769	93.3	90.0
II	1.8180	7.4130	1.4628	1.5331	90.9	87.6
III	1.8861	8.0151	1.4768	1.5037	93.7	90.2
IV	1.8907	8.2185	1.4676	1.4914	94.9	91.7

[1] Value is U.S. dollars per pound.
[2] Adjusted by changes in consumer prices.

Source: Board of Governors of the Federal Reserve System.

TABLE B–111.—*Growth rates in real gross domestic product, 1975–93*

[Percent change]

Area and country	1975–84	1985	1986	1987	1988	1989	1990	1991	1992	1993[1]
World	3.3	3.7	3.6	3.9	4.6	3.4	2.2	0.6	1.7	2.2
Industrial countries	2.5	3.3	2.9	3.2	4.3	3.2	2.3	.5	1.7	1.1
United States	2.5	3.2	2.9	3.1	3.9	2.5	1.2	−.7	2.6	2.7
Canada	3.2	4.8	3.3	4.2	5.0	2.4	−.2	−1.7	.7	2.6
Japan	4.0	5.0	2.6	4.1	6.2	4.7	4.8	4.0	1.3	−.1
European Community	2.0	2.5	2.9	2.9	4.2	3.5	3.0	.8	1.1	−.2
France	2.1	1.9	2.5	2.3	4.5	4.3	2.5	.7	1.4	−1.0
Germany[2]	1.8	1.9	2.2	1.4	3.7	3.6	5.7	1.7	1.9	−1.6
Italy	2.5	2.6	2.9	3.1	4.1	2.9	2.1	1.3	.9	.0
United Kingdom[3]	1.5	3.8	4.3	4.8	5.0	2.2	.4	−2.2	−.5	1.8
Developing countries	4.5	5.2	4.9	5.7	5.3	4.1	3.7	4.5	5.8	6.1
Africa	2.3	3.7	1.9	1.3	3.9	3.6	1.9	1.6	.4	1.6
Asia	6.3	7.3	7.0	8.1	9.0	5.5	5.7	6.1	7.8	8.7
Middle East and Europe	3.6	2.9	2.4	5.9	.7	3.6	4.2	2.4	7.8	3.4
Western Hemisphere	3.2	3.5	4.0	3.2	1.1	1.6	.3	3.3	2.5	3.4
Countries in transition[4]	3.9	2.1	3.6	2.6	4.3	2.3	−3.5	−12.0	−15.4	−10.2
Central Europe	3.3	3.1	3.7	1.9	1.5	.2	−7.1	−12.6	−9.1	−1.8
Former Soviet Union[5]	4.1	1.7	3.6	2.8	5.3	3.0	−2.3	−11.8	−17.8	−13.7

[1] All figures are forecasts except data for United States.
[2] Through 1990 for West Germany only.
[3] Average of expenditure, income, and output estimates of GDP at market prices.
[4] For most countries included in the group, total output is measured by real net material product (NMP) or by NMP-based estimates of GDP.
[5] Data beginning 1990 are weighted averages of separate estimates for the 15 states of the former U.S.S.R.

Sources: Department of Commerce (Bureau of Economic Analysis) and International Monetary Fund.

NATIONAL WEALTH

TABLE B-112.—*National wealth, 1946-92*

[Billions of dollars]

| End of year | Total net worth [1] | Private net worth [2] ||||||| Government net financial assets |||
| | | Total | Tangible wealth [3] ||| Financial wealth ||| Total [7] | Federal | State and local |
			Total [4]	Owner-occupied real estate	Consumer durables	Total [5]	Corporate equity [6]	Noncorporate equity			
1946	533.7	755.5	220.1	149.6	53.2	535.4	102.6	200.1	−221.8	−221.6	−0.6
1947	624.1	831.6	260.7	175.5	65.1	570.9	100.2	236.1	−207.5	−207.4	−.5
1948	673.9	872.9	294.7	197.1	76.3	578.2	99.0	245.1	−199.0	−198.8	−.7
1949	706.8	909.6	323.5	214.7	86.6	586.1	108.1	244.6	−202.8	−202.4	−.9
1950	816.9	1,015.4	373.1	239.7	108.2	642.3	132.0	276.3	−198.5	−195.1	−3.9
1951	918.8	1,112.9	419.1	266.8	124.4	693.8	154.6	297.3	−194.1	−189.7	−5.0
1952	954.5	1,167.6	455.2	291.6	134.0	712.4	156.3	299.6	−213.1	−203.2	−10.5
1953	979.0	1,204.5	486.3	312.6	143.0	718.2	150.2	301.2	−225.5	−212.1	−14.0
1954	1,076.5	1,311.2	514.4	335.4	147.1	796.8	218.9	303.3	−234.7	−217.5	−17.9
1955	1,186.2	1,421.7	557.9	364.8	157.3	863.8	268.2	312.0	−235.5	−215.1	−21.1
1956	1,282.2	1,515.0	603.2	391.9	171.9	911.8	288.4	327.4	−232.8	−209.4	−24.1
1957	1,302.4	1,537.0	634.3	416.3	176.2	902.7	254.3	337.7	−234.6	−206.7	−28.7
1958	1,452.6	1,702.5	664.1	438.8	182.0	1,038.4	358.0	351.1	−249.9	−216.5	−34.2
1959	1,526.9	1,784.0	699.1	464.4	189.0	1,084.9	385.4	354.5	−257.1	−219.4	−38.6
1960	1,570.9	1,828.9	730.0	488.2	193.7	1,098.9	381.5	356.4	−258.0	−217.0	−41.9
1961	1,727.5	1,995.3	761.2	512.5	196.8	1,234.1	487.8	365.0	−267.8	−223.1	−45.7
1962	1,715.0	1,990.6	794.5	535.9	202.3	1,196.1	423.0	374.1	−275.6	−227.8	−48.8
1963	1,855.5	2,135.8	833.0	559.2	212.8	1,302.8	497.3	383.6	−280.3	−229.9	−51.5
1964	2,010.1	2,297.3	874.9	584.6	223.7	1,422.4	572.2	396.1	−287.2	−233.8	−54.5
1965	2,182.8	2,474.2	919.2	609.6	236.1	1,550.0	649.8	417.8	−291.4	−235.7	−57.0
1966	2,239.0	2,537.6	991.8	651.9	258.5	1,545.8	581.7	441.3	−298.6	−239.0	−60.9
1967	2,513.8	2,825.2	1,059.4	688.2	283.2	1,765.8	724.2	460.6	−311.4	−247.0	−66.0
1968	2,847.8	3,172.0	1,182.0	768.7	314.2	1,990.0	863.8	496.5	−324.2	−255.5	−70.5
1969	2,891.4	3,216.7	1,282.8	826.7	343.7	1,933.9	655.5	524.1	−325.3	−249.2	−78.2
1970	3,018.4	3,364.0	1,363.9	867.4	372.4	2,000.1	638.6	546.2	−345.6	−260.7	−87.3
1971	3,331.3	3,706.9	1,478.1	945.7	393.7	2,228.8	730.1	592.8	−375.6	−282.3	−96.2
1972	3,762.9	4,153.7	1,667.7	1,085.5	424.7	2,486.0	810.5	666.2	−390.8	−298.9	−95.1
1973	3,942.4	4,333.8	1,887.8	1,234.9	470.5	2,446.0	607.0	799.9	−391.4	−305.2	−90.6
1974	4,090.1	4,493.6	2,146.8	1,395.2	544.2	2,346.8	387.8	877.6	−403.5	−316.2	−93.9
1975	4,636.0	5,119.4	2,391.1	1,572.1	595.7	2,728.3	515.6	958.6	−483.4	−392.9	−99.0
1976	5,328.1	5,871.9	2,683.8	1,790.4	652.8	3,187.9	721.1	1,071.4	−543.6	−452.9	−100.8
1977	5,784.6	6,396.6	3,088.3	2,094.7	725.5	3,281.3	620.4	1,195.1	−585.2	−507.7	−88.1
1978	6,615.9	7,232.6	3,601.3	2,478.2	815.2	3,631.3	631.4	1,398.6	−616.7	−545.3	−83.0
1979	7,734.5	8,365.6	4,178.7	2,897.2	924.4	4,186.9	764.3	1,632.0	−631.1	−566.5	−77.3
1980	8,958.9	9,650.6	4,703.0	3,289.4	1,014.3	4,947.6	1,021.0	1,863.6	−691.7	−626.7	−79.2
1981	9,531.1	10,307.6	5,096.5	3,572.6	1,086.2	5,211.1	926.1	2,016.2	−776.5	−702.8	−89.3
1982	10,099.5	11,021.4	5,358.5	3,758.4	1,133.7	5,662.9	999.1	2,015.1	−921.9	−848.3	−90.9
1983	10,860.8	11,961.8	5,672.8	3,983.9	1,193.8	6,289.0	1,158.7	2,059.1	−1,101.0	−1,041.7	−77.8
1984	11,421.5	12,697.7	6,160.0	4,349.4	1,281.5	6,537.7	1,099.8	2,026.8	−1,276.2	−1,223.9	−73.6
1985	12,474.0	13,942.3	6,603.2	4,650.1	1,391.1	7,339.1	1,453.5	2,049.6	−1,468.3	−1,429.8	−59.3
1986	13,468.6	15,158.5	7,100.4	4,978.2	1,527.5	8,058.1	1,754.8	2,107.2	−1,689.9	−1,663.7	−48.1
1987	14,249.3	16,122.7	7,656.1	5,368.9	1,659.5	8,466.6	1,757.0	2,224.6	−1,873.4	−1,845.4	−51.8
1988	15,146.6	17,216.2	8,102.8	5,619.6	1,808.4	9,113.4	1,900.0	2,353.0	−2,069.6	−2,037.8	−59.1
1989	16,683.5	18,955.6	8,708.6	6,058.5	1,929.6	10,247.0	2,264.9	2,508.1	−2,272.1	−2,212.9	−90.2
1990	16,425.2	18,933.1	8,738.7	5,979.0	2,047.1	10,194.8	2,190.4	2,440.6	−2,507.9	−2,406.0	−136.6
1991	17,949.8	20,731.8	9,248.3	6,440.7	2,141.9	11,483.5	3,073.4	2,344.6	−2,782.0	−2,646.5	−173.2
1992	18,569.3	21,749.9	9,534.1	6,671.7	2,232.1	12,215.8	3,665.5	2,266.6	−3,180.6	−2,998.2	−226.0

[1] Sum of private net worth and government net financial assets.
[2] Referred to as household net worth in the *Balance Sheets*.
[3] Held by households and nonprofit organizations.
[4] Also includes nonprofit organizations' real estate.
[5] Also includes credit market instruments, life insurance and pension reserves, security credit, and miscellaneous assets, and is net of liabilities.
[6] Includes households and nonprofit organizations' direct (or through mutual funds) holdings of corporate equity. Equity held through pension and life insurance reserves is not included.
[7] Also includes sponsored credit agencies and the Federal Reserve. Some tangible wealth is included for these agencies.

Note.—Data are from *Balance Sheets for the U.S. Economy, 1945-92*, September 1993, with updates for recent years from *Flow of Funds Accounts, Flows and Outstandings*, December 1993.
Data are measured at market value where available. For example, corporate equity and land are measured at market value, but bonds are measured at par value.

Source: Board of Governors of the Federal Reserve System.

TABLE B-113.—*National wealth in 1987 dollars, 1946–92*

[Billions of 1987 dollars]

End of year	Total net worth [1]	Private net worth [2]							Government net financial assets		
		Total	Tangible wealth [3]			Financial wealth				Total [7]	Federal	State and local
			Total [4]	Owner-occupied real estate	Consumer durables	Total [5]	Corporate rate equity [6]	Non-corporate rate equity			
1946	3,195.8	4,524.0	1,318.0	895.8	318.6	3,206.0	614.4	1,198.2	−1,328.1	−1,326.9	−3.6
1947	3,200.5	4,264.6	1,336.9	900.0	333.8	2,927.7	513.8	1,210.8	−1,064.1	−1,063.6	−2.6
1948	3,336.1	4,321.3	1,458.9	975.7	377.7	2,862.4	490.1	1,213.4	−985.1	−984.2	−3.5
1949	3,551.8	4,570.9	1,625.6	1,078.9	435.2	2,945.2	543.2	1,229.1	−1,019.1	−1,017.1	−4.5
1950	3,871.6	4,812.3	1,768.2	1,136.0	512.8	3,044.1	625.6	1,309.5	−940.8	−924.6	−18.5
1951	4,313.6	5,224.9	1,967.6	1,252.6	584.0	3,257.3	725.8	1,395.8	−911.3	−890.6	−23.5
1952	4,358.4	5,331.5	2,078.5	1,331.5	611.9	3,253.0	713.7	1,368.0	−973.1	−927.9	−47.9
1953	4,450.0	5,475.0	2,210.5	1,420.9	650.0	3,264.5	682.7	1,369.1	−1,025.0	−964.1	−63.6
1954	4,805.8	5,853.6	2,296.4	1,497.3	656.7	3,557.1	977.2	1,354.0	−1,047.8	−971.0	−79.9
1955	5,091.0	6,101.7	2,394.4	1,565.7	675.1	3,707.3	1,151.1	1,339.1	−1,010.7	−923.2	−90.6
1956	5,320.3	6,286.3	2,502.9	1,626.1	713.3	3,783.4	1,196.7	1,358.5	−966.0	−868.9	−100.0
1957	5,294.3	6,248.0	2,578.5	1,692.3	716.3	3,669.5	1,033.7	1,372.8	−953.7	−840.2	−116.7
1958	5,741.5	6,729.2	2,624.9	1,734.4	719.4	4,104.3	1,415.0	1,387.7	−987.7	−855.7	−135.2
1959	5,895.4	6,888.0	2,699.2	1,793.1	729.7	4,188.8	1,488.0	1,368.7	−992.7	847.1	−149.0
1960	6,018.8	7,007.3	2,796.9	1,870.5	742.1	4,210.3	1,461.7	1,365.5	−988.5	−831.4	−160.5
1961	6,494.4	7,501.1	2,861.7	1,926.7	739.8	4,639.5	1,833.8	1,372.2	−1,006.8	−838.7	−171.8
1962	6,328.4	7,345.4	2,931.7	1,977.5	746.5	4,413.7	1,560.9	1,380.4	−1,017.0	−840.6	−180.1
1963	6,747.3	7,766.5	3,029.1	2,033.5	773.8	4,737.5	1,808.4	1,394.9	−1,019.3	−836.0	−187.3
1964	7,153.4	8,175.4	3,113.5	2,080.4	796.1	5,061.9	2,036.3	1,409.6	−1,022.1	−832.0	−194.0
1965	7,552.9	8,561.2	3,180.6	2,109.3	817.0	5,380.6	2,248.4	1,445.7	−1,008.3	−815.6	−197.2
1966	7,463.3	8,458.7	3,306.0	2,173.0	861.7	5,152.7	1,939.0	1,471.0	−995.3	−796.7	−203.0
1967	8,109.0	9,113.5	3,417.4	2,220.0	913.5	5,696.1	2,336.1	1,485.8	−1,004.5	−796.8	−212.9
1968	8,735.6	9,730.1	3,625.8	2,358.0	963.8	6,104.3	2,649.7	1,523.0	−994.5	−783.7	−216.3
1969	8,429.7	9,378.1	3,739.9	2,410.2	1,002.0	5,638.2	1,911.1	1,528.0	−948.4	−726.5	−228.0
1970	8,361.2	9,318.6	3,778.1	2,402.8	1,031.6	5,540.4	1,769.0	1,513.0	−957.3	−722.2	−241.8
1971	8,766.6	9,755.0	3,889.7	2,488.7	1,036.1	5,865.3	1,921.3	1,560.0	−988.4	−742.9	−253.2
1972	9,430.8	10,410.3	4,179.7	2,720.6	1,064.4	6,230.6	2,031.3	1,669.7	−979.4	−749.1	−238.3
1973	9,168.4	10,078.6	4,390.2	2,871.9	1,094.2	5,688.4	1,411.6	1,860.2	−910.2	−709.8	−210.7
1974	8,647.1	9,500.2	4,538.7	2,949.7	1,150.5	4,961.5	819.9	1,855.4	−853.1	−668.5	−198.5
1975	9,108.1	10,057.8	4,697.6	3,088.6	1,170.3	5,360.1	1,013.0	1,883.3	−949.7	−771.9	−194.5
1976	9,866.9	10,873.5	4,970.0	3,315.6	1,208.9	5,903.5	1,335.4	1,984.1	−1,006.7	−838.7	−186.7
1977	10,007.6	11,020.1	5,343.1	3,624.0	1,255.2	5,677.0	1,073.4	2,067.6	−1,012.5	−878.4	−152.4
1978	10,518.1	11,498.6	5,725.4	3,939.9	1,296.0	5,773.1	1,003.8	2,223.5	−980.4	−866.9	−132.0
1979	11,307.7	12,230.4	6,109.2	4,235.7	1,351.5	6,121.2	1,117.4	2,386.0	−922.7	−828.2	−113.0
1980	11,866.1	12,782.3	6,229.1	4,356.8	1,343.4	6,553.1	1,352.3	2,468.3	−916.2	−830.1	−104.9
1981	11,637.5	12,585.6	6,222.8	4,362.1	1,326.3	6,362.8	1,130.8	2,461.8	−948.1	−858.1	−109.0
1982	11,812.3	12,890.5	6,267.3	4,395.8	1,326.0	6,623.3	1,168.5	2,356.8	−1,078.2	−992.2	−106.3
1983	12,189.5	13,425.1	6,366.8	4,471.3	1,339.8	7,058.4	1,300.4	2,311.0	−1,235.7	−1,169.1	−87.3
1984	12,307.7	13,682.9	6,637.9	4,686.9	1,380.9	7,044.9	1,185.1	2,184.1	−1,375.2	−1,318.9	−79.3
1985	13,020.9	14,553.5	6,892.7	4,854.0	1,452.1	7,660.9	1,517.2	2,139.5	−1,532.7	−1,492.5	−61.9
1986	13,687.6	15,405.0	7,215.9	5,059.1	1,552.3	8,189.1	1,783.3	2,141.5	−1,717.4	−1,690.8	−48.9
1987	14,011.1	15,853.2	7,528.1	5,279.2	1,631.8	8,325.1	1,727.6	2,187.4	−1,842.1	−1,814.6	−50.9
1988	14,262.3	16,211.1	7,629.8	5,291.5	1,702.8	8,581.4	1,789.1	2,215.6	−1,948.8	−1,918.8	−55.6
1989	15,057.3	17,107.9	7,859.7	5,468.0	1,741.5	9,248.2	2,044.1	2,263.6	−2,050.6	−1,997.2	−81.4
1990	14,196.4	16,364.0	7,552.5	5,167.7	1,769.3	8,811.4	1,893.2	2,109.4	−2,167.6	−2,079.5	−118.1
1991	15,020.8	17,348.8	7,739.2	5,389.7	1,792.4	9,609.6	2,571.9	1,962.0	−2,328.0	−2,214.6	−144.9
1992	15,121.6	17,711.6	7,763.9	5,433.0	1,817.7	9,947.7	2,984.9	1,845.8	−2,590.1	−2,441.5	−184.0

[1] Sum of private net worth and government net financial assets.
[2] Referred to as household net worth in the *Balance Sheets*.
[3] Held by households and nonprofit organizations.
[4] Also includes nonprofit organizations' real estate.
[5] Also includes credit market instruments, life insurance and pension reserves, security credit, and miscellaneous assets, and is net of liabilities.
[6] Includes households and nonprofit organizations' direct (or through mutual funds) holdings of corporate equity. Equity held through pension and life insurance reserves is not included.
[7] Also includes sponsored credit agencies and the Federal Reserve. Some tangible wealth is included for these agencies.

Note.—See Note, Table B-112.
Deflated by the GDP implicit price deflator. (The deflator was averaged for fourth quarter of year shown and first quarter of following year.)

Sources: Board of Governors of the Federal Reserve System and Department of Commerce, Bureau of Economic Analysis.

SUPPLEMENTARY TABLE

TABLE B-114.—*Selected historical series on gross domestic product and related series, 1929–58*

[Billions of dollars; except as noted]

Year	Gross domestic product					Constant (1987) dollars						Saving as percent of disposable personal income [1]	Population (thousands) [2]
	Current dollars	1987 dollars	Implicit price deflator (1987=100)	Percent change from preceding period			Personal consumption expenditures	Gross private domestic investment	Net exports	Government purchases	Disposable personal income			
				Current dollars	1987 dollars	Implicit price deflator					Total	Per capita (dollars)		
1929	103.1	821.8	12.5				554.5	152.8	1.9	112.6	585.8	4,807	3.0	121,878
1930	90.4	748.9	12.1	−12.4	−8.9	−3.2	520.0	107.2	−.3	122.0	542.2	4,402	2.5	123,188
1931	75.8	691.3	11.0	−16.2	−7.7	−9.1	501.0	67.2	−2.3	125.5	519.7	4,186	2.1	124,149
1932	58.0	599.7	9.7	−23.5	−13.3	−11.8	456.6	25.0	−2.4	120.5	449.8	3,600	−3.1	124,949
1933	55.6	587.1	9.5	−4.1	−2.1	−2.1	447.4	26.6	−3.0	116.1	437.0	3,477	−3.9	125,690
1934	65.1	632.6	10.3	17.1	7.7	8.4	461.1	41.1	−1.0	131.4	462.0	3,652	−1.1	126,485
1935	72.3	681.3	10.6	11.1	7.7	2.9	487.6	65.2	−7.2	135.7	505.2	3,967	2.3	127,362
1936	82.7	777.9	10.6	14.4	14.2	.0	534.4	89.9	−5.1	158.6	565.9	4,415	4.4	128,181
1937	90.8	811.4	11.2	9.8	4.3	5.7	554.6	106.4	−1.9	152.2	585.5	4,540	4.0	128,961
1938	84.9	778.9	10.9	−6.5	−4.0	−2.7	542.2	69.9	4.2	162.5	547.6	4,213	−.3	129,969
1939	90.8	840.7	10.8	7.0	7.9	−.9	568.7	93.4	4.6	174.0	590.3	4,505	2.4	131,028
1940	100.0	906.0	11.0	10.2	7.8	1.9	595.2	121.8	8.2	180.7	627.2	4,747	3.8	132,122
1941	125.0	1,070.6	11.7	25.0	18.2	6.4	629.3	149.4	2.8	289.1	713.9	5,352	10.7	133,402
1942	158.5	1,284.9	12.3	26.8	20.0	5.1	628.7	81.4	−11.1	586.0	824.7	6,115	23.1	134,860
1943	192.4	1,540.5	12.5	21.3	19.9	1.6	647.3	53.5	−28.1	867.7	863.8	6,317	24.5	136,739
1944	211.0	1,670.0	12.6	9.7	8.4	.8	671.2	59.8	−29.0	968.0	901.8	6,516	25.0	138,397
1945	213.1	1,602.6	13.3	1.0	−4.0	5.6	714.6	82.6	−23.9	829.4	890.9	6,367	19.2	139,928
1946	211.9	1,272.1	16.7	−.6	−20.6	25.6	779.1	195.5	26.5	271.0	860.0	6,083	8.5	141,389
1947	234.3	1,252.8	18.7	10.6	−1.5	12.0	793.3	198.8	41.9	218.8	826.1	5,732	3.0	144,126
1948	260.3	1,300.0	20.0	11.1	3.8	7.0	813.0	229.8	16.6	240.6	872.9	5,953	5.8	146,631
1949	259.3	1,305.5	19.9	−.4	.4	−.5	831.4	187.4	17.3	269.3	874.5	5,862	3.7	149,188
1950	287.0	1,418.5	20.2	10.7	8.7	1.5	874.3	256.4	3.2	284.5	942.5	6,214	5.9	151,684
1951	331.6	1,558.4	21.3	15.5	9.9	5.4	894.7	255.6	11.1	397.0	978.2	6,340	7.3	154,287
1952	349.7	1,624.9	21.5	5.4	4.3	.9	923.4	231.6	2.3	467.6	1,009.7	6,433	7.2	156,954
1953	370.0	1,685.5	22.0	5.8	3.7	2.3	962.5	240.3	−7.1	489.8	1,053.5	6,603	7.0	159,565
1954	370.9	1,673.8	22.2	.2	−.7	.9	987.3	234.1	−2.3	454.7	1,071.5	6,598	6.2	162,391
1955	404.3	1,768.3	22.9	9.0	5.6	3.2	1,047.0	284.8	−5.2	441.7	1,130.8	6,842	5.7	165,275
1956	426.2	1,803.6	23.6	5.4	2.0	3.1	1,078.7	282.2	−1.2	444.0	1,185.2	7,046	7.1	168,221
1957	448.6	1,838.2	24.4	5.2	1.9	3.4	1,104.4	266.9	1.6	465.3	1,214.6	7,091	7.2	171,274
1958	454.7	1,829.1	24.9	1.4	−.5	2.0	1,122.2	245.7	−14.9	476.0	1,236.0	7,098	7.4	174,141

[1] Percents based on data in millions of dollars.
[2] Population of the United States including Armed Forces overseas; does not include data for Alaska and Hawaii.

Source: Department of Commerce, Bureau of Economic Analysis.